SCHUBERT

SCHUBERT
A MUSICAL WAYFARER

LORRAINE BYRNE BODLEY

YALE UNIVERSITY PRESS
NEW HAVEN AND LONDON

This book is financially supported by the National University of Ireland, 49 Merrion Square, Dublin 2, DO2 V583, Ireland

Copyright © 2023 Lorraine Byrne Bodley

All rights reserved. This book may not be reproduced in whole or in part, in any form (beyond that copying permitted by Sections 107 and 108 of the U.S. Copyright Law and except by reviewers for the public press) without written permission from the publishers.

All reasonable efforts have been made to provide accurate sources for all images that appear in this book. Any discrepancies or omissions will be rectified in future editions.

For information about this and other Yale University Press publications, please contact:
U.S. Office: sales.press@yale.edu   yalebooks.com
Europe Office: sales@yaleup.co.uk   yalebooks.co.uk

Set in Adobe Garamond Pro by IDSUK (DataConnection) Ltd
Printed in Great Britain by TJ Books, Padstow, Cornwall

Library of Congress Control Number: 2023933148

ISBN 978-0-300-20408-7

A catalogue record for this book is available from the British Library.

10 9 8 7 6 5 4 3 2 1

For Seóirse, my other favourite composer

CONTENTS

List of Illustrations		*xiii*
List of Tables		*xv*
List of Musical Examples		*xvii*
Acknowledgements		*xxiii*
	Prologue: Becoming Schubert	1

I BEARINGS

1	*The Family before Schubert*	21
2	*The Origins of a Composer (1797–1813)*	33
	Early Musical Contexts	34
	Musical Life at the Stadtkonvikt	36
	The Aesthetics of Patricide	46
	Memoriae Matris Sacrum	51
	Regrouping	55
3	*Salieri, Partimento and the Beginnings of Creation*	57
	Early Exercises	59
	Fugue and the Search for Self-Realization	66
	Canon and the Beginnings of Intellectual Life	70
	Solfeggio and Schemata	76
	The Aesthetics of Resetting	80

CONTENTS

4	*The Makings of a Composer (1812–1813)*	87
	Early Steps in Composition: Success and Failure	87
	The Growth of Imagination: Schoolhouse String Quartets	88
	Schubert's Family Play their Part: A Forgotten History	98
	The Allure of the Symphony	100
	Leaving the Stadtkonvikt	106
5	*Place and Displacement (1813–1814)*	108
	Innocent Guilt: Teacher or Artist?	108
	Schubert's Arrangements: Notturno in G (D 96)	111
	Turning the Tide: Opera Composer or Church Musician?	114
	Private and Public Revolutions: 'The Liberators in Paris'	118
	Ad meliora: First Symphonies	121
6	*Schubert as a Church Music Composer*	125
	The Sacred Within and Without	125
	Apprenticeship at Lichtental, 1813–1816	126
	Intermezzo: The Other Schubert	128
	Schubert's *Marienbild*	130
	Stabat Mater: Rivalry and Recomposition	139
	Preoccupations: *Tantum Ergo*	141
	Stepping Stones: Kyrie Resettings	143
	Muses in Lichtental: Schubert's Mass in F major (D 105)	145
	From Tradition to Truth: Schubert's Latin Masses	149
	Stile Antico	151
	Sacred and Secular Scriptures: 'Am Tage aller Seelen' (D 343)	152
7	*Awakenings*	155
	'Quorum pars minima fui': 'Gretchen am Spinnrade'	155
	The Stolen Child: 'Erlkönig' D 328	166

CONTENTS

	Schubert's *Liederjahr* and the Romance of Creation	172
	Annus Mirabilis: Composing Goethe	174
	Between Realism and Idealism: Setting Schiller	178
	Recomposition, Variant, Version	188
	From *Ursprung* to *Fassung letzter Hand*: 'Meeresstille'	189
8	Unsung Schubert: Apprenticeship in Opera	191
	A Glimpse of Fulfilment? Schubert's Theatrical Calling	194
	Dramma per musica? *Claudine von Villa Bella* (D 239)	199
9	*The Promise of Freedom (1816–1818)*	207
	Preoccupations, 13–17 June 1816	207
	First Commission: The Lost *Prometheus* Cantata	210
	Things Fall Apart	212
	In the Crucible of Convention? Symphonies 4, 5 and 6	217
	Speculum mentis: Symphony in D (D 615)	232

II FRIENDSHIPS

10	Ars Amicitia: *Art of Friendship*	237
	In the Closet of the Stadtkonvikt?	238
	Epistolary Friendships	242
	Aesthetic Educations	244
	Some Select Circles	247
11	Ars Amicitiae: *Art Born of Friendship*	253
	The Good of Friendship: Josef von Spaun	253
	Rivalry or Reciprocity?: Anselm Hüttenbrenner	254
	Other Selves? Johann Baptist Mayrhofer	257
	Crediting Schober	271
	Vogl and the Civility of Friendship	276
	The Aesthetics of Friendship in Schubert's Musical Practice	278

CONTENTS

12 *Art Born of Improvisation* — 281
    Between Society and Solitude: Schubert's Improvisations — 282
    Schubert's Dances — 288

III CRISES

13 *In the Doldrums (1817–1818)* — 303
    Clearances: Schubert's Father — 309
    Muses in Zseliz: Uneasy Paradise, 1818 — 315
    'Hermit Songs' — 318

14 *Schubert's 'Double Nature' (1819–1822)* — 321
    Confidence and Indeterminacy: Schubert's Male-Voice Settings — 323
    Declaring his Genius: 'Erlkönig' (D 328), op. 1 — 332
    Tension and Riddles — 335
    Islands of the Mind: Multiple Fragments — 337

15 *Secrets of the Self* — 340
    The Watershed: *Annus Catastrophicus* — 340
    The Gardens of Alcinous: Schubert's Dream and Non-Dream — 341
    'Death and the Maiden': Schubert's *femme inconnue* — 347

16 *The Watershed (1822–1824)* — 358
    The Grace of Friendship: Moritz von Schwind — 358
    Turning the Tide: Illness and Hospitalization — 359
    Beauty and Brokenness: Schubert Confides in Kupelwieser — 369
    Et in Arcadia ego: Schubert's Minor-Key Quartets — 373
    Schubert Unmasked — 375
    Nietzschean Decay and Conquests of the Soul — 379

17 *'Art Born of Sorrow': Schubert's 'Unfinished'* — 381
    Tragedy and Symbolism: The 'Unfinished'? — 382

CONTENTS

	Ownership and Controversies: Schubert's 1823 Letter to Graz	392
	Finders Keepers? Josef and Anselm Hüttenbrenner	396
18	*Songs of a Wayfarer (1822–1824)*	404
	Paradise Lost, Goethe Regained	404
	Innocent Guilt: Schubert's Op. 12	406
	'Quorum pars magna fui': *Die schöne Müllerin*	411
	Schiller's Pilgrim	414
	Goethe's Wanderer	417
19	*High Windows of Zseliz*	420
	The Flight Path: Schubert as Teacher	420
	Everyday Renewals: Schubert's Piano Duets	422
	The Local and the Universal	428

IV ESSENCE

20	*After the Crises: The Spirit of Beauty and its Fate*	433
	Old Friends and New: Eduard von Bauernfeld	433
	In medias res: Portrait of an Artist	435
	summer in Upper Austria and the Apprehending of Beauty	437
	Schubert's 'Sommerreise' (D 944)	441
	After Liberation	453
	From the Dust-Cloud of a Passionate Empiricism into the Pure Circle of Historical Light: Schubert and his Publishers	458
21	*Late Sacred Music as a Site of Theology?*	465
	Revolution and Renunciation: Final Masses	465
	Stile Antico Fugues in Vocal Style	471
	Lichtentalesque: *Tantum Ergo* in E flat (D 962) and *Intende Voci* in B flat (D 963)	473
	History and Hermeneutics: Schubert's Credo	476
	Intimations of the Transcendent	481

CONTENTS

22	De Profundis: *Final Songs*	486
	Human Chain: *Winterreise* (D 911)	488
	Gathering up Fragments: Schubert's *Italianità*	498
	Schubert's Women	504
	Gifts of Graz	507
23	*The Final Year (1828)*	511
	Alarms Within, the Universe Without	511
	Redefining the Public: Schubert's Benefit Concert	514
	Songs on the Threshold: 'Glaube, Hoffnung und Liebe' (D 945 and D 955)	516
	Mysticism, Ecstasy and the Sublime: String Quintet in C (D 956)	518
	New Territory, New Directions: Symphony in D (D 936A)	524
	Final Journeys, Final Gifts	525
	Lightnings: 'Die Taubenpost' (D 965A) and 'Der Hirt auf dem Felsen' (D 965)	526
	Patri antevertens: Illness and Death	529
24	*Lacrimae Rerum*: Burial at Währing	537
	De Brevitate Vitae: Memorials and Reburials	543
	Chronology	546
	Notes	606
	Select Bibliography	653
	Index of Schubert's works	671
	Index	678

ILLUSTRATIONS

1. *Schubertiade*, by Julius Schmid, 1896. © Shim Harno / Alamy.
2. *Franz Schubert*, by Wilhelm August Rieder, 1825. © The Picture Art Collection / Alamy.
3. *Franz Theodor Florian Schubert*, by Karl Schubert. © Foto: Wien Museum.
4. Statue of Christ on the Mount of Olives, Neudorf. Photograph by the author.
5. Church of the Most Blessed Trinity, Neudorf, exterior. Photograph by the author.
6. Church of the Most Blessed Trinity, Neudorf, interior. Photograph by the author.
7. Schubert's mother's home, no. 51, Zlaté Hory. Photograph by the author.
8. Church of the Assumption of the Virgin Mary, Zlaté Hory. Photograph by the author.
9. Schubert's family home and inner courtyard, Nussdorferstrasse no. 54. Photograph by the author.
10. Jesuit Church Vienna. Photograph by the author.
11. Portrait of Ferdinand Lukas Schubert, 1840. © Foto: Wien Museum.
12. *Antonio Salieri*, by Joseph Willibrord Mähler, 1815.

ILLUSTRATIONS

13. *Elizabeth Vietz.* © World History Archive / Alamy.
14. *Therese Grob*, by Heinrich Hollpein, c. 1835.
15. *Franz von Schober*, by Leopold Kupelwieser, c. 1822. © A. Dagli Orti / © NPL – DeA Picture Library / Bridgeman Images.
16. Schubert's original gravestone in Währing Cemetery, photograph by HeinzLW. © Creative Commons Attribution-Share Alike 3.0 Austria.

ONLINE

lorrainebyrnebodley.com/schubert-a-musical-wayfarer/

17. Franz Theodor's family home.
18. Schubert's diary entry, 17 June and 8 September 1816.
19. *Johann Mayrhofer*, by Moritz von Schwind.
20. Schubert's letter to Graz, 1823.
21 a and b. Franz Theodor's letter to Ferdinand, 19 November 1828 and Ferdinand's letter to his father, Franz Theodor, 21 November 1828.
22 a and b. Franz Theodor's hand, 1828 and 1830.

TABLES

IN TEXT

1.3a	Franz Theodor Schubert's Children with Elisabeth Vietz	31
1.3b	Franz Theodor Schubert's Children with Anna Kleyenböck	31
2.1	Schubert's First Poem and First-Anniversary Memorial for his Mother, 'Die Zeit' ('Time', May 1813)	54
3.1	Schubert's Text for his Contribution to the 50th Anniversary Celebrations of Salieri (D 407)	58
3.2	Teenage Keyboard Fugues, 1812–1813	66
4.1a	Schubert's Schoolhouse Quartets, 1810/11–September 1813	88
4.1b	Schubert's Schoolhouse Quartets, November 1813–1816	89
4.2	String Quartets, 1820–1826	89
4.3	Schubert's Text, 'In Honour of My Father's Name Day' (D 80)	99
6.2	*Salve Regina* Resettings	131
6.3	*Tantum Ergo* Resettings	142
6.4	Stepping Stones Towards a Mass: Early Kyries	143
6.5	Schubert's Latin Masses, 1814–1816	149
6.6	Key Relations in Schubert's Latin Masses, 1814–1816	150
7.1	Therese Grob Songbook	158
8.1	Schubert's Apprenticeship with Salieri (Singspiele 1811–1816)	195

TABLES

8.2	Schubert's Apprenticeship on the Viennese Stage and Fragmentary Stage Works (1819–1823)	196
12.1	Piano Dances Published During Schubert's Lifetime	289
12.2	Piano Compilations Published During Schubert's Lifetime to Which the Composer Contributed	289
12.3	Tonally Closed Waltz Cycle (D 145), op. 18	291
14.1	Schubert's Cappi & Diabelli Publications, op. 1–18	333
15.1	Schubert's 'My Dream' (1822)	342
16.1	Schubert's 'Mein Gebet' (My Prayer, 1823)	360
16.2	Schubert's Poem, 'Klage an das Volk' (Complaint to the Nation, 1824)	365
16.3	Schubert's Letter to Leopold Kupelwieser, 31 March 1824	371
17.1	Schubert's Letter to the Styrian Music Society, 20 September 1823	393
19.1	Schubert's Marches for Piano Four Hands	424
19.2	Schubert's Complete Piano Duets Published During his Lifetime	429
23.1	Programme for Schubert's Benefit Concert, Wednesday, 26 March 1828	515

ONLINE

lorrainebyrnebodley.com/schubert-a-musical-wayfarer/

- 1.1 Schubert's Family Tree
- 1.2 Repertoire that Franz Theodor Schubert Performed in the Brno Gymnasium, 1770–1778
- 5.1 Schubert's Text 'Auf den Sieg der Deutschen' (To the Victory of the Germans, D 81)
- 6.1 Schubert's Sacred Music (1814–1816)

MUSICAL EXAMPLES

IN TEXT

2.1	Opening of 'Eine Leichenfantasie' (D 7), bars 1–44	47
2.2	'Der Vatermörder' (D 10), bars 1–36	50
3.2a	Sanctus (D 56), bars 18–24	60
3.2b	Sanctus (D 56), bars 71–86	61
3.3a	Schubert's Figured Bass Exercises with Salieri (D 25)	63
3.3b	Schubert's Figured Bass Exercises with Salieri (D 25B)	63
3.4a	Three Cantus Firmi which Salieri Set for Schubert	64
3.4b	Schubert's Realization of Cantus Firmus 2, Exercise III (D 25B)	65
3.4c	Schubert's Realization of Cantus Firmus 1, Exercise I (D 25B)	65
3.5	Fugue no. 6 in F (D 25C)	68
3.7	'Ein jugendlicher Maienschwung' (D 61)	72
3.8	'Dreifach ist der Schritt der Zeit' (D 69)	74
3.9	'Solfeggio' (D 619)	77
3.10	Lamento Bass Schema	78
3.11	Fugue in C major (D 24D), subject	78
3.12	String Quartet in C major (D 46/i), bars 1–7	78
3.13	'Der Vatermörder' (D 10), bars 125–8	79
3.14	'Hagars Klage' (D 5), bars 223–8	79

MUSICAL EXAMPLES

3.15	Piano Sonata in A minor (D 845/i) op. 42, bars 32–9	80
3.16a	String Quartet in G major (D 887/i), first subject, bars 15–24	81
3.16b	String Quartet in G major (D 887/i), bars 168–77	81
4.7	String Quartet in C major (D 46/ii), bars 1–2	95
5.2a	*Des Teufels Lustschloß* (D 84), bars 233–60	117
5.2b	Sketch for a Symphony in D (D 936A), bars 154–61	118
6.3	*Salve Regina* in F (D 223), soprano solo and continuo abstract, bars 16–60	133
6.5	*Salve Regina* in A major (D 676), bars 1–20	135
6.6	*Salve Regina* in C major (D 811), bars 1–13	137
6.7	Mass no. 1 in F major (D 105), Credo, bars 142–6	146
6.8	Mass no. 1 in F major (D 105), Kyrie, bars 28–36	147
6.10	'Am Tage aller Seelen' (D 343)	154
7.2	'Erlkönig' (D 328), bars 113–32	167
7.3a	'An Emma' (D 113A), bars 15–19	186
7.3b	'An Emma' (D 113B), bars 15–19	187
7.3c	'An Emma' (D 113C), bars 47–62	187
9.1	Symphony no. 4 in C minor (D 417/ii), first subject, bars 1–24	220
9.3	Symphony in D major (D 615/i), Adagio D minor Introduction and sequential modulations, bars 1–9	233
9.4	Symphony in D major (D 615/i), Allegro molto, first subject	233
9.5	Symphony in D major (D 615/i), Allegro molto, second subject	233
9.6	Symphony in D major (D 615/ii), second movement, first subject	233
12.2	Waltz from *Zwölf Walzer, siebzehn Ländler und Ecossaisen für Klavier* (D 145/6), op. 18	292
12.3a	Écossaises from *Zwölf Walzer, siebzehn Ländler und Ecossaisen für Klavier* (D 145), op. 18, nos. 1 and 2	293
12.3b	Écossaises from *Zwölf Walzer, siebzehn Ländler und Ecossaisen für Klavier* (D 145), op. 18, nos. 7, 8 and 9)	294

MUSICAL EXAMPLES

12.4	Ländler from *Zwölf Walzer, siebzehn Ländler und neun Ecossaisen für Klavier* (D 145/13), op. 18, bars 1–8	295
12.11	'Nähe des Geliebten' (D 162), bars 1–3	299
13.1	'Grablied für die Mutter' (D 616)	310
14.1a	'Das Dörfchen' (D 598), op. 11/1, bars 1–10	326
14.1b	'Das Dörfchen' (D 598), op. 11/1, canon, bars 97–132	327
17.1a	Symphony in B minor (D 759/i), introductory theme	386
17.1b	Symphony in B minor (D 759/i), introductory theme pitches	386
17.1c	Symphony no. 7 (D 759/i), introductory theme pitches transposed up a minor third	386
17.1d	Salieri, Partimento for Schubert D 25 (no. III in WB MH14421)	387
17.3	Symphony no. 7 (D 759/ii), second movement, second subject, bars 66–83	390
18.2	'Wandrers Nachtlied' (D 768), op. 96, no. 3	419
20.1	Symphony no. 8 (D 944/i), introductory horn call, bars 1–8	446
20.3a	Symphony no. 8 (D 944/iii), Scherzo, first subject, bars 1–4	449
20.3b	Symphony no. 8 (D 944/iii), Scherzo, second subject, bars 30–48	449
20.4	Symphony no. 8 (D 944/iv), Finale, second subject, bars 170–85	450
21.1	Mass no. 5 in A flat major (D 678/iii), Credo, 'Crucifixus', bars 157–62	470
21.2a	Bach, *Das wohltemperierte Klavier*, Book 2, Fugue no. 9, subject, bars 1–3	472
21.2b	Mass no. 6 in E flat major (D 950/ii), Gloria, fugue subject, bars 160–70	472
21.3a	Mass no. 6 in E flat major (D 950/vi), Agnus Dei, bars 250–6	475
21.3b	*Tantum Ergo* in E flat major (D 962), bars 29–33	475
21.3c	*Intende voci* in B flat major (D 963), bars 283–92	476

MUSICAL EXAMPLES

23.1a	Quintet in C major (D 956/ii), first subject, bars 1–9	519
23.1b	Quintet in C major (D 956/ii), bars 29–39	521
23.2	Symphony in D (D 936A/ii), revised first subject	524
23.4	Simon Sechter, Fugue in C minor on the name 'Schubert', op. 43, 'Dem Andenken des zu früh verblichenen Franz Schubert', November 1828, bars 1–15	531
24.1	'Pax Vobiscum' (D 551), to Schober's text, 'An Franz Schubert's Sarge', 21 November 1828	539

ONLINE

lorrainebyrnebodley.com/schubert-a-musical-wayfarer/

3.1a	*Beitrag zur fünfzigjährigen Jubelfeier des Herrn von Salieri* (D 407), opening, BN MS280
3.1b	*Beitrag zur fünfzigjährigen Jubelfeier des Herrn von Salieri* (D 407), canon, bars 1–28
3.6	Fugal Sketch in B flat major (D 37A)
3.17	'Quell' innocente figlio' (D 17), WB MH47
3.18	'Quell' innocente figlio' (D 17), bars 1–4, and 'Der Jüngling am Bache' (D 30), bars 1–4
3.19	'Der Jüngling am Bache' (D 30), WB MH3838
4.1	String Quartet no. 1 in G minor/B flat major (D 18), first violin part (in the composer's hand), WB MH125/c
4.2a	Overture in D (D 12), Cantilena from bars 108ff and 281ff
4.2b	String Quartet no. 2 in D major (D 94/i), bars 83–91
4.3a	String Quartet in C major (D 32/iii)
4.3b	Viennese Deutscher for Piano (D 128/12), bars 1–12
4.4	String Quartet in B flat major (D 36/i), bars 1–32
4.5	String Quartet in B flat major (D 68/i), bars 1–10
4.6	String Quartet in B flat major (D 68/iv), bars 1–12, rondo theme
4.8	String Quartet in D major (D 74/iv), bars 1–23
4.9	'Zur Namensfeier meines Vaters' (In Honour of My Father's Name Day, D 80), terzetto sketch for performance, WB MH53

MUSICAL EXAMPLES

4.10 'Zur Namensfeier meines Vaters' (In Honour of My Father's Name Day, D 80), tenor part in Schubert's hand, WB MH53, Inv 11357
4.11 Symphony no. 1 in D major (D 82/i), Adagio, bars 1–20, and Allegro vivace, first subject, bars 20–35
4.12 Symphony no. 1 in D major (D 82/iv), bars 1–35
5.1 String Quartet in E flat major (D 87/i), bars 1–27
5.3a 'Die Befreier Europas in Paris' (D 104), first version, WB MH68
5.3b 'Die Befreier Europas in Paris' (D 104), third version, WB MH68
6.1 *Salve Regina* in F major (D 27), soprano solo with clarinet obbligato, bars 183–214
6.2 *Salve Regina* in B flat major (D 106), tenor solo, bars 1–15
6.4 *Salve Regina* in B flat major SATB (D 386), bars 1–34
6.9 Mass no. 1 in F major (D 105), Credo, 'Qui propter' and 'Et incarnatus est', tenor solo, bars 75–91
7.1 'Gretchen am Spinnrade' (D 118)
7.4a 'Meeresstille' (D 215A)
7.4b 'Meeresstille' (D 216)
8.1 *Claudine von Villa Bella* (D 239), Overture, bars 1–8
8.2 *Claudine von Villa Bella* (D 239), Overture, bars 20–8
8.3 *Claudine von Villa Bella* (D 239/v), 'Es erhebt sich eine Stimme', bars 1–42
9.2 Symphony no. 4 in C minor (D 417/ii), transition theme, bars 94–103
9.7 Symphony in D major (D 615), WB MH189
11.1 'An die Musik' (D 547), BN, MS294
11.2 Vogl, 'Lied der Desdemona', opening bars 1–12
12.1a *36 Originaltänze* (D 365), WB, MH1864
12.1b '9 Incipits for Improvised Dances in A' (D 365), op. 9, on verso 'Ariette La pastorella a prato' (D 528), January 1817, WB M Mus. Autog F15
12.5 Gallop in C major (D 925), bars 1–24
12.6 Cotillion in E flat major (D 976), bars 1–24

MUSICAL EXAMPLES

12.7a Josef Hüttenbrenner, 'Tanz der Furien'
12.7b Teutscher für Josef Hüttenbrenner (D 643)
12.8a Folk tropes in Schubert's Ländler (D 980B)
12.8b Deutscher Tanz (D 365/36)
12.8c *Valses sentimentales* (D 779/12 and 13)
12.9a Folksongs in Schubert's Dances (D 146/5)
12.9b Folksongs in Schubert's Dances (D 529/8)
12.10 Trio from Deutsche (D 146/9), bars 1–8
14.2   'Gesang der Geister über den Wassern' (D 714), bars 1–15
15.1   'Sei mir gegrüsst' (D 741), bars 1–28
16.1   'Gebet' (D 815), soprano solo, bars 27–39
17.1e Salieri, Partimento for Schubert D 25 (no III in Original Exercise, WB MH14421)
17.2   Symphony no. 7 (D 759), first movement development, bars 114–50
18.1   'Wer nie sein Brot mit Tränen aß' (D 478/2), op. 12/2
19.1   Schubert's first composition, Fantasy in G major for Piano Four Hands (D 1, 1810) MH16237
19.2   Trio (B section) from Polonaise (D 824/3), bars 13–20
19.3   *March Militaire* (D 733/1), bars 1–22
19.4   Eight Variations on an original theme in A flat major (D 813), op. 35, Theme and Variation 1, 3, 7 and 8
20.2a Symphony no. 8 (D 944/ii), first subject, bars 8–16
20.2b Symphony no. 8 (D 944/ii), second subject, bars 93–97
20.5   String Quartet no. 15 in G major (D 887/i), bars 414–29
22.1   'Der Leiermann' (D 911/24)
22.2   'Il traditor deluso' (D 902/2), op. 83/2, bars 1–51
23.1a Quintet in C major (D 956/ii), first subject, bars 1–25
23.3a 'Die Taubenpost' (D 965A), MH4100
23.3b 'Die Taubenpost' (D 965)

ACKNOWLEDGEMENTS

The ability of books to transport us to another world has, perhaps, never been more evident. Writing this biography during the pandemic and at a time of great societal turbulence, I have often been reminded of Schubert's famous formulation, of music's ability to transport him to another realm. We reach back into past worlds partly to learn lessons, to view other lives with the benefit of distance. In his extraordinary life story we witness the tragedy and inspiration of an artist who died so young yet transcended all challenges to achieve his life's aim.

The biography of this remarkable individual has been many years in the making. This particular Schubertian journey began when I was invited to give a keynote lecture for the 25th Anniversary Celebration of the Franz Schubert Institute UK. As always, from my earliest lectures, my beloved Seóirse was there. So was Malcolm Gerratt, my now retired Music Editor of Yale University Press. At the end of that SIUK lecture in the Institute for Musical Research in London, he asked me if I had ever considered writing a biography of Schubert, an invitation for which I will be forever in his debt. It is wonderful to receive a commission like this but such a gift comes hand in hand with responsibility. In order to accept, I knew I would have to be clear on the contribution I would make. Two of the challenges in writing about Schubert is that so much has been written on him already and that he himself wrote so much. In order to gauge what I could add to the literature,

ACKNOWLEDGEMENTS

I spent a number of months re-reading Schubert biographies in English, German and French, and immersed myself in the marvellous work done by scholars who have gone before me and contemporary colleagues whose work I admire so much, perhaps even more now. I found a way in which gave me the courage to accept, and have been surprised by how many more emerged en route, and how much work remains to be done in Schubert scholarship.

It is always a pleasure to write about Schubert and always a pleasure to express my gratitude to those who have helped me to do so. The very first I must thank is Grazia Bitti (Radiologist), her husband, Renzo Caddeo, and Sergio Gemini (Emergency surgeon) at Azienda Ospedaliera G. Brotzu in Cagliari, Sardinia, for their generosity and grace. Had Grazia not intervened on 24 June 2014, I would not be here and this book would never have been written.

Later that year I relocated to Tübingen thanks to the generosity of the Deutscher Akademischer Austausch Dienst and Gerda-Henkel Foundation. The day after Seóirse and I arrived, Walther Dürr, Christine Martin and Rudolf Faber immediately stopped their work and sat chatting to us for hours around Walther's desk until the conversation closed naturally. The warmth of their welcome, despite the pressure of deadlines, the trust they afforded me in allowing me to borrow anything I needed, made me feel as if I were meant to write this book. That Walther is no longer physically with us deepens my regret that I cannot share with him the end result. In the final stages of writing the book, I felt the loss of his rich fount of knowledge which was only rivalled by the deep respect he afforded others working in the field.

In the Czech Republic I am glad to be able to thank staff at the Brno City Archives (Archiv města Brna); the District Museum of Local History in Šumperk (Okresní Vlastivědné Muzeum v Šumperku); the Regional Archive in Opava (Zemský archiv v Opavě); the Janowice State Archives (Státní Archiv Janovice) and Zlaté-Hory Holdings in Prague (Zlaté Hory-Archivní Správa Praha), which provided cadastral excerpts from the birthplace of the family of the mother Elisabeth Vietz in Zuckmantel. I am deeply appreciative of the warm hospitality the Palacký University,

ACKNOWLEDGEMENTS

Olomouc extended to me. I am deeply grateful to Jiří Kopecký for sitting with me for hours translating and discussing various Czech documents on our many exchange visits. It is thanks to Barbora Cupáková that I stood in the Church which Schubert's paternal grandfather had built in Vysoká. A next-door neighbour opened up the church and told us how to trace our steps through the nearby woods until we came upon the sandstone monument, Christ on the Mount of Olives, at the other side. On a different trip Barbora and Vašek drove me to Zlaté Hory to see Schubert's mother's home village, get a sense of her family's position in that village, and pay a visit to the church in which she was baptized.

In Vienna particular thanks are due to the manuscript collections of the Vienna City Library: two people in particular deserve special mention: Dr Thomas Aigner, Director, and Dr Karl Utz, who is responsible for reproductions and was incredibly helpful in arranging anything that I needed; my thanks too to Otto Biba during his time as Director of the Archives of the Gesellschaft der Musikfreunde and to the staff at the Austrian National Library (Österreichische Nationalbibliothek). Special thanks are due to Fr. Peter Fritzer, Rector of the Jesuit Church, Dr.-Ignaz-Seipel-Platz 1, who got more than he bargained for when he opened the door to me. After telling him about this biography, and finding common ground through the names of many Jesuit priests with whom Dan Farrelly had trained and that Peter knew, he paused his work to show me around the Stadtkonvikt, walk me through its historic gardens which Anton Bruckner's office overlooked, showed me the old oratory, took me into the neighbouring chapel and organ gallery where Schubert sang as a choirboy in Vienna, and even walked down Sonnenfelsgasse with me to show me buildings which had not been destroyed and retained their character from Schubert's day. On that same visit, at the height of summer, I walked the slow incline all the way from St Josef's Church in the Margareten suburb to the Church of St Lorenz and St Gertrud near Währing Cemetery to get a sense of the distance walked in the rain by Schubert's family and friends as they followed his cortege on Friday 21 November 1828.

ACKNOWLEDGEMENTS

By sheer chance, I find myself writing the acknowledgements for my book in an apartment on Sonnenfelsgasse on a return visit to the Schubert Research Centre at the Austrian Academy of Sciences (ÖAW), founded by its chair, Andrea Lindmayr-Brandl. I am very grateful to the board of the Schubert Research Centre for their warm reception of my work: in particular to Andrea Lindmayr-Brandl, a scholar of exceptional openness and optimism. I am especially thankful for the good grace of my fellow biographers: to Christopher Gibbs, who has warmly welcomed a new biography of Schubert, and for his collegial friendship over many years. Warm thanks too to Thomas Seedorf (Hochschule für Musik, Karlsruhe) for inviting me to be a member of the International Schubert Gesellschaft in 2014, and for our conversations on the shared joys and challenges of writing a biography of Schubert. I am also very happy to thank Hans Joachim Hinrichsen (Universität Zürich), Birgid Lodes (Universität Wien), Livio Marcaletti (Universität für Musik und darstellende Kunst Wien) and Katharina Loose-Einfalt (Austrian Centre for Digital Humanities and Cultural Heritage, ÖAW) for their support of my work at various stages. I am grateful to Julia Fuchs and Wolfgang Madl who assisted me with documents from the Hüttenbrenner collection in the archives of the Kunstuniversität Graz, and Elizabeth Giuliani, Directrice, Département de la Musique, who welcomed my scrutiny of many Schubert manuscripts housed at the Bibliothèque Nationale (BN), Paris.

In addition to the warmth of professional colleagues abroad, I enjoy an extraordinary supportive musicological community in Ireland through the Society for Musicology in Ireland, which is widely known for its warm embrace of international scholars. While writing this book I had the privilege of serving this community of scholars for two terms as SMI President (2015–2021) and working with two exceptionally engaged councils: founding President Harry White; Majella Boland; Anja Bunzel; Adele Commins; Joe Davies; Barbara Dignam; Damian Evans; Paul Everett; Eleanor Giraud; Una Hunt; Wolfgang Marx; Joseph W. Mason; Jennifer McKay; Hannah Millington; Christopher Morris; Denise Neary; John O'Flynn; Griff Rollefson; Ruth Stanley; Yo Tomita; Laura Watson; and Bryan Whitelaw.

ACKNOWLEDGEMENTS

Gabhaim buíochas ó chroí leo agus go rachadhdís go léir ó neart go neart (Heartfelt thanks to each of them and may they all go from strength to strength.)

One of the great joys of working in a university is to experience that great truth that we learn from our students as much as they learn from us, and in that spirit I want to thank the hundreds of students – international students too – who have been part of my Schubert courses at Maynooth University over the past decade. They have asked probing questions and forced me to think through these issues. They have endorsed my recognition that young adults need life stories that are reflective. They have learnt from experience that song provides an immediate and more detached form of contemplation during very stressful times. One student, Moriah Weir, wrote in an essay that Schubert's settings have no sell-by date: they are as relevant now as they were 200 years ago. Another, Lorenzo Charles Patti, recognized that Schubert did not just have a deep respect for music and poetry but also for the human condition. During the pandemic Jodie Moran drew a poignant parallel between Schubert alone in hospital at a time when his closest friends had departed Vienna with the experience of many Covid patients cut off from loved ones, 200 years later.

I have been richly blessed by my graduate students Anja Bunzel, Paul Higgins, Aisling Kenny, Niall Kinsella and Barbora Kubečkova, with whom I've spent hours talking about artsong or listening to their performances. I've been enriched by conversations with Barbara Strahan on Schubert's Fantasies, Nicolás Puyane on Liszt's resettings, Alison Shorten on Schubert's *Stabat Mater* and its textual relevance to contemporary society; Peter Shannon on Music and the Medical Humanities through the lens of Schubert's B minor and C major symphonies (D 759 and D 944), and Darragh Gilleece on the poetry and drama of Schubert's duets. All of my students at Maynooth's 'Schubert Music Institute' (as Mike Beckerman playfully renamed SMI at the Maynooth plenary in 2019) have been inspired by the presence and scholarship of Joe Davies, IRC Postdoctoral Fellow, and Marie Skłodowska-Curie, Global Fellow at Maynooth University and the University of California, Irvine.

ACKNOWLEDGEMENTS

To all my colleagues at Maynooth University I owe profound thanks for their support of me across many years. To work in an environment in which we feel our work is valued is a pearl beyond price. My deeply treasured friend, Gerard Gillen, as kind as he is wise, will always have my love and gratitude. No young scholar starting out could have been more fortunate. Warm thanks to my colleagues in the Department of Music, many of whom have been good friends to me: Adam Behan; Barra Boydell; Antonio Cascelli; Gordon Delap; Patrick Devine; Alison Hood; Victor Lazzarini; Michael Lee; Iain McCurdy; Darina McCarthy; Ryan Molloy; Christopher Morris; Fionnuala Moynihan; Estelle Murphy; John O'Keeffe; Martin O'Leary; Fiona Palmer; Francesca Placanica; and Adrian Scahill. I am deeply appreciative of the quiet acts of kindness to Seóirse by Grainne and John O'Keeffe, and Christopher Morris. I owe very special thanks to Antonio for his support of me during a very challenging semester and for introducing me to Giorgio Sanguinetti. When Giorgio first shared his research on partimento with us in Maynooth in 2009, he immediately alerted me to one possible explanation as to how Schubert could have written opera so quickly. Years later when I had written on Schubert's compositional training with Salieri, I invited Giorgio for a return visit in 2016, during which he spent hours talking to me, enthusiastically endorsed my findings, and gave an equally thought-provoking lecture on 'Working with Exemplars: The Stabat Cadence'. Hugh Murphy, Regina Richardson, Music Librarian, and Bernie Gardner at Maynooth University also aided my research by their willingness to interpret borrowing conditions in the most enabling way. A generous award from the National University of Ireland and the NUI Publications Committee chaired by the Registrar Patrick O'Leary enabled me to expand the biography beyond the initial word count. An award from the University Research Committee on Research at Maynooth University helped defray professional costs for the index.

Assembling the list of those who have actively supported and encouraged my work makes me realize, once again, how incredibly fortunate I am. I have been lucky enough to have been invited to share my research at many

ACKNOWLEDGEMENTS

universities in Austria, France, Germany, Ireland, the UK and North America which nourished many ideas in this book. Given that the book has been many years in the making, it is impossible to acknowledge all the interesting conversations I have had, all the email exchanges kindly sent after a lecture or paper, and all the advice and encouragement offered. The distinguished roster that follows is symbolic rather than exhaustive. Heartfelt thanks, therefore, to Nicolas Boyle (Schroeder Professor of German, Magdalene College Cambridge) and his wife Rosemary for their warm-hearted friendship across many years. I have drawn inspiration from the clarity and depth of Nick's writing on Goethe and benefited immensely from his endorsement of my own; Scott Burnham and Richard Kramer (City University of New York); Keith Chapin, Cameron Gardner, Clair Rowden (Cardiff University); Julian Horton (Durham University); Anne Hyland (Manchester University); Graham Johnson (Guildhall School of Music and Drama); Walburga Litschauer (NSA, University of Vienna); Su Yin Mak (The Chinese University of Hong Kong); Christine Martin (NSA University of Tübingen); Clive McClelland (SIUK, University of Leeds); Ian Partridge (Royal Academy of Music, London); Christiane Schumann (Deutsche Schubert Gesellschaft, Duisberg); James William Sobaskie (Mississippi State University); Glenn Stanley (University of Connecticut); Rolf Stehle (Goethe Institut Malaysia); Jürgen Thym (Eastman School of Music, University of Rochester); Yo Tomita (Queens University Belfast); Laura Tunbridge (St Catherine's College Oxford); Lorenz Welker, Hartmut Schick (Ludwig Maximilians Universität, Munich); and Susan Wollenberg (Lady Margaret Hall, University of Oxford).

I am incalculably indebted to two extraordinary women who looked out for me at the beginning of my career: Eda Sagarra – first female Professor of German at Trinity College Dublin (1975–1988) and first female registrar in any university between Ireland and Great Britain from 1981 to 1986 – was Pro-Chancellor of the University of Dublin (2001–2008) when I was beginning my academic career. Despite the many demands on her time, she looked out for me and endorsed my work in

ACKNOWLEDGEMENTS

ways that made a difference. Susan Youens, Schubert scholar extraordinaire, has since been an unstinting support and guide. In the twenty years I have known her, I have witnessed unremitting calls on her energy, countless official engagements and addresses. She too always made time for me, wrote stellar essays for volumes I have edited and delivered six inspiring keynotes in Ireland, all delivered with the same conviction, comprehension and passionate utterance. Her industry and intellect are a shining example for all of us writing about Schubert. For her many unselfish kindnesses to me, I owe a further entirely personal debt. I salute both women most warmly and thank them for their solidarity and example.

Two other women showed tremendous belief in me which was formative: Elizabeth Alberti and Stella Mew. The cloth these women were cut from was woven with generosity, dedication, infectious enthusiasm, and good humour. I will always be grateful to them as I am to Majella Boland; Sinéad Clarke; Therese Fahy; Amanda Geary; Aylish Kerrigan; Rosanne and James Maher; Rhona Clarke and Marie Hanlon; Claudia Mack; Hannah Millington; Sylvia O'Brien; Anne Marie O'Farrell; Linda O'Shea Farren and Brian Farren; Christiane Schumann; Noelle Tracey; Norma Sexton; Karen and Cormac Shaw, Katharina Uhde and Xiao Mei White, for their countless acts of friendship and love. I am deeply indebted to Frances Marshall and Sophie Light for photography and web design on the accompanying website.

During the course of writing this book, I have extended the reach of my research through public lectures, while attending rehearsals and performances at numerous Schubert festivals. It was a joy and a privilege to collaborate with Rada Jovicic, Director of Education for the Los Angeles Philharmonic, on a Festival of Schubert's Symphonies conducted by the brilliant Gustavo Dudamel in May 2017. A year later, I found myself at the Schubert Festival in Hohenems listening to Michi Gaigg conducting Schubert's complete symphonies and symphonic fragments performed by the L'Orfeo Baroque Orchestra in the Markus Sittikus Hall in May 2017. I am deeply indebted to Eugene Downes, Director of Kilkenny Arts Festival, for organizing a festival of Schubert's late works, 'Dreaming the

ACKNOWLEDGEMENTS

Sublime', in August 2017. I can mention with gratitude Sholto Kynoch, Artistic Director of the Oxford Lieder Festival, and several of his colleagues behind the scenes: Sarah Davies, Rebecca Homer and Zoe Lumsden, for the many invitations they extended to me. Many of the Oxford Lieder Festival audience have kept in touch with me, enquiring from time to time when the biography might be out. I can single out for explicit acknowledgement only a small handful: special thanks to Thierry Morris for sharing with me his photographs of Želiezovce (Zselisz). I gratefully acknowledge Chris Damerell, for his thoughtful exchange about Schubert as one of the historical figures whose life story can change lives for the better. Special thanks must go to Tom Empson whose lively mind raised many questions both at the end of my lectures and in many emails exchanged afterwards. I am grateful for his friendship and encouragement.

Many individuals have helped me with the preparation of this book. I owe a debt of gratitude to Julian Loose, Editorial Director, and his assistant, Frazer Martin, for guiding this work through to publication with such discreet and sympathetic professionalism. The good-humoured assistance of all at Yale University Press has been outstanding. Sincere thanks to my copy-editor Richard Mason whose tact and intelligence saved me from many errors, obscurities and fatuities which the readers will not see: those that remain on view are all my own work. I have been fortunate to have worked with two exemplary Maynooth doctoral graduates, Anja Bunzel and Cathal Twomey, who played an invaluable role in translating my many musical examples into legible copy. The majority of the examples were typeset by the indefatigable Cathal, whose help and first-rate work has enhanced my own efforts. It feels very special to have an original illustration of Schubert drawn by Yale's designer, Alice Marwick, for the front cover; I am also glad to be able to thank Amanda Speake who composed the index with professional expertise. Many thanks to Robert Sargant who thoroughly proofread the book and provided invaluable feedback. I owe special thanks to Rachael Lonsdale, Managing Editor and Design Manager who was superbly efficient in seeing the book through production, and to Meg Pettit,

ACKNOWLEDGEMENTS

Production Editor, whose meticulous reading of the manuscript made a real difference to the book. I am deeply indebted to her and to Jane Pickett, Yale's Senior Publicist.

I appreciate the assistance of many colleagues from archives, libraries, organizations and publishing houses who granted permission to use materials. The newly typed music examples from the works of Franz Schubert are taken, with the kind permission of the publisher, from the Neue Schubert-Ausgabe published by Bärenreiter - © Bärenreiter-Verlag Kassel Basel London New York Prague. I am grateful to Thomas Tietze, Legal Advisor to Bärenreiter Verlag, for his friendly assistance, also to Helmut Selzer, Wien Museum, for permission to reproduce the colour portraits of Schubert's father and brother, Ferdinand. I am grateful to Kate Brett, Music Editor at Cambridge University Press for permitting the republication of some paragraphs in chapters 12, 18 and 22 that first appeared in 'Music of the Orphaned Self' in *Schubert's Late Music: History, Theory, Style* (2016), ed. Lorraine Byrne Bodley and Julian Horton, and *Schubert's Piano* (2023) ed. Matthew Gardiner and Christine Martin, paragraphs which were stepping stones to a much fuller contemplation of *Winterreise* and Schubert's improvisatory practice here. Likewise, a chapter I wrote on 'Schubert's Sacred Music' for *A Musical Offering: Festschrift in Honour of Gerard Gillen* was the starting point for a much fuller development of the material in chapters 6 and 21: I am thankful to Michael Middeke at Boydell Press for granting permission. Thanks too to Oxford University Press for granting permission to publish part of my essay, 'A Place at the Edge: Reflections on Schubert's Late Style', which appeared in the special edition 'Writing *in extremis*', *Oxford German Studies* 44/1 (2015), 18–29, and which marked the beginnings of my research on Schubert's final illness in Chapter 23. I am grateful to Yale University Press for allowing me to dedicate 'The Gardens of Alcinous: Schubert's Dream and Non Dream' to Juergen Thym in Ulrich J. Blomann, David B. Levy, Ralph P. Locke, and Frieder Reininghaus, eds, *Music, a Connected Art: A Festschrift for Jürgen Thym on his Eightieth Birthday/ Die Musik - eine Kunst der Verknüpfungen*

ACKNOWLEDGEMENTS

und Verbindungen. Festschrift Jürgen Thym (Baden-Baden: Valentin Koerner, 2023).

Both of my parents died when I was in the final stages of writing this book. When writing my doctoral dissertation on Schubert's Goethe settings, my Dad, with his love of antiquarian books, turned up periodically with old biographies of Schubert as quiet gestures of support. At the time neither he nor I knew just how valuable those acts of remembrances would be until I began to trace the prosopological images of Schubert in the Prologue and found even the most obscure English-language biography of Schubert immediately to hand on my study shelves.

My deeply loved mother, Margaret, a woman of astonishing artistic creativity and quiet dignity, taught me much about the resilience of the human condition. When she took her leave of us earlier this year, after a long illness borne bravely, I was heartbroken but kept being grateful. Bláthnaid and I miss her wicked sense of humour, her quirky ways, but above all her great constancy and truth. Deep gratitude and love for Mary and her family, with whom we share our loss.

To my family with Seóirse: Blanaid and Peter, Ronan and family, Evelyn and family, Jennifer and John, Ruairi and Lie Shien, Dee and Albert, whose lively dinner conservations on their many visits have brought great joy to our home. I feel a deep debt of gratitude to Peter Staunton, J. J. Barry and Declan Lyons for their attentive care of Seóirse, and completely exceptional support of us both.

Gaby Smyth, one of my oldest and dearest friends, has been the most constant companion imaginable through the highs and lows of life's challenges as I wrote this book. He has looked out for me from the moment I met him.

I wish particularly to thank those who have given their time and attention to read and comment, often at greater length than I had any right to expect, on parts of the manuscript as it has developed. Among those who helped me personally with advice, criticism, assistance, with answers to questions, or indeed with questions, I should like to name the following:

ACKNOWLEDGEMENTS

Robert Hatten for reading chapter 3 critically; R. Larry Todd for his reading of chapter 3 and discussion of early nineteenth-century music education; Glenn Stanley for his friendship and critical encouragement of my writing on Schubert's Sacred Music which became chapters 6 and 21. Harald and Sharon Krebs for their warm friendship over many years. I shared parts of the unfinished manuscript with Harald, when he was working on 'Der blinde Knabe' (D 833), and he sent back deep thanks and thoughtful edits. I thank Andreas Dorschel for his uniquely probing comments on chapter 7. He is always a shining example of incisive, imaginative thought.

There are four more readers I must thank most deeply: Xavier Hascher focused on my early chapters with the kind of avidity you can only expect from a fellow Schubertian and exercised his razor-sharp acumen on what are now the first twelve chapters. He is a uniquely gifted reader of Schubert scholarship with an amazing eye for detail. He knows what a journey this book represents.

Michael Beckerman's willingness to read the entire manuscript epitomizes the exceptional generosity of spirit he extends to everyone who enters his orbit. It is one of many reasons why he is so widely and warmly loved, not only for his scholarly brilliance, and the intelligence of his wit, but also for his profound humanity. Mike's reading yielded many important comments.

Over many years when I was researching and writing this biography, Dan Farrelly proved indefatigably tolerant of Schubert-centric conversations. He has left his mark on my exposition of Schubert's liturgical music in particular, and the spirit of the book more generally. Eager to support me when I lost a second parent within two months, I asked him to read a chapter or two so we would have something to share other than the sorrow of recent months. He immediately accepted and read the entire manuscript with the same avidity with which he had read my doctoral dissertation. What Dan's support has meant to me is not the subject matter for an

ACKNOWLEDGEMENTS

acknowledgements section as without it my whole life would have been different.

Jorge Luis Borges once remarked that 'Great readers are rarer and more numinous than great writers', and Harry White belongs to this exalted company. It was Harry who first led me at the age of sixteen to think about music as an engagement with ideas. He is a natural assayer, who has the ability to put his finger on something problematical, a word or phrase that has me worried already. He too read chapters in gestation and the immediacy of his incisive and embracing critique of the entire manuscript in the final stages of writing the biography was particularly valuable to me and has left its mark on the revision. But beyond our support of each other's work, Harry has been my compass, steering me through rough waters, sharing his wisdom and experience, his unwavering support and deeply treasured friendship. No friend, no author, could hope for more.

My beloved Bláthnaid has been amazingly indulgent towards Schubert, who has been a constant presence in our home. 'How's Bertie doing today?', she'd quip with her gloriously irreverent sense of humour! For her love, her laughter and the sheer wonder of her, for her understanding of my engagement with life in a different time and place, for the joy she has given through the long hours and days of what has been a more demanding undertaking than I now hope is apparent, I owe the completion of this book.

At the very heart of this book is my husband, Seóirse, who has a composer's soul in the deepest sense of the word. Living with one composer facing his mortality at the end of a long and full life while writing about another whose life was so short has been incredibly poignant. I often found myself falling through the trapdoor of comparison. At a very basic level, when Seóirse was born in 1933 there was still no safe treatment for syphilis, Schubert's fatal illness: penicillin was discovered in 1947. Seóirse belonged to a generation who grew up in fear of infection: a number of his school friends died of tuberculosis; when I was writing this book during a

ACKNOWLEDGEMENTS

pandemic, his safety again felt placed in my hands. The courage he has shown with the travails of old age and Parkinson's disease has deepened his dignity. The gentleness of his spirit, the radiance of his smile, his deeply expressive eyes, his obvious joy in me and in any success that came my way, are all expressions of an incomparable love between us which bears quiet testimony to the beauty of the years we have shared. As I wrote this book by his side, his gentle presence cut through the isolation one needs to write, and mine through the increasing vulnerabilities of his old age. Those who have been moved by the profundity of Seóirse's music will sense something of the extraordinary man with whom I live. My indebtedness to him will, I hope, be evident not only in my dedication of this book to him but in everything I have written here. This book represents the very best of me. The love and gratitude I feel for him are immeasurable.

Lorraine Bodley
Vienna and Dublin, November 2022

PROLOGUE: BECOMING SCHUBERT

'Pro captu lectoris habent libelli sua fata'
('Books too have their experience')

Goethe[1]

I

Since the nineteenth century, Schubert has been subjected to considerable invention on the part of his biographers, acolytes and friends. Memoirs from some of Schubert's friends and contemporaries labelled him as a kind of cherubic idiot savant – a 'guileless child romping among giants', as Robert Schumann famously remarked.[2] He is depicted as a modest, relatively untutored *Schwammerl* (little mushroom), who frequented coffee houses and effortlessly improvised dance tunes for a coterie of friends, but who was unlucky in love, and who died young, impoverished and ignored. This highly sentimentalized image was reinforced by Schubert's first biographer, Heinrich Kreissle von Hellborn, in 1865 (the English translation swiftly followed in 1869)[3] and was embroidered with colourful detail by George Grove (1882).[4] What is important is not only what is true about Schubert's life and works but what has been taken for truth by those who were in the process of constructing an image of Franz Schubert. Oscar Wilde believed 'what is true in a man's life is not what he does, but the legend that grows up around him [. . .] you must never destroy legends. Through them we are given an inkling of the true physiognomy of a man'.[5] Such legends and anecdotal accuracy are also relevant to Viennese historians Ernst Kris and Otto Kurz in their seminal study of the intersections of artistic history and psychoanalytic theory, *Die Legende vom Künstler: Ein historischer Versuch*, where they claim: 'The only significant factor is that an anecdote recurs, that is recounted so frequently as to warrant the conclusion that it represents a typical image of the artist.'[6] In other words, public history claims its own reality: it functions as a counterpart to the historical life.

While Maynard Solomon's 1989 article, 'Schubert and the Peacocks of Benvenuto Cellini', attempted to restore the historical life by dispelling the sentimental image of the composer – which, as Scott Messing has cogently shown, permeated much of the nineteenth century[7] – in another sense it was replaced by a further aspect of the myth: that of a hedonistic artist, opposed to bourgeois culture and living on the edge of society. Eduard von Bauernfeld (1802–1890) was the first to portray Schubert as an outlaw who revelled in his rejection of conventional morality.[8] This image of Schubert as a marginal bohemian figure with an associated lifestyle of excessive drinking and free love was overlooked by biographers until it was resurrected by Fritz Lehner, whose revisionist filmic portrayal of Schubert in *Mit meinen heißen Tränen* (With my Hot Tears) casts a more knowing gaze on its subject than former films, though like its predecessors it did not stint on its speculations about the composer's life.[9] Since Lehner's film this postmodern image of Schubert has been developed in various ways by revisionist historians: most notably by Maynard Solomon[10] and the scholars who responded to his notorious article in a special edition of *Nineteenth-Century Music* in 1993,[11] and more recently by Susan McClary,[12] Lisa Feurzeig,[13] Rita Steblin,[14] Philip Brett[15] and Lawrence Kramer.[16] While this counter-image of Schubert undoubtedly brings us closer to the truth, such readings of Schubert's sexuality are also a product of our time. By unveiling the dark side of inspiration, they strikingly replace the myth of a divinely inspired composer, able to shake songs out of his sleeve, with the myth of a maverick artist, driven by malignant and demonic forces. Because these reactions are so extreme, and because other historical evidence contradicts them, we may want to relegate both images to the realm of myth. Like all good myths, however, they tell us something important and enduring about being human. They may not fully describe Franz Schubert but they do accurately portray aspects of the psychological realities in which he lived. To lift the veils of music history allows us to uncover the sources of these images, but it also leads us to ask, 'Who was Franz Schubert?'

II

Like many simple questions, 'Who was Franz Schubert?' is the hardest to answer and over the centuries many biographers have dismissed it as illegitimate and unanswerable.[17] Unanswerable as that may be, the human heart and mind can be counted on to disregard those dismissals and continue in our search to understand those that fascinate us the most.

Writing in the 1830s about the human empathy, abundance of detail and exacting scholarship that are essential for superlatively good biography, Thomas Carlyle spoke of catching the 'light-gleams' that make up a person's character.[18] One of the challenges of capturing Schubert's individuality is a responsibility to the truth which looks like a solid, unarguable rule until one realizes one of the challenges of writing a new biography of Schubert is whittling down the human being to human size from the mass of accumulated myth and surviving information (and misinformation). Some of his biographers have attempted to fill the lacunae in his life story by dramatizing their narrative with highly developed scene setting,[19] while others have gone further and invented meetings, imaginary episodes, hypothetical conversations. Examples of biographical tropes are the varied accounts of the composer's reported meetings with Beethoven in 1822 and 1827, which appear in the *Urbiographies* of Beethoven and Schubert, were endorsed by several of Schubert's surviving friends, and reappeared in subsequent biographies – George Grove,[20] Newman Flower,[21] Arthur Hutchings, for example[22] – though there is no definitive evidence that the composers ever met.[23] The story first appeared in the third edition of Anton Schindler's biography of Beethoven, in which a humble Schubert pays a visit to Beethoven accompanied by his publisher, Diabelli, in order to present to the master composer a copy of his Variations on a French Air (D 624) op. 10 for piano four hands, which he had dedicated to him in April 1822. According to Schindler the moment Beethoven pointed out a harmonic solecism, a blushing Schubert fled in panic.[24] While von Hellborn – like Josef von Spaun – immediately rejected Schindler's 1822 encounter and held the biographer 'answerable for the correctness of this episode, with all its rather improbable details, so humiliating to Schubert', it is interesting that von Hellborn should offer an alternative account of Schubert accompanied by Josef Hüttenbrenner and Josef Teltscher, visiting Beethoven on his deathbed in 1827 in Schindler's presence, an encounter which Beethoven's first biographer never even mentioned. Grove replaces Anselm Hüttenbrenner with Josef Hüttenbrenner, followed by Deutsch, whose account has been challenged by numerous biographers.[25] One of his most eminent critics was Maurice Brown, who concluded that the two composers had never met, though he himself had offered a conflated account of the 1827 encounter in his article for *Grove's Dictionary* just four years earlier.[26] When Grove's articles on Schubert, Beethoven and Mendelssohn were replaced by Brown in the fifth edition of the dictionary, they were republished in a monograph which kept the anecdote alive in the public domain for seventy years.[27] Brown's attack on earlier biographers also inadvertently invited a counter-attack on the authenticity of his own work, and so the trope continued to perpetuate in biographies until recently.[28]

An examination of contemporary records shows that Spaun believed 'Schubert would have considered himself fortunate had it been possible for him to approach Beethoven, but during the last years of his life the latter was quite unbalanced and unapproachable.'[29] As early as 1812 Goethe had predicted that Beethoven's increasing deafness would affect his social interaction rather than his composition, yet despite this distance in real life, Schubert's and Beethoven's lives have continually shadowed each other in musical biography. According to his brother, Ferdinand, Schubert invoked Beethoven on his deathbed and according to Schindler, Beethoven became acquainted with Schubert's songs on his deathbed when he gave them his laudatory blessing.[30] Even in death their fates are entwined: after Beethoven's funeral Schubert reputedly raised two toasts in the presence of his friends, Franz Lachner and Benedikt Randhartinger, at the Mehlgrube tavern[31] that evening: one to Beethoven and the second to whomever would follow him to the grave. Although the story was subsequently shown to be fiction, the episode remained an attractive way of enlivening Schubert biography through the fact that the composers died eighteen months apart, are buried and reburied in neighbouring graves.[32]

III

Such 'untruths gather weight by being repeated' and 'congeal into the received version of a life, repeated in biography after biography, until [. . .] they are unpicked'.[33] The first step in writing this biography was to spend time sifting through the prosopographical images of the composer by a broad constituency of biographers from Anglophone, French and Germanic contexts to uncover how in the past two hundred years history has rediscovered Franz Schubert numerous times with radically different results. These varied mythic and narrative structures reflect the problem of transference, which arises through the biographer's emotional involvement with Schubert's music. His music has inspired some scholars and performers to devote their entire lives to it; some even refer to the composer possessively as 'my Schubert'. 'So much careless love . . . and the recipient of so little intellectual respect', as John Gingerich has so wisely written.[34] The greatest challenge that Schubert's biographers have confronted, therefore, is not the absence of primary sources or the amount of secondary literature, or even the amount of music the composer has written, but the pitfall of dealing with themselves.[35] The key question – how to move beyond the autobiographical given that biographers must breathe life into Schubert's character – is, therefore, deeply problematic because biography is, in effect, a re-projection into a literary or semi-scientific, music-historical form of the primary sources reassembled by the musicologist. While laying bare the facts in a continuous and inquiring narrative, the musicologist becomes the informing mind without which the composer's character would enjoy, at best, only a flicker of an afterlife. As the novelist Joseph Conrad claimed, 'The dead can only live with the exact intensity and quality of the life imparted to them by the living.'[36]

It is fascinating to see how Schubert's biographers have risen to this challenge across the years. The first such undertaking was the two-volume biography by Heinrich Kreissle von Hellborn (1865), whose work bore witness to a high tide of musical biography and an entire series of endeavours to write a definitive life of the composer. Edward Wilberforce's reworking of Kreissle's biography – which condensed it from 590 to 250 pages – was the first substantial English-language work on Schubert to appear,[37] and it was replaced with a full translation of von Hellborn's biography in 1869, followed by George Grove's great portrait of 1882. Although not as popular as Grove's portrayal, Wilberforce's biography was immensely influential through its omission of the cultural, literary and intellectual context that von Hellborn had established for understanding Schubert's music and it placed a specific focus on the composer himself – a pattern which later biographers would continue. Wilberforce's portrayal of a feminine Schubert with somnambulant compositional gifts influenced numerous English-language biographies[38] including Henry F. Frost's *Schubert*, whose opening pages capture the tone of late nineteenth-century portraits of the composer:

> The world would be a loser had Schubert devoted the time occupied in writing down his beautiful thoughts to perfecting himself in foreign

languages or mathematics. He had a mission to accomplish, and the time allocated to him was short. Let us then be grateful that he fulfilled the task set before him so worthily and well.[39]

Sifting through such biographies of the age one immediately understands Grove's desire to write an objective biography. As outlined in his preface Grove's aim was 'to find out all the facts of the lives in which the works are produced [. . .] and to leave criticism alone',[40] yet his portrayal of a bourgeois, feminine Schubert and the imprint of Schumann's gendered Beethoven–Schubert dichotomy are evident throughout his biography.[41] Despite criticisms, Grove's *Schubert* became the standard English-language biography for many decades and, like Kreissle's biography, influenced many future accounts including George Lowell Austin's *The Life of Schubert*.[42] Such profiles as George Austin's – also those by Max Friedlaender[43] and August Reissmann[44] – reflect the nineteenth-century Romantic 'cult of genius', which overemphasized the biographical factor in creativity[45] and even advocated views of Schubert's music as his diary, a supposition put forward by Robert Schumann. Such 'tensions between expression and intellectual endeavour in music were sufficiently pronounced for biographers' at the turn of the century[46] – for example Richard Heuberger[47] and Willhelm Klatte[48] – to choose one over the other, and they collectively privileged the image of Schubert as a 'natural' composer. The early emphasis that Reissmann placed on Schubert's works rather than his biography became more commonplace in the twentieth century, when Schubert biographers emphasized the autonomy of his music or its place within a particular stylistic tradition, most notably Alfred Einstein (1951),[49] Hans Joseph Fröhlich (1978)[50] and John Reed (1987, r1997).[51] By the first half of the twentieth century most biographies recognized Schubert as the composer of several undisputed masterpieces still in the standard repertoire but mostly from his later years – the 'Unfinished' Symphony, the 'Great' C major Symphony, the String Quintet in C major, for example – yet balancing these appraisals were commonplaces of a different cast.

Schubert was a musician whose salon music betrayed a proclivity towards setting the poetry of his friends, whose songs and piano dances displayed a sentimental nature, an association which perpetuated stereotypes of the composer as one who evinced meekness and effeminateness, whose music buckled beneath the dramatic cogency of Beethoven.

In the English-speaking world Schubert's reputation suffered from endless charges of formal incompetence and latterly from antinomies in his character. Maurice J. Brown's *Schubert: A Critical Biography*[52] was among the first to redress such charges; Otto Erich Deutsch's documentary biography *Franz Schubert: Die Dokumente seines Lebens und Schaffens*[53] reflected the age of 'objective' musicology,[54] while his *Schubert: Die Erinnerungen seiner Freunde*[55] bore testimony to the ongoing interest in reminiscences and personal memoirs of composers. Deutsch's objective, documentary approach left its imprint on the three English-language biographies: Elizabeth Norman McKay's *Franz Schubert: A Biography*,[56] Brian Newbould's *Schubert: The Music and the Man*,[57] while Christopher Gibbs's *The Life of Schubert* comes closest to addressing ideological appropriations of Schubert.[58] Robert Winter, author of the *New Grove* entry on Schubert, did not depend on Deutsch's *Dokumente*, but responded to the lively, polemical debate about Schubert's sexuality which demanded a heavily revised image of the composer.[59] At the time of writing, it is forty-four years since Maynard Solomon's controversial article opened up this debate in Schubertian scholarship, nearly twenty-five years since these most recent English-language biographies appeared, twenty years since analysts began seriously to defend Schubert's handling of harmony and form, and twelve years since Hans-Joachim Hinrichsen's *Franz Schubert*[60] and Gernot Gruber's *Schubert. Schubert? Leben und Musik* were released.[61] There is an urgent need for a new biography of the composer, which reconciles the contradictory images of the man that are etched into our collective consciousness, and places him at the centre of his own story. A more nuanced portrait of Schubert which marks his gradual transition from a natural composer to a figure of authority and achievement is timely.

IV

Despite the numerous books written on him, despite our familiarity with his musical voice, therefore, Schubert's artistic career still presents a strange paradox. Apart from properties owned by his father and brother, there is no apartment like Beethoven's or Mozart's to visit, nor do we have a working library as we do for Brahms. Unlike Mendelssohn, who preserved his manuscripts and thousands of letters of his incoming correspondence in bound volumes, as if to save the record of his life for future scholarly inquiry, Schubert preserved nothing except his scores. Fewer than one hundred letters survive. His official papers run to one volume. Otto Erich Deutsch,[62] Walburga Litschauer,[63] Ernst Hilmar, Werner Bodendorff[64] and Till Gerrit Waidelich[65] filled another five with documentation and contemporary reports of him extracted from newspapers, correspondence and diaries of third parties.

But Schubert left monuments of a different kind: almost one thousand compositions – six hundred of which were written by the age of twenty-one – which have inspired an extraordinary amount of documentation for an individual achievement. The secondary literature about Schubert has long reached the point that no one could hope to encompass it; the primary sources are now not far behind through the valuable database Schubert-Online and ongoing publication of Schubert's works – in eighty-four volumes – released with full critical reports by the *Neue Schubert Ausgabe*. With the approaching 200th anniversary of Schubert's death in 2028, it is a natural time for reflection and reassessment, and a good time to attempt to situate this miraculous musical phenomenon in the broadest possible context. What makes Schubert special is the quantity, quality and individuality of the musical writing which caused this floodtide of interest in him and which perpetually expands our understanding of his inner life through its constant stream of reflection on the private and public events of his career.

There are many reasons for writing an intellectual biography of Schubert. Firstly, his compositions are the medium in which a prodigiously gifted and unusually well-placed observer determined and responded to numerous shifts in the bedrock of musical Europe, some of which led to earthquakes in his own time, others which we are only now beginning to appreciate. Schubert produced, with prodigious ability, music of unique form and character. But he was not just a composer, he was one of the most central European composers. The year he was born, 1797, was the year in which the first recognizably Romantic movements began. The two decades in which his works were written were a period of unparalleled richness in German music, literature and philosophy. By the time he died in 1828 he had left a legacy that would later establish him as a figure of global significance whose ultimate loyalty was avowedly to his art. To understand Schubert's significance is to adjust one's understanding of Romantic music, its course and derivation, and of Europe, and Vienna's place within it.

Secondly, in his music Schubert responded, as always, not to one single musical event, abstractly perceived, but to its reverberations throughout the personal, social and intellectual milieu in which he lived. The Viennese musical scene changed profoundly during his lifetime. The works in which he struggled to comprehend those developments are substantial enough anyway, but in order to trace the change in Schubert's understanding of his life and the purposes those works record one needs to explain their relation to their broader (turbulent) musical, social, personal, political, cultural and intellectual history. One of the ways of opening a pathway to the composer's concept of himself is to place him securely within the music-historical life of his times.

Schubert's short life bore witness to a whole series of intellectual and cultural innovations which were to have a powerful influence on the European mind of the nineteenth and twentieth centuries: Biblical criticism, re-interpretative theology, critique of philosophical idealism, neo-classical art and aesthetics, Weimar Classicism, early German Romanticism, Viennese cosmopolitanism, to name but a few. The extent of Schubert's achievement cannot be fully understood unless it is contextualized within these developments and measured against what was being attempted by the best of his contemporaries, with whom he was often in direct dialogue. However different his contribution, Schubert's ability to define himself in the face of challenges from the domineering presence of Beethoven and from an exceptionally demanding music-historical conjuncture is one of the themes of this biography.

Thirdly, past biographies have emphasized Schubert's uniquely iconic status as the only renowned composer of serious music who was born, spent his entire life and died in the capital of the Habsburg Empire – and have discussed Vienna's greatest musical son and his works in ways that reflected shifts in nationalist allegiances. This biography will radically reappraise this by retracing Schubert's heritage from Czech lands and relocating his musical training in *partimento,* a Neapolitan teaching tradition found in northern Italy, both of which, for musical and aesthetic reasons, illustrate the advantages of an interdisciplinary methodology that locates a composer within a broader historical, cultural and social context.

Fourthly, an important aspect of this research is to show how musical biography and historical analysis are inextricably linked, and how biographical studies offer an important tool for analysing historical questions. Building on recent analysis of Schubert's formal structures, which crystallize around the dichotomy between hypotactic and paratactic modes of formal planning – the former associated with the teleological processes of Beethoven's instrumental forms, the latter with Schubert's episodic alternatives – this biography will root Schubert's episodic handling of form in improvisatory practice and systematically explore the transformations of generic practices in neglected areas of his repertoire. Schubert's partimento training offers a new lens through which to view the freedom with which he treats chromatic thirds and semitonal relations and the significant role his music plays in the evolution of harmonic theory. This study will show how even in his early works these practices access an alternative triadic universe, governed by the logic of parsimonious voice leading and traceable to his improvisatory practice, and how his conception of bass degrees offers new insights into his use of harmony. By expanding our understanding of the cultural context of Schubert's musical training we are able to interpret more fully the meaning and trajectory of his inner musical life, the development of his musical intentions and ideals.

V

Within this framework, there are numerous challenges in writing a biography of Schubert, the first of which is reconciling the counter-images of the composer. Eduard von Bauernfeld was the first to point to the presence of 'opposing qualities' in Schubert.[66] Ten years later he again referred to the composer's double nature whereby 'a black-winged demon of sorrow and melancholy forced its way into his vicinity' and 'often brought out songs of the most agonizing beauty'.[67] Josef Kenner's hypocrisy is immediately evident in his identification of the composer's two souls 'of which the one pressed heavenwards and the other wallowed in mud'.[68] He made a similar observation a short time later when he priggishly observed: 'Anyone who knew Schubert knows how he was made of two natures, *foreign to each other*, how powerfully the craving for pleasure dragged his soul down to the slough of moral degradation'.[69] Whereas Kenner's perception of Schubert's personality, its binary language and moralizing tone, resonates with other remarks – and therefore must be taken seriously – his image of the polarity of the human soul also bears the imprint of an influential notion bequeathed to European culture by Goethe in *Faust I*. In 'Vor dem Tor', Faust expresses this very conflict between physical and spiritual desires, between earthly and heavenly ambition:

Zwei Seelen wohnen ach! in meiner Brust,	Two souls, alas, dwell in my breast,
Die eine will sich von der andern trennen;	Each seeks to rule without the other;
Die eine hält, in derber Liebeslust,	The one, with robust love's desires,

Sich an die Welt, mit klammernden Organen;	Clings to the world with all its might;
Die andre hebt gewaltsam sich vom Dust	The other fiercely rises from the dust
Zu den Gefilden hoher Ahnen.[70]	To reach sublime ancestral origins.

But even in *Faust* the image does not have to be interpreted in terms of depravity, rather a recognition that one has to live the side of the person who ends up in the dust. Kenner portrays Schubert as a Faustian man, one who would never happily settle for what ordinary existence seems to offer. Did he misunderstand the fundamental polarity at the heart of this Faustian metaphor? Or did Schubert scholarship misinterpret its context? There is a profound link between the highly destructive Faustian striving and the elemental striving that Kenner claims to have identified as Schubert's nature. Schubert's dark striving is not unique to him: it is part of the human condition to find ourselves torn between conflicting impulses, between reason and desire, duty and inclination, our purpose to ourselves and contribution to the greater good. Through his own striving – multifaceted as it is and Faustian in intensity – Schubert participated in this fundamental reality. His 'two natures, *foreign to each other*' are part of the same root, or in Goethean terms, part of Eternal Becoming.

Schubert's ability to reconcile these opposites through moral self-realization and escape from the pressures of everyday reality into a transcendent sphere through music is a tenet espoused in Schiller's *On the Aesthetic Education of Man*. Schiller identifies the aesthetic as a realm of experience that mediates between the physical and sensual, and unlocks this higher sphere by raising our consciousness, but only the aesthetic, Schiller believed, 'is a whole in itself'. [. . .] Here alone do we feel ourselves snatched outside time, and our humanity expresses itself with a purity and integrity as though it had not yet experienced any detriment from the influence of external forces.' Schiller's book on aesthetic education is a supreme statement of faith in the power of human creativity to heal and to restore to wholeness. It is a faith that Schubert's short life sorely challenged. Nevertheless, the nobility of this vision remains. One of the supreme truths of aesthetic education is that this ideal must always remain an ideal, something we approximate but never achieve. Another way of expressing this is that for Schubert – as for all of us – the whole is always partial and beauty is always imperfect. One of the ironies of Schubert's life is that he understood but refused to accept this truth.

In Schubertian scholarship these opposite images have not been reconciled and there has been a red thread across the centuries of what Joyce Carol Oates has defined as 'pathography',[71] memoirs and articles in which some scholars have fastened onto every loathsome detail of Schubert's life, with the result that he is not cut down to size but simply cut down. It is no coincidence that Kenner's unusually blunt remarks were made in order to assist in the first biographical project on Schubert. Although he had little contact with the composer in the 1820s, he obviously believed Ferdinand Luib should not write a panegyric whereby he should keep Schubert's vices out of sight, but a life represented as it really was. Do Kenner's remarks tally with Samuel Johnson's observation to James Boswell in 1773 that 'a man's intimate friend should mention his faults, if he writes his life'?[72] Or are they closer to Oscar Wilde's observation over a century later that 'every great man nowadays has his disciples and it is usually Judas who writes the biography?'[73] Whatever the answer to these musings, one thing is clear: Schubert was a mass of contradictions and one of the intriguing things about him is that he was able to reconcile these totally different qualities within himself and in his art. His was a divided, introspective nature, but behind that mask of human shyness resided a self-assured figure, who worked consistently to realize his potential. Although on the surface Schubert's life always seemed erratic, its central meaning was directed as consciously as his art.

Such paradoxes in human nature lie at the very core of life and art. In a letter to the composer Carl Friedrich Zelter in 1801, Goethe criticized the type of obituaries written by necrologists who, 'immediately after one's death, carefully balance the good and bad as perceived and applauded by

PROLOGUE: BECOMING SCHUBERT

the majority [. . .] touch up his so-called virtues and vices with hypocritical righteousness, and thereby are worse than death in destroying a personality, which can be imagined only in the living union of those opposing qualities'.[74] Later in the nineteenth century, when psychoanalysis and experiments in art forms produced a more indeterminate approach to individuality, the idea of a consistent self and identity that develops through the course of one's life began to break down. The existence of an essential self is there from Schubert's earliest traces: in the very first letter home he writes from boarding school, even in his earliest compositions. And yet when weaving the narrative of his life this sense of Schubert's innate, essential nature vies with the recognition that his character was also formed by his education and environment, accidents, contingencies. Such contrasting ways of describing Schubert overlap and conflict, rather than follow each other in a neatly chronological order.

The major events – rather than the day-to-day events – in his life are fully described in this book, but the main focus is on Schubert's intentions as a composer of images of the human condition. It is my aspiration that this biography will reflect the changing and conflicting concepts of what makes his self and its vicissitudes, what it consists of, how it expresses itself. I have consciously avoided a slavishly chronological approach, fostering variety and flexibility. If this has resulted in some anomalies, it is a price worth paying since the pay-off is more true to the manner in which life loops and meanders, advances and retreats, than any strictly chronological account could hope to be. While this book does not entirely conform to biographical convention, chronological biographies of famous figures almost inevitably become predictable once a composer's gifts have been recognized. The adoption of a thematic and works-based approach interwoven with chronology left me free to seek out the essential and emerging inner artist and explore his relationship to his own voice, his own place, his musical heritage, and his contemporary world.

A related and vital challenge in writing about Schubert is addressing the already vexed question in biography as to how – or whether – pathways between life and art can be mapped. What Edward Said calls the 'reticence' of music forewarns against drawing a direct analogy between art and autobiography, where meanings become masked in the process of creation. Even while problematizing the myth of a self-reflective art, it is nevertheless clear that Schubert's life carried vital meanings into his art, as he himself acknowledged repeatedly in his letters. At the time he wrote the famous letter to Leopold Kupelwieser portraying himself 'as the unhappiest and most wretched person in the world',[75] he produced the String Quartets in A minor and D minor ('Death and the Maiden'), two of the greatest works in the chamber music repertory. The pathos of these works points to a direct connection with his life and it is interesting to read a notebook entry of March of that year where Schubert makes the connection himself: 'What I produce is due to my understanding of music and to my sorrows.'[76]

In contemporary musicology, where interpretation and contextualization are favoured over positivism and formalism, the relationship between Schubert's life and music, therefore, cannot be ignored.[77] When attempting to answer such questions pertaining to the relationship between life and art, we are thrown back on the most important written memorials to Schubert, namely the compositions in which he sought to make individual occasions of his life into universal symbols of his age whose significance would speak to local audiences initially of his own day, but increasingly, and especially in his final years, to future listeners across the globe. The reader will see from the Contents page that chapters devoted mainly to Schubert's life alternate, on the whole, with chapters mainly devoted to his works. Not that the two subjects can be separated – on the contrary, it is the main theme of this biography that they cannot, and I will show how art throws light onto Schubert's life and vice versa. To make that orientation easier, and the biographical narrative more continuous, I have tried to reconsider the significance of his contribution to select genres in discrete sections. The biographical sections still contain discussion of some major and some lesser-known works, some fragments and resettings, enough to confirm the general principle of the inseparability of mind and matter.

PROLOGUE: BECOMING SCHUBERT

Some pieces are of significance for biographical rather than stylistically musical reasons. Genres engaged with over a long period of time – such as the symphony, for example – are treated as far as possible stage by stage in the course of their development. With Schubert's compositional output the biographical path has great analytical power. To abstract from the singular growth of his musical imagination and unfolding of his compositional gifts is the surest way of re-establishing those ideological preconceptions and conventional judgements which I am trying to challenge and, where possible, eliminate. For this reason I have sought the origin of Schubert's works in discrete occasions of the composer's life, which are given meaning and significance by their reference, explicit and implicit, to his self and the manifold catalysts that unleashed his musical creativity.

Finally, writing an intellectual biography which is accessible to an educated reader has been a vital aspect of my research. There has been so much magnificent scholarship about Schubert in English, German and French in the last fifty years, but most of it has been for a specialized audience, notable exceptions being Christopher Gibbs' *The Life of Schubert*[78] and Graham Johnson's monumental Hyperion recordings and *Franz Schubert: The Complete Songs*, both of whom consciously direct fine scholarship to a public audience.[79] This biography has also been written in the belief that different audiences can be reached in a study of Schubert and his music. In theory, this sounds viable but in practice it has been an immense challenge. Firstly, it is much easier to write a 'life-and-works' biography about a literary figure than about a composer, where the wider readership is not musically literate. This book is laden with musical and web examples not only for musicians and scholars: lecturing in Maynooth has convinced me that comprehension of concepts is deeper when the score is shown, whether the audience is literate or not. Then there are particular challenges in writing a biography of Schubert: for example, we know very little about Schubert's life in his final year at school, during his teacher-training year, but learn so much about his intellectual growth from close readings of his music. One of the reasons I used subheadings as signposts within chapters is so educated general readers with an interest in Schubert and classical music more broadly can, if they wish, leaf through analytical sections lightly and still grasp the key elements of the musical discussions and arguments, and thereby gain a deeper sense of what Schubert achieved. It is my hope that a serious scholarly audience will delight in the subtle discussions of musical form and idea as well as major historical arguments and details. Although cognizant of recent analytic readings of Schubert's work by music theorists, some of my discussions of his music are deliberately at a highly accessible level to make available current thinking to the general reader. The avid reader, whether specialist or not, will locate most of the compositions discussed on various streaming services, and thus have an opportunity to deepen their understanding of the music discussed. While of course, this book is intended to be read from start to finish, the use of signposts within chapters will, I hope, allow readers to pause and savour, study and listen to specific works.

Secondly, the book has been written from an interdisciplinary vantage point by a musicologist who has published on Goethe's lyric poetry and German cultural history. My hope is that the reader unacquainted with Austro-Germanic cultural traditions will find enough here to set Schubert's life in the context of his age, and his music in the context of his life. On the other hand, I hope those familiar with Schubert's works will learn something from seeing them presented against their biographical, social-historical, literary and philosophical backgrounds. My hope is that some of the themes raised and repertoire discussed will invite further dialogue and debate. For the scholar there may emerge a new image of Schubert as a figure of authority and exceptional achievement as well as a magnetic musical presence: a deeply thoughtful, superlatively intelligent thinker responding to the social, spiritual, cultural and intellectual demands of modernity, as they formed around him. For both specialist and non-specialist there will be the joy of new encounter with a remarkable individual: limited, ordinary even peculiar as we all are, but brilliant, courageous and exceptional as few of us are and as few of our musical forebears have been.

I

BEARINGS

1

THE FAMILY BEFORE SCHUBERT

'There's a divinity that shapes our ends.
Rough hew them how we will'.

Shakespeare, Hamlet (1601)

The name 'Schubert' is derived by genealogists from the Old German words 'schuoch wurhte' and the German 'schuowirt' meaning shoemaker. The name originated in Bohemia, which in the Middle Ages was part of the Holy Roman Empire characterized by feudalism. Before this time, people were only granted one name, but as the population increased and people began to travel, it became necessary to adopt a second name with which to identify themselves. Many families adopted the name of their feudal occupation as their surname: the name 'Schubert' was a German and Jewish (Ashkenazic) occupational name, signalling the profession of a cobbler and the symbol of the traveller. The motto on the family coat of arms, *diligenter et fideliter* (diligently and faithfully), was part of a lived inheritance handed down through many generations.

The composer's given name, Franz, was not new in the family. Over a century earlier, Schubert's grandfather, Karl Josef Schubert, named his second and third sons Franz. This Ur-Franz Schubert, who was the father of the composer, gave his name to five of his children. It was also the name of Schubert's maternal grandfather, Franz Johann (1720–1768).

Schubert's earliest known ancestor, Kaspar Schubert (1593–26 March 1657), was born in Waltersdorf in northern Moravia.[1] His second son,

Christoph Schubert (5 December 1632–1693), moved with his family in 1669 to the village of Neudorf (Vysoká, Malá Morava) at the foot of the Spieglitzer Schneeberg (Králický Sněžník) mountain in the Altstadt district of northern Moravia.[2] There, with the help of his wife, Sibille, he established himself as a farmer. The youngest of Christoph's nine children, Johannes 'Hans' Schubert (17 December 1678–27 November 1760), was Schubert's great-grandfather.[3] A lumberjack by trade, living at the edge of the Hochwald, Neudorf, Hans was a regimental musician who travelled widely through Europe and brought his wife home from Flanders. His marriage to Elisabeth (d. 5 July 1751) granted him one son,[4] Karl Josef (6 May 1723–24 December 1787), Schubert's grandfather, who inherited his father's gifts and also practised as a regimental musician. A farmer by profession and magistrate of his local community, Karl Josef married Susanne Möck (19 January 1733–2 August 1806), with whom he had five sons (Table 1.1 online).

Prayer was an important part of Karl Josef's habits and history, and he was strict and ardent in the practice of his own and his family's faith. His preoccupation with religion in the last decade of his life inspired him to erect a life-size sandstone monument of Christ on the Mount of Olives,[5] depicting the emotional torment of Christ in the garden of Gethsemane prior to his crucifixion (Figure 4). This humanistic portrayal of Christ's suffering built in 1780 was intended as a resting place for travellers passing between the two villages. In the same year Karl Josef funded a new organ in Vysoké Žibřidovice for which he had signed a contract on 8 August 1779.[6] In 1782 he oversaw the building of an oratory, Kapelle der heiligen Dreifaltigkeit (Chapel of the Most Blessed Trinity), so that weddings and funerals of his fellow parishioners could take place in their mountainous village of Vysoká.[7] The chapel, which is dedicated to the patron saint of the Czech Republic, St Ludmila (c. 860–921), still stands today and was renovated in 1997 to memorialize his grandson (Figures 5 and 6).[8] Something of Karl Josef's zeal for religion and desire to succeed also survived in the next two generations. His innocent piety found its way genetically to Schubert and the composer's extraordinary sensitivity to everything natural and spiritual.

THE FAMILY BEFORE SCHUBERT

Of Karl Josef's thirteen children, five sons survived.[9] His eldest and third sons, Johann Karl Alois (3 April 1755–29 December 1804) and Franz Theodor Florian (11 July 1763–9 July 1830), Schubert's father, were accepted as boarders at the Jesuit Gymnasium school in Brno, which had a rich musical tradition.[10] The Gymnasium, which had been founded by the Jesuits in 1578, was located in the Jesuit College near the Church of the Assumption of the Virgin Mary (kostel Nanebevzetí Panny Marie), popularly known as the 'Jesuit church' (U Jezuitů) on Jesuitská Street.[11] In autumn 1770 the two brothers left the family home (Neudorf, no. 41, see Figure 17 online), which their grandfather had built in 1759.[12]

Despite an eight-year age difference, the two brothers were registered in the Gymnasium's first class (*Rudimentarista*).[13] Schubert's father, then aged seven, had difficulties keeping up with written German and Latin and so in the following years, 1771–73, his elder brother, 'Carlus Schuberth', registered alone. In 1774 when he was ten, 'Franciscus Schubert, Moravus Neudorfensis', Schubert's father, re-registered as 'Principista' (Year 2). By then the school had 371 students, more than half of whom came from outside Brno.

Franz Theodor was proud of the education he received at this Brno Gymnasium with its emphasis on classical training. The year before Franz Theodor resumed his studies, Emperor Joseph II had censored the Jesuits' old-fashioned teaching methods – in particular their emphasis on rote learning and neglect of the national language – when the underlying political reason was the suppression of their power. By the 1770s the Order operated nearly 700 colleges and 200 seminaries across Europe. Although the Jesuits had many wealthy and influential benefactors, they had equally formidable enemies among senior ministers and aristocrats who sought to prevent the intervention of the Catholic Church in state affairs.[14] The State officially took over the Gymnasium,[15] but much of the teaching remained the same, due to a shortage of instructors, which meant, in fact, that many ex-Jesuits were retained. During Franz Theodor's school years, the Jesuits' *Ratio Studiorum* was freely adapted so that the students would continue to do well in state examinations. It was during this time that Schubert's father acquired his interest in philosophy through reading Aristotle as a primary study and through the school's systematic emphasis on scholastic philosophy and Christian apologetics, in particular Thomas Aquinas's proofs for the existence of God.

The seminary had a strong tradition of musical training. An excellent choral practice along with a very strict schedule of rehearsals meant annual performances were characteristically well prepared.[16] Sacred music was an integral part of this performance tradition and the liturgy Franz Theodor experienced every day can be found in the *Hymnodiae a Scholastica Juventute* (1741), the first example of manuscripts preserved in the *Gymnasio Brunensi Societatis Jesu* in the second half of the eighteenth century.[17] Although four-part polyphonic settings in Czech have been sourced,[18] Latin was the language spoken in church and during recreation.

Music performed followed the liturgical year. Popular repertoire from the *Manuale Marianum*[19] included the *Lauda Sion Salvatorum* sequence for Holy Thursday, the *Stabat Mater* for Marian celebrations, the hymns *Adoro Te devote* and *O Salutaris hostia*, as well as anthems in honour of Ignatius of Loyola (1491–1556), *O! Deus! ego amo te! Nam prior tu amasti me*, and the canticles of St Francis of Assisi, *O! Deus! ego amo te! Nec amo te, ut salves me*. The full repertoire that Schubert's father sang at the Brno Gymnasium is included in Table 1.2 online.[20]

Only scholarship students sang in the seminary choir, usually poor boys with special musical talent whom the Jesuits had earmarked as potential priests.[21] As was customary for choirboys, Franz Theodor learnt to play an instrument, the cello, and participated in the school orchestra.[22] A special list of scholarship students, who entered as postulants, were expected to enter the *Mariae in coelos assumptae* seminary.[23] As this list breaks off in 1770, we do not know whether that responsibility lay on Franz Theodor's young shoulders, though his passage through the school strongly suggests it did. Certainly Franz Theodor's whole way of thinking was structured by the discipline of boarding school, which was essentially preparation for a religious vocation. The ideal conclusion of his schooling would have been entry into a seminary. Neither brother lived up to that expectation. Karl, aged twenty, left after sixth class (*Rhetorika*) in 1775, and Franz Theodor graduated first in the humanistic class in 1778, aged fifteen.

Following in the footsteps of their great-grandfather who had relocated the family to Neudorf, Johann Karl and Franz Theodor migrated to Vienna where they established themselves as schoolteachers. Going to Vienna was a matter of going out into the world, a secular challenge, a testing ground, an entry into opportunity. Karl Schubert was the first to depart. With the help of another villager, Andreas Becker, who had secured a teaching position in the Carmelite elementary school in Leopoldstadt, Brunngasse no. 408 (today Taborstraße 21), he established himself as an assistant teacher. Eighteen months after Becker's death on 4 August 1776, the twenty-two-year-old Karl made an advantageous marriage to Becker's thirty-nine-year-old widow, Maria Anna, on 15 February 1778, and succeeded him as schoolmaster there.

Karl Schubert's position as headmaster of the Carmelite school enabled him to support his fifteen-year-old brother, Franz Theodor, who came to Vienna in the late summer of 1778.[24] On 19 November, Franz Theodor registered as a student at the University of Vienna.[25] Three years earlier on 16 November 1775 his brother, Karl, had registered as *logicus* (first class in philosophy).[26] That Franz Theodor reregistered for the preparatory class in philosophical studies in November 1783 – *Schubert Franc. A[ustriacus]. Neudorf. Logicus Pauper*[27] – suggests he had taken a break in his studies to complete the obligatory *Praeparandie* teaching course at the Normalhauptschule, Annagasse 3, before becoming an assistant to his brother at the Carmelite school,[28] where he earned between 70 and 80 Gulden per annum.[29] On 13 June 1786 he was appointed to his own school in Himmelpfortgrund, a suburb in the parish of Lichtental, the smallest Viennese district.

In Lichtental, Franz Theodor met and fell in love with Maria Elisabeth Catharina Vietz (30 October 1756–28 May 1812), a cook and servant girl living in the area. In the same year as he reregistered as a philosophy student at the University of Vienna, Elisabeth gave birth to their first child, Franz Ignaz, on 12 April 1783 in the Lichtental home of their future landlord, Ignaz Wagner (1756–12 February 1826), who stood as godfather when the baby was baptized in the Lichtental Parish.[30] Two days later the baby was handed into an orphanage and, as was the fate of poor foundlings, he died of *epilepsia puerilis* within a fortnight, on 27 April 1783.[31] Franz Theodor was nineteen when he fathered and forswore his first child. His application for a copy of his baptismal certificate in Hohenseibersdorf (Mähren) on 19 November 1783 suggests he wanted to marry the woman he loved. As he was under age, he needed his father's permission. That they waited until 1785 to marry suggests he lacked the courage to ask his father or Karl Schubert made him wait until he came of age.

Elisabeth was expecting their second child when they set up home together in a tiny one-room apartment on the first floor of *Zum goldenen Ring* (At the Golden Ring), Lichtental no. 152 (Vienna 9, Badegasse 20), two streets behind the Lichtental Church. Their rent was 17 fl. per annum. As was the custom, their landlord, Ignaz Wagner, registered them as new residents in the parish: Franz Theodor was enrolled on 8 August 1784,[32] Elisabeth on 3 November 1784, the beginning of the school year.[33] His age was given as twenty-five though he was only twenty-one and his profession listed as 'Instructor' (a private teacher of Latin), which gave him a certain anonymity. Elisabeth's age was given as thirty though she was twenty-eight, and her place of birth listed as Engelsberg (Andělská Hora), a village twelve miles south of where she was in fact born.

Schubert's mother came from Zuckmantel (no. 51, Zlaté Hory, Figure 7), a mountain village in northern Silesia, which, like Malá Morava, is in the mountain area of Jeseníky. Elisabeth came from a family with keen musical interests. Her great-uncle, Johann Georg Vietz, had been a 'competent organist' for forty years in the parish church in Zuckmantel (Zlaté Hory, Figure 8), and his son was a *virtuosis fidicen*.[34] Her father, Franz Johann Vietz (4 October 1720–24 January 1772), was a lutenist.[35] He had learnt the trade of locksmith and gunmaker from his father and had risen to be master of the local guild. When the family fell into financial difficulties during the Seven Years War (1756–63), Franz Johann used some of the money entrusted to his care, which at that time was a capital offence, and he was subsequently charged with abuse of office. Clemency was shown in view of his family's straitened circumstances and he was peremptorily dismissed and imprisoned.

Disgraced, emotionally and physically weakened from his time in prison, Franz Johann set out with his wife, Maria Elisabeth (née Riedel, 1724–1772), and their three children, Felix (b. 1748), Maria Elisabeth (1756–1812) and Maria Magdalena (1763–1829),[36] to walk two hundred miles across the Silesian mountains to Vienna. Exhausted from the strain of events, Schubert's maternal grandmother died en route and was buried by her family, who continued on their journey to Vienna. A few hours after they reached the inner city on 24 January 1772, Schubert's grandfather died in the aftermath of the affair, leaving their three children destitute.[37] His son, Felix, a weaver by trade, found work in the Lichtental area. His sixteen-year-old sister, Elisabeth, set up home and tended to their nine-year-old sister, Maria Magdalena. Franz Theodor's falsification of Elisabeth's home town on the parish register was undoubtedly to dissociate herself from her father's crime.

Elisabeth's marriage to Franz Theodor took place in the Lichtental Church, 'Zu den Heiligen Vierzehn Nothelfern' (Of the Fourteen Helpers in Need), on 17 January 1785, witnessed by their landlord, Ignaz Wagner, and Franz Theodor's brother, Karl. Franz Theodor found in Elisabeth, as his father had found in Susanne Möck, a woman who could live evenly and support him in his work. The tragedy in her childhood and her independent spirit prepared Elisabeth for the siege she must have experienced in body and spirit in the first fifteen years of marriage – her constantly being pregnant, the grief of carrying ten children to the grave, three dying in 1788. Some reinforcement must have been required, which most likely came from prayer, in particular her identification with the suffering mother of Christ.

Who was the stronger of Schubert's parents? Their personalities and address to the world were so antithetical. Certainly the man whom Elisabeth married was no ordinary person. Karl Schubert later portrayed his father as a hale man with a well-knit figure and sharply inquisitive eyes. The self-possession that Franz Theodor exudes in this portrait came from his precocity and the success with which he had established himself professionally (Figure 3). His first teaching appointment on 13 June 1786 in the parish of Lichtental served the children of 3,000 residents who inhabited the eighty-six buildings.[38] The triumph of this appointment was tempered the following year by the death of his 'dearly-loved and venerated' father on Christmas Eve 1787.[39] The small inheritance he received of 96 fl. was spent on rent and equipment for the new school, which he established in a ground-floor apartment of a two-storey building known as *Zum roten Krebsen* (The Red Crayfish), Himmelpfortgrund no. 72 (today Nussdorferstrasse no. 54), in the ninth district of Vienna. Schubert's father rented two of sixteen apartments: one for his school and one for his family. In addition to his salary of 130 fl. per annum, he received a subsidy of 30 fl. towards accommodation. By the beginning of the 1790s his basic salary rose to 163 fl. As his reputation as a teacher grew, his school swiftly expanded from a handful of children to 174 students registered in 1796.

By the time Schubert was born, the numbers of students had risen so significantly that, without regard to age and ability, they were divided between morning and afternoon sessions, each for four hours. Franz Theodor received an additional 373 fl. per annum and was entitled to a paid assistant. By 1800, seventy people were living in *Zum roten Krebsen*, but by 1801 he was able to afford a larger house, *Zum schwarzen Rössel* (The Black Horse), Himmelpfortgrund no. 10 (today Säulengasse no. 3) for his family and school, a short distance from *Zum roten Krebsen*. When Elisabeth Schubert bought this house with him on 27 May 1801 for 3,300 fl., the couple made a down payment of 200 fl. and for three years, between 1805 and 1807, they paid 1,000 fl. per year. It is very likely that Karl Schubert was guarantor for the purchase of Franz Theodor's new home into which the family moved on 25 June 1801. Six weeks after writing his will on 15 November 1804, Karl died on 29 December 1804, leaving his brother a large inheritance. Franz Theodor's school increased to 300 students through attracting pupils from his brother's school and outlying suburbs, which enabled his son, Ignaz, in 1805 to become his paid assistant.

The school year ran from 3 November to 21 September, with five weeks' holidays for the harvest, in addition to Sundays and Church holidays. As many of the new parents were too poor to pay fees, Franz Theodor supplemented his income by giving private tuition in Latin, for which he received an additional 1 fl. 20 kr. per month per student. Parents who were unable to pay the fees defrayed a registration fee for their children, while more financially well-off parents paid for their children to receive special instruction. Each child contributed to the cost of heating by carrying wood to school in winter and those who were able brought payment from their parents every Friday. At that time between thirty-five and seventy children were attending without paying fees, for which an additional remuneration of 20–40 fl. was granted to Franz Theodor per season. Later this became an official payment for the instruction of the poor of 15 kr. per child or 2 fl. 40 kr. per annum.

Franz Theodor's generosity to orphans was officially recognized in 1803 when he was appointed civil servant of the schoolteachers' widows society in Vienna, for which he was granted an additional allowance. In the same year his benefactor, Josef Spendou, Chief Superintendent of state schools, officially rewarded Franz Theodor's exemplary 'moral standing' and service by naming him fifth owner of the school court. In recognition of his work for impoverished infants in the Lichtental Parish, Kaiser Francis I ratified his appointment as Imperial Almoner on 13 November 1807.[40] In this role Franz Theodor's quick attentive mind formed the habit of mastering all responsibilities for the poor and the blind in his area, advising on their ability to work, their morality and industry, as well as superintending the execution of basic entitlements such as clothing, bedding, food and per diem. In Vienna from 5,000 to 6,000 unemployed were grant-aided every month at a cost of between 8,000 and 10,000 fl. It is not known whether the position of Imperial Almoner came with remuneration; for certain it carried tremendous responsibility and Franz Theodor worked indefatigably.

After many unsuccessful applications for promotion and a long upward struggle for betterment, Franz Theodor was appointed headmaster of a new school in the Rossau district no. 147 (today Grünentorgasse no. 11), on Christmas Day 1817.[41] Here he remained with his family until his death.[42] On 9 February 1826 he was awarded citizen rights in the city of Vienna in recognition of his outstanding contribution as an educator, his compassion for the marginal and orphans in particular.[43] The nature of these awards acknowledged his incredible capacity for concentrated work, his dedication as a teacher and the progressive nature of his school, into which blind students were integrated with their sighted peers.[44] Coinciding with the death of his son, Franz, in November 1828, he was recommended by his superior officers for the award of the Gold Medal of Honour for Civilians.[45] As promotions, certificates of merit and honours took almost two years to process during the Sedlnitzky era,[46] he did not live to receive this award.

Franz Theodor Schubert applied himself with equal diligence to the begetting of children. Following the death of their first son, Franz Ignaz, he was soon solaced by another, Ignaz Franz (1785–1844), who prompted his parents' marriage on 17 January 1785. In their sixteen years of marriage, Maria Elisabeth gave Franz Theodor fifteen children (see Table 1.3a).

Between the birth of his two surviving sons, Ignaz and Ferdinand Lukas (1794–1859),[47] eight children were born, all of whom died in infancy. In 1788 three children died: Karl was the first to depart through diphtheria on 6 February. The same illness carried off their two-year-old, Elisabeth, and two-month-old Franziska on 13 August 1788. Following the arrival of Franz Karl (1795–1855), Franz Peter Schubert (1797–1828), their thirteenth child, was the next to survive. Known to be Elisabeth's favourite, he must have been a great source of solace when her five-year-old Josef died the

THE FAMILY BEFORE SCHUBERT

Table 1.3a: Franz Theodor Schubert's Children with Elisabeth Vietz

Franz Ignaz	(12 April 1783–27 April 1783)[48]	15 days
Ignaz Franz	(8 March 1785–30 November 1844)	59 years
Elisabeth	(1 March 1786–13 August 1788)	2.5 years
Karl	(23 April 1787–6 February 1788)	10 months
Franziska Magdalena	(6 June 1788–13 August 1788)	2 months
Franziska Magdalena	(5 July 1789–1 January 1792)	6 months
Franz Karl	(10 August 1790–10 September 1790)	1 month
Anna Karolina	(11 July 1791–29 July 1791)	18 days
Petrus	(29 June 1792–14 January 1793)	7 months
Josef	(16 September 1793–18 October 1798)	5 years
Ferdinand Lukas	(18 October 1794–26 February 1859)	65 years
Franz Karl	(5 November 1795–20 March 1855)	60 years
Franz Peter	(31 January 1797–19 November 1828)	31 years
Aloisia Magdalena	(17 December 1799–18 December 1799)	2 days
Maria Theresia	(17 September 1801–7 August 1878)	77 years

following year. There were no more surviving children until Maria Theresia was born in 1801, four months before Schubert's fourth birthday. The total was nine boys and six girls.

Franz Theodor's second marriage to Anna Kleyenböck (1783–1860) brought him five more children, the names of whom were carefully chosen.

Table 1.3b: Franz Theodor Schubert's Children with Anna Kleyenböck

Maria Barbara Anna	(22 January 1814–1835)	21 years
Josepha Theresia	(8 April 1815–1861)	46 years
Theodor Kajetan Anton	(15 December 1816–30 July 1817)	8 months
Andreas Theodor	(7 November 1823–1893)	70 years
Anton Eduard	(3 February 1826–1892)	66 years

One of the hallmarks of Franz Theodor's life was his capacity for firm friendship. His best friend, Ignaz Wagner, who also came from Moravia, stood as godfather to Franz Theodor's first two sons, and Franz Theodor was godfather to Ignaz Wagner's second son, Franz Wagner (22 June 1785–27 January 1786). Each friend supported the other through the loss of several children: all of Ignaz Wagner's six sons died, his third son most tragically, aged six, on 7 May 1793. In the early years of friendship the two families lived together and Ignaz's first wife, Elisabeth Wagner, who came from Silesia, delivered many of Elisabeth Schubert's children. Elisabeth Wagner was godmother to their first daughter in 1786 and when her only surviving child,[49] Klara Wagner, married on 4 August 1799, Franz Theodor again bore witness. Ignaz Wagner was there for his friend when Elisabeth Schubert died on 28 May 1812; four days after her death and two days after her burial, Franz Theodor bore witness to Wagner's second marriage on 3 June. The fellow feeling lasted until Ignaz Wagner's death on 12 February 1826 in *Zum schwarzen Rössel*, Säulengasse no. 3, which Franz Theodor and Elisabeth had bought in 1801 and which they rented after moving to the Rossau district. Since then the value of the house had risen from 3,200 to 6,600 fl. C.M. That Franz Theodor waited to sell it until after Ignaz Wagner died was one of his many quiet acts of kindness and dedication.[50] It was no little life that he led. His extraordinary industry and achievement, his capacity for friendship were passed down to his son, who would claim his entitlement to imagine a different, better reality, just as his father had freed himself from the generational weight of his own history.

2

THE ORIGINS OF A COMPOSER (1797–1813)

'Be proud of your possession, and reflect:
of all that the gods bestow on mortals,
This is your highest gift!
And you will not abuse it.'

       Schubert, 'Lebenstraum' (D 39, 1810)

Franz Schubert was born on the kitchen floor in front of an open fire that led to the anteroom of a one-room, first-floor apartment on 31 January 1797 at 1.30 in the afternoon. He was lucky to survive. His forty-year-old mother, who had lost eight children, greeted his arrival with the astonishment reserved for miracles. Their cramped apartment was one of sixteen in a two-storey courtyard building known as *Zum roten Krebsen* (The Red Crayfish) that was home to fifteen other families. Who was with Schubert's mother when he was born? Who kept the fire alight? For a composer known for his elusiveness and resistance to biography, we are immediately forced to question everything beyond the most basic facts of his birth. We do know that he was the thirteenth child and the youngest son in Franz Theodor's first family – an accident of fate which was to shape his life. In folklore it is always the youngest son who succeeds in the quest: the happy-go-lucky one, the fortunate one marked by fate. In Schubert's childhood it gave him a huge advantage, enabling him to harness the supportive environment of his home to his own developing genius, but it also made him different. He did not naturally belong to a family of schoolteachers and was always the one apart.

The following day Father Johann Wanzka baptized him at the Lichtental Parish in the presence of his parents and his godfather, Karl Schubert. As Schubert was seven when his uncle died, his memories of him would have been selective, but his aunt Maria Magdalena, and their daughter, also Maria Magdalena (24 August 1797–9 October 1820), were very much part of his upbringing.

EARLY MUSICAL CONTEXTS

In the spring of 1801, Franz Theodor and his wife jointly bought the house *Zum schwarzen Rössel* (The Black Horse), situated diagonally opposite their previous residence. When Schubert was four the family moved from his birth house and relocated the school in the autumn of that year. When he was six he was enrolled in his father's school 'where he became distinguished invariably as the first of his peers'.[1] Schubert's confidence in a familiar environment is immediately evident from his father's memoirs, which provide the earliest records of the composer's conviviality. His father's claim that 'from early childhood he delighted in companionship and was never happier than when at his play-hours in a circle of merry schoolfellows' is very much the Schubert we know. It contradicts, however, the trance of loneliness with which Schubert most likely remembered his childhood.[2]

His father's classical training influenced the education that Schubert received, as did the 1805 Education Act which insisted instructors teach by the book and encourage rote learning. During his first two years Schubert applied himself happily to spelling, reading, arithmetic and catechism. During his second two years he developed his literacy skills through reading, dictation, penmanship and the rigours of orthography. Mathematics was never his best subject, but he successfully worked it up. Religion, which was taught by the clergy, was the one course of study that

THE ORIGINS OF A COMPOSER (1797-1813)

escaped his zeal. That music was already his particular specialism gave hints of the composer's later self.

There were two centres of musical activity in Schubert's early life: his family and the church. Two of his siblings had a hand in Schubert's musical upbringing: his elder brother Ferdinand (1794–1859) marvelled at his early musical development and became a lifelong advocate of his work. Schubert's eldest brother, Ignaz (1785–1844), who was responsible for his first piano lessons, admitted that his younger brother quickly outstripped him. In his memoirs he writes, 'I was astonished when after only a few months he announced to me that he had no further use for my teaching and would continue on his own. In fact, within a very short time he progressed so far that I myself had to recognize in him a master who far excelled me and whose standard I would never reach.'[3] Schubert thanked Ignaz for this early instruction with thirty minuets (D 41).

The other person in his family responsible for his musical training was Schubert's father, who taught him violin and played duets with him.[4] Franz Theodor was not slow in forming the highest opinion of his son and grandly determined to give him the best music education in Vienna. Having himself been a scholarship student at the age of seven, he saw no reason to delay. In 1804, when Schubert was seven, Franz Theodor arranged for his son to take lessons in voice, organ and ground bass with Michael Holzer (1772–1826), choirmaster at the Lichtental Parish.[5] Holzer, like Beethoven, had studied counterpoint with Johann Georg Albrechtsberger (1736–1809) and was later described by Anton Holzapfel (1792–1868) as 'a bibulous but competent contrapuntist'.[6] Holzer quickly spotted Schubert's fine treble voice and first employed him as a solo singer in the Lichtental Parish Choir. In Schubert's early years he commissioned from him church music for performance and offered him occasional experience as an organist between 1810 and 1820. That Schubert dedicated to Holzer his Mass in C (D 452, op. 48) – privately on the manuscript in July 1815 and publicly through its publication on 3 September and its premiere on 8 September 1825 – illustrates a characteristic loyalty that was shared by his teacher. 'If I ever wished to teach him anything new,' Holzer famously exclaimed, 'I found he had already mastered it. Consequently, I cannot be said honestly to have given him any lessons at all but merely talked with him and looked at him with mute astonishment.'[7]

Whereas Holzer and Ignaz romanticize Schubert's youthful originality, their accounts are consolidated by his achievements. The first of these accomplishments was an audition with Antonio Salieri (1750–1825), who was court music director and one of the most eminent musicians in Vienna. The interview was most likely arranged by Schubert's father, who, aware of his son's musical promise, sought the advice of a leading figure in music education. Salieri placed Schubert sixth on a list of nine singers auditioned on 28 September 1804 whom he found fit to sing for services in the Imperial Court Chapel.[8] Beside Schubert's name Salieri added the additional remark 'mezzo soprano' and recommended that he re-audition when he was eleven.

MUSICAL LIFE AT THE STADTKONVIKT

The opportunity to do so presented itself in the *Wiener Zeitung* on 28 May 1808 when an audition was announced for 30 September to fill two vacancies for choristers in the Wiener Kaiserliches-königliches Stadtkonvikt, the Imperial and Royal City Seminary, 796 University Square (today Dr.-Ignaz-Seipel-Platz 1).[9] The scholarship granted admittance to the academic Gymnasium, a place the recipient could retain after his voice broke, on the condition that he had distinguished himself academically. A second vacancy for a boy soprano was advertised on 3 August 1808 with auditions scheduled for 1 October.[10] Both auditions were conducted by the choirmaster Philipp Korner (1761–1831), Vice-Kapellmeister, Josef Eybler (1765–1846), with Salieri chairing the board.[11] Schubert wore a pale grey suit for the audition and was mistaken for a miller's son by the other candidates,[12] who surmised he would be accepted on those grounds. It was the exceptional nature of his singing and musicianship that secured Schubert his scholarship as chorister in the Royal Chapel and as pupil at the Stadtkonvikt. He and Franz Müllner (b. 20 August 1797) were declared the best sopranos and also 'placed first in elementary knowledge', with the alto, Maximilian Weisse (1798–1863), next in line. All three were admitted to the seminary.

When his father took him there in November 1808, Schubert was dressed in the school uniform: a dark brown coat with brass buttons and a small gilt epaulette on the left shoulder. Seminarians also wore short trousers and a waistcoat covering the abdomen, along with buckled shoes and a tricorne hat.[13] The sword of sorrow swung widely on the day Schubert entered as boarder. This was a definitive moment. Nothing prepared him for what was happening. His father was consigning him to boarding school. The real meaning of what was unfolding inevitably came when his father said goodbye and Schubert was left there alone,[14] inhabiting a place that was separate, for sure, and not a little sorrowful.

The Stadtkonvikt, a large five-storey building with its courtyard square and adjoining Jesuit chapel, inspired its students with thoughts of grand ambition and great suffering. Founded in 1802 by Emperor Francis I as a new educational institution, it was intended to replace the earlier Imperial Seminary, run by the Jesuits, which had been dissolved by Emperor Joseph II in 1773. Like the Löwenberg Seminary, which educated the nobility in the Josefstadt district, it was run by the Piarist Order, *Fratres piae scholae*. Teaching was conducted by seminarians, many of whom were graduates at the university, or by two older singers who were supported by special endowments and whose duty it was to furnish musicians to the local church, 'Am Hof'. The seminarians shared the same living quarters as the choirboys. The very name 'Stadtkonvikt' – derived from the Latin *convictorium* (boarding house) – signified a communal environment that was home to about 130 boarders. By 1813 it housed forty-eight theologians, twenty philosophers, thirteen Jurists, two medical students, along with fifty-two grammar school students and eight prefects divided into seven houses, each containing a large dormitory of twenty iron beds with a private room for the house prefect.[15]

Franz Innocenz Lang (1752–1835) had been Director of the Stadtkonvikt since 1803. A stern and high-minded individual, he was respected by the students but 'they could not feel any love for him, since he inspired too much fear in them'.[16] Among the benefits that Schubert retained from his scholastic education was a respect for his Piarist masters who had brought the curriculum in line with government requirements. One of these Piarists, Josef Tranz, published a treatise, *Versuch eines Leitfadens der christlichen Religion*, which offers a comprehensive view of the religious teachings that Schubert received at the Stadtkonvikt.[17] In Schubert's time state-authorized instruction books, *Institutio ad eloquentiam* (1779–1848), were used as a basis for teaching rhetoric and poetics, which placed a special emphasis on literature of the Enlightenment, in particular the writings of Klopstock and Lessing. The classes that Schubert attended for the first four years were conducted in Latin, with Greek studied in year four. Four more years, two in the humanities, were followed by two final years in philosophy, which prepared students for entry to the University of Vienna.[18] Josef von Spaun (1788–1865) paid tribute to Lang's educational leadership of the Stadtkonvikt, and observed that he lacked only one quality: 'the ability to judge a pupil's character'.[19] According to Holzapfel, a fellow chorister in the Court Chapel, Lang was bereft of any real musical understanding.[20] Whatever the truth of this claim, he clearly valued the art and took steps at an early stage to establish a student orchestra. In addition to purchasing musical instruments and scores, he attended rehearsals daily and paid for students' instrumental tuition.

When he entered the Stadtkonvikt, Schubert was already a well-behaved little boy in adult company, with a pale face and eyes of a light-brown hue which lent an impenetrable depth, an odd self-sufficiency, to otherwise regular, unremarkable features. His immediate response to the seminary is less clear than one would expect. His brother Ferdinand portrays a very happy Schubert there,[21] while Bauernfeld and Spaun both claim he was miserable.[22] That a boy of his age, suddenly removed from his family, could have been untroubled is hardly conceivable. The snobbery of small boys

THE ORIGINS OF A COMPOSER (1797–1813)

that he had experienced at the audition was new to him, but he countered this difficult start by distinguishing himself. At the end of his first year he was especially commended in music. At the end of his second, he was at the head of his class in music and impressed Ignaz Franz Mosel (1772–1844) so strongly that he sent a report to the Imperial Kapellmeister, Johann Ferdinand Graf Küfstein (b. 1752), requesting that 'especial care should be given to the musical training of Franz Schubert, since he shows so excellent a talent for the art of music'.[23]

The seminary, which the music critic Eduard Hanslick later described as 'a miniature music conservatoire',[24] gave Schubert an entrée into a new musical and social environment which had the air of liberty to care for intellectual and musical matters. Two traditions especially delighted him. The first was singing at the Chapel Royal, where church services were a pleasure rather than a penance;[25] the other tradition was playing in the school orchestra, conducted by Wenzel Ružička (1785–1823). Josef von Spaun, a law student, was leader of the second violins and deputy conductor when Ružička was working as violist at the Court Theatre. Spaun recalled his first encounter with the eleven-year-old Schubert in all his solitude and singularity: 'I noticed how the normally quiet and indifferent-looking boy surrendered himself in the most lovely way to the impressions of the beautiful symphonies we played.'[26] 'His delight in the music and zeal with which he took part made me notice him.'[27] Schubert's memory was retentive. He could quickly commit music to memory, and even keep whole pieces in his head undiminished.[28] Spaun made him his orchestral assistant, 'which involved looking after the stringing of instruments, lighting the tallow candles, putting out the parts, and keeping the instruments and music in good care and condition'.[29] Spaun was only there for Schubert's first year, but the friendship they formed was lifelong. When he returned to Vienna in March 1811, he kept Schubert under his wing and became his mentor in artistic matters. Although as a junior civil servant his salary was low, Spaun was still willing to share the little he had with him, bought him manuscript paper and took him to the theatre.[30] A memorandum in Spaun's hand acknowledges the closeness of their friendship:

'Schubert, at that time, poor and neglected, was for weeks and months supported by a friend at a small tavern.' The feelings that led Spaun to 'share his room – and even his bed – with him' need not have been simply fraternal.

In his reminiscences published in the *Österreichisches Bürgerblatt für Verstand, Herz und gute Laune* in Linz in 1829, Spaun recorded his memories of the seminary orchestra in which Schubert played an increasingly important role. The composition of the orchestra was classical: two flutes, two oboes, two clarinets, two bassoons, two horns, two trumpets, timpani and strings (six first and second violins, three violas, two cellos, two double basses).[31] Schubert swiftly moved from second to first violin; other violinists included Anton Hauer (b. 1796) and Johann Leopold Ebner (1791–1870). Holzapfel and Max von Spaun (1797–1844) both played cello. Georg Franz Eckel (b. 1797) played first flute, Josef Kleindl (b. 1796) first clarinet, and Benedikt Randhartinger (1802–1893) played the timpani. The *status quo* at rehearsals every evening was to play an overture (usually by Luigi Cherubini (1760–1842), Joseph Weigl (1766–1846), Étienne Méhul (1765–1817) or Wolfgang Amadeus Mozart (1756–1791), followed by a symphony – often by Joseph Haydn (1732–1809) or Amadeus Mozart – and conclude with another overture. During Schubert's first year, rehearsals were only cancelled once, when Napoleon laid siege to Vienna on 12 May 1809 at 9 p.m. A howitzer shell fell in University Square; another came through the seminary's roof, eventually landing on the first floor.[32] In later years Spaun recalled the spectacle of the evening with 'glowing cannon balls curving across the night sky' and 'many fires reddening the sky'.[33]

According to Spaun and Georg Thaa, a fellow student of Schubert, the orchestra was good enough to perform early masterpieces of Haydn, Mozart and Beethoven. Of the standard repertoire performed at Thursday evening concerts, Mozart's Symphony no. 40 in G minor and Beethoven's Symphony no. 2 in D major stayed with Schubert for a lifetime,[34] becoming sounding lines out to the world and into himself. During these formative years he developed a taste for symphonies by composers who came from Czech lands, preferring works by Leopold Kozeluch (Jan Antonín Koželuh,

THE ORIGINS OF A COMPOSER (1797–1813)

1747–1818) to those of Franz Krommer (František Vincenc Kramář, 1759–1831), whose works had more popular appeal.[35] He knew dozens of symphonies by contemporary Bohemian composers Adalbert Gyrowetz (Vojtěch Matyás Jírovec, 1763–1850) and Wenzel Pichl (Václav Pichl, 1741–1805), the Moravian composer Paul Wranitzky (Pavel Vranický, 1756–1808) and the German composer Bernhard Heinrich Romberg (1767–1841), all of whom animated and instigated something in his musical imagination.[36] On special occasions such as the birthday or name day of the Emperor (12 February and 4 October) or name day of the Director (1 February), gala performances took place in the aula maxima, one of the most important concert halls in Vienna around 1800 (today part of the Akademie der Wissenschaften, Dr.-Ignaz-Seipel-Platz 2).

Two concerts of note were arranged in Schubert's fourth year, a performance of choral settings from Collin's *Polyxena* set to music by Albert Stadler, which took place on Sunday 15 December 1811 at University Hall and was intended to raise money for the Austrian poet and dramatist, Heinrich von Collin (1771–1811), with a repeat performance given on Christmas Eve. On such formal occasions all boarders were expected to wear the school uniform of dark brown woollen material with epaulettes. Most of the winter concerts were private performances on Thursday evenings, but on fine summer evenings the windows were opened and the sound of the orchestra attracted a considerable audience. Listeners gathered in such crowds that traffic was completely disrupted in neighbouring streets, and Hanacek, the artisan who lived opposite, made available every chair in his house for the women to sit down. Without question these joyful and well-organized amateur evenings gave Schubert a considerable stimulus to compose and contributed greatly to his early precocity. The choice of key and orchestral forces for Schubert's earliest orchestral compositions, his fragmentary sketches for an Overture in D (D 2a) and first movement for a Symphony in D (D 2b) suggest that they were conceived with the school orchestra in mind. His Overture in D minor (D 12, 1811 or 1812) and Overture in D (D 26, 26 June 1812), the parts for which are in private possession, were most likely rehearsed by his fellow students and included in their Thursday concerts.[37] All of these early works attest to a connection between the young Schubert's experiences as a student and his future development as a composer.

In addition to his role as first violinist and assistant conductor of the seminary orchestra, Schubert was head chorister. He experienced the liturgical year in a very intense way, beginning every morning with a Latin mass. On Sundays and feast days, Schubert found himself in the impressive surroundings of the Stadtkonvikt's Baroque chapel, which was designed by the Jesuit brother, Baroque painter and architect Andrea Pozzo (1642–1709). The majesty of the church interior, with its colourful and heavily gilded marble columns, ornate altar, fresco ceiling and side chapel bays, captured his childhood imagination.[38] In contrast to Schubert's fellow choristers – Holzapfel, Kleindl, Weisse and other choirboys who endured the services – Spaun records how Schubert's 'child's mind, already led by nature on the right path, was delighted by those church compositions which were distinguished by intrinsic worth and religious inspiration rather than by outward effect'.[39]

The impact of musical life at the Imperial Court Chapel on Schubert was no less important. Repertory of the Court Chapel for the period 1808–13 when Schubert was chorister was largely a home-grown affair of instrumental masses, offertories, vespers and hymns by composers from Vienna.[40] Schubert sang masses by Georg Reutter the younger (1708–1772) and his students, Joseph Haydn (1732–1809) and his younger brother Michael Haydn (1737–1806). He knew Joseph Haydn's *Heiligmesse* in B flat major and was well versed in the *missa brevis et solemnis* tradition cultivated by Viennese composers. He sang Michael Haydn's *Missa Solemnis in honorem St Francisci* in D minor and an array of masses by Joseph Haydn including his *Missa Brevis* in F, *Missa in honorem Beatissimae Virginis Mariae*, *Missa Santae Caeciliae*, *Missa Sancti Nicolai*, *Missa Brevis St Joannis de Deo* and *Missa Cellensis*. Beyond Vienna, Schubert was exalted by the masses of Wolfgang Amadeus Mozart but also those of

THE ORIGINS OF A COMPOSER (1797–1813)

Joseph Leopold Eybler (1765–1846). Through singing the masses of Salieri's students, Peter von Winter (1754–1825) and Franz Xaver Süssmayr (1766–1803), he became well versed in the tradition of *missae solemnis* on feast days where trumpets and timpani were added to the instrumentation of *missae mediocres* on ordinary days. His knowledge of composers from the Czech lands included the masses and vespers by the Bohemian composer Adalbert Gyrowetz, and a Mass in E flat by Antonín Vranitcký (1761–1820).[41] Schubert sang well-known works by Albrechtsberger, including his *Missa* in D, which introduced him to the Viennese *a cappella* mass that was not necessarily unaccompanied but without independent instrumental parts. Like all young composers, Schubert was eager to find a style of his own and turned for this, in part, to the *a cappella* masses by Leopold Hofmann (1738–1793) and Georg Christoph Wagenseil (1715–1777), which explains his early knowledge of vocal polyphony. The precepts of *stile antico* had relevance for Schubert; his own works embody a complex and fascinating tension between old and new, conservative and progressive.

Schubert entered the world of church music under the best auspices in Vienna. He had a very delicate talent and was writing music which was remarkable for a boy of his age. But he also had the qualities of character to succeed: self-belief, patience, adaptability and the gift of growing by experience. During his four years at the Stadtkonvikt, Schubert sang numerous vespers, graduals, offertories, orchestral masses, cantatas and oratorios by Salieri, who had returned to church music composition after his only son died in 1805 and his wife passed away in 1807.[42] Schubert took part in the first performance of Salieri's Mass in B flat major,[43] his mass in D minor,[44] his 'Lauda Sion Salvatorem' (July 1810),[45] his 'Assumpta est Maria' (December 1811),[46] his 'Magna oper Domini' (12 September 1812), and his Kyrie in C major composed on 22 September 1812. In 1809, Salieri also embarked on numerous offertories: the 'Si ambulavero';[47] 'Audite vocem magnam dicentem';[48] 'Magna et mirabilia' (June 1809); 'Gloria et honor' and 'O altitude divitiarum' (July 1809) and 'Laudate Dominum' (October 1809), all of which his pupil studied and performed.

By the end of his third year, October 1811, Schubert was very much part of Stadtkonvikt life. This is evident from an order sent by the Imperial Secretariat on 28 September asking the Court Music Director to 'convey to Franz Schubert particular satisfaction at his excellent progress in all subjects' and at the same time 'to give due credit to those music-teachers mentioned by the Headmaster and especially to his piano teacher, Wenzel Ružička', from whom Schubert took over as conductor of the orchestra. By 1811 he was also leading the Stadkonvikt orchestra,[49] and he was the leading treble in the chapel choir. Most of the boarders, who had larger social expectations, more money and more confidence, did not perceive his early discontent, probably because Schubert precociously kept it to himself.[50] His friends' recollections of Schubert as a young child capture a stronger sense of his earliest self and bring us closer to the composer's unsatisfied, desiring, lonely, inner core which never left him but dwelt further within behind all kinds of socialized defences. Already as a child, he learnt to put up barriers in order to keep the inwardness intact, which ultimately had the effect of inuring him to sad feelings. Holzapfel, who was in school with Schubert, remembers him as 'one of those deep, quiet natures who [. . .] often seem to have little talent. But even in those days his intellectual activity was far in advance of his years.'[51] Many memoirs of Schubert – such as Georg Franz Eckel's insight into his introspective nature – suggest this childlike gravitas:

> Even in his boyhood and youth Schubert's life was one of inner, spiritual thought, and was seldom expressed in words but, I would say, almost entirely in music. Even with us [. . .] he was silent and uncommunicative, except in matters which concerned the divinity to whom he dedicated his entire life, and whose darling he was. A measure of innate seriousness and calm, friendliness and good nature in him admitted neither friendship nor animosity of the kind usually to be found among boys and youths in educational establishments, and all the less so since, apart from the study and leisure periods, Schubert

almost always spent the leisure hours we were allowed in the music room and generally alone [. . .] Even on the walks which the pupils took together he kept mostly apart, walking pensively along with lowered eyes and with his hands behind his back, playing with his fingers (as though on keys), completely lost in his own thoughts. Violent I never saw him, lively always, although this was more shown in manner and movement than in words, which were mostly short and to the point and revealed a good measure of humour. I seldom saw him laugh; more frequently I saw him smile, sometimes for no apparent reason as if it were a reflection of the inner life of the soul.[52]

Such antinomies in Schubert's character of conviviality and isolation suggest how even from the beginning he was fostering self-contradictory inclinations. For the first time we meet a particular duality characteristic of Schubert's whole life and indeed of his posthumous reputation. Those who were distant to him and only knew him slightly passed over a deep quiet nature whose genius was hidden. Those who were close to him saw beyond this quietude and were irresistibly attracted by the warmth and energy of an independent and unspoiled personality.

While Holzapfel is firm that Schubert 'was by no means among the special favourites of [his] reverend teachers',[53] Eckel believed 'teachers and colleagues loved him because of his quiet and steady behaviour', and 'everyone respected him for his extraordinary musical talent which was already apparent at the time'.[54] The recollection of Schubert's classmate, Albert Stadler, sketched for Ferdinand Luib in 1858, differs from these others, perhaps because he only came to the school in 1812. Stadler remembers with particular interest how Schubert composed during these years: 'he very seldom made use of the pianoforte while doing it. He often used to say it would make him lose his train of thought. Quite quietly, and hardly disturbed by the unavoidable chatter and din of his friends around him, he would sit at the little writing table, bent over the manuscript paper and book of poems (he was shortsighted), bite his pen, drum his fingers at the same time, trying things out, and continue to write easily and fluently, without many corrections, as if it had to be like that and not otherwise.'55 Josef Kenner also remembers how 'he frequently came after lunch to the unheated pianoforte room, where he used to go over Beethoven's and [Johann Rudolf] Zumsteeg's songs with Albert Stadler [. . .] and Anton Holzapfel [. . .] I constituted the lay public and, in this room, too, his first song compositions were run through and underwent their first criticism, and on the occasions when he did not sing and accompany himself, Stadler took his place at the piano and Holzapfel sang.'56 Johann Leopold Ebner was included in such gatherings and remembers how he 'like everyone else [. . .] was electrified by the infinite charm of Schubert's compositions and songs'.57

His elder brother Ferdinand claimed Schubert was writing from the age of ten. Certainly from 'Hagars Klage' (Hagar's Lament, D 5), composed on 30 March 1811, his first Lieder were songs of tension.58 Schubert modelled this episodic setting on Zumsteeg's (1760–1802) 'Hagar's Klage in der Wüste Bersaba' based on Genesis 21, where Abraham's concubine laments over her dying Ishmael in the wilderness before eventually turning to prayer. Zumsteeg's ballads had an almost magic effect on the young composer and were like a plant growing inside him. The older composer's influence on Schubert is evident in the alternation between *arioso* and *recitative*, expressive treatment of the vocal line and *recitativo accompagnato*. Despite a genuine desire to imitate, Schubert's deeper need was to find his own way. His early predilection for passing through many keys to illustrate the protagonist's emotions reveals that his appetite for dramatic presentation has been whetted. The precocity of this melodramatic scene attracted Salieri's attention and inspired him to give Schubert lessons in ground bass.

THE AESTHETICS OF PATRICIDE[59]

Paternity is a powerful motif in Schubert's early Lieder. From his earliest songs onwards, as in a setting of Schiller's 'Leichenfantasie' (A Corpse Fantasy, D 7), his father's presence is keenly felt.

THE ORIGINS OF A COMPOSER (1797–1813)

Example 2.1: Opening of 'Eine Leichenfantasie' (D 7), bars 1–44

The song augurs, with the ghastly clarity of a nightmare, a father's passionate sense of loss at the burial of his child. This vivid evocation of love between father and son called forth some of the most arresting music of Schubert's teenage years and is an example of the composer's early fascination with the macabre. The expressive leading motif, with its chromatically descending ground bass and syncopated, staccato chord groups, heralds a sense of foreboding. The opening gesture of an insistent pulse in a minor key to convey the idea of a nameless fear or threat, the composer's instinctive feeling for the emotional associations of this pulse, the piercing minor seconds and sudden shifts in key to match an infinite complexity of mood and situation, lend the song its dramatic effect and are early signals of Schubert's style (see Example 2.1).

THE ORIGINS OF A COMPOSER (1797–1813)

Many of Schubert's patriarchal songs invite us to contemplate the analysis of the work and play of psyche within them. The energy with which Franz Theodor faced the world was imparted to his son: the decisiveness of thought, the intensity of feeling, the sheer force of his will, all belong to the picture. Although his father presented himself as 'a highly moralistic teacher of young people', he appeared to his children much more 'genuine and humanely distinguished'.[60] This stern but ultimately kind-hearted father, if conservative Catholic, became associated in his son Franz's mind with something like the life-force itself. We hear this in Schubert's music, where his father's presence echoes in settings of Goethe's companion poems, 'Prometheus' (D 674) and 'Ganymed' (D 544, op. 19, no. 3), in which Schubert renders with equal force his father's shortcomings and merits, to the outright defiance voiced in his setting of Gottlieb Conrad Pfeffel's 'Der Vatermörder' (The Parricide, D 10), composed on St Stephen's Day 1811 when Schubert was an adolescent home for Christmas, and family tensions were rife. How might we construe such a setting? 'Der Vatermörder' – which is blazing with rage – tells us something of Schubert's frame of mind, of an aesthetics born of some private rebellion. The syntax of the setting tells us about the surface of the music – we hear in this song Schubert's favourite harmonic sequence, a lamento bass, combined with a syncopated rhythm to produce a hurl of rage and powerful image of flight (see Example 2.2).

A careful analysis of 'Der Vatermörder' shows how skilfully the rhythm is varied to match the mood and sense, but it tells us nothing of the song's essence or its importance in terms of its autobiographical content. Its music 'tells us something about the relationship of the son to the father, in this complex language of signification, at once abstract and concrete, that is the deepest reflection of feeling'.[61] What one hears conforms closely to what we have come to know, through Freud, as the archetypal ambivalence in the son's response to the father. We sense in Schubert's setting the assertion of individualism against authority: the desire for freedom or the instinct of self-preservation, the absolute need to affirm his own essence.

Example 2.2: 'Der Vatermörder' (D 10), bars 1–36

THE ORIGINS OF A COMPOSER (1797–1813)

MEMORIAE MATRIS SACRUM

While Schubert was strengthening his position at the Stadtkonvikt, his mother's health was deteriorating at home. On 28 May 1812 at 4 o'clock in the afternoon she died from *Nervenfieber* – likely typhoid fever – at the age of fifty-five. Schubert was fifteen. It is, of course, impossible to gauge the effect upon the composer. He may, or may not, have been inconsolable. Being taciturn and brought up in a strict regime, he most likely repressed what he felt and kept going. His childhood had been dominated rhetorically by his father, but emotionally by his mother with her down-to-earth nature, her constancy, her tenacity. On his fortnightly visits home, she had always been glad to see him, but how long had it been since he had seen her? Josef von Spaun, with his usual sweet temper, records how Schubert 'had enjoyed but few happy days in his parents' house' but 'nevertheless clung to it with deep affection'.[62]

In an allegorical short story, written on the tenth anniversary of her death (1822) – which Ferdinand posthumously entitled, 'Mein Traum' (My Dream) – Schubert 'remembers' being unable to partake in family festivities and feasting, whereupon his father became angry and banished him from his sight. Real or imagined, the story echoes domestic tensions and the hegemony of the father suggested in 'Der Vatermörder' (D 10), and puts forward the idea that Schubert had been exiled from home before his mother's death.[63] In his allegorical tale he tells us:

> I turned *my footsteps* and, my heart full of infinite love for those who disdained it, I wandered into far-off regions. For *long* years I felt torn between the greatest grief and the greatest love. And *so* the news of my mother's death reached me. I *hastened* to see her, and my father, mellowed by sorrow, did not hinder my entrance. Then I saw her corpse. Tears flowed from my eyes. I saw her lie there like the *old happy past*, in which according to the deceased's desire we were to live as *she had done herself*. And we followed her body in sorrow, and the coffin sank to *the* earth. – From that time on I again remained at home.[64]

How must it have felt to have returned home to see his mother laid out? What can it have meant to a fifteen-year-old boy to have been witness to such a scene? His mother was part of the stable world he had been engaged in renouncing: how could he not have felt desolate at this deeper separation? When her body was laid to rest on 30 May 1812, Schubert wept inconsolably for his mother and himself.

Franz Theodor's heart was no doubt broken, but he was soon consoled by Anna Kleyenböck, to whom he would be married by the first anniversary of Elisabeth Schubert's death, by which time Anna was pregnant. Schubert's composition catalogue suggests he sought refuge from grief in hard and relentless work.⁶⁵ The works of this period have never been interpreted in the light of his dead mother, though many evoke her presence. One month after her death, on 28 June 1812, Schubert wrote his first *Salve Regina* in F (D 27) for soprano, two oboes (or clarinets), two horns, strings and organ. That the parts rather than the autograph exist suggests it was performed as a parting gift in the Lichtental Church, observing the Catholic tradition of the month's mind.⁶⁶ From then on, allusions to his mother run like a red thread through Schubert's settings, from the beautiful 'Hier umarmen sich getreue Gatten' (D 60, 3 October 1813) with its subtle suggestion of a love that transcends death, right through to the May memorials, especially those of 1815: the *Stabat Mater* in G minor (D 175, April 1815), written leading up to the third anniversary of her death, to the mournful first setting of Ludwig Hölty's 'Auf den Tod einer Nachtigall' (D 201, 25 May 1815), written just before her anniversary, to the second setting (D 399, 13 May 1816) recast a year later, which shows the young Schubert at his purest and most concentrated:

Sie ist dahin, die Maienlieder tönte,	She is no more, the songstress
Die Sängerin,	who warbled May songs,
Die durch ihr Lied den ganzen Hain verschönte,	who adorned the whole grove with her singing
Sie ist dahin!	She is no more!
Sie, deren Ton mir in die Seele hallte,	She whose notes echoed in my soul,
Wenn ich am Bach,	when I lay among flowers
Der durch Gebüsch im Abendgolde wallte	by the brook that flowed through the undergrowth
Auf Blumen lag!	in the golden light of evening.

All of Schubert's nightingale songs of May 1815 – the rapturous Hölty setting, 'An die Nachtigall' (D 196) and Seufzer (D 198) composed on the same day, 22 May – link first loves back to his mother and suggest that Schubert may have been dropping back through his own trapdoors.[67] The songs that provided consolation are those in which his private possessions are turned into public images. But songs save as much as they show.

That Schubert's reaction to this bereavement was powerful is evident from his first poem 'Die Zeit', written in May 1813 to commemorate the first anniversary of his mother's death, a reflection on life's transience, an awareness which darkened many Mays.

Schubert's identification with his mother and her Silesian roots was deeply ingrained from childhood. It is certain he would have grown up speaking a Silesian dialect, though his father's Gymnasium training and aspirations would have ensured his sons were instructed in contemporary

Table 2.1: Schubert's First Poem and First-Anniversary Memorial for his Mother, 'Die Zeit' (May 1813)

Die Zeit	Time
Unaufhaltsam rollt sie hin Nicht mehr kehrt die Holde wieder Stät im Lebenslauf Begleiterin Senkt sie sich mit uns ins Grab hernieder.	[Time] flies unrelenting, Once departed, it cannot be retrieved. This fair companion of our days, Will sink with us into the grave.
Nur ein Hauch! – und er ist Zeit Hauch! schwind' würdig ihr dort nieder Hin zum Stuhle der Gerechtigkeit Bringe deines Mundes Tugendlieder!	But a breath! – for such is Time. Let this breath dignify her! Go forth to the throne of justice, Voicing songs of virtue!
Nur ein Schall! und er ist Zeit Schall! schwind' würdig ihr dort nieder Hin zum Sitze der Barmherzigkeit Schütte reuig Flehen vor ihm nieder!	But a sound! – for such is Time. Let this sound dignify Time! Go forth to the seat of mercy, Pouring prayers of repentance!
Unaufhaltsam rollt sie hin Nicht mehr kehrt die Holde wieder Stät im Lebenslauf Begleiterin Senkt sie sich mit uns ins Grab hernieder.	[Time] flies unrelenting, Once departed, it cannot be retrieved, This fair companion of our days, Will sink with us into the grave.

orthography. In Viennese dialect his name 'Franz' voiced 'Franzl' became 'Franzle' in Moravian-Silesian dialect, which was most likely how his mother addressed him. Elisabeth was one of many Silesian immigrants, known locally as 'Schlasinger', who were not so popular in Vienna and settled in ghettos on the outskirts of the city like Lichtental. Schubert's lifelong identification with marginal figures came from his mother, who was the first wanderer he had known. Given the shameful circumstances under which her family had departed,[68] Schubert's mother could hardly have visited her home town and would have understood the experience of being 'chased out' which her son later evoked so vividly in *Winterreise*. That Schubert's mother sang to him is also engraved as an emblem in the Lied, 'Der Tod und das Mädchen' (D 531) and the string quartet (D 810), which cites four bars from the Silesian song of death, 'Gute Nacht, o Welt'. A further example is the song 'Der Wanderer' (D 489, op. 4, no. 1) with its luminous and telling four-bar phrase from the Silesian folk song 'Es jagte ein Jäger'. If history tends to obliterate his maternal lineage, Schubert makes certain that his mother has her place within the legacy of his musical imagination.

REGROUPING

Schubert's first surviving letter was written on 24 November 1812, six months after his mother's death, in which he asks his brother Ferdinand for some monthly money with the appetite of a teenage boy:

> Straight out with what troubles me, and so I will come to my purpose the sooner, and you will not be detained by any precious beating about the bush. I have long been thinking about my situation and have concluded that, although it is satisfactory on the whole, it is not beyond some improvement here and there. You know from experience that we all like to eat a roll or a few apples sometimes, the more so if after a middling lunch we have eight and a half hours to wait for a mediocre evening meal. This wish, which has often become insistent, is now

becoming more and more frequent, and I had willy-nilly to make a change. The few Groschen I get from Father go to the deuce the very first days, and what am I to do the rest of the time? 'Whosoever believeth in Him shall not be put to shame.' Matthew iii. 4. I thought so too. – How if you were to let me have a few Kreuzer a month? You would never miss it, while I in my cell should think myself lucky, and be content. I repeat, I take my stand upon the words of the Apostle Matthew: 'He that hath two coats, let him give one to the poor', etc. Meanwhile I hope that you will give ear to the voice which calls unceasingly to you, the voice of your loving, poor, hopeful and again poor brother Franz.[69]

In contrast to the person we think of as Schubert (his genius, his tragically short life, his prolific output), we are confronted here with a decidedly unromantic corrective of reality. Hunger, poverty and lack of money are the principal themes of his letter and for the second time he referred to his dormitory as an icy prison cell.[70] Life at the Stadtkonvikt was spartan: the old building was freezing in winter and food was insufficient at a time of severe economic deprivation in Vienna. With the loss of their mother, Schubert had sought out Ferdinand as his new emotional and material provider. Ferdinand willingly accepted that mantle.

3

SALIERI, PARTIMENTO AND THE BEGINNINGS OF CREATION

'A teacher affects eternity:
he can never tell where his influence stops.'

Henry Brooks Adams

After Schubert's mother died, Salieri took him under his wing as a private student in his home in the inner city, no. 1154 (today Göttweigergasse 11), on 12 June 1812 (Figure 12).[1] In the privacy of Salieri's home, lessons in thoroughbass and composition, which were free, were held twice weekly, for which Schubert had 'special concession [. . .] as it was contrary to the school rules for a pupil to go out by himself'.[2] Whereas Leopold von Sonnleithner (1797–1873) and many musicologists after him believed Salieri was incapable of teaching Schubert,[3] Salieri's tutelage was in fact extremely pivotal for the composer. The generosity of his guidance during Schubert's four-year apprenticeship from June 1812 to December 1816, three years after he left the Stadtkonvikt, is subtly felt in Schubert signing his early manuscripts in Italian. That Salieri was the only teacher Schubert ever acknowledged is a measure of the importance of his relationship to the composer. On numerous manuscripts between 1813 and 1815 Schubert repeatedly announced himself as a 'Pupil of Salieri', including the title pages of *Des Teufels Lustschloß* (The Devil's Pleasure Palace, D 84, 10 October 1813), *Fernando* (D 220, 27 June 1815), *Claudine von Villa Bella* (D 239, 26 July

1815), *Die Freunde von Salamanka* (D 326, 18 November 1815), as well as on the String Quartet (D 74, 22 August–September 1813) and the ten variations for piano (D 156, completed 15 February 1815). Schubert's gratitude to him is also evident in the musical tribute *Beitrag zur fünfzigjährigen Jubelfeier des Herrn von Salieri* (Contribution to the 50th Anniversary Celebrations of Salieri, D 407), a tripartite cantata for male voices composed for the festivities in Salieri's home on the evening of 16 June 1816. Schubert's text also throws light on his relationship with his teacher.

Table 3.1: Schubert's Text for his Contribution to the 50th Anniversary Celebrations of Salieri (D 407)

Gütigster, Bester!	O you, wise one!
Weisester, Größter!	Most eminent, most gracious!
So lang ich Thränen habe,	As long as I have tears,
Und an der Kunst mich labe,	And feed on art,
Sei beides Dir geweiht,	I dedicate both to you,
Der beides mir verleiht.	Who gave me both.
So Güt' als Weisheit strömen mild	Kindness and wisdom flow from you
Von Dir, o Gottes Ehrenbild,	As God's own image, you are to me,
Engel bist Du mir auf Erden	An angel on earth
Gern' möcht' ich Dir dankbar werden,	I am heartily grateful to you.
Unser aller Großpapa,	Grandfather to us all,
Bleibe noch recht lange da!	Remain with us for a long time!

His love for his teacher is also patent in the reverential tone of the opening two sections arranged for male-voice quartet, followed by a tenor aria with piano accompaniment (Example 3.1a online). The closing section, a canon *a 3*, which pays tribute to Salieri's teaching, is a fine example of Schubert's musical humour where he underscores the words 'Unser aller Großpapa' by impersonating the syllabic sing-song of a child. The tribute concludes with a humoristic prolongation of its final line in the coda, bestowing a blessing of longevity and musically mirroring its sentiment (Example 3.1b online).

Despite Schubert's obvious gratitude to his teacher, his friends continually failed to acknowledge Salieri's influence on him, and the image of the teacher-student relationship that has endured is one largely dominated by Schubert's precocity. Sonnleithner's disparagement of Salieri as an outmoded, mediocre composer of Italian opera with little understanding of church music is completely unfounded. While Salieri dominated Italian opera in Vienna, he moved away from opera in 1805 as a result of the political, social and cultural upheaval in the city, confounded by the personal loss of his only son. His position as Hofkapellmeister at the Imperial Chapel inspired a sheaf of sacred music compositions, many of which Schubert performed. According to Sonnleithner, 'what Schubert lacked was a really accomplished composer to act as teacher and music counsellor, and a fatherly friend to regulate his mode of living, and it was the lack of these which prevented him from attaining that greatness to which nature seemed to have destined him'.[4] But this uncharitable belief is as misguided about Schubert as it is about Salieri. Johann Mayrhofer (1787–1836) similarly misrepresents Schubert as being 'devoid of a more profound knowledge of composition and ground bass' and terms him 'a natural artist'. He interprets Schubert's decision to take lessons with the supreme contrapuntalist Simon Sechter (1788–1867) as proof 'that the famous Salieri did not subject him to any strict schooling',[5] an opinion which has been handed down. Holzapfel also believed that the instruction Schubert received was 'very scanty [. . .] and that, on the whole, it consisted only in the superficial correction of small exercises in part writing, though most of it, and this may have been the most successful part, consisted in the reading and playing of scores'.[6]

EARLY EXERCISES

When one examines Schubert's early exercises, it is immediately obvious that counterpoint formed a central part of his compositional training and Holzapfel's dismissal of 'many incredibly boring old Italian scores'[7] provides the key to Schubert's composition classes. Schubert had studied figured bass with Wenzel Ružička in 1811 and took up this strand with Salieri, whose corrections are evident in the two-part exercises, including the canon, Sanctus (D 56, 21 April 1813). Here Schubert's ambition and experience shine through: from the Allegro (Pleni sunt coeli et terra) he writes in 2/4 against 3/4, already knowing that by putting 2 against 3 he can get the Sanctus sung in a pointed manner (Example 3.2a).

Example 3.2a: Sanctus (D 56), bars 18–24

Despite the grand *fortissimo* cadential closure and codetta-like figure which strives towards a heroic ending, the concluding phrase is undermined by the peculiar IVb-I cadence. IV, which spans bars 79–82, is a major chord (E flat major), and V-I in bb. 71–77 is not conclusive either. There is no perfect cadence, no V-I in root position (and no V chord to conclude). Instead it resolves via a common-tone diminished-seventh chord (bar 84) to a I in first inversion which, along with the absence of a cadence, makes it sound unfinished despite doubling note values in the last five bars (Example 3.2b). Schubert's Sanctus is a good example of his youthful experimentation.

Example 3.2b: Sanctus (D 56), bars 71–86

Salieri's corrections are already evident in the short vocal exercises 'Quell' innocente figlio' (D 17, 1812), 'Entra l'uomo' (D 33), 'Serbate, o Dei custodi' (D 35, also in the choral edition), and in 'Pensa, che questo istante' (D 76). It is not known whether the many revisions of *Der Spiegelritter* (D 11, December 1811) were encouraged by Salieri.[8] He did, however, take a demonstrable interest in Schubert's church music compositions, and his watchful eye is evident in the Kyrie (D 66, 12 May 1813), where many improvements are suggested. The emendation of parallelisms, cross-relations, awkward voice crossings, and other instances of non-idiomatic part writing are also evident in Schubert's instrumental works, including the Overture in D (D 26, 26 June 1812) and the String Quartet in D (D 94, 1811 or 1812).

The various didactic exercises in formal counterpoint which Schubert worked through with Salieri – fugues, imitation exercises, canons – tell us much about Schubert's compositional training and his persistence in mastering the intricacies of imitative writing. The exercises clearly represent only a portion of Schubert's youthful work in the tradition, though no other similar manuscript material has survived.[9] This, however, does not detract from their value as an important record of a teenage prodigy, and it is not Salieri's corrections but rather the methodology behind these early exercises that holds the more intrinsic interest. When the value of Salieri's teaching has, on rare occasion, been acknowledged, his grounding in Johann Joseph Fux's *Gradus ad Parnassum*, through Florian Theodor Gassmann (1729–1774) and the influence of Albrechtsberger's composition manual, *Gründliche Anweisung zur Komposition* (1790), are always recognized,[10] while the Italian tradition is completely overshadowed.[11] While Salieri was a leader in eighteenth-century Italian opera, he was also a much more cosmopolitan composer than is traditionally represented, as is evident in his ability to write operas in three languages. His compositional training was eclectic, but its roots were firmly grounded in the Italian tradition.

Salieri began his own music studies in his home town of Legnago in the province of Verona, where he was taught by his older brother Francesco Salieri, a former student of the composer and theorist, Giuseppe Tartini (1692–1770). He took organ lessons in Legnago Cathedral with Giuseppe Simoni, a pupil of Padre Giovanni Battista Martini (1706–1784), the celebrated Bolognese theorist and pedagogue who was interested in counterpoint and wrote a treatise on partimento,[12] a Neapolitan teaching tradition found in northern Italy. During his years as a choirboy at St Mark's Basilica in Venice, Salieri studied with the organist and opera composer, Giovanni Battista Pescetti (1704–1766), a student of Antonio Lotti (1667–1740), to whom a manuscript containing forty-eight partimenti is attributed[13] and which is beholden to a separate partimento tradition in Veneto.

Everything in Schubert's exercises and early work points to Salieri's knowledge of partimento, an instructional tool that encouraged improvisation as the path to musical fluency. That Salieri practised it as a teacher is evident in his partimento treatise, *Libro di partimenti di varia specie per profitto della gioventù*. Holzapfel's recognition that the most successful part of Salieri's teaching consisted in the reading and playing of scores bears testimony to the kind of compositional training Schubert received. Teachers would assign students partimenti that they would develop at the keyboard (from the nineteenth century onwards also in written form) and explain orally what they had to do. How to realize the partimenti has not been written down, but it is clear Schubert knew how, not only from the five pages of ground bass exercises which have been preserved but also from his manner of composition, where this conception of bass degrees and of modulation is evident even in his latest compositions and offers new insights into his harmony.[14] Here, Examples 3.3a and 3.3b are laden with Salieri's corrections, but Schubert's early manuscripts – especially his first opera and first mass – bear testimony to Salieri's solutions.

Example 3.3a: Schubert's Figured Bass Exercises with Salieri (D 25B)

Example 3.3b: Schubert's Figured Bass Exercises with Salieri (D 25)[15]

Partimento has its roots firmly in musical practice, and more precisely in keyboard improvisation. Schubert's gifts as an improviser of piano dance music and his ability to compose opera so quickly clearly points to this tradition. Given the nature of the partimento tradition, it is impossible to reconstruct the transmission of sources (of which there are three types – partimenti, rules and realizations), which has made the chronology of some of Schubert's early exercises and compositions difficult to determine. For numerous early works there is no surviving autograph. Even where autographs are extant they are not consistently dated nor is contextual evidence always available, despite the advantages of recent paper research. One particular challenge is the loss of Salieri's partimento manual, but the imprint is undeniably there, and we see it predominantly in the steps which are taken from counterpoint to imitative and fugal writing, first as exercises and free composition, to the writing of solfeggios and setting texts by Pietro Metastasio (1698–1782).

From the earliest exercises and compositions preserved from June 1812, it is clear that Salieri's imprint is based on two principles: partimento and counterpoint, in particular a scale-based counterpoint (using scales as part of a *cantus firmus*). Here we see Schubert adding a melodic line to a cantus firmus which Salieri set (Example 3.4a), first with two voices, then starting over with three, then with four, which are grounded in partimento practice. The most striking thing about these exercises is their emphasis on a singing line: the dictum, *chi canta suona* (if you can sing, you can also play) being central to the tradition. This emphasis on line bears testimony to a musical concept, well known among Italian composers, of *il filo*, a (cognitive) thread, like Ariadne's thread which leads Theseus through the Minotaur's labyrinth and guides the listener through the musical composition.[16] Here in these exercises, as in later works, we see Schubert adopting *il filo* as a guiding principle. In two of the three cantus firmi Salieri sets, we see him exploring ways of harmonizing an abridged scale to encourage smooth cantabile voice-leading:

Example 3.4a: Three Cantus Firmi which Salieri Set for Schubert

This partimento principle is at play in the two-part setting of D 25B, Exercise III:

Example 3.4b: Schubert's Realization of Cantus Firmus 2, Exercise III (D 25B)

The three-part setting, D 25B, Exercise I, on the other hand, where Schubert adds a series of 7-6 suspensions in the upper voice resolving on a 6/3 chord against the same cantus firmus, is reminiscent of the 7-6 descending examples by Fedele Fenaroli and Giacomo Tritto:[17]

Example 3.4c: Schubert's Realization of Cantus Firmus 1, Exercise I (D 25B)

Here we see Schubert learning how to think in separate parts and how to keep the music moving. D 25C bears testimony to Schubert's skilful handling of a migrating cantus firmus, a type of counterpoint exercise from Johann Kirnberger (a student of J. S. Bach), for example; of the three possible rotations, moving the pre-existent melody to the bass voice posed, without doubt, the most challenging exercise for Schubert. These cantus firmus exercises are strongly reminiscent of the various species of counterpoint in Fux's *Gradus ad Parnassum*. Example 3.4b is an example of invertible counterpoint while Example 3.4c looks like an exercise in the 4th species (syncopation). Such comparatives not only point to the eclecticism of Salieri's own educational experience but to the overlap between both schools and does not undermine the vital practice of Italian partimento training in Schubert's compositional development, an influence that has virtually gone unnoticed by music historians. This Italian compositional practice represents the true link between Schubert's early pedagogical exercises and fully fledged works of art.

FUGUE AND THE SEARCH FOR SELF-REALIZATION

The highest point of partimento training was instrumental and vocal fugal writing, which was the arrival point of time-consuming written exercises in imitative and invertible counterpoint, and the supreme test of a composer's contrapuntal stamina. In Neapolitan fugal partimenti there are two types of fugue: the easier kind of fugue is the instrumental fugue, usually in fast-moving dance rhythms and idiomatic keyboard textures. The most demanding type is a fugue in vocal style (or *stile antico*), solemn and slow.

Schubert's early keyboard fugues with their fast-moving dance rhythms and idiomatic harpsichord textures are part of the proficiencies of partimento playing and fundamental discipline of learning to improvise fugues. In the summers of 1812 and 1813 Schubert sketched nine keyboard fugues which stand out for their directed but carefree energy, to which training, or the lack of it, is scarcely relevant.

Table 3.2: Teenage Keyboard Fugues, 1812–1813

Fugue no. 1	D 13	fugue à 4	D minor	1812	
Fugue no. 2	D 24a	fugue à 4	C major	summer 1812	
Fugue no. 3	D 24b	fugue à 4	G major	summer 1812	
Fugue no. 4	D 24c	fugue à 4	D minor	summer 1812	Fragment
Fugue no. 5	D 24d	fugue à 4	C major	summer 1812	Fragment
Fugue no. 6	D 25c	fugue à 2	F major	summer 1812	Fragment
Fugue no. 7	D 37a	fugue à 4	B flat major	1813	
Fugue no. 8	D 41a	fugue à 2	E minor	July 1813	
Fugue no. 9	D 71b	fugue à 2	E minor	July 1813	

What is surprising about these fugues is, at first, the scant evidence of Salieri's guiding hand, especially since guidance is in order. The fugues are uneven in quality, the product of a greenish boy struggling to gain experience in fugal composition. One explanation of their episodic nature and absence of a countersubject is that Schubert had not yet appropriated fugal principles which link with his compositional development more broadly. Their lack of a frame and Salieri's lack of corrections can also be explained by the Neapolitan keyboard fugue being an improvised tradition.

Schubert was less solidly trained in writing the much more challenging vocal fugues for which there are no extant exercises. His ability to write *stile antico* fugues is clear from the closing fugue of the Gloria of his first Mass in F major (D 105), but the other three masses he wrote under Salieri's apprenticeship were in the missa brevis tradition (in which there are no extended fugues), which is another reason why the *stile antico* fugue did not become part of his native language. That fugue and double counterpoint were two weaknesses in Salieri's pedagogy casts a doubt on the customary practice of linking his teaching to Albrechtsberger's composition manual which moves from species to free counterpoint, imitation, fugue and double counterpoint, in which Sechter was trained. The superb grounding Salieri passed on to Schubert was anything but dogmatic, and rigidly rooting him in one school is easy prey to over-interpretation. The key point is that Schubert's technical training was rooted in late eighteenth-century Italian theory and aesthetics and that for all the polemics, the basic conception of harmonic structure held by eighteenth-century theorists – Italian, German and French – was a great deal more unified than we have formerly acknowledged. One of the outcomes of partimento training is the prolificacy which we have come to associate with the Italian tradition, and with Schubert, though the connection between the two has never been made.

A third reason, worth considering, is that Schubert was writing fugues in a different tradition. The fugal sketch in E minor (D 41A) is an example of a *fuga regolare* where the answer imitates the subject at the fifth in a complete exposition (which ends at bar 12) that does not contain a real countersubject. The fugue in F (D 25C) also starts off like a regular partimento fugue;

in the exposition, the answer imitates the subject at the fifth and again does not have a real countersubject.

Example 3.5: Fugue no. 6 in F (D 25C)

In D 25C it becomes clear by bar 7 that this is a *ricercata*, a free fugue in which the imitations of the subject may take place at any interval, but generally at the octave, as in bar 23, where the voices enter in stretto. This fugue is also exemplary of Salieri's subjects which usually require uncomplicated transposed (or real) rather than tonal answers. Like the Neapolitan fugues it has an *alla breve* signature, and from the very first answer it is clear that the entries are subject to modification.

Following this preliminary engagement with the fugue, Schubert progressed to vocal fugue writing in the Mass in F (D 24E), a fragmentary score that contains the last 147 bars from the Fugue Cum Sancto Spiritu from the Gloria, though from bar 55 it is no longer texted.[18] The *NSA* connects the fugue with D 24A because Schubert uses this fugue in a simplified and abridged form, but it is also an example of Schubert trying out different solutions to the same subject. The vocal fugue is an example of a *fuga libera*, where the strict imitations are interspersed with free episodes. As is characteristic of partimento fugues of the vocal type, the subject is almost invariably accompanied. The subject of this fugue is quite long (six bars) and its rhythmic drive makes it memorable.

Schubert's keyboard fugue in B flat major, D 37A, is also an example of a *fuga libera* where strict imitations open up into free episodes and, as is common with Schubert's early instrumental fugues, there is no real countersubject. As is characteristic of the Neapolitan fugue, it contains dance-like elements and idiomatic harpsichord textures. The four entries are in ascending order – a convenient arrangement especially for an instrumental partimento fugue. The freedom with which Schubert approaches the fugue swiftly becomes evident after the first exposition, where a second exposition immediately begins (bar 15) with the final two entries in stretto (bar 23). A third increasingly free exposition (bar 26) leads into a fourth fantasia-like exposition on the thematic material. The nature of the section that follows the exposition is anything but clear. To summarize: the long section between the fourth exposition (bar 34) and the final appearance of the theme (bar 52) cannot be described as middle entries separated by episodes, because after the entry in bar 35 there are no complete entries until the recapitulation in bar 53. In this long stretch Schubert's fugal design is neither a formal scheme nor a generative response to the subject; instead, the fragmentation of the subject, together with the continual chromatic shifts and tonal meandering, bring it closer to the fantasia.[19] Schubert deploys cadences, sequences and prolongational harmony in the fourth exposition, but the issue as to how these functions can be analysed as formal determinants is problematic.[20] D 37A is a good example of how attempts to analyse Schubert's early fugues in terms of formal schemes susceptible to architectural description are likely to be insufficient (Example 3.6 online).

Is Schubert already searching for autonomy in writing fugues or identifying techniques and processes beyond their social function? His fugal exposition exercises and tonal answers that he wrote for Simon Sechter in

November 1828 do not corroborate the idea of a lack of formal training but rather his search for a more complex integration of rhetorical, expressive, stylistic and contrapuntal devices from seventeenth- and eighteenth-century theory from Matthisson's stylistic schemes to Fux's models of invertible counterpoint. Counterpoint has always been associated in the thinking of musicians with the profound and the serious, and this gesture is indicative of the gravity of Schubert's musical thought and continual search for self-realization.[21]

CANON AND THE BEGINNINGS OF INTELLECTUAL LIFE

Even before he began his studies with Salieri, the canon had been something of an artistic preoccupation for Schubert, as is evident from his transcription of nine canons by various composers in 1810, including four by Michael Haydn, a four-part canon by Johann Rudolf Zumsteeg, 'Hoffnung Kind des Himmels' from the Singspiel *Elbondocani*, an 'Alleluja' by Mozart (K 553), and two canons on themes by Mozart: 'Laß immer in der Jugend Glanz' (K 484d, D 92) and 'Selig alle, die im Herrn entschliefen' (K 382b).[22] It is clear from the four imitative exercises, which are also canonic in nature, that Schubert achieved fluency very quickly. As is characteristic of partimento training, he made his first attempts at *obbligo* canonical settings with a 'Sanctus' (D 56, 21 April 1813), a canon in three parts 'con coda', and an 'Alleluja' (D 71A, July 1813), where he focuses on the technical task that he must observe for the duration of a composition.

In the partimento tradition, canon was considered the touchstone of harmonic aptitude, a primary test of musical prowess. Schubert's Schiller canons are illustrative of this pedagogical principle, but perhaps more interestingly they are steeped in iconographical references to philosophical practices, which raises many questions about the role of canonic writing more generally in the intellectual life of the period. Musical historiography has generally overlooked Schubert's canons, considering them trivia and unconnected with his development. In recent scholarship on his teacher Salieri, canonic repertoire has also been overshadowed by the prominence given to opera. Yet Salieri's composition of over 180 canons places his work on a spectrum of contrapuntal compendia that can be traced from 1800 to 1819.[23] It is possible, indeed very likely, that canon occupied a much more vital position in musical culture of Vienna and the *Hofkapelle* than has yet been recognized.

From his earliest Schiller canon, 'Schmerz verzerret ihr Gesicht' (D 65, 11 May 1813), Schubert's settings to texts by Schiller show how canon, for Schubert – as for Salieri – served as a central avenue of artistic expression. In his sixteenth year, between 15 April and 15 July 1813, he composed fourteen male-voices settings (TTB) for his lessons with Salieri, most of which are fragments from Schiller's poems, *Elysium* and *Triumph der Liebe*, and all of which give the impression of vignettes by a talented youth in free, declamatory style. The range of dynamics is always expressive and sometimes extreme, varying from *pp* to *fff*.

Schubert's early Schiller settings are a musical realization of an aesthetic philosophical theory in Schiller's *Über die ästhetische Erziehung des Menschen in einer Reihe von Briefen* (1794), which espouses a dialectic interplay between man's material, sensuous nature – or *Sinnestrieb* – and *Formtrieb*, his drive to impose conceptual and moral order on the world. Schiller resolved this dialectic through the concept of *Spieltrieb* which is synonymous with artistic beauty, or 'living form'. In Schubert's Schiller settings this aesthetic regime of art is underpinned by ten harmonic tercets occasionally animated by counterpoint. Scrupulous attention has been paid to the choice of key: the Epigram is in C major; there is a Pastorale (D 57, 'Hier strecket der wallende Pilger' from Schiller's *Elysium*, 29 April 1813) in B flat and a hymn-like tercet (D 55, 'Selig durch die Liebe' from Schiller's *Triumph der Liebe*, 21 April 1813) in A major. Among the most interesting are the canonical settings (three canons à 3): 'Unendliche Freude durchwallet das Herz' (D 54, 19 April 1813) and 'Ein jugendlicher Maienschwung' (D 61, 8 May 1813), which is the one real canon that is lyrical and passionate in style (see Example 3.7):

Example 3.7: 'Ein jugendlicher Maienschwung' (D 61)

A very typical feature of Neapolitan teaching is the search for alternative solutions, whereby the same bass, or the same text, was set several times in different ways. In his three settings of 'Dreifach ist der Schritt der Zeit' from Schiller's *Sprüche des Konfuzius*, we see Schubert searching continually for new and original solutions to the same problem. The second setting of 'Dreifach ist der Schritt der Zeit' (D 69, 8 July 1813) is singular. Treated almost entirely in free polyphonic style, full of shifting, even violent contrasts of light and shade, it is an early example of Schubert's compositional style, even opening on a C major chord when the main key is E minor. The words 'eternally the past stands still' are symbolized by a change of time, from 4/4 to 4/2, and the effect bears testimony to Schubert's familiarity with *a cappella* works of the sixteenth century, to which he was introduced by Salieri (Example 3.8).

Schubert also shared his teacher's skill in reimagining what he learnt from others: the songs recall Mozart's *Gesellige Lieder* and Haydn's canons, and one of Schubert's tercets, 'Zwei sind der Wege, auf welchen der

Example 3.8: 'Dreifach ist der Schritt der Zeit' (D 69)

Mensch', seems to establish this link, as does his third fragmentary setting of 'Dreifach ist der Schritt der Zeit' (D 70, 8 July 1813), which in bar 17 of the manuscript is marked 'Imitatio ad Haydni consuetudinem [in the manner of Haydn], den 8. Juli 1813'. That these settings were part of a living tradition in the musical culture of Vienna is suggested through the existence of a bass part for seven Schiller tercets and the canonical setting, 'Ein jugendlicher Maienschwung' (D 61),[24] and later evidenced in the memoirs of Anselm Hüttenbrenner (1794–1868):

> At the same time as Schubert and I enjoyed Salieri's instruction, the composers Stuntz from Munich, Panseron from Paris, Aßmayr, Randhartinger and Mozatti also took part. [. . .] Schubert, Aßmayr, Mozatti and I agreed to sing a new quartet for male voices, which each of us had composed, every Thursday at Mozatti's who kindly acted as host. On one occasion Schubert came without a quartet but, as he received a slight reprimand from us, he immediately wrote one in our presence; Schubert attached very little importance to these small *pièces d'occasion* and scarcely six of them can still be in existence.[25]

Hüttenbrenner's estimate of a half-dozen polyphonic choruses – as opposed to the one hundred male-voice settings Schubert composed – illustrates how little Schubert's friends realized the extent of his achievement, even in a genre with a remarkably high percentage of premieres in his lifetime. That Schubert was the most important Viennese representative of the *Liedertafel* tradition, founded in 1809 in Berlin by Carl Friedrich Zelter (1758–1832), perhaps explains Hüttenbrenner's unwillingness to acknowledge it.

SOLFEGGIO AND SCHEMATA

Once students achieved a certain fluency in partimento and counterpoint, they were allowed to make their first attempts in free composition. A widely used method was to begin with a short solfeggio, a vocal exercise for one or more voices and basso continuo which, like partimenti, were a very popular Neapolitan speciality. Although none of Schubert's youthful solfeggi have survived, a later singing exercise for two voices and figured bass (D 619), composed for Marie and Karoline Esterházy (1805–1851) in Zseliz, July 1818, is a clear example of an exercise that could have been developed into a work of art; it bears testimony not only to Schubert's familiarity with the genre, but also to a different kind of mastery.

Example 3.9: 'Solfeggio' (D 619)

In his early compositions we also find evidence of Schubert internalizing standard bass schemata from partimenti exercises which he then uses as basses for his written compositions. One harmonic schema which recurs frequently in both the songs and instrumental works can be represented as follows:

Example 3.10: Lamento Bass Schema

Here the chromatically descending bass line, which is also used as an independent motif in, for instance, the Fugue in C major (D 24D) and in the first movement of Schubert's String Quartet in C major of March 1813 (D 46), derives from a familiar ground bass, the lament tetrachord, used by Baroque composers:[26]

Example 3.11: Fugue in C major (D 24D), subject

Example 3.12: String Quartet in C major (D 46/i), bars 1–7

The association of this trope with death is long established by Purcell in *Dido and Aeneas* ('When I am laid in earth'), Pergolesi's *Stabat Mater* and Bach's B minor mass (Crucifixus). It is significant, then, that Schubert uses the lamento topos in various forms and tempi in four episodic songs, all of which are associated with death: 'Hagars Klage' (D 5), 'Des Mädchens Klage' (D 6), 'Leichenfantasie' (D 7) and 'Der Vatermörder' (D 10, Example 3.13).

Example 3.13: 'Der Vatermörder' (D 10), bars 125–8

In 'Hagars Klage (D 5, Example 3.14) the harmony is quite striking, modulating from E major to F sharp minor (the 6/4 on C sharp) followed by a Neapolitan 6th instead of V.

Example 3.14: 'Hagars Klage' (D 5), bars 223–8

A diatonic version, the Phrygian tetrachord, forms the opening gesture of his canonical sketch, 'Das Grab'. This association of the lamento bass with Death continues in Lieder composed after his lessons with Salieri; examples include 'Harfenspieler I' (D 478); 'Fahrt zum Hades' (D 526); 'Der Jüngling und der Tod' (D 545); 'Gruppe aus dem Tartarus' (D 395); 'Mignon I' (D 394 and D 726); 'Mignon II' (D 395 and D 727); 'Lied der Mignon' (D 489 and D 877); 'Der Wegweiser' (D 911); and 'Kriegers Ahnung' (D 957).

The pattern pervades Schubert's sacred and instrumental works. It functions very prominently, for example, in the 'Crucifixus' in the A flat major mass (D 678) and the subsequent 'judicare vivos et mortuos' sections of the Credo;[27] the lament descending tetrachord which opens the Quartettsatz (D 703, C^1–Bflat–Aflat–G) dominates the entire movement. A similar progression, in which chromatic lines move in the opposite direction, is found in Schubert's Piano Sonata in A minor (D 845), op. 42, first movement:

Example 3.15: Piano Sonata in A minor (D 845/i) op. 42, bars 32–9

In later years we see Schubert deviating from this pattern. An example is found in the falling chromatic fourth bass of the principal idea for the G major Quartet (D 887, Example 3.16a) harmonized as G–D^6–F–C^6–E flat–D, where the dominant harmony is simply delayed by a 6-4 chord and which Schubert continues indefinitely in the development (bars 168–77, Example 3.16b, and 189–98, transposed up a semitone and spanning a tenth). What is striking in this harmony are the F and E flat perfect chords and the subdominant 'embellishment' in the major.

THE AESTHETICS OF RESETTING

The next step in partimento training was the composition of ariette, usually on texts by Metastasio. Of Schubert's early settings of texts from Metastasio's operas and oratorios, eleven choral settings in different styles have survived, as well as one bass aria and three ariette for soprano in which Schubert had to write the voice part in the old-style clef in strict accordance with the rules. While Spaun believed Metastasio's texts 'left the intensely ardent composer, who scarcely understood the language, cold and his efforts in this line had but little success',[28] Salieri's influence on the composer is much more significant than he suggests.[29] Salieri was one of the most important

Example 3.16a: String Quartet in G major (D 887/i), first subject, bars 15–24

Example 3.16b: String Quartet in G major (D 887/i), bars 168–77

teachers of his generation; that Beethoven sought his advice when contemplating writing an opera bears testimony to his acknowledged expertise in text setting. Spaun's belief that 'Salieri entirely disapproved of the very form of composition to which Schubert was drawn, namely German song'[30] should not be taken at face value. Although Spaun is a reliable witness, it shows his ignorance of Salieri's encouragement of the Schiller settings and his belief that Schubert should apply what he had learnt to original compositions. Spaun's remark that 'Salieri begged Schubert [. . .] no longer to concern himself with compositions of this kind but rather to husband his melodies until he was older and more mature'[31] shows Spaun did not realize Salieri himself composed Lieder and that Schubert had studied Salieri's settings very carefully and imitated them in his own works. 'Trinklied' (D 148) not only shares the same text by Ignaz Franz Castelli as Salieri's setting[32] but also the same C major tonality, strophic form and forces: solo tenor, male-voice choir, which Schubert expands with two tenors and a bass. 'Der Zufriedene' (D 320) shares the same text by Christian Ludwig Reissig as Salieri's rendering, but also the same A major tonality, 2/4 metre, strophic form and triplet accompaniment motifs.[33]

Spaun's comment, however, unwittingly touches on the importance of the series of exercises in text setting which Schubert undertook with Salieri and the role they played in diverting his attention away from Zumsteeg and the academic *Gesang* to more Italian melodic forms. While Schubert's early Metastasio texts are conventional rhetorical pieces that lack the freedom of his later Italian works in which he parodies the Italian musical idiom, their sense of line, *il filo*, is central to partimento pedagogy and Schubert's development. He made nine versions of an aria, 'Quell' innocente figlio' (D 17, one soprano solo, one duet, three tercets and four SATB quartets, Example 3.17 online),[34] from Metastasio's oratorio *Isacco*, the first of which shares melodic and harmonic gestures with his first lyrical song, 'Der Jüngling am Bache' (D 30) composed as early as September 1812 (Example 3.18 online).

This first Schiller setting marks the evolution of a new lyricism in Schubert's style and shows a sensibility which is at once energetic and intensely reactive, but is still a long way from achieving the highly individual idiom that has become so closely associated with Schubertian song (Example 3.19 online).[35] In 1821 Schubert acknowledged the personal and musical influence that Salieri had on his development of this style when he dedicated the opus 5 Goethe Lieder 'most respectfully' to his teacher.

As with the Schiller canons, we see Schubert setting the same text repeatedly in search of different solutions, and Salieri's numerous corrections in textual declamation. In addition to the nine settings of 'Quell' innocente figlio' (D 17), there are six settings of 'Entra l'uomo allor che nasce' (D 33, one soprano solo, one duet, one tercet and three SATB quartets), two settings of 'Serbate, o Dei custodi' from Metastasio's *La Clemenza di Tito* (D 35, for SATB and one tenor solo), two soprano settings of Timante's aria 'Misero pargoletto' from *Demofoonte* (D 42), and two versions for bass of Fronimo's aria 'Pensa, che questo istante' from *Alcide al bivio* (D 76). This practice of recomposition is found in one of the last exercises Schubert completed with Salieri in December 1816. Schubert's 'Vedi quanto adoro' (D 510), an aria and recitative for soprano and piano, is a setting of a text from Metastasio's *Didone abbandonata* (Act 2, Scene 4) which presents a similar scene to Donna Elvira's scene in Mozart's *Don Giovanni* (Act 2, Scene 4d): here Dido feels deeply that a life without Aeneas would be meaningless and implores him not to leave her. The melodic gestures of Schubert's setting suggests he was familiar with Salieri's 1803 setting of Dido's aria which he had published as number 9 of his *Dodici Divertimenti Vocali*.[36] Salieri had Schubert practise the art of Italian declamation in Dido's aria[37] no fewer than four times and the manuscripts of the first three contain numerous corrections in Salieri's hand.[38] The great emphasis Salieri placed on textual declamation is evident from his corrections and confirmed by Mosel in his memoirs:

> When they were alone, Metastasio allowed [Salieri] to declaim large scenes from his opera and oratorio 'which' Salieri admitted, 'had served as a completely useful schooling in declamation', a school which – as

Metastasio intended – to everyone, who wants to educate themselves in song composition, is completely necessary.

When Schubert transcribed the fourth and final fair copy of 'Vedi quanto adoro' (D 510) and gave it to Salieri in the final month of his apprenticeship, in December 1816, it was a gesture of gratitude for all he had learnt from him, in particular the practice of resetting, which would prove one of the most enduring layers of influence.

Salieri very cleverly encouraged resettings not only of Italian texts but of texts that his precocious and productive student loved. Even very early Lieder were revisited many times and there are more multiple settings of Schiller than for any other poet. Schiller's intellectuality inspired Schubert as he strove to match the poet's challenges in multiple settings of 'Des Mädchens Klage' (D 6, 1811/12; D 191, 15 May 1815; and D 389, March 1816); 'Der Jüngling am Bache' (D 30, 24 September 1812; D 192, 15 May 1815; and D 638, April 1819); 'Thekla' (D 73, 22–23 August 1813, and D 595, November 1817); and 'Das Mädchen aus der Fremde' (D 117, 16 October 1814, and D 252, 12 August 1815). Many resettings were composed on the same day or one day after the next. The three settings of Schiller's 'Dreifach ist der Schritt der Zeit' (D 43 TTB; a canon D 69 and a tercet D 70) were all composed on 8 July 1813. Goethe's 'Meeresstille' (D 215a and D 216) were composed on 20 and 21 June 1815, and Ludwig Kosegarten's 'Abends unter der Linde' (D 235 and D 237) on 24 and 25 July 1815. The TTB setting of Hölty's 'Totengräberlied' (D 38) was most likely composed in January 1813 shortly before the Lied (D 44) on 19 January 1813. And his TTB setting of Schiller's *Elysium* ('Unendliche Freude durchwallet das Herz', D 51) and canon D 54 were composed on 15 and 19 April 1813, respectively.

As is characteristic of partimento training, it was not merely a matter of multiple settings but settings for different voices: Schiller's 'Frisch atmet des Morgens lebendiger Hauch' (D 67), composed for TTB on 15 May 1813, was reconceived as a Lied (D 402) on 18 March 1816. The setting of 'Auf den Sieg der Deutschen' ('Verschwunden sind die Schmerzen', D 81), composed for solo voice, two violins and cello in autumn 1813, was reimagined as a TTB canon (D 88) on 15 November 1813. Likewise, Schubert's solo settings of Matthisson's 'Erinnerungen' (D 98) and 'Andenken' (D 99) were reconceived in May 1816 as TTB settings: 'Andenken' (D 423) and 'Erinnerungen' (D 427). An interesting example of returning to texts is Schubert's TTB setting of Hölty's 'Mailied' ('Grüner wird die Au', D 129), composed between March and May 1815, reimagined as a Lied (D 503) in November 1816 and in between as a duet for two voices or two horns (D 199) on 24 May 1815. Two days later Schubert reconceived his Lied fragment for Theodor Körner's 'Der Morgenstern' (D 172) from 12 March 1815 as a duet for two voices or horns (D 203) on 26 May 1815.

Although most of Schubert's resettings date from his years of 'apprenticeship' with Salieri, this practice of multiple settings as one of the hallmarks of partimento training remained with him throughout his life, though his motivation obviously changed. Famous examples include his two settings of Goethe's 'An den Mond' (D 259), from 19 August 1815 and (D 296) which was reimagined after February 1820; his multiple settings of Mignon and the Harper's songs from *Wilhelm Meisters Lehrjahre*; his five settings of 'Gesang der Geister über den Wassern' (D 484, D 538, D 704, D 705, D 714, op. posth. 167) and six settings of 'Geistes-Gruß' (originally composed as D 142 in March 1816 and newly revised for publication as op. 92/3 in July 1828). In particular, poems by Schiller and Goethe invited multiple settings, but Schubert also returned to Matthisson and Hölty texts in his early years. Interesting examples of how this partimento practice remained with him long after his lessons with Salieri include his setting of Franz von Schober's 'Frühlingsgesang' (D 709) originally composed as a TTB setting before 1822 and reimagined as D 740, op. 16/1, for TTBB in early 1822; and the two settings of Johann Pyrker's 'Die Allmacht' (D 852, op. 79/2, August 1825) and (D 875A, January 1826), the second sketched for SATB with piano. Additional examples include his four settings of Schiller's 'An den Frühling' (D 283), composed on 6 September 1815 before the TTB setting (D 338) in 1816, and two versions of D 587 in October 1817. A further example is his return to Schiller's 'Hoffnung' ('Es reden und träumen die Menschen viel', D 251), composed on 7 August 1815 and reimagined as D 637, op. 87/2 in 1819.

Beyond his early exercises with Salieri and the practice of resetting, Schubert's engagement with the Italian tradition spans his entire compositional career more selectively but also more explicitly over the years. Recent research has traced the beginnings of this reception in the two overtures in Italian style from November 1817,[39] but it actually reaches further back in his compositional training. Spaun's belief that Metastasio's texts 'left the composer cold'[40] is contradicted by Schubert's return to Italian texts in the four canzone (D 688) to texts by Vittorelli and Metastasio which he composed without commission in January 1820 – ironically for Franziska Roner von Ehrenwerth, Spaun's future wife. Schubert returned to Metastasio again in his *Drei Gesänge für Baßstimme mit Klavier* (D 902) op. 83, written in 1827, and his selection of the Italian text 'Al par del ruscelletto chiaro' for his *Kantate für Irene Kiesewetter* (D 936), for TTB, SATB Choir and Piano Four Hands, composed on 27 December 1827, his final Christmas, in celebration of the recovery of the daughter of Raphael Georg Kiesewetter von Wiesenbrunn (1773–1850).

What Spaun fails to recognize, and what is only coming to light in recent research, is Schubert's versatility as a composer, a significant part of which embraces Italianate reception. His *Drei Gesänge* (D 902) op. 83 reveal Salieri's imprint not only through Schubert's embrace of a stylistic curve from opera seria, oratorio and opera buffa, but also through the recent discovery of early versions of the first two songs (in an auction catalogue listing) which date from Schubert's lessons with Salieri. The song set is a characteristic example of Schubert returning to sketches and reworking them for publication, a practice which is in keeping with the aesthetics of resettings that he had learnt from his teacher.[41]

4

THE MAKINGS OF A COMPOSER (1812–1813)

'sic itur ad astra'
('thus one journeys to the stars')

Virgil, Aeneid

EARLY STEPS IN COMPOSITION: SUCCESS AND FAILURE

The Stadtkonvikt supplied Schubert with the necessary distance to develop. As his soul threw off his boyhood he went through a series of violent changes: the sudden loss of his mother, which was a catalyst in the unfolding of his own compositional truth, and a very gradual unshackling from his father's influence. He emerged from this period sombre and more inward, except with his close friends to whom he exhibited his candour and youth. Although he enjoyed the frivolity of friends, Schubert was already showing that proclivity for aloneness which characterizes many composers, a need for deep silence in which creativity can arise. Anton Holzapfel remembers his exceptional powers of concentration as being 'far in advance of his years'.[1]

The marginalia in his hand on the alto part of Peter Winter's first mass – 'Franz Schubert crowed for the last time, 26 July 1812' – marks the end of an era as head chorister and a decisive moment in his psyche and physical development when boyhood changed to adolescence. As he was no longer under obligation to attend rehearsals, he had extra time for composition and began exploring various genres at high speed. The day after leaving the choir Schubert began work on a Piano Trio in B flat (D 28), which preoccupied him from 27 July to 28 August 1812. By September of that year, he had to his credit an impressive number of compositions. His earliest completed works present us with stylistic dilemmas. Some reveal fresh stylistic influences, others reveal the imprint of Salieri's teaching; all offer a lens through which we can view his development.

THE GROWTH OF IMAGINATION: SCHOOLHOUSE STRING QUARTETS

Around September 1812 Schubert also began to write string quartets, which are a substantial achievement of his boyhood.[2] Ferdinand played his part in the evolving mythology surrounding these works, claiming Schubert started composing string quartets for Michael Holzer when he was a boy soprano in Lichtental. Two of these quartets, D 19 and D 19a from 1810/11, survived until the end of the nineteenth century when they were not considered worthy of inclusion in the old Complete Works edition and both manuscripts have been lost since then. But the remaining quartets have been preserved and there is a notable growth in technique from D 32 and D 36 when he began taking lessons with Salieri (Table 4.1a and b). In the aftermath of his mother's death, Schubert turned to composition

Table 4.1a: Schubert's Schoolhouse Quartets, 1810/11–September 1813

String Quartet no. 1	D 18	G minor/B flat	1810/1811
String Quartet no. 2 (no. 7)	D 94	D major	1811?
String Quartet no. 3 (no. 2)	D 32	C major	Sept/Oct 1812
String Quartet no. 4 (no. 3)	D 36	B flat major	19 Nov 1812–21 Feb 1813
String Quartet no. 5 (no. 4)	D 46	C major	3–7 March 1813
String Quartet no. 6 (no. 5)	D 68i/iv	B flat major	8 June–18 Aug 1813
String Quartet no. 7 (no. 6)	D 74	D major	22 Aug–Sept 1813

THE MAKINGS OF A COMPOSER (1812–1813)

Table 4.1b: Schubert's Schoolhouse Quartets, November 1813–1816

String Quartet no. 8 (no. 10)	D 87	E flat major	Nov 1813
Quartet movement	D 103	C minor	23 April 1814
String Quartet no. 9 (no. 8)	D 112	B flat major	5–13 Sept 1814
String Quartet no. 10 (no. 9)	D 173	G minor	25 March–1 April 1815
String Quartet no. 11	D 353	E major	1816

as he would in later times of crisis. These works document a journey out of grief, an apprenticeship, an adventure of a musical mind in the making.[3]

Quartets written between November 1813 and 1816 (Table 4.1b) show a heightened degree of linguistic craftsmanship and are stepping stones to the three masterly quartets of 1824–26:

Table 4.2: String Quartets, 1820–1826

Quartettsatz (no. 12)	D 703	C minor	Dec 1820
String Quartet no. 13	D 804	A minor	Feb–beg. Mar 1824
String Quartet no. 14	D 810	D minor	Mar 1824
String Quartet no. 15	D 887	G major	20–30 June 1826

In between, Schubert would write the Allegro assai in C minor (Quartettsatz, D 703), an unfinished quartet, whose bold design and intensity of expression is rich illustration of his development.[4]

From his very first quartet Schubert handles the ensemble with the familiarity of lived experience. His quartets were tailored to the family ensemble: Franz Theodor played cello, Ferdinand first violin, Ignaz second violin and Franz Schubert viola.[5] This family quartet was typical of the practice of domestic quartet playing which flourished in the early nineteenth century, especially in musical Vienna. *Hausmusik* was an important part of life for the professional classes, part of home erudition and a social pastime exclusively among men. Intended for domestic settings, these works were performed *prima vista* by Schubert's family quartet on Sunday afternoons on his fortnightly visits home. The challenge of writing for a medium performed in a domestic forum, where every note counts, enabled him to gauge the impact of what he had written.

These early quartets, in all their variety, are distinguished by their structural ambiguity, inventiveness and a marked leaning towards monothematic processes. It is fascinating that the inner movements consistently follow convention, while the outer movements consistently defy tradition. Do these string quartets exude inexperience or experimentation? Does their sovereignty of expression mark the end of a period of rapid growth or a conscious break with youthful experimentation? Do they look back to Baroque precedents in their preference for a unitary conception of musical form? Or do they reach towards the dialectic of tonal contrast that characterized classical thought? However one answers these questions, their exhilaration and brazen originality offered Schubert an escape from grief after his mother's death and a concomitant disengagement from academic life. The year 1812–13 was, for Schubert, a period of immense change.

Much has been made of Schubert's later claim about paving his way to a symphony by writing string quartets, whereby the A minor and D minor quartets (D 804 and D 810) are proposed as preparatory works for the 'Great' C major Symphony (D 944).[6] But the key to understanding this much debated passage in his 1824 letter to Leopold Kupelwieser is found at the very beginning of his compositional career in these early string quartets – and D 74 in particular – where preliminary studies lead to Schubert's First Symphony (D 82) and the process became associated with raising the bar of achievement. Domestic music making in Schubert's family typically crossed generic boundaries. Sometimes his family were a close-knit quartet, and when a friend joined they became a quintet. On other occasions when a group of friends gathered they became a chamber orchestra, opening up the choice of performance repertoire. That the family quartet played arrangements of Haydn and Mozart symphonies explains the orchestral conception of several passages in his early quartets.[7] Schubert himself crossed generic boundaries in his earliest writings, composing an overture for string quintet (D 8) and dances for string quartet (D 86 and D 89). Ferdinand partook in this familial and social practice by arranging Schubert's earliest violin sonatas for orchestra

(D 384, D 385 and D 408). This breadth of sonority would remain a hallmark of his chamber music up to his very last quartet in G major (D 887).

There is very little documentation of Schubert's day-to-day life from 1811 to 1814, yet we can tell so much about the unfolding of his creativity from a careful reading of these early quartets. String Quartet no. 1 in G minor/B flat major (D 18) dates from the second half of 1810 when Schubert was thirteen years old and already imagining music hovering between keys. Its opening bars announce this tonal instability as the introductory Andante masquerades in C minor before establishing the Presto vivace subject in G minor. This monothematic movement, the theme of which is reprised with a sequence of unfolding transitions (from bar 175ff) through E flat minor, G flat major, B minor and E flat minor, concludes on two D major chords. Only in the coda is the music pointedly tonicized.[8] That the form of this movement has been described as a chain of variations, or compared to the opening movement of a suite, is entirely characteristic of Schubert's early string quartets. At this stage of his development Schubert does not have a firm grasp of the principles of tonal contrast and synthesis at the heart of sonata form.[9] Nonetheless, the unfolding of musical materials, however unconventional, is not arbitrary and unveils a very accomplished development of the main motif. If anything, the inner dynamic is closer to J. S. Bach, whose influence is apparent not only in the contrapuntal framework, but in its allegiance to an essentially unitary conception of musical form and a remarkable intensification through harmony and line.[10] This is apparent in the thematic economy of Schubert's movement and its unorthodox tonal argument. In the final rondo movement, D flat colours the movement significantly, with the main tonality, B flat major, established through the introduction and coda. Most intriguing is the way in which Schubert frames this string quartet with contrapuntal themes, a canon in the first movement and again in the finale, which evince a young, eclectic composer drawing on a wide range of repertoire. More than this, his early efforts were encouraged and performed: parts dated 1812 exist in an unknown hand, but the third-movement parts for first and second violins and viola are in Schubert's hand (Example 4.1 online).[11]

String Quartet in D major (D 94), written in the summer or autumn of 1811, is the earliest example of Schubert's self-borrowing when the cantilena from bars 108ff and 281ff of his Overture in D (D 12, Example 4.2a online) re-emerges at the end of the exposition of D 94/i (Example 4.2b online). Both Schubert's handwriting and unfolding of musical material place these neighbouring works much closer together than the original Deutsch catalogue number suggests. D 94/i also poses the question as to how far Schubert was consciously engaging with sonata form. The second subject resonates in the tonic (bar 83) and it is the first subject, rather than the second, which is restated in the subdominant towards the end of the exposition. The three statements of the main theme (bars 1–28, 29–44 and 45–53) are reordered in the recapitulation (bar 168ff) which opens in the key of C major, ♮natural VII (or more generally, ♭flat VII). Schubert bypasses the second subject in favour of reordering and reimagining the expositional material (bars 168–196, 251–302 and 348–356), which he interspaces with new episodes and material. That the second subject is treated in exactly the same way in D 12, but restated in the dominant, is one of many invitations to a comparative analysis of Schubert's early works.

String Quartet in C major (D 32), composed in September/October 1812, is a further act of retrieval where the trio of the third movement is borrowed from a suite of piano dances (D 128, Examples 4.3a and 4.3b online). In contrast to the unified rondo form of D 94/iv, this opening movement takes on aspects of a ritornello as the main motif is continually reprised in the tonic.[12] The eclecticism of Schubert's quartet and improvisatory embrace of a sonata-form principle is announced through an unexpected excursion into the subdominant from which the main motif metamorphoses into a second subject in the key of IV (bar 40), swiftly returning to the tonic where it dallies before veering to the dominant. Already Schubert's ability to surprise is putting his audience to the test. Any allusions to sonata form are immediately cancelled out in the reprise of D 32/i, where an expositional structure plays no role. Haydn's C minor Symphony no. 78/i – readily available and arranged for string quartet – serves as a touchstone for Schubert's minor-mode finale, as it does for his Overture for String Quintet (D 8). Schubert's assimilation of Haydn's form affirms a deeply held reverence for the work, yet there is no sense of his musical forefather as lawgiver.[13] Instead, monothematicism – where the second subject characteristically evolves from the first – combined with inscrutable harmonic originality, augur Schubert's ability to forge a new aesthetic which challenges that legacy.

Six or seven weeks later, on 19 November 1812, Schubert commenced his fourth String Quartet in B flat major (D 36), which he completed on 21 February 1813, just three weeks after his sixteenth birthday. It may have been performed at his father's wedding to his second wife, as its first violin part is dated 5 April 1813. But even if it were written for a public occasion, the privacy of Schubert's language raises tantalizing analytical questions. Does his first movement merge monothematicism with sonata-form principles? Is its second subject related to the main fanfare motif or is this one of those very rare movements that are based entirely on only one theme (Example 4.4 online)? If so, are the exposition, development and recapitulation of this theme ritornello variations or a breach in the sonata aesthetic?[14] The Allegretto finale, which combines a rondo with sonata-form principles, is altogether freer and more personal than the opening movement. The thoughtful Andante in 6/8 time and B flat major essays a recognizable Schubertian trait when it shifts into the remote key of C flat major (bars 29–30) and the intensity of the gesture is keenly felt. Similarly, the transition in the Trio which relocates from D major to the flattened sixth, B flat, pivoting on a repeated octave D (Trio, bars 1–2), augurs the composer's mature manner in D 944/iii.

A few months after completing his fourth String Quartet in B flat major (D 36) Schubert composed an opening Allegro and a Finale that are usually regarded as a separate, incomplete work. Given Schubert's critical sense and patterns discernible in his work habits, it is worth reconsidering the historical position of the catalogued String Quartet in B flat major (D 68).[15] Isn't it much more characteristic that its two exiled movements were intended to replace the cornerstone movements of D 36, to which they are superior? The three sketches for an Andante D 36/ii and later addition of a third movement, Minuet in D major, support this proposal of ongoing revision.

The two orphaned movements composed between 8 June and 18 August 1813 and catalogued as D 68/i and iv, show Schubert casting around for a new voice (Example 4.5 online). The gravity of the opening movement is declared in Schubert's unfolding of the first and second subjects (bars 1–9, 53–60). Derived from the principal theme, it reaches the dominant (bar 60) via the relative minor, G minor (bars 29–30): an axiomatic tendency in Schubert's unfolding of the musical material. It also heralds his unique contribution to the development of form whereby two harmonious cornerstones are expanded into three, thereby neutralizing Beethovenian polarity as a construction principle. Schubert's rondo theme imprints his final movement with a bold sense of articulation (Example 4.6 online). His entwining of two couplets – which ascend harmonically in a circle of fifths through F major and C major – with a refrain continually recast in the tonic, are illustrative of the composer's early decision making. His structural 'two couplets and a refrain' is metaphorical of Schubert's melody writing whereby he is engaging musical form through the prism of poetic structures. His exchange of chamber with orchestral soundscapes is also increasingly evident across the rondo's bold, labyrinthine pages as exemplified in the exceptionally grand tremolo octaves and concluding chords.

String Quartet in C major (D 46), composed between D 36 and D 68, is a fine example of Schubert's rapid development and has a particular status in his reception history.[16] Written in March 1813, the first movement was completed on 3 March, its second three days later; the finale and entire manuscript were ready on 7 March, and an accompanying set of parts on 13 March. Schubert takes as his motto theme the chromatically descending fourth isolated deep in the bass as a fugal exposition:

Example 4.7: String Quartet in C major (D 46/ii), bars 1–2

He exploits the fragility of this opening Adagio in a manner strongly reminiscent of Mozart's 'Dissonance' Quartet in C, and then enlists it as a counterpart to the dancing triplets of the Allegro con moto which takes some time to arrive at the full brightness of C major. The locution of this theme, the chromatic labyrinth it weaves, and use of anxious silences between the penultimate phrases of the exposition all affirm Schubert's dramatic sense. In the development section this introductory chromaticism yields music of uncommon subtlety and effect. The most successful of the two inner movements, which are reversed in the score, is the Minuet in B flat, a bold shift in narrative from the simple Andante in G. The composition of the finale can be explained as a veritable sonata rondo, the vitality of which endorses Schubert's melodic gift.

The elaborate celebration of birthdays and name days was, and still is, a feature of the highly personalized and private nature of Austrian middle-class life. Schubert's promotion of this habit is exemplified in two occasional works composed in the aftermath of his father's fiftieth birthday on 11 July 1813. The first is his String Quartet in D major (D 74), an intensely autobiographical piece which seeks to understand the significance of this occasion in the wake of his mother's death. The beginning of the score is dated 22 August 1813, the end of the first movement is dated 3 September 1813, and the end of the finale, September 1813. A first violin part preserved in the Spaun family collection is proudly given two calligraphic inscriptions, the first in French – 'Trois Quatuors composés par François Schubert, écolier de M. de Salieri' – and on the second folio 'Zur Namensfeyer meines Vaters, Franz, Sohn'. We detect in this dedication not only the fashionable tradition of French works: *quatuors concertants et dialogués*, elegant and easy-to-play pieces by Vachon and

Bréval in the family repertoire, but also Franz Theodor's preference for aesthetic accessibility.[17] We also sense Schubert's recognition of his calling, his faith in his own ability and ambition to contribute to Viennese and Parisian quartet culture.

The String Quartet in D major (D 74) unwittingly captures a fundamental opposition in Schubert's life: on the one hand there is a deep desire to please his music-loving father and on the other, there is a consciousness of his own claim to musical genius which declares how remote he is from any notions of a self-justifying art. We hear this in its opening movement which is a constellation of his musical heritage from works in the family repertoire – Mozart's String Quartets no. 20 in D major (K 499) and no. 21 in D major (K 575) – and Beethoven's Symphony no. 2 in D major op. 21, which Schubert played at school. Others have heard the Andante from Mozart's 'Prague' Symphony in Schubert's Andante in G, and the Haydnesque ring in Schubert's Minuet and Finale. Far from imitating his musical forefathers, Schubert essays a new sonata form with no development where the second half moves from dominant (bars 243ff) to tonic, a form to which he would return in the G minor String Quartet (D 173) of 1815. What is most interesting is to hear Schubert wander from the precipice of more secure chamber writing into a symphonic sound world. Bars 205–245 of the opening movement masquerade as an orchestral work while the Finale with its fanfares and *tremoli* seems to have been conceived more in a symphonic spirit (Example 4.8 online). In between bars 160 and 161 of the finale autograph Schubert crossed out a quasi-orchestral passage. Bars 209–223 of the final movement are exactly the same as in a fragmentary orchestral work of the same period (D 966A), and an attentive listener will also hear reminiscences of this work in his First Symphony.

There is no doubt whatsoever that Schubert's early chamber music paved the way to his First Symphony and that D 74 in particular is a preparatory work that marks the end of a period of youthful experimentation. After the preceding quartets, one might finally expect the analogue of a first-movement exposition that moves from the tonic to the dominant and a recapitulation that reverses it. D 74/i characteristically bypasses traditional thematic and tonal regularity, this time leaping straight into the dominant in the second subject group (bars 175–189), without any real transition, and opening the recapitulation in the dominant. Such deviations, so carefully integrated into the larger design, along with the symmetry of both outer movements, affirm Schubert's conscious study of musical technique. The result of his diligence was that every work after the First Symphony engages with sonata-form principles.

String Quartet in E flat major (D 87) marks a bold shift in narrative and is the first of Schubert's quartets to be widely recognized as an important contribution to the genre. The work has a firm grasp of the concertante interplay of forces, which makes for good chamber music and essays unprecedented textures. Equally unorthodox is the Andante of String Quartet in B flat (D 112) which moves from its tonic, G minor, to F major for a new theme (bar 39). From there, Schubert transitions easily into D minor, transplants the F major music in E flat and moves back to G minor via B flat. His early quartets show him exploring new harmonic relationships and forms, but his most successful movements are the more conventional ones, especially the minuets in which he was well rehearsed.

If we are willing to acknowledge the authority of Schubert's schoolhouse quartets, then we must see them within a contextual web and live with their complexities. Unravelling their contradictions, we must venture beyond their opaque forms in pursuit of what Richard Kramer calls their 'truth content'.[18] At stake is their value as an extreme expression of what might be called Schubert's 'early style' in which traditional harmonic functions are challenged. But these works also illustrate how Schubert had to appropriate sonata-form principles and understand what he had inherited before he could reinterpret and transpose them into a truly personal style. More broadly, they are part of a double trajectory at play during Schubert's formative years: partimento exercises for Salieri and string quartets for the family as the joint basis for his emergence as a composer of instrumental music.

SCHUBERT'S FAMILY PLAY THEIR PART: A FORGOTTEN HISTORY

In these formative years 'occasional' music governed everything Schubert wrote. Domestic venues gave rise to pieces for other chamber-music combinations and to a continuing pattern of piano trios, quintets, octets, overtures, all written for a particular purpose or performance. 'Die Advokaten' (D 37, 25–27 December 1812), a humorous TTB terzetto arranged for performance over Christmas, or cantatas composed for family friends such as 'Zur Namensfeier des Herrn Andreas Siller' (D 83), or later the orchestral cantata in honor of Government Councillor and Chief Inspector of Elementary Schools, Josef Spendou (D 472), patron and supporter of Schubert's father, are examples of Schubert's response to opportunity around him.

Schubert's Wind Octet in F (D 72, 18 August 1813) or seldom-performed Wind Nonet in E flat (D 79, 19 September 1813) were composed as an ornament to some social occasion in the Stadtkonvikt. The self-irony of the latter's title, 'Franz Schuberts Begräbniß-Feyer' (D 79), suggests he composed it around the time his final report arrived home, by which time he had already decided to leave school. It is a good example of the tension between the impersonal constraint of a conventional genre and a musical imagination which is striving to make the work a response to the personal state of the composer.

Circumstance links Schubert's String Quartet no. 7 in D major (D 74) to its companion cantata for two tenors and a bass: 'Zur Namensfeier meines Vaters' (In Honour of My Father's Name Day, D 80, Example 4.9 online). Composed on 27 September 1813, the cantata is a cheerful setting in mock-heroic style which expresses Schubert's hope that his 'beloved father' will enjoy a long and happy life. This musical encomium

Table 4.3: Schubert's Text, 'In Honour of My Father's Name Day' (D 80)

Ertöne Leyer	Resound, lyre,
zur Festesfeyer!	for this festive occasion!
Apollo steig hernieder,	Apollo, come down and
begeistre unsre Lieder!	inspire our songs!
Lange lebe unser Vater Franz!	Long live our father Franz!
Lange währe seiner Tage Chor!	Long may his chorus of days continue!
Und im ewig schönen Flor	And in eternal beautiful flowering
blühe seines Lebens Kranz.	may his life's wreath blossom.
Wonnelachend umschwebe die Freude	Laughing with delight may joy surround
seines grünenden Glückes Lauf.	his ever greener course of fate.
Immer getrennt vom trauernden Leide,	For ever separated from sad pain,
nehm' ihn Elysiums Schatten auf.	take him to Elysium's shades.
Endlos wieder töne, holde Leyer,	Ring out again endlessly, lovely lyre,
bringt des Jahres Raum die Zeit zurück,	bring this time of year round again
sanft und schön an dieser Festes-Feyer	gently and beautifully to this festive event.
Ewig währe Vater Franzens Glück!	May father Franz's happiness continue forever!

is the only work by Schubert arranged for guitar obbligato accompaniment and gives a good indication of the composer's abilities as a guitarist and of music making in his family home. Characteristically, Schubert wrote both the text and music, which signal a subtle identification with his father with whom he shared the same name day (see Example 4.9 online).

As vocal parts have survived in Schubert's hand (Example 4.10 online), the terzetto was presumably performed at home on the evening of Monday, 4 October by Schubert and his three brothers, Ignaz, Ferdinand and Karl, with Schubert accompanying on the guitar. As it was performed before his official withdrawal from the Stadtkonvikt, Schubert's musical gift to his father may have been intended to soften the blow of his decision to leave school. Did Franz Theodor realize that Schubert had lost all interest in academic work the year after his mother had died?[19] Or was he dealing with too much to notice what was going on? Both of them were grieving in different ways. With Franz the father remarried, Schubert turned again to composition.

THE ALLURE OF THE SYMPHONY

'non est ad astra mollis e terris via'
('there is no easy way from earth to the stars')

Seneca the Younger, *Hercules*

As he emerged as the author of numerous string quartets during his final year at the Stadtkonvikt, Schubert began to think of himself as a symphonist. Writing a symphony is a touchstone for many composers. Another pathway to trace how strategically and systematically Schubert approached this aim are the three unsigned and undated sketches for symphonic movements and overtures.

Schubert's first three symphonic sketches, D 2A (65 bars), D 2B (30 bars) and D 2G (47 bars), were originally dated 1812, but it is now believed they were sketched in 1811 before Schubert's lessons with Salieri.[20] The reciprocity between these three attempts can be traced in their musical unfolding, each of which is broken off at different stages of their development. Schubert laid out bars 1–17 of D 2A in pencil, which was then over-written in ink. Only in the subsequent Allegro can we see the apprentice composer at work through the various revisions he makes, until he gives up at bar 65. He takes up this thread of thought in a further sketch of 30 bars (D 2B), which he grandly entitles a 'symphony'. A short while later he changed course and attempted to write an overture: D 2G (47 bars), which combines the two previous manuscripts. A detailed comparison of D 2G with D 2A suggests D 2A was the last of these three manuscripts and that its perfectly achieved Adagio (in pencil) was the result of considerable revision. The fact that Schubert breaks off the transcription in the middle of a page is a sure indication, not only in this

THE MAKINGS OF A COMPOSER (1812-1813)

manuscript but in all three fragments, that these are his first symphonic sketches. The sketches are important because they show Schubert coming to terms with orchestration and the orthography of writing an orchestral score.[21] That he was unwontedly focused on this is one explanation of their free conception of form, a feature which is characteristic of his early works.

While the Deutsch Catalogue dates his D major Overture D 4 to 1812, on compositional grounds it is closer in time to the fragments D 2A and D 2B, composed one year earlier. Schubert wrote D 4 for a private performance of *Der Teufel als Hydraulicus*, a comedy written by the German physician and writer Johann Friedrich Ernst Albrecht (1752–1814), whose plot is based on Paul Weidemann's *Der Bettlerstudent*. One of the most striking things about this overture in relation to Schubert's development is that it remains in the tonic key of D major, despite some detours over the course of its 357 bars. As in his orchestral fragments, his priority seems to have been orchestration, as opposed to working out harmonic nuances of form.

Manuscripts which have been catalogued together do not necessarily refer to the same work, as is the case with the two fragments D 74A (15 bars) and D 71C (151 bars), which are identical in their composition and arrangement of voices but are two separate orchestral works, both in D major. Identical watermarks show that they were drafted around the same time. The single sheet on which D 74A is written belongs to the period prior to Schubert's Symphony no. 1 in D major (D 82), after the completion of his String Quartet no. 7 in D major on 3 September 1813. The fragmentary orchestral score D 74A is an orchestration of bars 209–233 of his String Quartet in D (D 74/i). Another preliminary study to his First Symphony, presumably composed in the spring or summer of 1813, can be derived from the 151 bars of D 71C which we now recognize as an *Überlieferungsfragment*, a work which was once complete but whose outer folios have become separated and lost to time. Although we cannot approach the fragment's meaning when we do not possess the outer folio that would convey it, the motivic and thematic gestures of D 71C suggest it was once an overture, though its connection with any of Schubert's theatrical works is not immediately obvious. The overall proportions of the work and wind orchestration of its opening bars give the impression that the fragment opens at the beginning of a development and breaks off in the middle of a coda. Its evocation of what has been sequestered is a slow introduction, an exposition and conclusion of the coda.

We do not know exactly when Schubert began writing his First Symphony because the place on the top right-hand side where he typically signed his name and commencement date has been cut out. We do know that he completed it on 28 October 1813, just three months before his seventeenth birthday. One of Schubert's earliest gestures of loyalty is his dedication of Symphony no. 1 in D major (D 82) to Dr Franz Innocenz Lang, headmaster of the Stadtkonvikt, who founded and financed its orchestra. Whether the symphony was performed by the school orchestra on 28 November 1813, as Schubert's first biographer originally claimed, is no longer certain.[22] The corrected parts – which have been handed down by Josef Doppler and are dated 1816 – suggest he heard his symphony performed by the chamber orchestra which grew out of the family string quartet. This date on the envelope is extremely important for understanding Schubert's development as a composer because it suggests he heard this symphony by the chamber orchestra *after* he had composed his second and third symphonies. The key question is whether the information Kreissle von Hellborn provided was correct: that the symphony was also performed at the Stadtkonvikt. Significantly, there are no signs of substantial revisions, which are characteristic of Schubert to show he was dissatisfied with what he heard. Also significant to his development would have been what he heard played alongside his work and the comparisons he, his fellow performers and audience would have made among themselves. Stepping back from this, the anticipated premiere of his First Symphony – knowing family or friends would be performing or listening to it – determined Schubert's logical construction of his musical materials and deployment of orchestral forces in exciting ways. Schubert wanted to prove his mettle by writing a symphony, the most prestigious of all instrumental genres.

Schubert's First Symphony was written for a similar orchestral combination – with a single flute – to Mozart's final symphonies. Beethoven also wrote several symphonies for one flute – his Fourth, for example – but the solo flute and wind doublings may reflect the availability of players and how performance determined his composition. The various inherences that have been heard in Schubert's First Symphony – from Mozart's 'Prague' Symphony to Beethoven's Second Symphony, *Prometheus* overture and ballet – attest to his ambitious assimilation of his forebears. Such comparisons paradoxically acknowledge Schubert's legitimate place among this Viennese symphonic pantheon – Haydn, Mozart and Beethoven – and downplay his own significance as a symphonist. Even recently it has been argued that Schubert's symphonies 'trace not a public path [. . .] but a private and interior world of half lights and self-doubts whose technical musical language is often not far removed from the lied'.[23] 'Self-doubt' no more describes the music of Schubert's First Symphony than it does his last. Whatever criticism has been levelled at his early works, they affirm a novice's strategic engagement with the genre, his willingness to experiment and his search for successful solutions to formal challenges. Although his symphonies share structural affinities, their basic conception distinguishes them radically from each other, and Schubert's own development across the genre is palpable.[24]

Analysts pondering the mysteries of Schubert's symphonies need to resituate them in a broader environment of intertextual resonance with a broader range of Viennese contemporaries and forebears, whose influence he absorbed through performing their work. The D major symphony by the Bohemian composer Johann Baptist Wanhal (Jan Křtitel Vaňhal, 1739–1813) is never evoked in the list of D major symphonies associated with Schubert's First Symphony, nor is his propensity for interrelation between themes traced back to the symphonies of Salieri's teacher and predecessor, Florian Leopold Gassmann (1729–1774). Schubert's subdominant recapitulations and digressions into the minor mode are never traced back to the symphonies of Georg Christoph Wagenseil (1715–1777), nor is his use of shared motifs between movements ever linked to the symphonies of Wenzel (Václav) Pichl (1741–1805), Michael Haydn (1737–1806) or Adalbert Gyrowetz (1763–1850), whose symphonies were performed in Vienna well into the 1820s. New narrative frameworks for understanding and interpreting Schubert's symphonies are needed to place his work in dialogue with prominent Czech symphonists in Vienna such as Franz Krommer, or popular symphonies such as the C major 'Jena' symphony attributed to Beethoven but composed by Friedrich Jeremias Witt (1770–1836), or the E flat major symphony by Anton Eberl (1765–1807) which engages in remarkably imaginative formal innovations and was widely performed in Schubert's day. An exhaustive summary of representative influences is not feasible in a biography; this practical overview is at once a starting point and an invitation to explore hitherto unassimilated influences on Schubert's symphonies.[25]

Schubert's resolve to exercise complete control over the genre is immediately audible in his First Symphony (D 82), the intellectual concentration of which must have astonished his fellow students and teachers. The imprint of Leopold Hofmann's D major symphony (D 4) is in the opening of Schubert's First, in which the cantabile character of his Allegro vivace with its clear periodic phrasing and tonal logic is contextualized by a preceding Adagio of considerable *gravitas*. Schubert's exhilarating opening with its slow semitone descent to the dominant which lingers there for bars 9–20 is a rhetorical gesture that derives from the social function of the Viennese symphony where rhetoric was expected of his listeners (Example 4.11 online). Despite the clear contrast of the main themes in D 82/i, the monothematicism of his early quartets determines the character of Schubert's 'singing Allegro'. A good example of this is his sequential exploration of the second subject in both exposition and development. Already his disruption of expectations in the reprise of the slow introduction in an Allegro tempo at the beginning of the recapitulation (bars 314–344) reveals the introduction as part of a broader antecedent and consequent and holds particular significance in the unfolding of the musical material. Schubert's poetic use of the wind ensemble at the beginning of the recapitulation and shrewdly provocative opening movement are clear harbingers of later directions.

D 82/ii, an Andante in G major in 6/8, has the character of a cavatina. Here too Schubert subtly subverts convention, interrupting its principal theme by two episodes in E minor: the first heralds the composer's sense of drama, the second is pastoral and plaintive. Already in this movement Schubert shows his ability to develop strategies for creating unity through motivic exploration and to make use of the expressive sonority of a wind chorus.

Although Schubert's minuet takes its cue from Mozart's 'Jupiter' Symphony no. 41 which he had transcribed shortly before, his mastery of this compact binary form through improvising keyboard minuets for Salieri explains his ability to play with parameters like rhythm and texture in this short, unpretentious minuet. In typical fashion, Schubert chases the first minuet with a concertante trio which, with its slower tempo and nostalgic character, is more like a Ländler and thereby contrasts with the reprise of his opening minuet.

The dramatic Allegro vivace fourth movement is very much in the spirit of Schubert's sonata-like calibrations and speaks with great personal force (Example 4.12 online). An early example of his ability to surprise is evident in the restlessness of the exposition which urges the need for tonal closure, which the woodwind phrases endorse through their deceptive allusions to the first subject. Instead of the anticipated expositional repeat, Schubert shifts to an F major development where he exploits the second subject and a variety of textures including canon. This intensity is maintained through the restatement of both subjects in a theatrical recapitulation, the first subject in the tonic major and minor, the second in B flat, before Schubert's return to the tonic drives his finale to a dramatic close. This full recapitulation with thematic and tonal contrasts, digression in the minor mode and submediant recapitulation, show his precocious proficiency in formal and thematic segmentation. Clearly, Schubert's knowledge of the symphonic repertoire provided a stimulus and a framework which he commands with astonishing mastery, while also playing on those conventions and the expectations of his peers. Writing a symphony is a touchstone for many composers, most of whom approach it far later in life. Whatever imbalances can be heard in it, Schubert's First Symphony is a rich affirmation that the sixteen-year-old composer was uncannily gifted.

LEAVING THE STADTKONVIKT

During the summer months of 1813, when Schubert was working on this symphony, one of his older colleagues at the Academic Grammar School, Johann Bacher, was suspected of political intrigue and imprisoned on this account. A petition for his release was led by two of Schubert's older boarding-school friends: Michael von Rueskäfer (1794–1872) and Johann Senn (1785–1857). Josef Kenner later recalled in 1858 that Rueskäfer left the Stadtkonvikt voluntarily at this time while Senn, who was dependent on a scholarship for his studies in Vienna, lost his foundation award, and became a prime suspect in the case.[26] That Schubert was deemed 'an excellent youth' whose 'superior musical talent' was rewarded with a further scholarship shows he did not support his schoolmate.

For choristers whose voices had broken, continuing scholarships were available dependent on the moral conduct and academic distinction of their recipients. As he had 'lapsed into second rank' in mathematics Schubert was deemed to have failed but was offered a Meerfeld Endowment on 22 October 1813, on the condition that he would resit an examination in mathematics.[27] The Emperor signed the Imperial resolution laying down the foundations that 'singing and music are but a subsidiary matter [. . .] good morals and diligence in study are of prime importance and an indispensable duty for those who wish to enjoy the advantages of an Endowment'.[28] But music was no subsidiary matter for Schubert, who had

THE MAKINGS OF A COMPOSER (1812-1813)

outgrown all the Stadtkonvikt could offer him. At the beginning of his schooldays he had written the piano fantasy for four hands in G major and at the end he had composed his First Symphony. One week after he received the offer of an endowment on 22 October, he completed his farewell symphony. When he signed 'finis et fine' on the last page, childhood ties were broken. Two days later he began his first opera, renounced his scholarship, and resigned from the Stadtkonvikt.[29] As aesthete and composer, Schubert left the cocoon of a Catholic boarding school but he took with him the excellent training and decorous backdrop with which the Stadtkonvikt had supplied him for his unfolding gifts. If he retained anything from his time there, it was his conviction of the integrity of those who had educated him.

5

PLACE AND DISPLACEMENT (1813-1814)

'We are as great as the peaks of our desires.'

Plato

INNOCENT GUILT: TEACHER OR ARTIST?

For three years, from autumn 1813, Schubert lived at home with his father, stepmother, maternal aunt Maria Magdalena, and his brother Karl in the Säulengasse schoolhouse. One year had passed since his mother's death so Schubert must have felt a strange absence. Although his father was eager that his son might succeed where he had failed, and continue on to university, Schubert was to prove himself by the same history his father's son. Upon leaving the Stadtkonvikt, Franz Theodor had imposed one condition: that his son perforce must enter the teaching profession as a way of making a living and preventing him from being conscripted into military service. Schubert did not put up a fight and embarked on his teaching studies, though not very assiduously. Like his father and his brother Ferdinand, he entered the k.k. Normalhauptschule, the Imperial and Royal teachers' college as a 'secular' student, almost three months before his seventeenth birthday. Whatever favour he enjoyed as a trainee teacher came from his industry in German language, grammar, spelling and handwriting. Unlike his father, his worst subject was still religion, but as a secular student this did not affect his grades.[1] Having tolerated the ten-month course, he passed his final examination with relative ease on 19 August 1814, qualifying as an assistant elementary schoolteacher.

What life was like for Schubert during this year can be gathered from two occasional incidents at home. The New Year began with the birth of Maria Barbara Anna to Schubert's parents on 22 January 1814, the first baby to enter the Schubert household after more than twelve years. While Schubert loved his stepmother and her five children loved him, the most apparent kinship he had with his siblings during these years was with his elder brothers, Ferdinand and Karl.

The Schubert brothers, staunch and true, were beginning to attain separate individualities. Ferdinand was a serious, slim young man, taller by several inches than Schubert, and was already giving signs of the steadiness and determination that were to characterize his life. The next brother, Karl, two years older than Franz, was to prove an artist of true talent. Just after his sixteenth birthday he had entered the Academy of Fine Arts in Vienna to study landscape painting in November 1811 and he spent several years in full- and part-time courses there. As the Academy was in the same building as the Imperial teacher-training college in Annagasse, the two brothers may have shared the same route many times. They also shared the same social circle. It is telling that Franz Schubert did not make a single friend at the Imperial teacher-training college. Instead, he made friends with Karl's fellow students, most notably Leopold Kupelwieser (1796–1862), who had lost his father in 1813 and lived with his brother, Josef, who, a decade later, would write the libretto for what has become Schubert's most popular opera, *Fierabras*. An exceptionally gifted painter and graphic artist, Leopold had been accepted by the Academy at age twelve and was later appointed professor in 1836. During 1813–1814 Leopold was a classmate of Karl's, who studied copper engraving as well as drawing and painting at the Academy. At the end of this academic year Franz Theodor proudly recorded in his diary that his son Karl was awarded first prize for figure drawing. Among the Schubert boys, however, the emphasis still fell on Franz, in whom his father recognized an immense musical talent. Even in these early years, Ferdinand, three years older than Franz, already trailed him worshipfully.

Like Karl, Franz had his special manner too, which was evident in the music he wrote. His return to the schoolhouse in the autumn of 1813 had revived the practice of music making in their home and many of the chamber works from this period are somehow connected with his father.[2] A series of occasional works signal a passing identification with Franz Theodor, who had relinquished the final years of his scholarship and into whose profession he was now entering. Many pieces were written in gratitude to his father, who supported his departure from the Stadtkonvikt and wanted his most educated and gifted son to teach at his school.

Just how unlikely this would be is evident from the extraordinary musical strides Schubert was making, as is immediately apparent in his String Quartet in E flat major (D 87), op. 125/1, which he began composing in November 1813 (Example 5.1 online). As the autograph is incomplete, we do not know its date of completion. For many years it was believed that the quartet belonged to 1824 (and it is interesting to ponder how far that belief influenced its fate). Its harmonic range is significantly more moderate than the earlier quartets, but above all what gained the work its critical acclaim is that three of its movements are in sonata form.

Even here Schubert makes a raid on predictability, as exemplified in this work's tonal uniformity. That all four movements are composed in E flat major places immediate pressure on him to individualize them. Schubert does this by reversing the order of the Adagio slow movement and Prestissimo scherzo and trio – a magnificent disorder with which he had experimented in his String Quartet in C major (D 46) and which he would further explore in his A major Violin Sonata (D 574) of 1817. In the first movement he brazenly ignores both subjects in favour of a brief exploration of its transition material, through which he also successfully circumvents the challenges of motivic development. In the second movement his curtailed reprise of the second subject is also unorthodox. This parade of divergent qualities, with a view to their ultimate reconciliation, is the method of D 87. While it is distinguished by its contrapuntal, chamber-music texture, perhaps its most defining feature is its display of symphonic brilliance, which is even more pronounced than in previous quartets. Ultimately what the string quartet shows is that Schubert outmanoeuvred everyone. He did what his father expected of him by becoming a teacher but remained his own person and – again and again throughout his life – did what nobody expected. He played the role of dutiful son teaching at his father's school and writing *pièces d'occasion*. But he retained the freedom to pursue his own private path.

SCHUBERT'S ARRANGEMENTS: NOTTURNO IN G (D 96)

Schubert's early development as a composer was rooted in this extraordinary dual trajectory: domestic music making at home in Lichtental, and his apprenticeship with Salieri. The mastery of the early symphonic and sacred works with Salieri is subsumed by his stylistic promiscuity and exploration of so many genres in close succession. In his schoolhouse years we see the beginnings of his distinction between higher and lower aesthetic levels. At the same time there was something startlingly retrogressive about some occasional works he wrote during this year.

One such work is Schubert's Guitar Quartet (D 96), the second of two manuscripts with guitar accompaniment.[3] In his eighteenth year, Schubert was already capable of writing a far more profound composition. Yet the popular nature of Wenzel Matiegka's popular Notturno op. 21 for flute, viola and guitar spoke to him so directly that he decided to transcribe it into a quartet on 26 February 1814, rewrote significant portions, and added a cello part that transforms the entire work.

Schubert's quartet is interesting because it offers an insight into his relationship with the guitar of which we otherwise know very little. It also opens a window onto a particular school of guitar playing that gave a distinctive character to domestic music making in Schubert's Vienna. Following the lead of Simon Molitor (1766–1848), a group of outstanding players – Leonhard von Call (1767–1815), Wenzel Matiegka (1773–1830), Mauro Giuliani (1781–1829), Anton Diabelli (1781–1858), Franz Tandler (1782–1806) and Luigi Legnani (1790–1877) – all extended the facilities of the instrument and brilliantly blended the language of Viennese classicism with emerging elements of early Romanticism.

Already through its instrumentation, D 96 holds a special place in this school and in Schubert's chamber-music repertoire. But what inspired this particular arrangement? And for whom did he write the transformative cello part? Even in Schubert's day the addition of a cello to Matiegka's combination of instruments was extremely rare. Carl Friedrich Whistling's *Handbuch der Musik. Literatur oder Verzeichnis der bis zum Ende des Jahres 1815 gedruckten Musikalien* lists dozens of serenades, variations and dances by Arnold, Boecklin, Bornhardt, von Call, Diabelli, Küffner and Matiegka, all for flute, viola and guitar, but the only other quartet for guitar, violin or flute, viola and cello is von Call's Quartet op. 57. What distinguishes Schubert's arrangement from von Call's is the commanding cello writing, the certainty with which all four various instruments are handled, and Schubert's exploration of their unique sonorities. His masterly writing for every instrument, each of which plays a special role within the ensemble, suggests he had particular players in mind when he arranged it.

Who these performers might have been can be traced through the discovery of the manuscript in the attic of Karl and Marianne Feyerer's Zell am See country home. A family member on Feyerer's side, Ignaz Rosner, was a close friend of the soprano, Therese Grob (1798–1875). Rosner was an accomplished musician who played flute and cello. But he was also friends with Josef von Spaun through a fellow civil servant, Friedrich Stenzl, who was violist in the orchestra of the Gesellschaft der Musikfreunde. Stenzl's sister was a gifted guitarist to whom Schubert most likely dedicated the quartet because it was through her that the manuscript came into the Feyerer family's possession. An engraved page included with the manuscript bears the title 'Written in Franz Schubert's hand'. There is not even the slightest doubt about the authenticity of this manuscript:

from beginning to end it is clearly in his hand and already reveals the firm purposeful strokes which are recognizable in later manuscripts. Unfortunately, all we possess is a sizeable discoloured *Überlieferungsfragment* of thirty-two oblong pages, each containing twelve systems (in two folios). On the fragment's third page, the handwriting reveals a change to a finer, more delicate quill, and the manuscript is laden with minor corrections and performance directions.

Who played the guitar part is part of the intimate history of this piece. Estate records show that Schubert had two guitars in his lifetime: a guitar made by Bernard Enzensperger in 1805 and a second made by Johann Georg Staufer in 1815.[4] Although his personal interest in the guitar is famous, it is uncertain whether he ever mastered the instrument. From this quartet we can gauge that he was a master of the violin, and well versed in writing for the guitar. His handling of the instrument affirms his understanding of contemporary guitar notation, which he adopts and develops with purpose.

Although this arrangement now belongs to Schubert's large portfolio of incomplete compositions and small portfolio of arrangements, it is so much more than an historical curiosity.[5] Firstly, the directions in Schubert's hand tell us so much about his ability to refine occasional works through performance. Secondly, it is one of the earliest pieces we have in which Schubert makes the distinction between music composed for the pleasure of a small circle of connoisseurs and popular music intended to be enjoyed by a less endowed public. Thirdly, it is the first time Schubert's attraction to Hungarian music can be heard in his music through the Zingara melody in the penultimate movement. Fourthly, and ultimately what is most intriguing, is the question of whose legacy hangs over the eloquent cello solo? Schubert transformed the third movement into a disquisition on the cello. The domestic performance of this work in Schubert's family home – perhaps even in Therese Grob's – the concentration of occasional works for his father during this period, and the long lines of this quartet's Lento e patetico, all suggest a deeply held obligation to his father.

BEARINGS

TURNING THE TIDE: OPERA COMPOSER OR CHURCH MUSICIAN?

At the same time as Schubert was arranging his Guitar Quartet, Salieri was moulding his student into a composer of opera or church musician, the two ways an aspiring composer could make a living. By 1814 Schubert was an ambitious young composer who wanted to write everything he could. As he vaulted from genre to genre, trying on new selves, he aimed for a higher ethics in which artistic freedom and full expression of personality were possible. In the dead of night at Himmelpfortgrund 10, his father's school, he soared above the teaching profession for which he was training.

Two days after he finished his First Symphony on 28 October, he began his first complete Singspiel, *Des Teufels Lustschloß* (The Devil's Pleasure Palace, D 84), to a text of August von Kotzebue, which he composed under Salieri's tutelage. Salieri was receptive to his student's talents and Schubert respected his critical judgement. It is significant that he began his first complete opera on his mother's birthday and when he finished his first complete draft on 16 March 1814, Salieri read it with delight. Just how seriously teacher and student took his opera is evident in the extent and nature of the revisions which Schubert completed on 22 October 1814, after six months of intensive work. As Act 2 of his revised manuscript was destroyed in Huttenbrenner's keeping, Schubert's definitive version of his three-act *Zauberoper* relies on both manuscripts.[6] This is the second Singspiel that Schubert set, but his first complete operatic work.[7]

So what plot attracted Schubert's attention? And what can we discover in him from the opera he composed? *Des Teufels Lustschloß* tells the tale of a knight, Oswald, who is put through the hoops by his devilish father-in-law as a test of his fidelity, only to be reunited with his beloved, Luitgarde, at the end. Kotzebue's libretto relies heavily on Joseph-Marie Loaisel de Tréogate's *Le château du diable* (1792) and had already been set to music by Ignaz Wagner and Johann Friedrich Reichardt.[8] Schubert's first opera forms an imaginary line between the stage machinery of Baroque opera and examination rituals for budding couples, which form a precarious tradition of probation plots in German opera from Mozart's *Die Zauberflöte* to Beethoven's *Fidelio* and Weber's *Der Freischütz* to Wagner's *Die Meistersinger*. It is often said that Schubert was far too young to portray Kotzebue's parody of the fashionable genre of fairy tale and magic plays, but already at seventeen he declares his scepticism about finding domestic bliss in marriage. In the final denouement he exchanges the rejoicing of Kotzebue's chorus, 'Heil dem mächt'gen schönen Triebe' (Hail the powerful beautiful instinct), with a quartet of soloists from the chorus and soprano solo, probably texted by himself, which bears the moral of the tale: 'Heil dem stolzen, kühnen Paare, das sich jedem Kampfe weiht!' (Hail to the proud, bold couple who dedicate themselves to every fight!). Kotzebue's denouement, where all suffering is resolved and domestic harmony restored, is also marked by hesitation through Schubert's dramatic use of silence in the *fortissimo* Vivace – a moment of withdrawal and musical critique of the lovers' rapture.[9]

One of the most extraordinary aspects of Schubert's *Zauberoper* is his early knowledge of contemporary opera. Salieri gave Schubert a good grounding in the operas of Gluck, Mozart and his Italian contemporaries, and Schubert assumed his cosmopolitanism. The portrayal of the storm scene in the overture to *Des Teufels Lustschloß* transitions into an introduction with its Gluckian orientation from *Iphigénie en Tauride*. His finale to Act 1 – when the Amazon and statues of Oswald crash into darkness – again bears the hallmarks of the orchestral unisono *sforzandi* which distinguish Don Giovanni's entry into hell but more importantly the lamento bass schema, the chromatically descending tetrachord (bars 379–392). Schubert finished the final draft of his opera one week before he attended the premiere of Beethoven's third and final version of *Fidelio* on 23 May 1814, but the similarities between Leonore and Florestan's duet and Schubert's own ecstatic B flat major duet of the reunited spouses 'Hab' ich dich wieder/Seliger Traum' (no. 21) bear the imprint of a framework that both composers received from lessons with Salieri. Schubert's F major trio of lovers, 'Ich lach', ich wein' (no. 22) – where Robert's exuberant friends are juxtaposed with the pair's internalized happiness – flows into a three-part B-flat major canon (bar 68ff), just like the *Fidelio* canon 'Mir ist so wunderbar', and his anniversary tribute to Salieri *Beitrag zur fünfzigjährigen Jubelfeier des Herrn von Salieri* (D 407), a formula which would re-emerge many times, most famously in 'Das Dörfchen' (D 598). Quite apart from the melodic similarity between these two numbers, Schubert handles the orchestra in the same way with an increase of orchestral instruments at each vocal entry, a *diminuendo* after the last vocal entry with closing orchestral gestures voiced *fortissimo*. Schubert's acquisition of musical dialects was richly eclectic and his ironic handling of Kotzebue's finale not only echoes the finale from *Fidelio* but also that of *Die Zauberflöte*. Finally, his impressive closing *decrescendo* – where the violas, first supported by the cellos, play in rhythmic augmentation from quavers to crotchets to minims in a chromatic ascending and descending stepwise sequence of a sixth (bars 375–392), while the lower strings hold a *pianissimo* pedal point in C until the music fades (bars 383–392) – bears testimony to his familiarity with Cherubini's *Lodoïska*.

For all the homage he pays to tradition, Schubert learnt at an early age the importance of being himself. The *crescendo* timpani roll opens the overture in F major, which suddenly stops before the music resumes in E major – a gesture that depicts the art of rapture in a way that does not happen in opera before or after Schubert. *Des Teufels Lustschloß* is Schubert's earliest programmatic overture. The 28-bar chorale which concludes its development section, voiced by three trombones, is one of many musical gestures associated with dying and codifies the threat that hangs over Oswald. This trope would turn up in a symphonic sketch, D 936A, which commemorates Beethoven's passing, and is one of the most striking examples of Schubert's self-borrowing late in life (Examples 5.2a and b).

This trial piece was a culminating episode in Schubert's apprenticeship. He had not spent much time on his pedagogical studies, but he had composed his first complete opera, a sure-fire indication that the industrious torpor of the schoolroom and parish church could never contain Schubert himself, except when he was forced to return to the family circle as a matter of survival. There was not much tension with his father during his teacher-training year: he saw him in the evenings and for all appearances was taking on his mantle.

Example 5.2a: *Des Teufels Lustschloß* (D 84), bars 233–60

Example 5.2b: Sketch for a Symphony in D (D 936A), bars 154–61

PRIVATE AND PUBLIC REVOLUTIONS: 'THE LIBERATORS IN PARIS'

Franz Theodor, stern and sociable by turns, kept the family's life from becoming either too comfortable or too tedious. Something of his overbearing nature can be detected on 16 June 1814, when Emperor Francis was welcomed back to Vienna from Paris, and the *paterfamilias* publicly proclaimed his patriotic fervour with a banner displayed outside his house for all to see:

> 10 Himmelpfortgrund in the Säulengasse,
> House of Herr Schubert, Schoolteacher,

O could I, as I would
Do honour, as we all should
To the best of emperors, Franz!
Only candles are burning here
But sprouting from my heart
Are sprigs of laurel.
FRANCIsCo MAGNO, VICTORI
REDEVNTI![10]

Codifying the year, 1814, by counting up the roman numerals, Schubert's father was displaying his intellectual prowess with a Latin inscription and mathematical computation. But behind the obsequious attitude to authority displayed by this Habsburg loyalist lay a deep-seated insecurity and lifelong desire for respectability.

The patriotic fervour for Francis I in Schubert's household expressed itself in two settings which are rare examples of Schubert's engagement with political events.[11] The first, 'Auf den Sieg der Deutschen' (To the Victory of the Germans, D 81), commemorating the battle at Leipzig, 16–19 October 1813, is composed to a hopelessly prolix text, most likely one of Schubert's long odes to which Holzapfel refers (Table 5.1 online). This song of victory in praise of the Emperor was composed after his father's name day tribute and clearly under his influence.[12] It suggests a very similar blend of political conservatism and personal insecurity as Franz Theodor's welcome-banner in praise of the returning Emperor. Taken together these two songs offer a fascinating glimpse at what Schubert might have become had he, like Ferdinand, been able to live a more orthodox life. This voice and string trio setting (D 81) was written for Schubert's family to perform: the violin part played by Schubert or Ferdinand, and the very simple cello part by Franz Theodor. That Schubert wrote this setting as part of his twice-weekly lessons with Salieri is evident in his recomposition of the first stanza as a canon for two tenors and bass on 15 November 1813 when he reimagined it for his father Franz Theodor, Ferdinand and Ignaz (D 88). Schubert invested a great deal in this setting but was clearly alert to the dangers of introversion by rarely treading this path. Was he trying to fit in at home and please his father? Or was he consciously contributing to a long lineage of political settings which emerged during the Wars of Liberation, 1806–1815? Schubert would have known Haydn's 'Volkslied' (Gott erhalte Franz den Kaiser), Beethoven's 'Österreich über Alles' and *Wellington's Victory* performed in a charity concert at University Hall in December 1813 to raise money for the soldiers who had taken part in the Battle of the Nations. Did he believe when he attempted these domestic and potentially commercial settings that an ideal allows even the historical and political to be subsumed into art?[13]

Schubert's only other foray into political settings was composed on 16 May 1814 when allied armies (the Austrians under Francis I, the Prussians and Russians) entered Paris on 15 April 1814 forcing Napoleon to abdicate and causing his banishment to Elba. A jingoistic poem by Johann Christian Mikan (1769–1844) celebrating this victory – declaimed by the actress Sophie Schröder at the Redoutensaal on 13 April 1814 and subsequently published in the Viennese periodical *Der Sammler* on 16 May – resulted in three versions of 'Die Befreier Europas in Paris' (The Liberators of Europe in Paris, D 104). The ballad captures being on the threshold of a new social order and the balance of power in Europe. There are eight verses in Mikan's original, of which Schubert only transcribed the first:

Sie sind in Paris!	They are in Paris!
Die Helden! Europa's Befreier!	The heroes! Europe's liberators!
Der Vater von Österreich, der Herrscher der Reussen	The father of Austria, the ruler of the Russians,
Der Wiedererwecker der tapferen Preussen.	He who aroused again the brave Prussians.
Das Glück ihrer Völker – es war ihnen teuer.	The happiness of their nations was central to them.
Sie sind in Paris!	They are in Paris!
Nun ist uns der Friede gewiss!	Now we are assured of peace!

That the song caused the composer much pain is evident in the impassioned crossings-out on the first two versions (Examples 5.3a and 5.3b online). All three versions are on the same folded sheet of manuscript paper. Was Schubert consciously writing from a nationalist perspective? Were his three drafts an experiment in the partimento practice of resetting? Or did his struggle reflect discomfort at violating artistic purity for the purpose of political statement? Even at this early age Schubert shows he is capable of civic commentary through his patriotic setting with *pomposo* fanfares and military dotted rhythms, its *pianissimo* ending expressive of a contemporary desire for Europe to be at peace. Truth to one's feelings, activist or not, is not only required in song, but is what drives us to song. These settings are pondered constructions rather than a spontaneous communication of feeling. But for all they communicate, they leave much unsaid.

AD MELIORA: FIRST SYMPHONIES

The very next day after composing 'Die Befreier Europas in Paris' (D 104), Schubert set to work on his first Mass in F major (D 105). His first mass was commissioned for the Lichtental centenary celebrations by Michael Holzer, who was looking out for Schubert who, along with Ferdinand, was still actively involved in the musical life of the parish. The mass was written between 17 May and 22 July. Its premiere on 16 October 1814 was a landmark performance which launched Schubert's professional career. It also marked the end of his teacher-training year at the Imperial college and a highly successful apprenticeship year as Kapellmeister.[14] Under Salieri's tutelage he had composed his first complete symphony, first opera and first mass, the precocious mastery of which is astonishing evidence of Schubert's stylistic originality

Following his ten-month course of studies, Schubert took up employment at his father's school as sixth assistant teacher in charge of the infants. Schubert was, by nature, a disgruntled teacher and too strict a disciplinarian with the children. He was quick to clout students on the side of the head, subjecting them to the same petty tyranny with which his lean, dried-up choirmaster, Philipp Korner, had discommoded and disciplined him.[15]

Schubert made anticipation of the new term bearable by composing his String Quartet in B flat (D 112), op. 168, in one week, 5–13 September 1814. He proudly recorded that the first movement was written in four and a half hours: imitation of the father, which was to mark the rest of his emotional life, had begun in more ways than one. The methodological discipline of his father is embedded in Schubert's meticulous dating of his schoolhouse manuscripts. His Symphony no. 2 in B flat (D 125) was composed between 10 December 1814 and 24 March 1815.[16] Its first movement was written in seventeen days from 10 to 26 December 1814; the middle movements are undated and the finale was written between 25 February and 24 March, during which time he also composed his second Mass in G major (D 167) between 2 and 7 March. The day after completing his Second Symphony, he began a new String Quartet in G minor (D 173), which he finished on 1 April 1815.

Although the Second Symphony was written only one year after his first, the difference is extraordinary and bears testimony to just how much Schubert had developed since he left the Stadtkonvikt. In between the composition of his first and second symphonies he had revised the parts for *Des Teufels Lustschloß*, written and conducted his first mass. The revisions to both manuscripts – and to the score of the F major mass in particular – shows he very much benefited from the experience. In his Second Symphony, Schubert is so much more assured and any occasional imbalances in orchestration in the opening movement of his First Symphony are ironed out.[17] The orchestral forces and accompanying set of orchestral parts, with a dedication to Dr Franz Innocenz Lang on the envelope, suggest Schubert's first two symphonies were performed in the Stadtkonvikt. The 1816 parts in Doppler's possession suggest he also benefited from a private performance in Franz Frischling's apartments.

What is novel in this symphony and in Schubert's development is that it is the first time we have a three-key exposition. The tonal map is rearranged where B flat transitions into the second subject in the subdominant, E flat, and reaches to the dominant F major only at the end of the exposition. The second movement in E flat is the only time Schubert uses variation form in any of his symphonies: the fourth variation of the five-bar theme is not in the expected tonic minor but the relative C minor. No less radical is the minuet in the relative C minor. Was Schubert consciously experimenting with conventional classical tonal planning? Or was he imitating Beethoven's Seventh Symphony (1812)? Whatever the answer, the middle movements share a common key-focus, the C minor–E flat–C minor is the antithesis of the second movement's E flat–C minor–E flat. Only in the final movement does the tonic return with a memorable finale subject answered with the second subject in E flat major underscored by a tonic pedal for 48 bars. If Schubert's love of key contrasts deviates from classical norms in this symphony, we also have a new concentration of ideas and proportional balance found in the Viennese symphony. The work solidified his resolve to look beyond the classroom which threatened his compositional integrity.

A few months after he completed his Second Symphony, Schubert marshalled all his forces to commence his Symphony no. 3 in D major (D 200), on 24 May 1815; he took up at bar 65 on 11 July, completing the first movement the following day; he began the second movement on 15 July and completed the symphony four days later. Most of the symphony was notated in little over one week and his confidence and new-found serenity are evident in his writing. Parts in Ferdinand Schubert's possession show the symphony was performed. The score, which is more modest than his second, suggests it was written for smaller forces, most likely for the family orchestra.[18] Even if written for domestic performance Schubert was modulating his old aspiration as a symphonist.

In terms of length and scope, this 'little' D major symphony, at first glance, seems to have taken a step back from his ambitious First Symphony in a quest to correct anything he was unhappy with in the opening movements of his previous two symphonies. D major has a particular place in

Schubert's symphonic lexicon as the tonality of experimentation. D 200/i, distinguished by its rhythmic energy and grand gestures, is much more congruent with classical principles than his earlier symphonies. Schubert introduces an element of suprise into the recapitulation by stating the second theme in the subdominant before retreating to the tonic. The second movement is a lied-like Allegretto in the subdominant, G major, with a contrasting theme in C major, which breaches convention in the reprise. Although its form is shared with previous symphonies, this symphony distinguishes itself by the nobility of its instrumentation. D 200/iii is a lively minuet and trio in D major, with the trio in the style of a Ländler, as in his First Symphony. The triumphant finale is a sonata rondo with many surprises in the harmonic, orchestral and thematic narratives such as the recapitulation of the first subject in the dominant or the dynamic motif which closes not only this movement but the entire work. Upon its conclusion Schubert, at eighteen, had consolidated what he had learnt from his Viennese predecessors. Different as his first three symphonies are in their local strategies, together they convey an assurance which would lead in future directions.

6

SCHUBERT AS A CHURCH MUSIC COMPOSER

'There is another world, but it is in this one.'

W. B. Yeats

THE SACRED WITHIN AND WITHOUT

Church music was part of the Edenic and everyday dimensions of Schubert's childhood. Its certainty and security, calendar customs, feast days and ecclesiastical rites were part of the tradition and values that Franz Theodor had inherited from his own schooling, and part of the cultural and religious bonds of bringing up children. For a long time Schubert played along with his father obediently – even quite happily – running around the corner and down the steps to take organ lessons from the local maestro, Michael Holzer, and to sing in the choir. In the Lichtental Parish he first became acquainted with the sacred music of Michael and Joseph Haydn, Johann Wanhal and Johann Albrechtsberger (Holzer's teacher), and his lessons served as a propaedeutic.[1]

Schubert's student days as head chorister at the Imperial Chapel and municipal Catholic boarding school in Vienna deepened his knowledge of sacred music. His prestige among his peers is recounted by Spaun, who also recognized his enjoyment of singing at the Chapel Royal, which other choirboys only endured (Figure 10).[2] The refinements of ritual captured his imagination: he was drawn to the artistic side of the church, while treating its dogmas with reserve. That he developed a delight in the forms of Catholicism rather than its content is evident in his early liturgical works, which are founded on his intimate acquaintance with the church music tradition and at a profound level a recognition of the socially constructive function of Catholic festivals.

Schubert's apprenticeship with Salieri was central to his training as a church musician, one of the expected career paths for which he was prepared.[3] Through his selection of music performed at the Chapel Royal, Salieri introduced Schubert to a wide range of influence including *stile antico* as practised by composers of the late Baroque and early classical periods who used controlled dissonance and modalities to heighten the expression of textual meaning. A central part of Neapolitan training is mastering a technique and applying it in original compositions. Schubert's lessons with Salieri, coupled with performance opportunities in Lichtental, afforded him the perfect grounds for personal and professional growth.

APPRENTICESHIP AT LICHTENTAL, 1813–1816

Lichtental was formative not only during Schubert's childhood but for the performance opportunities it afforded him during his studentship. Much of his sacred music composed in the period autumn 1813–1816 was for the Lichtental Parish. For the average Viennese, church services offered the most accessible form of live music making, offering Schubert a distinct, captive audience and valuable experience, neither of which were available to him in opera. But Lichtental also provided much more than a performance outlet and was a cornerstone in Schubert's musical imagination as he strove to fulfil local needs.

We can tell so much about contemporary practice from the sacred works Schubert composed in these years. Many of the solo soprano lines of his Lichtental liturgical works were written for Therese Grob (1798–1875). We hear this in his first four masses and occasional works, especially the Offertorium in C (*Totus in corde langueo*, D 136) described on the fair copy as an 'Aria with clarinet solo',[4] the *Salve Regina* in F major (D 223) for soprano and strings, as well as the *Tantum Ergo* in C major (D 460) and 'Auguste jam coelestium' (D 488), a duet for soprano and tenor. At the time Schubert wrote these works, women were precluded from performing in chapels – a law which could be bypassed to include relations of the *Regens chori* or local schoolmasters. As the daughter of a silk factory owner, Therese Grob was not officially permitted to perform, yet her premiere of many of Schubert's sacred works in the Lichtental Parish is a good indication of the slippage between law and practice.[5]

We can also tell a great deal about contemporary praxis from Schubert's organ parts which are sketched rather than fully realized. The part was always written out in transcription and even when a figured bass is omitted it indicates the tradition of playing from an unfigured partimento. It is inconceivable that these works were performed without the organ: when Schubert wanted this effect in particular passages he marked them 'senza Organo'. Occasionally in rehearsal he crossed out the organ part. A further example is found in Schubert's autograph for the *Salve Regina* in B flat major (D 106) where the 'Basso' line is intended for cello, bass and organ. Schubert later pencilled in a figured bass notation which Ferdinand interpreted differently. On the envelope for his set of parts Ferdinand noted 'Die Orgel ist nur in Ermangelung der Blas-Instrumente [zu] spielen' (the organ is only used in the absence of wind instruments), which he characteristically realized for two oboes, two bassoons and horns. The same practice occurs in Schubert's *Tantum Ergo* in D major (D 750), the parts for which Ferdinand transcribed in 1822, later adding a new organ part 'zur Supplirung einiger Blas-Instrumente' to supplement the wind instruments. Depending on the nature of the parish ensemble, a professional organist was expected to voice a flute or violin solo, for example, or missing wind parts. We find an example of this practice in the publication of

Schubert's Mass no. 4 in C (D 452), where passages for the oboes or bassoons are added above the organ continuo in smaller notation.

The rich repository of liturgical music for the Roman Catholic Church written between 1814 and 1816 bears testimony to Schubert's apprenticeship as a composer of sacred music and his ambition to secure a position as Kapellmeister (Table 6.1 online). The extensive revisions to Schubert's manuscripts – especially the scribbled pencil markings – are the refinements made at rehearsals. The abrupt halt in liturgical compositions in 1816 coincides with leaving the Lichtental Parish. Ferdinand's distinction as a church organist and curatorship of Schubert's sacred music was established during these Lichtental years. Through Ferdinand many of Schubert's sacred works after 1816 not only came into existence but became established in church music repertoire. Numerous sets of parts are in Ferdinand's hand: he was responsible for conducting at least eight premieres during Schubert's lifetime and at least seven posthumous performances.

INTERMEZZO: THE OTHER SCHUBERT

The way in which Ferdinand and Franz collaborated in Lichtental consolidated their training as church musicians (Figure 11). It was entirely natural for Franz Theodor, whose father had built the church and funded an organ in Vysoká, to witness his sons' ambition and active involvement in the musical life of the parish. This working relationship between siblings very naturally continued when Ferdinand became responsible for the music education of pupils at the orphanage of the *Normalhauptschule* in 1816. Three of Schubert's works with German text were written for Ferdinand's new position: the German *Salve Regina* (D 379), *Stabat Mater* (D 383) and *Deutsche Requiem* (D 621). When Ferdinand was appointed teacher and choirmaster of a boys' school in the Alt-Lerchenfeld suburb in 1820, Schubert wrote the *Sechs Antiphonen zum Palmsonntag* (D 696) for him and forgave Ferdinand's 'sin of appropriation' when he passed off his when he passed off his brother's *Requiem* (D 621) as his own.[6] Did Ferdinand embark on a long course of self-humiliation? His solid musicianship is evident in his imaginative realization of the figured bass and skilful orchestration of Schubert's *Salve Regina* in B flat (D 386), which he published as his own composition with Anton Diabelli in 1834, even going as far as dedicating it to Sigismund Schultes, Abbot of the Schottenstift.[7] But before jumping to conclusions about opportunism, dishonesty, and what must have been a painful recognition of his own inferiority, it is important to consider to what degree Ferdinand's actions are culturally dependent. Whereas the extreme side of his borrowing would today come under the rubric of 'plagiarism', Schubert himself not only borrowed but was introduced to the technique of *imitatio* by Salieri, where material from earlier or contemporary composers (or oneself) was used as a starting point for original work. This was standard practice at the time when the idea of intellectual ownership did not exist. Nietzsche went as far as claiming that 'life itself is *essentially* a process of appropriating ... "exploitation" does not belong to a corrupted or imperfect, primitive society; it belongs to the essence of being alive'[8] – a principle that is echoed in Heidegger's *immer schon* (always already) or Jean-Louis Chrétien's *Call and Response* which opens with a quote from Joseph Joubert, 'in order for a voice to be beautiful, it must have many voices in it'.[9] How does Ferdinand's recycling of Schubert's Kyrie in B flat (D 45) and other works in his 'Pastoral Mass' (1833) compare to Schubert's citation of his or other's work? Is Ferdinand's orchestration of *Salve Regina* in B flat (D 386) any different to Schubert's arrangement of Matiegka's Guitar Quartet (D 96) or Czerny's arrangement of Schubert's 'Trauerwalzer' in A flat op. 9/2? One half of the answer is found in John Milton – 'For such a borrowing as this, if it be not bettered by the borrower, among good authors it is accounted Plagiare' – the other half in the tyranny of custom and care.[10] Through Schubert, Ferdinand had formed the ambition to be a composer and had doggedly tried his hand at composition while working at the orphanage and wasting the ability he hoped he possessed. If marriage into the middle class offered him constriction, obscurity and forgetfulness of those dreams, it also preserved his love of his brother who had taken the more difficult path.

SCHUBERT'S *MARIENBILD*

The frame through which we view Schubert as a church music composer is crucial: the retrospective pattern-recognition by which we wrest his personhood from his experience. Sifting through cause and effect in his life, experiences connect across time and many connections emerge, one of which is his allegiance to the *Marienbild*. That Schubert's mother, Maria Elisabeth, died in May, the month that is traditionally dedicated to the Blessed Virgin Mary, heightened his association. The same affective devotion, showing Mary not just as a woman but as an ideal to which humanity should aspire, re-emerges in his songs at times of crisis. In the latter half of 1818 it appears in 'Das Marienbild' (D 623, August 1818) and in a setting of a poem of Aloys Wilhelm Schreiber, 'Blondel zu Marien' (Blondel to Mary, D 626, September 1818, text anonymous); it re-emerges in 'Vom Mitleiden Mariä' (D 632), text by Friedrich Schlegel, December 1818, and 'Marie' (D 658), to a text by Novalis, May 1819. The most popular example is 'Ellens Gesang' III (Ave Maria, D 839), a setting Schubert describes as spontaneous prayer in 1825:

> People are very surprised at the piety which I have expressed in a hymn to the Blessed Virgin and which, as it seems, stirs all hearts deeply and moves everyone to a feeling of devotion. I believe that happens because I never force myself to pray and, apart from when I am instinctively overcome by a feeling of devotion, I never compose such hymns or prayers, so [when I do], the right kind of devotion comes about.[11]

Schubert's sacred and secular Marian hymns are a vessel of true religious feeling, and an important step in his discovery of a musical art that is at once autobiographical and objective.

Of the four antiphons of the Blessed Virgin Mary, *Salve Regina* captured Schubert's imagination. At a time of immense loss, there is something deeply connective in his resetting of the *Salve Regina* text, which has been prayed by believers for hundreds of years. The text was usually sung at the end of the

Compline from Trinity Sunday until the first Sunday of Advent. Victoria, Palestrina, Josquin and Lassus wrote numerous *Salve Reginas*, as did Vivaldi, Handel and Joseph Haydn, though it is likely that Schubert would only have known the Palestrina, Haydn and Salieri settings. As with his multiple settings of the *Tantum Ergo* text, Schubert's sevenfold settings allow us to witness his gradually gained mastery. The very same principle at play in prosody and varied part writing in his nine partimento resettings of Metastasio's 'Aria dell' angelo' ('Quell' innocente figlio', D 17) underpins his *Salve Regina* resettings:

Table 6.2: *Salve Regina* Resettings

			Composed	Premiere	Scoring
1	*Salve Regina* in F	D 27	28 June 1812	1812?	S and clarinet obbligato, orch., org.
2	*Salve Regina* in B flat	D 106	28 June - 1 July 1814	1814?	T, orch., org.
3	*Salve Regina* in F	D 223, op. 47	5 July 1815 rev. 28 January 1823	1815? 8 September 1825 St Ulrich's	S, orch., org.
4	Deutsches *Salve Regina* in F	D 379	21 February 1816	1816?	SATB, org.
5	*Salve Regina* in B flat	D 386	March 1816		SATB *a cappella*?
6	*Salve Regina* in A ('Offertorium')	D 676	November 1819/1822		S, string orch.
7	*Salve Regina* in C	D 811	April 1824	September 1824 Melk Abbey	TTBB

In his earliest setting in F major (D 27), dated 28 June 1812, the steadying hand of Salieri is felt in the aftermath of Schubert's mother's death, guiding him away from a commemorative Mass (D 24E, D 31) and into a setting which creates an immediate counterpoint between art and life. Schubert could easily have been lost in grief: to counteract this, Salieri gave his musical intentions a limiting form and firmness by using the clearly defined figures and ideas of the Christian Church. D 27 is Schubert's first sacred music composition, ambitiously scored for soprano, obbligato for two clarinets (or two oboes), two horns, strings and organ. The tessitura of the soprano line and envelope containing the parts inscribed 'Del Signore Franz Schubert e C.R. Convictu, composite Die 28 Juny anno 1812. Ad usum T.G. 1812' confirms that it was written for his mother's *commemorationis dies* at the Lichtental Parish. To premiere it Schubert had Theresa Grob in mind.[12] Salieri's guiding hand is present in the comparative brevity of the text, which did not overtax the abilities of his student composer, and in the Italianate colour of Schubert's setting, in particular the coloratura *Salve Regina* at the song's close (Example 6.1 online). Deep emotion is hidden here behind Schubert's mask of ambition. When the setting passionately implores the 'Mater misericordiae' not to abandon him to suffering, the diction of the text becomes the diction of the music. This expressiveness is most apparent in the second section, B, where Schubert turns to rhetorical gestures to express his loss and grief.

Schubert's second Marian setting, composed two years later on the very same day, contains similar expressive tropes with key moments of *Erinnerungsmotive* from *opéra comique*, to which Schubert was introduced by Salieri. This Italianate resetting, with its intimate orchestration, modernizes the image of Mary as a tender, accessible woman, who will protect those who seek her care. As with his boyhood setting, this *Salve Regina* in B flat (D 106) observes the Catholic practice of prayer as petition and the aspiring composer's deployment of conventions. His salutation deprecatonia is expressed in an elegant tenor solo, imploring the Madonna of Mercy for relief (Example 6.2 online). Through the rondo's *Grundmotiv*, a falling or rising whole or half tone (A, bars 8–11), this dramatic prayer apostrophizes Mary as an agency of intervention, each repeated request individualized and intensified. The date of the setting again connects the interceding Mary with Schubert's mother, bringing Catholic theology into contact with human culture. We cannot distinguish the human and the divine in Schubert's mind, but we can hear in his music the purity and simplicity of his encounter with a creative Absolute.

One year later, during one of the most prolific months of his life, Schubert wrote his most striking *Salve Regina* setting in F major (D 223), op. 47:

Example 6.3: *Salve Regina* in F (D 223), soprano solo and continuo abstract, bars 16–60

D 223 liberates the Biblical person of Mary into the nineteenth century in a musical celebration of her as a symbol of divine embodiment and agency. Distinguished from earlier settings in its refinement of feeling and harmonic underpinnings, this impassioned musical narrative is still conceived for Therese Grob but its conceptional world is new.

As is characteristic of Schubert's small-scale liturgical prayers, it can be mapped out in binary form, but an unorthodox one which bears testimony to how much Schubert has now made this text his own. The three invocations of section A are tonally distinguished in F major (bars 1–25), A flat major (bars 32–36) and F minor (bars 43–45) as the soprano proclaims her opening prayer. Schubert omits the quintet beginning 'Eia ergo, advocata nostra' in favour of restating the prayer's final intercessions, 'O clemens, o pia, o dulcis Virgo Maria' (bars 43–60) and a short codetta in C minor–C major (bars 61–74). An irregular recapitulation begins at bar 75 with varied intercessions in F major (bars 75–84), D minor (bars 87–88) and G minor (bars 89–90), the final supplications (bars 103–123) concluding with an F major coda (bars 125–131). Years later Ferdinand copied out his brother's memorial to their mother into which Schubert very skilfully added wind parts on 28 January 1823. A month after the publication of this second version, the work was performed for the first time in Maria Trost Church on 8 September 1825 with the Graduale in C (Benedictus es, Domine, D 184) as companion works to his Mass in C (D 452).

The fourth and fifth *Salve Reginas*, written for mixed chorus, were composed within a short time of each other. The *Deutsches Salve Regina* (D 379), composed on 21 February 1816, returns to F major, a key which holds a special place in the tonal lexicon of Schubert's sacred music. This simple, homophonic setting, now in ABCA form with codetta, is framed by an imaginative tonal spectrum – F major, C minor (bar 14), D minor (bar 30), F major (bar 46) – the chromatic colouring of the interior sections intensifying the choir's invocations of Mary.

The fifth, SATB resetting in B flat major (D 386), composed in March 1816, is usually performed *a cappella*, although Schubert wrote a figured bass line for organ continuo as with his earlier settings (Example 6.4

online). Listening to Schubert's setting, it is hard to believe it was parsimoniously composed into the unfilled staves of the *Stabat Mater* manuscript (D 383).[13] The setting is remarkable for its hymnal decorum. Its self-possessed calm erupts for a moment at the *sforzando* on 'et spes nostra' (bar 17), transcending the formal constraints of the text in urgent solicitation. Characteristically, Schubert's ability to surprise is ever present: the locution of 'lacrymarum valle', underscored by a German sixth which he unexpectedly brings to a dominant seventh in D minor (bars 31–34), is typical of Schubert's harmonic invention as is the brazen shift to F major at 'Eia, ergo, advocata nostra' as the choir turns to a compassionate mother in search of comfort (bars 37–42). As is characteristic in his handling of this text, the B section of this ternary setting, the chromatic voicing of the choir's supplication, 'illos tuos/misericordes oculos ad nos converte', is answered by a harmonic trajectory which traverses through D minor, G minor and F major (bars 58–64). In this setting the short sequences leading to D minor ('ventris tui') are echoed in remembrance of an exile ('nobis post hoc exilium ostende'), which hovers over a dominant pedal (bars 64–69), building tension before the closing intercession. As the choir raise their voices to the Madonna of Mercy ('O clemens, o pia, o dulcis Virgo Maria'), their cry culminates in one final prayer set squarely over a tonic pedal, a musical affirmation of the mercy that Mary offers those who suffer.

Example 6.5: *Salve Regina* in A major (D 676), bars 1–20

The sixth and seventh resettings (D 676 and D 811) possess great moral depth and sincerity. By the time he composed both, Schubert had suffered greatly. This intimate A major setting (D 676, 1819) addressing an earthly and heavenly queen, is written in the familiar binary form, each unorthodox half recalling the three sections in the F major setting of 1815. Supplication is again voiced harmonically as well as melodically in B (bars 45–82) through its reach for distant tonal relationships. Performed in the Lichtental chapel and still written for Therese Grob, the sensuous beauty of the solo part emulates the sound of the human voice soliciting comfort.

SCHUBERT AS A CHURCH MUSIC COMPOSER

In a time of great suffering and isolation, Schubert wrote one final, exquisite setting of the *Salve Regina* (D 811, 1824) for *a cappella* male voices, rich in feeling and harmonic resource. Innovative in terms of church settings, this triple-time C major setting is challenging to perform. In modified rondo form, the principal theme of Schubert's nocturnal setting is posited in the tonic followed by two episodes that are free and inventive.

A simple parsing of the descending thirds on 'dulcedo' (bars 6 and 10) decorates this part of the theme with Monteverdian-like interpolations. The first emotional climax is reached at the choir's apostrophe to Mary, 'ad te suspiramus gementes et flentes in hac lacrymarum valle', sending up their prayers in antiphonal textures which circle from E minor (bar 17) through E major (bar 19), D major (bar 20), C major (bar 20), and back

Example 6.6: *Salve Regina* in C major (D 811), bars 1–13

to E minor (bars 23–24). Schubert's supplication of the Mother of Mercy is reinforced by a subtle use of the pedal bass line to announce the incarnation of Christ in C major (bars 35–39), restating it in D major (bars 41–42), before returning to G major for the three invocations, 'O clemens, o pia, o dulcis Virgo Maria' (bars 42–50). The eloquence of the discourse is evident in the *pianissimo* return of the melody with newly inflected harmonies, such as the very effective use of the French sixth to apostrophize the Divine Mother (bar 62), its dissonance prolonged in a *pianissimo* repetition (bar 63). A further example is found in the elocution of 'lacrymarum valle' on an E major chord (bar 74), masquerading as the dominant of A minor before boldly shifting to G major and C major to apostrophize the noble advocate (bars 75–78). The final restatement of 'O clemens, o pia' led by the tenor and bass soli is intensified by the striking intervallic figure of the augmented second in the bass part on 'Virgo Maria' (bar 98). The final reprise of the opening gesture reaches a climactic A flat on the parting 'Salve Regina' (bar 115), with fading echoes played *piano* and *pianissimo*.

Schubert's resettings of the *Salve Regina* illustrate his growing professionalism as a composer of church music when settings of this text were in regular demand for performance at an offertory, before a rosary, or even a recessional. By his third setting he had clearly transcended the functionality of a more traditional liturgical setting into an independent artistic statement as exemplified in his final setting (D 811). The key question is, can Schubert's settings for the Blessed Virgin be successfully performed today or does his portrayal of women betray their historical position? The medieval image of Mary is at best problematic: a model of womanhood conveying impossible ideals. Such images contribute to our social reality and Schubert would have been the first to agree that what we proclaim in song is connected to our self-understanding. It is significant that the morally exemplary characters with whom he identifies – a transfigured Gretchen and the Blessed Virgin of the Salve Regina – are females whose ethics are ethics of the heart and whose moral values reflect a middle-class conception of virtue. When Schubert composed these teenage settings he brought his own gendered experiences and expectations to this cultural metaphor. Beyond the obvious identification with his own mother as an agency of intervention – a role reassigned to Ferdinand in the aftermath of her death – there are the themes of divine embodiment, of love between mother and son, and a Madonna of mercy who offers consolation. In Schubert's *Salve Reginas*, Therese Grob, mother and church are all bound up as one.

Beyond Lichtental's liturgical rituals, there is the complexity of Mariology to consider and a devotional image whose meaning is not fixed in its medieval origin. Therese Grob's role in performing Schubert's nineteenth-century settings raises the broader question about the role of women in consciously reinterpreting these images. A very immediate connection can also be made between performances today and the *Salve Regina* text of the Middle Ages which, in the aftermath of the Black Death, emerged as an image of the potential of love for transcending distance between people at a time of great suffering and isolation. Salve Regina is a traditional image of feminine agency but more profoundly it is an image of human vulnerability: an icon of the importance of love and compassion in helping others. The *co-passio* of Mary as a universal embodiment of compassion compels us to recognize the human capacity for mercy, both given and cultivated.

STABAT MATER: RIVALRY AND RECOMPOSITION

That the image of the suffering mother of God, the Mater Dolorosa, had equal resonance for Schubert as an interceding madonna is again audible in his *Stabat Mater* (D 175 and D 383).[14] Here again is a musical reminder – an image of selfless love to emulate – and a statement of ambition as he resolved to write a new (and comparatively rare) German-language setting of the famous Latin text set by Giovanni Pergolesi. Even if a copy of this score had not been found in the Lichtental archives,[15] portentous signals of Pergolesi's significance are evident in Schubert's D 383 setting: the same F minor tonality, the same formal mapping in twelve numbers with a fugue concluding both parts, the same placing of solo numbers except that the duets are replaced by choruses. Pergolesi's presence is also inscribed in the sigh-motifs of 'Wer wird Zähren sanften Mitleids', one of four movements to contemplate the terrible image of crucifixion, which Schubert salts with chromatic dissonance. And yet for all its classical poise Schubert's score is decidedly un-Pergolesian: the instrumental prelude to the opening number which begins with a long sustained F minor chord in the oboe and trumpets immediately evokes a different sound world. The Romantic colouring of the orchestration, which carries the intimacy of a chamber music setting, the minor–major modalities of 'Wer wird sich nicht innig freuen', the rhetorical symbol of the Cross in the opening movement and the closing *fuga libera*; the shift from Jacopone's Latin text to Klopstock's German text and accompanying shift in perspective from the *Stabat Mater* to the suffering figure of Christ, all evince a breach in the aesthetic. If in Pergolesi's *Stabat Mater* there is a diction that intrigues him, Schubert responds in his own voice and assimilates that influence within his own origins. Those origins are richly rooted in a partimento tradition where the *cadenze finte*, the feigned 'Stabat' cadences which switch to the minor mode – a series of at least three deceptive authentic cadences or evaded cadences deliberately manipulating desire for tonal closure – are a partimento topic used to depict sorrow and loss. In throwing down the gauntlet to Pergolesi, Schubert is illustrating his intimate knowledge of the *Stabat Mater* tradition employed by Neapolitan composers from Domenico Scarlatti (1715) and Alessandro Scarlatti (1723) – which was commissioned by the same Neapolitan confraternity, the Confraternita di Cavalieri di San Luigi di Palazzo, and influenced Pergolesi's setting – and his mastery of a recurring partimento topic in the introduction to Girolamo Abo's *Stabat Mater* (1750), for example, in Joseph Haydn's 'Fac me vere tecum flere' from his *Stabat Mater* (1767), and in Mozart's 'Dalla sua pace' from *Don Giovanni*.[16]

Nothing is more basic to Schubert's existence than the call and response structure which was part of the very structure of his creative life. Just how eclectic that creative influence is, is evident in the tenor aria with oboe obbligato, no. 6, 'Was hätten wir empfunden', where Bach's trio sonata style has woven itself into Schubert's thought as early as 1816.[17] But to imagine that Schubert needed such models in a technical sense is decidedly not the point. What is played out beneath the surface of D 383 is neither an act of homage nor an example of historicism but something much more obscure. Schubert's *Stabat Mater* is about Schubert in 1816 and all this signifies about a critical juncture in his development. Pergolesi's and Bach's legacies live on here, not in imitation of form or style but in the deeper currents of their aesthetic: as models of an immediacy of expression in sacred music composition which Schubert responded to, even sought to emulate, an apprenticeship which rapidly transformed into rivalry and re-composition. The foundations of historicism laid in his apprentice years would reverberate in later works.

PREOCCUPATIONS: TANTUM ERGO

Schubert's *Tantum Ergo* settings demonstrate further the demand for smaller liturgical pieces in the daily office from Trinity Sunday until the end of the church year. The *Tantum Ergo* text plays an important part in the Rite of Eucharistic Exposition and Benediction of the Blessed Sacrament. Written by St Thomas Aquinas the hymn pays homage to the idea of transubstantiation, which honours Christ's presence in the Eucharist. It was sung as part of the *Pange Lingua*, during processions of the Blessed Sacrament such as at the Feast of Corpus Christi, when the faithful walk behind the monstrance carried by the priest. It was also sung before Benediction when the priest blesses the congregation who worship the Host in silent meditation.

Many settings of this Eucharistic hymn written by Schubert's contemporaries were written for Benediction, including the two SATB settings with orchestral accompaniment by Schubert's brother, Ferdinand, op. 5 no. 1 (for two oboes, two horns, two trumpets, timpani, strings and organ) and no. 2 (for two horns, strings and organ), published by Diabelli.[18] Schubert's six songs of eucharistic veneration respect this custom and tradition. They exemplify the composer's ability to avail himself of performance

Table 6.3: *Tantum Ergo* Resettings

			Composed	Premiere	Scoring
1	*Tantum Ergo* in C	D 739	1814	1822? St Ulrich's, 8 September 1825	SATB, orch., org.
2	*Tantum Ergo* in C	D 460	August 1816	St Ulrich's, 1825	S, SATB, orch., org.
3	*Tantum Ergo* in C	D 461	August 1816	St Peter's, 1826	S,A,T,B, SATB, orch., org.
4	*Tantum Ergo* in B flat	D 730	16 August 1821	St Peter's	S,A,T,B, SATB, orch., org.
5	*Tantum Ergo* in D	D 750	20 March 1822	1822?	SATB, orch., org.
6	*Tantum Ergo* in E flat	D 962	October 1828	Dreifaltigkeits-Kirche, 4 October 1829	S,A,T,B, SATB, orch.

opportunities in the Catholic liturgical year in various churches around Vienna and to write swiftly to commission (see Table 6.3). One of the ways he achieved this in the *Salve Regina*, *Tantum Ergo* and male-voice settings was by using a foundational frame. A good example is the tripartite form of Schubert's first Lichtental *Tantum Ergo* (D 739, 1814), which re-emerges in his B flat major setting (D 730, 16 August 1821) dedicated to Josef Mayssen, *Regens chori* in the Viennese suburb of Hernals. Related keys and dates suggest he conceived the service symphonically, composing additional items to be performed within the mass. While working on the Credo and Sanctus from *Missa solemnis* in F major (D 105), *Salve Regina* in B flat major (D 106) was composed for performance perhaps at the offertory or Communion, with the customary performance of *Tantum Ergo* in C major (D 739, 1814) at Benediction.[19] D 739 was repeated – along with the Gradual, *Benedictus es, Domine* in C major (D 184) and Offertory, *Tres sunt, qui testimonium dant in coelo* in A minor (D 181) – at a second performance of the F major Mass in the Lichtental Church on Trinity Sunday (25 May), for which Schubert also wrote an alternative 'Dona nobis pacem' (D 185).[20] He again drew on this experience by composing the *Tantum*

Ergo in C major (D 460 and D 461) as companion pieces for the Mass in C major (D 452), performed in St Ulrich's Church in 1825, with an alternative *Tantum Ergo* in C (D 461, August 1816) performed in St Peter's Church the following year. Even in Schubert's final Mass he would observe this practice.[21]

STEPPING STONES: KYRIE RESETTINGS

As part of his lessons with Salieri, and as stepping stones towards his first Mass, Schubert also composed a number of Kyrie movements, of which the first, with its description 'Missa in partitura', is the most salient. The absence of a slow introduction in any of Schubert's Kyries aligns him with the Stadtkonvikt masses of Salieri, Michael Haydn and Eybler. Salieri composed his fourth and final Mass in 1809, which Schubert performed in his first *Hofkapelle* year. Since then his teacher had only composed movements for the Mass Ordinary. On 22 September 1812 he completed a Kyrie, three days later Schubert wrote his.

In the first of these Kyries, Schubert's ambition is boldly announced: *Missa in Partitura von Franz Schubert*. The self-conscious nature of this undertaking is demonstrated in the vocabulary of this ambitious, dark-toned setting (D 31), scored for orchestra, including trombones and timpani.

Table 6.4: Stepping Stones Towards a Mass: Early Kyries

Kyrie no. 1	D 31	D minor	25 September 1812	S, T, SATB, 1 fl., 2 ob., 2 bsn., 2 trb., timp., strings, org.
Kyrie no. 2	D 45	B flat major	1 March 1813	SATB
Kyrie no. 3	D 49	D minor	Dated beginning April, at end 15 April 1813 (the last page is torn in half)	S,A,T,B, SATB, 2 ob., 2 bsn., 2 trb., timp., strings
Kyrie no. 4	D 66	F major	12 May 1813	SATB, 2 ob., 2 bsn., 2 trb., timp., strings, org.

This movement for the mass proper is written in the traditional 'Austrian' form: the 'Kyrie' in the theatrical D minor, the 'Christe' in the relative major (bar 61) and characteristically containing solo passages for soprano and tenor (bars 79–100). The 'Kyrie', however, is not simply repeated (bars 111ff) but is enriched with new features. Already we see Schubert experimenting with traditional forms in this ambitious setting composed at the age of fifteen.

Partimento principle is very much at play in March, April and May 1813 when Schubert reset the Kyrie three more times. The second of these, the Kyrie in B flat major (D 45), is a short *a cappella* movement already showing a solid grasp of vocal writing. It is possible that the April Kyrie, no. 3 (D 49, 15 April 1813) in D minor, the key of Mozart's *Requiem*, was intended as mourning music for Schubert's mother as he approached the first anniversary of her death. This movement for the mass proper is scored for a different combination of wind instruments: oboes, bassoons, table 6.4 suggests trombones as well as timpani. With its flourish of trumpets in the first movement and rushing figures on the violins, it is much more superficial and ostentatious than the first, and a true piece of 'Baroque' church music.

The May Kyrie (D 66), written in the weeks leading upto the first anniversary of his mother's death, is much more intimate in character. Its absence of soloists is unusual, a gesture Schubert does not revisit until his E flat major Mass. The second 'Kyrie' bears the imprint of Kyrie II in Michael Haydn's *Missa solemnis in honorem St Francisci* in D minor (1803) and Joseph Haydn's *Missa Sanctae Caeciliae*: it is an orthodox Allegro choral fugue, with *stretto*, pedal point, and shows a solid grasp of fugue though there is only one real episode (9 bars). The extent of what Schubert was learning at the Stadtkonvikt under the watchful Salieri is evident in the extraordinary technical mastery of these Kyrie settings, but even more telling is the conviction with which they were composed. These early transvaluations of Christian images of God's mercy declare early Schubert's allegiance to the Church, which is part of the world in which he was living in the aftermath of his mother's death.

SCHUBERT AS A CHURCH MUSIC COMPOSER

MUSES IN LICHTENTAL: SCHUBERT'S MASS IN F MAJOR (D 105)

Schubert's resettings of the Kyrie prepared him for his first commission, a festive *Missa solemnis* for the centenary Jubilee of the Lichtental Church on 25 September 1814. Schubert was seventeen. As *Regens chori*, Michael Holzer was responsible for the Lichtental celebrations, Ferdinand Schubert played the organ, Therese Grob was the solo soprano, and Joseph Mayseder (1789–1863), well-known composer and first violinist in the Kärntnerthortheater orchestra, led the orchestral players. Even given Emperor Joseph II's desire to strengthen the national Church with great displays of splendour, the size of the choir and orchestra with a string section of twenty players (6+6+4+2+2), wind (11–13 players), soloists and choir (25–30 singers) is still astounding. We know from Ferdinand's memoirs that the musicians 'consisted of none but friends of [Schubert's] youth or people among whom he had grown up'.[22] From this it can be assumed that Josef von Spaun and Anton Holzapfel were among the players.

Despite his shyness, Schubert had the ambition, musical authority and charisma to conduct a public performance of his first Mass in F major (D 105). The premiere took place on 16 October 1814 to a packed church which included many dignitaries.[23] A further performance, which Schubert conducted, took place in the Augustinian Church on 26 October near to the court where celebrations for the name day of Emperor Francis I were ongoing, perhaps also as part of the court celebrations for the Vienna Congress. It was in the close confines of the Lichtental chapel that the sincerity of Schubert's setting led Franz Theodor to an intense awareness of the significance of his son's talent. Following the performance, he bought him a five-octave fortepiano, not in anticipation of his becoming a professional performer but in recognition that the instrument lay at the heart of Schubert's creativity.

Less devout than his father but devout enough, Schubert wanted to please in this first commission. The praise he received – which Ferdinand records in his memoirs, 'If he had already been Court Kapellmeister for thirty years, he couldn't have done it any better'[24] – is especially poignant when one realizes Salieri, who was at the performance, had been in this position for twenty-seven years. He too had written his first Mass at seventeen and his own words of praise – 'Franz, you are my student and you will bring me further honour'[25] – reflects the fatherly interest he took in this Mass. Salieri's corrections are still pencilled in Schubert's score: in the opening bars of the Kyrie, for example, he alters Schubert's *colla voce* accompaniment so that the second violin underscores the alto voice as it does in Beethoven's C major Mass, op. 86, which was published in 1814 as Schubert was beginning his first Mass. Salieri's influence is also evident on the intimate and soloistic settings of the Mass – the 'Kyrie eleison' and 'Gratias agimus'; in the operatic character of the Gloria and Benedictus; the coloratura passages at 'Qui propter nos homines' in the Creed; and in the Pergolesian tenor solo with oboe and string quartet which opens the Agnus Dei. The imprint of Schubert's partimento training is in the *Laudamus te* canon and Cum Sancto Spiritu fugue which closes the Gloria and proves his ability at seventeen to write a formal fugue, and so he opts not to close the Credo with its customary fugue. The expression of textual meaning is discernible in Schubert's deployment of the *passus duriusculus* that drives the bass up at 'cujus regni non erit finis' (his kingdom will have no end; see Example 6.7), where it is used to great dramatic effect:

Example 6.7: Mass no. 1 in F major (D 105), Credo, bars 142–6

and downwards in the Crucifixus where it becomes a vivid metaphor of suffering and sadness, and augurs Schubert's handling of this passage in future masses. We hear it too in the Benedictus to which he lends the strength of *stile antico* by scoring it as an SSTT canon, though his original sketch for this cantibile theme, jotted down on 29 May 1814 and held in the National Library, is indicated *Canon a tre voci*.

Schubert's extensive revisions – some in ink, some in pencil – show the pains his first Mass (like his first opera) cost him. It also shows the opportunity it afforded him because many of the pencil revisions, including numerous tempi changes, were hastily made in rehearsal. Even Ferdinand's hand is evident on the score where, as organist, he pencilled a figured bass into the Kyrie. Schubert's own handwriting differs throughout the score: for example, the Cum Sancto Spiritu fugue at the end of the Gloria is an almost immaculate copy, suggesting he wrote out a final version after earlier sketches. The 'Crucifixus' in the Creed evidently gave Schubert considerable difficulty as the manuscript is laden with changes: at bar 103, à la Salieri, he pasted in a second piece of manuscript paper over the original two bars; he also crossed out three repetitions of the 'Crucifixus', pasting over ensuing passages. The final part of the Benedictus also cost him extensive revisions. Even after the work's closure Schubert was an inveterate reviser, as he composed an entirely new 'Dona Nobis' for a festive performance of the Mass in April 1815.

At the age of seventeen, Schubert clearly strove for authority. He may not have achieved the sublime degree of *autoritas* he envisaged when he wrote his first Mass, but it is so much more than an apprentice piece. Its stylistic assurances are astonishing not because this is the work of a seventeen-year-old composer, but because it so radically departs – in its expressive topoi, and extremely unconventional word-setting – from the court masses with which Schubert was familiar. The genius exhibited in his first masterpiece, 'Gretchen am Spinnrade', is already latent in the extraordinarily personalized diction of the Mass (D 105). It is no coincidence that the first soloist to emerge at the opening of the Kyrie is the soaring soprano line for Therese Grob (bars 14–18 and 28–36) for whom this part was conceived:

Example 6.8: Mass no. 1 in F major (D 105), Kyrie, bars 28–36

In this opening movement Schubert combines the Neapolitan lyricism of the soprano solo (bars 14ff and 28ff) with dialogue between the soloists and chorus, and concertante soloists (bars 43ff and 51ff), all of which became part of Viennese church style (bars 36–41). To both he adds the 6/8 metre of the Pastoral tradition and opening reminiscence motifs of a *Gesamtkunstwerk* which subtly unify his Mass and put his own stamp on tradition. Just how far he has come since his first Kyrie (D 31) – when he first experimented with the third part taking up the first Kyrie in a varied way – is evident in the varied chromatic soprano lines with which the chorus announce the Kyrie as a cry for redemption (bars 7ff and 64ff). Above all what is so immediately communicated in this opening Kyrie is the work's emotional intelligence and Schubert's musical sincerity.

The work's structural intelligence is even more remarkable in the soft invocations of the Credo where Schubert again shows his ability to surprise. In lieu of traditional changes of tempi and time signature, he observes the text's structure through the alternation of choral, solo and orchestral textures. The Credo opens with an intimate avowal of faith in an Andantino tempo and hushed *piano* dynamics (bars 7–27). Schubert brings out the drama of the liturgy through choral proclamations of the incarnation of man (bars 64–75), their hushed account of the 'Crucifixus' (bars 103–109) and drama of the resurrection (bars 115–135). Even at traditional points where his Viennese forefathers closed off a section and began afresh with a new tempo, texture, time, key, scoring, material, Schubert extends the confessional tone of this movement with an Italianate tenor solo 'Qui propter' (bars 75–82) and continuation of it at 'Et incarnatus est' (bars 83–91) (Example 6.9 online). Autonomy of person was Schubert's primal need and from his earliest setting scriptural infallibility is surrendered. The precocity of this youthful work provides astonishing evidence of Schubert's early stylistic originality as he bridges the gap between sacred and secular, German and Italian traditions.

SCHUBERT AS A CHURCH MUSIC COMPOSER

FROM TRADITION TO TRUTH: SCHUBERT'S LATIN MASSES

Under Salieri's tutelage Schubert wrote four liturgical masses in the Neapolitan tradition, the combined choral and orchestral movements with sections in which a limited group of instrumentalists accompanied one or more vocal soloists. Masses 2–4 were *Missae breves*, designed for regular Sunday services:

Table 6.5: Schubert's Latin Masses, 1814–1816

		Composed	Premiere	Mass Type	Scoring
1	Mass in F	D 105	16 October 1814	Lichtental	*Missa solemnis*	S, A, T, B, SATB, orch., org.
2	Mass in G	D 167	2–7 March 1815	Lichtental	*Missa brevis*	S,T,B, SATB, strings, org.
3	Mass in B flat	D 324	11 November 1815	September 1824, Hainburg, Lr Austria	*Missa brevis*	S,A,T,B, SATB, orch., org.
4	Mass in C	D 452	June–July 1816	8 September 1825, St Ulrich's Maria Trost	*Missa brevis*	S,A,T,B, SATB, strings (no viola), org. ('cl, timpani ad libitum' written into score by Schubert)
5	Mass in A flat	D 678	1819–22 rev. 1825/26		*Missa solemnis*	S,A,T,B, SATB, orch., org.
6	Mass in E flat	D 950	6 October 1828	4 October 1829, Church of the Holy Trinity	*Missa solemnis*	S,A,T,B SATB, orch.

Smaller in scale than his *Missa solemnis* in F, Schubert's Mass in G (D 167) was professionally written in five days from 2 to 7 March 1815. Originally scored for STB soloists, mixed chorus, strings and organ, Ferdinand later wrote into the spare lines of Schubert's manuscript trumpets and timpani parts for festival occasions. That Schubert still conceived the high soprano-solo part for Therese Grob is immediately audible in the Christe eleison. His contrasting of soprano and bass solos in the Dominus Deus section of the Gloria (bars 40–58) and Agnus Dei (bars 6–10, 20–24) shows his familiarity with Austrian Mass traditions to which he would return in the choruses of the A flat major Mass. How on top Schubert is of writing for local needs is subtly observed in the choral settings of the Incipit of the Gloria and Credo movements which are usually intoned by the priest, but which Schubert sets to protect the ears of those gathered.

Six months after completing this second Mass, Schubert began his third on 11 November 1815, again a *Missa brevis*, with the orchestration of a *Missa solemnis*, into which Ferdinand posthumously added two horn parts as orchestra; his practice developed. Schubert's final *Missa brevis*, in C, written in June and July 1816, is the last of three *Missae breves* to be written in sixteen months. Schubert's thorough knowledge of Viennese and Italian Mass traditions is evident in his observance of tonal structures in the Lichtental Masses (see Table 6.6).

Tradition required that certain sections of the Mass are contrapuntal or more precisely, fugal, but in the *Missa brevis* there are no extended fugues, which again explains why the *stile antico* fugue did not become part of his native language.

Table 6.6: Key Relations in Schubert's Latin Masses, 1814–1816

	Kyrie	Gloria	Credo	Sanctus	Benedictus	Agnus Dei
Mass in F	I	V	I	I	IV	I minor–I major
Mass in G	I	V	I	V	I	VI minor–I major
Mass in B flat	I	I	I	I	V	VI minor–I major
Mass in C	I	I	I	I	IV	I
Mass in A flat	I	#5 (E major)	III	VI major	I	VI minor–I major
Mass in E flat	I	V	I	I	IV	VI minor–I major

STILE ANTICO

One of the benchmarks of Schubert's sacred music is its late flowering of the *stile antico* style, which is evident from his earliest sacred music compositions, especially when setting Latin texts. Examples are his homophonic settings of *Salve Regina* for mixed choir (D 379 and D 386) and male-voice choir (D 811), but also his *Sechs Antiphonen zum Palmsonntag* (D 696), where his style is reminiscent of Palestrina and the four-part *a cappella* movement, with its melodic asceticism, avoidance of leaps, and chaste harmonies. When setting texts in the vernacular Schubert understood *stile antico* as a four-part strophic chorale which, along with a *colla voce* organ part, is melodically simple, as exemplified by the *Deutsches Salve Regina* (D 379), the *Deutsches Requiem* (D 453) and the *Deutsche Messe* (D 872).

In his late Latin Masses, when he composes the Credo in conservative style, it shows Schubert's interest in the deeper currents of liturgical aesthetics through which he could highlight fundamental lines of the text. Mostly – and from his very first Mass in F major (D 105) – he knew to set the Credo in long note values with stepwise movement in the vocal line as found in the C major Mass (D 452) in which words which hold less meaning are curtailed, and in the late A flat and E flat major Masses where the vocal line is almost intoned like a psalm (D 678, bars 5–15, and D 950, bars 3–33). The most striking example is the *stile antico* Credo of the G major Mass in the characteristic *alla breve* time where the long notes of the vocal line are in contrast to the marching bass. Here, the soaring profession of faith in Christ which moves in an ascending direction at 'in unum Dominum, Jesum Christum/Filium Dei unigenitum/ex Patre natum ante Omnia saecula' (bars 21–32) and 'qui cum Patre et Filio simul adoratur et conglorificatur/qui locutus est per Prophetas' (bars 153–165) is proclaimed antiphonally between the upper and lower voices at the unison. A further example of expressive word painting is heard in the crucifixion scene in B minor, a terrifying example of how Schubert perceived that key (bars 73–89). It is answered with a transition to D major at 'et resurrexit' to music of uncommon subtlety and dramatic effect (bars 97–137). What plays out in Schubert's handling of such passages is neither an act of homage nor a conscious revival of an historical style. Tradition is a value and a hallmark of Schubert's early sacred music which increasingly displays a dialectic of liturgical function and emancipated aesthetic.[26]

SACRED AND SECULAR SCRIPTURES: 'AM TAGE ALLER SEELEN' (D 343)

Schubert's consciousness was dominated by Catholic pedagogies and practices: death and everlasting life, prayers for the dead, were part of this. Funerals and memorial services were part of the culture which formed the composer, part of the ethic of respect. His very first sacred music compositions – the Kyrie for a *Missa* in D minor (D 31) and *Salve Regina* (D 27) – were composed in memory of his mother. Even after he moved away from the Lichtental Parish, Schubert's secular songs are laden with the Christian preoccupation with death and its time-honoured conviction, *memento mori*: two examples are his B minor 'Grablied für die Mutter' (D 616, 1818), which offered comfort to a former school friend, Josef Ludwig von Streinsberg, when he lost his mother, and 'Schwestergruss' (D 762, 1822), in memory of Sybille, the sister of Franz Seraph Josef Vincenz von Bruchmann (1798–1867).

Schubert's commemoration of all the faithful departed, and a further example of his feeling for religious sentiment in secular texts, is found in the long legato lines of 'Am Tage aller Seelen' (D 343, 1816), written for All Souls' Day, 2 November, the last day of Hallowtide (Example 6.10). This 12-bar musical prayer is a fine example of Schubert's reconciling interchange of what is sacred and what is secular, what is inside the law and outside the law, where the differences are even more important than the connections. The song's theological premise is the doctrine that the souls of the departed who have not been perfectly cleansed from venial sins, or who have not fully atoned for past transgressions, can be helped by the prayers of the faithful on earth. Schubert's observance of this holy day of obligation is evident here and in his practice of visiting the cemetery with his brothers to pray for the beloved in heaven, an annual gesture Schubert made in the last weeks of his life which coincided with his last supper. The pious poet Friedrich Heinrich Jacobi's secular litany invokes all souls who have departed, young or old, those who lived and died bravely, those who found love, those who didn't, those who died suffering or peacefully. All invocations end with the same consolation: 'all souls rest in peace'.

Schubert's response to Jacobi's six-line strophe becomes the carefully plotted ground plan whereby the music for the first line of poetry becomes the last (bars 1–2, 8–9). Within this noble chiasma, Schubert's song of sorrow unfolds in lines 2 to 5, mirrored in the modulation into the relative minor via the descending tetrachord, a musical depiction of death (bars 3–4). The sigh-motifs remembering 'those barely born who have left this world' rise up in supplication to a vocal climax and carefully prepared return to E flat major via a cadence in the dominant (bar 8–9). The gently supportive accompaniment, steadiness of the bass which tolls like a bell on the Day of the Dead, and reappearance of the memorable opening theme remembering the deceased, are Schubert's musical tropes of consolation. The valedictory solo (bars 10–12), its threefold rising sequences – an antecedent raised in prayer and supplication and a consequent offering hope of consolation – acknowledges life's transience before acceptance is reached. Art teaches us truths about life. 'Am Tage aller Seelen' (D 343) offers a deep understanding of human life as love and trust, desire and loss, despair and supplication, remembrance and consolation. The depth and sincerity of Schubert's setting, his peerless declamation of Jacobi's text and novel handling of harmony, transforms suffering into Divine revelation for the souls of the departed. For those who are left behind, Schubert offers familiar consolation: transcendence of suffering in art through the process of expressing it.[27]

Example 6.10: 'Am Tage aller Seelen' (D 343)

7

AWAKENINGS

'If art teaches us anything,
it is that the human condition is private.'

Joseph Brodsky

'QUORUM PARS MINIMA FUI': 'GRETCHEN AM SPINNRADE'

Three days after the premiere of the F major Mass (D 105) in the Lichtental Parish Church on 16 October, Schubert wrote his first masterpiece, 'Gretchen am Spinnrade' (D 118) on 19 October 1814. Since its inception, this lied has been continually promoted as 'revolutionary', which made the song seem all the more remarkable. However innovative 'Gretchen am Spinnrade' is, it is still strongly dependent on tradition. To borrow the philosopher Hans-Georg Gadamer's words, 'Even where life changes violently, as in ages of revolution, far more of the old is preserved in the supposed transformation of everything anyone knows, and it combines with the new to create a new value.'[1] Even the avant-garde, Pierre Boulez, acknowledged that composing always takes place within a tradition, 'The composer is exactly like you constantly on the horns of the same dilemma, caught in the same dialectic – the great models and an unknown future.'[2] So too the writer Ralph Waldo Emerson acknowledged in 1876, 'Our debt to tradition through reading and conversation is so massive, our protest or private addition so rare and insignificant [. . .] All minds quote. Old and new make the warp and woof of every moment. There is no thread that is not a twist of these two strands.'[3]

The two strands woven together in Schubert's 'Gretchen am Spinnrade' are the Italian and German traditions. What *sounds* so new is strongly grounded in Italian tradition which he inherited from Salieri and his Viennese forefathers, whose forays into song are much closer to Italian opera than anything else.[4] It is no coincidence that Schubert was setting dramatic scenes by Metastasio before he set a German scene for Salieri, who alerted his student to that intimate union of genius and tradition. Salieri recognized in Schubert someone who could combine the inspiration of antiquity with the demands of modern musical life to produce something quite novel: a work rooted in reality but suggestive of an ideal fulfilment; a work that has 'truth' in the fullest sense for it is true to what is, as well as what ought to be.

Another catalyst of Schubert's creativity was the soprano who premiered Schubert's Mass in F three days earlier. Therese Grob had an alluring voice, round and soft, full of variety and expression. Holzapfel, who met her in 1816, characterized her prosaically, recalling that she 'was by no means a beauty, but had a fine, fairly full figure, a fresh complexion, and a wholesome face, plump like a child's', rather similar in character and status to Schubert's mother (Figure 13).[5] From the few accounts that survive we have an impression of a self-sufficient, competent, honest, naturally open sixteen-year-old girl, socially on a par with Schubert's family. Although they knew each other beforehand,[6] her performance at the Lichtental Church may have been the agent of Schubert's awakening to a new energy of sexual desire. 'Gretchen am Spinnrade' was not the direct consequence of meeting her; the pump was primed as much by other music as by other people, but there definitely was a new charge, a quicker flow. Holzapfel confirms this by recognizing that 'Schubert's feelings were intense and kept locked within himself and were certainly not without influence on his first works, as the Grob household was given to serious music making'.[7]

AWAKENINGS

According to Anselm Hüttenbrenner a very crestfallen Schubert later confessed to him, 'I loved someone very dearly and she loved me too [. . .] in a mass, which I composed, she sang the soprano solos most beautifully and with deep feeling. She was not exactly pretty [. . .] but she had a heart of gold. For three years she hoped that I would marry her, but I could not find a position which would have provided for us both [. . .] she then bowed to her parents' wishes and married someone else, which hurt me very deeply. I still love her and there has been no one who appealed to me as much as, or more than, she. She was just not meant for me.'[8] Hüttenbrenner's belief that Grob laid claim to Schubert's heart rings too true and certainly for a couple of years Schubert was pleased to match Grob's hopes. His application for a teaching position in Laibach (now Ljubljana) on 14 April 1816, his composition of the Adagio and Rondo Concertante in F for Piano Quartet (D 487) for her self-assured brother, Heinrich (1800–1855), or such settings he wrote for her as 'Stimme der Liebe' (D 187, May 1815), all suggest his silent, secret wooing. A hint of Schubert's mental intoxication can be gleaned from the eight songs (D 302–9) which he wrote on her name day, 15 October 1815, for a musical celebration in her home that evening, including an impassioned invocation of the power of love in 'An die Geliebte' (D 303).[9] The same agitation of frustrated desire runs through the entire song set, and so does the parallel discovery (more tentatively) that the self can form the subject matter of song. The collection confirms an abrupt transition from objective, plastic verse to a rapturous diary of his relations with Therese Grob.

Schubert gifted her sixteen songs for her eighteenth birthday in November 1816, which she later had bound together in an album entitled Lieder (Manuscripts) by Franz Schubert which I solely possess' (see Table 7.1).[10]

Seven of the songs – 'Andenken' (D 99), 'Lied aus der Ferne (D 107), 'Litanei auf das Fest aller Seelen' (D 343), 'Am ersten Maimorgen' (D 344), 'Klage an den Mond' (D 436), 'Zufriedenheit' (D 501) and 'Mailied' (D 503) – only exist in this album, which immediately illustrates how

Table 7.1: Therese Grob Songbook

	Song	Poet	Date	Page
1.	'Edone' (Edone, D 445)	Klopstock	June 1816	1r–2v
2.	'Klage' (D 512 =I, 28, Lament)	Adapted Hölty 'Der Leidende' no. 5.		3r–4v
3.	'An die Natur' (To Nature, D 372)	Stolberg-Stolberg	15 Jan 1816	5
4.	'Pflügerlied' (Ploughman's Song, D 392)	Salis-Seewis	Mar 1816	6r
5.	'Der Leidende' (The Sufferer, D 432, entitled 'Klage')	Hölty	May 1816	6v
6.	'Gott im Frühling' (God in Spring, D 448)	Uz	June 1816	
7.	'Ins stille Land' (To the Land of Rest, D 403)	Salis-Seewis	Mar 1816	8r
8.	'Der Herbstabend' (Autumn Evening, D 405)	Salis-Seewis	Apr 1816	8v
9.	'Am Grabe Anselmos' (At Anselmo's Grave, D 504)	Claudius	4 Nov 1816	9r–9v
[17.]	'Am ersten Maimorgen' (On the First May Morning, D 344)	Claudius	Text, V.2–4	10r
10.	'Andenken' (Remembrance, D 99)	Matthisson	Apr 1814	10r–11r
11.	'Am Tage aller Seelen' (Litany for the Feast of All Souls, D 343)	Jacobi	Aug 1816	11r
12.	'Lied aus der Ferne' (Song from Afar, D 107)	Matthisson	V1: Jul 1814, V2?	11v
13.	'Zufriedenheit' (Contentment, D 501)	Claudius	Nov 1816	12
14.	'Klage an den Mond' (Lament to the Moon, D 436/437)	Hölty	12 May 1816	13r–13v
15.	'Mailied' (May Song, D 503)	Hölty	Nov 1816	13v
16.	'Trauer der Liebe' (Love's Sorrow, D 437)	Jacobi	Aug 1816	14r
17.	'Am ersten Maimorgen' (On the First May Morning, D 344)	Claudius	1816?	14v

valuable the collection is.[11] The album contains an assortment of paper types and three songs – 'An die Natur' (D 372), 'Zufriedenheit' (D 501) and 'Lied aus der Ferne' (D 107) – are in transposed versions for Therese Grob. The difference between the songs in this collection and their printed versions offers a rare insight into Schubert's compositional life. A slow introduction is added to 'Ins stille Land' (D 403) and 'Der Herbstabend' (D 405), while 'Am Tage aller Seelen' (D 343) omits the one-bar introduction of the first published version. As one would expect, 'Edone' (D 445), 'Pflügerlied' (D 392), 'Gott im Frühling' (D 448), 'Am Grabe Anselmos' (D 504), 'Andenken' (D 99), 'Klage an den Mond' (D 436) and 'Trauer der Liebe' (D 437) all contain nuanced amendments in the published editions. One song, 'Klage' (I, 28), is not by Schubert but is scored in a very unpractised hand. It is possible that Therese Grob, like Marianne Willemer in Goethe's *Westöstlicher Divan*, responded artistically to Schubert's setting of Hölty's 'Der Leidende' (D 432) and her parody became part of the collection. The mirrored Klagelieder and such songs as 'An die Natur' (D 372) offer us a self-portrait of the artist and songs of a personal physical love. Certainly a new and unconcealed personal note is sounded: a call to separateness, to be more himself.

Such musical offerings bear testimony to ecstatic hours shared, with 'Mailied' closing on a note of marriage: 'Like the dove, you too should take a wife and be happy.' Schubert's reflections in his diary on 8 September 1816 confirm he was contemplating marriage: 'Happy is he who finds a true friend. Happier still is he who finds a true friend in his wife.' But marriage had its financial as well as its emotional side and as the imperturbable Grob guessed, there was opposition. It came in the form of the Marriage Consent Law introduced in 1815, which required that all men give proof of an adequate income to support a wife and family.[12] Members of the aristocracy, property owners, professional people and higher state officials were exempt, but permission for assistant schoolteachers was deemed necessary. In his diary Schubert admits the despondency of a lover who anticipates his own failure and uncannily his own future, as he prays these laws will be lifted 'without harmful consequences'.[13] The real obstacle was precisely that such difficulties were not insuperable. Grob was completely available and very suitable, and there were no great social or financial disparities. There was a strong and mutual attraction and the match would have been a good one and that no doubt is why from the start Schubert was uneasy. Therese Grob presented him with the fully real possibility of marriage and for that reason the crisis in which he rejected her was the most decisive of his life. Grob meant marriage and marriage meant Lichtental. Grob represented the security of home, family, the lure of the world where he knew he would be valued, but those limitations were all too apparent to him. Even the omission of his age and marriage status on his application letter to Laibach – which were requested on the application and left the Directorate of Laibach guessing that he was very young – is an equivocal augury.

But there is no doubt that Schubert conceived a small, rich passion for Therese Grob. For several years she queened his imagination in a way that, modest and discreet as she was when she met Kreissle von Hellborn in 1860, she could not have revealed. Aside from her voice, she had a good deal of common sense and her marriage to Johann Bergmann in 1820 led to much happiness later in life. In the years they were together Therese's voice held Schubert under a spell: the raw energy of 'Gretchen am Spinnrade' communicates intense desire unsettled by reservation. Through his art, Schubert transformed himself from an adolescent suffering from unrealized love to an empowered subject – a composer who shapes a world of aestheticized love. So much has been written about the metaphorical spinning wheel, the dual significance of Schubert's piano accompaniment, the psychological realism of the first climax, even the extraordinary understanding of love at seventeen. But what makes the song so magnetic is that it is a nineteenth-century song of erotic compulsion sung by a woman, and its censored subject gave the song its notoriety and originality. The contours of Schubert's setting were neither written for or by an ingénue; the song is uncompromisingly erotic: directly concerned with the most powerful source of individual volition and uninhibited display of feeling. What constitutes the birth of Schubert's unique musical genius (as opposed to the fluent talent which he already obviously possessed) is the moment when self and form are not simply counterbalanced but are synthesized into a new unity in which self is no longer expressed directly but mediately and form is no longer an alien discipline but is bent to the needs of the individual occasion. All talk of the significance of the spinning wheel or the psychological realism of its marvellous first climax, 'sein Kuss', or even the German Lied being born on 19 October 1814, misses a central point – that Schubert was making the most decisive innovation of his entire musical career. This song takes an important step towards Schubert's discovery of a musical art that is at once autobiographical and objective, and marks the eruption of an altogether new kind of Lied.

The lyrics of 'Gretchen am Spinnrade' are especially interesting when considering Schubert's sexual orientation (Example 7.1a online). The text Schubert composed his music to expresses the physical love the protagonist has for a man, culminating on the climax 'and his kiss'. Did the song provide an outlet for latent desire he had towards the same sex without confirming outright his bisexuality? Whether Schubert experimented with two forms of sexuality, love of women and love of men, the song is still premonitory of his own tragedy. Why did he set Gretchen's solitary song in D minor? The tenor of the song suggests he was not entirely at ease in his wholly real – and so for him at this stage impossibly difficult – relationship with Grob, even as he was initially swept away in the hope of being with her.

This theme of tragic love is first announced in the polyrhythm between the accompaniment figure and the vocal line, which suggests Gretchen is all too distracted by her obsession with Faust to think straight (bars 2–11) (Example 7.1b online). The physicality of the spinning wheel represents the monotony of everyday life versus Gretchen's sexual delirium. She recalls Faust so vividly that he almost stands before her. Schubert underscores the ascent of her passion with a rise in harmonic tension as the song moves from F through G minor (bars 55–56), A flat major (bars 57–58) and B flat (bars 59–60). Tension has been mounting over an augmented sixth chord on B flat, the voice seeming paralysed and clinging to high D and F (bars 63–66); the chromatic transformation of the chord into a diminished seventh and the further rise to a first inversion dominant seventh, of which the root, A, ascends to B flat in the top of the accompaniment (a typical Schubertian effect) to form another diminished seventh, allows the voice to leap up to high G (bar 68). Gretchen's heaving sigh, 'and o, his kiss' (bars 67–68), approaches the despairing outburst of emotion in an operatic aria. The bass, which had been suspended during her cry, is then reinstated, the chord being transformed into a minor dominant ninth over A (bar 70). The fissure in the accompaniment as Gretchen's memory of Faust arrests her is one of the most celebrated moments of psychological realism in music. Time stands still within time as the changing material world symbolized by the spinning wheel is reconciled with the human heart's demand for the absolute. Love and beauty have in common with ethical obligation that they render irrelevant all anxiety as symbolized by the cessation of the spinning wheel and the absence of a terra firma symbolized by the accompaniment. At this point the accompaniment forgoes the bass which is re-established with the 9-7 chord on A (bar 68). This moment of psychological realism as Gretchen is lost in remembrance, this moment of sexual realization in Schubert's setting, crystallizes one of the peaks in Faust's experience which is revealed to him through Gretchen, of a good that transcends the wager.[14]

While this song became the *locus classicus* of Romantic song, one abounding criticism from the earliest writings on this lied is Goethe's rampant *animus* towards Schubert's setting.[15] The belief that Goethe would have hated what Schubert did always hinges around its through-composed form and the composer's recapitulation of the opening *ritornello*, which is not in the poet's original scene. But the song is a dramatic scene and the critique overlooks Goethe's lively interest in music theatre and his lifelong wish that *Faust* would be set to music.[16] Even if one merely examines the scene as a poetic text, Schubert's combined use of short vocal phrases in a high register with continuous harmonic movement, whereby a lasting tonic is never established, exquisitely mirror the irregular stanzaic divisions and irregular cadences through which Goethe poeticizes Gretchen's sexual unrest. Contrary to received opinion, Schubert *does* observe the cessation of Goethe's scene through the perfect cadence (bars 111–12), which marks the song's closure. His subsequent recall of Goethe's opening couplet is possible because the song is completely static, but it also clinches the crux of Goethe's play. Schubert's portrayal of an obsessive love as Gretchen reverts to her mantra is premonitory of her tragedy and captures the cruel irony at the heart of Goethe's play. As in Goethe's *Faust*, the form of love is rendered as corrupt: Gretchen is destroyed by the man she loves excessively. Schubert's first Goethe setting not only affirms an immediate understanding of the poet, but also an uncanny understanding of the dramatic and social context in which the scene was conceived.

Who was Schubert's Gretchen in 1814? Who is she today? In order to answer this we need to ask who Gretchen was in 1774. Goethe based his heroine on the story of Susanna Margaretha Brandt (8 February 1746–14 January 1772), a serving-maid who worked at the Frankfurt inn 'Zum Einhorn'. Three or four weeks before Christmas 1770 she was seduced by a goldsmith from Holland, who on his travels stayed as a guest in the inn. When he departed to Russia she neither knew his exact name nor address. She concealed her pregnancy from her two sisters and her landlord, and the two physicians, whom she visited, 'failed to notice' anything. When, on 31 July, however, she went into labour, the landlord's wife, threatened her with dismissal. On the evening of 1 August 1771 she gave birth to her son. According to her later statement, it was a precipitate delivery: the child was born headfirst onto the stone floor and already his breathing was laboured. In her delirium she grasped his neck with her left hand, scratched his face with her right as she cut the umbilical cord, and abandoned her child in the stable behind the house. As soon as the city gates opened she fled to Mainz. Entirely weak and without means she returned to Frankfurt the following day, was arrested at the city gates and imprisoned 200 yards from Goethe's family home. On 3 August she was admitted to hospital. Five days later her baby was found. When questioned, she broke down and acknowledged he was hers. After eight weeks' preparation the court sojourned from 8 to 12 October 1771. On 12 October the first death sentence was issued. On 7 January 1772 death by execution was confirmed. A request for grace was immediately rejected. On 14 January at 10 a.m., aged twenty-six, Brandt was led to the scaffold at the police headquarters, where the executioner, Johann Hoffmann, was waiting for her. He led her by the hand to the execution chair, sat her on it and bound her to it in two places, firmly fixing her neck and head in place. On the steady count of the *locum tenens*, she was decapitated with one blow.[17]

At this time Johann Wolfgang Goethe had concluded his law studies and was working as an attorney in Frankfurt from August 1771 until May 1772. He knew many people directly involved in the process: the clerk of the court, Johann Heinrich Thym, had been a house tutor to him and his sister, Cornelia, for nine years. One of the two physicians who treated Brandt in hospital was his family doctor, Mertz. Goethe's uncle, Johann Jost Textor, worked for the court; his friend and future brother-in-law acted for the executioner, who claimed he was too old to decapitate with one blow and passed that responsibility on to his son. As a lawyer Goethe had access to and had copies of the entire case made. Brandt's public execution and the way in which the case was handled deeply stirred the civic community, especially since her defender specified many mitigating circumstances in his final speech. The child had been born at eight months: the survival rate for premature children was, at that time, very low, and there was also the question as to whether the child had ever lived. Goethe was so deeply disturbed by the case that the tragedy became a central motive in *Urfaust*. A copy of the prison scene written in prose, the oldest part of *Urfaust*, dates from a short time after Brandt's execution.

Schubert instinctively understood the plight of Goethe's Gretchen from experiences within his own family home. The two women closest to him, his mother and his maternal aunt with whom he had grown up, had both abandoned children by the men they subsequently married. Within his immediate family, his parents had forsaken their firstborn. Schubert's maternal aunt, Maria Magdalena Vietz, produced a baby for Karl Schubert five years before she married him. Karl's wife, Maria Anna, was still alive at the time. Less than three months after Maria Anna's death on 14 February 1792, Karl married the twenty-eight-year-old Magdalena. But their first child had shared the same fate as the first Franz Vietz. Weak and jaundiced from his birth on 4 August 1787 he was abandoned in an orphanage and died a fortnight later on 18 August 1787. Of 3,010 children handed into the orphanage, only 173 (5.7 per cent) survived.[18] That Schubert and his siblings knew something of their parents' experience is suggested in Ferdinand's autobiography where he acknowledges being one of fourteen children.[19] The year after Franz Ignaz's death, Emperor Joseph addressed this social issue by opening the orphanage in the Alservorstadt (today Boltzmanngasse 7–9) where Ferdinand worked and lived for several years. Their two sisters married teachers who taught in orphanages: Matthias Schneider and Johann Bitthan. Schubert wrote numerous works for orphans including his 'Gratulations-Kantata' (D 294) which Ferdinand performed on the name day of the orphanage director, Franz Michael Vierthaler. He also composed his *Deutsches Salve Regina* (D 379) in 1816 and *Deutsches Requiem* (D 621) in summer 1818 for the orphans to sing in the vernacular, which Ferdinand passed off as his own in a publication by A. Diabelli & Co. with a dedication to Johann Georg Fallstich, the orphanage vice-director. The work was sung by the orphans in the k.k. Waisenhaus and by the students of the k.k. Normalschule in Vienna. Even in his summer of discontent, Schubert sketched a Kyrie (D 755) for the orphans in Ferdinand's school.

So perhaps not only Therese Grob but something of Schubert's mother survives in 'Gretchen am Spinnrade'. Schubert's family secret appears in his work in thin disguises: it explains the composer's fascination with the marginalized Mignon, Goethe's famous orphan, who also raises the theme of variable sexuality, through whom Schubert explores feelings of loss, grief and the desire for stability. In his Mignon and Gretchen settings Schubert explores notions of sexual belonging and separation very poignantly. At the deepest level 'Gretchen am Spinnrade' illustrates the belief that emotions are infinite, their limits defined only when exceeded. Mephisto provides Faust with the means of attaining the peaks of human experience, but it is also the mechanism by which he destroys what he attains. It unites him with Gretchen but ultimately brings about her death: their dead child, a symbol of the cruel irony which the ancient tragedians called Nemesis.[20]

No song worth its salt is unconcerned with the world it answers for and sometimes answers to. That answering function is what makes a song like 'Gretchen am Spinnrade' in the deepest way responsible – capable of offering a response, but a response in its own terms. If the sharp vicissitudes of fortune that destroyed many women was hardly the sole *raison d'être* for 'Gretchen am Spinnrade', it nevertheless runs like a red thread through Schubert's setting. As the earliest reviews show: everything is different after this lied, and people comprehend song differently.[21] *This* is what makes 'Gretchen am Spinnrade' undeniable and indispensable, making it a happening in and of itself. Listening to the lied we recognize Gretchen's experience as part of the human condition and at the same time the privacy of the human self.

THE STOLEN CHILD: 'ERLKÖNIG' D 328

Another transcendent masterpiece of the young Schubert, 'Erlkönig' (The Erlking, D 328, op. 1), is proof positive of a powerful, concrete, impersonal imagination taking the field against its time and place. Spaun records the speed at which this deeply autobiographical song crystallized. Somewhere in the private region of his soul, where music had its wellsprings, Schubert acknowledged the prosaic cheeriness and industry with which he was cementing over an unfulfillable relationship with Therese Grob and his hidden anguish escaped in a moment of intense musical imagination. Very probably in October 1815, perhaps the preceding winter, Schubert wrote the most terrifyingly erotic song of his life. The father in 'Erlkönig' rides with his sick son in his arms through a symbolic world of death – night, wind, streaming mist, dry leaves, grey, bare willows – and out of this dead, dark spectral landscape arise spirits of perverted lust. They whisper golden promises but in reality it is the voice of desire speaking to a boy with a directness unparalleled anywhere in Schubert's songs:

Example 7.2: 'Erlkönig' (D 328), bars 113–32

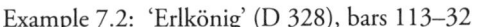

'Ich liebe dich, mich reizt deine schöne Gestalt,
Und bist du nicht willig, so brauch' ich Gewalt.'
Mein Vater, mein Vater, jetzt faßt er mich an!
Erlkönig hat mir ein Leids getan!

'I love you, your beautiful form excites me,
And if you are not willing, I will use force.'
My father, my father, now he is taking hold of me!
The Erlking has hurt me!

Death brooks no refusal and 'Erlkönig' is one of a phantasmagoria of black songs – 'Der Tod und das Mädchen' (D 531), 'Der Fischer' (D 225), 'Heidenröslein' (D 257) – where the beautiful, the strong and the innocent have no extraordinary claim to immunity. The simple childishness of the boy's last phrase makes the death with which the song ends unbearably poignant.

By the time Schubert published his opus 1, Franz Theodor had buried ten of his twenty children. What role, if any, does this play in Schubert's setting? What aspects of human experience does the song represent? Why did it speak so immediately to Schubert's contemporaries?

The answers to some of these questions are found in the song's mythography as each retelling has added some variations to its theme. Goethe's text is a rhythmical parody of the Danish ballad 'Sir Olaf and the Elf-King's Daughter', which was translated into German by Herder.[22] In Herder's translation it is Sir Olaf who is on horseback and on the threshold of being married. Riding to greet his wedding guests, he is entranced by the music of the Erlking's daughter, who invites him to dance with her. When he refuses, she casts a spell on him and he returns home to his mother, deathly pale. The following morning, on his wedding day, his bride finds him dead under a red mantle.

Goethe's poem distances his ballad from the Norse legend in four significant ways. In the Northern tradition, the tragedy takes place between protagonists of the opposite sex and comparable age; Goethe's *Erlkönig* seduces a child. In Danish mythology, the elf who ensnares human beings is female: an *ellerkone*, an *Elfenweib*. Goethe not only changes the gender, but assigns this character a new role: the *Ellenkonig*, king of the elves, becomes an *Erlkönig*, king of the alder trees, which are associated with Death. Thirdly, Goethe adds a measure of rationality to the superstition surrounding sprites: while the boy actually sees the Erlking, it is possible that the figure is a figment of his fevered imagination. Finally, in Herder's translation the elves are motivated by desire, jealousy and revenge, whereas the incentive of Goethe's Erlking remains unclear.

In the transformation of this tale from oral to written to poetic to musical traditions, an ethical phase is reached whereby the characters and incidents of Goethe's poetical narrative are realized as abstract symbols, intensely characteristic examples of moral or spiritual conditions.[23] Exactly as in 'Der Sänger' (D 149), his first setting to a ballad by Goethe, Schubert sets the musical stage for the first of these symbols before the narrator asks: 'Wer reitet so spät durch Nacht und Wind?' ('Who rides so late through the night wind?'). The authority with which the father is announced is immediately undermined. The boy he holds is anything but 'safe', an irony Schubert underscores with grace notes. In a gesture of extreme musical irony, the father's adoption of the traditional role as lawgiver is musically voiced in the measured phrases, dull back vowels and rising fourths with which he tries to appease his child's fear (bars 36–37, 80–81, 105–106). And yet precisely at the moment of greatest remove from the G minor tonic (into C sharp major, bar 104) Schubert stretches the early nineteenth-century tonal system to pinpoint the father's awareness of his own failing.

This outcome is already augured in the piano introduction where the kinetic image of the horse, as the instrument of a higher providence, is associated with the boy's destiny – the inevitable destination is, of course, death. In Goethe's *Egmont* – as in 'An Schwager Kronos' (D 369) – the horse is a symbol of the mysterious life force in nature and in man:

> As if whipped by invisible spirits, the sun horses of time go through with our fate's light chariot; and there is nothing left for us but to courageously grasp the reins and steer the wheels away, soon to the right, soon to the left, from the stone, here from the fall there. Where it goes, who knows? He scarcely remembers whence he came.[24]

Goethe lends this image eloquent force by placing these words at the end of his autobiography.[25]

The child's terror is central to the portrayal of his innocence because Goethe recognized the importance of keeping fear in its place. One of his strongest objections to Christianity is his belief that it is a 'religion based on fear' and he distinguishes sharply in his description of the *Pädagogische Provinz* between the traditional Christian kind of fear and the reverence in which he believes.[26] In 'Erlkönig', neither the father nor the child demonstrate this reverence for Nature. The child voices his fear to his father in minor keys. The father does not recognize his son's terror as absolute fear because he does not face reality until it is too late. The child's fear of the forces of nature is not dormant but undeveloped and so he is unable to exorcise his fear. Schubert brilliantly depicts the child's terror through repetition: his staccato phrases are an appeal for protection, an expression of rising fear and frustration at his father's inability to see what is taking place. The Erlking's increasingly insistent speeches rise up in B flat major (bars 57–72), C major (bars 86–96) and D minor (bars 117–123). His rising lines as he is drawn up by the sinister seductive phrases of the wraith is a secular realization of the soaring principle in the Neapolitan fugue tradition whereby the voices climb up with an almost mystical effect. This alienating reversal of tropes, whereby a sacred tradition depicts the ascent of evil – a subtle acknowledgement of good and evil sharing the same source – is accompanied by familiar rhythms of the Erlking's waltz played too fast and the reversal of the traditional use of recitative to confirm the child's dance with death.

'Erlkönig' is unique among Schubert's songs of stolen children. One of his most sensitive readings is a text from de la Motte Fouqué's novel, *Undine*: 'Mutter geht durch ihre Kammern' (D 373, 15 January 1816). It tells the story of a wounded and wounding couple who have lost their child, and Schubert composed it when his father and stepmother were mourning their eight-month-old, Theodor Kajetan Anton (15 December 1816–30 July 1817). This theme is revisited from a mother's perspective in Schiller's 'Klage der Ceres' (D 323, 9 November 1815–June 1816), a song coeval with 'Erlkönig' (D 328, October 1815). Like its companion setting, 'Erlkönig' renders with unprecedented force the incomprehensibility of losing a child, which was why it spoke so immediately to Schubert's contemporaries and why it is so relevant today. Children find their worst nightmare come to life:

forced abduction from a parent at the hands of a stranger; adolescents can ponder the experience of initiation that they themselves may be going through or may anticipate as forthcoming; adults find in the ballad a representation of their own experiences of tragic loss and grief. Ostensibly, the story symbolizes the loss that awaits all children and their parents: the loss of childhood innocence and the parent's loss of a child to time.

The undeniable sexual undercurrents – the Erlking does not seduce, the child is taken by force – render the story, like Proserpina, an example of mythic rape. The Erlking coaxes an innocent child, addressing him intimately as 'du liebes Kind' and, in imposing his will on the boy, he transgresses all moral laws. The story is not about abduction but violation, a typical example of pursuit and struggle, of supernatural beings assaulting mortals. The child is shown as vulnerable to assault, only able to escape through death. The portrayal of the father as a helpless agent against the soft and sinister beseechings of death is typical of the enthroned fathers in Greek popular culture who are unable – or unwilling – to intercede to prevent the rape. In an uncanny way, the boy in 'Erlkönig' is like the women in the parthenoi myths who reject marriage and so are denied male protection and pursued by the gods for sex.

In Schubert's settings of 'Gretchen' and 'Erlkönig' we see him testing the limits of how sexual desire is represented in the salon, how provocative depictions of sex and violence could be. His friends' enthusiastic response to the latter song and financial support of its publication say something of the personal and cultural code of Schubert's circle. It is often remarked how precocious his understanding of Gretchen's desire is when what is extraordinary about both settings is how alive he was to the destructive side of passion at age seventeen. Privately, the setting can be read as an avowal of Schubert's anguish over conventional sexuality (marriage) against his own impulses and an uncanny symbol of the inevitability of his fate. In 'Leichenfantasie' (D 7) Schubert conceives his own death and his father's regret when it is too late. Here again the child that Franz Theodor is losing is him. The song is an avowal of the uselessness of nurture against the claims of nature and circumstance, a musical affirmation that the Lichtental schoolhouse and parish church could not contain him.

SCHUBERT'S *LIEDERJAHR* AND THE ROMANCE OF CREATION

Between 1814 and 1817 Schubert composed more than 320 Lieder, over half of the settings he wrote during his lifetime. In this three-year period he composed fifty of his seventy-four Goethe settings; thirty-one of his forty-four Schiller settings; seven of his eight settings by Jacobi; his twenty-one Kosegarten songs; twenty-two of his twenty-three Hölty settings; twenty-six of his twenty-nine Matthisson settings; thirteen of his fourteen Körner settings; thirty-one of forty-seven Mayrhofer settings; his thirteen Claudius settings; his thirteen Klopstock settings; his ten Ossian songs; his thirteen Salis-Sewis settings; his seven Jacobi settings; and seven of his nine Stolberg-Stolberg settings. Half of these texts were prescribed poems from his school anthology *Institutio ad eloquentiam*, his resulting settings were musical ricochets and chain reactions. As only one poem by Goethe was included in the *Institutio ad eloquentiam*, Schubert's Goethe settings were drawn from his own voracious reading. His habit was very systematic, reading a poet's work widely and responding to that individual voice, before moving on to seek inspiration from another. His appetite for setting material is evident in the ambit of settings from eighteenth-century writers to the perennial Goethe and Schiller settings, to modern poems by friends. His settings of Austrian provincial poets – the Viennese Josef Stoll and Styrians Johann Fellinger and Johann Kalchberg – reveal his desire to create a national song style. But they also exemplify the many-sidedness of his mind and his stirring modernity which is evident in his eclectic embrace of the world around him. Unlike Hugo Wolf, he did not limit himself to canonical writers.

A new air of confidence runs through the increasingly hectic activity of Schubert's *annus mirabilis*. In 1815 he composed four Singspiele, a symphony, a string quartet, nine solo piano works, eight sacred music compositions with orchestra, twenty-four part songs and 150 songs, sometimes as many as nine in one day (D 267–275 on 25 August 1815). Schubert was buoyed up and charged up with a powerful will to deliver. There was an air of optimism in Vienna, the Gesellschaft der Musikfreunde had been founded and there was a new sense of enthusiasm and purpose in the post-Napoleonic period. Once he opened those channels, he definitely got a surge: *Der vierjährige Posten* (D 190, The Four-Year Sentry Duty), a light-hearted Singspiel by the late poet and dramatist, Theodor Körner, took Schubert just twelve days to complete (8–19 May 1815), during which time he was also setting poems by Hölty and Schiller. He also composed a short one-act Singspiel, *Fernando* (D 220), to a libretto by another friend, Albert Stadler, between 3 and 9 July.

Song crept up on Schubert, and the period between July and October in particular was replete with Lieder, including eight Goethe settings of 18–21 August 1815; nine settings of miscellaneous poems on 25 August; eight Klopstock settings, 12–15 September; eight love songs on Therese Grob's name day (15 October); and seven Kosegarten settings on 19 October. One cannot expect all of the 150 songs of this year to be masterworks – many were by their nature experimental – but the compositional current flowing in his veins, coupled with the arrival of the piano his proud father had gifted him, helped to catalyse a spontaneous liberation in the piano's role in his songs which felt given and also discovered itself gradually. Inevitably he composed a wide variety of songs: some beautiful, some still neglected, and some unquestioned masterpieces.

Schubert's *Liederjahr* is marked by a new confidence and, on the whole, a continuity with the past which is otherwise characteristic of the period. There had been good grounds for confidence, through the compositional strides of the previous years; the new-found freedom of leaving school and embarking on a professional career; the premiere of his first Mass and in the spring of 1815 a new and firmer footing seemed to be established in his relations with Therese Grob. In the songs he wrote out of his association with her, a counter-current to the inspiration of Zumsteeg's ballads had begun to flow. A number of opuscula, as rhythmically inventive and memorable as ever, grasp at the mood of the moment in the attempt to assimilate this new love to the pattern of its predecessors. The Grob songbook forms a large part of his inner dialogue with Therese but, more than that, it makes poetry a part of its subject matter in a way that is new in Schubert's songs. It is this cultivation of subjectivity – of their revelation of the inner man – rather than their objectivity that distinguishes the songs of 1815.

ANNUS MIRABILIS: COMPOSING GOETHE

There are twin dangers in identifying a composer's early influences: one either overstates or understates their effect. But Goethe's poetry was part of the air the composer breathed. It was, in 1815, at once a nurture and invitation to be true to song as a solitary calling. It reserved its right to reach for the stars. The question was whether Schubert had risen to that challenge.

Josef von Spaun certainly thought he had when, in the early months of 1816, he persuaded Schubert to make fair copies of his finest Goethe settings so that he might bind the manuscript and send it to the poet in the hope of procuring his blessing. The speed at which the book was assembled and the chance order of its contents does not suggest a premeditated organization of the material:

Title	Page
'Jägers Abendlied' (D 368)	1
'Der König in Thule' (D 367)	2–3
'Meeresstille' (D 216)	3–4
'Schäfers Klagelied' (D 121)	5–8
'Die Spinnerin' (D 247)	9
'Heidenröslein' (D 257)	10
'Wonne der Wehmut' (D 260)	11
'Wandrers Nachtlied' ('Der du von dem Himmel bist', D 224)	12
'Erster Verlust' (D 226)	13–14
'Der Fischer' (D 225)	14–15
'An Mignon' (D 161)	16

'Geistes-Gruß' (D 142)	17
'Nähe des Geliebten' (D 162)	18–19
'Gretchen am Spinnrade' (D 118)	20
'Rastlose Liebe' (D 138)	21–24
'Erlkönig' (D 328)	25–31

But Schubert surely appreciated Spaun's energetic involvement on his behalf, including his long, respectful letter to Goethe in Weimar requesting that the songs should be dedicated to the poet, closing with the greeting 'Your Excellency's most obedient servant' and his signature:[27]

> Your Excellency,
>
> The undersigned dares with these lines to steal a few moments of your Excellency's valuable time and he takes this enormous liberty upon himself only in the hope that Your Excellency may consider the enclosed collection of songs a not unwelcome gift.
>
> The poems contained in the present collections are set to music by a 19-year-old composer named Franz Schubert, whom from the earliest years nature endowed with exceptional musical abilities, gifts which Salieri, the Nestor among composers, brought to full maturity with the most unselfish love of art. [. . .]
>
> The composer now wishes to dedicate these songs most submissively to Your Excellency, to whose glorious poetry he is indebted not only for the origin of a great part of them, but also, in all essentials, for his development into a Lieder composer. Being too modest himself, however, to regard his works as worthy of the great honour of bearing a name so highly celebrated wherever the German language is spoken, he lacks the courage to request so great a favour of Your Excellency in person, and I, one of his friends, enchanted by his melodies, dare to ask Your Excellency on his behalf. [. . .] I refrain from any further recommendation of these songs, which speak for themselves, but will only add that [. . .] the pianist who is to perform them for Your Excellency should lack nothing in dexterity and expression.

Should the young artist be so fortunate as to obtain the approval of one whose praise would honour him more than that of any other person in the world, may I dare to request that the solicited permission may be graciously granted in a few words,

I remain in boundless admiration,

Your Excellency's most obedient servant,

Josef Edler von Spaun

Vienna, 17 April 1816. Resident at Landskron-Gasse, No. 621, 2nd floor

While anxiously waiting on word from Weimar, the composer began work on a second suite of songs, *Lieder von Goethe componirt von Franz Schubert. 2tes Heft*, which tells us as much about Schubert's usual effort and anxiety as it does about his favourite settings:[28]

Title	Page
'Sehnsucht'	
('Was zieht mir das Herz so?', D 123)	1–5
'Wer kauft Liebesgötter' (D 261)	6
'Trost in Tränen' (D 120)	7–8
'Der Gott und die Bajadere' (D 254)	9
'Nachtgesang' (D 119)	10
'Sehnsucht'	
('Nur wer die Sehnsucht kennt', D 310)	11–13
'Kennst du das Land?' (D 321)	14–16
'Bundeslied' (D 258)	17–18
'Tischlied' (D 234)	19–20
'An den Mond' (D 259)	21
'Der Rattenfänger' (D 255)	22–23
'Der Sänger' (D 149)	24–32

The return of the first *Liederbuch* by Goethe's secretary, F. J. Kräuter, was the first of many blows Schubert was to receive in 1816. Doubtless, the rejection was a shock and, as his letter nine years later suggests, one that he never forgot.

Goethe's silence is still cited as proof of the poet's musical conservatism, but if one examines *inter alia* the political and personal backdrop to the album's arrival in Weimar, many reasons crystallize.[29] In April and May 1816 the political aftermath of the Wars of Liberation, the Congress of Vienna, and in particular the new democratic constitution weighed very heavily on the poet. In particular, his anxiety over the planned public demonstration in Wartburg in 1816 – which he knew would antagonize Prussia and Austria – along with his personal situation filled him to the brim with despair.[30] At the time he received Spaun's consignment of Schubert's songs, Goethe's wife, Christiane, was critically ill and died on 6 June 1816. What then could a suite of songs from an unknown composer have meant to him at the time? Now more than ever was a time to step back from the pressures of a life in which literary acclaim was accompanied by the gall of people making massive claims on his time. Postage records in Weimar of daily requests, invitations, proofs, academic enquiries, personal letters, manuscripts in progress and new books, to a house through which passed a constant stream of visitors, gave Goethe strong grounds for reservation. His husbandry of the private self in response to his wife's death is recorded in his diary.[31]

Carl Friedrich Zelter gets the blame for misadvising Goethe but Schubert is never mentioned in their correspondence, nor was Zelter in Weimar when the songs arrived. Even if Goethe considered Schubert's songs independently, it was inevitable that he judged them by the aesthetic principles that governed what he himself produced.[32] In his hands the German lyric had achieved a higher perfection than ever before. The unprecedented emotional and musical power of Goethe's lyric poetry galvanized Schubert into new realms of song. Goethe was a catalyst in Schubert's genius and through him Schubert established a new site in the human soul in his songs. In his hands the German Lied became the absolute condition of poetry, the furthest reach of which the poetic spirit was capable. That is a daunting thought for poets per se. Goethe's recognition of this lay at the heart of his initial reticence.

BETWEEN REALISM AND IDEALISM: SETTING SCHILLER

That Schubert's *Liederbuch* arrived during an immensely difficult period in Goethe's life is one of those extraordinary vicissitudes of fate, which remind us how our circumstances are shaped by accident and contingency. Schubert continued to regard Goethe and Schiller as twin stars or Dioscuri, the Castor and Pollux of German literature, and patron saints in his development as a song composer. Between D 6 and D 801 there are forty-three Schiller settings: next to Goethe he is Schubert's most frequently set poet and in a very different way he was equally susceptible to Schiller's voice.

It was Schiller's love for music and its effects that first drew Schubert to his verse. Before 1786 Schiller was preoccupied with musical metaphors which pepper his early poems. It was not until the beginning of 1793 that he became interested in music's intellectual aspects, most famously illustrated in his letters to Christian Gottfried Körner, posthumously published as his *Kalliasbriefe*, but also in his correspondence with Zelter (1796). Schiller's most influential work on aesthetics, *Briefe über die ästhetische Erziehung des Menschen* (1794), which had a profound impact on Schubert and his circle, was strongly influenced by Johann Sulzer's *Allgemeine Theorie der schönen Kunst*. In the twenty-second of these letters, the only one in which music receives more than a passing mention, Schiller extends Sulzer's ideas on intersection of the arts, even postulating that interdisciplinary boundaries be dissolved:

> Music in its loftiest and purest form must become shape, and act upon us with the tranquil power of antiquity; [...] the plastic and graphic arts in their highest perfection must become music and move us through their immediate sensuous presence; poetry in its most perfect development must, like musical art, take powerful hold of us,

but at the same time, like plastic art, surround us with quiet clarity. Perfect style in any art [is] capable of removing the characteristic limitations of that art without however removing its specific excellence, and of lending it a more general character by a wise employment of its proper nature.[33]

The philosopher's preoccupation with form as the basis for evaluating the fine arts offers an insightful lens through which to view Schubert's settings of Schiller's poetry. Musical form meant many things to Schiller. He gives it a semi-mystical meaning in an essay on Matthisson's poetry:

> Every beautiful harmony of form, tone, and light which delights the aesthetic sense satisfies at the same time the moral sense; every consistency with which lines follow each other in space or tones follow each other in time is a natural symbol both of the inner harmony of the spirit itself and of the ethical coherence of action with feeling, and in the beautiful harmony of a painting or piece of music there is the even more beautiful [harmony] of the ethically disposed soul.[34]

His aesthetic theory re-emerges in his poetry, most notably 'Die Künstler', where he concedes, 'Creations arise/From harmonies, harmony'.[35]

True to his age, Schiller did not align form with structure but with content when he claimed 'if you take all form from music it loses all its aesthetic power but not its musical power', which, for Schiller, was physiological and sensual.[36] Schiller's separation of the *Gestalt* from the *Gehalt* is paradoxical – even profoundly unmusical – because nothing that is experienced is without form.[37] Schiller's identification of an inner form is more convincingly explained by Goethe, who does not separate form and content but recognizes them as different aspects of one artistic truth. For Goethe in art the internal form, the artist's individual experience, is given a general/universal form, or to borrow his words, 'Poetry points to the secrets of nature and tries to solve them by images.'

Schubert was deeply inspired by Schiller's belief that 'the musician expresses the emotions of the form',[38] an idea which Schiller develops in his essay on Matthisson's poetry:

> The whole effect of music (as a beautiful and not merely agreeable art) [is] to accompany the inner moving of the spirit through analogous external movements. [. . .] If only the composer and the landscape painter will penetrate into the secret of every rule which governs the inner movement of the human heart, and if he studies the analogy which exists between these movements of the spirit and certain external phenomena, he will arise from a depicter of common nature to a true painter of souls. From the realm of the arbitrary he enters into the realm of the necessary, and can appear if not on the side of the plastic arts which depict the external man, then on the side of the poet who takes the inner man as his object.[39]

Several years earlier the poet had aired the same idea in an essay on contemporary German theatre (1782), in which he acknowledged how 'music overcame the rough destroyer of Baghdad [Tamerlane] where Mengs and Correggio would have exhausted all their creative arts in vain [. . .] The path of the ear is the most direct and closest to our hearts.'[40] Schiller's belief in music's singularity is representative of a broader intellectual and philosophical backdrop into which Schubert's art was born. 'The path of the ear is the most direct and closest to our hearts,' wrote Wilhelm Heinrich Wackenroder (1773–1798), one of the founders of German Romanticism, who was one of the most important figures to articulate a new aesthetic of listening and to explore the fluidity of thought through which ideas reside in the work and in listeners' minds. Friedrich Schlegel's belief that hearing is 'the most noble of the senses' echoes the dignity that Schiller ascribes to the allegorical figure, Music, in his last completed dramatic poem, *Die Huldigung der Künste* (1804), an occasional work in which the seven arts greet their sovereign.

From his earliest years we see Schubert responding to such social, philosophical and intellectual debates as they formulated themselves around him. Schiller's lofty idealism on the moral effect of art had a profound influence on his musical thought. 'Art that is merely agreeable' was, in Schiller's canon, 'not only aesthetically unworthy but also meretricious'. In his final symphonies Schubert would advance a corollary that great art must carry a 'message'. Schiller's identification of the emotional resonance of a single note as a means of musical expression casts in a new light one of Schubert's favourite rhetorical effects, most famously found in Schubert's 'Great' C major Symphony D 944/ii (bars 148–160) when the *pianissimo* horns, which 'seem to come from another sphere', call everything into question with the repeated tolling of a single note, harmonically reinterpreted by the subtly shimmering strings.[41] Such passages can, of course, be traced to Schubert's exemplars with whom he was in direct musical dialogue – the trombone E flats in Mozart's *Die Zauberflöte* or the sustained dramatic Fs in the slow introduction to Beethoven's *Egmont* overture – and yet all accrue a different colour when placed against this backdrop of contemporary cultural politics.

In the late eighteenth century, lyric poems were perceived as musical works in their own right. Christian Körner recognized that the philosophical content of Schiller's prosody presented a particular set of compositional challenges when he observed, 'Up to now you have never made it easy for the musician, and many things have gotten into [your poems] which can be better read than sung' adding that 'not to destroy the melody [. . .] is a special difficulty for the musician.'[42] Songs from the plays, which were intended to be sung, were relatively straightforward. Responding to the unorthodox metrics and line-construction of philosophical poems was a much more formidable task. Such challenges are there even in ballads and 'social songs', where, as Körner observed, 'the long lines and the construction of the strophes as a whole do not make [the organizing of] musical periods easy'.[43] So much of Schiller's poetry lends itself more to declamation than to song and it is fascinating to sift through Schubert's solutions.

Schubert responded to Schiller's poetry between 1811 and 1824, but only five of his forty-three settings were composed after 1817. In addition to pithy poems and the customary lure of lyric poetry, he selected songs from Schiller's theatrical works, but was more especially drawn to ballads and philosophical poems. His dramatic songs are rarely, if ever, performed in productions of Schiller's plays: vocally, they are too technically demanding for most actors but they also rise above their original atmospheric function. This is as true of popular settings like 'Des Mädchens Klage' (D 6, D 191 and D 389) as it is of lesser-known operatic settings such as 'Hektors Abschied' (D 312) – an alternating duet between Andromache and her husband Hector from Homer's *Iliad* – or the arioso introduction which opens up into a recitative setting of Amalia's 'Schön wie ein Engel' (D 195) from *Die Räuber*.

Schubert's early declamatory settings of Schiller's ballads bear Zumsteeg's imprint, which is so interesting considering how closely Schiller worked with the composer. This influence is best illustrated in 'Die Erwartung' (D 159) where the brilliance of Schiller's prosody with its dactylic trimetre and trochaic quadrimetre alternating with ottava rhyme lines call forth the alternating arioso and recitative sections of Schubert's setting, which in turn is influenced by the pace and form of Zumsteeg's setting. But Schubert's operatic realizations of Schiller's ballads also bear the imprint of Italian scenes such as 'Der Jüngling am Bache'. A comparison of his resettings of 'Sehnsucht' (D 52 and D 636) allows us to see how he settles on a solution in his second operatic scene, which throws down the gauntlet even to experienced singers. Another lesser-known aria, 'Der Kampf' (D 594, a favourite of Johann Michael Vogl's, 1768–1840), is Schubert's last solo Schiller setting. One of the eight Laura odes, this Werther-like lied which contemplates the love of a married woman, was opposed by the censors in 1829. 'An essay in symphonic song-writing', Schubert's 'Der Kampf' – like his other lengthy Schiller ballads 'Die Bürgschaft' (D 246 or D 435) and 'Der Taucher' (D 77) – is an exercise in recitative and a grand aria inspired by Schiller's musical metrics and inner form.[44]

In one of his finest Schiller settings, 'Gruppe aus dem Tartarus' (composed in three versions D 65, D 396 and D 583, September 1817), Schubert answered the challenge of setting a philosophical poem (laden with classical allusion) with rising chromaticism: first melodically in rising semitones below a pedal point (bars 1–3 and bars 4–6), then harmonically throughout the song.[45]

Another way Schubert answered Schiller's complex prosody was by composing short, epigrammatic choral settings. Among the most popular are Schubert's drinking song, 'Punschlied' ('Vier Elemente', D 277) for male chorus and piano, and short, strophic setting of 'Hymne an den Unendlichen' (D 232) for mixed chorus with an independent piano part. Another solution was to set parts of Schiller's longer poems as male-voice canons, which Schubert wrote into the albums of friends who could appreciate their polyphonic ingenuity. Among the most performed are 'Unendliche Freude durchwallet das Herz' (D 54) from *Elysium*, 'Liebe rauscht der Silberbach' (D 983A) from *Der Triumph der Liebe*, and 'Dreifach ist der Schritt der Zeit' (D 69) from Schiller's *Sprüche des Konfuzius*.[46]

One of the ways in which Schubert cut the Gordian knot of Schiller's complex prosody was by composing declamatory settings with unconventional phrase patterns. The changing metres and cataclysmic images of 'Laura am Klavier' (D 388, March 1816) is a good illustration of Schiller's use of metre in a virtuosic way to capture the turbulence he describes. Despite the debt Schiller's lyric ode owes to Klopstock's ability to capture in monumental terms the evanescent, or Wieland's *via media* of a rational sensual life, the lied pays deep homage to Italian literature. The poet's tormented love for Luise Fischer takes on the poetic namesake of Petrarch's Laura in the same courtly tradition and is a cerebral celebration of feminine charm – at a distance.

'Laura am Klavier' (D 388) is a poetic realization of Schiller's belief that 'even the most ethereal music, by reason of its matter, has a closer affinity with the senses than true aesthetic feeling allows'.[47] The very title signals a tradition of women accompanying themselves at the piano – 'Lieder am Clavier zu singen' rather than songs 'mit Clavier Begleitung'. There are two versions of this song, both of which date from March 1816. When Schubert rallied his ideas into the second version, he added an exquisite prelude which transforms the song by portraying Laura as a gifted *dilettante* of the 1780s rather than a modern virtuoso. Both poem and setting accord with Schiller's celebration of the sensuous effect of musical performance as outlined in his *Schema über den Dilettantismus* (1799). In Schubert's second version the narrator is inspired by the beauty, grace and sincerity of the pianist rather than her musical mastery. Does Schubert's prelude ironize the exaggeratedly enthusiastic response of the poet in stanza one? Does the poet's apostrophe of stanza two – 'Sorceress! You use notes, in the same way/That you use glances on me, to control them' – raise the question as to whether the prelude is artifice or an expression of sincerity? Is it an example of Schiller's gendering of emotion? Or did Schubert know in 1816 that Schiller valued a melodic line which observed the basic rhythmic declamation of his poetry and a simple accompaniment which did not overshadow his text? Questions of this kind can never prove Schubert's musical intent. Certainly he knew Schiller's encomium belonged to the eighteenth-century tradition of celebrating women at the keyboard: his only other song at the piano, the 1785 version of Christian Friedrich Schubart's 'An mein Clavier' (D 342) – later published as 'Serafina an ihr Klavier' – also dates from 1816 and was also composed in A major. 'Laura am Klavier' (D 388) is illuminated and deepened by this pairing.[48]

Even if we could assert with confidence Schubert's intention, harder questions about definitive versions remain. To ignore them is to overlook the richness of Schubert's compositional process. The first version, with its underlying harmonic motion from E major to B flat major, is one of a number of songs, mostly from 1815–17, whose final strophe closes away from the tonic. Schubert's final redaction (transposed to A major), more tightly organized with a single tonal centre, shows how far he was prepared to adapt his initial musical ideas in the remaking of his songs.

'Das Geheimnis' (D 250), a philosophical love poem, originally set in 1815 and later revised for publication (D 793), is one of Schubert's most distinguished Schiller settings. The poet himself revisited the lyric between 1775 and 1805. Although Schubert's second version is catalogued as an entirely different song from D 250, the matrices of thought and feeling between these settings suggest the first is the seed from which the later version grew. The connection with its *Entstehungzeit* and reworking of ideas implies that the composer was much more strategic than history has allowed. The concept of revision is first announced in the vocal line which is more or less based on the earlier version, but beautifully reimagined in the second setting. The accompaniment idea which opens D 250 is at first retained: quavers alternating with rests to suggest the shy questioning of the opening lines, its hushed, harmonically secretive prelude never settling anywhere. It is really in the second stanza that the concept of revision begins to be tested: the natural setting for the lovers' tryst inspires a new accompanying pendulum figuration, rooted on a low C dominant pedal (9 bars). Subtle emendations are consistently made to the melody, which is beautifully decorated with a G sharp under auxiliary on bar 15 enhanced by the E flat climax to accentuate the word 'Liebenden' (bar 20), or unsettled by D flat (bar 22), underscoring the world's negativity. The emendations that filter into the piano interlude (with chromatic shiftings over a tonic pedal) are either harmonically very adventurous (bars 26–27) or textually expressive. Examples are the finely-tuned sextuplet accompaniment figure that evokes Schiller's 'empty buzz of voices' or the efficacy of the left-hand crotchets depicting hammer beats heightened by their preceding grace notes. Other minutiae are changed here and there to mirror the elocution of Schiller's text. It is noticeable, for example, that the unsettling D flat which is dispelled by the lovers' happiness in bar 46 announces itself at 'overtaken by envy' (bar 70), thereby heightening the shift of scene. On first hearing, D 793 sounds utterly strophic; only closer examination reveals how much work the composer has done to individualize each stanza in a modified strophic setting. On the final page, for example, he splits the opening chords for the first time (bars 79–81) and in bar 91 the E flat is now sounded on the accent, which gives greater definition to the words.

One of his most original Schiller settings, 'An Emma' (D 113), was written by the poet in 1797, the year in which Schubert was born. Schubert's three versions of this song are so dazzling in their beauty, we have to remind ourselves that the first rendering is dated 17 September 1814. Schubert relived the emotions of his youth and recast their musical expression in a second version prepared for a supplement to a magazine on 30 June 1821, but subsequently altered it again when the song was published as part of his op. 56 Schiller settings on 6 April 1826. All three versions offer insight into Schubert's compositional ambivalences and document not only his reflection upon textual minutiae but his evolution as composer from apprentice. That the metre troubled Schubert is evident across the three versions until he found a way of notating *arioso* and *recitative* with enough precision and freedom.

Schubert's compositional process was as much a syntactical one connected with the grammar of relationships as with the substance of thought and idea. In the first version in 2/4 the accompaniment plays itself out in flowing triplets. The repeat of the words 'ist es nur der Schein der Nacht' hovers on A, the dominant of the relative minor. When Schubert transcribed the song on a second occasion he brazenly changed the time to 6/8, interrupting the triplet movement here and there. This time at the words, 'ist es nur der Schein der Nacht', the music sinks into the darker regions of the relative minor:

Example 7.3a: 'An Emma' (D 113A), bars 15–19

Example 7.3b: 'An Emma' (D 113B), bars 15–19

In the published version Schubert reverts to 2/4 and elongates the vocal line with dotted notes which makes it sound more improvisational, more natural, thereby liberating it from the accompaniment. The song is *vollendet*. The composer gives it its finish in such details as the efficacy of voice and piano in contrary motion as a synecdoche for starlight and its reflection, or the Italianate vocal line of 'Deckte dir der lange Schlummer' accompanied by *a bel canto* triplet figuration (bars 20–23). Although the confirmatory cadence is pointedly tonicized, the voice gives nuance to Schiller's haunting question with which the song refuses to end:

Example 7.3c: 'An Emma' (D 113C), bars 47–62

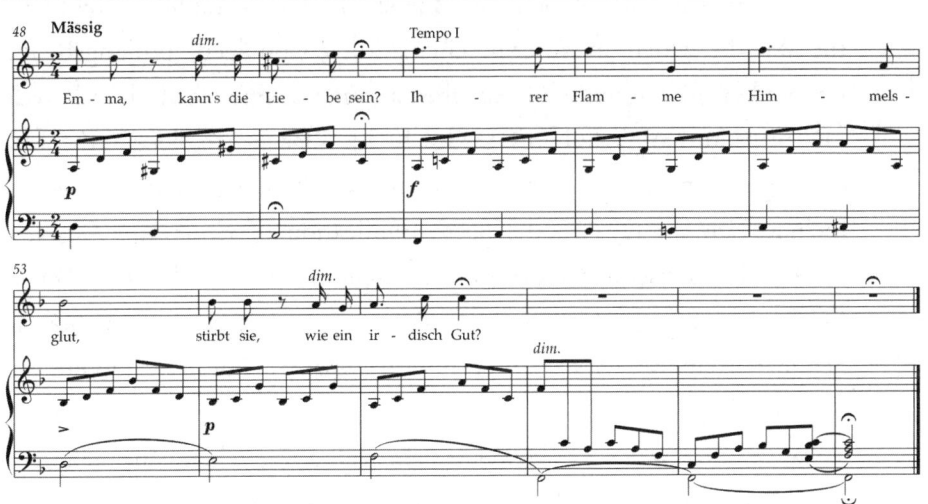

RECOMPOSITION, VARIANT, VERSION

Such detailed preparation of music for publication affected nineteenth-century philosophical thought. The gradual emergence of a *Werktreue* ideal led to the devaluation of works with a fluid nature while 'divinely inspired' works like 'Gretchen am Spinnrade' and 'Erlkönig' were much more immediately celebrated in the composer's circle.[49] Yet multiple versions were part of Schubert's compositional training and creative practice, and the process of re-reading texts is central to our understanding of him as an intellectual and artist. It is not just the breadth of texts Schubert set which defines him as a major reader but that he was an active and creative re-reader. While his revisions, variants or recompositions stemmed from his own creative impulse they were also an innate part of his performance practice. With manuscript dissemination of Schubert's songs among friends, each newly created copy of a score opened up the possibility of incorporating alteration and 'improvements', so that it carried with it a sense of individuality that was largely removed by dissemination in print. The frequently complex relationships between different handwritten copies of Schubert's songs – as illustrated by Vogl's arrangements of Schubert Lieder in his songbooks – highlight the way in which manuscript circulation encouraged, prolonged and repeated creative activity.[50] Even when a song was published, the relatively low print run of Schubert's Lieder in his lifetime challenges the idea of song as a fixed text. Even a seminal text like Goethe's *Faust* – which includes *Urfaust* (1774), the poet's publication of *Faust. Ein Fragment* (1790), his subsequent revision and republication of *Faust I* (1808), followed by a revised 1828–29 version – is a good example of how in Schubert's day creativity as a process with a clearly delineated endpoint was questionable.[51]

With such songs as 'Heidenröslein' (D 257), where one definitive version was written in 1815 and published in 1821, it is likely that Schubert would have improvised a short piano prelude in a private drawing-room performance.[52] Peering behind the scenes, one discovers the poem by Goethe combines self-discovery with a literary model for which no definitive version survives. Written in June 1771, the version Herder published in 1773 was written down from memory, but the version Goethe published in 1778 has an entirely different conclusion, suggesting a sexual encounter between near equals. Goethe had written the parody for Friederike Brion which Schubert uncannily set for Therese Grob, where the affective nature of his charming melody disguises a violent loss of innocence. But Goethe's and Schubert's 'Heidenröslein' is as much a song about thinking as it is a song about sensual experience. It is a reminder that the experience in song comes to us not pure but already shot through with literary and other pre-formed symbolic patterns. It is a reminder that artists do not create *de novo* and from their own resources the 'symbolic' component of their existence.

FROM *URSPRUNG* TO *FASSUNG LETZTER HAND*: 'MEERESSTILLE'

A really interesting example of a fluid text is found in Schubert's 'Meeresstille' (D 215A) composed on 20 June 1815 and the quiet, spare, haunting eloquence of D 216, op. 3, no. 2, recast a day later (see Examples 7.4a and 7.4b online). By smoothing out the original daring harmonies – eliminating the first version's tonic cadence at the end of the first stanza (bar 16), the very intense ninth chord at 'Weite', the chromaticized voice-exchange at 'regret', and the melodic tritone at 'keine' – something is gained in textual clarity, but something essential in the original inspiration is also lost.[53]

Do the two settings of 'Meeresstille' have a continuing identity? Are Schubert's changes improvements or alternatives? How much does one version need to differ from another in order to be considered a separate work? How we answer this reflects our ontological intuitions and our values. The traditional route is to have a *Fassung letzter Hand*, which enables us to make more confident assertions about Schubert's motivations as the final version can be viewed as a point of arrival. Schubert prioritized 'D 216' when he published it with Cappi & Diabelli in 1821 and his destruction of drafts suggests that he concurred with the idea of a *Fassung letzter Hand*. But 'Meeresstille' D 215A and D 216 are proof positive that he was an inveterate reviser. Although catalogued as separate works, D 216 deals with the exploration of the possibilities implicit in the music of D 215A, and characteristically, Schubert's revisions are interested in advancing the poetic impulse.

8

UNSUNG SCHUBERT: APPRENTICESHIP IN OPERA

'Whither is fled the visionary gleam?
Where is it now, the glory and the dream?'
William Wordsworth, *Intimations of Immortality*

Revision was part of everything Schubert wrote. One only has to look at the number of resettings during his lifetime to see how willing he was to fine-tune through performance. The manuscripts for the F major and A flat major masses – at both ends of his career – are laden with corrections. Refining and resetting were part of his training and practice where nuances of tempi and dynamics were adjusted at rehearsal and entire movements sometimes rewritten. One sovereign exception are Schubert's stage works and this lack of opportunity had a long-lasting impact on his career.

Only on three occasions was Schubert granted the experience of watching his own stage works in performance (see Table 8.2). He rarely benefited from dissension at rehearsals that lead to solutions worked up in the theatre rather than imagined in the writing of a score.[1] Two of Schubert's most successful operatic contemporaries, Meyerbeer and Donizetti, both recognized the necessity of this experience. When revising *Le prophète*, Meyerbeer openly acknowledged the difference between an opera perceived when writing its score and the end result realized in the theatre.[2] Most of Donizetti's operas exist in multiple versions presenting a challenge to editors deciding on a 'base text'.³ Most of Schubert's operatic scores are 'base texts', which is completely at odds with his performance practice in every other genre. That he was rarely afforded the opportunity to work with a cast and revise through rehearsals seriously hindered the success of what he wrote.

Who remembers today that Schubert wrote eighteen works for music theatre, six of which are complete? When did he begin to imagine himself as a composer of opera? Did he perceive it as a popular or high-minded form? Do his Singspiele (usually referred to as operettas) have bound identities to his particular time and place in cultural history or can they be successfully reimagined on stage and screen?⁴ Which of his stage works even merit such lavish attention?

Schubert's first hypnotized visits to the opera were with Spaun, who brought him to see Josef Weigl's *Die Schweizerfamilie* (*The Swiss Family*, 1809).⁵ Weigl was one of the most influential Singspiel composers of Schubert's day and one of several theatre composers who turned away from the frivolous tastes of Viennese audiences, preferring idyllic subjects with pastoral elements. The visit had a formative influence on Schubert's choice of libretti and marked the beginnings of his love of music theatre. The two friends sat regularly in the fifth gallery of the Kärntnertortheater (Carinthian Gate Theatre) where they listened to Cherubini's *Médée* (1809), Nicolas Isouard's *Cendrillon* (1810), François-Adrien Boieldieu's *Jean de Paris* (1812) and Mozart's *Die Zauberflöte*. Seasonal performances included Gluck's two *Iphigénie*s; Cherubini's *Faniska* – to a libretto by Josef Sonnleithner – Mozart's *Die Entführung aus dem Serail* and *Don Giovanni*; Ferdinando Paër's *Sargino*, *Camilla* and *Leonore*, and Weigl's *Das Waisenhaus*⁶ (*The Orphanage*, 1808).⁷ The highlight of these opera trips was an 1813 production of Gluck's *Iphigénie en Tauride* over which 'Schubert was totally beside himself [. . .] and declared that there could be nothing more beautiful in the world'.⁸ It was here he first heard Anna Milder Hauptmann as Iphigénie and Johann Michael Vogl as Orestes, with both of whom he would later work.

Fired up by these early visits to the theatre, Schubert began composing his first opera at the age of fourteen: an ambitious *Singspiel, Der Spiegelritter* (The Looking Glass Knight, D 11, December 1811). Work on it was interrupted by his mother's death in May 1812 but gradually resumed under the guidance of Salieri, whose pencil corrections are evident in the overture.[9] His first libretto by the Weimar playwright, August von Kotzebue (1761–1819), immediately calls into question the cliché: that his failure was due to the poor quality of the text. Kotzebue's prolific work for the theatre was hugely popular in early nineteenth-century Vienna and he brilliantly assessed what the local burghers would like. The libretto Schubert set is a parody of the *Zauberstücke* that were fashionable at the time. Most of the stock characters of the magic play are present – the heroic knight, the comic squire and the magician – but Kotzebue makes it clear on stage and in the foreword to his published libretto (1792) that his intention was to parody this type of Romanticism rather than confirm it. The whole libretto, with its exotic stage-sets, abrupt scene changes and brilliant dramatic effects, is a send-up of chivalrous drama which no doubt was what attracted Schubert's attention. The extravagance of his musical gestures hint at Kotzebue's ironic objectives so much that Schubert's very first attempt at opera shares Kotzebue's campaign against mediocrity in Vienna's suburban theatres beyond the city walls: Theater in der Leopoldstadt, Theater an der Wien, and to a lesser degree, Theater in der Josefstadt.

Already *Der Spiegelritter* contains some really interesting music and Schubert's first attempts at musical characterization. The unfinished ensemble No. 2 reveals his interest in developing longer musico-dramatic structures incorporating different stylistic devices such as recitative, dialogue, arioso and chorus. Most interestingly, the opera allows us to witness the formation of Schubert's work methods: after fifty-one bars, Schubert's scoring changes from full orchestration to keyboard short-scores, which is precisely how he leaves the sketches to his last operas, *Sakuntala* (D 701) and *Der Graf von Gleichen* (D 918). The Singspiel also yields up the first example of self-borrowing in Schubert's operas: the music for the comic quintet (No. 3), a chiding exchange between Schmurzo and the four ladies of the court, was later transposed from D to C major for the women's chorus of *Der vierjährige Posten* (D 190): a practice which would become commonplace in Schubert, most especially with his overtures.

Since opera was the fastest and most certain way to fame and success, Salieri encouraged Schubert to continue composing opera and helped him to complete his first Singspiel during his teacher-training year.[10] A central part of partimento pedagogy involved learning to compose opera very quickly, which explains Schubert's ability to compose four Singspiele (and so much else) in 1815. His double infatuation with opera and Therese Grob were part of his search to make a living, which explains his dogged obsession with the stage after a career in teaching failed. Between the ages of sixteen and twenty-six he wrote eighteen works for music theatre, ten of which were complete, six of which have been handed down to us. He spent the springtime of his life striving to be a commercial success: Schubert harboured dreams of being Salieri's successor in German opera (see Tables 8.1 and 8.2).

A GLIMPSE OF FULFILMENT? SCHUBERT'S THEATRICAL CALLING

Each of the 1815–16 Singspiele composed during Schubert's years of apprenticeship with Salieri were selected to give him an experience of different styles. *Claudine von Villa Bella* is an Italianate German opera, *Der vierjährige Posten* (The Four-Year Sentry Duty, D 190) is a light-hearted, comic Pastoral, and Schubert duly ignored both librettists' rhyming verse. *Fernando* (D 220) – based on the 'lost child' theme popular in contemporary Viennese theatre – is his first attempt at serious opera. The remaining two Singspiele show Schubert in search of classical themes: *Die Freunde von Salamanka* (The Friends of Salamanka, D 326) is inspired by

Table 8.1: Schubert's Apprenticeship with Salieri (Singspiele 1811–1816)

		Libretto	Genre	Composed	Premiere	MSS
1	*Der Spiegelritter* D 11	August von Kotzebue	Three-act Singspiel	December 1811–1813	Radio Beromünster 11 Dec 1949	Fragment
2	**Des Teufels Lustschloß** D 84	August von Kotzebue	Three-act Singspiel	30 Oct 1813–15 May 1814 r. 22 Oct 1814	Musikverein, Vienna 12 Dec 1879	Overture and 23 numbers Two workings Act II of revised version (12–7) destroyed by Josef Hüttenbrenner
3	**Der vierjährige Posten** D 190	Theodor Körner	One-act Singspiel	8–19 May 1815 Overture 13–16 May 1815	Dresden, 23 Sept 1896	**Complete** (Overture and 8 numbers)
4	*Fernando* D 220	Albert Stadler	One-act Singspiel	9 July 1815	Vienna, 13 April 1907 (Concert performance) 18 Aug 1918 Magdeburg	**Complete** (7 numbers)
5	*Claudine von Villa Bella* D 239	J. W. von Goethe	Three-act Singspiel	26 July 1815 (begun)	Vienna, 26 April 1913 (Concert performance) Dublin, 5 April 2003	Acts II and III destroyed by Josef Hüttenbrenner
6	**Die Freunde von Salamanka** D 326	Johann Mayrhofer	Two-act Pastoral Singspiel	18 Nov–31 Dec 1815	Nos. 4, 8, 9, 12 19 Dec 1875, Musikverein Vienna (Johann Herbeck) Scenic realization 6 May 1928, Halle	**Complete Score** (Overture and 8 numbers) Libretto lost or destroyed by Mayrhofer
7	*Die Bürgschaft* D 435	After Schiller	Three-act Opera (16 numbers) Act III incomplete	2 May 1816 (begun)	Schubertbund 7 March 1908	Fragment

Table 8.2: Schubert's Apprenticeship on the Viennese Stage and Fragmentary Stage Works (1819–1823)

		Libretto	Genre	Composed	Premiere	MSS
8 *Die Zwillingsbrüder*	D 647	Georg von Hofmann	One-act 'Farce with Music'	? January 1819	**Kärntnertortheater, Vienna 14 June 1820 (ran for 6 nights)**	**Complete** (Overture and 10 numbers. Parts: Ferdinand Schubert)
9 *Adrast*	D 137	Johann Mayrhofer	Opera	1819/20	Musikverein, Vienna, 14 November 1875	Fragment (8 complete, 5 incomplete numbers) Libretto lost or destroyed by Mayrhofer
10 *Lazarus oder die Feier der Auferstehung*	D 689	August Hermann Niemeyer	Three-act Oratorio (2 Acts)	February–March 1820	Easter Sunday, 11 April 1830, St Anna Kirche, Vienna	Fragment (as far as the resurrection scene in Act II)
11 *Die Zauberharfe*	D 644	Georg von Hofmann	Singspiel	April–August 1820	**Theater an der Wien, 19 August 1820 (ran for 8 nights)**	**Lost libretto** 2 Prologues (6 of 13 numbers are melodrama)
12 *Sakuntala*	D 701	Johann Philipp Neumann (after Kalidasa)	Three-Act Opera	October 1820–April 1821	Vienna, 12 June 1971	Fragment (Sketches for 11 numbers in Acts I and II[11]
13 *Das Zauberglöckchen*	D 723	Friedrich Treitschke	Operatic Aria and Duet	1821	**Kärntnertortheater, Vienna, 20 June 1821**	Commissioned Aria and Duet for Viennese premiere of Hérold's *opéra comique*

14 **Alfonso und Estrella**	D 732	Franz von Schober	Three-act through-composed Opera	20 September 1821–27 Feb 1822	Abridged version, Weimar, 24 June 1854	**Complete** (Overture and 35 numbers)
15 **Die Verschworenen** (*Der häusliche Krieg*)	D 787	Ignaz von Castelli (after Aristophanes)	One-act Singspiel	Feb–April 1823	Private performance in Schubert's lifetime in Giannatasio del Rio's home.	**Complete** (11 numbers)
16 **Fierrabras**	D 796	J. Kupelwieser	Three-act Chivalric Opera with spoken dialogue	25 May–2 Oct 1823	Overture, Musikverein, 6 January 1829, cond. Ignaz Schuppanzigh Concert performance Theater in der Josefstadt, 7 May 1835, cond. Konradin Kreutzer, Karlsruhe, 9 February 1897	**Complete** (Overture and 23 numbers)
17 **Rosamunde, Fürstin von Cypern**	D 797	Helmina von Chézy	Four-act Play with Incidental Music, Last theatre commission	Nov–Dec 1823	**Theater an der Wien, 20 December 1823 (with overture for *Alfonso und Estrella* premiered)**	**Complete** (Overture and 10 numbers)
18 *Der Graf von Gleichen*	D 918	Eduard von Bauernfeld	Two-act Opera	19 June 1827–March 1828	Redoutensaal, Vienna, 15 December 1865 (cond. Johann Herbeck)	Sketch (for 20 numbers)

Shakespeare's *Twelfth Night* whereas the sketches for *Die Bürgschaft* (The Pledge, D 435) make clear his ambition to compose a grand opera.

Shortly after he completed his training with Salieri, Schubert began a second operatic apprenticeship in Viennese theatres. Vogl negotiated the first of four theatrical commissions: a one-act farce, *Die Zwillingsbrüder* (D647), by Georg von Hofmann, secretary at the Kärntnertortheater who translated foreign-language opera libretti into German. Of the ten vocal numbers in the operetta, the best five were tailor-made for Vogl, who cast himself in the title role. Despite this performer-composer collaboration, Hofmann's uninspiring libretto ensured the Singspiel was dropped after six performances.

Two further commissions followed: a melodrama by Hofmann, *Die Zauberharfe* (The Magic Harp, D 644), which ran for eight nights. Schubert's melodrama is hugely engaging, but Goethe's *Proserpina* to music by Carl Eberwein – a composer lacking Schubert's genius for musical invention – is a much stronger melodrama. Firstly, the text is a forgotten and timeless masterpiece through which Goethe levels criticism at society's treatment of women. Secondly, for Goethe music was the defining element:

> It is now time to think of music, which in this context is to be regarded as the sea on which that artistically decorated boat is carried, as the favourable breeze which gently but sufficiently fills the sails and obeys the sailor in all her movements in whatever direction.[12]

Thirdly, Goethe understood the theatre event as a *Gesamtkunstwerk* in which the most varied practical elements along with music were engaged. He not only collaborated intensely with Eberwein, but also worked on costume and stage design, drew a distinction between declamation and recitative, and from Amalia Wolff, their first Proserpina, requested stylized gestures à la Lady Hamilton right down to the final tableau.[13] Schubert did not have Goethe's pragmatism or power as a man of theatre. In the hope of getting his foot in the door, he applied for the position of *répétiteur*, supported by glowing testimonials from Salieri and Josef Weigl. Timewise he was a disaster – and not very good at his job – but the theatre management still commissioned two numbers for insertion into *Das Zauberglöckchen* (The Magic Bell, D 732), another *Zauberoper* based on the story of Aladdin.

The operatic fragments of his second apprenticeship show Schubert determined to raise the bar and make his own way in opera as in other things. *Adrast* (D 137) is his only attempt at a tragic opera and his first opera in which aria emerges from recitative. A strikingly original approach to recitative with lyrical interjections can be heard in his fragmentary Easter oratorio, *Lazarus* (D 689). His most successful work, *Die Verschworenen* (The Conspirators, also known as *Der häusliche Krieg*, Domestic Warfare, D 787), is a sparkling one-act comedy based on two plays, *Lysistrata* and *Ekklesiazusae* (The Parliament of Women), adapted by a clever and popular Viennese dramatist, Ignaz von Castelli (1781–1862). After Schubert's death the operetta was enormously popular, performed all over Europe and translated into many languages. In Schubert's day it was not the grand opera that the Kärntnertortheater was looking for. Neither were *Alfonso* nor *Fierabras*.[14]

DRAMMA PER MUSICA? CLAUDINE VON VILLA BELLA (D 239)

It is much more difficult to assess Schubert's achievement as a composer of opera than in the symphony or the mass because of the number of operatic fragments and the range of genres, popular and serious. Schubert was a wayfarer whose improvisatory personality moved through many genres, in comparison to contemporary opera composers who dedicated their life to it. But something of the early promise he showed in his first operatic apprenticeship can be detected in *Claudine von Villa Bella*, whose natural and lively prose is perfectly suited to the Viennese court theatre and transfers well to a modern stage.

Goethe's light-hearted romance was originally published in 1776 as a *Schauspiel mit Gesang* to indicate how spoken prose dialogues alternate with songs. The libretto that Schubert set is Goethe's radically revised version of *Claudine,* which he worked on extensively during his Italian journey in 1786–87 and published with Göschen in 1788.[15] When rewriting the text, Goethe aligned his libretto with the dramatic principles of Italian opera buffa, replaced spoken dialogues with verse recitatives, substituted songs with arias, duets and ensembles, and closed all three acts with the customary finale.[16] Although Goethe modestly entitled this work as a Singspiel, it was as he once referred to it in a letter, 'a really fat opera'.[17] The unusual amount of musical numbers and literary originality of Goethe's libretto were what attracted Schubert's attention. It is the only North German libretto with anything remotely approximating Bretzner's abduction scene in *Die Entführung aus dem Serail* and the grand finale to Act 2 is the first real finale in North German opera. The sentimentalist Sicilian family of minor nobility and the theme of rival brothers popular in *Sturm und Drang* plays were both new to German music theatre, and it was the first time Romantic bandits make their appearance on the Viennese stage.[18]

By revising his libretto to suit the composer's needs, Goethe uncannily sacrificed dramatic content, diminished the psychological depth of his characters, and thereby limited the emotional range of Schubert's Singspiel.[19] In the first version Claudine dresses up as an Amazon and rides off with sword in hand to rescue her lover, Pedro. Both Pedro and Crugantino are in love with her and this rivalry in love – and social critique – gives Goethe's *Ur-Claudine* its grit.[20] Goethe's self-awareness of what he had lost 'in order to make the work singable' has not spared the opprobrium of *literary* critics who are generally agreed that the revised version is inferior.[21] This criticism, which is the product of German literature studies, misses the fact that Goethe's insertion of Lucinde was to fulfil the obligatory final 'Coro', the last solo SATB ensemble, where at least two female parts are required.[22] It fails to acknowledge Goethe's awareness of opera as a collaborative art and that the naturalistic dialogue and rhythmic variety of his new recitative version of *Claudine* is historically and musically one of its most defining and distinguished features. Of the ten original numbers only three are retained: the new arias are all carefully crafted in iambic tetrametre (the metre most frequently employed in opera buffa), ensembles juxtapose various metres, and finales close (as expected) in trochaic tetrametre. Goethe's deviation from iambic pentametre in two places to accentuate suffering or strife – in verses 704–12 (for the duel between Pedro and Rugantino) and verses 1115–39 (where Rugantino holds a dagger at Claudine's breast) – at once observes and departs from the strict treatment of metre in the Italian tradition where the librettist leaves it up to the composer to interrupt the rhythm as he pleased.

Using the revised edition of Goethe's text published by Anton Strauss in Vienna in 1810, the seventeen-year-old Schubert set about composing *Claudine* on 26 July 1815, which was one of the most prolific months of his career. He completed Act 1 by 5 August, finished the Singspiel the following month, but the music for Acts 2 and 3 was destroyed by Josef Hüttenbrenner, who acquired the score on the pretext of securing a performance, but not for one second would he have promoted an opera by Schubert that his brother also set.[23] In addition to the two fair-copy volumes (Overture and Act 1) which have been handed down, vocal parts (in Schubert's hand) for Rugantino's tenor arietta, 'Liebliches Kind' from Act 2, and Claudine's soprano part for her duet with Pedro, 'Mich umfängt ein banger Schauer' from Act 3, have survived, which supports Otto Biba's claim that *Claudine* was performed in a domestic context.[24] At that time Vienna's vibrant theatrical scene spilled over from public to private performance. Works like *Claudine* were a distraction from political tensions and part of the fun-loving character of Vienna.

Whether or not *Claudine* was intended for private or public performance, Schubert's choice of libretto immediately signals his ambition. The Singspiel belongs to a period in his life when he was intensely engaged in setting Goethe's works. The timely flood of publication of the poet's works in the Habsburg capital after the Congress of Vienna contributed enormously to his favourable reception in the Restoration era. Given his popularity with Viennese audiences, the absence of a public performance during their lives was all the more regrettable when one realizes that Schubert was the composer who came closest to realizing Goethe's musical ambitions for his libretto. Had Schubert sent Goethe his Singspiel instead of his *Liederbuch* in 1816 – or had he been the kind of person who could just show up in Weimar with his score under his arm as Johann Reichardt did in 1789 – the setting would have undoubtedly piqued the poet's interest. As Director of the Weimar Theatre from 1791 to 1817, Goethe had arranged for 131 Singspiele to be performed and Schubert's *Claudine* perfectly fulfilled local expectations.

Goethe's revised libretto, which aspired to establish a German literary opera through remodelling Italian practice, was tailor-made for Schubert's apprenticeship. On the title page of his score, Schubert acknowledges his debt to Salieri whose experience of writing Italian operas for the Viennese Court Theatre positioned him perfectly to help Schubert achieve this aim. Enough survives to prove that Schubert, at seventeen, could write successfully for local audiences.[25] The opening gesture of the Adagio introduction exhibits some fine contrapuntal invention and masterly orchestration (see Example 8.1 online). The imprint of Italian opera is immediately heard in the vivace section of Schubert's overture where there is a real feeling of the theatre, a sure handling of orchestral forces (Example 8.2 online). An early example of Schubert's theatrical abilities is his use of silence as a dramatic event when he calls the audience to attention in the overture (bars 135–36). Schubert already knew how to individualize character through skilful orchestration: Claudine's appearances (nos. 4 and 6) are accompanied by wind and strings, which subtly distinguishes her title role from Lucinde's, whose aria (no. 3) is serenaded only by strings.

That Schubert was well versed in the aesthetic conventions of opera buffa is clear from his arias. He entitles his female solos Italian *ariette*, yet neither Claudine, Lucinda nor Pedro have showy theatrical bravura material to sing. Instead of technical virtuosity he seeks from his characters an expressive interpretation of cantabile lines which he underpins with rhythmically active and carefully orchestrated accompaniments. In Pedro's aria no. 5 (Example 8.3 online), details of articulation, dynamics and texture are all carefully variegated with the aim of drawing attention to the text (bars 1–19). The relatively restricted harmonic vocabulary of the aria renders the music memorable: cadential phrases are almost always repeated and the music is in general quite repetitive (bars 19–42).[26]

When setting *Claudine*, Schubert had already acquired from Salieri a solid understanding of Italian music theatre and how to synthesize contemporary operatic styles. His *Introduction* (no. 1) is a cheerful Italian terzetto for Lucinde (soprano), Pedro (tenor) and Alonzo (bass). The Italianate Ensemble (no. 2), 'Fröhlicher, seliger herrlicher Tag', with its graceful solo for a child, is a typical Singspiel ensemble setting with alternating choral and solo episodes. The ensemble can also be defined in pastoral terms where clear articulation of sections typically involves thematic contrast between paragraphs; its ternary structure, steady rhythm and uncomplicated harmony are all characteristic of four-part homophonic writing in this repertoire.[27] This hybridity of styles is evident in the closing choruses where Rugantino's bandits' Chorus, 'Mit Mädeln sich vertragen' (no. 7), is scored antiphonally following French-German practice. The influence of Paisiello's operas – whose finales often recreate a play within a play – is evident in Goethe's double chorus. When at the end of Rugantino's revised scene with the bandits a quarrel breaks out between Rugantino and Basco, who opposes the plan to kidnap Lucinde, Goethe creates a textual basis for a second great action finale, 'Deinem Willen nachzugeben' (no. 8). Schubert responded in a strong, rhythmically pulsing Allegro ma non troppo finale, underscored by rising dynamics, the double choir edging up the dramatic tension by musically pitting the two choruses of robbers against each other.

Understanding how carefully Goethe set the stage for the composer of *Claudine* allows us to appreciate Schubert's precocious understanding of Italian music theatre and how skilfully he already uses various languages of the repertoire. Even his choice of libretto tells us something about Schubert at seventeen. Its theme of infidelity – or fidelity to oneself against the conventions of society – was undoubtedly one of the threads that drew him in. The two rival brothers offer an intriguing parallel between Ferdinand and Franz and their theatrical counterparts, Pedro and Rugantino, who symbolize different reactions to the way in which they were raised. The play's central conflict focuses upon the artist Rugantino, whose antisocial behaviour expresses an inability to take conventional pathways in life and thereby usurps the operetta's most memorable role. But it is on the closeness between composer and libretto rather than the composer and Rugantino's character that *Claudine*'s special status among these early Singspiele is grounded. As with his handling of Kotzebue's *Der Spiegelritter*, Schubert's literary discernment is again evident as he recognized Goethe's conciliatory spin on a tragically irreconcilable *Sturm und Drang* theme. In Goethe's finale the tension between the two temperamentally contrasted brothers is resolved through Rugantino's inheritance of his patrimony of Castelvecchio and Pedro's marriage to Claudine, whereby the continuation of a feudal, patriarchal order is guaranteed. One bitterly regrets that the music for Acts 2 and 3 did not survive so we could see what Schubert made of Goethe's celebration of married love in this final tableau. His handling of Kotzebue's *Des Teufels Lustschloß* suggests he would have shared Goethe's ironic deflation of this *lieto fine* when Basco declares, 'if only one could find a way of getting away from these people who are boring me'.

In weighing up the Schubert-Goethe constellation in opera, three conclusions can be drawn. Firstly, *Claudine von Villa Bella* is a deceptively simple text. Without the kind of collaboration afforded to Reichardt, Radziwill and Eberwein, Schubert could not have known that gesture was a crucial aspect of Goethe's music theatre or that the final passage before the last finale of *Claudine* requires a substantial pantomime to music in which the tying and unravelling of the dramatic plot takes place before the last chorus brings the work to a close:

This whole development, which poetry can only hint at and which the music will execute more fully can only really come alive through the performance of actors. Alonzo's astonishment and the way he gradually composes himself as the situation is explained to him; the way he goes from one state of amazement to another and eventually becomes calm; the tenderness of Pedro and Claudine; the more lively passion of Carlos and Lucinde which is no longer contained; the gestures of Pedro as he introduces his brother to Alonzo; the annoyance of Basco at not being able to leave the scene – all this the players must express in a lively, appropriate and harmonious manner and animate the performance with studied pantomime.[28]

Secondly, Schubert was too inexperienced to take up the gauntlet that Goethe had thrown down to the composer of *Claudine*. As spoken dialogue was the *sine qua non* of German operetta, Schubert did not respond in *secco recitative* but kept the dialogue in verse form.[29] He was not ready to see the opportunity that Goethe's metrical dialogue offered him to highlight a harmonious passage and make it his own.

Thirdly, when set against the incontrovertible genius of 'Gretchen am Spinnrade' and 'Erlkönig' in the previous chapter, it is already clear that *Claudine von Villa Bella* is an apprentice-piece and that the intimacy of song was Schubert's true métier. But before conclusions are too swiftly drawn about Schubert's operatic endeavours, it should be remembered that the intensely dramatic 'Gretchen am Spinnrade' and harmonic daring of his 'Cathedral Scene from Goethe's *Faust*' (D 126) were the natural next step in Schubert's partimento training with Salieri who had him setting Metastasio's scenes. Schubert harboured dreams of being the German Salieri and, in searching for a German text to apply what he had learnt, it was entirely natural that he would turn to *Faust*. Although gradual changes in perceptions of the spoken text across the nineteenth century have led to the reception of Goethe's *Faust* as a purely literary text, in Schubert's day it was perceived as a literary and musical text. Numerous composers collaborated with Goethe on *Faust*, including Eberwein who conveyed to us that it was Goethe's idea to treat the scene where Faust consults the book of Nostradamus as musical melodrama.[30] Goethe also collaborated with Reichardt on *Claudine* and Radziwill on *Faust*, undertaking textual changes or additions according to each composer's wishes. Beethoven's unfulfilled desire to compose *Faust* was the result of daily conversations he enjoyed with Goethe in Teplitz.

Biography is not just about reality but the realm of possibility – everything that Schubert was capable of becoming – and what he achieved in opera must be understood in such terms. Had Schubert collaborated with Goethe on *Claudine*, had he realized that his temperament was more suited to tragedy, had he continued to compose *Faust*, both artists' ambitions in music theatre would have taken a very different course, less problematic and less neglected. But acknowledging the historical contingency of Schubert's life as it was rather than musing on what might have been, Goethe's influence on Schubert's development of the lied through setting an entire scene from *Faust* led to the drama of *Gretchen* and ultimately to his most radical operatic work. In Schubert's day melodrama led an exciting life of experimentation: the reduction down to one single protagonist, the emotional shifts in music and text, and lack of short tragedies on the German stage were all part of the cultural climate that would come to shape *Winterreise* as a through-composed, experimental and incredibly modern musical monodrama.[31]

9

THE PROMISE OF FREEDOM (1816-1818)

'The cause of freedom, or rather of one's own energy,
has to be the cause of every cultivated man.'

Wilhelm von Humboldt

PREOCCUPATIONS, 13-17 JUNE 1816

Schubert scarcely maintained any sort of diary beyond dating most of his manuscripts. From whatever journal he may have written, only a few pages have survived which allow us a rare glimpse of the composer's life. The conscious effort to take himself in hand, discipline his life, and make himself an efficient social being was already evident in a more meticulous dating of manuscripts during this period. His 1816 journal reveals a new resolve to observe and record the rhythms of his mood, but his inability to maintain it beyond a few entries shows that the one thing his mind could not do was to conduct a monologue. His creative intellect, like his music and his friendships, was in constant dialogue: to exist it needed reaction.

In the first entry Schubert records a series of prosaic notes over five days between 13 and 17 June 1816. The next record is dated 8 September 1816, with the final memorandum on 24 March 1824. The June 1816 entries especially capture a burgeoning inner freedom, an increasingly quizzical attitude to everything he experienced. His appetite for self-reflection is whetted and many predilections are patent. On Thursday 13 June Mozart fires his mind and his search for analogues is also clear:

> A light, bright, fine day will remain through my entire life. As from afar the magic notes of Mozart's music still gently haunt me. How unbelievably vigorously, and yet again how gently, was it impressed deep into the heart by Schlesinger's masterly playing. Thus does our soul retain these fair impressions, which no time, no circumstances can efface, and they lighten our existence. They show us in the darkness of this life a bright, clear, lovely distance, for which we hope with confidence. O Mozart, immortal Mozart, how many, oh how endlessly many such comforting perceptions of a brighter and better life you have brought to our souls! – This Quintet is, so to speak, one of the greatest of his lesser works. – I too had to show myself on this occasion. I played variations by Beethoven, sang Goethe's 'Rastlose Liebe' and Schiller's 'Amalia'. Although I myself think my 'Rastlose Liebe' better than 'Amalia', I cannot deny that Goethe's musical genius contributed much to the success. I also made the acquaintance of Mme Jenny, an extraordinarily fluent pianist, who however seems to be somewhat lacking in true and pure expression.[1]

The following day, 14 June, the wayfarer records one of many walks he took with his brother, Karl:

> I took an evening walk for once, as I had not done for several months. There can scarcely be anything more agreeable than to enjoy the green country on an evening after a warm summer's day, a pleasure for which the fields between Währing and Döbling seem to have been especially created. In the uncertain twilight and in the company of my brother Karl, my heart warmed within me. 'How beautiful' I thought and exclaimed standing still in sheer delight. A graveyard close by reminded us of our dear mother. So, talking sadly and intimately, we arrived at

THE PROMISE OF FREEDOM (1816–1818)

the point where the Döbling road divides. And, as from the heavenly home, I heard a familiar voice coming from a halting coach. I looked up and it was Herr Weinmüller, just alighting and paying us his compliments in his friendly, honest way. In a second our conversation transformed itself to the polite sociability of other people's tone and language. How many attempt vainly to show their upright disposition by means of cordial, honest language; how many would thereby only expose themselves to derision. Such a thing may not be regarded as an acquisition, but a natural gift.

The evening after, 15 June, Schubert attended an exhibition at the Academy of Fine Arts, where his brother Karl was a student. The public display of Austrian paintings prompted him to reflect:

> It is quite common to be disappointed in one's expectations. This happened to me when I saw the exhibition of Austrian paintings held at St Anna's. Among all the pictures a Madonna and Child by Abel appealed to me most. The velvet cloak of a prince deceived me completely. For the rest, I admit that it is necessary to see such things several times and at leisure, if one is to discover the proper expression and receive the right impression.

On 16 June, Schubert recorded the fiftieth anniversary of Salieri's arrival in Vienna (D 407). His celebration of his teacher and Salieri's admiration for Gluck prompted the twenty-year-old to touch gingerly on the vexed question of Beethoven's influence:

> It must be beautiful and refreshing for an artist to see all his pupils gathered about him, each one striving to give of his best for his jubilee, and to hear in all these compositions the expression of pure nature, free from all the eccentricity that is common among most composers nowadays, and is due almost wholly to one of our greatest German artists;

that eccentricity which joins and confuses the tragic with the comic, the agreeable with the repulsive, heroism with howlings and the holiest with harlequinades, without distraction, so as to goad people to madness instead of dissolving them in love, to incite them to laughter instead of lifting them up to God. To see this eccentricity banished from the circle of his pupils and instead to look upon pure, holy nature, must be the greatest pleasure for an artist who, guided by such a one as Gluck, learned to know nature and to uphold it in spite of the unnatural conditions of our age.

Herr Salieri celebrated his jubilee yesterday having been fifty years in Vienna and nearly as long in the imperial service; he was awarded a gold medal by his majesty and invited many of his pupils, male and female. The works written for the occasion by his composition students were performed from top to bottom, according to the order in which they came under his tuition. The whole was framed by a chorus and an oratorio, 'Jesu al Limbo', both by Salieri. The oratorio is worked in a genuinely Gluckian manner. The entertainment interested everybody.[2]

FIRST COMMISSION: THE LOST *PROMETHEUS* CANTATA

The final entry on 17 June refers to the lost *Prometheus* Cantata (Figure 18 online). In the spring, Spaun had moved from his apartment in the inner city (Landskronegasse) into Professor Heinrich Josef Watteroth's home in Landstrasse no. 97 (today Erdbergerstrasse 17, Vienna 3), a suburb southeast of Vienna, where his friend and former fellow student Josef Wilhelm Witteczek was also living. Aware of the pressure Schubert was under at home and anxious for his well-being, Spaun invited him to spend a few days with him during Whitsuntide in May. During this visit, Spaun and Witteczek in youthful high spirits locked him into his room with an order to complete a composition before they would release him. That Schubert received the barb in good part shows that one of his most attractive characteristics was his enjoyment of jokes at his expense. The resultant Six

THE PROMISE OF FREEDOM (1816–1818)

Écossaises for piano (D 421) bore the inscription on the title page (now lost), 'Composed while confined to my room at Erdberg, May 1816 – thank God!' His throwaway comment reveals his attitude to inspiration and raises the unanswerable question as to what extent the will can do the work of the imagination.

Heinrich Josef Watteroth, a much-loved Professor of Law and Political Science at the University of Vienna, taught several members of Schubert's circle including Spaun, Schober, Stadler, Mayrhofer, Schlechta and Sonnleithner, all of whom were influenced by his liberal views. One of his students, Josef Witteczek, decided with some other pupils of the professor, to celebrate Watteroth's name day with a cantata for which Schubert was enlisted to write the music. The text was by a law student, Philipp Dräxler von Carin. The commission was a stimulus and Schubert discovered a way of responding that brought the libretto to life. The premiere took place in the courtyard and garden of his home: the first performance planned for 12 July had to be postponed until 24 July. Schubert's one-act cantata, which opened the programme, lasted approximately forty-five minutes. According to Sonnleithner, the solo sections consisted largely of 'solemnly delivered recitatives, which recounted the tragic fate of Prometheus and its cause'. In addition to one elaborate duet for the two soloists, the rest of the work consisted of three choruses of considerable variety. The opening ensemble had that Promethean spark; the second, in the form of a slow funeral march, is a chorus of Prometheus's pupils, a poetic allusion to Watteroth's students; and the third an impassioned chorus of triumph.

The performance was an incredibly meaningful occasion for Watteroth's students, one of whom, Franz Schlechta, recorded his appreciation in an enthusiastic poem, 'To Herr Franz Schubert (On the performance of his Cantata Prometheus)', published a year after the event in the *Allgemeine Theaterzeitung* on 27 September 1817. Composed for soprano and bass soloists, chorus and orchestra, *Prometheus* (D 451) was Schubert's first commission. 'Today I composed for money for the first time,' he wrote in his diary on 17 June 1816. 'The fee is 100 florins WW [40fl. KM]'. Even more significant is its theme, for *Prometheus* is the very type of a solitary creator. Aware of the exceptional power of the symbol he had been given, the cantata was clearly one of the most searching of Schubert's early works, perhaps even an early contemplation on the limitations of secular literature. Prometheus is, after all, an Antichrist figure. In setting Dräxler von Carin's text Schubert imagined with deep seriousness the replacement of God by human creativity. His supreme satisfaction to make something blessedly, actively independent of himself was fulfilled in this first commission.

THINGS FALL APART

Schubert's last diary entry on 8 September 1816 follows on directly from his record of 17 June, which proves there are no missing pages (see Figure 18 online). It was written the day after receiving notification of the rejection of his application to Laibach and makes dispiriting reading. It was also written in the recognition that any thoughts of marrying Therese Grob were now out of the frame unless he followed in his family's footsteps. We bear witness to his rejection of conformist behaviour, more fundamentally the destruction of his hopes which augurs the beginnings of a deeper crisis.

The September aphorisms, which aspire to Goethe's *Maximen und Reflexionen*, testify to a nineteen-year-old Schubert grappling with existential issues such as the role of suffering in life and the state's refusal to permit the marriage of men without means, forcing them into unwilling celibacy or towards commercial sex. We witness a man possessed by an inner energy which he himself does not fully understand. We see him struggling to come to terms with his troubled circumstances and resolve his own contradictions, which in time he would see as a source of strength. It marks the onset of great suffering for Schubert caused by a conflict to live outside or beside the law – perhaps even in contravention of law and custom – and at the same time we sense his need to maintain equilibrium within himself, with others, and with the moral order of the world. What Schubert cannot yet see here was just how essential this conflict was to his spiritual and emotional survival. On 8 September he writes:

Man resembles a ball, to be played with by chance and passion.

This sentence seems extraordinarily true to me.

I have often read authors to the effect that the world is like a stage on which the human being plays a part. Applause and censure follow in the next world. – But as a stage part is assigned, so is our part assigned to us, and who is to say whether he has played it well or ill? – Is it a bad producer who gives his actors parts they are unable to play? Neglect is unthinkable here, for the world has no example of an actor who was dismissed for bad elocution. If only he is given an apt part, he will play it well: whether he receives applause or not will depend on a public subject to a thousand different moods. Up there, praise or disapproval depends on the stage-manager of the world. Thus public censure is suspended.

Natural disposition and education determine mankind's mind and heart. The heart *is* the ruler, but the mind *ought* to be. Take people as they are, not as they should be.

Blissful moments brighten this dark life; up there these blissful moments become continual joy, and happier ones still will turn into visions of yet happier worlds, and so on.

Happy is he who finds a true friend. Happier still is he who finds a true friend in his wife.

To a free man matrimony is a terrifying thought these days: he exchanges it either for melancholy or for crude sensuality. Monarchs of today, you see this and are silent. Or do you not see it? If so, O God, shroud our senses and feelings in numbness; yet take back the veil again one day without lasting harm.

Man bears misfortune without complaint, but feels it the more keenly. Wherefore did God give us compassion?

Light mind, light heart. Too light a mind usually means too heavy a heart.

Urban politeness is a mighty antithesis to the sincerity of human relationships.

The greatest misfortune of the wise and the greatest fortune of the foolish rests upon convention.

To be noble and unhappy is to feel the full depths of misfortune and happiness, just as to be noble and happy is to feel happiness and misfortune.

I can't think of any more now. Tomorrow I shall think of something more. Why is that? Is my mind duller today than tomorrow because I am sated and sleepy? – Why does my mind not think when the body is asleep? – It goes for a walk, no doubt? For surely it cannot sleep? –
>
> What are all these questions?
> 'Twill not do to dare it.
> No, 'tis not enough:
> We must grin and bear it.
> And so to bed
> Till morn shines red.[3]

Was Schubert ever seriously intent on marrying Therese Grob and securing a full-time teaching position? The notice in the *Wiener Zeitung* of 17 February 1816 invited applications for the 'Filling of the Music Master's Post at the German Normal School Establishment at Laibach' by 14 March 1816.[4] Motivated by his desire to leave home, by a salary of 450 florins A.C. – six times the pittance that he was receiving at his father's Säulengasse schoolhouse – motivated by the hope of personal advancement and by a teaching position that was closer to his own vocation than his father's, Schubert threw his hat into the ring. His letter of application answers most of the musical requirements outlined in the first paragraph of the advertisement – his training as a singer, his abilities as an organist and violinist, his exceptional musical training as a Kapellmeister – but he fails to address any of the requested details such as his age, birthplace, teaching qualifications and experience, whether he is single or married, a parent, and if so of how many children. In addition Schubert's letter of application arrived on 14 April, exactly one month after the closing date. Salieri's one-line testimonial:

> I, the undersigned, assert that I support the application of Franz Schubert in regard to the musical post at Laibach
> Antonio Salieri,
> First Musical Director of the I. & R. Court
> 9 April 1816[5]

suggests he had a hand in the late application, knowing Schubert was 'the most suitable of all the applicants'.

The board's decision on Schubert's case supports this reading as they added him to their list of recommendations of Peter Anton Hanslischek and Josef Wöss which they had made on 3 April, noting that Salieri's 'judgement greatly honours Schubert'.[6] In their notes on Schubert's petition on 26 May they acknowledge a second favourable reference from Josef Spendou, Schubert's family's patron and an important figure in the Austrian school system, who extolled the composer's rapport with young children. Schubert's knowledge of wind instruments and birthplace are all marked 'unknown', with a comment that he 'may be supposed to be still very young'. But the net had been cast wide when they advertised the position in Vienna, Graz, Prague, Klagenfurt and Laibach, and Salieri was only responsible for Viennese and Lower Austrian candidates. Salieri had also written for Peter Anton Hanslischek, Josef Wöß and Jakob Schauff. Despite being 'highly recommended by the civic authorities and the School Inspectorate in Vienna', Schubert was notified on 7 September that his application had been unsuccessful and that Franz Sokoll – seventeen years older than him – had been appointed.

Knowing that his own financial state prohibited him from marrying Therese Grob was humiliating for Schubert even if he perceived matrimony as an 'exchange of freedom for melancholy'. What is most interesting about the diary entry is his staid, conservative view of marriage at the passionate age of nineteen. The passage is one of the most important documents we have for Schubert because it shows a fear of the constriction of marriage as a fixed state. That Ferdinand got married around the time of this diary entry suggests Schubert was comparing himself with others around him and suggests that for a while he considered that intention. This shows that Schubert was not in love with love or a mere possibility. Therese was no phantom: she was a person of such charm and character that Schubert could love her, and she could and did love him. The temptation she offered was to regulate his life and so the music, which fed on his life, to a defined role within an existing social order. But possession, fixity, was something which, in 1816, his character was not yet mature enough to accommodate. The relationship with Therese had felt wrong from the beginning, not least the disproportion between the 'bourgeois' world in Lichtental which she represented, and the breadth and celerity of his own nature. Schubert had never been properly moulded into the Lichtental ground. There was always a degree of at-homeness missing – not just inside his family house but within the social milieu. This out-of-placeness of these in-between years mattered as much for his compositional life as the in-placeness of his early childhood. His diary entry catches for a moment this emotional ambivalence of a young man who, balanced between vitality and earnestness, does not want the complete sexual and social fulfilment of a state of life – the bourgeois bond of marriage – no longer open to change and ambition. What he wanted was to perpetuate what he discovered in 'Gretchen am Spinnrade': a music animated by desire, but a desire that never rests in full possession.

Since Schubert shied away from a serious bond with Therese Grob for reasons which were not only social and financial, the relationship became a pointless affliction on them both. Not being appointed to Laibach meant he remained unaccountable, unpredictable and uncommitted. But the temptation was also physical, and resisting it, for whatever purpose, exacted

THE PROMISE OF FREEDOM (1816-1818)

a physical cause. But we miss the true importance of Schubert's flight in 1819 if we think of it simply as an escape. Unlike his father, Schubert may have shrunk from a bond that would have made marriage almost inevitable, but in sexual matters motives are never straightforward and the degree of sexual intimacy that Schubert and Therese reached is also insignificant. What is significant is the momentous consequence of his encounter with her, which opened the way for the peculiar, if not unique, symbiosis of life and art that characterizes Schubert's subsequent career.

IN THE CRUCIBLE OF CONVENTION? SYMPHONIES 4, 5 AND 6

Much of the music written during these years was chamber music for friends and family. Schubert's eight Ländler in F sharp minor for violin (D 355) and his nine Ländler in D for violin (D 370) were most likely charivari written for Ferdinand's marriage on 7 January 1816. Ferdinand had been assistant teacher at the orphanage from 1810 but his promotion from assistant to teacher in 1816 had allowed him to marry. The Ländler may have been occasional works although another set in B flat major followed in the spring of 1816. Around this time Schubert composed three concise Sonatas for violin and piano which Diabelli published as Sonatinas. Although No. 1 is in D major (D 384), the following two – No. 2 in A minor (D 385) and No. 3 in G minor (D 408) – were clearly an exploration of the expressive harmonic colours available from the minor mode before Schubert began his Fourth Symphony in April and concluded it within the same month. Who were Schubert's violin and piano works imagined for? For Therese Grob's brother, Heinrich? For Ferdinand or Otto Hatwig? The Rondo in A for solo violin and string orchestra (D 438) which followed in June 1816 was most likely premiered by Ferdinand at the orphanage or at least read through by the local orchestra.

When Schubert remarked in 1824 – during a period of depression – that his first ten years had brought nothing of significance, he was not doing his earlier self justice. We must be careful not to give too much importance to his withering dismissal of early work. Even with works that he felt were of a conventional stamp, practically nothing he published appeared in the form in which it was first written. Privately, the 4th Symphony had strong personal associations for on its manuscript the ever self-aware Schubert later appended the sobriquet, 'Tragic'. The gesture is powerfully suggestive of his private depression in the wake of the Therese Grob affair and an affirmation of music's ability to take refuge to the inner life.

Written in April 1816, the same month in which Spaun wrote to Goethe and Schubert applied to Laibach, the 'Tragic' Symphony no. 4 in C minor (D 417) dwarfs its predecessors. The presence of a local orchestra no doubt helped to stimulate his orchestral imagination, but with this symphony there is no record of a premiere or even a reading in the 1815–18 concerts led by Otto Hatwig. The first performance of which we know took place on the twenty-first anniversary of Schubert's death in Leipzig in 1849. Eduard Hanslick's 1860 review determined its subsequent reception history, and it is only in recent years that its considerable individuality has begun to be recognized.[7] Despite the absence of parts, Schubert's sobriquet and subsequent withdrawal into more popular styles suggest the experience of a failed performance.[8] Emotionally exposed and technically demanding, it is a statement of personal ambition and Schubert never wrote anything like it again.

It is probably the tonal innovation that strikes the listener most when we first hear the 'Tragic' Symphony. The temptation to write a minor key symphony, which has a greater expressive function, must have held enormous appeal for a composer used to probing harmonic colour and now striving to mark a turning point in his own musical development. It was also a measure of Schubert's ambition as C minor was Beethoven's favourite minor key, prompted by his admiration for Mozart's C minor movements, in particular his Piano Sonata (K 457) and Piano Concerto (K 491).[9] Schubert's Adagio molto immediately announces a very different symphonic tone in the longest of his symphonic introductions. Its *lamento* motif with its dissonant suspensions, chromatic lines – including a transition into G flat major (bar 10) – and broad melodic gestures point to a tragic situation from which the symphony will free itself. The symphony shares the same psychology as Schubert's famous letter written to Leopold Kupelwieser eight years later, in which he opens with a description of himself as the unhappiest man on earth but closes with plans to arrange a public concert of his music, in the course of which he appears to write the depression out of himself. The first subject of Schubert's Allegro vivace in C minor emerges as a liberation, its first statement bearing the intimacy of a string quartet, its sigh figures leading to a powerful outbreak (bar 39). Schubert's lyrical second subject surprises in A flat major rather than the expected E flat major. Though it is the classic two-key exposition, it passes through a myriad of harmonic associations through E major (bar 89) and C major (bar 97) and from A flat major brings the music to the threshold of C minor (bars 31–34). The 42-bar development section is the furthest thing from Beethoven's influence. Schubert is not interested in the motivic unfolding but in establishing his own code of repetition and variation. He states the first subject twice in B flat minor in such a way that its third restatement in G minor (bar 177) disguises the beginning of the recapitulation so there is no sense of tonal homecoming. Schubert's recapitulatory response is extremely daring and original. After reprising the first subject in the dominant, the second subject in E flat (bar 214), he returns to the tonic in the closing section (bar 248). Schubert's solecism is strategic: by ending his first movement in the major variant, which is common in the Finale, he transcends the tragic and affirms his originality.

D 417 is the only one of Schubert's youthful symphonies that does not have a subdominant slow movement. Although Schubert follows the tendency of Mozart's and Beethoven's C minor sonatas by composing the slow movement in A flat,[10] it is less a portentous signal of Beethoven's influence in the *Pathétique* or Fifth Symphony than a reflection of Schubert's assimilation of Vienna's cosmopolitan classicism and his own personal penchant for the submediant. The artistry by which the romance theme emerges arrests the listener (bars 1–24, see Example 9.1), its consequent phrase stated by the oboe followed by wind dialogue with the strings (bars 25–32, 33–40) and a *tutti* closing section (bars 41–52).

Example 9.1: Symphony no. 4 in C minor (D 417/ii), first subject, bars 1–24

The sublime vocality of this theme is beautifully offset by the dark rhetoric of the second subject in F minor (bar 53), which gives the kind of harmonic jolt listeners have come to expect with Schubert. The same tonal liberalism is at play in the unfolding of the second subject as the music migrates into E flat minor and F flat major (bar 71ff), settling into C flat minor (bar 80). The movement is in ABABA song form and the extraordinary transition into the reprise of A is the most daring in a Schubert symphony. Once again he draws on the descending tetrachord, the semiquavers moving progressively higher while the bass descends (Example 9.2 online). In the subsequent reprise of the second subject in B minor (bar 162), the pulsing semiquaver figuration and sigh figures, tossed between the first violins and wind, create a sense of longing and expectation (bars 178–188). Schubert grants the opening melody the final say (bar 256) in this gloriously long second movement.

Although Schubert marks the manuscript for his Allegro vivace movement *Menuetto*, it is a major key scherzo in E flat major rather than the expected C minor minuet. While the form belongs to the classical symphony – A (bars 1–14), B (bars 15–38) with varied repeat of A (bars 39–54) – the most striking characteristics of the scherzo are its extraordinary chromatic lines and daring displacement of accents, heightened by constant alteration between staccato and legato articulation. It is counterbalanced by a very simple, dance-like trio, with pizzicato string accompaniment, the period and phrase structure of which belongs to the Classical period.

Teleologically, the most important movement of D 417 is the Allegro finale, which is unusual for Schubert as the symphony moves from C minor[–C major]–A flat–E flat–C minor[–C major]. A study of the manuscript shows that what sounds like an improvised four-bar prelude with its ascending bass was an afterthought leading back into the expositional repeat. Schubert accompanies his breathless, restless first subject in C minor (bar 5), driven by a flight motif in the strings racing through E flat major (bar 31), landing back on the tonic (bar 43). He then crescendos into a powerful *fortissimo* passage whose *sforzandi* chords lead into a jubilant second subject in the submediant (bar 85). Schubert's two epilogues (bar 129) land us into E flat major with a characteristic harmonic diversion into C flat major. His ruse here is to climb up from C flat major through C, D flat and D to re-establish E flat major (bar 163). The recapitulation recasts this broad expositional key-scheme (C minor–A flat major–E flat major) as C major–A minor–F major–C major. His harmonic diversions to the tonic major are as symbolic as his recollection of jubilant cries that are called into question by unrestful modulations.

Schubert's Janus-faced Symphony no. 4 is a singular work led by what Robert Lowell called 'the incomparable wandering voice' of inspiration. The work weaves an abundance of carefree lyric action into a bleaker perception of life. It tells us much about the emancipation of Schubert's imagination as it does about the radical changes in contemporary aesthetics of the symphony. Far from being wary of Beethoven's inheritance, Schubert knew music's impulse to outstrip the given. Specifically his singular lengths, countless repetitions, abrupt, attention-grabbing harmonic shifts, and more generally his ability to hew to the symphonic possibilities of his own musical language, all bear the hallmarks of Schubert's 'late' style.

In tracing Schubert's development from symphony to symphony, one witnesses a nineteenth-century pilgrim's progress. Five months after he composed the 'Tragic', Schubert began his ever-popular chamber Symphony no. 5 in B flat (D 485) and the last of his teenage symphonies. Written in less than a month in September 1816, Schubert's Fifth transmutes the genre into a private, domestic medium, thereby opening up an entirely new sound world. Even the very notion of a 'chamber symphony' is at odds with concepts of symphonic style and monumentality. Was it a reaction against the genre's excesses or the experimentation of his Fourth? Or a response to the sociability of the symphony? Certainly Schubert's personal development as a symphonist reflects broader trends. Just as A. B. Marx's 1824 essay on Beethoven's symphonies rests on a premise of Hegelian unfolding,[11] Schubert's symphonies stand out by virtue of their variety. In the Fifth he builds on the symphony's history as a metaphor for exploration, even resolution, of psychological and social contrast.

The symphony's new aesthetic at the beginning of the nineteenth century witnessed a gradual shift from private to public performances. The public concerts given by the Gesellschaft der Musikfreunde began in 1814, two years before this symphony was conceived. In seeking to understand its roots, it is essential to remember that very few European cities had a standing civic orchestra: Leipzig's Gewandhaus was an exception and the Vienna Philharmonic Society was not founded until 1842. Most of the orchestras in which Schubert played were private orchestras, such as the chamber orchestra which had expanded from the quartet evenings in his home. As the orchestra outgrew available space, rehearsals relocated first to Franz Frischling's larger residence within the city walls in Dorotheergasse and then the Schottenhof home of Otto Hatwig (1766–1834), a musician at the Burgtheater whose concerts supported symphonic repertoire. Leopold von Sonnleithner recalled in some detail the orchestral complement which amounted to a total of thirty-five players: one flute, two oboes, [three clarinets], three bassoons; two horns; [two trumpets], [timpani] and strings (seven first violins including Otto Hatwig, Eduard Jaëll and Ferdinand Schubert; six second violins including Heinrich Grob; three violas including Schubert; three cellos and two double bass).[12] Schubert's chamber symphony tells us less about the size of Hatwig's orchestra than about the abilities of its 'amateur' players. The Fifth is unique from the rest of Schubert's symphonies because it is delicately scored for an early-Classical ensemble with only one flute, no clarinets, trumpets or timpani. That the wind parts were performed by single instruments endorses the (semi-)professional abilities of the players who premiered it in autumn 1816. The private, chamber-music-like character of the symphony tells us much about the gradual changes in the social function of the symphony, but also the changing perceptions of the role of the listener. This is music for an educated audience, away from Beethoven's influence, for Schubert's playing with conventions demands a sharpness of attention suited to chamber music performances rather than the symphony proper. The work and its listenership are embodiments of the aesthetic idealism symbolized by Goethe in his description of the orchestra in *Wanderjahre*.[13]

Along with some of his overtures, Symphony no. 5 in B flat (D 485) was premiered at Hatwig's, at the Schottenhof in the autumn of 1816. Schubert's experience as leader of the Stadkonvikt orchestra and his insider's knowledge of this local ensemble allowed him to capitalize on its existing strengths. Schubert was well acquainted with the symphony's communal tone, and the acoustical results of this house orchestra would have varied considerably depending on the venue and number of players. His knowledge of the Viennese symphony influenced the colour of his own. Scored for an orchestra of the same size and constitution as Mozart's Symphony no. 40 in G minor (K 550), Schubert's Fifth is as compact in structure as it is in instrumentation. While its formal articulation is continually expressed in relation to Mozart – from its orchestration to the concise sonata-allegro design of its opening movement – its origins can also be traced to other rhetorical models. Prominent examples include Pasquale Anfossi's *Sinfonia* in B flat which was also widely known in Vienna for its ingenious disruption of convention, and Leopold Hofmann's B flat major chamber symphony, which Schubert knew from its Catholic liturgical contexts where it was performed in celebration of the Eucharist. Both influences again show Schubert retreating from the public condition of Beethoven's symphonic discourse in this semi-private salon symphony.

Schubert's clearly articulated themes are announced by a four-bar prefatory idea, a seemingly nonchalant gesture he had used in the finale of his Fourth Symphony. The Classical imprint is immediately recognized in the triadic flourishes of the first subject designed to summon attention. Schubert's canonically exchanged triads are voiced by the first violins, echoed by the cellos and basses (bars 5–18), and answered by the flute on the restatement (bar 25ff). The expositional second key theme, in the dominant, also comprises the Classical antecedent and consequent phrases (bars 65–72). Following a characteristically succinct development which reminds us of the prefatory motif (bar 120ff), his subdominant recapitulation (bar 168ff) bears the hallmark of Wagenseil's symphonies. The lyricism of both themes is beautifully contrasted by dramatic *tutti* passages laden with dynamic contrasts (bars 45–64, 80–117, 134–170, 203–230). Schubert's mastery of orchestral writing is also affirmed in the spacious soaring climax (bar 276).

Mozartian cross-referencing is very much part of the symphony's reception history, with Donald Tovey hearing in Schubert's elegant E flat major melody in the second movement vestiges of Mozart's Violin Sonata in F (K 377), and Mosco Carner identifying a memorial trace of the Andante of Mozart's G minor Symphony in Schubert's second section (bars 27–56). If by breaking free of the Beethovenian model, Schubert is looking back to Viennese masters, he not only lightened his burden but found a unique symphonic voice in the process. The short modulatory link between subjects (bars 24–26) and bold tonal excursions from E flat to C flat (bar 27), gently landing on G flat the second time around (bar 93), epitomizes the audacious harmonic and tonal twists for which he is famed. Schubert characteristically plays with audience expectations to the end by continually deferring cadential closure, tonal and expressive resolution. His experience as a symphonist is evident in his ability to vitalize the ABABA formal strategy with local-level contrasts and very effective woodwind writing. This use of tonal contrast marks a gradual change in his attitude to second movements in the symphony: after the Fifth he composed them in sonata form.

Expressive choices are not limited to Schubert's second movement. One of the wonders of the minuet is his transformation of the opening theme into a flowing cantabile in the second section where the wind are in subtle interplay with violins and lower strings. Schubert returns to Classical diatonic practice from which he had departed in his Second Symphony – one which Beethoven never introduces into any of his symphonies – and grants his major-key symphony a minor-key minuet, this time tonicizing the relative minor.[14] Although entitled 'Minuet', its Allegro molto tempo and character bring it a step closer to the scherzo in Schubert's lyrical style. Orchestration plays a significant role in Schubert's manipulation of the Trio's thematic and textural procedures where drama hinges on contrasts of dynamics and register, reminiscent in character of other famous G minor symphonies, most obviously Haydn (Hob I: 39) and Mozart's 'little G minor' no. 25 as well as no. 40 but also by Dittersdorf, who makes equally prominent use of tone colour. This dramatic process commences when the upper wind answer the violins in exact canon and the symphony's periodicity is extended from a four-bar to six-bar phrase, momentarily departing from the Trio's Classical style.

Whether or not one hears the imprint of Mozart's string quartets K 387 in G major, K 458 in B flat major and K 465 in C major, which Newbould traces in Schubert's Allegro vivace Finale, Schubert's symphony stems from a much broader environment of intertextual influence. Certainly, the dynamic shaping of Schubert's first subject bears testimony to his first-hand knowledge of Haydn's finales, while his decision to precede the lyrical second subject by a short silence reflects more broadly his intimate knowledge of Vienna's cosmospolitan classicism. In terms of formal strategy, the finale is unique among Schubert's symphonies. Composed as a regular sonata-allegro, it is the only one of more than twenty sonata-form movements in his symphonies in which he ends the movement the same way as he ended its exposition.[15] One of the most engaging elements of this symphony is not only what it tells us about Schubert's compositional development but his larger place in society. In direct contrast to the traditional image of Schubert, we see a composer availing himself of opportunities around him and in complete mastery of symphonic conventions.

The orchestral works of these crowded years culminated in a Sixth Symphony (D 589), which Schubert began to compose in October 1817 and drew the final double bar a few days after his twenty-first birthday in February 1818. The genre's aesthetic prestige invited him to mark his birthday with a symphony, a paradigm of artistic ambition and autonomy. The symphony's unusually long gestation period was in part due to the family move to Rossau and partly due to his experimentation with genre. The conflict is resolved, aesthetically speaking, in a work which is very different from the Fifth and the symphonies that follow.[16] Originally entitled *Grosse Sinfonie*, it was later nicknamed the 'Little C major' to distinguish it from his final symphony, a *cognomen* that is misleading about the work and role it plays in Schubert's development. The Sixth is a public statement of ambition which greatly contrasts with the intimacy of his Fifth. It too is scored for a full late-Classical orchestra, this time including clarinets, trumpets and timpani.

Schubert's coming of age was crowned by the spring premiere of this *Grosse Sinfonie* – either in Otto Hatwig's Gundelhof home (Bauernmarkt no. 4/5 Brandstätte) or in Anton von Pettenkofer's apartment (Bauernmarkt no. 1) – along with a chain of Italian overture performances in the first half of 1818.[17] A decade later the symphony would be performed to the wider public that Schubert imagined on 14 December 1828, just four weeks after his death, in the Redoutensaal of the Imperial Palace under the direction of Johann Baptist Schmiede. An account of this memorial concert published by Eduard von Bauernfeld in 1829 suggests that Schubert knew of the Gesellschaft der Musikfreunde's decision to perform the symphony in their Sunday concerts series and had discussed the work with him: 'A Symphony in C Major, performed soon after his death at one of the concerts of Vienna's Society of the Friends of Music and composed as early as 1817, was counted by Schubert himself among his less successful works. Yet the work certainly justified expectations, for even though it is written almost throughout in the manner of a master highly esteemed by the young composer, even that master himself would have had no cause to be ashamed to rank it among his own works.'[18] Schubert's adoption of key and inter-movement strategies of Beethoven's First Symphony[19] – in particular the formal logic and tonal planning of his first movement and scherzo – could also be read as the twenty-one-year-old's ambitious rivalling of his famous contemporary. His Sixth pays homage to and refutes Beethoven with the blitheness of youth. Long before Beethoven entered the arena the symphony had established itself as the most demanding and prestigious of genres, and his own contribution added an even greater aura of insuperability. Beethoven himself was thirty-one when he wrote his First Symphony, Bruckner was thirty-eight, Brahms was forty-three. By the time he was twenty-one Schubert, in the wisdom of youth, had written six symphonies which stand out all the more for their variety.

One of the most engaging aspects of Schubert's Sixth Symphony is his synthesis of German and Italian influences, and in particular his dialogue with Neapolitan conventions. While D 589 shows the close attention that he paid to stylistic and aesthetic resonances of Rossini's works – perhaps another attempt to guarantee success after the 'Tragic' – it also testifies to a much deeper engagement with Italian tradition. This intention is signalled by his title *Sinfonie* which reminds us of the origins of the Viennese symphony in the operatic overtures of Sammartini, Jommelli and Galuppi, and the symphonies of the Italian-trained, operatic composer Georg Christoph Wagenseil. The humour in Schubert's *Sinfonie* is also imprinted by the *Dramma giocoso* tradition which he knew through Salieri. Salieri's *Falstaff, ossia le tre burle* is laden with musical humour from the opening Sinfonia through the various acts, including Falstaff's Act 1 patter aria, the quartet or duettino 'La stessa, la stessissima' in Act 1, the technically brilliant 'laughter' trio, canonical duet of Mr and Mrs Ford in Act 2 and the grand finale of Act 2. Schubert was very familiar with Salieri's parody of *opera seria* conventions; for a start *Falstaff* was performed continually at the Kärntnertortheater and Beethoven even deployed one of its duets, 'La stessa, la stessissima', in his variations, WoO 7.[20] The cheerful character and thematic construction of Schubert's Sixth shares the light-hearted character of Italian comic opera and expects the liveliness of an attentive audience.

The solemn chords of the slow introduction – a distinguishing feature of the 'great symphony' tradition – announces Schubert's intention to experiment with symphonic form. Although Schubert reverts to the slow introduction that he had composed for all his symphonies up to his Fifth, this opening is different to those which have gone before. As is characteristic of Italian overtures, it is made up of multifarious elements: the traditional slow introduction ternary form (ABC with a cantabile B phrase); the dramatic restatement of its opening gesture (bar 8), the surprising *sforzati* (bar 8/9), the pivotal turn from C major to C minor in the cantabile theme (bar 10), the triplet motif (bar 12), clarinet solo (bar 18) and horn fifths (bar 23). Schubert stamps all of these with his own signature the moment he catches us off guard with a sudden shift to A flat and return to the tonic via an augmented sixth.[21] This intention for novelty is announced in the Italianate character of the Allegro: its theatrical turn of phrase, sparkling orchestration, and Schubert's knack for configuring the orchestra in unexpected ways. We hear it in the canonic wind writing before the end of the exposition or the subtle change of sonority where the wind play *colla parte* with the strings in an epilogue that truly emphasizes the movement's theatrical implications. The delicacy and finesse of his wind writing testify to Schubert's direct knowledge of the music of Italian emigrants, Gaetano Brunetti and Luigi Boccherini, but also the Bohemian symphonists, Johann Stamitz (1717–1757) and Antonio Rosetti (1750–1792), all of whom are known for their imaginative and varied use of wind instruments. Like the closing movement of Schubert's Fifth, the opening Allegro is in conventional sonata form and yet sounds as if it were conceived for the stage. One of the reasons is that it is the first of Schubert's symphonic movements to have a coda faster than the main body of the movement: a device common to Italian overtures which would resurface in his 'Great' C major Symphony.

The theatricality of Schubert's Sixth is continued in the refined artistic spirit and balletic *character* of a second movement which is lighter than his earlier Andante movements, in particular in his Fourth and Fifth Symphonies. His inclusion of trumpets and timpani in this slow movement augurs his use of full brass and drums from his Eighth Symphony onwards. Episodic in form, the Andante is a kaleidescope of dance scenes whose melodic grace glides seamlessly into a beautifully articulated Italianate middle section (bars 41–75), laden with *fz* and *fp* accents and staccato triplets. When Schubert recapitulates this romance theme (bar 82), he enlivens it by an Italianate triplet rhythm. Whether it is the falling tritone or carefully articulated answer of the antecedent, or the very simple harmony or rapid sextuplet figuration in the consequent, the simple construction of periods in this AABA romance perfectly complements the themes of the opening movement. The light-hearted nature of the Andante also arises from the unexpected as the music wanders off into mediant transitions C–A flat–C (bars 41–70) and F–D flat–F (bars 82–107). The movement contains a whole spectrum of imitation from Schubert's gentle pastiche of the Italian middle-section melody with its triplets, to the very playful wind and strings dialogue (bar 115ff). This parody of Italian musical styles brings us back to the orchestra and occasion, for he was writing this occasional symphony to mark his twenty-first birthday with family and friends. The humour of this symphony is immediately understood in and beyond these social and systemic contexts.

The first time Schubert deploys a Beethovenian scherzo is in his Sixth *Sinfonie*. Cast in a traditional binary form, which he enlarges with an extended development section, his scherzo is prophetic of his Ninth and merits his designation of this work as a 'Great Symphony'. The vivacity of his dance-like Presto is enlivened by his thematic carnival, subtle orchestration and wind usage which delineate structural function. From the very beginning the movement is laden with intricacies from the unexpected turn to E minor (bar 8), its subsequent correction in the dominant (bar 16), both unexpectedly voiced in a *tutti* outburst. Tension is maintained by off-beat *fp* accents (bars 20–31) as the wind and strings chatter away in humorous play with the metre before the playful dynamic and key changes of the middle section (bar 65). The music migrates into the mediant major for the più lento Trio, an intra-movement strategy shared with the Assai più lento of Beethoven's Seventh.

Schubert's Allegro moderato finale is thematically abundant and beautifully orchestrated. Composed as a divertissement, the movement is a kaleidoscope of prismatic scenes, a synthesis of diverse textures, in which many themes come to the fore and drop back to make room for others. The light-hearted ABA subject is playfully answered by the wind (bars 2–11), which wanders off unexpectedly into A flat (bar 15ff). The humoresque restatement of the main theme and its *tutti fortissimo* development (bar 47ff), semiquaver string motif (bar 53ff) and carnivalesque second subject (bar 91ff), first in A major then in G major, all brilliantly parody the Italian tradition. The movement's motivic patterning includes double paralleled thirds (bar 129ff, for example), dotted rhythms tossed back and forth as the musical narrative glides from one image to the next, gaining unstoppable momentum. Schubert's ebullient style and adventurous episodic technique has metaphorical as well as thematic significance. Its theatricality bears testimony to the composer's ability to conflate public and private modes of thought: a grand symphony brilliantly written for Hatwig's chamber orchestra employing a brilliant pastiche of Italian techniques: *sforzandi, crescendi,* string tremoli, and the use of wind for both sonic and harmonic reinforcement. The movement is a network of thematic transformations which continually command audience attention as the music grows in dramatic intensity.

This theatricality is also part of a serious aesthetic whereby Schubert's experimentation with symphonic form leads him to abandon finale contexts. He closes D 589 with a movement employing the standard bipartite pattern of the Italian overture in which individual thematic episodes are set off against each other in the manner of a rondo. With the exception of a standard slow introduction, the form is the same as an Italian overture: an exposition and recapitulation (bar 246) without development but with a colourful coda (bar 467) that deflates audience expectations to accelerate the tempo. The Italian model remains recognizable through the rhythmically offset upper and lower voices, harmonic twists, dotted rhythms, dynamic variety, including *sforzati,* string tremoli and drum basses which build in suspenseful anticipation of the firm conclusion.

Why does Schubert specifically ask for three bars, rest after the last chord of the Sixth Symphony? Does he want the players to sit still or its listeners to delay their reaction? Certainly, the rests have a post-cadential function which signals to the audience to withhold applause until the end. This closing gesture is less a light-hearted play with rituals than a serious request for contemplation, which tells us much about performance customs in Schubert's day. It also affirms the presence of an actual audience in Otto Hatwig's home, actively engaging with his music. Contrary to the belief that Schubert never heard these works performed, the expressive rhetoric of his symphonies was significantly shaped by his audiences. Already by the age of twenty-one, his attention to orchestral effects demonstrates the synergy of compositional environment and style that is so central to understanding not only Schubert's symphonies but symphonic repertoires in early nineteenth-century Vienna.

SPECULUM MENTIS: SYMPHONY IN D (D 615)

Schubert's Sixth is usually grouped with the first five symphonies as marking the end of a period of youthful engagement, but it also marks the beginning of a new period of experimentation. Schubert composed six complete symphonies between 1813 and 1818 and four incomplete symphonies between 1818 and 1822: two in D major (D 615 in 1818, D 708A in 1820), one in E major (D 729), and one in B minor (D 759).[22] His Symphony in E major (D 729), which is complete in piano score though only 110 bars are fully orchestrated, was until recently classified as his Seventh, but shortly after finishing his Sixth he sketched a Symphony in D (D 615) in May 1818. This 120-bar piano particell contains an Adagio introduction in D minor (33 bars), an Allegro molto first movement in D major (86 bars) and a principal Andante first subject (28 bars), which reveal a very different Schubert. The urgency with which the introductory theme transitions through A minor and D flat into a cantabile sequential passage in D flat and G flat major creates an even greater contrast between the D minor introductory theme (Example 9.3) and D major Allegro molto first subject (Example 9.4).

The magisterial slow introduction dramatically complements the lyricism of Schubert's opening subject whose *pianissimo* restatement looks back to the introductory theme in its motivic material and uncharacteristic

Example 9.3: Symphony in D major (D 615/i), Adagio D minor Introduction and sequential modulations, bars 1–9

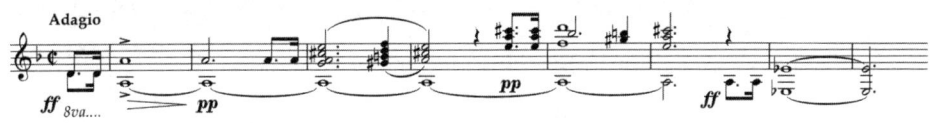

Example 9.4: Symphony in D major (D 615/i), Allegro molto, first subject

chord chains. The second subject is also linked by motifs with the slow introduction. Directly voiced in the dominant it builds to a beautiful cantilena before breaking off (Example 9.5).

Example 9.5: Symphony in D major (D 615/i), Allegro molto, second subject

Although the second movement first subject is a characteristic slow movement primary theme, its absence of repetition and a tonic key surprises us (Example 9.6).

Example 9.6: Symphony in D major (D 615/ii), second movement, first subject

As this 120-bar map of symphonic knowledge breaks off, we see Schubert wrestling with musical thought, but offering the public nothing except what he has won from his own intensely felt experience. The fragmentary sketch is a 'mirror of Schubert's spirit', an example of 'perfect freedom reserved for the [composer] who lives by his own work and in that work does what he wants' (Example 9.7 online).[23]

II

FRIENDSHIPS

10

ARS AMICITIA: ART OF FRIENDSHIP

'Only through Beauty's morning gate
Can you enter the land of knowledge.'

Schiller, *Die Künstler*

The sentimental image of 'Schubert and his friends' in music history has misunderstood, trivialized and subverted the role of friendship in the composer's life. It has missed how one of the gifts of friendship was that it humanized and educated him in the Platonic sense – that is, it drew out of him what was innate but unrealized and unrecognized. In recent years friendship has proved a magnet to Schubert literature, as scholars have begun to re-evaluate the intellectual interests of his circle and learn from it the nature of who Schubert is.[1] One thing in common between traditional and contemporary images of his *Freundeskreis* is seeing Schubert as a social and relational being who needed others in order to flourish and develop.

In order to understand the significance of friendship in Schubert's life, it is essential to realize how people perceived friendship at that time. By the early nineteenth century, the discourse of friendship was so ingrained in German cultural life that terms such as *Freundschaftskult* are frequently used to describe the age into which Schubert was born. During the Enlightenment, German concepts of friendship had become so emotionally and ideologically charged that it extended far beyond conviviality. Two factors played a tremendous role in this: Pietism – a movement within Lutheranism with its emphasis on personal transformation – and the rational philosophy of the Enlightenment, both of which cast a completely different light on friendship and led to the development of individual consciousness.[2]

This newly found interest in friendship as an historical phenomenon is reflected in numerous treatises and published letters of the time.[3] In 1748 two friends, the theologian, Samuel Gotthold Lange (1711–1781), and the philosopher and art historian, Georg Friedrich Meier (1718–1777), published a weekly paper that explored newly defined concepts of *Freundschaft und Geselligkeit* and took a leading philosophical and socio-ethical position in the eighteenth century.[4] Virtue and truthfulness are the topoi of friendship in Johann Wilhelm Ludwig Gleim's (1719–1803) four-volume *Freundschaftliche Briefe* (1746–71),[5] while Herder's *Ideen zur Philosophie der Geschichte der Menschheit* (1784/85) focuses on the development of friendship in society. Christian Fürchtegott Gellert created a utopia of male friendship in his popular novel, *Das Leben der Schwedischen Gräfin* (1747), and his *Moralische Vorlesung*,[6] both of which were influenced by Aristotle's *Nicomachean Ethics*. Arguably, the most original take on friendship was put forward in Johann Joachim Winckelmann's (1717–1768) *Gedanken über die Nachahmung der griechischen Werke in der Malerei und Bildhauerkunst* (1755). In the opening paragraphs he authoritatively links friendship with the process of learning to appreciate great works of art and achieving greatness as an artist.[7] Goethe recognized the profound influence this essay had on the study and perception of art in the section on 'Friendship' in *Winckelmann und sein Jahrhundert* (1805). Equally telling, he describes Winckelmann as having felt himself born to an idealized form of male friendship as propagated by the Greeks.[8]

IN THE CLOSET OF THE STADTKONVIKT?

The same could be claimed of Schubert and his circle, where male friendship was the key to acceptance into manhood by one's peers. In the nineteenth century becoming a man lay in the gift of one's male friends after the *cursus honorarium* of life in boarding school or an apprenticeship such as Schubert's teacher training which characteristically began at a very early age. The all-male environment of the Stadtkonvikt and its codes were extremely formative for Schubert, so it is inevitable that – in the way of those unconscious, undirected developments that so often perpetuate social inequities – a literature of direction should have emerged, extolling the virtues required for masculine life.

Schubert's older Stadtkonvikt friends, who were grammar school graduates of the Kremsmünster seminary in Linz, formed a literary circle in 1811. The core of Schubert's circle included Josef von Spaun, Anton Holzapfel (1792–1868), Josef Kenner (1794–1868), Albert Stadler (1794–1888), Johann Senn (1795–1857), and later other like-minded Viennese intellectuals and artists such as Johann Baptist Mayrhofer (1787–1836), Franz von Schober (1796–1882) and Leopold Kupelwieser (1796–1862). This Viennese group was modelled on the all-male literary circles of northern Germany, most famously Klopstock's *Bremer Beiträger*, Gleim's 'friendship temple', and the coterie of young male poets around the Swiss author Johann Jakob Bodmer (1698–1783). Like their German counterparts, Schubert's circle was cultivated along the lines of classical friendship espoused by Aristotle, Cicero and Montaigne, all of whom signalled the tradition of friendship to be a male one.

In accordance with Classical writers and Enlightenment thinkers, Schubert's friends perceived the generous nurturing of younger male talent as part of a deeply moral sense of duty towards society. The preface to volume one of their short-lived yearbook, which they high-mindedly entitled *Beyträge zur Bildung für Jünglinge* (Contributions towards the education of young men), explains this emphasis on youth: through diligent study of the good, the true, and the beautiful, gifted adolescents would mature into men who were manly, noble, and beneficial to society.[9] Their perception of a person as an artwork in progress was not unique to their circle but can be traced back to the Stoic philosopher Epictetus (c. 55–135 AD), who believed exposure to the Classics would produce exemplary beings, their raw humanity moulded and filed away by a double discipline, at once ethical and aesthetic.[10] When Schubert was invited into this society of idealistic young men, it was a major turning point in his life. Within five years, considerable advances in his intellectual development were made, important aspects of his style crystallized, crucial friendships and artistic relationships firmly established.

Whether these friendships were sexually consummated or not is a topic of recent debate. Certainly, recent writings about Schubert's circle tell us as much about today's evolving sexual and relationship taxonomies as they do about Viennese society that produced these stories. Intimate friendships between nineteenth-century middle-class men were confined to youth and in some ways seen as rehearsals for marriage and tests for manhood when men were expected to make a lifelong commitment to a woman, to share secrets, lend emotional support, and be physically affectionate – just the kinds of behaviours in which they engaged with their male friends. The fact that many of Schubert's circle married and had children is irrelevant. It is more pertinent to ask whether sentimental expressions of affection without literal implications of homosexuality were acceptable during this period.[11]

Any attempt to answer this can scarcely escape speculation about the degree to which nineteenth-century homosociality was, in practice or in latency, a form of homosexuality. As the actual letters and diaries of many of Schubert's circle show, intimate friendships of this era are not limited to fictional accounts. In line with the Romantic privileging of intense feeling, friendships in Schubert's circle were arm-in-arm, full of openly expressed affection as exemplified in Anton von Ottenwalt's letter to Schober on 1 January 1816:

> Anton [von Spaun] sat at the piano in Frau von Brandt's room, and while darkness fell he played his variations on the Almerlied, the new ones on the Russian folksong, the theme of which I love so, because it

is in the minor, and the melancholy Traunerlieder and some others. The tones carried me away [. . .] Suddenly I realized the Kremsmünster students would have to leave the next day; I was driven to them [. . .] Then I remained standing there between them, gave friend Kahl my right hand and put my left around our beloved Ferdinand, *who sat arm in arm with Kenner*. He drew me closer with his right arm, and as the tones thus spoke directly into the soul, I felt the gentle, fervent press of their hands, and I had to look back and forth into their faces and their beloved eyes. They sat so still, pleasantly moved by the music, but yet so peaceful and cheerful, and I gazed at them so, thinking: oh, you good souls, you are indeed happy in your innocence. Music makes you gentler, but not sad, not upset; what your heart desires you grasp in the hand of a friend, and you know no other wishes, you whom the melody gives only loftier waves.[12]

The sensuality of this scene makes it hard to imagine psychological intimacy did not spill into physical intimacy, and it is likely that some of these relations had sexual components. What is immediately conspicuous is Josef Kenner's position at the centre of this scene because of the moralistic stance he took about Schubert's 'two natures'.[13] It raises the question as to whether the most outspoken of his friends was homosexually inclined and outed Schubert compulsively. In the immediate aftermath of the composer's death, Kenner admitted to Spaun that had he not 'unmerited pleasure in his wife and children, [he] would have gladly died for Schubert, and would have done so unhesitatingly'.[14]

Nineteenth-century culture allowed for more varied interpretations of manhood which are closer to today than to the post-Freud era, when male friendships became more limited in scope as issues of homosexuality, masculinity and sexuality entered public discourse. In Schubert's day the concept of friendship included a range of erotic, sexual and platonic possibilities.[15] The German word 'Freund' often referred to a lover and 'Freundschaft' to an 'erotic-affectional relation, either hetero- or homosexual'.[16] In the writings of this period, passages about friends and friendship replace explicit descriptions of same-sex sexuality and contain euphemisms for sex, romantic-emotional relationships or 'just' friendship.[17]

It was not until later in the nineteenth century that literature on same-sex 'friendship' verged on being more explicitly homosexual. Henry Clay Trumbull's 1892 *Friendship the Master-Passion or The Nature and History of Friendship, and its Place as a Force in the World* focuses on same-sex relationships in the Bible, in ancient Greece and in contemporary literature,[18] and Elisar von Kupffer's 1900 anthology of German poetry, *Chivalric Affection and Love between Friends in World Literature*, presents homosexual literature that many saw as an important contribution to a rising German gay-liberation movement.[19]

EPISTOLARY FRIENDSHIPS

Despite the fodder such letters provide for queer readings, interpreting male-male desire as the wellspring of Schubert's creativity may, therefore, not be the best explanation of the forces at play. In his memorial for Winckelmann, Goethe recognizes letters as 'among the most important memorials which an individual can leave behind', because they offer deep insight into the psyche of the writer. In Schubert's letters this truth is complicated by censorship in Metternich's Vienna whereby letters could be opened and read, unless carried between friends. Despite Ottenwalt's account of linking arms, holding hands and caressing, scant evidence exists in the letters of Schubert's circle about sexual relations between members in these romantic friendships.

What is evident is the deep emotionality of Schubert's correspondence with his friends. In a note sent to Josef Hüttenbrenner on 21 February 1818 he addressed him as 'Dearest friend', spoke of his 'most devoted friendship' to him and expressed the wish to 'become closer friends'. Early in 1819 when living with Mayrhofer, he assured Josef, 'I am and remain yours'. To his brother in art, Anselm Hüttenbrenner, he closed a letter on

21 January 1819: 'Remain my friend and do not forget your Schubert.'[20] Nine years later he still employed the language of tender friendship and fidelity to '[his] dear old Hüttenbrenner', promising to 'remain [his] faithful friend until death'.[21]

The exact same sentiments are found in Schubert's correspondence with his family, where the relatively static relation between friendship and fraternity, which his father and grandfather had found in the church, becomes secularized in Schubert's letters. When he writes to Ferdinand and his parents on 8 August 1818 he expresses his fidelity to his family – 'I remain, with true affection for you all, your sincerely faithful Franz' – and to Ferdinand from Zseliz he signs himself off with accustomed affection, 'your ever devoted brother Franz'. This practice of family letters which were read *coram publico* is found in his letter from Zseliz on 3 August 1818 in which he collectively addresses Spaun, Schober, Mayrhofer and Senn as his 'best and dearest friends'. On 8 September 1818 he again addresses his absent friends – Schober, Spaun, Mayrhofer, Senn, Streinsberg, Weisse and Weidlich – and closes 'in eternal affection, your faithful friend'.[22]

What emerges most in Schubert's correspondence is his need to connect with others and his admission that he would have become misanthropic without their letters. He tells Ferdinand on 16 July 1824 that he is hurt by the silence at home. When his father gently addresses Franz's withdrawal from family in a letter dated 8 June 1825, any hint of criticism is muted by Schubert's reluctance to jeopardize their reconciliation and he immediately echoes Franz Theodor's pledge of love.[23] Present or absent, friends and family eased the burden of writing and provided emotional support. Ferdinand's central role in his reception history is already in the making as Schubert enlists his brother to further various artistic projects. In his travel letters on 12 and 21 September 1825, and on 16–18 July 1824, he recognizes Ferdinand as his 'truest friend, bound to my soul with every fibre', the subordination of younger to older brother balanced out by the dynamic of the more gifted to the less talented.[24]

FRIENDSHIPS

Within and beyond his own family, friendship was deeply liberating for Schubert, who did not fit easily into society's stereotypical structures. Lack of a permanent position and lack of marriage prospects made friendship all the more important for him. What he missed out in terms of permanent relationships was largely compensated for by friendship networks, especially with Franz von Schober, who became a de facto family and on a daily basis provided material and emotional support.

AESTHETIC EDUCATIONS

It has long been recognized that the study of literature with its emphasis on the Classics was a key tenet of Schubert's circle.[25] What is much more central is the extent to which the topology of friendship intersects with literature, music and aesthetics, and the composer's aspirations for achieving artistic greatness. Schubert's circle bore the imprint of Immanuel Kant's perception of moral friendship as mutuality between men of excellent character and the exchange of private ideas for the improvement of each individual.[26] Self-improvement through learning and artistic activity was zealously sought[27] and there was an abiding mistrust of inactivity among its older members.[28]

Much of this rubbed off on Schubert, who began to redirect his energies as his creative imagination matured to a pyrotechnic productivity it would not surpass until his final year. Between November 1814 and September 1816, while he was working as his father's teaching assistant, Schubert wrote some 360 of his 936 works. Behind this creative outburst lies the nurture of friends who could motivate and support his aspirations. Their motto – 'determine yourself from within', most famously discussed in Schiller and Christian Gottfried Körner's *Kalliasbriefe* – was passed on directly to Schubert by Körner's son, Theodor (1791–1813), who advised Schubert to 'live only for Art', for only in music would he find true fulfilment.[29]

Senn attributed this desire to escape into art to the oppressive political climate in Restoration Austria where the German struggles for liberation, from 1813 to 1815, left in their aftermath a significant spiritual upheaval. At a time when traditional religious commitments were in retreat, Schubert's contemporaries looked to art for spiritual dividends previously sought elsewhere. Although, at first glance, the rhetoric of Romanticism in 'An die Musik' (D 547) conjures a sense of *Schwärmen* on all levels, Schubert did not adopt the Romantic tendency to invest art with the kind of unanchored religious sentiment which burdens it with intoxicating expectations that are inevitably disappointed.[30] In 'An die Musik' art offers balm for the spirit but if this is not religious balm, what sort of balm is it?

One of the most ardent attempts to answer this was made at the end of the eighteenth century by Schiller (1759–1805) in his *Über die ästhetische Erziehung des Menschen in einer Reihe von Briefen* (On the Aesthetic Education of Man in a Series of Letters, 1794), an essay which played a central role in Schubert's intellectual development. Schiller's treatise was a project of social betterment which he hoped would help establish the freedom that the French Revolution had conspicuously failed to achieve. Schiller's vision of the centrality of aesthetic experience to daily and political life resonated within Schubert's circle and directly shaped the composer's artistic thought. The poet's insistence on aesthetic experience as 'a condition of the highest reality' and his association of aesthetic experience with moral freedom is evident in 'An die Musik', where music transports Schubert 'to a better world'. Schubert symbolizes the role music plays in this other, higher world through the 'wondrously lovely sound' circles which close his short story, 'Mein Traum', into which 'eternal bliss [is] gathered together in a single moment'.[31] In a fleeting moment of grace, music, love and nature are means of access to a transcendental sphere. Schubert's association of aesthetic experience with higher consciousness was not only profoundly influenced by Novalis but also Schiller's *Aesthetic Education*. On the one hand, Schiller defines the aesthetic as that which leads us from the life of sensuous appetite to the life of moral freedom, a step on the pilgrim's journey to moral self-realization. On the other hand, he recognizes the aesthetic as a realm of experience that mediates between the moral and the physical, resolving the tension between them in a higher unity that is both physical and moral, sensuous and intellectual. In this sense, an aesthetic education is an end in itself: an experience of freedom that relates 'to the totality of our various functions without being a definite object for any single one of them'. That Schiller never really resolves this tension in one sense underscores his point: the aesthetic both points the way towards freedom and is an instance of it.

A second tenet in Schiller's thinking that influenced Schubert's circle is his identification of *Geselligkeit* as the concept by which, together with friendship, man attains wholeness. An issue devoted to friendship from the mid-century moral weeklies, *Der Gesellige*, not only illustrates the degree to which these concepts were bound to each other in Schubert's time, but how friendship was seen as a regulating principle. Prior to assigning a regulating function to friendship *that leads to an aesthetic state*, Schiller had endowed friendship with this power in a short allegorical prose work that mirrors the rhapsodic vision of equality with which he culminates the reader's journey through the *Ästhetische Briefe*. Here, Schiller summarizes how, 'in the realm of aesthetic appearance, the ideal of equality is fulfilled, which the enthusiast wishes to see realized in essence'.[32] He closes the *Ästhetische Briefe* by questioning: 'Does such a state of aesthetic appearance exist? And if so, where can it be found?', to which he responds, 'According to need, it exists in every finely tuned soul and according to deed, one would like to find it – like the true church and the true republic – in a few chosen circles.'[33] The *Bildungskreis* was one such circle, Sonnleithner's salon another in which Schubert experienced friendship as a 'living form' that was bound up with the process of achieving artistic greatness. Whether Schiller's vision of equality was fulfilled in Schubert's closest friendships will be addressed in the following chapter. Even at this formative age, Schubert knew that the growth of an artist's mind was a solitary affair, in spite of all the help it could receive from its context and company.

Thirdly, Schiller's essay, *Über naïve und sentimentalische Dichtung* ('On Naïve and Sentimental Poetry', 1795–96), which seeks to define the modern human condition, played a central role in Schubert's reception history. Schubert's friends' portrait of him as a *Genie* displaying a naïvety that is at one with nature was very much influenced by Schiller's portrait of an artist. For Schiller, such artistic genius often exhibits a kind of naïvety: he is 'guided solely by nature or instinct' and acts with 'simplicity and ease', unconcerned with social connotations or norms.[34] That Schiller had Goethe in mind immediately qualifies this kind of innocence. While Schubert's circle characterized his naïvety by such simplicity, naturalness, directness and ease, his strength of character, creative independence and extroverted need to share his music with others, which they also recognized, gradually became overshadowed. Even before his involvement with the *Bildungskreise*, Schubert knew that the freedom to make choices consonant with his talent was a precondition of a good life. This freedom to think and act informed his decision to give up his scholarship at the Stadtkonvikt, and he exercised the same freedom to use reason publicly in his handling of the Nicene creed.[35] Years later Anton von Ottenwalt acknowledged his exceptional mind in a portrait of a very loquacious Schubert, which is very different to the sentimental image of the composer.[36]

SOME SELECT CIRCLES

While Schubert's circle nurtured him, the way to know what sort of person he was is to examine more closely the kinds of friendships he maintained throughout his life. Friendship is not a singular, easily characterized thing: it gave depth to Schubert's life and took many forms, including non-standard ones such as his friendship with Ferdinand and Elizabeth Traweger's five-year-old son, Eduard,[37] whose memory of Schubert staying in his parents' house in Gmunden in 1825 allows us to glimpse Schubert's affection for young children, of which there are many accounts. 'I was hardly awake in the mornings when, still in my nightshirt, I used to rush in to Schubert [. . . who] in his dressing-gown, with his long pipe, used to take me on his knee, puffed smoke at me, put his spectacles on me, rubbed his beard against me and let me rumple up his curly hair, and was so kind that even us children could not be without him.'[38] Seen through five-year-old Eduard's eyes, Schubert's life took on a happier aspect.

The sheer variety and nuance of these more general relationships shaped Schubert's social persona. In his early years he sought friends with whom he could share musical activities and interests rather than face-to-face support. A close friend at the Stadtkonvikt who is often overshadowed is Albert Stadler to whom Schubert played new songs on his visits to the boarding school after he left. Stadler was responsible for Schubert's Honorary Membership in Linz in 1823. A gifted pianist and composer in his own right, Stadler also made copies of all of Schubert's manuscripts to which he had access. His collection – along with copies made by Johann Leopold Ebner (1791–1870), another school friend, and Karl Pinterics (d. 1831), and first editions by Josef Witteczek (1787–1859) – was of central importance for the first edition of Schubert's Complete Works.

At the Stadtkonvikt, Schubert began his lifelong practice of setting poetry by friends, a good example of which is the Singspiel, *Fernando*, by Stadler, who later supplied the text of *Kantata zum Geburtstag des Sängers Johann Michael Vogl* (D 666). Moritz von Schwind's sepia drawings of Schubert's Kenner setting 'Der Liedler' (D 209) in 1823, intended for publication with Schubert's dedication of the song to his school friend in 1825, also illustrates the rich exchange of poetry, visual arts and music in Schubert's friendship circle. A government official in Linz, Kenner was an amateur painter and poet and these three Kenner Lieder illustrate Schubert's personal identification with the texts he set. Like Beethoven and Brahms, Schubert composed numerous settings of now mostly forgotten poets, many of whom were well regarded in their day. This does not display a lack of literary discernment but rather the creative exchange in Schubert's friendship circles where poetry was part of the fabric of everyday life. The Viennese poets he met and set helped form the composer's world view and shape the nature of his music with respect to genre choices, style and content. One such poetic friendship within a political, sociological and ethical context was with Spaun's cousin, Matthäus von Collin, whose three settings are among Schubert's most important ones of 1822. At the poet's musical evenings at 7 Teinfaltstrasse, Schubert's songs and piano duets were also introduced to some of the most influential and distinguished Viennese music lovers as early as 1820.

Much more central was his friendship with Leopold von Sonnleithner (1797–1873), who actively promoted Schubert's music in soirées at his family residence at the Gundelhof (Bauernmarkt no. 4/Brandstätte no. 5), one of Vienna's most distinguished salons.[39] Many important landmarks in Schubert's career took place at these Friday evening concerts which ran from 26 May 1815 until 20 February 1824. When 'Erlkönig' was premiered there by August von Gymnich and Anna Fröhlich, friends clubbed together to finance its publication and launch Schubert's public career. Sonnleithner was also closely connected with the Gesellschaft der Musikfreunde, established by his uncle Josef, who was employed in Emperor Joseph II's private office. Leopold von Sonnleithner conducted important premieres of Schubert's works there, including the Overture in E minor (D 648), 'Geist der Liebe' (D 747) and *Am Geburtstage des Kaisers* (D 748), which he commissioned for a concert in celebration of Emperor Francis I in 1822. Equally important are Sonnleithner's musicological writings which provides extensive and reliable biographical details such as Schubert's appearance, compositions and interpretation of his songs. Through him we know about the regular Sunday string-quartet sessions in Schubert's home. Sonnleithner clearly wanted his own role to be remembered as he provided a wealth of information to Wilhelm Böcking, who wrote a detailed account of Sonnleithner's contribution to Schubert's career.

A number of Schubert's friendship circles were linked with location and profession. One of his most important friendships from Zseliz was Baron von Schönstein (1797–1876), one of the most admired singers of Schubert's Lieder of his time, whose influence is overshadowed by Schubert's musical partnership with Vogl. Sonnleithner considered him 'one of the best, if not the best Schubert interpreter' he had heard.[40] Anselm Hüttenbrenner admired his 'exceptionally beautiful rendering of Schubert's songs', which frequently moved him to tears, a response echoed by Spaun and Liszt.[41] Schubert wrote to Jenger how much he enjoyed hearing Schönstein sing and he dedicated *Die schöne Müllerin* (D 795) to him.[42] Schönstein not only played an important role in the reception of this cycle but also in introducing Schubert's music to the Viennese aristocracy.

Another admired interpreter of Schubert's songs and one of the many Czech musicians with whom Schubert associated is Ludwig Tietze (1797–1850). Leopold von Sonnleithner praised his simple and unaffected manner of singing Schubert's Lieder which he considered infinitely preferable to the subtle and declamatory interpretation favoured by certain persons 'who are forever searching behind the musical idea' (which they do not comprehend and accordingly disdain) for another, poetic or philosophical, idea.[43] Tietze premiered numerous Lieder in Schubert's lifetime, including 'Rastlose Liebe' (D 138) on 29 January 1824, 'Der Einsame' (D 800) on 23 November 1826, 'Normans Gesang' (D 846) on 8 March 1827, 'Im Freien' (D 880) on 6 May 1827, and 'Gute Nacht' (D 911/1) on 10 January 1828, all at the evening entertainments of the Gesellschaft der Musikfreunde. Schubert had him premiere 'Auf dem Strom' (D 943) at his private concert at the Musikverein and dedicated the 'Offertory in C major' (D 136) 'to [his] friend Ludwig Tietze'. Tietze continued to promote Schubert's music after his death, giving many more premieres: 'Der blinde Knabe' (D 833) on 8 January 1829, Jenger's orchestration of 'Mirjams Siegesgesang' (D 942) at Schubert's memorial concert on 30 January 1829, 'Drang in der Ferne' (D 770) on 19 February 1829 and 'An mein Herz' (D 860) on 7 February 1833. His performance of Schubert's 'Liebesbotschaft' (D 957/1) and 'Erlkönig' with Franz Liszt was reviewed in the *Wiener allgemeine Theaterzeitung* on 1 May where Friedrich Adami wrote, 'I do not believe that this accompaniment has ever been played so brilliantly. It is to Herr Tietze's credit that he held his own so successfully against such a brilliant performance.'

Another accomplished pianist in Schubert's Graz circle was Johann Jenger (1793–1856), who secured Schubert's honorary membership of the Styrian Society in 1823. After he moved to Vienna, Jenger was appointed Musical Director of Kiesewetter's salon, which explains Schubert's increased involvement in these musical evenings from 1827. A sensitive accompanist, Jenger was much in demand as a pianist and performed Schubert's songs in all circles of Viennese society and eventually the highest. He continued to promote Schubert after his death and administered the funds – with Grillparzer and Schober – for Schubert's memorial concert on 23 December 1828 and for the erection of his tombstone in 1830. His friendship with the composer is memorialized in the famous triple portrait with Anselm Hüttenbrenner and Schubert by Josef Teltscher.

Throughout his career Schubert befriended many painters and graphic artists including August Rieder, Moritz von Schwind and Leopold Kupelwieser (1796–1862). Schober commissioned Kupelwieser to paint two watercolours of the *Bildungskreis* at Atzenbrugg Castle: the first an excursion to Aumühle Castle, the other engaged in a game of charades with Schubert seated at the piano. Kupelwieser also contributed numerous portraits of Schubert's circle including Schubert himself, Schober, Bruchmann, Schwind, Spaun and Vogl.

One of the forgotten musical friendships in the last two years of Schubert's life was with the composer and conductor Franz Lachner (1803–1890), organist at the Lutheran Church and from 1827, Kapellmeister at the Court Theatre. The two composers met at the Haidvogel restaurant (30 Graben) where they had lunch every day and shared compositions.[44] Premieres in Lachner's home (12 Marxergasse) included Schubert's String Quartet in D minor (D 810) and F minor Fantasy (D 940), and Hartmann's diaries often mention Lachner's presence at gatherings at the 'Zum Anker' restaurant (10 Grünangergasse). Lachner and Schubert travelled to Baden and Heiligenkreuz in Schubert's final summer, where Lachner inspired Schubert's Fugue in E minor for organ duet (D 952) and his preoccupation with tonal answers. As Lachner studied with Simon Sechter, he may have recommended him to Schubert for private lessons. After Schubert's death Lachner completed the composer's plans for an orchestral arrangement of *Mirjams Siegesgesang* (D 942).

All of these friendly relations played an important role in shaping Schubert's social persona. Explicitly intimate relationships in his life, which are fewer in number, played a deeper role in forming Schubert's individuality.[45] Each one of his friends pushed him in rather different directions, so friendship made him, in a way, more complicated. His sense of self, like all of us, was a composite of influences and reactions to such influences, not least the sway of people whom he admitted into his confidence. One of the recurring motifs in nineteenth-century philosophical writings on friendship – first explored in Xenophon's *Memorabilia* and taken up in Augustine's *Confessions* – is the belief that the most central, formative friendships do not enter our lives accidentally, but providentially. Augustine interprets such relationships as the gifts of God's grace and often surprising sources of love in our lives. Even if we don't agree with Augustine, we can still appreciate the great significance of friendship when we consider how different Schubert's life would have been if certain friends had never entered into it. Not only would his biography have been different, but he too would have been different. So, which friends shaped Schubert's character? Who challenged him and gave him hope? Who influenced his attitudes, values and perceptions?

11

ARS AMICITIAE: ART BORN OF FRIENDSHIP

'There the magic veil of poetry's youth
Lovingly wound itself around the truth.'

Schiller, *Die Götter Griechenlands*

THE GOOD OF FRIENDSHIP: JOSEF VON SPAUN

Nine years older than Schubert, Josef von Spaun (1788–1865) was one of the first to strike up an acquaintance with Schubert in 1808, which quickly ripened into a sincere friendship. One of the many graces of Spaun's friendship lay in the succour he offered Schubert during his Stadtkonvikt years – arranging his first visits to the opera and supplying manuscript paper – thereby helping him to reach his fullest potential. The number of contacts to whom Spaun actively introduced Schubert affirms their friendship as a social process, embedded in a society's institutions, cultural norms and opportunities.[1] Only at the height of Schubert's crisis did Spaun show the slightest disaffection when he admitted how it 'cut him to the soul that Schubert had ceased to sound for him'.[2] Still the friendship held. He had more than enough inner freedom and confidence to retain his dignity no matter what hurts he endured.

Spaun loved Schubert for his own sake and seems to have regarded the good he did for him as valuable in its own right. Their friendship was altruistic in that it advanced Schubert's happiness and this was an end in itself. According to consequentialism, Spaun's actions were only valuable in relation to something extrinsic to their friendship: Schubert's creation of music as the greatest aggregate of human welfare.

RIVALRY OR RECIPROCITY? ANSELM HÜTTENBRENNER

Beyond the confines of the Stadtkonvikt, Schubert wove social threads of his own, including a new web of relations with musicians. One such composer, Anselm Hüttenbrenner (1794–1868), had been an organ scholar of Matthäus Gell at Graz Cathedral before arriving in Vienna to study composition with Salieri, who was the agent in his meeting with Schubert. When Hüttenbrenner and Schubert met, they were operating with the same inner compass but were on different paths. Hüttenbrenner was wealthy and clever: he excelled at piano and took his law studies seriously. Schubert was training to be a teacher but a friendship with another composer was a field of force. Between 1815 and 1821 there was mutuality, a happy shadowing and colouring of minds as they awoke to different things in each other and in themselves. Schubert's power over Hüttenbrenner came from his superior musical mind and his habit of refraining from comment. Hüttenbrenner's overweening ambition struck like waves against Schubert's taciturnity, who listened to his friend's confidences and offered some of his own. The wide berth that Hüttenbrenner gave Schober and the literary circle suggests he needed no other friend as much as Schubert.

When Schubert lived with Mayrhofer, Anselm would wait for his friend to finish his morning's composition, so that in the afternoon or evenings he might capture that receptive ear for new musical disclosures. For his part, Schubert was as fascinated by Hüttenbrenner's unabashed speech as Hüttenbrenner was by his friend's intimidating silences. The two men may have been temperamental opposites, but they had great respect for each other's talent.

For Schiller, the presence of one's creative spirit – one's genius – is a precondition for receptivity to friendship.[3] Certainly, this was the sounding note of Schubert's friendship with Hüttenbrenner and a decisive element in the unfolding of each other's gifts. Hüttenbrenner wrote over 250 male-voice settings and found inspiration in the poetry of Karl Gottfried von Leitner, Goethe, Bürger, Uhland and Heine for more than 200 Lieder. He also composed several operas, at least two of which were later produced in Graz: *Armella oder Die beiden Viceköniginnen* on 6 February 1827 and *Leonore*, based on Bürger's famous ballad, on 22 April 1835. Like Schubert, Hüttenbrenner composed numerous overtures and six symphonies, the first of which was performed in Graz in September 1819. His pianistic gifts called forth over sixty solo piano works, twenty of them for piano four hands.

Both composers understood the importance of being viewed as having shaped his world as well as having been shaped by it, and they shaped each other through music and friendship. Direct evidence of this is found in the male-voice settings which they both composed for the Thursday evening gatherings with two of Salieri's other students: the composer and organist, Ignaz Assmayr, and the tenor, Josef Mozatti.[4] Originally, the quartet met at Mozatti's to sing through the male-voice quartets of Carl Maria von Weber, which were very popular at that time, as well as those of Konradin Kreutzer, whose music Schubert admired. Hüttenbrenner devised an amusing test of each of their abilities to bring something new to sing.[5] His memoir suggests the three composers got involved in a kind of vying that is not quite rivalry, more an aspiration to outdo. The desire to have something terrific to pull out of their pockets when they met suggests a kind of trumping and self-trumping enjoyed by all; no begrudging of achievement per se. Schubert did not consider himself in competition with anyone else but he may have been the cause of it, which only means he was raising the standard without trying.

It is evident from Hüttenbrenner's memoirs that he considered himself the more elegant pianist, but he also willingly lent his performance abilities to Schubert's success. At the Roman Emperor Inn on 12 March 1818 the two friends performed one of Schubert's overtures (D 590 or D 591), which the composer had transcribed for piano four hands. Anselm contributed to two significant events in Schubert's career: the first was a musical soirée hosted by Matthäus von Collin in 1820, 7 Teinfaltstrasse, which was attended by a distinguished company of Viennese music lovers. On this occasion Hüttenbrenner performed with Vogl 'Der Wanderer' (D 489) and with the composer his *Eight Variations on a French Song* (D 624). The second occasion was the first public performance of 'Erlkönig' (D 328) with Vogl at the Kärntnertortheater on 7 March 1821. In Graz, Hüttenbrenner arranged for Schubert's 'Das Dörfchen' (D 598) and 'Die Nachtigall' (D 724) to be performed, and accompanied 'Erlkönig' (D 328) numerous times.

While none of Schubert's works published in his lifetime were dedicated to Anselm Hüttenbrenner, the special place his friend had in his affections is evident in his thirteen Piano Variations (D 576) on a theme in A minor from the third movement of Anselm's String Quartet in E major op. 3, on which Schubert wrote four variations. In May 1819, half in jest, he wrote to his friend, 'It will be a decade before I see you again [. . .] you may, of course, say like Caesar, you would rather be first-rate in Graz than second-rate in Vienna.'[6] Was he saying the same thing musically by outdoing him with thirteen variations? His validation of his friend is also obvious in the inscription on a copy of D 365/ii, the so-called *Trauerwalzer* on 14 March 1818, which he 'transcribed for [his] dear fellow, coffee, wine and punch drinker, Anselm Hüttenbrenner, the world-famous composer'. Schubert's double mention of artistic standing, coupled with Anselm's need to befriend great figures, are clues to his friend's insecurity and ambition.

The son of a wealthy landowner, Hüttenbrenner was able to avoid many of the struggles Schubert faced as his means and temperament lured him into a lazy, hermitic domesticity in Graz, where his world turned around a family axis. But he was also aesthete enough to feel that his own life had not been wasted, as he bore witness to Schubert's posthumous fame.

Although acquisitive of honour, Anselm and his brother were negligent in their handling of the B minor Symphony, also Act 2 of Schubert's revised version of *Des Teufels Lustschloß* and of the final two acts of *Claudine von Villa Bella* which were burnt while in their care. Taking for granted that the writing environment is never free from resentment and that there are rights of way for everyone, we are still tempted to ask: Did Hüttenbrenner seriously compete with Schubert? Or did he befriend him, as he had befriended Beethoven, to feel special by association? Why did he compose a new setting of 'Erlkönig' when he had premiered his friend's masterwork? Did he withhold the score of the Unfinished Symphony to retain his position as first-rank in Graz? Why were three of Schubert's major manuscripts and none of Hüttenbrenner's used as kindling? When attempting to answer these questions one stands at a crossroads where different truths intersect. On the one hand the facts are capable of revealing that even friends can betray and there are lapses in every human relationship, however well intentioned. On the other hand they testify that both men kept up sincere and devoted relations with each other, as attested by Schubert's final letter to his 'dear old Hüttenbrenner' in which he signs off promising to remain a true friend until death.[7]

OTHER SELVES? JOHANN BAPTIST MAYRHOFER

I	I
Für Franz	To Franz
Du liebst mich! tief hab ich's empfunden,	You love me! Deeply have I felt it,
Du treuer Junge, zart und gut:	You faithful youth, tender and good;
So stähle sich denn, schön verbunden,	Then let our courage never falter,
Der edle, jugendliche Muth!	So beautifully united between the two of us!

Wie immer auch das Leben dränge,	However life troubles us,
Wir hören die verwandten Klänge.	We hear kindred sounds.
Doch, Wahrheit sei's womit ich zahle:	But it is truth with which I reckon:
Ich bin nicht, Guter, wie du wähnst	I am not, beloved, as you imagined
Du sprichst zu einem Ideale,	You perceive an ideal
Wornach Du jugendlich Dich sehnst, –	For which in your innocence you long for, –
Und eines Ringer's schweres Streben	And you perceive the grapplings of one who
Hältst Du für rasch entquoll'nes Leben.	Strives as overflowing life.
Was ich gelallt mit schwacher Lippe, –	I have but lisped with weak expression, –
Hab' ich das Wahre auch erkannt?	Did I ever perceive the truth?
Ich schuf – er war ein arm Gerippe;	Whatever I wrote, was but poor skeleton;
Hab' ich den Geist je festgebannt?	Have I ever caught the spirit?
Konnt' ich den Sinn der Weltgeschichten	Did I ever grasp the sense of history
Erscheinen lassen in Gedichten?	And rendered it in poetic form?
Doch laß uns treu, bis sich dem Willen	But let us faithfully, while desire
Die Bildung und die Kraft gesellt,	Joins knowledge and imagination,
Als Brüder redlich bau'n im Stillen	As brothers quietly united

An einer schönern, freien Welt.	Strive for a more beautiful, freer, world.
Sie ist es nur, der ich gesungen, –	I have only sung of this, –
Und ist sie, – sei das Lied verklungen.[8]	And when it comes to pass my song will cease.

For the recipient of these lines, Franz Schubert,[9] there was nothing more valuable than a poem from his friend, Johann Baptist Mayrhofer (1787–1836).[10] The artist, who offered this emotional recognition of love, was neither a young adolescent nor a hopeless romantic. Mayrhofer was an unstable, depressive, deeply complex character with a remarkable gift for introspection.[11]

The 'dark anxiety about life'[12] which underlay Mayrhofer's character may have been awakened when he was eleven by the death of his father, Matthias Remigius. In accordance with his father's wishes, Mayrhofer entered the Augustinian monastery in St Florian near Linz where he was a novice from 5 October 1806 to 18 October 1810. After studying law at the University of Vienna (1810–13), he held a lifelong position as a census official from 1814 until his death in 1836, where, contrary to his oppositional, national and liberal sentiments, he earned the reputation of being a very strict book censor.

A distinguished intellectual and poet in his own right, Mayrhofer was an influential personality in the contemporary literary scene when, in December 1814, Spaun brought the eighteen-year-old Schubert to visit his old friend in the third-floor apartment in the inner city no. 420 (today Wipplingerstrasse no. 2, Vienna 1). Four years later Schubert moved into Mayrhofer's single room, which they shared from November 1818 until the end of 1820. The bond between these two brilliant souls was full of work and storms, the balance between the two shifting to the latter as time passed. Mayrhofer's poetry suggests an erotic relationship, but above all it was an intellectual and artistic friendship, in which each encouraged the other, directly and by example, to produce some of their finest work.

One of many things to enjoy in this record of high achievement is that Mayrhofer's poems are 'fragments of a great confession'. Even while acknowledging the enigmatic nature of poetry, Mayrhofer was 'his own most frequent subject'[13] and Schubert's understanding is immediately palpable. In his poetry, libretti and even in his editorship of *Beiträge zur Bildung für Jünglinge* – such as his Raphael dialogues in volume two – Mayrhofer extols the highest ideals of friendship from antiquity.[14] Equality features prominently in Mayrhofer's aesthetics of friendship that bear the influence of Books Eight and Nine of the *Nicomachean Ethics*, in which Aristotle considers equality a necessary condition for true friendship. This ancient adage of a friend as another self, Aelred of Rievaulx identifies as 'spiritual friendship', Montaigne 'perfect friendship', and Schiller, a view of ourselves in another glass – processes which he believed were part of forming another artistic character.[15] Mayrhofer's notion of mutual respect in friendship carries a very different implication: one recognizes a friend as a different self, not another self in the Aristotelian idealization.

Was Schubert's artistic collaboration with Mayrhofer one of equals who grew in common vocation? Or was this one of a number of seemingly submissive relationships with men – romantic and otherwise – in which Schubert was involved? At one level Mayrhofer deeply desired the friendship in a way that arises from an acute sense of lack, which is more characteristic of erotic love. But he also recognized friendship as a virtue to be exercised when he took Schubert in and frequently placated Franz Theodor about his son. Nine years Schubert's senior, Mayrhofer took full advantage of his attentive mind and influenced him in considerable ways. His misogynistic attitudes may have severed any residue of hope Schubert harboured about marrying Therese Grob. It is no coincidence that after one of his visits to the poet, Schubert expressed in his diary some decidedly pessimistic thoughts on life in general and marriage in particular.[16] Mayrhofer's anti-clericalism did not impinge on Schubert, who was not an apostate, but no doubt he kept him up to the early hours of the morning talking about church institutions and rituals, teaching him much about antiquity, and broadening his taste in philosophy and neo-classical literature. In particular he shared with him his love of Heraclitus, Herodotus, Horace and the Stoics, especially the writings of Marcus Aurelius. His deep sense of suffering was an important source of the melancholy so characteristic of Schubert's greatest work.

In his obituary for Schubert published in the *Neues Archiv für Geschichte, Staatenkunde, Literatur und Kunst* on 23 February 1829, Mayrhofer portrayed himself as the ringleader in the artistic process: 'Love of poetry and music made our relationship more intimate. He composed what I wrote.'[17] In reality Schubert offered Mayrhofer spiritual stimulation and increased motivation for production. In his forty-seven settings of Mayrhofer's texts – including one vocal quartet, 'Der Gondelfahrer' (D 809) and two Singspiele, *Die Freunde von Salamanka* (D 326) and *Adrast* (D 137) – Schubert created a monument to their friendship. Most of the songs were written between 1816 and 1817 before he moved in. While they lived together Schubert witnessed such poems as 'Die Sternennächte' (D 670), 'Nachtstück' (D 672) and 'Freiwilliges Versinken' (D 700) form under Mayrhofer's hand, and they collaborated so closely that their songs became as alive to him as to Mayrhofer.

Mayrhofer's mind had a subtlety and a strangeness that attracted Schubert to set his poetry most frequently after that of Goethe and Schiller. Behind these songs lie trends in European thought exemplified in the exaltation of freedom and nature by Rousseau and Herder, and the ethereal nature of the sublime. Mayrhofer's lyrics are laden with the *Weltschmerz* of the Metternich era, from which he escapes into a Utopian life in art. During their years together Mayrhofer was searching for a theory of art that would be a philosophy of life. For a while he thought he had found it in poetry: art alone could be trusted so he became for Schubert a cause as well as a friend. It was also a time for both men to be experimental and Mayrhofer invested his revolution in language which is rich in form from *Rollengedichte* ('Der Schiffer', D 536), to songs of nature ('Am See', D 746), to poetry of longing ('Iphigenia', D 573), to ballads ('Wie Ulfru fischt', D 525). His agile mind so evident in 'Erlafsee' (D 586), the first Schubert setting to appear in print, led to tonal radicalism and harmonic experimentation on Schubert's part.[18] 'Auf der Donau' (D 553), 'Freiwilliges Versinken' (D 700) and 'Orest auf Tauris' (D 548) all belong to a group of songs which end in a different key to the opening tonality.

Mayrhofer's songs of antiquity are especially interesting because they are a composite of incompatibilities between his double life as censor and poet. The poet used his experience as censor to codify the themes of the *Bildungskreise* – the nature of art and role of the artist; the sun as redemptive; the hostility of society to productive activity – and he drew on classical myths to capture the changeless laws of human nature. One of his most interesting disclosures is his unmasking of 'der Alte', Goethe's Harper, a modern-day Orpheus figure, with whom Mayrhofer shared the same tormented condition and fate. The codification of his love for the composer is also intriguing because his emotions for Schubert were for himself, whom he saw reflected in Schubert. Mayrhofer's quest for the ultimate good was founded on such self-knowledge, which involved a recognition of deficiency and a determination to remedy it. Time and again we see him reaching for the sun as codified in 'Heliopolis I' (D 753). One of his most interesting representations of the composer is found in his Orestes songs – 'Orest auf Tauris' (D 548) and 'Der entsühnte Orest' (D 699) – where he portrays Schubert in the image of Orestes, whom Kant singled out – together with his companion Pylades – as having represented friendship conceived in its purity or completeness. The fame of Lucian's dialogue *Erotes* ('Affairs of the Heart') in the nineteenth century, as well as the well-known tradition of Greco-Roman heroic homoeroticism – such as Achilles and Patroclus from Homer's *The Iliad* – meant audiences of Schubert's time would have recognized Orestes and Pylades as the principal representatives of homoerotic love. This theme is developed in songs of experience which were omitted from his first collection and remained unpublished until the edition of his poetry in 1843. In his *Xenien* – satirical comments on life in the manner of Goethe and Schiller – another legend long invested with homoerotic significance, 'Hiacinth' tells the tale of a beautiful youth loved by Apollo: the first time a man loved another man.[19] Similarly 'Erhebung' commemorates love lost for an unnamed and unknown friend:

Ernst schwärmte ich trunken	Once I revelled, enraptured,
Im Augen des Freundes	In the eyes of a friend
Wir träumten uns frei!	We dreamed ourselves free!
Froh schwanden die herrlichen	The glorious hours sped by
Stunden, – noch glüh' ich,	Happily – I still glow
Gedenk' ich des Traum's!	When I think of the dream!
Nun ist es wohl anders!	Yet now it is different!
Doch hab' ich gewonnen,	Still, I have won
Und preise mein Glück.	And treasure my happiness.
[. . .]	[. . .]
Das Herz, das einst jubelnd,	The heart that once exulted
Für Freundschaft geglüht,	In friendship's flame,
Das Herz, das voll Sehnsucht	The heart that full of yearning love,
Für Eine gelebt, –	Lived for One –
Es hat sich erweitert:	It has expanded:
Nun ruhen in ihm	Now the stars, the worlds,
Die Sternen, die Welten,	The rivers and seas,
Die Ströme und Meere,	And all peoples,
Und all Geschlechter,	United in love,
In Liebe vereint.	Repose within it.
D'rum hab' ich gewonnen	Therefore have I won
Und preise mein Glück![20]	And treasure my happiness!

By the end of the poem whatever peace of mind is celebrated by the poet's embrace of *caritas* – the most excellent of the seven virtues extolled by Thomas Aquinas – it is clear such consolation has been very hard won. Although Mayrhofer presents passion as a perturbation that has been overcome, thereby showing the influence of the stoics, everywhere else in his oeuvre he laments love's loss.

In 'Tillisberg':

Zerschnitten sind der Liebe zarte Faden,	Love's delicate thread, on which
An denen froh die Seele hing, –	The soul hung happily, is broken –
Ach, unersetzlich scheint was ich verloren.²¹	Alas, what I have lost seems irreplaceable.

In 'An Eccho' his alter ego broods:

Mancher Ton dringt schmeichelnd an die Ohren	Many sounds caress the ear
Einer nur vereinte das Zerstückte,	Only one united the fragmented
Einer wär' es, der mich noch beglückte	Only one could still make me happy
Aber ach, ich habe ihn verloren?²²	But oh, I have lost him?

And in 'An die Geliebte' he suffers the agonies of being separated from the person he most loves and cannot have:

Von Dir entfernt, streb' ich zu Dir zu kehren,	Distanced from you, I strive to return to you,
Hat ohne Dich das Leben Werth?²³	Does life have any value without you?

In reality Mayrhofer and Schubert did not sustain the complete fusion of wills that the poet attributed in art to their friendship, which is exceedingly rare and a function of grace. Instead they were lovers of substance and significance – a beautiful bond in its own right but inevitably riven when they revealed themselves to be something other than they first appeared. In Mayrhofer's words, 'While we lived together our idiosyncrasies could not but show themselves; we were both richly endowed in that respect and the consequences could not fail to appear.'

A man of spartan habits, Mayrhofer lived like a stoic. A bed, a writing desk, some books, a pipe, and a guitar adorned his home. The very incongruity of ambition in such a setting helped to sustain it in him. In this austerity he prepared to become great. His regular routine – a nap after dinner and a daily walk his simple pleasures – returned day after day in the same order. Even Mayrhofer's portrait shows a most penetrating gaze, a set stubborn mouth and an unyieldingly serious appearance which bore something of the same rigidity that a lonely person often owns, though on occasion it was interrupted by bright laughter (Figure 19 online).

Their dwelling place provided a pleasant setting for flamboyant tomfoolery. Roistering with Schubert, Mayrhofer adopted a tone of bantering affection that the composer reciprocated: 'We teased each other in many different ways and turned our sharp edges on each other to our mutual amusement and pleasure. His gladsome and comfortable sensuousness and my introspective nature were thus thrown into higher relief and gave rise to names we called each other accordingly, as though we were playing parts assigned to us. Unfortunately I played my very own.'[24] Each took pleasure in puncturing the other's armour, but the game was too finely played for Schubert's taste. Being the kinder hearted, he was usually worsted, and the ground was prepared for later quarrels.

Long before Schubert moved in, Mayrhofer was a valetudinarian. His anxious disposition and self-loathing manifested itself in 'persistent abdominal problems' which 'plagued [him] for many an evil hour', halting the flow of creativity. 'The worm of my spleen gnaws at my life, eating the blossom. Can any fruit follow?', Mayrhofer asked.[25] In their early years of friendship Schubert anchored his imagination, but as he grew older

Mayrhofer contemplated the world from an increasingly melancholic and misogynistic perspective until he became suspended between the despair in which he wallowed and a refined intellectualism that touched the limits of asceticism. His moral tenderness to the point of pathology and his gloomy, acerbic character were the positive and negative poles of his extreme states of mind. The poem 'Mephistopheles', found in his literary bequest, expresses exquisitely his bitterness. For such moods he even invented a form of poetry which he called 'Sermone', audacious 'lectures' in which he allowed his misanthrophic bile to overflow.

A wayfarer by nature as well as by necessity, Schubert had sufficiently complicated his life with Mayrhofer by the time he moved out in 1820, but he preferred to loosen the knot of friendship than to break it. For two years he had lived with Mayrhofer gratis, but he felt this dependency could not be a permanent arrangement and, with Vogl's financial help, he withdrew from his lodgings. Mayrhofer's life had been inseparable from Schubert's, his fellow conspirator, correspondent, poet, friend, and he had been generous in every way. But Schubert always had a measure of innocence and never more so than when dealing with someone who was cruel, because cruelty was not in his own nature. According to his chroniclers, Mayrhofer was deeply disturbed by the loss and his poetic production suffered as a result of it.[26]

Schubert stopped setting Mayrhofer's verse when he moved out in 1820, but in April 1822 he set three songs from the *Heliopolis* cycle, the manuscript sheaf of six epigrams and twenty poems the poet dedicated to Schober in 1821. The collection bears the imprint of *Über die ästhetische Erziehung des Menschen* (1795), though the poems show little of Schiller's optimism that art would ultimately better society.[27] In his op. 21 dedication of the Mayrhofer settings 'Auf der Donau' (D 553), 'Der Schiffer' (D 536) and 'Wie Ulfru fischt' (D 525), announced on 19 June 1823, Schubert refers to himself as a 'friend' of the poet, at once placing friendship at the centre of their creativity and making it clear how he wanted it to be perceived. Through Mayrhofer he had written a music he intuitively knew to be possible: a music of objective feeling. Mayrhofer, by contrast, made his love for Schubert explicit in his *Gedichte* (1824), an anthology which gathered stages of his spiritual experience together in a connected pattern. On the subscription list for its publication, Schubert's name is not listed, despite one of the poems, 'Geheimnis', being dedicated to him.[28]

After a hiatus of two years – during which there were no Mayrhofer settings for the first time since 1814 – Schubert finally took leave of the poet with five of his best settings from the newly published *Gedichte*: 'Der Sieg' (D 805); 'Abendstern' (D 806); 'Auflösung' (D 807); and two settings of 'Der Gondelfahrer' (D 808 and D 809), a lied and TTBB-setting with piano.[29] Unlike earlier collaborations, where Schubert had access to Mayrhofer's manuscripts before they were edited for publication, there are very few discrepancies between Schubert's songs and Mayrhofer's texts, which make it clear he was now working from the printed edition.[30] The settings were composed between the A minor and D minor quartets in March 1824, the same month as Schubert wrote to Leopold Kupelwieser describing himself as the most wretched of men. The existential and emotional loneliness the composer experienced around this time is also expressed in a wistful diary entry of 27 March 1824: 'There is no one who understands the pain or joy of others! We always imagine we are coming together, and we always merely go side by side. O what torture for those who recognize this!'[31] In 'Resultat' the poet speaks *in propria persona* seeking to alleviate his despair and no hope is forthcoming: 'Who will dry the tears I have wept for myself? Where is the friend with anxious desire to comfort me?' Were Schubert's settings composed in lieu of a financial subsidy at a time when his purse was under great strain? Were they a parting gift? Did he outgrow the poet not out of ingratitude or indifference but simply because Mayrhofer had given to him all he had to give? Or did he turn to Mayrhofer knowing he was the poet who could best give voice to the kind of despair he himself felt? However one answers these questions the settings mark the end of a very significant artistic collaboration. Schubert never set a word of Mayrhofer again.

Mayrhofer withdrew too, but in his own way. Although he remained isolated from Schubert, they did occasionally see each other in salons. Mayrhofer was at Bruchmann's Schubertiad on 2 December 1823; in June 1826 Anton von Spaun wrote to his wife from Karlsbad that Mayrhofer 'sang many Schubert songs' and he also attended Josef von Spaun's Schubertiad on 15 December that year. According to Adam Haller, a close friend of Mayrhofer's, Schubert's death had a traumatic effect on Mayrhofer's mental health, intensifying his melancholia and despair over the human condition. On the day of Schubert's *Requiem* he returned to his apartment and commemorated him in an ecstatic elegy, addressing him in breathless lines one final time as his Apollo, the sun, the source of all that is creative:

Nachgefühl. An Franz Schubert	Emotion afterwards. For Franz Schubert
	(19 November 1828)
Von eines Birnbaums Zweige	A little bird sang
Da sang ein Vögelein;	From a pear-tree branch;
Der Herbst, er geht zur Neige,	The autumn draws to a close –
Es muß geschieden sein!	I must depart!
Ich flatt're von hinnen	I fly away
Zu wolkigen Zinnen	To the cloudy pinnacles,
Weit über das Meer;	Far over the ocean;
Die Winde von Norden	The north winds
Sie wüten und morden	Rage and kill
Hier Alles umher!	Everything here, all around!
D'rum eil' ich zu Auen,	Therefore, I hurry to the meadows
Wo unter dem lauen	Whose fragrances, consecrating me,
Gekose der Lüfte	And flowers,

Mich segnende Düfte	Under the breezes' mild caresses
Und Blüten erfreu'n:	Gladden me:
Wo ewige Lenze	Where eternal springtime
Nur welkende Kränze	Extravagantly strews
Verschwenderische streu'n!	Garlands which never wither!
Wie will ich dort singen,	How I want to sing there,
Wie soll es nicht klingen	Why shouldn't my peaceful song
Mein friedliches Lied, –	Resound –
Wenn jubelnd die Seele	When the soul, rejoicing,
Aus schwellender Kehle	Issues forth from the swelling throat
Verstandener zieht!	In full understanding!
O selige Wonnen!	O blessed rapture!
Ihr leuchtenden Sonnen	You shining suns,
Ich fliege zu Euch!	I fly to you!

It was not Schubert's death that crushed Mayrhofer so much as self-accusation. Long before Mayrhofer threw himself from the third storey of his office building on 5 February 1836, his life seemed to withdraw inside him until he was the most *fermé* of men. He stayed in that role best suited to his personality, that of a perpetual critic and overweening malcontent. The suicide, which he had contemplated many times in life, in art was a blunt admission of the futility he felt. Although no doubt the outbreak of cholera in Vienna triggered his hypochondriasis to a point of unbearable psychological distress, it was not the cause as is commonly claimed. His despair went far beyond what he felt in that moment and in a deeper sense was a manifestation of the loss of self. As poet and censor, Mayrhofer did not act in accordance with his true essence. Eduard von Bauernfeld hated him for this[32] and it probably was one of many sources of Mayrhofer's own self-hatred. He expresses the same existential angst in 'Tillisberg' when he asks 'Why do I flee the river, that so faithfully promises me peace in its blue depths?'[33] In 'Nachtstück' he identifies what it is that holds him back:

the desire to find meaning, to live into old age. But Mayrhofer lived his life in a way which put him in perpetual danger of having everything meaningful break down. Goethe, whom he revered, continually warned of such dangers of emotional self-destruction:

Ach, wer heilet die Schmerzen	Ah, who will heal the pains
Des, dem Balsam zu Gift ward?	Of one for whom balm has turned to poison?
Der sich Menschenhaß	One who drank misanthropy
Aus des Fülle der Liebe trank!	From the brimming cup of love.
Erst verachtet, nun ein Verächter,	First despised, now a despiser
Zehrt er heimlich auf Seinen eignen Wert	He secretly consumes his inner worth
In ung'nügender Selbstsucht.[34]	In unsatisfying self-addiction.

In this dilemma of a life of the heart that could not be sustained without external support, and a social life that was too insubstantial to support it, Mayrhofer took his own life. His desire to leave no trace behind was expressed in 'An die Freunde' (D 654) of March 1819, where he requests a dwelling place:

Im Walde, im Wald da grabt mich ein,	Bury me in the forest,
Ganz stille, ohne Kreuz und Stein:	Silently, without cross or stone;
Denn was ihr türmet, überschneit	For whatever you raise up,
Und überwindet Winterszeit.	Winter time will cover with snow.

If he was to be forgotten, what then was the point of all his work? When Mayrhofer took leave of himself and the world, he believed he had not written enough to preserve him from oblivion. He confesses this in 'Am Eingang des Avernus', where the poet is not admitted to paradise because 'his life lacked direction' and 'fearfully conscious of it' he longs to 'create a great, daring work that will conquer the grave's night and time'.[35] The Viennese dramatist and poet Franz Grillparzer (1791–1872), who wrote Schubert's epitaph, augured that Mayrhofer would be remembered for his *poetica per musica*.[36] Mayrhofer himself locates the source of his immortality in the lonely garret where he had known self-abandonment and was one of life's celebrants:

In trauter Stube eingeengt	Enclosed in a cosy room
Von Ihrem Hauch belebt,	Given life by your breath
Weiß ich kaum, daß ich gedrängt,	I hardly recall that I, driven
Von Wünschen einst gestrebt!	By desires, once strove . . .
Gestrebt – nach Ruhm, nach Wirksamkeit	Strove – for fame, for effectiveness
Nach Glück, – und es nie fand.	For happiness – and never found it
Bis es in diese Einsamkeit	Until, in this solitude,
Die zarten Blüten wand![37]	I entwined tender blossoms![38]

In his intense and passionate pursuit to give meaning to his life, Mayrhofer came closest to knowing himself through Schubert, who granted to his life: love, loss, meaning, music – and ultimately immortality.

CREDITING SCHOBER

Schubert's friendship with Franz Adolf Friedrich von Schober (1796–1882, Figure 15) is much more nebulous. Schubert and Schober became acquainted in 1815. Schober was a close neighbour of Spaun and had, since 1813, been in close contact with Spaun's circle, in particular his brother Anton, Kenner, Mayrhofer and Ottenwalt, all of whom engaged in a sometimes polemical, epistolary debate about matters of aesthetics and morality. Being a man of culture and verbal force of nature, Schober was quickly accepted into this circle. His mother, Katharina (1762–1833), was wealthy, and together with her and his sister, Sophie, he lived a luxurious lifestyle. Being a dandy of great *attrattiva* he quickly became one of Vienna's socialites and his home a popular meeting place. Schober was Schubert's best friend, an additional family member, a 'brother' who acted as a lover and was to keep a permanent place in Schubert's life.

Much has been written about the philosophy of hedonism in Schober's character as drawing Schubert into shameless immorality.[39] Certainly Schubert's friendship with Schober had a double face: it was in many ways positive but not an unalloyed good. Schober was in some respects an undisciplined narcissist, with grandiose ideas of himself. A splendid talker and a handsome man, he was a voluptuary, who trod a delicate line between social prestige and opprobrium. He sought admiration, preferred to talk than write, and left too little of his genius behind him – a few brilliant poems in two small collections of poetry, poetic fragments, suggestive, sometimes insightful, but too often disorganized.[40] For far too long the reasons why this was so have been overlooked. The tragedy of Schober's life – the trauma of losing his father, Franz von Schober (1760–1802), when he was six and subsequent loss of his three siblings before he turned thirty – not only casts light on his career but also on his relationship with Schubert. Three years before Schober entered Schubert's life, his sister Ludwiga (1790–1812) was accidently shot by her husband, the Italian tenor Giuseppe Siboni (1780–1839), in circumstances which were never fully explained. Schober's eldest brother, Axel (1789–1817), a lieutenant serving in the Austrian army, fell ill with tuberculosis on the way home to Vienna from Dillingen in the district of Saarlouis and died on 6 September 1817. His only surviving sibling, Sophie (1795–1825), who married a land surveyor, Johann Ignaz Zecheneter, passed away in 1825. Having lost everyone except his mother, Schober knew how precious friendship is and how fragile life is.

Recent research has traced bouts of depression in Schubert's life, though Schober's life and artistic output bear the imprint of depression much more obviously than Schubert's. What Bauernfeld blamed as 'idleness' was an inability to lead a focused life.[41] His immatriculation was formally cancelled by the University of Vienna in September 1819 after he signed up to read philosophy, before switching to law, then considering medicine but ultimately failing to realize his talent. Although Schober knew Schubert longer and better than anyone else outside his family, he never set down a single sentence of reminiscence. 'I would very much have liked to write a small book about him and our life together, but have never managed to do so,' he confessed of the tantalizing might-have-been biography he proposed to Bauernfeld in 1869: 'How could I ever make you, who writes so easily and so excellently, understand the insurmountable incapacity to write which has, to my despair, afflicted me throughout my life and has been a veritable misfortune to me.'

Anton von Spaun claimed Schober took advantage of Schubert, but the young lay-abed was also extremely good to him.[42] Firstly, it was his intellect and the way his particular intelligence manifested itself that caught Schubert's imagination. Schober and his mother regularly hosted Schubertiads and held reading parties which considerably widened Schubert's knowledge of contemporary literature. When he acquired the Lithographisches Institut in Vienna in 1826, Schober published Schubert's op. 96 and op. 106 in 1828, containing first editions of the songs 'Das Weinen' (D 926), 'Die Sterne' (D 939), 'Fischerweise' (D 881), 'Gesang: Was ist Sylvia' (D 891), 'Heimliches Lieben' (D 922), 'Jägers Liebeslied' (D 909) and 'Vor meiner Wiege' (D 927). Was he cashing in on Schubert's success or actively furthering his career? His private purchase of manuscripts and safeguarding of fair copies suggest he had Schubert's best interests at heart.

Schober also helped Schubert out at various crucial points in his life, most especially the break from home in Autumn 1816 when his mother's generosity enabled Schubert to give up the burden of teaching and provided an environment conducive to furthering his creativity. One of the many invaluable gifts Schober gave Schubert at this time was the ability to imagine a more hopeful, more authentic way of life. From Autumn 1816 until August 1817 Schubert lived in their apartment 'Zum Winter' no. 592 (today Tuchlauben no. 26, Vienna 1), and he was to benefit from their support and hospitality on many more occasions. In 1820–22 Schubert was among the guests whom Schober entertained on the summer escapades to Atzenbrugg Castle, a property owned by Klosterneuberg Monastery and administered by his uncle, Josef Derffel. In 1822 Schubert moved back in with the Schobers, who were now living in less imposing surroundings at the Göttweigerhof (today 9 Spiegelgasse, Vienna 1). Apart from a period from late 1822 and spring 1823 when he returned home, Schubert remained their guest until the summer of 1823, as he did for much of the last three years of his life. When he moved into Ferdinand's home at the beginning of September 1828, he did so with the evident intention of returning to Schober's apartment, where he enjoyed the luxury of a music room with a six-octave piano, and two other rooms where he left nearly all his manuscripts.

Between 1815 and 1827, Schubert set sixteen poems by Schober, mostly for solo voice including 'Am Bach im Frühlinge' (D 731), 'Pilgerweise' (D 789), 'Todesmusik' (D 758) and 'Schiffers Scheidelied' (D 910). In the best known of these settings, 'An die Musik' (D 547), a poetic parody of Schulze's 'Die bezauberte Rose', Schubert asserts music to be constitutive for happiness through its ability to transform reality.[43] This musical miniature, written into the family album of his friend, became Schubert's signature theme, which he transcribed on many occasions for friends. Deceptively simple and laden with musical sincerity, the setting is difficult to perform well because of the profundity of its message. Composed in March 1817, 'An die Musik' took on a new meaning when he published it a decade later when it became a song of thanksgiving for a life transfigured through art (Example 11.1 online).

Schubert and Schober's complete commitment to *Alfonso und Estrella* (D 732) is one example of how hard work together in pursuit of a common dream can forge some of the strongest bonds of friendship. Schober was naturally indolent and needed a contrary spirit to stir him into creative action. The remarkable ascendancy over Schubert's mind that he achieved in these years is perhaps most tellingly endorsed in the indignant response of Schubert's friends who were true to him. While they recognized Schober as a solipsist, what they failed to see was his tendency for introspection. Years later in a letter to Schubert's nephew Heinrich, Schober was very critical of his part in this project. 'From the association with your immortal uncle and myself you have picked out the very most unfortunate moment, when I was in Ochsenburg writing the opera *Alfonso und Estrella* for him which, indeed, earned me great praise, as a poem, from such renowned authorities as Friedrich Schlegel, Ludwig Tieck and Matthäus von Collin but which, as an opera libretto, was such a miserable, stillborn, bungling piece of work that even so great a genius as Schubert was not able to bring it to life.'[44]

This was the first of a number of occasions where Schober reneged but at no point in his rake's progress did Schubert ever disown him. His departure from Vienna during Schubert's illness, 1823–25, may have been for medicinal as well as professional reasons because his own remission (and return to Vienna) coincided with Schubert's. The last letter Schubert wrote to his absent friend shows him holding onto friendship for dear life: 'I am ill. I have eaten nothing for eleven days and drunk nothing, and I totter feebly and shakily from my chair to bed and back again. [. . .] If ever I take anything, I bring it back up again at once.' He continues, entrusting himself to Schober in the confidence that he will not betray him, 'Be so kind, then, as to assist me in this desperate situation by means of literature. Of Cooper's I have read, *The Last of the Mohicans*, *The Soy*, *The Pilot* and *The Pioneers*. If by any chance you have anything else of his, I implore you to deposit it with Frau von Bogner at the coffee house for me. My brother, who is conscientiousness itself, will most faithfully pass it on to me. Or anything else.'

According to Schober's wife, Thekla, Schober did, in fact, visit him in Schubert's last days: 'but the dying man no longer recognized him, he lay in wild feverish delirium and Schober used to tell of the painful impression he received when the eyes, once familiar, looked strangely and wildly at him'.[45] From his description of their last encounter, Schober was called when Schubert was dying, which is characteristic of their brotherhood and Schubert's unconditional love for him. Certainly, Schubert remained on the best of terms with Schober right to the end, and had good reason to do so. Their friendship was of a special nature that exceeded the degree to which most can approach an ideal between permanence and balance based on complementarity. Their mutual efforts to fashion themselves as an aesthetic pair so evident in *Alfonso* (D 732) would culminate in Schober's struggle to adequately memorialize the partner to whom he had related so closely. The refined versions of 'An Franz Schuberts Sarge' for Schubert's *Requiem Mass*, the prologue 'An Franz Schubert' declaimed at the opening of his best friend's memorial concert, his design for a tombstone at Schubert's first resting place, are all testaments to his love. Does genuine friendship depend more on our intentions, feelings and attitudes than the results of our behaviour? However you answer this question, Schober had a privileged role in Schubert's lifelong process of self-construction, not because he was a good person, moral, wise, or generous – much of which he was – but primarily because Schubert loved him.

VOGL AND THE CIVILITY OF FRIENDSHIP

When Montaigne extolled friendships rooted in the everyday, customary relations between people – which are not bound up with the dignity of perfect friendship – he was very much ahead of his time. By the late eighteenth century such notions of reciprocity were an accepted part of the learned conventions of friendship.

Schubert's reciprocal friendship with the egotistical, sublime Johann Michael Vogl (1768–1840) began as a public – even political – phenomenon.[46] A man of affairs and the world and of no illusions, Vogl had reluctantly agreed to meet Schubert at Schober's apartment (26 Tüchlauben) in March 1817 where Schubert was living at the time. The difference in age, height and reputation, not to mention Vogl's histrionic streak and piercing intelligence, must have given him an appearance of imposing maturity in Schubert's eyes. A brilliant raconteur, with a sense of humour as pungent as his sense of classical antiquity, Vogl became enamoured of Schubert's Lieder as the baritone once sang *mezzo voce* through Mayrhofer's 'Augenlied' (D 297), 'Memnon' (D 541) and Goethe's 'Ganymed' (D 544), but he departed without promising anything. On the way out he clapped Schubert on the shoulders and observed of his sensitive inarticulateness: 'You have something in you but you are too little a comedian, too little a charlatan: you squander your fine thoughts without making the most of them.'[47] To others, the baritone freely expressed his admiration, declared 'Lied eines Schiffers an die Dioskuren' (D 360) to be a magnificent song, and said it was incomprehensible how such depth and maturity could emanate from such a young man. Recognizing Schubert's ability to create symbolic vignettes in song – images at once of the self and of a tendency of the age – Vogl invited the composer to his home to rehearse with him. Overwhelmed by the respect and applause their performance together elicited, Vogl used his prominent position in Viennese musical life to further Schubert's career by performing his music at private salons at which he was always a welcome and admired guest. While he rarely sang Schubert's songs before a wider public, he was a leading exponent on two important occasions in 1821 and 1828. The first was the first public performance of 'Erlkönig' (D 328) at the Kärntnertortheater on 7 March 1821 which helped to establish Schubert's reputation as an exceptionally gifted song composer. The second was Schubert's own concert on 26 March 1828, at which Vogl premiered five songs: 'Der Kreuzzug' (D 932); 'Die Allmacht' (D 852); 'Die Sterne' (D 939); 'Fischerweise' (D 881) and 'Fragment aus dem Aeschylus' (D 450). His most poignant premiere was 'Die Taubenpost' (D 965A), at a memorial concert on the eve of the composer's thirty-second birthday. It was the first time since Schubert's death that he had premiered his friend's songs in public without him, and he was visibly overcome.

While both artists gained professionally and privately from the collaboration, their friendship blossomed into the kind of empathy that was closer to nineteenth-century camaraderie than to the learned conventions of friendship of previous centuries. When Schubert met Vogl, he had parted company with Salieri and urgently needed someone of similar culture and comparable intellect with whom he could endeavour to make sense of this new stage of his life. He willingly put himself under his musical and intellectual tutelage, and being treated as an equal by a singer he especially honoured affected Schubert inestimably. It fed his confidence and made him feel creative. The thirty-four-year age gap and great difference in their artistic and social standing also meant in the early years Vogl served as an experienced and trusted advisor to the composer, perhaps providing him with sexual encounters,[48] but certainly with the skills, contacts and information valued by the professional operatic world. Vogl helped Schubert obtain a commission for *Die Zwillingsbrüder* in 1820 in which he himself appeared. The only serious disagreement they ever had was over the quality of Schober's libretto for *Alfonso und Estrella*, which he believed was unworthy of Schubert's talents. Schubert enjoyed three vacations in Upper Austria in Vogl's company in 1819, 1823 and 1825, where the singer's support of Schubert extended beyond the financial to the aesthetic. During the first visit Schubert composed his cantata (D 666) to celebrate 'the Greek Vogl's' birthday. In 1821 he dedicated to him his op. 6: 'Am Grabe Anselmos' (D 504), 'Antigone und Oedip' (D 542) and 'Memnon' (D 541), whose classical texts reflect the baritone's knowledge of classical culture. Vogl's wide reading and intelligence were evident in his reading of authors as diverse as Epictetus, Thomas à Kempis, Marcus Aurelius, his favourite poet Walter Scott, and his immediate apprehension of how Schubert's songs touched the nerve of his age. What is less known is that Schubert was also a formative influence on Vogl, who was a composer of three Masses, an offertory and a collection of fifteen songs which are not rooted in the everyday but offer evidence of a strong sensibility (Example 11.2 online).

THE AESTHETICS OF FRIENDSHIP IN SCHUBERT'S MUSICAL PRACTICE

Schubert's works offer an insight into the intimate connections between friendship and the aesthetics of the period, not only due to the extent that such discourses resonate in his musical output, but also because of how uniquely he regarded musical activity as friendship. Despite his shyness, Schubert's ability to acquire the lasting friendship of many colleagues and patrons with whom he came into contact enabled him to create music that can effectively move his listeners. Many of his friends belonged to the professional middle class, who together with the less numerous aristocracy and professional musicians themselves, made up the majority of the musically literate Viennese public.[49] Bauernfeld, a competent pianist, played duets with Schubert, Schwind was an excellent singer and pianist who performed Schubert's early songs, while Leopold von Sonnleithner was an accomplished composer whose services of friendship and musical discernment had great consequence for Schubert's career.[50] Publicly, Sonnleithner premiered many of Schubert's works at the Gesellschaft der Musikfreunde concerts and privately at his father's soirées. The first salon performance of 'Erlkönig' was so enthusiastically received at his home that he and three friends there that evening decided to defray the cost of publication. The occasion gave rise to a further pivotal friendship with the pianist, Anna Fröhlich, whose growing affection is also evident in the many choral works she commissioned, including the occasional work, 'Ständchen' (D 920), for the birthday of one her pupils, Louise Gosmar. Even the inception of this song tells us a great deal about Schubert's ability to tailor-make music for particular audiences:

> At Fräulein Fröhlich's request, Franz Grillparzer had written for the occasion the beautiful poem, 'Ständchen' and she gave this to Schubert, asking him to set it to music as a Serenade for her sister Josefine (mezzo soprano) and women's chorus. Schubert took the poem, went into an alcove by the window, read it carefully a few times then said with a smile: 'I've got it already, it's done and it's going to be quite good'. After a day or two he brought the composition and it really had turned out quite good. [. . .] The effect of the first performance on a beautiful summer's night in the open was also magnificent.[51]

Schubert's part-songs, songs, piano dances and duets offer an understanding of how friendship and aesthetics intersect with and fundamentally affect one another with particular intensity in his musical practice and production. This intimate ability to shape his listenership along the lines of friendship lies at the heart of Schubert's music, just as friendship is a prominent trope in his texts. If 'Die Geselligkeit' (D 609) and 'Ständchen' (D 920) are obvious examples of conviviality, so are the many *Trinklieder* and TTB canons he wrote alongside Hüttenbrenner, which exemplify how the realities and practicalities of life make friendship a down-to-earth business, with laughter, music, food and wine. *Die Freunde von Salamanka* (D 326) – a dramatic presentation on friendship set in allegorical and historical mode – *Alfonso und Estrella* (D 732), *Fierabras* (D 796) and *Der Graf von Gleichen* (D 918) all point to the central role friendship plays not only in the exchange of ideas but in works of art that arose from the emotional and aesthetic sensibilities shared by friends.

12

ART BORN OF IMPROVISATION

'Caminante, no hay camino, se hace camino al andar.'
('Wanderer, there is no road, the road is made by walking.')
Antonio Machado, *Campos de Castilla*

However we define Schubert's life – whether examining his creative and professional life or personal loves and friendships – we are looking at two decades of extraordinary richness. One side of his life that is overlooked is his skill as an improviser, which points back to his partimento training and forward in anticipation of late works. During this 'middle' period his pianistic skills and self-confidence as a professional performer unfolded in the drawing rooms of his friends. Fewer major works were written down, yet no comparable period shows so well his genius for making the best of fleeting opportunities, for improvising dances, composing songs, using uncompleted fragments, and the long slow haul on a magnum opus like the A flat major Mass, to advance into territory unknown to any but the most keen-sighted of his contemporaries.

Our perception of improvisation and the written score differs radically from Schubert's world. In the eighteenth century, composition and improvisation belonged to a continuum of 'music-making', and while the two worlds were perhaps not synonymous, they occupied a shared conceptual territory. As the authority of the written text increased with nineteenth-century publication and criticism, composition and improvisation became split apart conceptually and set into hierarchical tension. The increasing proclivity to privilege the written text placed improvisation in a separate category of music making to composition, but in Schubert's day the two traditions co-existed.[1] Beethoven, whose compositions have been the effective cornerstone for the work concept, was simultaneously admired by his contemporaries for a level of improvisational brilliance that exceeded what his written works could capture.[2]

BETWEEN SOCIETY AND SOLITUDE: SCHUBERT'S IMPROVISATIONS

Schubert acquired the art of improvisation from Salieri, who had trained him in the old school of a Kapellmeister or *maître de chapelle*, who was a keyboard player expected to fulfil a variety of musical roles in which improvisation was essential. According to Ferdinand, Schubert was improvising minuets at the keyboard before composing his earliest piano fantasy (D 1).[3] Josef von Spaun also recalls twelve missing Minuets and Trios for piano (D 22), which Schubert wrote and lent to friends at the Stadtkonvikt.[4] Here he learnt to lead an orchestra, accompany a singer or instrumentalist, play the organ for a solemn service or for a private musical gathering. In order to fulfil these demands at short notice, Salieri trained him to be a highly capable keyboard improviser who would be able to compose, in a short space of time, a festive mass, symphony, or opera, and to furnish publishers with songs, chamber music and piano repertoire. Salieri himself was a wonderful extemporizer. Ignaz Moscheles records a summer-night gathering with Salieri, Hummel and Meyerbeer in a house outside Vienna where 'walks were taken, tableaux arranged, all sorts of musical trifles composed and performed on the spot'.[5] Around the time that Schubert's friends labelled his teacher's theoretically grounded practice of keyboard improvisation old-fashioned, numerous treatises lamented its disappearance from musical pedagogy.[6] Ironically, his friends failed to see the pragmatic value of

Saleri's ideal of an all-round musician, skilled in performance, composition and theory alike,[7] though their own educational philosophies – which supported the development of a well-rounded, remarkably cultivated artist rooted in society – supported the same ideal under a different regime.

Schubert's success in improvisation was also directly linked to the intimate nature of the Viennese drawing rooms in which he played, which assured him of a select audience. Whereas pianists of the early to mid-nineteenth century played for a vastly expanded concert audience with a lower level of musical education, and Vienna had its complement of well-travelled virtuosi, Schubert's improvisations were exclusively in private, elite company, where he was sure to be understood. Accounts of his extemporizing celebrate the spontaneity and immediacy of his playing. The actor Heinrich Anschütz recalls Schubert's spontaneous improvisation of piano dances being broken up by a police inspector knocking on the door because it was Lent, to which Schubert humorously quipped: 'They do this to me on purpose because they know I love playing dance music so much.'[8] In later years the Hartmann brothers' diaries document Schubert's multi-levelled improvisation at Schober's Sunday circle.[9] When he tried out his *Valses nobles*, some friends danced in other rooms undistracted by his pianistic skills, while others gathered around the piano listening attentively as he satisfied simultaneously popular and learned tastes.[10]

Professional accounts of Schubert's pianism emphasize the charm and nuance of his playing. The pianist Ferdinand Hiller, who first heard Schubert perform in Katharina Buchwieser's home, recalls:

> Schubert's piano playing, in spite of not inconsiderable fluency, was very far from that of being a master. And yet I have never heard the Schubert songs sung as they were then! Vogl was able to make one forget his lack of voice by means of the utmost fervour and aptness of expression, and Schubert accompanied, as he could not help accompanying. One piece followed another – we were insatiable – the performers indefatigable. I can still see my portly master [Hummel] [. . .] with

tears running down his face. My own feelings I am unable to describe. It was a revelation.[11]

Ferdinand's obituary aligns with this impression: 'Although Schubert never represented himself as a piano virtuoso, any connoisseur who had the chance of hearing him in private circles will nevertheless attest that he knew how to treat this instrument with mastery.'[12] Even Hüttenbrenner's rivalry forces him to admit Schubert's fluency and natural ease at the piano: 'Schubert was not an elegant pianist but he was a very safe and fluent one; [. . .] he read all clefs with ease and even in the mezzo-soprano and baritone clefs no notes escaped him, just like our Papa Salieri who was a remarkable score player, as indeed he had to be having written 52 operas.'[13] Hüttenbrenner's acknowledgement of Schubert being just as facile and flexible an extemporaneous player as Salieri is central to our understanding of Schubert's pianism. He was not a virtuoso but his ability as an improvisational pianist is not merely a question of technique: it is also about the social and political impact of his performance and his ability to draw a community together.

Many eyewitness accounts reveal how many of Schubert's compositions began as improvisations at the keyboard not only in public but also in private. Louis Schlösser recalls visiting the composer in his humble lodgings in the Rossau suburb:

> . . . where he received the most distinguished visitors in particular the Hungarian gentry, whose national airs he was so frequently able to weave into his compositions. I had heard sounds of the piano from outside and therefore opened the door very softly so as not to interrupt him; when, in spite of this, he noticed me and hurried towards me I pressed him to continue and finish the work he had begun, whereupon he immediately sat down at the instrument again and soon afterwards played me the variations of the Impromptu in B flat major, 2/4 time. Much as I liked the pieces I should not care to say for certain whether

they were published exactly as he played them on this occasion from the sketch, improvising, as it were, rather than actually playing from the music. How spontaneous it sounded! How his eyes shone. I listened to the sounds with indescribable excitement – and yet, from the standpoint of virtuoso performance, this piano playing could not in any way compete with the world-famous Viennese master pianists. With Schubert, the expression of the emotions of the world within him obviously far outweighed his technical development. But who could think of this when, carried away by some bold flight of imagination, oblivious to everything around him, he recited the mighty C minor Fantasia or the A minor sonata![14]

Schlösser's description of Schubert's Impromptu variations captures the pleasing, popular side of the composer's improvisations – in this case his choice of Hungarian tunes which he elaborated in ways that kept the melody clearly in the listener's ear. By selecting a national theme for improvisation in these pre-Lisztian *Hungarian Rhapsodies*, Schubert was clearly framing the performance as an event geared toward the audience's ear, while simultaneously claiming the right to deconstruct the theme. This way of improvising was one of a myriad of ways in which he established a direct rapport with his audience.

In Schubert's day, public extemporizations were usually on a theme by someone else, of which there are numerous examples in his compositions. An interesting example is his duet variations on a French song in E minor, op. 10 (D 624), composed in Zseliz in September 1818, which he dedicated to Beethoven on 19 April 1822, thereby honouring the composer's reputation as an extemporizer. The thematic treatment of these exultantly virtuoso variations is characteristic of an improvisatory style, where the theme is played straight and then varied in many ways, with primo or secondo sharing of the material. An earlier example is his Variations on a theme by Anselm Hüttenbrenner in A minor (D 576), composed in August 1817: a stylized improvisation on the dactylic theme from the slow movement of his friend's String Quartet in E major, op. 12, which had been published earlier that year. Whereas Hüttenbrenner's movement uses four variations, Schubert outdoes him with thirteen, the harmonic inflections of nos 5, 6 and 9 being the most striking. In both cases borrowing is what makes art possible. Schubert's Hüttenbrenner variations are conceived in the spirit of the theorist Johann Mattheson (1681–1764), who believed 'borrowing is permissible, but one must return the thing borrowed with interest, that is one must so construct and develop imitations that are prettier and better than the pieces from which they are derived'.[15]

Schubert's proclivity for self-borrowing, whereby a pre-existing song becomes the basis of an entirely different work, is one of his hallmarks and in his fantasies in particular, the genre exhibiting the greatest continuity from his earliest to late works.[16] At the age of fourteen Schubert used the theme of his very first composed lied, 'Hagars Klage' (D 5), composed on 30 March 1811, to 'get the ball rolling' in the opening and concluding section of his second four-hand fantasia in G minor (D 9, 1811). This freevariant mode of elaboration is again evident in his 'Wanderer Fantasy' in C major for piano solo (D 760), where a popular theme from an earlier lied, 'Der Wanderer' (D 489/D 493, 1816), is audibly subjected to 'developmental' techniques such as reharmonization, modulation, diminution. Here Schubert welds the fantasy's four movements into a continuous and unified whole whose conscious improvisation brilliantly blends a learned style (which consists of first-movement sonata form, final fugal or quasi-fugal passages) with a more pleasing style (which consists of variations). He arrives at such fugal playing in the fourth movement after freely varying the song melody in the second movement, so that the concentrated density of the fugal playing feels like the culminating point of a linear process.

This twin aesthetic of serious and light is present in Schubert's final fantasies (D 934 and D 940) where the private–public distinction holds a particular primacy. The 'private' pole is aligned with connoisseur values – learned style, counterpoint, extended forms, rational control and intellectual satisfaction – while the 'public' pole was aligned with mixed audiences

– pleasing style, popular melodies, variation, and audience delight in dazzling virtuosity. Schubert's ability to bridge private and public worlds with this combination of styles means his fantasies cannot clearly be labelled as learned or popular because they are both at once. In his 'Wanderer Fantasy' (D 760) and Fantasy for Violin and Piano (D 934), also in C major, he does not merely juxtapose learned and pleasing styles, but transitions imperceptibly from one to the other, as though the distinct styles belonged to a single underlying 'substance' rather than an order of discrete and hierarchized differences. Like many of Schubert's works, D 934 plays on preconceived notions associated with various genres and directly evokes one of his own compositions in its centrepiece: a series of four variations on his 1822 setting of 'Sei mir gegrüsst!' (D 741), one of his most popular songs. The three bravura variations, opening violin cantilena which soars over a piano tremolo, Hungarian-style Allegretto in A minor–A major with the two instruments playing in canon and March militaire finale intended to display Slavík's virtuoso technique, are examples of Schubert very consciously creating a diverse array of effects in order to heighten the effect of his composition. His final Fantasy in F minor for Piano Four Hands (D 940) plays on preconceived notions associated with the genre and even directly evokes Mozart's F minor Fantasia (K 608) as it too shifts unexpectedly into F sharp minor and incorporates a fugue into its final section. Schubert's opening melody with its expressive agogic appoggiaturas and Hungarian speech-rhythms, his intertwining of a scherzo and march in improvisatory sketches, the final return of the work's opening theme in a new, chromatically enhanced harmonization, ask us to reconsider: Is it really possible to separate 'Schubert the improviser' from 'Schubert the composer'?

In attempting to answer this question, it is especially interesting to ponder the connection between improvisation and personality because Schubert's artistic identity is homologous with the musical results. Had he been capable of being a predictable and dependable individual – securing and holding down a full-time position, marrying Therese Grob, seeking out a permanent place to live, turning up punctually to rehearsals and salon engagements – it seems unlikely that his music could have remained unpredictable and innovative. But the ebb and flow of Schubert's life had improvisation at its very core, so it is unsurprising that his particular type of temperament expressed itself in music which appears to prefer spur-of-the-moment decisions to carefully considered choices, where unpredictability is part of his personal style.

SCHUBERT'S DANCES

Josef Kenner's lament that Austria only extolled Schubert's dances when he was alive acknowledges how the composer's private improvisations were integral to his public reputation.[17] As early as 1818 Hüttenbrenner confirmed the widespread popularity of Schubert's dances: 'one of his waltzes in A flat [op. 9/2 'Trauerwalzer'] was long accepted as a work of Beethoven's but, when asked about it, he denied authorship [. . .] Quite by chance I learnt that Schubert had composed this waltz and asked him to put it on paper for me because there were so many divergent copies in existence.'[18] Josef Gahy helped popularize Schubert's dances in private salons and public dance halls. In 1823 Carl Czerny published an arrangement of one of Schubert's dances and in 1825 the dance composer Johann Baptist Schiedermayr (1779–1840) arranged Schubert's *Deutsche Tänze* for orchestra.[19] Hartmann's diary entry about Schubert composing his Polonaise 'when he needed money to travel and received from Haslinger 60fl. in exchange (24 fl. A.C. or 25 kr Austrian currency)' is illustrative of the market Schubert was able to exploit.[20] In most years from November 1821 he brought out sets of dances in Carnival (*Fasching*) and contributed to dance compilations (see Tables 12.1 and 12.2). An interesting example is the collection of Austrian Ländler which Sauer and Leidesdorf published under the title *Halt's enk z'samm* (Hold it together), which contained D 146/2 and D 366/6, the title page of which Schwind illustrated.[21] During his lifetime Schubert published eight dance cycles and approximately 200 dances which reflect the fashions of his day and are stamped with his personal style.

Table 12.1 Piano Dances Published During Schubert's Lifetime

	Dance Cycles	Dance	Publication Market
1.	36 Waltzer	D 365, op. 9	Christmas 1821
2.	12 Waltzer, 17 Ländler und 9 Écossaisen	D 145, op. 18	Carnival 1823
3.	16 Deutsche und 2 Écossaisen	D 783, op. 33	Carnival 1825
4.	Galopp und 8 Écossaisen	D 735, op. 49	Christmas 1825
5.	34 Valses sentimentales	D 779, op. 50	Christmas 1825
6.	17 Ländler und 2 Écossaisen	D 734, op. 67	Christmas 1826
7.	12 Valses nobles	D 969, op. 77	Carnival 1827
8.	12 Grazer Walzer	D 924, op. 91	Carnival 1828

Table 12.2 Piano Compilations Published During Schubert's Lifetime to Which the Composer Contributed

	Dance Cycles	Dance	Publication Market
1.	Sammlung original deutscher Tänze	D 971	Carnival 1823
2.	Album Musicale	D 769/2	Christmas 1823
3.	Halt's enk z'samm. Sammlung original österreicher Ländler	D 366/6, D 146/2	Carnival 1824
4.	Musikalisches Angebinde. Eine Sammlung 40 neuer Walzer	D 366/17	Christmas 1824
5.	Terpsichore. Eine Sammlung von 50 der neuesten Deutschen Tänze	D 779/8, D 779/9	Carnival 1825
6.	Ernst und Tändeley. Eine Sammlung verschiedener Gesellschaftstänze	D 976	Christmas 1825
7.	Seyd uns zum zweytenmal willkommen! 50 neue Walzer	D 978	Christmas 1825
8.	Moderne Liebes = Walzer	D 979	Christmas 1826
9.	Neue Krähwinkler Tänze	D 980	Christmas 1826
10.	Krähwinkler Tänze	D 980D	Carnival 1828

There is every reason to think that these published sets of piano dances began as keyboard improvisations. The dances are prime examples of how a great deal of intricate composition went on in Schubert's head before he produced any manuscript copies.[22] Legend has it that his eloquent exposition of these dances took place in the evening, and the following morning he wrote his favourite ones down (Example 12.1a online).[23] These recorded improvisations – which Maurice Brown called 'notes' in a musical 'journal' – were functional dances, where he worked under clear technical constraints of four- or eight-bar phrases in AB form, with the accompanying binary opposition of freedom and constraint. Brown would have us think Schubert was actually composing his dances while performing them and on that point he seems right (Example 12.1b online). What appears implausible is the suggestion that, in writing a dance down, Schubert was merely being his own copyist, recording in notation from his memory of what he had played. Assuming that Schubert could have written down exactly what he had played, without any variation whatever, is there any reason to think he would have?[24]

Schubert's thirty-six 'Original Dances' for Piano (D 365), op. 9 (written between March 1818 and July 1821), give a very immediate impression of what it must have been like to be at a Schubertiad when the composer improvised for his friends. Listening to this set it is hard to imagine that the closed position of the waltz, with bodies and faces touching, still caused a scandal in Schubert's day.[25] The dances place Schubert at the heart of a living tradition improvising at the keyboard for a musical gathering, fulfilling one of the roles for which Salieri had trained him. But the music he wrote transcends this performative function and he was the first major composer to produce Viennese waltzes. His first collection of dances – published after his songs, op. 1–7 – is a compilation of his favourite dances: nos. 2, 3, 5, 6, 7, 32 and 33 recur in later publications.[26] His waltzes are harmonically adventurous and the cycle foreshadows the form adopted by major dance composers: a tonally rounded chain of Viennese waltzes whose closing variations refer to earlier realizations. This nascent process would materialize into exceptional waltz cycles published later in his career, including the two commercial volumes of his thirty-four *Valses sentimentales* (D 779, op. 50, 1825), of which nos. 8, 9, 12 and 14, composed during February 1823), which stand out for their originality and variety of invention, energetic rhythms and soaring melodies above characteristic waltz-like accompaniment figures. Similarly, the majesty and refinement of invention in the twelve *Valses nobles* (D 969), op. 77, announce Schubert's innate feeling for these wonderful rhythms, his professed and obvious enjoyment of the *joie de vivre* expressed by dance.

The local spirit of the thirty-eight dances in the two volumes of his twelve Waltzes, seventeen Ländler and nine Écossaises for piano (D 145), op. 18, offer an equally telling glimpse of Schubert's abilities as an improviser. Even in this early opus his multi-levelled improvisation is evident in the way he sets up formal, textural, dynamic and harmonic contrasts as he moves between dances and dance sets. The imprint of improvisation on D 145 extends beyond these surface features of the score to the genres he used and recurrent features of the music's large-scale organization. Their characteristic binary structure, whereby an antecedent sets up the expectation of an answer in the consequent, is a distinguishing feature of all his dances from the earliest minuets (D 30) composed for his brother Ignaz to the 'Grazer Walzer' (D 924), op. 91, performed at Schober's on 16 January 1826.[27] Characteristically, the tonally closed waltz cycle of his first published set (D 145) is more chromatically coloured than the Ländler and Écossaises chains, as he cascades through a series of keys:[28]

Table 12.3 Tonally Closed Waltz Cycle (D 145), op. 18[29]

1.	E major	16+16
2.	B major	16+8
3.	A minor–A major	24+24
4.	C# minor	8+8
5.	E minor–G major	8+8
6.	B minor–B major	16+16
7.	E flat major	8+16
8.	E flat minor–G flat major	8+8
9.	F sharp minor	8+16
10.	B minor	8+8
11.	B major	8+16
12.	E major	16+16

Before *Die schöne Müllerin* (D 795, November 1823), Schubert is already thinking in cycles as he compiled his thirty-eight dances in two volumes for the Carnival of February 1823.

The three Atzenbrugger Deutsche (nos. 1, 2 and 4), which open the cycle, announce Schubert's authority as a composer of innovative dance music.[30] The cycle contains some of his favourite dances: D 145, nos. 2, 5 and 8, also Écossaise D 145/8 (which recurred as D 735/6 and D 977/1).[31] The most popularly played dance is D 145/6, one of his glorious minor-key waltzes, composed in the Viennese custom of accentuating the second beat, which conveys a faster, lighter rhythm, and also breaks off the phrase:

Example 12.2: Waltz from *Zwölf Walzer, siebzehn Ländler und Ecossaisen für Klavier* (D 145/6), op. 18

Although the dances are best realized as a carefully constructed cycle, there are hidden gems that merit equal attention.

The second set are Écossaises, lively contradances in duple-metre (8+8), characteristically coloured with *pianissimo* and *fortissimo* dynamic contrasts, as well as sudden shifts of key and register, which contribute to their unique dynamic energy. Played without a break, the dance set gradually gathers momentum generated by these sequential models which 'get the ball rolling'. By the time we reach the final Écossaises, nos. 7–9 (4+4), Schubert's imagination has soared far from the opening and there is no doubt that their harmonic exploits were directly inspired by his improviser's fingers (see Example 12.3a and b).

Example 12.3a: Écossaises from *Zwölf Walzer, siebzehn Ländler und Ecossaisen für Klavier* (D 145), op. 18, nos. 1 and 2

The Écossaise cycle contrasts beautifully with the framing Waltz and Ländler sets. As is characteristic of Schubert's Ländler, there is an emphasis on major keys with nine of the seventeen Ländler characteristically in the same key, as for example the chain of dances in D flat major (nos. 4–12).[32] Schubert's consistent use of block chords and a simple harmonic progression in the left hand to support a varied figuration

Example 12.3b: Écossaises from *Zwölf Walzer, siebzehn Ländler und Ecossaisen für Klavier* (D 145), op. 18, nos. 7, 8 and 9

or successive melodic variations in the right hand is a typical improvisatory gesture, as is the inner chordal pattern, both found in Ländler no. 13:

Example 12.4: Ländler from *Zwölf Walzer, siebzehn Ländler und Ecossaisen für Klavier* (D 145/13), op. 18, bars 1–8

With the luminous exception of Écossaises nos. 7–9 (4+4) and Ländler no. 2 (8+16), both sets are similarly constructed in short symmetrical binaries of 16 bars each (8+8). Played without repeats – with the exception of repeats for the first dance to remind us of their formal function – Schubert's Ländler cycle can still hold audiences rapt by their invention. In order to do so, it is essential for pianists to recapture the spirit of improvisation at the heart of these dances by avoiding a four-square tempo and metronomic rigidity. This does not mean an excess of rubato: these works were written to be danced to and accounts of Schubert's own playing is characterized by a surface freedom and underlying temporal logic. One of the best ways to recapture this essential synergy is to observe the partimento principle at the heart of this courtship dance: if you can sing, you can also play.

The wide variety of dance music that Schubert wrote offers exciting performance possibilities. His dances are energetic, as they were performed at both public and private balls: his op. 9 and op. 18 waltzes were rehearsed in Linz on 7 February 1824.[33] The most popular nineteenth-century dances along with waltzes and quadrilles were gallops but surprisingly Schubert only wrote two (D 735 and D 925). Both gallops were included in compilations: D 735 by Diabelli in 1825, D 925 in Haslinger's compilation of *Favourite Gallops* in 1828. Both are characteristic of the time: an 8-bar binary form (with repeats) followed by a similarly structured trio, a framework shared with the Austrian dance music composers Josef Lanner and Johann Strauss Senior. Melodically and rhythmically, the impetus is maintained by continuous dotted rhythms and semiquaver runs to energize the footwork of the dancers (Example 12.5 online).

Schubert only wrote a single Cotillion, a fashionable contradance performed by eight couples as the finale to a Viennese ball. D 976 first appeared in the popular dance compilation *Ernst und Tändeley* (Serious and Dalliance) in 1825. The set changes in Schubert's Cotillion are 16 bars long: the second 8+8 allows the dancers to return to their places on the repeat (Example 12.6 online). As D 976 borrows the second subject from Schubert's Sonata for Violin and Piano in A (D 574), it was either composed around 1817 and revised for this compilation, or is another example of the composer's favourite tunes and self-borrowing. Certainly Schubert's friends were familiar with this dance: it closed Schober's sausage ball on 10 February 1827[34] and various performances are recorded in Spaun's family journal, 1822–1825, in Linz.[35] The Hartmann diaries on 26 February 1827 record Spaun dancing a Cotillion,[36] and on 19 February 1828 the performance of two Gallops, two Deutsche and five Cotillions. Bauernfeld remembers Schubert playing his waltzes over and over again until they developed into an endless Cotillion.[37]

Although Deutsche are hardly mentioned in Schubert's *Bildungskreis*, he commonly gifted his German Dances to close friends. In Schubert's circle birthdays were celebrated with Deutsche and dancing, as Hartmann documents on 13 February 1827.[38] Schubert's *12 Wiener Deutsche* (D 128) were written when he was at the Stadtkonvikt (1812); already D 128/12 borrows the Trio from his String Quartet (D 32) and his six Atzenbrugger Deutsche were written for friends in 1821. Deutsche are indistinguishable from Ländler and Waltzes, but Schubert used the title to indicate tempo – a slow waltz but quicker than a minuet – which explains why he used the titles interchangeably on various transcriptions of D 365, nos. 2 and 3.

One of his most interesting Deutsche, in C sharp minor (D 643), was composed for Josef Hüttenbrenner in 1819. The unusual tonality, accompanying figuration, and intermittent *furioso* character all take their cue from 'Tanz der Furien' composed by Hüttenbrenner on the reverse side (Example 12.7a online). The manuscript is creased as if Josef had thrown his work away. When Schubert discovered it, he flattened it out and wrote this virtuoso character piece in C sharp minor and the Écossaise in D flat on the reverse side of Hüttenbrenner's sketch. Interestingly, he composes a furiant, a rapid and fiery Czech dance in triple metre (Example 12.7b online).

Schubert also dedicated a Waltz in A major to Anselm Hüttenbrenner and Baron Karl von Schönstein.[39] Two undated Deutsche in E flat are inscribed at the beginning of the second version of 'Rastlose Liebe' (D 138), with a dedication to Countess Karoline Esterházy which Schubert carefully crossed out. It is very likely that the manuscript was transcribed for an evening's entertainment at the Esterházys, as the manuscript which bears Schönstein's name remained with him.[40]

Bauernfeld's comment on Schubert's double nature has become so sexualized that its continuation which acknowledges the folk-like element in Schubert's art is always cast aside.[41] Nowhere is this heritage more evident than in Schubert's dances that share the emotional variegation and gestures of Moravian and Silesian folk songs, which the boy composer had learnt from his mother. Such tropes are woven across Schubert's dances: his Ländler (D 980B) and his Deutscher Tänze (D 365/36 and D 779/12 and 13) (Examples 12.8a, 12.8b and 12.8c online). Schubert's great-grandfather, grandfather, father and uncle, Karl, were well known as musicians in Vysoká: their family string quartet played for dances in their home village just as Schubert's father continued this tradition with his boys. The Moravian folk tunes in D 146/5 and D 529/8 may have been passed down through his family (Examples 12.9a and 12.9b online).[42]

The improvisatory gestures of 'Der Leiermann' (D 911/24) – its plaintive melodic line, minor tonality and natural vocal qualities – are all melodic, rhythmic, harmonic and formal gestures of Silesian-Moravian folk music. This hurdy-gurdy topic recurs in Schubert's Dances; in the trio of D 146/9 the left hand turns the imaginary wheel (Example 12.10 online).

The appearance of such harmonic sequences in many of Schubert's early and late works clearly stems from improvisatory practices to help improvisers 'get the ball rolling'. Features arising from the music's origins at the keyboard include chains of parallel harmonies, both chromatic and diatonic, which have been programmed into Schubert's fingers, as can be found in D 790/5 and 6, or the passages based on thirds in D 790/4 and the *Valses sentimentales* D 779/1, 2 and 5. But the imprint of improvisation on Schubert's dances extends beyond these surface features to the genres he used and recurrent features of the music's large-scale organization. Many of his works play on preconceived notions of genre and style in order to create a diverse array of effects. An example of his subversion of generic conventions is found in his handling of the French overture topic in the slow movement and fugue of his F minor Fantasy (D 940), which he and Franz Lachner played for Bauernfeld on 9 May 1828.[43] In terms of the music's large-scale organization, the characteristic binary structure of his dances, whereby an antecedent sets up the expectation of a varied repetition or an answer in the consequent, is a distinguishing feature from his earliest minuets (D 30) to the 'Grazer Walzer' (D 924), op. 91. In the latter, Schubert's use of block chords in the left hand to support varied melodic variation in the right is a mature handling of the same improvisatory gestures in D 145. The figuration in *Moments musicaux* (D 780) no. 3 clearly has practical origins, as does the characteristic lyricism of Schubert's impromptus, which are fantasies of the freest kind and an example of the counterpoint of genres that he built into the substance of his musical thought. Like many contemporaries Schubert increasingly sought to capture this spirit of improvisation in his works in the brilliant style. The Impromptus (D 899 op. 90 and D 935, op. post. 142) and the three Klavierstücke (D 946) are Schubert's pianistic reinterpretation of the *bel canto* singing line in which a free-flowing melody floats above an arpeggiated accompanimental figuration, such as the inner chordal pattern in the Impromptu in G flat major (D 899/3).

Between 1816 and 1826 Schubert wrote down over 500 dances from those he improvised – about 130 Ländler, 160 Deutsche, 130 Waltzes, sixty Écossaises, two Gallops and a single Cotillion – from which he published about 200 between 1823 and 1828. These deceptively simple dances help us to understand how Schubert navigated himself through society, not only in friendship circles but also commercially, and offer unique insights into his 'improvisatory' compositional technique, his close contact with the piano while composing and his exploration of harmony at both local and structural levels. There can be little doubt that Schubert's very individual approach to harmony and form – two of the most intriguing aspects of his music – was influenced by his ability to improvise at the keyboard.

Many of his harmonic exploits were discovered by his improviser's fingers as they freely traversed and explored the timbre of the instrument. This point is central since Schubert's basic ideas are frequently harmonic as well as melodic. We hear this immediately in the preluding figuration of an early setting, 'Nähe des Geliebten' (D 162), which immediately shows Schubert exploring deeply expressive and novel sonorities to indicate the entrance of the text. The two-bar piano introduction of 'Nähe des Geliebten' – which does not begin in the main key (G flat major) but with a perfect cadence in E flat minor and rises chromatically in both treble and bass – tells us much about his performance practice, where many introductions were improvised to lead the singer in:

Example 12.11: 'Nähe des Geliebten' (D 162), bars 1–3

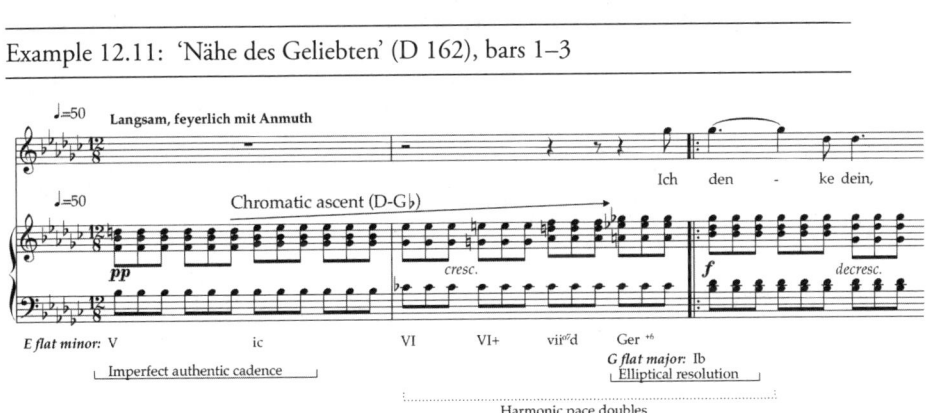

Publicly, improvisation earned Schubert a living, while privately it offered a distinct channel of communication and escape. The outpouring of dances in his middle period is in itself a statement about the central role they played in self-expression during a very difficult period in his life.[44] For a person who was reputedly very socially reserved, and may have had particular difficulty expressing himself verbally at this time, the freedom provided by musical improvisation may well have offered a cathartic release and made it a healing process.[45] Antonio Machado's poem *Campos de Castilla* about the fundamental freedom to improvise, as with each step we arrive at new choices, making decisions as we go, applies as much to Schubert's life as it did to his art.

III

CRISES

13

IN THE DOLDRUMS (1817–1818)

'If way to the better there be, it exacts a full look at the worst.'
Thomas Hardy, 'De Profundis' (1902)

The years 1818–23 are generally accepted as 'years of crisis' in Schubert's life. But neither the timeframe nor the term adequately explains the events of these years, and the trying period in Schubert's young life that intervened needs to be considered in more detail. It was a time of mistakes and failures, none greater perhaps, or so it must later have seemed, than his years as a schoolteacher and his relationship with Therese Grob, both of which must have been painful to look back on. Yet it is possible on the basis of letters and reminiscences of friends, his own letters and musical works, to identify several distinct phases within these years of crisis, which we shall consider in turn in the next four chapters. While the period as a whole has a character of its own, certain themes run through it from beginning to end and its coherence would be misrepresented if we did not first consider these separately. The period raises central questions about the extrinsic value of intense psychological distress and its significance for Schubert's music. It also invites us to make important distinctions between adversity – such as lack of financial means or illness – and suffering, but more significantly the relationship between negative affect and creativity in Schubert's life.

CRISES

There were two distinct crises: the first great crisis of his life – physical, emotional, musical – was one of identity in the period 1816–19. Three factors in particular dominate these years: the steadily increasing burden of his teaching, his relationships with Therese Grob and his father, and finding his true métier as a composer. The second existential crisis came to a head in 1822–25 when he contracted syphilis, with its sudden immediacy of ultimate questions. The roots of the first genuine, and at least potentially tragic, dilemma began as early as 1816 when Schubert was only twenty. Already feeling trapped by life choices such as his school teaching job and the claustrophobia of living at home after five years at boarding school, the growing feeling of being 'locked in' and needing to get out gradually propelled a feeling that change was not only possible but necessary.

Feeling stuck and downcast, Schubert, as always, turned to friends. Recognizing Schubert's distress at his life in the Säulengasse schoolhouse, Schober was the first to offer a lifeline by releasing him from the time constraints of teaching and restrictions in his father's home, and encouraging him to take the pivotal step to be a freelance composer. His first year living with Schober and his mother in their apartment (26 Tuchlauben) from Autumn 1816 until August 1817 was a 'time out' period which essentially pushed the crisis back to 1818. His flight to the tranquillity of their home set the pattern for numerous future flights, some of which would have more serious consequences.

Equally significant was Schubert's break with his teacher, Salieri. When Schubert was green and malleable Salieri had trained and harnessed his genius to be a Kapellmeister, an opera composer, a symphonist and a church music composer, and in the early days of Schubert's departure from the Stadtkonvikt Salieri had been one of the tiny audience for which he wrote. But by December 1816 Schubert knew his four-year apprenticeship was over and it was time to strike out on his own. What followed was a period of confused identity, a time of painful adjustment, as he decided in which direction he wanted to go. Without the regularity of lessons, Schubert's confident mood left him, his compositional output dropped

IN THE DOLDRUMS (1817-1818)

drastically, and the seclusion of Schober's home proved wholly unproductive. In 1816 he composed 270 works and over 100 songs; in 1817 he wrote eighty-three complete works; and in 1818 twenty-eight complete works. Ironically, when he was freed from the regularity of his teaching position, his output dropped significantly, and it was teaching in Zseliz that lured him back to composition.

During this unusually indolent period, the presence of a full six-octave piano in Schober's home gave impetus to a new artistic aspiration. One of the first works Schubert wrote there, in October 1816, was an Adagio and Rondo Concertante in F for piano quartet (D 487), which Therese Grob later claimed was written for her brother. In the spring and summer of 1817 numerous piano pieces ensued, more especially further attempts at the sonata. Schubert began a cascade of piano works in February 1817 with eight Écossaises in E flat for Piano (D 529). The following month he composed a three-movement Sonata in A minor (D 537), which he entitled his fifth although we only know of three predecessors (D 157, D 279 and D 459). In June he completed his Sonata in E minor (D 566), which he entitled Sonata no. 1 though it is commonly accepted that he had written four. His Sonata for Piano in D flat major (D 567), composed in June 1817, was later transposed into E flat and revised for publication (D 568) most likely in 1826–28. It is also probable that Schubert completed his Sonata for Piano in B major (D 575) in 1828 when preparing it for publication. In between, Schubert sketched three further fragmentary works: a Piano Sonata in A flat (D 557) from May 1817, an *Überlieferungsfragment*, whose final movement is missing at least 28 bars. The incomplete Scherzo and Trio in D and Allegro in F sharp minor for Piano (D 570) is most likely part of his Sonata in F sharp minor (D 571) composed in July 1817, for which we have 142 bars of the opening movement. For all his endeavours and rapid progress, Schubert's struggle to formulate his piano-sonata principles is evident in these fragments.

Schubert's reliance on friends is never more apparent than during these dog days. In the lethargic aftermath of a five-year exertion crowned by the success of his *Liederjahr*, he composed Spaun's 'Der Jüngling und der Tod' (D 545) and his thirteen Variations on a theme by Anselm Hüttenbrenner (D 576). Schubert's seventeen Mayrhofer settings, composed between January and September 1817, bear testimony to the poet's true resourcefulness, writing lyric poems for Schubert while assuaging his father's anxiety. Mayrhofer marked Schubert's coming of age by arranging for 'Erlafsee' (D 586) to appear as a supplement to an art and nature lovers' almanac on 29 January 1818, just before Schubert's twenty-first birthday.[1] Has ever a major composer been launched so modestly? As early as 1811, he had been on the verge of the momentous discovery that he could compose songs out of the material of his own life but had always held back from making the transition from private experience to printed score, perhaps waiting to see how his talent developed. In 1818 these inhibitions were overcome, and the classical nature of many of his Mayrhofer settings – 'Uraniens Flucht' (D 554, April 1817), 'Iphigenia' (D 573, July 1817) and 'Atys' (D 585, September 1817) – and likewise the Schiller settings of this period – 'Gruppe aus dem Tartarus' (D 583, September 1817), op. 24 no. 1; 'An den Frühling' (D 587, October 1817); the episodic 'Der Alpenjäger' (D 588, October 1817); the rhetorical 'Der Kampf' (D 594, November 1817) and lyrical 'Thekla: Eine Geisterstimme' (D 595, November 1817) – were inspired by Schubert's collaboration with Vogl. During this compositional crisis, he conceived many masterworks, including the first versions of 'Die Forelle' (D 550), op. 32, 'Der Tod und das Mädchen' (D 531) and Schober's 'An die Musik' (D 547, March 1817), op. 88 no. 4, a manifesto of serenity in the midst of chaos. It was during this first stay that the two friends also produced 'Pax Vobiscum' (D 551, April 1817), which would be performed at Schubert's Requiem. It was also a period of subtle but undeniable experimentation evident in his Sketch for a song without words in A minor (D 555), his orchestrated 'Lied ('Brüder, schrecklich brennt die Träne', Anon, D 535) and his third dramatic scene from Goethe's *Faust*: 'Gretchen im Zwinger' (D 564).

After settling in with Schober as a 'freelance' artist, Schubert suddenly had to vacate the room for Schober's brother, Axel, who, while serving in the Austrian army, became ill and needed to be brought home from France. On 24 August 1817, Schubert bade Schober farewell in a song of deep sincerity. 'Abschied' (D 578, 'Lebe wohl! Du lieber Freund!') shows how integrated into Schober's family he had become, and how alone he must have felt in the aftermath of his departure. The prospect of finding affordable lodgings was beyond his means. The only conceivable course of action was to go back to being his father's teaching assistant – a position he hated – in order to pay for his keep and ensure a sense of purpose in the months ahead. For Schubert this meant a revival of the trauma from which he had only just escaped. His return to the schoolhouse in August 1817 marked the beginning of a restless period. His main struggle was a lack of complete commitment and a lingering feeling that he was straying off course. Initially, he sought solace in composition – a Duo Sonata in A major for Violin and Piano (D 574), op. post 162, for which individual parts exist that suggest it was privately performed. His Polonaise in B flat for Violin and Orchestra (D 580) was also written for Ferdinand in September 1817 and premiered by him in the orphanage the following year. With the onset of teaching, however, Schubert laboured under the burden of working in a professional non-musical environment that was privately exacerbated by living in a strained and unhappy family atmosphere.

One of the biggest changes came in December 1817 when Schubert's father was finally promoted to director of the elementary school in the Rossau district. The new position meant there were now three points on the family compass: Himmelpfortgrund no. 72, where Schubert was born, Himmelpfortgrund no. 10, where the family moved when he was four, and Grünentorgasse no. 147, a much bigger apartment into which they all moved in January 1818. The improved financial circumstances of his father and stepmother could not compensate for the independence Schubert craved and were in stark contrast to the state of his composition that was dwindling and withering. After a winter of almost complete unproductivity, he was in the very worst temper. The year was portentous: January brought his twenty-first birthday. His inability to recapture his earlier fluency, to harness effectively on paper the ideas that still flowed readily enough at the piano, must have played a role in his imprisonment. In the first half of 1818 his spirits and creativity plummeted. Apart from the completion of his Sixth 'Little' Symphony in C major (D 589) and the two Overtures in the Italian Style (D 590–1), hardly anything of importance survives from this period.[2] Indeed from January 1818 a spell of real sterility appears to have set in, which to some degree justifies the severity of his later judgement. One explanation is that the effect of Schubert's ultimately fruitless search for a conventional life during this time was so damaging that his artistic conscience could not finally be satisfied with anything that he had written during the course of it.[3]

In the early months of 1818, and possibly at the instigation of his father, Schubert sought membership of the Gesellschaft der Musikfreunde, one of the most prestigious music societies in Vienna which held a seasonal orchestral concert series on Sundays at noon in the Redoutensaal of the Imperial Palace and was now introducing a new chamber music series to include performances of song and part-song. The application itself is interesting as the first evidence of the attraction that social advancement held for Schubert, which was at least rooted in the social marginality of his family and may explain both his application and its rejection. This adversity in itself did not trigger his ensuing depression, which was an amalgam of many things. His application was made with the urgent restlessness of a youth convinced that he was destined for that position. The letter of rejection he received, like the letter of rejection he had received in September 1816 and subsequent break with Therese Grob, were all part of the black period that led to a complete exhaustion of the musical vein. As the months wore on, the increasingly insistent prospect of a life of unrewarding and small-scale teaching left Schubert feeling lost, and increased tension at home. Even before moving house to Grünentorgasse no. 147, there was a lot going on: the loss of his mother in 1812, his father's remarriage in 1813, three small children born between 1814 and 1816. One month before Schubert moved home, his eight-month-old baby brother died on

IN THE DOLDRUMS (1817–1818)

30 July 1817. Schubert's return home to an atmosphere of grief cannot have been easy on anyone.

For all the sterility of this time Schubert's extraordinary empathy for sorrow and loss still shines through these songs. A little-known example is his commemorative B minor setting of 'Grablied für die Mutter' (D 616), a poetic version of the reconciliation scene of 'Mein Traum', for which he most likely wrote the text (see Example 13.1). D 616 commemorates Maria Anna Streinsberg – mother of Schubert's school friend, Josef Ludwig von Streinsberg – who died on 26 June 1818. As the manuscript remained in Josef's possession, there seems little doubt about the origins of this *pièce d'occasion* which has many layers of truth. Schubert's compassion and recollection of his own bereavement suggest he was sufficiently moved to give time to composing a short setting which he sent to Josef as a spontaneous expression of comfort. The song is an incredibly insightful little masterpiece which presents at least three different sides of death: opening as a kind of lullaby which plays on ancient associations of sleep and death, then moving to a 'proper' staggering funeral march rhythm on 'Bleich und stumm' (bar 14), yet the key to the song is the incredibly heart-wrenching move from B minor to B major at the angel's call (bar 33). The haste in which the manuscript was written suggests he wrote the song impromptu, but its musical sophistication and human understanding had been hard won.

CLEARANCES: SCHUBERT'S FATHER

What role did Schubert's father play in his son's crisis? Fathers have a long tradition of being demonized in music history and Franz Theodor is no exception. Even in his lifetime he was maligned by his son's friends and has since been presented as at worst dictatorial and at best dyspeptic, his relation with his son fraught and tense. It is time that this one-dimensional portrait of Schubert's father is replaced by a more nuanced, more humane account.

Franz Theodor's methodical manner may have made him seem to his sons Ignaz, Ferdinand, Karl and Franz as pedantic, and he was undoubtedly

Example 13.1: 'Grablied für die Mutter' (D 616)

IN THE DOLDRUMS (1817–1818)

Hauche milder, Abendluft,	Breathe more mildly, evening breeze,
Klage sanfter, Philomele,	Lament more softly, nightingale;
Eine schöne, engelreine Seele	A beautiful soul, as pure as an angel,
Schläft in dieser Gruft.	Sleeps in this tomb. |//

Bleich und stumm am düstern Rand, Pale and mute, at the gloomy edge of the grave,

Steht der Vater mit dem Sohne, A father stands with his son,
Denen ihres Lebens schönste Krone Their lives' fairest crown
Schnell mit ihr verschwand. So swiftly disappeared with her.

Und sie weinen in die Gruft, And they weep into the grave,
Aber ihrer Liebe Zähren But their tears of love
Werden sich zum Perlenkranz Will be transfigured into a wreath of pearls
 verklären,
Wenn der Engel ruft. When the angel calls.

infuriating. But no pedant could have selected the kind of music education which he decided upon for his son, and the melancholy from which he suffered was not the malady of an unimaginative man. It was not an uninspired act to present his son with a piano after the premiere of the F major Mass, despite many calls on his earnings. From the emphasis he placed on music in particular and the arts more generally it should be obvious that Franz Theodor's intense concern for his sons' education was not limited to laying the foundation for solid teaching careers. It was through education that Franz Theodor became who he was and everything suggests that he plainly intended for his sons – and Franz in particular – to follow the same academic path, but further and with greater ease. Franz Theodor valued Franz's natural gifts all the more for lacking them himself, for he had achieved everything through inexpressible industry, assiduity and repetition. In many ways he lived for and through his family: his meticulous family records and letters, the many times he took Franz home show his ongoing commitment to his son's well-being.[4] What else but the flexibility of his love explains his continuing support of his son? What else explains his patience, manifest in the worry he confided in Mayrhofer, about an adolescent Schubert who, at times, must have been vexatious and 'difficult'?[5] Although we first encounter Franz Theodor as the typical *paterfamilias* in the veiled parricidal drama of 'Der Vatermörder' (D10), Schubert's music is swiftly freed from that particular obsession and quite different, more natural relations between parents and their children are expressed in his eight cradle songs.

In a very different way to his son Franz, struggle determined Franz Theodor's entire life. Responsibility for three young children, dealing with his wife's grief at the death of their eight-month-old son, the no less real task of combining two families (with Ignaz, Karl, Franz and Maria Theresia still living at home) and an ongoing search for professional advancement were just some of the domestic challenges he faced in 1818. How desperate Franz Theodor was for success is suggested in the contract he signed for the Directorship of the Rossau school on 28 October 1817 in which he offered his sons to provide church music services in Rossau gratis – an extension of their Lichtental apprenticeships – which amounted to a savings for the parish of several hundred Gulden annually. This obstinate ambition and self-determination was offset by Franz Theodor's unfailing responsibility and goodness. When the family moved into the new schoolhouse, he delayed the sale of Säulengasse 3 in support of his best friend, whose only living child, Klara Wagner, had died on 12 January 1818 leaving three young children destitute. As District Director for the Poor in Lichtental, Franz Theodor was in a prime position to give financial aid to the grandchildren of Ignaz Wagner, to whom he gave shelter until his death.[6] The reversal in their circumstances transpired through Franz Theodor's austerity and ingrained work ethic as he tried to inculcate a regime of respectability and conformity in the Rossau school and devoted all his frustrated ambition into making the new appointment a success. The acute emotional stress of all this made everyone's life unbearable. The source of this sadness is found in Franz Theodor's roots, as his whole way of thinking and feeling, from the age of seven, had been structured by the discipline of a Catholic boarding school. The thing that originally tormented him became his delight and he ran his own home in the same way. What one encounters in his family records – the scrupulousness and religious ordering of the mind – was part and parcel of the childhood world in which he had lived.[7] This whole theology of suffering and centrality of sacrifice was the very thing in him against which his sons rebelled.

So, against this backdrop one must revisit the reasons for Franz Theodor's hostility to visits from Schubert's friends – Albert Stadler and Anton Holzapfel – which may have been a way of protecting his grieving wife who was looking after two young children. At the same time Schubert, with his huge talent and unpredictable energies, was struggling to survive: visits from friends, with whom he played and sang through his songs and male-voice trios, was one of the few avenues of escape from professional and private hardship. The dissolution of the family string quartet through Ferdinand's marriage and his father's preoccupation with young children meant there was no longer an audience of systematically educated musicians in Grünentorgasse, no artistically active milieu to provide support and stimulate his efforts. It had been two years since Schubert had composed the last of his schoolhouse quartets, String Quartet no. 11 in E major (D 353). The absence of an objective human world to support his imagination meant the disintegration of his music. Composition had been the one consolation for his moments of very real loneliness, but even now that failed him. The culmination of tension and deteriorating relations between him and his father brought about what would be described today as a near nervous breakdown in Schubert. He became increasingly impatient to be out of his home and into a new life, but he could see no means of escape into artistic freedom. If he failed to keep open the vein of composition, Schubert was no more than just another schoolteacher.

After an emotionally difficult winter for everyone, wounding words were seemingly spoken by the embittered father whose patience was fraying at last. Franz Theodor's black moods had their own complexity; they expressed not only his disappointment at Schubert's departure from the Stadtkonvikt and failure to go to university – a step to which he himself had aspired. His bitterness also sprang from a deep fear for his son's future: it was anxiety and vanity born of insecurity rather than malice that made him irascible. The winter of 1817–18, the family's most difficult year, shifted the emotional foundations of their home: the four brothers grew even closer. When Ferdinand escaped into marriage on 7 January 1816 and had children of his own, Schubert witnessed inspiration in his brother weighed down by the cares of marriage. The two artistic brothers found different ways of freeing themselves from their father's company. Karl departed that summer and travelled to Gmunden and Linz,[8] leaving Ignaz labouring under domestic tensions.[9] Being fond of his family, Schubert could not abjure its members, but nor could he sacrifice himself by conforming to their standards. In 1818 the twenty-one-year-old Schubert made the final break with schoolteaching, and moved away from home to devote himself to composition. He would be granted one decade in which to complete his life's work.

IN THE DOLDRUMS (1817–1818)

MUSES IN ZSELIZ: UNEASY PARADISE, 1818

The abject blackness of Schubert's evolving relations with his father pointed him towards Johann Karl Unger, who knowing that Count Esterházy of Galánta was looking for a piano teacher for his daughters (Karoline, thirteen, and Marie, sixteen), recommended the twenty-one-year-old composer to him. When in July 1818 the family moved to their country residence in Zseliz (now Želiezovce in Slovakia), Schubert, on receipt of his permit, travelled with them. One of many reasons for his high spirits on leaving Vienna was that he felt he had been forced into accepting this position. 'You happy creature! How enviable is your lot!', his eldest brother Ignaz wrote about the unhappy family atmosphere under their father's rule. But unlike Ignaz, Schubert was a traveller by nature as well as necessity. When he had sufficiently complicated his life in one place, he preferred to move on and allow time to heal old wounds.

Now that he was liberated from the oppressive confinement of his father's home, in receipt of board and lodgings, and generously paid for work he loved, Schubert's happiness was a direct consequence of his move. 'Thank God I live at last,' he wrote to his friends, 'it was high time, otherwise I should have become nothing but a thwarted musician.'[10] In this open letter to Spaun, Schober, Mayrhofer and Senn which is reflective of the spirit of his time, he presents himself as a demiurge: 'I live and compose like a god, as though that were as it should be', as he alludes to the creative barrenness of the last six months at Rossau.[11] Here in Zseliz a new wave of musical production began in a very different form. In the summer of 1818, as Schubert recovered from the ruins of his relationship with his father, he started to write piano duets for the count's two daughters, who were clearly very competent pianists. Some duets are typically didactic and may have been intended for him to play the more demanding primo part. In others the musical material is shared, extending the parameters of the duet in this and in his embrace of many genres: sonatas, Deutsche, Ländler, polonaises, overtures, fantasies, divertissements and marches. Among the most significant are the Four Polonaises (D 599), op. 75; Trois Marches Héroiques (D 602), op. 27; the B flat Major Duo Sonata (D 617); Deutscher in G with two trios and two Ländler in E for Piano Four Hands (D 618); and Eight Variations on a French Song (D 624), which he later dedicated to Beethoven.

But there were also enough brambles to ensure he had chosen the right path. In retrospect, the journey in mid July 1818, over deteriorating roads, seemed to Schubert to have something of the character of a flight, offering the opportunity to cut himself off from family tensions. He became a hermit living only for his own devotions, but his isolation was not complete. Whenever the consequences of seclusion became serious, contact was restored with the rest of the world and his letters continually prodded friends and family for companionship.

Going from Vienna to Zseliz must have been like leaving the city for a protracted house-party on a country estate. Zseliz lay on a route of the mail-coach 146 miles east of Vienna. The most notable monument was the medieval church of St James the Greater, situated in the town centre, richly decorated with murals including the Man of Sorrows and a fresco depicting the celestial trial for the departing soul of George Besci who commissioned the paintings.[12] At first Schubert stayed in the Neoclassical residence of the Esterházy family before moving into a quieter house in the neighbouring park.

In a second letter to his friends on 8 September, after having spent two months in Zseliz, Schubert wrote home enthusiastically about the new sights and company in which he lived:

> Our castle is not one of the largest, but very pretty. It is surrounded by a most beautiful garden. I live in the manager's house. It is fairly quiet, except for some forty geese, which sometimes cackle so loudly that you cannot hear yourself speak [. . .] All the people around me are decent. It must be rare for a count's retinue to fit so well together as they do. The inspector, a Slavonian, is a good guy and has a great opinion of his former musical talents. He still plays two German dances in 3/4 time

on the lute with great virtuosity. [. . .] The steward fits his office perfectly: a man with an extraordinary insight into his pockets and his bags. The doctor, who is really accomplished, ails like an old lady at the age of 24. A lot of oddity around! The surgeon, whom I like best, is a venerable old man of 75, always cheerful and happy. May God give everyone as happy an old age. The magistrate is a straightforward, pleasant man. A companion of the count, a merry old fellow and a capable musician, often keeps me company. The cook, the lady's maid, the chamberlain, the nurse, the manager etc and two grooms are all good people. The cook [is] a bit of a lad; the lady's maid 30 years of age; the chamber maid very pretty and often my companion; the nurse a good old sort; the manager my rival. The two grooms are more fit for the company of horses than human beings. The count is rather rough, the countess haughty, but more sensitive; the little countesses are nice children. So far I have been spared dining with the family. Now I cannot think of any more; I hardly need to tell you, who know me, that with my natural candour, I hit it off quite well with these people.[13]

This, then, was the world into which he entered in July 1818. Although good relations were established, Schubert neither had the diplomat's desire nor ability to talk with zest to locals about secondary issues. If he had the reputed frisson with the chambermaid, emotionally it left little mark on him. Instead, the sombre solitude in which he lived among such a gathering is acknowledged in the section of the correspondence addressed to Schober, where he lamented the lack of intellectual and musical possibilities:

Here in Zseliz I am obliged to rely wholly on myself. I have to be composer, author, audience, and goodness knows what else. Not a soul here has any feeling for true art, or at most the countess now and again (unless I am wrong). So I am alone with my beloved [Muse] and have to hide her in my room, in my pianoforte and in my bosom. Although this often makes me sad, on the other hand it elevates me all the more.[14]

What heightened his loneliness was that the majority of the population of Zseliz spoke Hungarian, with the exception of the count and his household who were German-speakers as were a small number of families who had settled in Zseliz at the count's encouragement. For the biographer a number of features in his letter to Ignaz, three weeks before he left, are revealing: that Schubert understood Hungarian by the end of his sojourn is evident in his ability to lampoon a series of sermons he had heard the Hungarian priest, Nikolaus Horvath, deliver in Zseliz.[15] The letter also tells us that the supposedly irreverent Schubert was at mass at the nearby Gothic Church. It shows how a different mixture of irony and affection pertains in Schubert's relations with each of his siblings. It also shows a perfect adaptation to each recipient.

'HERMIT SONGS'

In addition to the rift at home, Schubert's summer escape contained a solitude that required all his energies to overcome. His music grew out of his letters and his letters into music, as reflected in 'several songs that materialized' over the summer, 'very good ones', Schubert believed.[16] In July 1818 he detonated a little time bomb left in his keeping by Mayrhofer before the composer took his leave. His long setting of Mayrhofer's 'Einsamkeit' (D 620) is a letter to posterity which asks what human life is when reduced to its simplest terms. The song is far more than a confessional understanding of the experience of enforced solitude, or a testament to his understanding at the age of twenty-one of the human inclination to withdraw when we are at our lowest ebb. The setting, which was first given written shape during this extraordinary summer of 1818, shows the solitary Schubert protesting at this sad alienation in a solo cantata,[17] which has been repeatedly recognized as his first song cycle.[18] 'Einsamkeit' is the first of a series of philosophical poems that Schubert set between 1818 and 1820, which reflect the Pietist cult of interiority. His setting of Aloys Wilhelm Schreiber's 'Das Abendrot' (D 627), written as a parting gift to the count, evinces a similar eremitic otherworldliness and the composer's natural inclination towards transcendental modes of thought.

The erotic force, frustrated by isolation, was sublimated into compositional fervour. It expresses itself in sensuous interest in a sheaf of *Marienbild* songs inspired by four different poets – Schreiber's 'Das Marienbild' (D 623) and the anonymous 'Blondel zu Marien' (D 626) in which Schubert turns a physical need into spiritual perfection. Later, in his December 1818 setting of Friedrich Schlegel's *Stabat Mater*, 'Vom Mitleiden Mariä' (D 632), and Novalis's 'Marie' (D 658) in May 1819, he associates the religious motive with the force of Eros, of personal desire. Schubert's self was secluded but the seclusion was overcome, as far as possible, through his inner dialogue with a distant beloved in the sensual, obsessional Petrarchan sonnets of solitude (D 628–D 630), written in Zseliz while he was longing to go home. For whom are these songs of veneration written? D 623, D 632 and D 630 are masterworks. Schubert's Marian settings – his *Salve Reginas* (D 27, D 106, D 223, D 379 and D 386), his *Stabat Mater* settings (D175 and D 383) and Magnificat (D 486) – were all written for and premiered by Therese Grob. In 1818, Ignaz's October letter acknowledges that Schubert would not be around so much at the Grobs anymore and for the first time Therese was not the soprano solo in a premiere of sacred work by Schubert.[19] Was this out of fidelity to Franz because Ferdinand was passing off his brother's German *Requiem* (D 621) as his own?[20] Or did Therese have her own reasons for thinking that an epoch had ended?

Schubert's last letter from Zseliz shows his burning desire to escape back into the company of family circles. He sends kisses to Therese, her brother Heinrich, their Hollpein neighbours, whose youngest son Karl was the namesake of his godfather, Schubert's brother. Whatever rifts had driven Schubert to Zseliz, the links to home remained strong: his love for his three- and four-year-old stepsisters, Maria and Pepi, is palpable in Ferdinand's account of how much they miss him, and his affection for their younger sister, Therese, is evident in the confident exuberance of his greeting: 'You dear Resi, you often think of me'. He anticipates his return to Vienna and the happy reunion he wished to have with family and friends, a wholly middle-class affair untouched by the formalities of rank in which he had lived since July.

Fundamentally, it had been a lonely summer with one nascent friendship, but the Esterházys had been kind to him. After the long bone-shaking days in their carriage, it was evidently a pleasure to arrive in Vienna on 19 November 1818. Schubert had exactly one more decade to live. The goal in reaching Zseliz turned out to symbolize the need for a new start and a new way of life. The experiences that lay before him were to frustrate his father's calculations, but they were to define for Schubert himself a new kind of music. By moving him closer to the mainstream of Austro-Germanic culture, ultimately they were to change its future course.

14

SCHUBERT'S 'DOUBLE NATURE' (1819-1822)

'And I wish to enjoy in my inner self
What is allotted to the whole of humanity
To grasp with my spirit the height and depth,
To heap on my bosom its weal and woe,
And so expound my own self to its self
And like itself at last be shattered too.'

Goethe, Faust I

By the age of twenty-one Schubert was already aware that he was an uneasy amalgam of two people. From his earliest years in the Stadtkonvikt his life had taken on a characteristic pattern: among a small circle of initiates, either school friends or fellow musicians, he was fully at ease, unpretentious and willing to talk freely, but to the rest of the world he remained monosyllabic. He existed in this state of private disclosure and public reserve: a condition that was not confined to his post-Zseliz years. He was a genius – a mystery not only to others but also to himself – but during this period the polarity was perhaps greater than usual.

Schubert identified these extremes of human behaviour and artistic expression within himself. When he acknowledged these Goethean counterparts – 'whenever I attempted to sing of love, it turned to pain. And again, when I tried to sing of pain, it turned to love'[1] – he was echoing a proverb from 'Klärchens Lied' (D 210), which was commonly cited by European intellectuals as being characteristic of the Romantic soul:

Freudvoll	Full of joy
und leidvoll,	and full of sorrow,
gedankenvoll sein;	Full of thoughts;
Langen	Longing
und bangen	and trembling
in schwebender Pein,	in uncertain anguish,
Himmelhoch jauchzend	Rejoicing to heaven;
zum Tode betrübt,	grieving to death
Glücklich allein	Blessed alone
ist die Seele, die liebt.[2]	is the soul that loves.

This fluid duality is at the very core of Schubert's life's work. He knew that the sources of our greatest joys lie awkwardly close to our greatest pains and how our most fulfilling projects are inseparable from a degree of torment. In 'Mein Traum' he identifies his music as a working synthesis of these ferocious contradictions within himself and 'the dark' as a positive element from where his music originates. But there is also a sense of the dark as something he needed to traverse in order to arrive at some reliable light or sight of reality: the dark night of the soul, the dark wood of creative endeavour, even dark sexual gods.

Eduard von Bauernfeld was the first to identify this dark side of Schubert's double nature.[3] Josef Kenner was gifted with a tongue sharper than his mind when he identified the composer's two souls, 'of which the one pressed heavenwards and the other wallowed in mud'.[4] His detachment of Schubert's physical nature from his ethical principles admits little understanding of the psychological paradox of these permanently opposed forces, little understanding of Schubert, and is completely at odds with the contemporary conception of the individual as being whole. 'Everything spiritual,' Wilhelm von Humboldt believed, 'is only a more refined blossoming of the physical'.⁵ Although Humboldt was drawing on contemporary science, his thinking unveils an older pattern of metaphysics: the monadic individualism of Leibniz with its definition of the soul as a self-propelling force, at once physical and spiritual, developing in accordance with its own inner law.

Even a post-Kantian reading of Schubert's storm and stress years as a deviation into what Kant calls heteronomy – allowing himself to be determined by something other than his rational self – raises questions about the circumstances of the composer's life and his ability to rise above them. There is no rational explanation of a choice to be irrational: these years are radical and go to the root of his humanity. In his *Bildungskreis* era he seemed to have a claim to moral centrality but loses it in this period, so that his vacillations attract our interest even more. In endeavouring to understand Schubert's character what distinctions can we make before and after this time? What were his public and private selves?

CONFIDENCE AND INDETERMINACY: SCHUBERT'S MALE-VOICE SETTINGS

Schubert's public self was very much bound up with his friends, who continued to aid him financially, actively support and inspire his art. On his return to Vienna on 19 November 1818, Schubert moved in with Mayrhofer. He was delighted by the news that while he had been in Zseliz, Vogl had negotiated his first operatic commission at the Kärntertortheater: a one-act opera *Die Zwillingsbrüder* with Vogl in the dual role as the twin brothers. Leopold von Sonnleithner was rehearsing a second performance of *Prometheus* at the Gundelhof on 8 January 1819. Schubert crossed over into the New Year with a feeling of success.

When we consider the composer's professional life beyond the private salon, performances of his works increased rapidly in 1819–22 and his music was received with critical acclaim in Vienna and beyond. In the early months of 1819 music by Schubert was included in four public concerts. Three of these featured 'Schäfers Klagelied' (D 121), which was Schubert's first song to be publicly performed. The premiere was given by the Kärntnertortheater's operatic tenor Franz Jäger at the Roman Emperor Inn on 28 February. The concert mounted by the Society of Amateurs on 14 March included one of Schubert's orchestral overtures, most likely the Overture in E minor (D 648) completed the previous month and performed three times in Vienna before its public premiere at the Gesellschaft der Musikfreunde the following year.

During the 1820s Schubert was one of the most widely published and performed Viennese composers; reviews continually refer to him as a 'popular composer' and he became known as a master of musical miniatures which began to be published as supplements in local journals, the *Wiener Zeitschrift für Kunst, Literatur, Theater und Mode* but also in the *Taschenbuch zum geselligen Vergnügen* in Leipzig in 1821. In January 1820 'Erlkönig' and 'Der Wanderer' marked his debut at the Musikalischen Abendunterhaltungen (musical evening entertainments), a prestigious concert series organized by the Gesellschaft der Musikfreunde, the most prominent venue for the performance of his songs and part-songs during the 1820s. Between 1825 and 1828 Schubert was the most frequently performed composer in this series.[6] His Lieder and part-songs were regularly programmed in public concerts in the largest public venues in Vienna: the Großer Redoutensaal (Large Assembly Hall) seated up to 3,000 listeners;[7] the Kärntnertortheater had 670 seats, with standing room for an additional 200; the Theater an der Wien held between 1,000 and 1,500, the Baroque Landhaussaal (County Hall) between 500 and 800.

By 1820 the prospect of Schubert's career as an operatic composer was beginning to bear fruit. The comic Singspiel, *Die Zwillingsbrüder* (D 647), was first performed at the Kärntnertortheater on 14 June 1820, and received six performances between June and July. At the premiere Schubert's friends formed a claque, calling for the composer, but Schubert refused to go up on stage and acknowledge their applause, perhaps realizing in performance what he had misjudged in rehearsal. Leopold von Sonnleithner helped procure the premiere of his melodrama, *Die Zauberharfe* (D 644) at the Theater an der Wien on 19 August 1820, with a further seven performances in October before it fell from the repertoire. In the nine weeks between the two premieres Schubert seems to have attempted no work other than the revision of this score. Although the success of both was extremely short-lived, Schubert had his foot in the door of two of Vienna's most important theatres which would lead to two commissions: *Fierabras* (D 796) and the incidental music to *Rosamunde* (D 797), which would be premiered at the Theater an der Wien on 20 December 1823, after which he never completed another stage work.

One of the genres for which Schubert was becoming better known was his male-voice settings composed in the Austrian custom of one voice per part. All but one of his nineteen part-songs published during his life were written for male voice.[8] Long before these settings were published or publicly premiered, Schubert was writing small-scale works for the pleasure of family and friends, trying out new compositional possibilities which pushed the limitations of the genre.[9]

One such setting, 'Das Dörfchen' (D 598), op. 11, no. 1, conceived in December 1817, was leavened in 1821 in the interest of popular style. The setting is a fine example of Schubert's ability to make his own a formula which he had inherited from Salieri: a Sentimentalist text set for male voices in square-cut phrases, conventional harmonic progressions, mostly homophonic but unfolding into a simple canon toward the end as each singer comes forward for a curtain call (Examples 14.1a and b). The setting was premiered at the Kärntnertortheater on 7 March 1821 with a repeat performance on 8 April 1821 at the Gesellschaft der Musikfreunde, but before that it enjoyed numerous private performances.

The Lusatian singers, who premiered the setting, were well known as an ensemble. Like Schubert's parents, all of them had been born in Bohemia or Moravia and had come to Vienna to make a living. The first tenor, Josef Barth (1781–1865), was a professional tenor at the court chapel to whom Schubert dedicated the published setting. The second tenor, Johann Karl

Example 14.1a: 'Das Dörfchen' (D 598), op. 11/1, bars 1–10

Umlauff (1796–1861), was one of Vogl's singing students. The first bass, Josef Götz (1787–1822), was a professional opera singer. The second bass, Wensel Josef Nejebse (1796–1865), was a dedicated amateur singer and founder member of the Vienna Männergesang-Verein. Their *a cappella* performance of 'Das Dörfchen' pleased the audience so much it had to be repeated.[10] The following year D 598 was published with obbligato guitar or piano

Example 14.1b: 'Das Dörfchen' (D 598), op. 11/1, canon, bars 97–132

accompaniment as op. 11, no. 1, with 'An die Nachtigall' (D 497) and 'Geist der Liebe' (D 747). These three published part-songs – and 'Frühlingsgesang' (D 740) from Schubert's op. 16, no. 1 – dominated public performances (1821–24) and were one of the media through which he conversed with distant friends.

The concert at which 'Das Dörfchen' was officially premiered opens a window onto Schubert's compositional world. The annual benefit concert for blind, deaf and orphaned children, organized by the Gesellschaft adeliger Frauen zur Beförderung des Guten und Nützlichen (the Noblewomen's Society for the Advancement of Good and Benevolence), was one of a series of performances on Ash Wednesday when theatres were closed. The second part of the programme included a performance of 'Erlkönig' (D 328) by Vogl and Anselm Hüttenbrenner, and the premiere of another choral work, 'Gesang der Geister über den Wassern' (D 714) performed by Josef Götz, Josef Barth, Josef Nejebse, Johann Karl Umlauff, Johann Michael Weinkopf, Josef Frühwald and two choristers.[11] In comparison with 'Das Dörfchen', the premiere of D 714 was a fiasco and the condescending review by one of the *Allgemeine musikalische Zeitung*'s favourite jackdaws was distinctly unfavourable:

> On the other hand, the eight-part chorus by Herr Schubert was received by the audience as an accumulation of musical modulations and tonal subversions, without meaning, order and purpose. In such works the composer resembles a coachman, drawn by eight horses, who steers right, then left, so moves forward, then reverses and plays this game constantly, without ever arriving at a particular street.[12]

The musical scene in Vienna in 1821 was not so bright that Schubert's setting required so much excoriation. Just how seriously he took this polemic can be seen in a letter to Leopold von Sonnleithner where he declined a subsequent offer to perform a part-song in one of the Gesellschaft der Musikfreunde concerts:

You know yourself how the later quartets were received: people have had enough of them. True, I might succeed in inventing some new form, but one may not count with certainty on anything of the kind. But as my future fate greatly concerns me after all, you, who take your share in this, as I flatter myself, will yourself admit that I must go forward cautiously and that I cannot therefore by any means accept such an invitation, much as it honours me.[13]

The letter shows a very strategic Schubert unwilling to risk reputational damage, alert to the preoccupations of his time. It is also a threadbare attempt to cover up his humiliation. The music confirms his original expectations had been considerably higher, and his disappointment correspondingly more intense than his cool and tactical assessment of 1821 written to a fellow composer might imply.

'Gesang der Geister' (D 714) is not in the first instance an exploration of the pathology of the public mind, but the response his ambition met on this occasion tells us much about Schubert's Vienna. Did Schubert expect to find an audience of enlightened individuals: a broader world than the cognoscenti gathered in Sonnleithner's home? It is tempting to think that the function of Sonnleithner's salon as a deliberately chosen instrument of musical enlightenment was in direct contrast to the Ash Wednesday concerts. Sonnleithner himself did not consider the audience a factor but believed the piece had received too little rehearsal.[14] His letter to Josef Hüttenbrenner on 26 March 1821 stresses the need for Schubert to attend rehearsals for a subsequent private performance, which he successfully mounted at his father's home on 30 March 1821.[15]

In comparison with the public press, Victor Umlauff von Frankwell wrote stirringly in private praise of the setting and acquitted Schubert on the strength of the originality of his composition:

[Johann Karl] Umlauf [my father] also participated in the evening of vocal works organized by The Noblewomen's Society for the

Advancement of Good and Benevolence on 7 March 1821, at the first public performance of vocal works by that great composer [. . .] and in the eight-part song 'Chorus of the Spirits [hovering] over the Waters' by Goethe, one of Schubert's greatest compositions. [. . .] The 'Chorus of the Spirits [hovering] over the Waters', a deeply thought-out, sublime tone poem, was performed by eight singers, thoroughly capable, trained musicians, was well rehearsed and well rendered, but the challenging music was incomprehensible to the audience, who were, in any case, unfamiliar with Schubert's output; they remained cold, no hand was raised in applause, and the singers, who had been impressed by the sublime beauty of this piece of music, had expected the greatest success, retreated as if struck by a cold shower. Nevertheless, they had the courage to perform the same song a short time later, and it was so much appreciated that it had to be repeated.[16]

Frankwell's identification of audience incomprehensibility suggests how, in contrast to the select salons in which Schubert played, here in contrast to he played for a much larger audience with a lower level of musical 'education'.

Hans Robert Jauss's 'horizon of expectations' in literary theory refers to the preconceptions a listener has when they encounter a work shaped by their artistic experiences. Jauss posits that the 'aesthetic distance' between a reader's horizon of expectations and the text's fulfilment of these expectations or its failure to do so are central to our understanding of a work's contemporaneous reception. I am very grateful to Nicolas Puyane for drawing my attention to Hans Robert Jauss's 'horizon of expectations' in reception theory and *The Oxford Dictionary of Literary Terms*, ed. Chris Baldick 4th edn (2015). This idea of 'aesthetic distance' or 'horizontal change' offers a valuable lens through which to view the reception of D 714 on 7 March 1821 and its audience's cultural values.

The most interesting thing about both concerts is the centrality of audience, revision and resetting in Schubert's compositional practice. Both part-songs, more especially the multiple settings of 'Gesang der Geister über den Wassern', are further examples of composition as a fluid process, whereby reworking and revision are inherent aspects of that activity, and multiple versions are a record of this process. Over a period of five years, Schubert continually returned to Goethe's poem, each resetting wrestling with different textual challenges. By examining its many settings we can chart the shifting intentions that formed each version, from the madrigalesque tendencies in his first part-song of Goethe's (TTBBB, D 538) to the 1821 premiere of this octet (D 714). First drafted in December 1820, the February 1821 version asserts Schubert's aspiration to compose an artistically ambitious concert piece. Composed for a double chorus of four tenors, four basses with instrumental accompaniment by two violas, two cellos and a double bass, D 714 redefines part-song into a more sophisticated and demanding genre (Example 14.2 online).

Schubert was an inveterate reviser, and each of the rival versions of 'Das Dörfchen' and 'Gesang der Geister' are a product of a particular time. Each offers us a glimpse into his compositional processes and evolving aesthetic principles, as well as the external forces that shaped their revisions. By highlighting his connection to society and the external forces it exerted upon him, motivations behind some of these revisions can be discerned. It shows Schubert as a social being, not only shaped by social pressures, but by his self-conscious attempts to find a relation to those pressures.

DECLARING HIS GENIUS: 'ERLKÖNIG' (D 328), OP. 1

During these years Schubert also made his debut in the world of commercial publishing with the appearance of 'Erlkönig' (D 328) by Cappi and Diabelli on 2 April 1821, dedicated to Moritz Graf von Dietrichstein. Following the first salon performance of 'Erlkönig' on 1 December 1820 by August von Gymnich and Anna Fröhlich at his home, Leopold von

Sonnleithner and three other friends – Johann Schönauer, Johann Nepomuk Schönpichler and Josef Hüttenbrenner – had advanced money for the song to be printed as Schubert's op. 1. By October over 300 of the 600 printed copies were sold. Three years earlier Schubert was someone who had one song published as a supplement to an art and nature lover's almanac. The moment 'Erlkönig' was published was a moment of change. He began to recover something of the sense that he had in his exhilarating teenage years that in the medium of print he could converse with or at any rate be performed by the best musicians of Vienna.

Between April 1821 and October 1823, Diabelli acted as agents for thirty-one of Schubert's songs, two Piano Dance Cycles (D 145 and D 365), three male-voice settings and one piano duet (see Table 14.1), for which they received a commission on sales. Grateful for his friends' support, Schubert poured his heart into publication, and emerged to the public with a new zeal:

Table 14.1: Schubert's Cappi & Diabelli Publications, op. 1–18

1.	'Erlkönig'	D 328	2 April 1821
2.	'Gretchen am Spinnrade'	D 118	30 April 1821
3.	'Schäfers Klagelied', 'Heidenröslein', 'Jägers Abendlied', 'Meeresstille'	D 121, 257, 368, 216	29 May 1821
4.	'Der Wanderer', 'Morgenlied', 'Wandrers Nachtlied'	D 493, 685, 224	29 May 1821
5.	'Rastlose Liebe', 'Nähe des Geliebten', 'Der Fischer', 'Erster Verlust', 'Der König in Thule'	D 138, 162, 225, 226, 367	9 July 1821
6.	'Memnon', 'Antigone und Oedip', 'Am Grabe Anselmos'	D 541, 542, 504	23 August 1821
7.	'Die abgeblühte Linde', 'Der Flug der Zeit', 'Der Tod und das Mädchen'	D 514, 515, 531	27 November 1821
8.	'Der Jüngling auf dem Hügel', 'Sehnsucht', 'Erlafsee', 'Am Strome'	D 702, 516, 586, 539	9 May 1822
9.	Original Dances	D 365	29 November 1821
10.	8 Variations on a French Song for Piano Duet	D 624	19 April 1822

11.	TTBB: 'Das Dörfchen', 'Die Nachtigall', 'Geist der Liebe'	D 598, 724, 747	12 June 1822
12.	Harper Trilogy	D 478	13 December 1822
13.	'Der Schäfer und der Reiter', 'Lob der Thänen', 'Der Alpenjäger'	D 517, 711, 524	13 December 1822
14.	'Suleika I' and 'Geheimes'	D 720, 719	13 December 1822
15.	'Wanderer Fantasy'	D 760	24 March 1823
16.	TTBB: 'Frühlingsgesang' and 'Naturgenuß'	D 740, 422	9 October 1823
17.	TTBB: 'Jünglingswonne', 'Liebe rauscht der Silberbach', 'Zum Rundetanz', 'Die Nacht'	D 983, 983A, 983B, 983C	9 October 1823
18.	38 Walzer, Ländler, Ecossaisen	D 145	5 February 1823

When Diabelli realized the exceptional profits being made, he went behind Josef Hüttenbrenner's and Leopold von Sonnleithner's backs (knowing full well they would reject him) and made a private offer to Schubert of a one-off cash payment in return for the plates, remaining print run and future rights of op. 1–12. Desperate for money, Schubert agreed. He earned a meagre sum of 2,000 Gulden, approximately 800 Gulden in Assimilated Coinage, an average of 166 florins for each work, a price he never commanded again.[17] His actions caused an eruption of anger in Sonnleithner who had made significant strides in furthering Schubert's career. He and the other friends who had his works engraved at their expense were horrified when they realized the composer had sacrificed his future security for immediate cash in hand, in a sale which they considered far too small. This is the well-known account, which is too often taken as evidence of financial ineptitude and Schubert's tactlessness as horrendous. When his friends rightly believed he had been improvident, even ungrateful,[18] what they did not determine were the conditions that led Schubert to make this decision. The real motor forces in Schubert's decision were desire and psychological distress. He had not inherited his father's instinct for conserving capital, was in dire financial need, and paying the price for his private amours and guilts.

TENSION AND RIDDLES

Schubert's public success as a professional composer coincided with a period of personal crisis. During these years more than one of his friends commented on his potentially debilitating lifestyle. Gerhard von Breuning and Josef Hüttenbrenner both mention an evening where good wine flowed, conversation sparkled, and after hours of performing the composer was so drunk 'we had to carry our Schubert into another room'.[19] Whatever mishaps Schubert's clumsiness brought on himself, Leopold von Sonnleithner offers a very balanced perspective:

> What Schindler says about his propensity to drink is probably rather exaggerated; under no circumstances should too much attention be paid to this matter in his biography. But unfortunately, I must confess that I saw him in a drunken state several times. On one occasion I was with him at a party, in one of the suburbs, where there was a great deal of music making and feasting. I went home at about 2 o'clock in the morning; Schubert remained still longer and the next day I learnt that he had to sleep there as he was incapable of going home. This happened in a house where he had not long been known and where he had only been introduced a short time previously. This note, by the way, is only for the biographer and not for the biography.[20]

It does belong to this biography, however, as does the regret Schober expressed in later years that 'Schubert let himself go to pieces; he frequented the outskirts of the city and roamed around in taverns, at the same time admittedly composing his most beautiful songs in them, just as he did in hospital too where he found himself as the result of excessively indulgent sensual living and its consequences'.[21]

In 1821–22 Schubert was an unbridled, immoderate man, and for a while something slightly crazed entered his conduct. When Schubert was living with Mayrhofer, Josef Hüttenbrenner, who admired the composer inordinately, moved into the apartment a floor below and became his amanuensis and long-suffering factotum. Tired of pestering letters, Schubert began to treat him inconsiderately. He was nicknamed 'The Tyrant' at first good-humouredly by his friends, but many of them felt themselves discountenanced as he continued to act thoughtlessly. With the barbarity of an offhand remark or an ill-mannered friend, he trampled on Viennese conventions in which Spaun, Vogl and Sonnleithner had educated him. He succeeded in alienating those who had taken his genius under their wing and there was a growing resentment at what they believed to be Schober's influence.

Certainly, the focus of his friendship narrowed with Schober, who for a while inherited and absorbed his other close relationships. In Autumn 1821 they spent a month together at St Pölten in Lower Austria, as guests of the bishop, Johann Nepomuk von Dankesreither, who hosted them while they worked on *Alfonso und Estrella* (D 732). Vogl was apoplectic with rage when he heard Schubert was wasting his time on Schober's libretto and there may have been an element of jealousy on his part. His annual tour with Schubert in Upper Austria was replaced by holidays with Schober, who was dabbling in Vogl's profession.

Schubert's preoccupation with *Alfonso* was more than a case of his puzzling instinct for mediocrity. It formed in part the basis for his new rush of self-confidence, but there was also a touch of unrealism about this period. History has shown the emptiness of the plans Schubert was forging, his double infatuation with Schober and their scheme for a through-composed opera. Both men's obsession with the theatre was a diverted and misapplied *eros*. Schubert shared Schober's grandiose perception of their opera and for a while became inaccessible to other friends.

The real reason for his remoteness was a mental detachment from his earlier life. In 1820–22 Schubert was living too isolated a life and

SCHUBERT'S 'DOUBLE NATURE' (1819-1822)

his productivity spiralled downwards. If his music was to recover it would have to find its way back into company; but until then, and in order to survive, he had to suffer the ultimate severance of self from society.

ISLANDS OF THE MIND: MULTIPLE FRAGMENTS

Between 1818 and 1822 very few of Schubert's major compositional projects came to completion. Two dramatic works – the one-act Singspiel, *Die Zwillingsbrüder* (D 647, January 1819) and *Alfonso und Estrella* (D 732, September 1821 to February 1822) – and the *Deutsches Requiem* (D 621, August 1818) composed for Ferdinand in Zseliz, the A flat major Mass (D 678, November 1819 to September 1822), the Sixth Symphony (D 589, October 1817 to February 1818) and numerous exiguous works were all evidence that he was not lapsing into impotent silence. Apart from unpredictable moments of lyric inspiration which kept the creative vein open, any works he completed were for immediate consumption. The other works, in which a new form of expression is attempted, were nearly all fragments which he kept to himself. In the symphonies, chamber music, operas and church music that Schubert wrote during these years, we find a depiction of his situation and of the conflicting factors in it. After five years of astonishing growth and productivity, Schubert was burnt out. Given his circumstances it is remarkable that he wrote as much as he did. What followed was Schubert's own variety of the storm and stress period in which his spirit wandered aimlessly. The oppressive stagnation which he had depicted in 'Meeresstille' (D 215a and D 216) in 1815 – whereby musical syntax coagulates into a frightening stasis – took on symbolic meaning during this period. In 1822 a whole summer wore away: between April and August of 1822 he produced nothing new other than a sketch for a Kyrie (D 755), the lied 'Du liebst mich nicht' (D 756), and a piece for female voices, 'Gott in der Natur' (D 757). Presumably these months saw a sustained spell of work on the A flat Mass (D 678) which hung on from November 1819.

One of the things that was missing during this period of compositional incapacity was a secure understanding of his role as composer and the next steps to take. He acted as if he knew what he wanted and appeared to be going after a career in music theatre, but fundamentally there was a part of Schubert that was lost. The period between 1818 and 1823 was marked by protracted difficulties with several genres. Between 1810 and 1816 he composed twelve string quartets but did not complete another until 1824. He composed six symphonies between 1813 and 1818 and four incomplete symphonies between 1818 and 1822. At first glance his piano literature appears to have suffered most. He made next to no significant progress on his 1818 preoccupation with the piano sonata, but wrote over 500 piano dances for publication and developed enormously as a pianist.

The unfinished works of these fallow years are also among Schubert's masterworks and herald a new age not only in his own compositional development but in Romantic music in general. Islands of concreteness in this sea of abstraction include the Quartettsatz in C minor (D 703), composed in December 1820, a work that marks his first maturity in instrumental music, or the 'Unfinished' Symphony in B minor (D 759), begun in October 1822. His cautious approach is manifest in his failure to complete the dramatic oratorio *Lazarus* (D 689, February 1820) or to score the four-movement particell for his Symphony no. 7 in E major (D 729, August 1821), a work which reveals Schubert going well beyond the classical models of his first six symphonies.

The years between the ages of twenty to twenty-five, which for many might be their most productive, were for Schubert a period of beginnings. From the amount and the quality of fragmentary works, it is clear he tried very hard to settle down to composition but for a while it became a painfully slow process. During this long directionless period he became intensely self-critical as a composer, but part of his creative anguish was a result of putting his head above the parapet. Being unable to finish compositions must have felt paralysing, but however meaningless, however impossible it felt to fulfil the promise in his ideas, Schubert 'violated' that negative place. Unlike St Augustine's metaphor, *subtracto fundamento in aere aedificare*, he was not 'building castles in the air', grandiose fragments that were impossible for him to realize. His fragments are where he was aspiring to be, and he was laying foundations for the time when he could concentrate on future projects. What appears to be a degenerative phase in Schubert's output is regenerative: it was a time of disquieting, transformative stirrings.

During these years Schubert learnt that withdrawals are part of writing and that waiting is sometimes part of the work. There are so many different ways of explaining this 'unproductive' period: his entire creative life fits the pattern of starting out, taking stock, and the new freedom that follows. Schubert's contemplation of marriage in his diary is part of the desire to be settled but only as far as he was unsettled was there any hope for him. Had he cut short the floundering, the stumbling about, had he sought certainty and resisted the discomfort from which self-transcendence springs, he would have robbed himself of possible creative outcomes.

Another reason for this long directionless period is his assiduity and obsession with the publication of his works. Much effort had to go into the task of revising and completing works for publication to the apparent exclusion of composition. It was one of the means by which he preserved an impassive divine silence. One could even argue convincingly that for a while he stood apart from a state of constant activity and learnt that leisure is just as essential to growth. But leisure and ease are the opposite attributes for this period. Everything that he wrote bore the marks of restriction, of the brutal division of his public and private life, and of a mind that was properly destined to live in subtle and manifold interaction with its surroundings. His works of this dry season are traditionally characterized by 'crisis' when what is really meant is that the relation between self and world, precariously balanced, had been further destabilized. With such complete failure of self-understanding during these years, it is no surprise that Schubert lost the power to write as much as he had before.

15

SECRETS OF THE SELF

> '"How many secrets do you know?" – "Three", replied the old man. "Which is the most important?" asked the silver king. "The open one," replied the old man.'
>
> Goethe, *Das Märchen*

THE WATERSHED: *ANNUS CATASTROPHICUS*

1822 was the year that altered the composer's whole conception of himself: Schubert contracted syphilis. Just how devastated he was is evident in his letters. He was twenty-five: the limits of his life had been marked out and whatever eternity it possessed had henceforth to be found within them.

In Schubert's day syphilis belonged to the vocabulary of dread. Many of his contemporaries had died of it and fear of contagious disease haunted his generation. It was also a highly stigmatized disease: it marked the person as a social pariah and was a sign of sexual deviancy. It was a scandal that set tongues wagging in his circle and left Schubert in an isolation which would have demoralized a person of lesser tenacity.

What is immediately striking is that many of his friends moved away from Vienna. Spaun had already moved to Linz in 1821. Painful for a different reason was Schober's move to Breslau, Silesia's liberal capital, in July 1823, which may have had a medical as well as a professional purpose.

Either way he does not emerge from the whole affair with credit. Schober's attraction was to the art of theatre, where as an actor he could pretend to all the attributes he did not possess in reality. He could not be an artist, but he could act the part. This is surely the oldest argument ever put forward for running away to go on stage, but in Schober's case, musicologists have overlooked its absurdity because of the grain of sociological truth it contains. During Schubert's crisis years Schober became a living Wilhelm Meister.[1] There is nothing to say about the waste of life and opportunity which is all that his theatrical mission amounted to. Schober achieved nothing specific, learnt nothing tangible and gained experience of the world only in the sense that his life was now interwoven with guilt. He had deserted his dearest friend in his hour of need. The best that can be said is that Schober survived. On his return to Vienna in 1825 he did the only thing that survivors ever do: he started all over again, this time with his Lithographic Institute.

Schubert's loss of friends coincided with a certain ostracism in society, for when he contracted syphilis his career was directly affected. Prior to this he had been in the public eye for two and a half years. Public and semi-public performances of his music fell from eighteen in 1821, and fifteen in 1822, to just seven in 1823. Schubert was alone and in the darkness he had to find his way. He had done so in his first crisis when he turned his suffering into artistic works. In 1822 he began to repeat that cure.

THE GARDENS OF ALCINOUS: SCHUBERT'S DREAM AND NON-DREAM[2]

On 3 July 1822, shortly after the tenth anniversary of his mother's death, Schubert wrote an allegorical short story, 'Mein Traum' (My Dream), the title of which was added in ink by his brother, Ferdinand, to the composer's extant pencil sketch.[3]

Schubert never set his scholars a puzzle more openly than in this allegorical tale. The question as to why he wrote it is the most interesting one that can be asked.

Table 15.1: Schubert's 'My Dream' (1822)

I was the brother of many brothers and sisters. Our father and mother were good people. I was deeply and lovingly devoted to them all. Once my father took us to a feast. There my brothers became very cheerful. I, however, was sad. Then my father approached me and ordered me to enjoy the delicious dishes. But I could not, whereupon my father, becoming angry, banished me from his sight.

I turned my footsteps and, my heart full of infinite love for those who disdained it, I wandered into far-off regions. For long years I felt torn between the greatest grief and the greatest love. And so the news of my mother's death reached me. I hastened to see her, and my father, mellowed by sorrow, did not hinder my entrance. Then I saw her corpse. Tears flowed from my eyes. I saw her lie there like the old happy past, in which according to the deceased's desire we were to live as she had done herself. And we followed her body in sorrow, and the coffin sank to the earth. – From that time on I again remained at home.

Then my father once more took me to his favourite garden. He asked whether I liked it. But the garden wholly repelled me, and I dared not say so. Then, reddening, he asked me a second time: did the garden please me? I denied it, trembling. At that my father struck me, and I fled. And I turned away a second time. And with a heart filled with endless love for those who scorned me, I again wandered far away. For many and many a year I sang songs. Whenever I attempted to sing of love, it turned to pain. And again, when I tried to sing of pain, it turned to love. And so love and pain were divided in me.

And one day I had news of a gentle maiden who had just died. And a circle formed around her grave in which many young and old men walked as though in everlasting bliss. They spoke softly, so as not to wake the young woman. Heavenly thoughts seemed for ever to be showered on the young men from the maiden's gravestone, like fine sparks producing a gentle rustling. I too longed sorely to walk there. Only a miracle, however, can lead you to that circle, they said. But I went to the gravestone with slow steps and lowered gaze, filled with devotion and firm belief, and before I was aware of it, I found myself in the circle, which uttered a wondrously lovely sound; and I felt as though eternal bliss were gathered together into a single moment. I saw my father too, reconciled and loving. He took me in his arms and wept. But not as much as I.

Franz Schubert[4]

One reason why Schubert's *Traumbild* grabs our attention is because it presents many biographical parallels: the death of his mother, an authoritarian father, many brothers and sisters, the death of a young woman, and the portrayal of the protagonist as a solitary Romantic artist. The short story allegorically describes his father inviting him to a feast and tempting him into the gardens of Homer's Alcinous. How do we imagine and interpret such scenes? Schubert's brother, Anton, was among the first to suggest that the two banishments by the father disclose Schubert's two periods of exile from the family home.[5] Chronologically, the first was before his mother died. The second could be Autumn 1816 when he moved in with Schober, but more likely it was the summer of 1818 when he fled to Zseliz. The allegory was written six months before Schubert's first written acknowledgement of the syphilitic copper rash that did 'not permit [him] to leave the house.'[6]

The story is written in the poetic, aphoristic tradition of Novalis, Hölderlin and Friedrich Schlegel, writers who were central to the programmatic social liberalism of the reading circle.[7] Schwind's and Schober's transcriptions made during Schubert's life and shortly after his death bear witness to their identification with his tale.[8] By the time Schubert wrote it, he had set a handful of Novalis's poems from the *Geistliche Lieder*, the most obvious resonance being in 'Nachthymne' (D 687), the fourth of Novalis's *Hymnen an die Nacht* (*Hymns to the Night*), where the grave is the scene of mystical revelation. Ilija Dürhammer has identified a direct correlation between 'Mein Traum' and the allegorical fairy tale 'Hyazinth und Rosenblüte' from Novalis's fragmentary novel *Die Lehrlinge zu Sais*.[9] Both storylines portray a pilgrim's journey to self-knowledge – a quest which the father does not understand – happy siblings of a protagonist who is sad and isolates himself, as well as a mysterious young woman who lies at the end of this path. The Neverland setting, bright schematic figures and magic circle is like Goethe's *Das Märchen*, which for Novalis was like 'a narrated opera'.

The father figure as a point of departure and homecoming leading the protagonist back to his inner self are common tropes in the nineteenth-century *Bildungsoman*. Both literary tropes have resonances with many early Romantic texts including Ludwig Tieck's *Herzensergießungen eines kunstliebenden Klosterbruders* (1796) and Wilhelm Heinrich Wackenroder's novella *Das merkwürdige musikalische Leben des Tonkünstlers Joseph Berglinger* (1797), where the protagonist is the prototype of the Romantic wanderer, whose isolation from his father, his contemporaries and society are illustrative of the conflict between a musical spirit and a prosaic life. This journeying trope is a common quest for truth and inner peace in Schubert's songs. The most striking parallel of parting with family and wandering far away is in 'Drang in die Ferne' (D 770) composed in the early months of 1823: 'Let me go,' Schubert sings, 'I must ask for a parting kiss. Father and mother, you must not be angry. I love you dearly, but a wild urge drives me to the forest and beyond, far from home.' While many enigmatic symbols of Schubert's story all have precedents in Novalis – the virgin, the grave, the forbidden nature of the realm, the reunion with the father, the bond of tears; the efficacy of music, wonder of a fairy tale and oneiric narrative – Schubert's *Traumbild* moves beyond these literary tropes to embrace the metaphysical.[10]

In order to see the real connection to Novalis in 'Mein Traum' one has to remember that he was not an artist in an ivory tower but a scientist engaged in mining. As is clear from his *Hymns to the Night*, he, like many a contemporary scientist, had studied the findings of astronomers and was aware of the vast expanses of our universe and beyond. He was fascinated by the sources of light and by the vast dimensions of the universe from which it originates. For Novalis there is a still more important dimension to life. In his work in mining, he spends time under the earth – in the inside of things. Here is a dimension of reaching into the memory of humanity by digging into the earth and, by correlation, a descent into the 'interior' of the human psyche 'in which truth dwells'.[11] 'We dream of journeys through the cosmos – is the cosmos, then, not within us?' The mysterious path leads inwards. Within the self, in one's own conscious life, one finds fundamental meaning. For Novalis, there is an exterior world in which he lives and an inner world where ultimate meaning is to be found. It is at the grave of the deceased beloved, Sophie von Kühn, that he gains a higher understanding of the world and ascribes to her universal significance.

As in classical iconography and nineteenth-century German literature, the grave in Schubert's story is related to the feminine: a place of safety, birth and growth, a loving symbol embracing sadness. The grave in 'Mein Traum' and 'Ihr Grab' (D 736), also composed in 1822, represents a graveyard within: lost love, repressed desire, memories of happier times. The young woman made her way to the grave when life closed in with real existential conflicts from which there was no apparent issue.[12] Ferdinand Schubert's designation of the story as a dream codifies some secret desire or life for the person Schubert has lost. The story's protagonist first seeks an answer by the tomb of his mother, who carried his life into the depths and darkness of the earth. Here, as in his music, his mother's image haunts him because it is connected with the deepest and oldest emotions he can remember. The second answer he seeks is by the graveside of his beloved. Once again Schubert's 'dead' are extremely powerful.

Much has been made of the young woman in 'Mein Traum', who has been read as St Cecilia, patroness of music[13] and a recognition of the composer's true calling.[14] Without making too trim a fit between Schubert and his tale, there are many possible scenes of familial reconciliation: his mother's burial being the most obvious, less obvious the Lichtental funeral of Klara Wagner, who died in the darkest days of January 1818. But it is much more likely that 'Mein Traum' symbolizes the embrace of domestic kindness in the physical crisis of 1822. It is clear that Schubert could not do without the love and security that he received from family whenever he was unwell. It is equally clear that at a certain level of his existence he needed to be an outcast: this was one of the motives which brought him to the young woman whom Schubert represents as a watershed in his life and art. At the grave of his beloved, he experiences some kind of initiation, the arrival of knowledge of an ultimate reality, the principal turning point in his life. It is an image of what must vanish, the inevitable evolution of things. The story codifies an important development in the transformation of Schubert's self: a near encounter with death, grief and inescapable destiny. *Mors janua vitae*: death as a door to understanding life, his life's purpose and accompanying intimations of immortality. In his story Schubert draws around him a circle into which nothing can intrude but music and those most loved. It is a circle to the spirit, a gateway to regeneration with love as its vital, transforming force. As in Rousseau's *Émile*, love of the young woman symbolizes the arrival of wisdom (*philosophia*), but what is most interesting is how Schubert entwines this image with music and uses it to his own end. Here, as in his songs, music is a symbol of a natural order to which humanity aspires.

One thing that is certain in 'Mein Traum' is that, unlike *Winterreise*, it ends: the time comes, prophecies are fulfilled, loved ones are united, the world is changed. Do we stand on the brink of apotheosis or renunciation? If in its final lines we look into a new epoch, that is a formula with which all fairy tales properly conclude. The narratives of ordinary individual lives, which begin in chance, can only end in renunciation or a miracle that provisionally and artificially anticipates the resolution of contradictions in divinity and death. Schubert recognizes what can only be ideal. In the circle, men possess this ideal but only in the form of an inaccessible secret which is impossible to release into the public world. The end of 'Mein Traum' points us to the Ideal because that is the goal to which we are all bound, and only stories can end with that goal achieved. 'Das offenbare Geheimnis', 'the open secret' or 'the mystery revealed', in 'Mein Traum' is that autonomy is an illusion constructed out of all its partial interpretations. By resolutely remaining a puzzle, by continually provoking scholars to decipher it, 'Mein Traum' – like *Winterreise* – reminds us that the material of art is meaning and from this seed has grown two centuries of intriguing interpretation.

One possible interpretation is that the story marks a watershed in Schubert's life: the beloved enters a realm of sacred darkness (the grave of 'Mein Traum') in which the only prospect of life is the hope for her glorious re-emergence in song. Such renunciation, the allegory suggests, is the act of an artist who believes his happiness is dependent on a power beyond his control. Schubert's *Pilgrim's Progress* is an allegory of a spiritual journey which acknowledges the inscrutability of fate and contingency of circumstance.

'DEATH AND THE MAIDEN': SCHUBERT'S *FEMME INCONNUE*

'O rose, thou art sick!
The invisible worm
That flies in the night,
In the howling storm,

Has found out thy bed
Of crimson joy:
And his dark secret love
Does thy life destroy.'

William Blake

The sexual continence Schubert had contemplated in his diary on 8 September 1816[15] had proved impossible and driven him into the arms of some berserk passion that could only have occurred in a clandestine world of partial disclosures. Whether or not that dance of death was prostitution or an illicit affair, Schubert's encounter had momentous consequences. He underwent a personal physical and moral experience of such intensity that it left traces in major works he conceived in the remaining years of his life. Who is the *femme inconnue* of Schubert's 'Mein Traum'? And what happened after he left Therese Grob?

Therese married Johann Bergmann (1797–1875), a baker, on 21 November 1820.[16] The event whipped up again Schubert's quiescent desire for her: the woman for whom he once seemed destined was marrying someone else. The pain of her departing from him had somehow to be made his own, accommodated to his personality so that it might eventually issue from him in musical form. Schubert had an unfinished past alive in his present and during the month of November he shied away from composition completely, except for a single song, a maudlin setting of Heinrich Hüttenbrenner's 'Der Jüngling auf dem Hügel' (D 702), op. 8, no. 1. The song is an epitaph of their liaison, a painful recollection of a particular happiness which neither of them would know again. Even from a biographical point of view there is something retrogressive about the work. Schubert's reminiscences of her sound distressed not shattered.

One possible *femme inconnue* hides herself in 'Der zürnenden Diana' (D 707), which he composed for Katharina Lászny von Folkusfálva (1789–1828), operatic soprano and daughter of the composer, Balthasar Buchwieser, Kapellmeister at the Theater der Wien from 1815. Katharina enjoyed a very successful career at the Theater an der Wien and Kärntnertortheater where she was 'almost unrivalled in integrating acting and singing'.[17] Among her most important roles were Susanna in Mozart's *Le nozze di Figaro* and the Princess of Navarre in Boieldieu's *Jean de Paris*. Before Schubert was formally introduced to her in 1819, she had lived a very full life, and it was hardly concerned with proprieties. Shortly after they were introduced, Schubert began performing at soirées at her Wieden suburban home (today Paniglstrasse no. 7). The manuscript of 'Der zürnenden Diana' (D 707, two versions, December 1820), which Schubert composed for her, is laden with pencil corrections. When news of Katharina's illness became known in 1825, Schubert published D 707 with 'Nachtstück' (Nocturne D 672), the first version of which he had composed in October 1819. 'Nachtstück' is Mayrhofer's Harper, who gives up on life when he loses his Sperata. Schubert revised it for publication on 11 February 1825 and dedicated it to Katharina as his op. 32. Against the backdrop of both their lives, it resonates as a song of empathy and shared understanding. The final section combines a very poignant piece of Schubertian scene-painting whereby a tonal descent from E flat through D flat to C major depicts death slowly taking the protagonist. The following

1. Julius Schmid's portrait of a musical evening of Schubert's music in a middle-class Viennese household, painted seventy years after Schubert's death. The prominence of women in Viennese cultural life is subtly suggested by the central position of the Fröhlich sisters, Anna, Barbara, Katharina and Josefine, immortalized in the operetta *Das Dreimädlerhaus* (The House of the Three Girls).

2. Wilhelm August Rieder's best-known and best-loved portrait of Schubert in 1825 is signed by both the painter and the composer, endorsing the watercolour as a realistic depiction of himself. Schubert's friends considered it to be an extraordinarily good likeness.

3. Oil painting by Schubert's brother Karl of their father Franz Theodor Florian Schubert, one of many fathers demonized in music history. A brilliant and difficult man who loved his son profoundly, Schubert's father deeply influenced his development.

4. Life-size sandstone monument of Christ on the Mount of Olives, Neudorf, designed by Schubert's paternal grandfather, Karl. This humanistic portrayal of Christ's suffering built in 1780 was intended as a resting place for travellers passing between Vysoke Zibridovice and Vysoká. The statue was restored by the Czech-Austrian Franz Schubert Society in 2004.

5 & 6. Church of the Most Blessed Trinity, Neudorf (Vysoká, Malá Morava), exterior and interior. The oratory was also designed and funded by Schubert's grandfather, Karl, so that weddings and funerals of his fellow parishioners could take place in their mountainous village of Vysoká. The chapel, which includes a choir balcony, is dedicated to the patron saint of the Czech Republic, St Ludmila, and still stands today. It was renovated by the Czech-Austrian Franz Schubert Society in 1997, to memorialize Karl Schubert's most famous grandson.

7. No. 51 on the main street in Zlaté Hory, a mountain village in northern Silesia. This was Schubert's mother's home, where her father was locksmith, gunmaker and master of the local guild. After being charged with abuse of office during the Seven Years War, Schubert's maternal grandfather was exiled to Vienna – and the family along with him.

8. Schubert's mother Elisabeth came from a family with keen musical interests. Her great-uncle, Johann Georg Vietz, was organist for forty years at the Church of the Assumption of the Virgin Mary, Zlaté Hory. Schubert's mother was baptised in her parish church.

9. Schubert's family home and inner courtyard, Nussdorferstrasse no. 54, where Schubert was born. Their cramped apartment was one of sixteen in a two-storey courtyard. Schubert was the thirteenth child and the youngest son in Franz Theodor's first family, an accident of fate that was to shape his life.

10. The nave, organ and choir gallery in the Jesuit Church, Dr.-Ignaz-Seipl-Platz 1, Vienna, where Schubert sang as chorister in the Imperial and Royal City Seminary. The scholarship granted admittance to the academic Gymnasium, a place the recipient could retain after his voice broke, on the condition that he distinguished himself academically.

11. Incomplete oil painting of Ferdinand Schubert, Schubert's brother. Ferdinand hoped to be a composer, but marriage forced him to forget those dreams. Schubert forgave Ferdinand when he passed off Schubert's *Trauermesse* as his own. Ferdinand played a central role in the promotion of his brother's work during Schubert's life and posthumously.

12. Antonio Salieri, Schubert's teacher, who took Schubert under his wing after his mother's death, and whose partimento training was pivotal. Salieri trained him to be a highly capable Kapellmeister and improvisor, able to compose quickly a mass, symphony, or opera, or furnish publishers with songs, chamber music and piano repertoire.

13. Schubert's mother, Maria Elisabeth Catharina Vietz. Her independent spirit prepared her for the turmoil of her first fifteen years of marriage – constantly being pregnant, and navigating the grief of carrying ten children to the grave. If history tends to obliterate his maternal lineage, Schubert ensures his mother has her place.

14. Therese Grob, whose solo soprano performance in Schubert's first Mass in F major at the Lichtenthal Church may have been the agent of Schubert's awakening to a sexual desire expressed in 'Gretchen am Spinnrade' composed a fortnight later. Schubert composed eight songs on her name day and was uneasily contemplating marriage.

15. Schubert's best friend, Franz von Schober, a dandy of great *attrattiva*, who kept a permanent place in Schubert's life. The tragedy of Schober's life – losing his father when he was six and the subsequent loss of his three siblings before he turned thirty – casts light on his career and relationship with Schubert.

16. Schubert's original gravestone in Währing Cemetery, designed by Franz von Schober with Ludwig Förster, is a memorial of Schober's friendship with the composer which incorporated love, material support and solidarity. The simply styled gravestone was carved by Anton Wasserburger, and the bust sculpted by Josef Alois Dialer.

year he dedicated his piano duet, *Divertissement à l'hongroise* (D 818, op. 54) in G minor to her. When she died on 9 July 1828, Schubert did not compose anything for a month.

In the vast array of research into Schubert's possible lovers, Katharina is never suspected because nineteenth-century sexism has portrayed Schubert as short and shy, as if any woman of substance would not see beyond that. Schubert scholarship is laden with sexist assumptions about the avenues in which syphilis was transmitted through prostitution or lower-class women such as the Zseliz chambermaid, Josefine (Pepi) Pöcklhofer (1797–1879), who lived to be eighty-two.[18] Syphilis was one of the most common causes of female (and infant) mortality in the nineteenth century: women were unprotected and uninformed by their doctors, who chose to guard their husbands' reputations.[19] Mercury was reputedly given for morning sickness and infants infected with syphilis were left in foundling homes.

The archetype of the *femme fatale* or 'poison woman' of nineteenth-century literature and art partly reflects the devastation of syphilis because women were stigmatized and blamed for the transmission of the disease. John Keats's 'La Belle Dame sans Merci' and *Lamia* are classic examples, and in Schubert's output 'Death and the Maiden' could be read as the sexual commerce of a sick man with a healthy woman or 'Der Fischer' as a song of fatal seduction.

Three days after the dedication of 'Der zürnenden Diana' and 'Nachtstück' to Katharina Lászny von Folkusfálva was announced in the Viennese papers on Valentine's Day 1825, the twenty-one-year-old Schwind wrote of Vienna's thirty-six-year-old *femme fatale*, 'What a woman! If she were not nearly twice as old as I am, and regrettably always ill, I would have to leave Vienna, for it would be more than I could stand. Schubert has known [Katharina] for a long time, but I only met her recently. She takes pleasure in my work and likes me more than anyone except yourself [. . .] I have not seen her lately, but we are to dine at her house tomorrow. Now I know what a woman looks like who is held in ill repute throughout the city, and what she does.'[20] Schober and Schwind recognized the deep and serious purpose of 'Mein Traum' and very likely knew the significance of Schubert's game of hide and seek. Why does Schwind's *Schubert Lunette* (1869) for the Hoftheater feature Diana as Huntress – with a crescent moon in her bow – and 'Der Fischer' in the same panel? Evidence is too tenuous to draw conclusions about Schubert and Katharina, but Schwind's painting symbolizes something in Schubert's experience. Goethe's Fisherman gazing into his own reflection – the solitary Narcissus – is a symbol of fatal attraction. Here – as in *Die schöne Müllerin* – the river is a death-dealing force which exercises a fatal attraction over the soul, a hybrid of eros and ego that brings the protagonist to his death. Schwind knew Schubert's work and what made it, better than anybody, and surely he knew how much the composer's own pained reactions to the great events they lived through was hidden in works that most people found so cryptic.

What difference would it make to our understanding of Schubert's music or his humanity if we knew that he embraced the agonized intimacy of prostitution? It would not even confirm the composer's orientation because male prostitution was long institutionalized in nineteenth-century Vienna despite same-sex relationships being forbidden by the church.[21] The end of legal sanctions against sodomy through the Napoleonic Code allowed the male sex trade to flourish in the capital of Catholicism in central Europe. Male prostitutes enjoyed a certain freedom from policing in comparison to female sex workers, not least because of the reduced recognition of male prostitution as a social phenomenon including steady relationships with varying forms of compensation: monetary, manuscript paper, food or shelter. Weren't Schubert's relationships with Vogl and Mayrhofer conceived along such lines? What difference would it make if we knew Schubert's love for Schober were consummated? What difference would it make if we knew he and Katharina were lovers rather than friends? Whomever he loved, we should respect his choice to allow the world to know what he became and achieved, but to cloak his experience in art.

Spaun's reaction to Kreissle von Hellborn's discussion of Schubert's private life was not nineteenth-century reticence but a recognition of privacy as a basic dignity and human right.[22] Schober guarded Schubert's privacy and left unanswered Luib's unpublished letter enquiring into 'the erotic side of Schubert's existence'.[23] Only to Bauernfeld did he allude to a 'love story of Schubert's which not a soul knows, as I am the only one in the secret and I have not confessed it to anyone'.[24] I can think of no compelling reason why Schober or the Pachlers or Anselm Hüttenbrenner should have revealed the more private and intimate details of Schubert's life. The real point is that Schubert did love, and loved deeply through his art. Baldassarre believes, 'Schubert was a person of public interest and that is why questions on his sexual orientation became as important as questions on formal strategies in his music.'[25] Is forfeiting the right to privacy a consequence of producing great works of art?

On the evidence left behind we cannot know Schubert's sexual orientation. Even in his music it is ambiguous. In 'Nähe des Geliebten' the beloved is masculine, whose absence is transformed into presence by the power of (musical) thought. Whether 'he' is human or divine is left unspecified. Was Schubert allowing himself to be inspired by instinct or by a more publicly acknowledged intellectual tradition? The androgyne, the fully bisexual human being, was, according to alchemists, one of the symbols of perfection. The goal of their activities, the Philosopher's Stone, was sometimes called 'the Hermaphrodite'. Behind Schubert's fascination with Goethe's orphan, Mignon, lay a transformative cultural tradition. Goethe's translation of Cellini's *Autobiography* gave liaisons (male and female) among the artists of sixteenth-century Italy an evident appeal and provided an intimation of an epoch in which world and artist and work of art made up a single harmonious image. Without making any allusions to alchemy, Wilhelm von Humboldt published essays in the earliest issues of the *Horae* in 1795 on the anatomical difference of the sexes and on the necessary hermaphroditic nature of the human ideal and its representation in Greek art: if the ideal was not to be exclusive to one sex but was nevertheless, as Schiller in his *Aesthetic Letters* demanded, to be attainable in the real world, it had to be represented as either asexual or bisexual. The consequence of

Schiller's *Aesthetic Letters* for Schubert's circle is apparent: the androgyne became a recurrent theme in Schubert's art. In 'Nähe des Geliebten' male and female are fused in a representation of the ultimately desirable goal. In his art as in his life, Schubert is concerned with the mysteries of life, of purpose and identity.

All we can really know is when Schubert contracted syphilis at the age of twenty-five, the embrace of a lover was denied him. Whatever adventures awaited him, the crowning of desire could not end in possession. Was his ultimate frustration tragic or transfigurative? No one has spoken of his vulnerability at this time, his first turning to introspection and back to celibacy. The personal devastation of grieving over a relationship is evident in the few songs he wrote in 1822 and 1823. The coincidence of artistic impotence with the emotional upheaval of tragic love becomes clear, as does the tragedy of Schubert demanding too much of himself. He had found and lost a happiness which did not owe anything to music, but ultimately in music he admitted it.

Song is never a medium of illusion for Schubert, but an instrument for the apprehension of truth. 'Geist der Liebe' (D 747) and 'Frühlingsgesang' (D 740) were both composed in January 1822, in the belief that fulfilment of the heart's desire is tenable, and that the real world, however limited and recalcitrant, can become the vehicle for the highest ideals of the human spirit. For the first time in his life Schubert portrays a love that is not unappeased desire. There is no doubt that he is expressing some intimate truths in his two Platen settings – 'Die Liebe hat gelogen' (D 751) and 'Du liebst mich nicht' (D 756) – in April and July 1822, which are, in a sense, the first songs of his adulthood. Graham Johnson is the only scholar to realize that the repetitions of the title phrase 'Du liebst mich nicht' 'suggest someone unhinged with the break-up of a relationship, and the harmonic excursions suggest someone tormented by deep and complex feelings'. Other than in music, Schubert's grief had no public acknowledgement. It was a high price to pay for the freedom he had experienced and he was, at least in two senses, drawing on material furnished by his own life.

By Autumn 1822 Schubert's setting of Senn's 'Schwanengesang' (D 744) – which was published a year later as his op. 23, no. 3 – encodes the wayfarer's struggle with solitude and mortality:

'Wie klag' ich's aus, das Sterbegefühl,	'How shall I lament the feeling of death'
Das auflösend durch die Glieder rinnt?	The dissolution that flows through my limbs?
Wie sing' ich's aus, das Werdegefühl,	How shall I sing of the feeling of new life
Das erlösend dich, o Geist, anweht?'	That redeems you, o Spirit, with its breath?'
Er klagt', er sang,	He lamented, he sang
Vernichtungsbang	Fearful of extinction
Verklärungsfroh,	Joyously awaiting transfiguration
Bis das Leben floh.	Until life fled.
Das bedeutet des Schwanen Gesang!	This is the meaning of the swan's song!

Once again Schober's 'Todesmusik' (D 758) proves the hidden merits of mediocrity and records the act that lifted him, both in reality and symbolically, above the confusion and frustration of his ordinary existence: 'At the solemn hour of death [. . .] descend one more time/to heal the deep wound of parting/within my heart./Raise my pure, anguished soul/from the earthly struggle/bear it on your wings/to be united with the light.'

Schubert was possessed and pursued by death: he grew up in a house which had lost ten siblings; the death of his mother proved pivotal and now the death of love threatened to destroy him again. Certainly, by July 1822 there is a sense that Schubert has enjoyed the last hours of an old world, half-knowing that love would not survive the winter. The three Matthäus von Collin settings of 1822 raise interesting parallels to 'Mein Traum': in 'Wehmut' (D 772) the same tension between countervailing forces prevails: within every being, at all levels of existence, death and life co-exist. Forsaken, Schubert's 'Zwerg' (D 771) loses his sense of purpose when he loses his terminally ill lady (verses 5–9):

Er spricht, 'Du selbst bist schuld an diesem Leide',	He speaks, 'You yourself are to blame for this
Weil um den König du mich hast verlassen;	Suffering, because you left me for the king;
Jetzt weckt dein Sterben einzig mir noch Freude.	Now only your death will awaken joy in me.
Zwar werd' ich ewiglich mich selber hassen	True, I will hate myself forever
Der dir mit dieser Hand den Tod gegeben	For having brought you death by this hand
Doch musst zum frühen Grab du nun erblassen.'	And now, pale, you must go to an early grave.'
Sie legt die Hand aufs Herz voll jungem Leben,	She lays her hand on her heart, full of youthful
Und aus dem Aug' die schweren Tränen rinnen	Life, and heavy tears flow from her eyes
Das sie zum Himmel betend will erheben.	Which she would raise to heaven in prayer.
'Mögst du nicht Schmerz durch meinen Tod gewinnen!'	'May you reap no sorrow from my death!'
Sie sagt's, das küsst der Zwerg die bleichen Wangen	She says, then the dwarf kisses her pale cheeks,
D'rauf alsobald vergehen ihr die Sinnen.	Whereupon she immediately loses her senses.
Der Zwerg schaut an die Frau, von Tod befangen:	The dwarf gazes at the lady in the grip of death:

Er senkt sie tief ins Meer mit eig'nen Handen.	He lowers her deep into the sea with his own hands.
Ihm brennt nach ihr das Herz so voll Verlangen.	His heart burns with such longing for her.
An keiner Küste wird er je mehr landen.	He will never again land on any shore.

In its sexual and emotional maturity, the song marks the return to a more decisive music, far more original and capable of development. Though Schubert masked his personal identity in his narratives, the songs of this period prove that a complete disengagement of an artist from his art is almost impossible. Schubert failed to elude his own demons in the labyrinths of song, but this union of imagination and raw humanity is what makes his songs so fascinating. One wonders whether Spaun's cousin, Matthäus von Collin, wrote 'Der Zwerg' for Schubert, who was caricatured as a dwarf in his circle, and most cruelly by Schober, who drew an image of a miniature Schubert trotting behind the statuesque Vogl. The three von Collin settings of this period called forth Schubert's most inspired and powerful settings of the Viennese Romantics.

Another of the most remarkable songs of this period is the first of six settings by Friedrich Rückert. The poem is a Persian *ghazal*, first introduced into German literature by Goethe and Friedrich von Schlegel.[26] Rückert's *ghazal* appeared in his new collection of poems *Aus den östlichen Rosen*, published in Germany at the beginning of 1822.

O du Entriss'ne mir und meinem Kusse! Sei mir gegrüsst!	You who were torn from me and my kisses! I greet you!
Sei mir geküsst!	I kiss you!
Erreichbar nur meinem Sehnsuchtsgrusse!	You, whom only my yearning greeting can reach,
Sei mir gegrüsst!	I greet you!
Sei mir geküsst!	I kiss you!

Du von der Hand der Liebe diesem Herzen	You who were bestowed on this heart
Gegeb'ne! du	by the hand of love,
Von dieser Brust	you who were taken
Genomm'ne mir! mit diesem Tränengusse	from my breast! With this flood of tears
Sei mir gegrüsst!	I greet you!
Sei mir geküsst!	I kiss you!
Zum Trotz der Ferne, die sich, feindlich trennend,	Defying the distance that, hostile and divisive,
Hat zwischen mich	has come
Und dich gestellt;	between you and me;
Dem Neid der Schicksalsmächte zum Verdrusse,	frustrating the envious powers of fate,
Sei mir gegrüsst!	I greet you!
Sei mir geküsst!	I kiss you!
Wie du mir je im schönsten Lenz der Liebe	As in love's fairest spring
Mit Gruss und Kuss	you once came to me
Entgegen kamst,	with greetings and kisses,
Mit meiner Seele glühendstem Ergüsse,	so with all the fervour of my soul
Sei mir gegrüsst!	I greet you!
Sei mir geküsst!	I kiss you!
Ein Hauch der Liebe tilget Räum' und Zeiten,	One breath of love dissolves time and space,
Ich bin bei dir,	and I am with you,
Du bist bei mir,	you are with me;
Ich halte dich in dieses Arms Umschlusse,	I hold you closely in my arms' embrace,

| Sei mir gegrüsst! | I greet you! |
| Sei mir geküsst! | I kiss you! |

One of the reasons why the significance of the song has been overlooked lies in its mawkish performance tradition: its chromaticism overworked, its *Langsam* tempo masking Schubert's sincerity. The song is an immensely dignified song of final parting, of radiant love which has absorbed and transcended a great deal of pain (see Example 15.1 online).

'The young woman's death' places us back at the metaphorical graves of 'Mein Traum'. Like Novalis's Sophie, Schubert's 'Entriss'ne' (the woman torn away) is on the other side of a Great Divide. The woman he apostrophizes is not a departed spirit but, in the classic tradition of the *ghazal*, a hopeless or forbidden love, most famously exemplified by Goethe's *Divan ghazals* for Marianne Willemer. As Graham Johnson detects, 'before this song is sung there has been a catastrophe which has given rise to the lyric — this is no commonplace lover standing with his lute beneath a balcony'. The song is an elegy of profound human feeling, expressed by someone who has faced reality and still loves. The heightened, barely controlled passion of the music and deep desire to relive that experience keeps the piece moving. The constant repetition of its key phrase becomes a litany, the obsessiveness of its many repeats reinforcing that he will never kiss her again. A sigh of desire transfigures longing into the miracle of a moment in which the Ideal enters reality once more and the powers that rule the world take on, however fleetingly, the constellation they had in Paradise. The heightened feeling of this music is controlled: it is this restraint that awards love its dignity and force. In the music he has still to write, Schubert can hope to glimpse again what he has renounced.

A remarkable burst of musical productivity followed this trauma of loss, just as it had followed the death of his mother. It is essential to Schubert's extraordinarily resilient creativity that in a crisis he was able to call on a restorative natural rhythm and to take deliberate, even harsh, command of himself in the months that followed.

16

THE WATERSHED (1822–1824)

'One goes down into the well
and nothing protects one from the assault of truth.'

Virginia Woolf

'We rarely find people who achieve great things without first going astray.'

Meister Eckhart

THE GRACE OF FRIENDSHIP: MORITZ VON SCHWIND

In these years of broken heart and health, Schubert needed love to lift his depression. The jets of affection in his friendship with Moritz von Schwind (1804–1871) made the world young for him again.[1] Schubert clung tightly to his rapport with the young artist seven years his junior who, in his late teens, was an incredible source of strength. During the desolate winters of 1822–23 when love and friends fled, Schwind's friendship with Schubert grew amid the leaf fall of dark years and daily visits.[2] To Schober in Breslau, Schwind reported, 'As far as I can, I share his whole life with him.'[3]

For warm-hearted men with artistic tastes, Schubert and Schwind were inevitable poles of attraction. Schwind's boyish face, controlled but passionate manner, already in 1821 gave a hint of an original and productive talent. He was immensely charming and even more immensely intelligent, and Schubert's partiality for him was patent. Schwind, in turn, responded to what was excellent in Schober and Schubert, the two men he loved excessively. Once again Schober's ability to inspire love had a mesmeric effect. 'The greatest things known to me on earth are love, beauty and wisdom. You have yourself ranked me with you and Schubert and I could not bear the delight of it. Thus has pain cleansed me, so that to be third among you means everything to me,' Schwind wrote meaningfully to Schober on 20 January 1822. Schwind worshipped Schubert, and music making bound them together. In his diary on 8 December 1826 Franz von Hartmann recorded Schwind singing Schubert's Lieder accompanied by the composer at an evening spent with Spaun. Hartmann praised Schwind's performances of Schubert's songs at Schober's on 4 March 1827 and of Schubert's piano dances in Ottenwalt's salon on 18 October of that year.[4]

TURNING THE TIDE: ILLNESS AND HOSPITALIZATION

Given the aura of secrecy surrounding Schubert's contraction of syphilis, evidence is gathered piecemeal. It is possible that he had carried the condition in him for a while but became aware of the primary infection by June 1822. As the incubation period typically took anywhere from nine to ninety days to rear its head, it is likely that he was infected by early summer when he had more or less stopped composing. Approximately three weeks after exposure, painless ulcers or chancres typically appear at the site of infection, but as the sores are firm, round and painless, he could have had them for a while without noticing or even overlooking them.

By the winter of 1822, however, there was an undeniable sense that the die was cast: Schubert had moved home in July and begun a period of sombre remorse. His letter to Spaun on 7 December 1822 was still written from Rossau, where he seems to have welcomed a release into a shared humanity.[5] The first mention of illness is on 28 February 1823, when he wrote to Ignaz von Mosel, *taedium vitae*, 'Apologies that once again I implore you by writing, but the circumstances of my health do not permit me to leave the house'.[6] In the spring of 1823 he began to suffer considerable pain and distress brought about by the onset of a particularly virulent phase of the disease. At this stage, six weeks to six months after exposure, with the primary genital ulceration healed or healing, the disease would have progressed to a fever and fatigue. Schubert would have suffered further ulcerations, a rough rash of reddish brown and livid colour on the palms of his hands and soles of his feet, perhaps even a secondary rash on his torso. In a letter to Anna Hönig he intimated the socially stigmatizing open sores that mark the infectious stage of secondary syphilis as being 'of *that* sort so as to make me totally unfit for every kind of company'.[7] In Beethoven's conversation books his nephew Karl wrote, 'Everyone speaks very highly of Schubert but they say he seems to have gone into hiding.'[8] To Schober, Schubert recounted his hermit-like existence and doubted he would ever be well again.[9]

So sequestered a life was wholly unusual for him. By 8 May 1823 Schubert's illness pushed him into one of those extreme states in which he turned to a supreme intelligence as both the origin of his physical existence and judge of his heart. He apostrophized 'Almighty God' in a thaumaturgic prayer, pleading that his suffering might abate:

Table 16.1: Schubert's 'Mein Gebet' (My Prayer, 1823)

Tiefer Sehnsucht, heil'ges Bangen	With deep longing and holy zeal
Will in schön're Welten langen;	I reach into a better world;
Möchte füllen dunklen Raum	I would want to fill this gloomy earth
Mit almächt'gem Liebestraum.	With love's almighty dream.
Großer Vater! reich' dem Sohne	Almighty God! Grant only your blessing
Tiefer Schmerzen nun zum Lohne,	To your sorrow's child,
Endlich als Erlösungsmahl	Send a ray of your eternal love
Deiner Liebe ew'gen Strahl.	As redemption.
Sieh, vernichtet liegt im Staube,	See, abased in dust,
Unerhörtem Gram zum Raube,	Scorched by agonizing fire,
Meines Lebens Martergang	My life's tortuous path
Nahend ew'gem Untergang.	Approaching eternal descent.

THE WATERSHED (1822–1824)

Tödt' es und mich selber tödte,	Take my life, take me,
Stürz' nun Alles in die Lethe,	Plunge everything into Lethe
Und ein reines kräft'ges Sein	And let me transmute, O Lord,
Lass', o Großer, dann gedeih'n.[1]	Into a purer, more powerful existence.

10 *Dok*, 192.

In the same month, in defiance of ill health, he began a period of almost ceaseless work on a new opera, *Fierabras* (D 796), to a text by Josef Kupelwieser, from 25 May to 2 October 1823.

Despite strained relations in 1821 and 1822, the *rapprochement* with Vogl offered respite when the singer's generous love took him back to his homeland in Upper Austria, which for Schubert was still a new and natural phenomenon. In the summer of 1823 he enjoyed the hospitality of the Hartmann family in Steyr and of Albert Stadler at Linz, where the duo performed for friends. Schubert assured Schober on 14 August that he was 'fairly well', living simply and walking regularly, and in regular correspondence with August von Schaeffer, his first physician, who treated two of Josef von Spaun's brothers.[11] But Count Anton von Doblhoff-Dier, a liberal politician, lawyer, and member of the composer's circle in the 1820s, detected the marks of these months on Schubert, whom he recognized as being 'seriously ill'.[12] Perhaps this is the reason Schubert and Spaun did not spend any real time together and only met at public events, the first of which was an evening at the end of August when Schubert and Vogl were invested with honorary membership of the Linz Musical Society. The second occasion was a small party hosted by the Ottenwalds (Anton and Marie, née Spaun), at the Schlossberg gardens on 23 August at which Schubert and Vogl performed. By mid-September the fragility of Schubert's health necessitated a return to Vienna, a passage eased by Josef Huber's generous invitation to stay with him at Stubenbastei 14 in the first district. As usual on his return journeys, Schubert sank into himself again, preparing himself for the shock of the metamorphosis to come.

By October, Schubert was seriously ill through the recurrence of an extremely virulent stage of syphilis. Too sick to stay in Huber's home, and unable to return to the schoolhouse – his stepmother having become pregnant in the spring of 1823 – it was probably at this time that he entered the General Hospital in the ninth district (Alserstrasse 4), almost opposite the Dreifaltigkeitskirche (Church of the Holy Trinity) where, in time, he wished to be commemorated. If Hölzl and Schober are both correct in their recollection that he worked on Wilhelm Müller's *Die schöne Müllerin* songs while he was there, it is most likely that he was hospitalized, bled and treated with a mercury salve and suffumigations in October 1823.[13]

In Vienna's General Hospital, Schubert lived on a knife-edge between ancient and advanced medical treatments. At that time mercury fumigations were typically administered over a fire, whereby patients were either steamed in a seat over hot coals or had their entire bodies – with the exception of their heads – enclosed in a sauna. The idea behind this sweating cure is that patients who developed high fevers were sometimes cured of syphilis. Bleeding and mercury inhalation therapy – with sessions repeated up to twenty times – were also commonly administered. Unlike Schober – who seems to have been more alert to the dangers of mercury treatments – Schubert allowed doctors to administer this hopeless panacea for a disease which he knew was incurable. The most pronounced physical effect of mercury on him was to discolour his teeth, but the mental effect was profound. He had already been subject to fits of melancholy; now there was a new warranty for them.

Schubert shut himself away in Huber's lodging and did not leave the house during November, even his own room. His baby stepbrother, Andreas Theodor, was born on 7 November 1823, the first child in six years after eight-month-old Theodor Kajetan had died in 1817. According to Schwind on 9 November, Schubert was 'ill in bed again' and unable to join the bacchanal on the eve of Kupelwieser's departure for Rome. Schwind added that both doctors, Schaeffer and Bernhardt, visited Schubert and declared he would recover within the month.[14]

THE WATERSHED (1822-1824)

During this time of reflection and convalescence Schubert completed *Die schöne Müllerin* (D 795) and put on a brave face to Schober on 30 November when he wrote, 'the state of my health (thank God) finally seems to be firmly restored'.[15] On 9 December, Johanna Lutz confirmed to her fiancé, Leopold Kupelwieser, 'Schubert is now pretty well and already begins to show a desire to give up keeping to his new regime. If only he does not destroy himself.'[16] On Christmas Eve, Schwind explained this differently to Schober, assuring him, 'Schubert is better, and it will not be long before he goes about with his own hair again, which had to be shorn owing to the rash. He wears a cosy wig. He is often with Vogl and Leidesdorf. The dratted doctor is often with him.'[17] On 7 January 1824 Doblhoff assured Schober, 'Schubert is almost completely well and in constant contact with Bernhardt and Leidesdorf.'[18]

Some weeks later, one year after the onset of secondary syphilis, Schubert suffered a serious relapse. He marked the anniversary with his 'Trockne Blumen' Variations (D 802), a song of fidelity from *Die schöne Müllerin* (D 795/18) in which the hero conjures up his own grave. During this time Schubert endured the typical tumours of scirrhus hardness all over the body, which induced terrible suffering. The common cure was mercury inunctions as well as dehydration, fasting and emetics.[19] By this time Schubert had placed himself in the care of the physician Jacob Bernhardt (1790–1846), who appears to have concluded that Schubert's disease was in his stomach, and reduced his diet accordingly. The destruction of the stomach's lining is a well-known consequence of mercury poisoning, which Schubert appears to have taken throughout the gloomy winter. Schwind records Schubert's slow and painful recovery, confinement to bed,[20] pains in his left arm,[21] and agonies of hunger which he suffered as a consequence of this strict regime.[22] There was little more for Schwind to do than write weekly letters to keep Schober informed and himself calm. On 13 February 1824 he recounted Schubert's stupendous industry with innocent cruelty, 'Schubert is keeping a fortnight's fast and confinement. He looks much better and very cheerful, and very comically hungry, and writes innumerable quartets, German dances and variations.'²³ On 22 February 1824 he assured Schober, 'Schubert is quite well. He has given up his wig and shows a charming trace of downy locks. Once again he has an abundance of the finest German dances.'²⁴ On 6 March 1824, Schwind again wrote briefly of Schubert's privations, his very restricted diet and need to keep hydrated: 'Schubert is already pretty well. He says how after a few days of the new treatment he felt a breakthrough in his illness and everything was transformed. He still lives one day on panada and the next on cutlets, overindulges in tea, besides that goes swimming a good deal and is prodigiously industrious.'²⁵ By this stage Schubert seems to have suffered the effects of syphilis sores that become ulcers which eat into the bones and extend into the mouth and throat. In another letter to Breslau, Doblhoff wrote, 'Schubert still complains of pains in his bones'.²⁶ When Schubert wrote to Leopold Kupelwieser on 31 March, he was suffering from laryngitis; his chronic sore throat, irritability and nervousness were all part of a protracted recourse to mercury. Kupelwieser related to Johanna Lutz on 8/12 May, 'The good, unique Schubert complains to me that he is sick again', but around this time Bernhardt seems to have brought about a decisive turn for the better. A long latent period began; his prayer of desperation had been heard.²⁷ His anxiety abated and his sense of purpose steadied.

In May 1824, Schubert had recourse for the second time to the device by which he had in 1818 sought clarity and relief from despair: he rode off in a carriage to the Esterházy summer residence in Zseliz. Once again his reason was that he was looking for a way forward. Once again he was questioning Fate. The flight to Zseliz was about the possibility of his transcending the restricted choices that circumstances seemed to offer him, to question whether he was, in fact, the beloved one, the 'darling' of the gods. As before, the assurance that Schubert had found in Zseliz was a feeling that he could survive. Through the lonely summer of 1824 he composed the 'Grand Duo' (Sonata in C, D 812) and the Eight Variations in A flat (D 813), two major works for piano duet. He also composed the Six Grandes Marches et Trios (D 819) for Piano Four Hands, which he dedicated to

THE WATERSHED (1822–1824)

Bernhardt. Though Schubert's second sojourn was essentially an interlude of cultured seclusion, it was a period with an unusual character of its own.

At first the only letters he wrote were to family, who were his true security. At the end of June, his father Franz Theodor rejoiced with him, 'We are all delighted that you are in good health', and on 3 July Schubert's brother, Ferdinand, begged reassurance, 'Now dear Schubert write to me (but expressly addressed to me) to let me know if you are well.' Schubert replied in a letter which is dense with worthwhile activity on 16 July 1824:

> Of course that happy time is over when everything seemed to us to glow with a youthful halo. Instead there is dire confrontation with a wretched reality which I try to brighten as much as possible with my imagination and for which I thank God. [. . .] We believe that happiness haunts that place where one has found happiness before, but, in fact, happiness is only found within ourselves. [. . .] I think that I am better able now to find happiness and peace within myself.[28]

Typically, Schubert looks back to Arcadia, the paradise of innocence and love lost. But he also looks forwards to Elysium, the paradise into which he is gathered each time he triumphs over his sorrows in art. Through music these divisions were healed and he was temporarily made whole. The sentiments of his letter are echoed, and generalized, in 'Nacht und Träume' (D 827) and 'Klage an das Volk' (Complaint to the Nation), written in Zseliz on 'one of those dark days', and yet his preoccupation with achievement is evident in the constant repetition of 'Kraft' (power) und 'Tat' (deed):

Table 16.2: Schubert's Poem, 'Klage an das Volk' (Complaint to the Nation, 1824)

O Jugend unsrer Zeit, Du bist dahin!	O youth of our time, you have fled!
Die Kraft zahlosen Volks, sie ist vergeudet,	You who squander the strength of countless folk
Nicht *einer* von der Meng' sich unterscheidet	Not *one* distinguished from the crowd

Und nichts bedeutend all' vorüberzieh'n.	And pass by in empty insignificance.
Zu großer Schmerz, der mächtig mich verzehrt	To great pain, which gnaws at my innards
Und nur als Letztes jener Kraft mir bleibet;	And only a last vestige of that power remains to me;
Denn thatlos mich auch diese Zeit zerstäubet,	These times are quickly bringing me to ruin,
Die jedem Großes zu vollbringen wehrt.	Prevents everyone from achieving great things.
Im siechen Alter schleicht das Volk einher	Sick and decrepit, people drag themselves around,
Die Thaten seiner Jugend wähnt es Träume	The deeds of their youth are perceived as dreams
Ja spottet thöricht jener gold'nen Reime,	And golden poetry, mocked as foolish,
Nichtsachtend ihren kräft'gen Inhalt mehr.	Robbed of its power
Nur Dir, o heil'ge Kunst, ist's noch gegönnt	But you, o sacred art, the gods will yet begrudge
Im Bild' die Zeit der Kraft u. That zu schildern,	In effigy to picture ancient glory,
Um weniges den großen Schmerz zu mildern	To soften somehow this great grief
Der nimmer mit dem Schicksal sie versöhnt.	With which fate will never be reconciled.

All letters written in August affirm Schubert was well. Franz Theodor's relief at his son's steps towards social advancement and getting himself together was patent when he wrote, 'I rejoice all the more in your present well-being because I see you planning a happy future.' Schubert's brother Ignaz followed suit on 14 August as he confided, 'I am unconscionably pleased that you are keeping well.' In August, Schubert assured Schwind, 'Thankfully, I am still well', and Schwind immediately reported to Schober on 20 August, 'Schubert has written. He is very well and industrious.' On 21 September, Schubert broke a year's apparent silence to Schober when

THE WATERSHED (1822-1824)

he heard his friend was unhappy and had to sleep off the frenzies of despair, most likely from his shattered literary and cultural ambitions:

> I have now been in good health for five months, yet my cheerfulness is often dampened by your absence and that of Kuppel, and I often live through days of great misery. [. . .]

Schubert's Zseliz letters are typical of his search to understand his life and its events at a time of deprivation. He nostalgically calls back the happy hours they spent together in stark contrast to his present situation where very little attracts him:

> Now I sit here alone in the depth of the Hungarian countryside, to where I unfortunately let myself be enticed a second time, without having a single person with whom I could speak a sensible word. I have hardly written any songs since you went away.

A window is opened on Schubert's isolation through his setting of 'Gebet' (D 815), rehearsed and performed on two September evenings in the Esterházy home. Baron Karl von Schönstein (1796–1876), who was by that time a senior official at the Hungarian court chamber, was an extremely gifted amateur singer, a student of Vogl and house guest in Zseliz during Schubert's stay. He nostalgically recounts the inception of this setting:

> Countess Esterházy invited Meister Schubert during breakfast, which we all took together, to write a four-part setting of a poem of which she was particularly fond [. . .] Schubert read it [. . .] took the book and retired forthwith, in order to compose. In the evening of the same day we were already rehearsing the finished song at the piano from the manuscript. Schubert accompanied it himself. If our joy and delight over the Master's splendid work were already great that evening, these feelings were still further enhanced the next evening, when it was

possible to perform the splendid song with greater assurance and certainty from the vocal parts, which had now been written out by Schubert himself, the whole thereby gaining in intelligibility. It is understandable that anyone familiar with this opus and its not exactly modest dimensions will feel skeptical of the truth of what I have said, when one realizes that Schubert produced this work in barely ten hours. [. . .] The composition was unknown to the public at that time, as it was written for the E. family, and the manuscript was acquired from Schubert on the condition that it was not to be published.

Schubert composed the vocal quartet (209 bars SATB with piano) for the Esterházy family and friends to sing: Schönstein sang tenor, the count stepped in as bass, while his daughters, countesses Marie and Karoline, took the two top parts, joined by their mother singing the contralto line with Karoline, with Schubert at the piano. His ability to write a very skilful setting of the long poem to suit social circumstances and the particular abilities of each singer bears testimony to a social decorum rarely attributed to him, and to Salieri's training of his student to step up to this role. Once again we detect Salieri's framework in Schubert's homophonic opening (bars 4–23) before he allocates a quatrain to each voice. He composes not only with an intimate understanding of each voice but also the social context: his singing student Marie is afforded a twelve-bar solo (bars 27–39) embellished with an ornamented vocal line which shows off her ability to sustain a high B flat (bars 37–38) (Example 16.1 online). Her passage concludes in D flat major, is answered by an alto solo for her mother in B flat minor (bars 41–49), followed by a baritone voicing (bars 52–58) and Schönstein's tenor solo (bars 59–70), which is not allowed to overshadow the count. Schubert's closing Andantino suitably allows the Esterházys' guest to take the curtain call, beautifully balancing tenor and soprano solos. Although brilliantly done, Schubert's music of sincerity is replaced by a certain musical decorum.[29]

If Zseliz was a distraction, it was also a reminder of how much his musical ambitions were at odds with his environment. Such 'carefree' scenes were disturbed by the composer's growing disconsolateness at his variable physical condition. His first delusions that he was poisoned marked his sudden departure from Zseliz on 12 October 1824 when in a state of agonized apprehension he set out with Baron Schönstein in his private carriage. As the coach pressed on to Vienna, Schubert smashed the rear window: a consequence of feeling asphyxiated with anxiety or dosing himself with mercury which typically produced violent fits of anger. Either way, on the road from Zseliz to Vienna, Schubert prepared himself for his second homecoming.

If Schubert was entering a new life in October 1824, as his carriage made its way to Vienna, the choice was not easy. Instead of returning to his lodgings with Josef Huber, the prodigal son went straight to his father's schoolhouse at Rossau on 16 October. Looking back on this peculiar period he concealed the traumatic effect on him of the suffering he had endured, but the urgency of his need to be in his childhood surroundings kept him with his family until the following year.

BEAUTY AND BROKENNESS: SCHUBERT CONFIDES IN KUPELWIESER[30]

The image of Schubert which emerges from friends' documentation of these years bears an uncanny resemblance to the narrative of an alienated Romantic musician. This image first emerged in E. T. A. Hoffmann's 'Johannes Kreislers, des Kapellmeisters musikalische Leiden' (1815) and made its way across the long nineteenth century to Romain Rolland's *Jean-Christophe* (1904–12), Jakob Wassermann's *Das Gänsemännchen* (1915), Hermann Hesse's *Das Glasperlenspiel* (1943), and most famously Thomas Mann's portrayal of a syphilitic composer in *Doktor Faustus* (1947). In real life Schubert's plight directly mirrored the fundamental connection between sickness and creativity that the syphilitic Nietzsche made, which influenced Thomas Mann's belief that disease is not to be regarded as wholly negative as explored in the character of Hans Castorp in *Der*

Zauberberg (1924). In his essay on Dostoyevsky, Mann conceded of such artists that 'in their case something comes out in illness that is more important to life and growth than any medical guaranteed health or sanity . . . in other words certain conquests made by the soul and the mind are impossible without disease, madness, crime of the spirit'.[31]

Did Schubert, like Mann's Hans Castorp, experience the opening of new spiritual possibilities in the midst of sickness? Like Schiller, he continued composing despite being unwell, but awareness of his mortality also deepened his thinking. Knowledge of impending death and recognition of one's mortality are entirely different things: the latter moves beyond knowledge of the human condition and is a philosophical position. To claim that Schubert's private life had no effect on the nature of his musical compositions is to deny any real significance to an apparent turning point in his life history.[32] We are able, on the empirical evidence of his letters, poems, short story and music, to show that his illness brought about a revolution in his thinking, not only how he approached the empirical world, but within the noumenal world, in an ideal and observable self.

In his most harrowing letter, to Leopold Kupelwieser on 31 March 1824, Schubert's sober confrontation with his own mortality is dramatized.[33] A grief-stricken Schubert opens with his most despairing admission that his health would 'never be right again'. He sketches a panoramic view of his situation and its discontents, and closes with a more sanguine review of his compositions and professional future. The tone of despondency with which his letter opens takes on a whole new meaning when we realize he was undergoing a course of mercury treatment when he wrote it and his whole system, mentally and physically, was depressed.

In this jeremiad we witness his ongoing struggle, with indifferent success, to regularize his life and restore his peace of mind. The letter is singular among Schubert's documents:[34] as the still-life painter Johann Carl Smirsch (1793–1869) was its bearer, Schubert wrote freely in the knowledge that it would not be intercepted – a luxury one could not assume in Metternich's Vienna, see Table 16.3:

THE WATERSHED (1822–1824)

Table 16.3: Schubert's Letter to Leopold Kupelwieser, 31 March 1824

31 March 1824

Dear Kupelwieser!

For a long time I have felt the urge to write to you, but I never knew where to turn. Now, however, [Johann Carl] Smirsch offers me an opportunity, and finally I can once again fully pour out my soul to someone. For you are so good and honest, you will be sure to forgive many things which others might take in very bad part from me.

In a word, I feel myself the most unhappy and wretched creature in the world. Imagine a man whose health will never be right again, and who in sheer despair over this always makes things worse and worse instead of better; imagine a man, I say, whose most brilliant hopes have perished, to whom the happiness of love and friendship have nothing to offer but pain, at best, whose enthusiasm (at least of the stimulating kind) for all things beautiful threatens to disappear, and I ask you, is he not a miserable, unhappy being?

'My peace is gone, my heart is heavy, I'll never, ever find it again', I may well sing again every day, and each morning but recalls yesterday's grief. Thus, joyless and friendless, I should pass my days, were it not that Schwind visits me now and again and shines on me a ray of those sweet days of the past.

Our [reading] society, as you probably know already, has done itself to death owing to a reinforcement of that rough chorus of beer-drinkers and sausage eaters, for its dissolution is due in a couple of days, though I have hardly visited it myself since your departure. [The pianist and music publisher Maximilian] Leidesdorf, with whom I have become quite well acquainted, is in fact a truly deep and good fellow, but so hugely melancholic that I am almost afraid I owe him more than enough in that respect; besides, my affairs and his go badly, so that we never have any money. The opera [*Fierabras*] by your brother (who did not do any too well by leaving the theatre) has been declared unusable, and thus no use has been made of my music. Castelli's opera, *Die Verschworenen*, has been set in Berlin by a local composer and received with acclamation. In this way I seem once again to have composed two operas for nothing. Of songs I have not written many new ones, but I have tried my hand at several instrumental works, for I wrote two string quartets and an octet, and I want to write another quartet; in fact, I intend in this manner to pave the way towards a grand symphony.

The latest in Vienna is that Beethoven is to give a concert at which he is to produce his new symphony, three movements from the new Mass, and a new Overture.

God willing, I too am thinking of giving a similar concert next year. I will close now, so as not to use too much paper, and kiss you a thousand times. If you were to write to me about your present enthusiastic mood and about your life in general, nothing could please me more.

Your faithful friend,
Frz Schubert

The honesty with which it is written and the whole psychological curve of the letter, from darkness to optimism, offers a unique insight into Schubert's psyche as he grapples with problems and attempts to make the best of things.

Perhaps the most remarkable thing about this letter is Schubert's recognition of the inseparability of hope and despair. Writing to Leopold Kupelwieser, he understands what hope is because he has grappled with despair. One could say the very same of his faith: the serious doubts he expressed when setting the creed were not a lack of faith but its opposite. All the reservations he expressed show that his faith never became a dogmatic formula, an orthodoxy, a way of evading the complexity of life rather than a way of engaging honestly with it. Schubert's engagement with both sides – hope and despair, faith and doubt, beauty and brokenness – is what keeps his letter to Kupelwieser honest.

In the same month as he described himself to Kupelwieser 'the most unhappy and wretched creature in the world',[35] Schubert composed his final five Mayrhofer settings (D 805–809), his Octet (D 803), and two String Quartets, in A minor (D 804) and D minor (D 810, 'Death and the Maiden'), in a projected set of three for publication. The pathos of these works points to a direct connection with his inner life which he makes in a notebook entry a few days earlier: 'What I produce is due to my understanding of music and to my sorrows.'[36] While the springtime hours of his life haunted him, Schubert recognized it was not in moments of happiness but in banishment from them that he could practise an art that was truly his own. This is a new theme in his letters but an old one in literature: the suffering in which music has its origin; the anguished yearning of a passionate soul irresistibly drawn into exile. The string quartets are evidence

THE WATERSHED (1822–1824)

of how art that takes beauty seriously is art that takes tragedy seriously. Like Schubert's 'Unfinished' Symphony, they bear witness to the horrors of this period. Their music is utopian: it recognizes that the world is not as it should be and it projects and transports him 'to a better world'.[37] Their music bears witness to his fallen world and his hope for its redemption.[38] It depicts both suffering and hope.

Ultimately the letter exemplifies how struggle of various sorts had become an existential principle in Schubert's life. Things tended not to come easily to him. He was undoubtedly a genius, but in social gatherings he lacked the effervescent ease that often attends a brilliant, magnetic personality. Instead, his was a divided, reflective nature whose art expresses two contradictory energies. On the one hand he preferred art's adoption of masks to conceal the truth. On the other there is a complete outpouring of the self, a covenant with the listener, an openness and availability: a music of sincerity.

ET IN ARCADIA EGO: SCHUBERT'S MINOR-KEY QUARTETS

We hear this sincerity in these minor-key quartets which once again were a repository for his most intimate thoughts. One expression of Schubert's privacy is self-citation. The D minor quartet (D 810) gains its sobriquet from the song 'Death and the Maiden' hidden in its grim G minor Andante. It is the only time Schubert composes a set of variations in his string quartets. It is also his first scherzo in a quartet and he uses both forms to great expressive effect. The arch-like structure of three movements in the tonic key with a slow movement in the subdominant brings us back to 1813, to String Quartet no. 7 in D major (D 74), which he dedicated to his father in the aftermath of his mother's death. It is unlikely Schubert was conscious of this but he knew what he was doing when he composed a Neapolitan tarantella finale in D minor, a courtship dance of Death and the Maiden, and a legendary dance of death.

Schubert takes an intimate theme from the B flat Act 3 Entr'acte (and bucolic scene) from *Rosamunde* as the starting point of the second movement of his String Quartet in A minor (D 804) and characteristically unsettles it in the opening bars of the minuet when he recalls an 1819 setting of Schiller's 'Die Götter Griechenlands' (D 677) with its anxious question, 'Schöne Welt, wo bist du?' Even the closing gestures of the quartet's final movement are codified. Its *style hongrois* and gypsy rhythms – accentuated second beats, dotted rhythms, drone harmonies, and quasi-improvised ritardandos – all intimate this wayfarer's longing.[39] The quartet's expressive nature is intimate and confessional: its song-like character invites the listener in. Its introspective nature explains Ignaz Schuppanzigh's criticism of the work because it is contrary to the emerging individuality of virtuosic voices in the new 'public' quartet, which had departed from the fictional dialogic quality of Classical quartets.[40] Had Schuppanzigh not returned from St Petersburg in 1823, Schubert might never have written these quartets. For the first time he was writing for a professional quartet in public performance but was still imagining an intimate audience.[41] The career violinist publicly premiered Schubert's A minor quartet (D 804) in 1824, and gave a private reading of his D minor quartet (D 810) and told the composer to 'go back to your songs'.[42] Beethoven's late string quartets, which are contemporaneous with Schubert's late quartets and intensely private in nature, were also beyond the comprehension of contemporary audiences. Both men wrote their quartets in failing health. In Beethoven's case it gave rise to the deeply felt slow movement of Quartet no. 15 in A minor (1825), which he called 'Song of thanks to the divinity, from one made well'.

Goethe is said to have known nothing of Schubert, yet a review of D 804 and D 810 in the Weimar *Musikalische Eilpost* in 1826, which recognizes Schubert's attainment of the highest perfection in art, bears testimony to the composer's growing international reputation:

> True to our journal's tendency, which forbids extensive reviews, we may very well combine the announcement of these two works, if we regard them from the point of view of the highest artistic endeavours, which are clearly expressed. Profound feeling, force and charm, significance

and vitality and poetic fire characterize both; whoever has appreciation for this species – *and it still survives in many* – will certainly enjoy them more than once, and each time with heightened interest.[43]

By locating their privacy in the past it acknowledges the new 'public quartet' and a new intimacy of expression that was becoming imaginable.

SCHUBERT UNMASKED

In his letter to Kupelwieser, Schubert drew a line under his operatic career after the rejection of three stage works (*Alfonso und Estrella*, *Die Verschworenen* and *Fierabras*) had left him utterly despondent. The idea of 'genius' – or even talent – has very little meaning when assessing Schubert's operatic career: the determining factors are disposition and temperament combined with timing and circumstance.

One factor which cannot be separated from Schubert's inability between 1815 and 1824 to bring any operatic work to the stage with complete satisfaction is the general state of contemporary operatic life. As eminent operatic composers dispersed or died, Schubert was caught in the shift in mood. For a while there came over German opera a sultry stillness, which could offer his reactive mind neither support nor stimulus.

A number of things also happened in Schubert's Vienna which were beyond the composer's control. When Domenico Barbaja, impresario at Naples and Milan, was appointed to the Kärntnertortheater on 1 December 1821, many leading German singers including Vogl soon resigned. The Rossini craze had already begun in 1816, coinciding with the start of a period of unprecedented Habsburg control of Italy.[44] Barbaja's appointment marked the ascent of Italian opera in Vienna and raised Rossini's status to that of a great celebrity. Though his initial contract lasted until 1825, it was renewed until 1828, the entire period of Schubert's mature compositional life.

A very difficult period in the librettist Josef Kupelwieser's life may also have played into some of the decisions made. In addition to his position at the Vienna Court Opera, Kupelwieser took over running the factory of his late father, who had become bankrupt in 1822. Josef subsequently became involved with the actress Emilie Neumann, for whom Helmina von Chézy's play *Rosamunde* was written at his request. When the affair became public, his wife, Anna Nödel, left him, took their five children with her and Kupelwieser lost his job. He was an excellent dramaturge and translator, not a librettist at the top of his game. He had written the first version of *Fidelio* which Beethoven had revised by two different librettists. A much younger Schubert did not have the social confidence or operatic know-how to do this.

Another unhappy coincidence of this time was Schubert's isolating illness, which did not lend itself to collaboration. For most of 1823 the Court Opera Theatre Management was waiting on his opera so as to include it in their 1823/24 season. It was a cruel twist of fate that he completed *Fierabras* three weeks before the costly failure of Weber's *Euryanthe* brought the curtain down on German music theatre. Once Kupelwieser lost his job at the Vienna Court Theatre, the only German-language opera commissioned in 1824 was given to the Court Music Director, Konradin Kreutzer. There were no German-language productions in 1825 and 1826. When audiences began to tire of Rossini, the theatre started to close for long periods: ten months from the summer of 1825, for much of 1827, and for most of 1828.

Opera was the great lodestone, the magnet towards which Schubert's ambition aligned itself especially in his crisis years, but was it also a false tendency? In his letter to Leopold Kupelwieser in 1824, Schubert recognized his operatic works as a misdirection of effort on a grand scale. While extremely ill in 1823 he had written two operas and incidental music for a play, and only had a single performance to show for it. He admitted to Kupelwieser his engagement with opera had been a hopeless cul-de-sac, but was he ever equipped to enjoy a theatrical career? Although Schubert had a strong dramatic sense and wrote beautifully for the stage, he lacked the roll-up-your-sleeves practicality and political acumen which Meyerbeer and Donizetti displayed. Both men devoted themselves entirely to opera, were heavily involved in the production and promotion of their work. After his lessons with Salieri, Meyerbeer had studied with numerous opera composers. The two years he spent with the Abbé Vogler at Darmstadt were of central importance: it was here he learnt about the business of music, organizing performances and dealing with publishers. When Meyerbeer's first opera *Die beiden Kalifen* (1814) was a disaster in Vienna, he immediately relocated to Italy for a decade. In nineteenth-century Vienna, Schubert lacked Meyerbeer's money, privilege, social skills and connections. Money still plays a crucial role in our reception of Schubert's operas – opera of course being the most expensive performing art to stage.

What role, if any, did subjectivity – emotion, illusion and self-deception – play in Schubert's desire to break into the Viennese operatic scene? Most of his works for music theatre were written during an unfavourable time in his life when he was least likely to succeed. His self-deception shows how badly he wanted to succeed as a composer of opera: in no other genre does the dogged determination of Schubert's father shine through as much as it does here. The 'why' of Schubert's self-deception is the most interesting question: financial gain and social standing are the most obvious reasons.

Alfonso und Estrella was written during Schubert's fallow years, when the theatre provided an escape into aesthetic illusion. Both he and Schober were seeing the world as they wished to see it, rather than as it really was. Schober saw it as an opportunity to make something of himself and did not realize that a writer for the theatre could not give full rein to his literary ambitions. Although the two friends collaborated, Schober did not submit to conditions dictated primarily by the music. As a result the plot is complicated, lacks dramatic impetus, there are numerous problematic scenes, and characterizations are undeveloped. The opera only contains one female role, which limits the possibilities for solo ensembles.[45] Some ensembles are exquisite, such as the emotional richness and dramatic contrast of the multi-tempo finale to Act 1 for soloists and chorus, or the music accompanying Alfonso's unwelcome suit for Estrella's hand. Above all, Schober's virtual avoidance of meaningful recitative, which resulted in the opera's long string of lyrical scenes without dramatic contrast, is highly problematic.

Where does Schubert's responsibility lie in all of this? What input did he have into the libretto so it would serve the music he wanted to write? Schubert knew the Court Theatre was looking for good German operas and was convinced *Alfonso* was exactly what they wanted. When Vienna and Graz rejected it, he spent 100 fl WW having the opera copied so that he could send it to Dresden and Berlin. But the audience for which he wrote *Alfonso und Estrella* was also a phantasm. It was conjured up in Schubert's mind to suppress the recognition that his genius was more suited to an autobiographical art of the emotions, the more intimate world of song than stage.[46] When Vogl was describing it as 'a disaster', 'a complete failure', and could see he was 'clearly on the wrong track', Schubert was claiming it was 'the best music he had ever written'.[47]

It was an aesthetic illusion that came crashing down when he worked on *Fierabras* with an experienced librettist, Josef Kupelweiser, general manager of the Vienna Court Theatre and passionate advocate of German opera. Despite being a gifted translator of libretti, well versed in the general principles of stage dramaturgy, Kupelwieser did not realize the dramatic necessities of a good libretto. The opera is rich in conflict, characters span an emotional range, poetry and prose are of sufficient variety and regularity, but there are also practical problems with Kupelwieser's libretto. It is a chivalric opera set in the reign of Charlemagne. Naming one character Roland and another Boland was not Kupelwieser's sexiest move. What is even more astonishing is that he overlooks Schubert's extraordinary gifts as a song composer: in two and a half hours of music there are only two arias. Instead, the whole opera is conceived in vast blocks of ensemble, which 'make it a total nightmare to stage'.[48] But the richness of Schubert's control and invention is evident in the duet between Florinda and Roland (no. 15), Florinda's aria no. 13 is a show-stopper, and the final allegretto is a tour de force with its varied vocal and orchestral textures.[49] Schubert's friendship opera – where

THE WATERSHED (1822-1824)

friendship and love overcome political differences – is potentially a great opera, but it needed the kind of cuts he routinely made in rehearsal. Without seeing a note of Schubert's score, Barbaja turned the libretto down. Kupelwieser resigned from the theatre. Schubert did not get paid.

Fierabras was written when Schubert was in the throes of syphilis; he did not have the headspace to weigh up the consequences before responding at top speed.[50] He needed the money. Even more, he needed the success. Composing opera was a psychological defence: it allayed anxiety and gave him hope.

NIETZSCHEAN DECAY AND CONQUESTS OF THE SOUL

In his letter to Kupelwieser, Schubert's prudence is revealed in his ability to weigh up the consequences of all the available courses of action. His ability to regulate his emotions and reason through a very difficult situation is apparent in his dawning realization of what now needed to be done and his subsequent ability to act on it. While scholars are unanimous about Schubert's change of style, some reject concepts of 'lateness' in one who died so young. But to dismiss the notion of a late style on the basis of age is to deny the significance of extreme suffering in Schubert's life. Perhaps it is the concept of 'lateness' which needs to be redefined, for the development of wisdom does not depend on age but on experience acquired through hardship and suffering, in particular through situations affording a reflection on life. Here in his letter to Leopold Kupelwieser, Schubert's balance in the middle of a complex life challenge could not be more evident. By the time he writes to Ferdinand in 1825 the despair he confides in his friend has transformed into calm acceptance of his struggle and what he will never have. His admission that he has found happiness within himself shows his understanding of why things are a certain way, which runs much deeper than merely knowing that things are a certain way.

Schubert's developing wisdom is related to the love of 'Sophia' in 'Mein Traum' as 'transcendent wisdom', 'ultimate reality', or knowledge of the ultimate truth of things. The woman in 'Mein Traum' signals the arrival of the kind of wisdom which includes a deeper understanding of subjective experience, including intuitive ways of knowing. That bedrock was laid in Lichtental, in the Stadtkonvikt, and in the simple piety he inherited from his paternal grandfather. Schubert's final period, however one defines it, is characterized by objectivity, an interest in the outer world – most markedly discussed in relation to the influence and example of Beethoven – but this turning outwards marks a new-found knowledge of our interconnectedness and it is the cultivation of *this* kind of subjectivity that distinguishes the music of Schubert's final years.

As Faust wishes it to be possible for him to be all that is open to humanity, Schubert shared Goethe's ambition to embrace all human experience. Why should he too not reflect within his own compass the wholeness of the universe, 'to heap on [his] bosom its weal and woe?' Ironically, while Josef Kenner identifies this Goethean polarity of Schubert's all-too-human soul, he misses the point of *Faust*. By contrast, Schober's acknowledgement of Schubert's illicit relations recognizes that his nobler ambition did not lose itself in the need for sensual gratification, but that he maintained his original vision and purpose. The assault by illness on his sensuous life in 1822–24 was the very condition for reigniting that power of mind whose activity produces pleasure. Observing Schubert triumph over his emotions and personal circumstances allows us not only to sympathize but to witness in him what is most impressive. Schubert's dignity in the face of such suffering, his ability to compose despite such physical and mental anguish, is the highest expression of his humanity.

17

'ART BORN OF SORROW': SCHUBERT'S 'UNFINISHED'

'And if man stays mute in his torment
A divinity let me say what I suffer.'

Goethe, 'Marienbad Elegy'/Tasso

Could Schubert have grown into the composer he is without weathering such storms, without the desolation and indignities of his illness, without the torture of self-mistrust during his 'crisis years'? Behind the Romantic image of Schubert as a musical maverick who shook songs out of his sleeves lies the ruinous belief that fulfilment came easily. It masks his extraordinary courage in overcoming challenges and his ability to withstand the kind of savagery of the spirit demanded by everything valuable, that is, the good that comes out of negative experience.

It was by enduring and transcending such suffering that he proved his worth. The only way in which he could deal with his sorrows – which by his own admission brings us to the root of who he is – was by protecting himself from them: by devoting his mental and emotional energies to expressing and transmuting them in his art. It would be quite wrong to suggest that he insulated himself from pain. On the contrary, to recall pain, to put up a musical, if often inscrutable, monument to it, was for him an obsessive need. It was a way of making sense of his suffering.

TRAGEDY AND SYMBOLISM: THE 'UNFINISHED'?

One emblematic work of this new epoch is Schubert's B minor Symphony (D 759). The volcanic originality of 'a masterpiece mid formation' offers audiences an enticing sense of mystery that has become part of the work's reception history. What has added to the cultural baggage attending this symphony is the confusion of dating and repeated renumbering of his final three symphonies: the 'Great' C major, once recognized as Schubert's Ninth, now no. 8, was originally thought to be no. 7. This misplacement led to the mythical association of D 759 as a death fragment, representative of the unfinished life of a composer who died so young.[1] Schubert was twenty-five when he composed it and had six more years to live. Death did not intervene, but it did play a defining role.

D 759 is unique among Schubert's symphonies in that it has been handed down in full score and piano-score sketches.[2] The particell consists of a draft of the Allegro moderato starting at bar 249 (before the modulation to the second subject in the recapitulation); a draft of the Andante con moto; 112 bars of the scherzo, marked Allegro, and the melody line for the first section of a Trio (16 bars). Only the piano sketch of the scherzo survives, apart from two pages of its orchestral realization. Complete in structure though not in texture, the scherzo has the character of a Ländler, like the third movement of Schubert's 'Tragic' Fourth Symphony, unlike the brisker pace of Schubert's Sixth (known as the 'Little' C major).[3] More importantly, the scherzo's existence proves that Schubert was planning a four-movement work.[4] Its continuation is also evident from the orchestral manuscript, the last page of which contains the first nine bars of the scherzo fully scored. The discovery of an incomplete orchestral page for bars 10–30 torn from the score has been taken as proof that Schubert abandoned the work.

Various reasons have been put forward as to why Schubert abandoned his B minor symphony.[5] In the year in which Schubert wrote it, the influential critic Amadeus Wendt threw down the gauntlet that 'the gigantic works of Beethoven appear to have scared off successors in this sphere'.[6] Two hundred years later, Martin Chusid and Maynard Solomon were still playing this card, arguing that Schubert was keenly aware of a debt to Beethoven in the scherzo and abandoned the plan for a four-movement work in favour of a two-movement work.[7] The belief that Schubert judged its two movements as sufficient is linked with Beethoven's two-movement Piano Sonata no. 32 in C minor, op. 111, which the latter completed on 13 January 1822, then published with Schlesinger in Vienna and Clementi in London later that year. Schubert's letter to Spaun on 7 December 1822, however, does not mention the B minor symphony in his list of recently complete works, nor had Beethoven's influence deterred him before.[8] On the contrary, he had openly challenged Beethoven in his Sixth Symphony. Here again, the B minor Symphony extrapolates different symphonic tendencies. Had Schubert a two-movement symphony in mind, it is much more likely that he looked back to the Italian 'Sinfonia', with which he entitles the work, suggesting his original intention for chamber orchestra. Two-movement symphonies – such as Mattei's Italian symphonies – maintained a lively presence in Schubert's Vienna.

Another reason put forward for Schubert's abandonment of the B minor Symphony was that he was stymied by compositional challenges and could not conceive a B major finale because of his increased use of brass. It is ludicrous to suggest he had not properly thought through the implications of using brass instruments until he reached the finale. Schubert would have found it hard to write for horns in B major: apart from asking the horn players to use B crooks, there was not a single regular crook available to him, and it would have been cumbersome with the orchestral resources of Hatwig's orchestra.[9] His awareness of this problem may also have been driven by market forces: most publishers preferred symphonies with instrumental requirements that most ensembles could offer.

Some scholars argue that the symphony is associated with the sexual encounter through which he contracted syphilis. But it is entirely uncharacteristic of Schubert to forsake a project because of its correlation to reality. On the contrary, he repeatedly acknowledged that his best-loved music grew out of his sorrows. The completion of the A flat major Mass (D 678) in September 1822 is a musical metaphor of everything of value that could be rescued from his storm and stress years. The B minor symphony, dated 30 October 1822, and the 'Wanderer Fantasy' (D 760) composed in November 1822, affirm a confident awareness of rare powers. Rossau was a genial and comfortable place to live, but the world outside was heading for a metaphorical winter; his health had collapsed by February 1823 and never fully recovered. It is more likely that the disruption of the move, other musical ventures, and extreme upheaval over the months that followed meant that the work was temporarily laid aside. It could not easily be brought under the shelter of some other work, as has been suggested with the Entr'acte from *Rosamunde*;[10] it could, however, be ignored. He had, after all, much else to occupy him. The vicissitudes of life have a way of deciding that something is finished – whether or not the artist is of the same opinion. Scores can be mutilated or mislaid and Schubert's oeuvre is replete with such examples. The incompletion of D 759 is, after all, in keeping with the experimental nature of other fragments from this period.

So much has been written about its unfinished state and so little on its mysterious origins. What prompted Schubert to write another minor-key symphony rather than orchestrate the four-movement particell for his Symphony in E major (D 729, August 1821)? As with his A flat major Mass, the B minor Symphony was not a commissioned work, but composing was never disconnected from Schubert's life. On the contrary, music flowed from it and reflected it in profound ways and there is a strong sense of music being the only available outlet for his deepest feelings. Even the choice of B minor – with its associations of 'Blute nur du liebes Herz' from Bach's *St Matthew Passion* or 'Es ist vollbracht' from the *St John Passion* – alerts us to his ability to invest the key with special significance. This is the tonality he chooses to depict the crucifixion in his G major

Mass.[11] In his Lieder he repeatedly associates B minor with absence and lost love, in 'Klage' (D 292), 'Der Unglückliche' (D 713) and 'Abschied' (D 578), which he composed in 1817 on his first parting with Schober. Over and over he expunges a longing for death in B minor as in 'Der Leidende' (D 432), 'Die liebe Farbe' (D 795/16), 'Grablied für die Mutter' (D 616), 'Vor meiner Wiege' (D 927), and originally the last song of *Winterreise*: 'Der Leiermann' (D 911/24). These songs – along with his designation of his only other minor-key symphony as 'Tragic' (no. 4) – tell us much about Schubert's ability to transfigure suffering. His desire to rebuild his life, to forget the past, is expressed in 'Am Flusse' (D 766) in December 1822 and 'Mein Gebet' in May 1823. This purging of memory, this willing himself through some process of catharsis, is played out in D 759. Too much memory and loss lay behind the bliss he had experienced. To understand this symphony is to understand Schubert's capacity for renewal.

From July 1822 we see Schubert seeking reconciliation in his own life and – insofar as his temperament would allow – with the forces in Austrian musical life with which he had felt in conflict. 'Mein Traum' symbolizes the restoration of friendly relations with Franz Theodor and reconciliation of his life's aim with his father's ambition, both evidenced in his return home and in their subsequent correspondence.[12] As the rift between his public and private life narrowed and his life again became more whole, he resumed serious composition. His desire to be consistent, especially with works begun but not yet completed, is signified in the completion of the A flat major Mass in September 1822 and his fulfilment of earlier symphonic ambitions in D 759.

For all its unfinished business, D 759 is the symphony in which the twenty-five-year-old Schubert's talent emerges from mere precocity into unique and lasting achievement. With the composition of this work, though no one knew it for another forty years, he changed the prospects of Austro-Germanic and European music. He also established the pattern by which, and without the involvement of a public, he would continue to write for his remaining six years. In October 1822 a new art re-emerged which could, in a highly refined sense of the term, be called autobiographical. In his own way Schubert took up his father's tradition of meticulously marking family dates, dating the symphony to 30 October 1822, his mother's birthday, ten years after her death. Once again he rediscovered that music could be made out of the crisis in his own life. With the 'Unfinished' he was not just on the brink of full stylistic maturity. He had already arrived there.

It is this quality – and not the 'unfinished' nature of composition – which renders D 759 the most direct and personal communication of Schubert's spirit.[13] The ethereal nature of its music, rooted in B minor, is unprecedented in a symphony. The key immediately announces Schubert subverting convention: the very act itself is an expressive choice. What is achieved in the crucible of this symphony is immediately evoked by its contrasting themes. Schubert's chant-like *cantus firmus* recalls one of Salieri's partimenti, D 25 (set on 18 June 1812), illustrating how a simple theme can be the plinth for everything from a two-voice solfeggio to an orchestral movement:

Example 17.1a: Symphony no. 7 (D 759), first movement, introductory theme

Example 17.1b: Symphony no. 7 (D 759), first movement, introductory theme pitches

Example 17.1c: Symphony no. 7 (D 759), first movement, introductory theme pitches transposed up a minor third

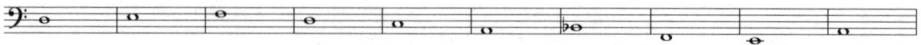

Example 17.1d: Salieri, Partimento for Schubert D 25 (no. III in WB MH14421)[14]

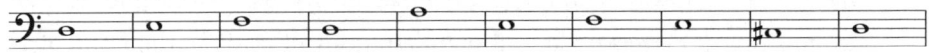

This partimento, essentially a thread, allows Schubert to transform his base and explore its possibilities as a compositional matrix precisely because it is not an iron-clad entity in the Fuxian tradition. This quasi-unconscious interiorization of compositional schemata and existence of a particell suggest that Schubert sketched realizations while composing at the piano (see also Example 17.1e online).

The dark rhetoric of this novel cello-and-bass entrée heralds a plangent first subject which Xavier Hascher describes as 'sylvan and nocturnal'.[15] An expressive chain of four bars leads from the end of the first big B minor paragraph to the magisterial entry of the famous cello second subject in G major, an Elysium on earth, which Eduard Hanslick identified as a Ländler.[16] Schubert's artistry lies in the exquisite care with which all three themes arrest the listener, being more concentrated in a two-key than a three-key exposition. The tragic nature of the first subject, the concision and lyricism of the submediant second subject, look back to the expositional i-VI plot in the first movement of Schubert's Fourth Symphony in C minor (1816) and look forward to the seamless transition from G major to B major in 'Der Musensohn' (D 764) a month later (Example 17.2 online).

One advantage of reintroducing the formality of an expositional repeat is that the opening cello-and-bass theme is so implanted in our minds after two hearings that when it is freshly resolved downwards to the low tonic and followed by two hushed steps as a portal to the development, its deepening mystery gains in impact. This ethereal opening – one of the most extraordinary mutations of Schubert's opening theme – coupled with its widely spaced orchestral weave evokes a sense of 'being outside time', which is the lynchpin of the symphony's extra-musical meaning.[17] Its sublime and *sforzando* passages are musical equivalents of Horace's 'black bolt' of terror. This is music of desolation.

The dynamic extremes and dramatic outbursts of the first movement have been variously codified as examples of Schubert's volcanic temper, expressions of extreme fear and manifestations of crisis.[18] The unpredictability of such passages can also be perceived as intimations of the sublime, which Edmund Burke locates in 'whatever is in any sort terrible, or is conversant about terrible objects, or operates in a manner analogous to terror', and produces 'the strongest emotion which the mind is capable of feeling'.[19] Schubert's dynamic outbursts are aural images of the thunderbolts which the German Romantic writer Jean Paul perceived as 'the quintessential emblem of the sublime in nature'.[20] When writing this symphony, Schubert was surely aware of the emphasis that E. T. A. Hoffmann had placed on the sublime in his review of Beethoven's Fifth. Before Hoffmann, Johann Sulzer had associated the sublime with the symphony as a genre not on account of its mass forces but its irregular 'transitions and sudden shifts from one key to another, which are the more striking the weaker the [harmonic] connection is'.[21] Building on Sulzer, Schiller recognized the sublime as a transcendent 'pathway out of the sensuous world'.[22] Conscious or not of this cultural *Zeitgeist*, Schubert's symphonic expression of the sublime is audible in the sheer force of his music, the sheer grandeur of the *tutti* which echo Edmund Burke's oft-quoted definition of the sublime as being 'vast in its dimensions'.[23] From its opening bars, Schubert's B minor Symphony sets in motion a new lever of the sublime and locates the listener's experience within the aesthetics of Idealism.[24]

Friedrich Schlegel's much-quoted aphorism that music has 'more affinity to philosophy than to poetry', a way of knowing beyond the expression of emotion or ideas, is exemplified in the exquisite second movement in E major, the key of 'Des Baches Wiegenlied' (D 795/20) and 'Elysium' (D 584), a place of perfect peace where the pilgrim finds rest. Schubert had already chosen E major to tell the tale of poisoned love in *Lacrimas* (Lied des Florio, D 857), for 'Erinnerung: Die Erscheinung' (D 229) and 'Auf dem Strom' (D 943), songs of separation where lovers are united in another world. It is his preferred key for the prose text of the Last Supper –

'Evangelium Johannes' (D 607), a Christian love-feast of bread and wine memorializing the Divine presence with its concomitant promise of return. Schubert acknowledges human limitations in E major in 'Grenzen der Menschheit' (D 716), expresses bliss in E major in the halls of heaven and in the beloved in 'Seligkeit' (D 433). The Divine is an essential component of the symbols Schubert used as he sought to interpret his world, understand the events of his life and the age in which he lived. The Romance tone of his earlier second movements gives way here to philosophical contemplation. The dynamic extremes, dramatic outbursts and key of 'Der Lindenbaum' (D 911/5) from *Winterreise*, a love song of remembrance and rest, are all echoed in the vocality of this movement.

The salient impression of the second movement is one of a heightened poetic feeling, where expressive intentions are allied with musical content. Schubert reverts to his beloved rondo form, ABABA, of the equivalent movement of the Fifth Symphony, another Andante con moto in compound time. In lieu of a periodically structured theme and contrasting *alternativo*, he assembles two thematic fields of moderate contrast: an entirely new intra-thematic strategy. Both subjects are in song form *aaba*. First subject *a* is composed of contrasting elements: a rising bassoon and horn gesture underscored by a partimento descending bass scale, answered by a lyrical motif in the strings. These opening gestures mutate into *b* (bars 33–44). The serenity of *a* contrasts with the passionate outburst of *b* where striding strings and bass trombone assume a *moto perpetuo* drive, above which the wind intone in jubilant counterpoint. The second subject, also *aaba*, is an elegiac clarinet *cantilena* in C sharp minor, the relative minor of E major (bars 66–83, see Example 17.3).

Characteristically, Schubert's musical idea is harmonic as well as melodic: below the clarinet's high A (bars 71–74), syncopated strings surprise us with sudden shifts to D major (bars 71–74) and F major (bars 75–76). Below the high G they taper to a triple *piano* resolution in C sharp major (bar 82) and an oboe restatement in D flat major (bar 84). Farewell flute and oboe gestures, voiced triple *piano* (bars 92–95) intensify the

Example 17.3: Symphony no. 7 (D 759), second movement, second subject, bars 66–83

musical drama, also our anticipation of *b* (bars 96–111), yet Schubert's polyphonic mutation of the elegiac cantilena still catches us by surprise. The *cantus firmus* in the bass, dramatic timpani and dynamic countersubject in the violin, intoned like a Kyrie, heavy, burdensome, pleading for mercy, is almost violently heightened by a further contrapuntal figuration, a frenzied demisemiquaver motif in a subsequent repetition recited like a chorale before taking refuge in D major (bar 111). These are outbursts into another world, laden with feeling, bound in strict counterpoint, voiced all the more strongly because of that restraint. The intimacy of the music opens up transcendent moments of almost unbearable beauty interrupted by dramatic themes made of one and the same substance. This generative process has its basis in the opening subject and the entire movement grows in a gradual refinement of its opening subjects. Everywhere Schubert is writing with a heightened sensitivity: we can literally hear 'the better world' to which he aspires.

Schubert's preference for seamless transitions in his symphonies finds some of his most beautiful solutions here. The opening bassoon and horn gesture between the first and second subjects is one of his most masterly transitions, heralding his cantilena with a single note (bars 58–64). The end of the second thematic complex concludes in C major (bars 128–129) where he again holds us in harmonic suspense until the horn's hollow octave leaps on E bring us seamlessly onto the keynote of E major for a recapitulation of the opening gestures (bar 142), and a recapitulation of both thematic complexes. The coda, another exquisite metamorphosis of the opening gestures, is twice interrupted by the unanimous *ppp* transition figure calling the second subject, which no longer appears (bars 280–286 and 290–296). Does Schubert's ruse signal unfulfilment or farewell? The movement concludes with a repeated farewell figuration and final bass descent, a farewell within a farewell, moving further and further away like Gretchen's ascent at the end of *Faust I*.

The Italianate tone of his Sixth Symphony in C major (D 589) has given way to a mystical seriousness in his Seventh. This is Schubert's world, with its particular topography, personal and public history, in which he pursues his task of interpretation and transformation, whether it brings him a vision of the life of the gods or the torment of guilt. When he wrote D 759 the conflict between the sense of being determined by events and the sense of being responsible for determining their meaning was extreme. By embodying this conflict in his struggle to extend music into the future, Schubert achieved a greatness that far transcended his local origins. Belief in the necessity of renunciation was forced upon him by personal circumstances in which he had his deepest experience of loss. It determined the character of his writing and a notion of symphonism that is quite different from that embodied in earlier symphonies.[25] Schubert was creating a new symphonic template in this symphony. Contrary to received opinion, it does not 'conform uneasily to early nineteenth-century expectations of the symphonic genre', it breaks them.[26] The symphony is decidedly un-Beethovenian and is a paradigm of artistic autonomy and utopian ambition.

OWNERSHIP AND CONTROVERSIES: SCHUBERT'S 1823 LETTER TO GRAZ

When Schubert composed these movements in October 1822, he could not have known that two hundred years later the symphony would be his most popular work. Forty-three years after he wrote it, thirty-seven years after his death, the premiere took place at a Sunday afternoon concert in the Großer Redoutensaal on 17 December 1865, conducted by Johann Ritter von Herbeck (1831–1877), and caused an absolute sensation.[27] It was not only the extraordinary beauty of Schubert's 'Unfinished' but the added scandal of 'hidden' treasure that piqued audience interest. In the Schubert biography released earlier that year, Kreissle von Hellborn blamed Anselm Hüttenbrenner for keeping an unknown symphony 'under lock and key'.[28] Hanslick seized the opportunity to decry *soi-disant* 'Schubert friends' by separating them into two groups: 'those without responsibility, who give away their treasures for a small sum to American music collectors – and those who lock their pearls into a suitcase and go to bed with the key, unwilling to share them with the public'.[29]

History would have us believe that Schubert had given the two completed movements of the 'Unfinished' Symphony to Anselm Hüttenbrenner, as a token of gratitude for the role his friend had played in obtaining Schubert's honorary membership of the Styrian Musikverein in 1823. It was not Hüttenbrenner but Johann Jenger, Secretary of the Styrian Music Society (1819–25), who officially proposed Schubert as honorary member. Hüttenbrenner was Secretary from 1825 to 1829 and 1831 to 1839.[30]

'ART BORN OF SORROW': SCHUBERT'S 'UNFINISHED'

The only 'proof' we have that D 759 was ever intended as a thanksgiving offering to Graz is the problematic letter Schubert wrote in 1823:

Table 17.1: Schubert's Letter to the Styrian Music Society, 20 September 1823

Honorable Music Society

I thank you most sincerely for the honorary membership diploma you so kindly sent me, which, due to my prolonged absence from Vienna, I only received a few days ago.

May my devotion to music render me fully worthy of such a distinction one day. In order to express my sincere gratitude also through music, I shall take the liberty, as soon as possible, of presenting your commendable society with one of my symphonies in full score.

With deepest respect to your honourable society, I remain your most grateful, most willing servant

Franz Schubert[31]

The words 'Löblicher Musikverein' and 'Eines löblichen Vereines' are written in bold calligraphy across the top of the letter, above Schubert's exaggeratedly formal signature in cursive script.[32] Neither the design nor obsequious opening and closing greetings are characteristic of the composer. Deutsch's 1954 edition of Schubert's correspondence acknowledged the letter as a copy and there have been many investigations into whose hand can be attributed to Schubert's *Dankschreiben*.[33] The chirography report by Gerth Neudert, Director of the Institute of Criminology at Graz University, on 30 July 1964, declared the hand to be neither Schubert's nor Josef Hüttenbrenner's.[34] In 1996 Werner Aderhold came to the opposite conclusion, believing that the facsimile of the *Dankschreiben* contained 'so many clear characteristics of Schubert's handwriting (not only in the German normal script, but also in the calligraphy) that the authenticity of the original cannot be doubted'.[35] Schubert complicates the issue further by writing to different types of recipients in three different scripts – he wrote to friends in *Schulschrift*;[36] he wrote formal letters in

Kurrentschrift;[37] and his letter of application to Laibach bears a letter heading in *Kanzleischrift*.[38] Nowhere in his correspondence does he sign any letter with this signature which is an exact copy of the signature on the title page of Schubert's manuscript.[39] David Montgomery reaches the conclusion that the letter was forged by Anselm Hüttenbrenner.[40] I believe that his brother Josef Hüttenbrenner was the culprit.

It is very difficult to prove this once and for all because the original letter is 'lost'; all we have is a copy from 1905.[41] Two further copies of the *Dankschreiben* in *Kurrentschrift* were handed down through the artistic director of the Styrian Music Society, Ferdinand Bischoff. One copy dated Graz, 27 August 1870 – presumably when Anselm Hüttenbrenner's papers were bequeathed to the Musikverein – is signed with an exact replica of the signature *manu propria* on the *Dankschreiben* and manuscript title page. The other copy in the same layout but with a handwritten signature is acknowledged on the reverse '*ad acta* Jenger/Sekretär, 15 October 1823'; a note in the bottom left-hand corner identifies the letter as Schubert's *Dankschreiben* (see Figure 20 online). The originals of both copies of Schubert's letter have since been 'lost'. At some point they were brought to Vienna by Bischoff's son, Ernst. Photographic reproductions were retrieved from Bischoff's descendants by Josef-Horst Lederer.

Even if we accept that one of these letters was in Schubert's hand, it still leaves unanswered questions. Why would Schubert dedicate half a symphony to anyone, let alone a distinguished Society? Why did Josef Hüttenbrenner have the manuscript? When did Anselm Hüttenbrenner acquire it? And why did the Hüttenbrenner brothers hold onto it for four decades?

Firstly, there is no evidence of any dedication to anyone on the manuscript. On 8 March 1860 Josef Hüttenbrenner first claimed the symphony was given to Anselm as Schubert's thanks for the Diploma of Honorary Membership.[42] In 1867 Josef added that Schubert gave him the manuscript outside the Schottentor and dedicated it to Anselm.[43] In 1868, the year in which Anselm died, Josef still maintained that the symphony was dedicated to his brother but for the first time acknowledged the Styrian Musical Society.[44] A note in the possession of his great-nephew Rudolf Weis insists that Schubert dedicated D 759 to Anselm.[45] This issue of the dedication – which is bound up with questions of manuscript ownership – continued into the twentieth century when the collector of Schubert manuscripts, Nikolaus Dumba, left 200 Schubert manuscripts in his will to the Gesellschaft der Musikfreunde. In a letter to Hermann Kundigraber, Roderich Mojsisivics (both former directors of the Styrian Music Society) asserted ownership of the manuscript of Schubert's 'Unfinished' and accused Eusebius Mandyczewski, director of the Gesellschaft der Musikfreunde, as being 'echt jüdisch' when he wisely refused to lend the manuscript for a Graz Arts Festival, anticipating it would never be returned.[46] Up until the 1970s Felix Hüttenbrenner was still defending his grandfather's honour.[47]

One hundred years earlier, following the publication of Kreissle von Hellborn's 1865 biography and the 1865 and 1866 performances of Schubert's 'Unfinished' Symphony, the Hüttenbrenner family were also concerned with saving face. The 1867 posthumous publication by Spina of Schubert's Thirteen Variations (D 576), composed on a theme from Anselm Hüttenbrenner's E major String Quartet, bore the dedication 'to my friend and fellow student, Anselm Hüttenbrenner'. This dedication, however, is not inscribed on Schubert's original autograph, which Anselm possessed. It is on the copy that Anselm made for Johann Herbeck.[48] We have no way of knowing whether the dedication 'to his friend Josef Hüttenbrenner' on the 1829 publication of 'Die Erwartung' (D 159) was Schubert's or Josef's because the autograph is also lost. The famous inkblot copy of 'Die Forelle' (D 550), transcribed by a tipsy Schubert on 21 February 1818 – which led Josef to claim the work was composed in Anselm's presence and dedicated to him – is also conveniently lost.[49]

Schubert was too honest to dedicate half a work to anyone and too astute to have sent a fragmentary work to a distinguished Society which counted Beethoven, Salieri, Moscheles, Diabelli, Kiesewetter and Josef

Sonnleithner among its honorary members.[50] True, the most he could have hoped for in Graz was a performance in part: aside from Beethoven, complete symphonies were no longer played there from 1823.[51] Had Schubert sent the two movements for performance – with the intention of finishing the work as the letter states – he would have recopied the final page of the Andante, the reverse side of which contains the scherzo in full score. It is risible to imply he would not have needed the scherzo's first page to pick up the weave of this orchestral thread.[52]

FINDERS KEEPERS? JOSEF AND ANSELM HÜTTENBRENNER

None of this explains how Josef Hüttenbrenner acquired the manuscript. After Anselm introduced his brother to Schubert in 1817, Josef undertook several tasks for him. In 1819 he arranged his Symphony no. 1 (D 82) and *Die Zauberharfe* Overture (D 644) for Piano Four Hands.[53] By early 1821 he had assumed the role of factotum, actively furthering Schubert's career by bringing his compositions to the attention of theatre directors and publishers. Josef rendered Schubert an even greater service when he covered the costs of publishing 'Erlkönig' (D 328) along with three other friends, and secured Cappi & Diabelli's 'sale or return' agreement.[54] When 'Erlkönig' and 'Gretchen am Spinnrade' (D 118) were published, Josef wrote the accompanying announcements and glowing reviews of both songs in *Der Sammler* on 31 March and 1 May 1821 respectively.[55] Then all of a sudden in February 1823 he called a halt to the biographical essay he was writing on Schubert,[56] stopped being his amanuensis, drew up two accounts of what he owed him, and cut off all professional ties.

Josef Hüttenbrenner's break coincides with the first reference to Schubert being unwell. It also occurs six months after Schubert's sale of the plates to Diabelli for op. 1–7 and op. 12–14, which must have frustrated Hüttenbrenner enormously. He had procured the contract with Cappi & Diabelli and arranged both dedications. According to an unpublished note written in 1860, he had also arranged an annuity for Schubert from

Leidesdorf. A long letter from Peters shows that Hüttenbrenner had also whetted the appetite of the Leipzig publisher.[57] For whatever reason, Schubert took over writing letters to Diabelli on 21 February and to Mosel on 28 February. The accompanying envelope to Mosel is in Josef's hand but after that there is no evidence of any continuing working relationship with him.[58] Schubert still asked Hüttenbrenner to deliver occasional messages: as late as 27 September 1827 he asked him to deliver a letter to Marie Pachler in Graz. As Josef delivered the Diploma to the composer when he was on the threshold of being admitted to hospital, Schubert may well have asked him to carry a reply to Graz.[59]

Schubert's illness provides the only clue as to why and when Josef Hüttenbrenner acquired the manuscript of D 759. According to Josef, Schubert gave it to him outside the Schottentor, Vienna's city gate in the old fortress walls and a halfway point between his apartment in Wipplingerstrasse 2 and Schubert's family home. This yields three possibilities. The first is that Schubert gave it to him in late 1822/early 1823 when he was living at home and Josef was actively promoting him. Andreas Hüttenbrenner, a lawyer of distinction, was one of the founding members of the Styrian Music Society in 1815; Anselm was an honorary member since 1820. Josef may have used his brothers' connections – even knowledge of this symphony – to procure Schubert's fellowship while advancing the Society's interests.[60] On the verso of Schubert's letter to Anselm on 19 May 1819, Josef advises his brother Heinrich to attach himself to Schubert, who would one day 'shine like a new Orion' and through whom he could become known across Europe.[61] Johann Jenger's proposal acknowledges that Schubert has already proved he will become a high-ranking composer; even before the motion was passed, a diploma certificate modelled on Beethoven's award was being prepared. Josef's first recognition of Schubert as 'a second Beethoven' is in his letter to Peters in 1822 and the second comparison is made in relation to this symphony in his letter to Herbeck in 1860.

Everything points to Schubert giving Josef Hüttenbrenner the manuscript in February 1823 in lieu of payment for the money he owed.

Schubert was in dire financial straits and had no means of paying the two bills with which Josef presented him. This uneasy mixture of payment in kind was already in Josef's and Schubert's wont. Josef's note on the revised manuscript for *Des Teufels Lustchloss* – 'this three-act opera purchased from the composer. Josef Hüttenbrenner Royal Court Registrar' – is part of Schubert's practice of selling manuscripts to friends, Schober included.⁶²

The only other possibility for a Schottentor exchange is that Schubert gave the manuscript to Josef when he moved back in with his parents' on his return from Zseliz in October 1824. Moritz von Schwind, the composer's closest companion in 1823–24, tells us twice that Schubert was working on a symphony in Zseliz. This makes more sense of the plan that Schubert reveals in March 1824 when he tells Kupelwieser that he is paving his way to a (B minor) symphony by composing (minor-key) chamber works.⁶³ It mirrors his work habits where the minor-key sonatinas – no. 2 in A minor (D 385) and no. 3 in G minor (D 408) – were an exploration of the expressive harmonic colours before Schubert wrote the 'Tragic' C minor Symphony. It confirms the authenticity of the *Dankschreiben* in September 1823 in which he promises to send a symphony in full score. It explains why he got sidetracked completing *Die schöne Müllerin*, prioritizing paid work – the 'Wanderer Fantasy' for Emanuel Karl von Liebenberg de Zsittin (1796–1856) and *Fierabras* for the Court Opera – while being overtaken by a harrowing year. It explains Franz Theodor's reminder of dedications on 14 August 1824, 'How do you stand about your honorary distinctions by diploma from the Styrian and Linz Musical Societies? If contrary to all expectation, you should not have done so, let me urge you most earnestly *to thank them in a worthy manner*. These noble societies show you exceptional love and respect, which may be very important for you.'⁶⁴ Schubert's father was not referring to a letter of acknowledgement but to the statutes of the Society, which Schubert received with the Diploma and which states that members are expected to do their best to further the Society's best interests.

So why did the manuscript remain in Josef Hüttenbrenner's possession for many years? At first glance Josef's actions are almost understandable given the composer's offhand treatment of him, which earned Schubert the nickname 'the tyrant'. Josef Hüttenbrenner had turned himself into a hardworking and disciplined amanuensis, but a report to Heinrich Kreissle von Hellborn claimed that Schubert found him 'almost repugnant' despite his seeming veneration and readiness to serve him.[65] The abruptness of Schubert's missives and consistent use of 'Sie' rather than 'Du' (which he offered Anselm) confirms that Schubert kept Josef at arm's-length.[66] When did the declaration of 'sincere friendship' in February 1818 turn into disdain? Probably when Schubert realized that Josef was Janus-faced or inconsistent at best. Schubert distrusted him – and with good reason.[67]

Through acting as his factotum, Josef had started a personal collection of over a hundred Schubert manuscripts, retrieving autograph copies from friends to whom the composer had lent his copy and keeping them 'safely' in his possession.[68] According to Anselm, 'This pleased our friend Schubert, who after that gave all subsequent works to my brother for safe-keeping, as long as they were living under one roof.'[69] To 'live under one roof', a legal term, can only refer to the period when Schubert lived with Mayrhofer, and Josef was in the flat above them in Wipplingerstrasse 2 in 1820. It is no coincidence that Anselm owned the autograph of 'Gretchen am Spinnrade' (D 118), for which Josef arranged publication. Perhaps he once possessed Schubert's final fair copy of 'Erlkönig', for which Josef had also arranged publication and which Anselm accompanied many times. This was how the manuscript of 'Der zürnenden Diana' (D 707) came into Anselm's possession after he performed it in Graz on 25 March and 7 April 1827. As Schubert's last letter to Anselm suggests, the composer may have held onto the manuscripts with the intention of publishing them in the *Musikalische Blumenlese des steiermärkischen Musikvereins* with Johann Lorenz Greiner.[70] Josef also acquired various manuscripts by casual means. *Des Teufels Lustschloß* (D 84) first came into his possession when he wrote a piano transcription of it for four hands. His promotion of Schubert's work with publishers brought other manuscripts into his bequest and he had no qualms in signing first editions with Schubert's name or initials. As he acted as Schubert's intermediary and worked so closely with Sonnleithner in the promotion of the composer's work, Josef is the most culpable unnamed 'bearer of instructions in Schubert's own writing' who collected the score of *Prometheus* from Sonnleithner a few weeks before Schubert's death, after which every trace of the music as well as the libretto disappeared.[71]

The irony of Josef Hüttenbrenner's harvest of manuscripts is the disappearance or destruction of numerous scores. Original manuscripts rather than copies were given to publishers who destroyed them. The autograph scores of two Schubert operas, *Des Teufels Lustschloß* (D 84) and *Claudine von Villa Bella* (D 239), in Hüttenbrenner's possession were originally complete.[72] Herbeck was also interested in them, but Josef refused to hand them over.[73] The discovery of more incomplete scores would have been a complete fiasco. Josef's subsequent claim that his servants used Act 2 of *Des Teufels Lustschloß* and Acts 2 and 3 of *Claudine von Villa Bella* as tinder has been accepted uncritically because until recently no one really cared about Schubert's operas. The possibility that Schubert's 'Unfinished' Symphony in B minor (D 759) was also once complete cannot be ruled out on the basis of one incomplete orchestral continuation: it is entirely characteristic of Hüttenbrenner's mishandling of Schubert's manuscripts. Typically, Schubert only wrote title pages for complete works ready for the publisher. The cover sheet for D 759 has the start date and unusually a place – 'Wien, den 30. Octob 1822. Sinfonia in H moll von Franz Schubert, manu propria' – indicating that the score was written in the composer's hand and not that of a copyist. The two movements are fully realized and in fair copy; all that remains is to produce parts.[74] What we have is not an unfinished symphony but an *Überlieferungsfragment* like *Claudine*: a fair copy which was once complete but whose last two movements became separated and lost.

So when did Anselm receive the B minor Symphony and why did the Hüttenbrenner brothers hold onto the manuscript for nearly four decades? It is one of the ironies of music history that the person who promoted

Schubert so actively and wrote so many letters on his behalf did not contact Schubert's brother in 1835, when Ferdinand listed seven symphonies in a published inventory of Schubert's works.[75] Considering the reception of Felix Mendelssohn's premiere of Schubert's 'Great' C major Symphony with the Gewandhaus Orchestra on 21 March 1839 – of which the Hüttenbrenners were aware – it is extraordinary that neither brother communicated the existence of the B minor Symphony to him. The first record of Anselm Hüttenbrenner having the 'Unfinished' Symphony is in a letter to his brother on 4 April 1842 in which he assures Josef that he had burnt the diary which he had kept for twenty years, because between 1815 and 1828 Schubert had appeared in it over a hundred times.[76] Although Anselm made an arrangement for piano four hands in 1853,[77] he did not mention the 'Unfinished' Symphony in his lengthy 'Fragments from the Life of the Song Composer, Franz Schubert' written for Franz Liszt in 1854. Nor did he mention it in his correspondence with the biographer, Ferdinand Luib, in 1858, in which he happily recounts the drunken 'dedication' of 'Die Forelle'.[78] Instead, Anselm waited until 1860 to mention the symphony, one year after Ferdinand Schubert's death. The only other person who could have known the manuscript was intended for Graz was Johann Jenger, who died in 1856. Jenger had written an account of Schubert's life, which Anselm gave to Marie Pachler (1794–1855) and Karl Pachler (1789–1850), who requested it should be destroyed after their deaths.[79] Renate Bozić's history of the Styrian Music Society suggests that Schubert had written the symphony in full but lost the second half on his 1827 trip to Graz when he and Jenger stayed with the Pachlers during Anselm's second term as secretary.[80] Perhaps Teltscher's famous portrait of Schubert with Jenger and Anselm Hüttenbrenner, which dates from this visit, was commissioned to commemorate this gift.

The year after Ferdinand Schubert died, Josef Hüttenbrenner wrote to Johann Herbeck on 8 March 1860, unequivocally recognizing the unperformed work as a masterpiece: 'Schubert's B minor symphony, which we place on a level with the great C major symphony, *his instrumental swan song*, and with any of Beethoven's'.[81] What is significant is that both Hüttenbrenner brothers knew the symphony was written before the 'Great' C major Symphony, a chronology which Schubert scholars took decades to discover.

Anselm was living in Graz when Schubert wrote his B minor Symphony. As scion of the Hüttenbrenner lineage, he had inherited the family estate in Styria in 1821 and married Elisa Picher, with whom he had nine children. After his wife's death in 1848, he lived in increasing isolation, withdrawing from concert life, rekindling his interest in theology through his encounter with the Christian mystic and visionary, Jakob Lorber (1800–1864). Unlike Schober, Anselm never acknowledged the inequity of his creative gifts in comparison with Schubert's. Right from the beginning he was far more interested in the promotion of his own work. Anselm cashed in on the success of Schubert's first publication by releasing his own *Erlkönig Walzer* with Diabelli on 13 August 1821. At Schubert's Memorial Mass on 23 December 1828, which Josef Hüttenbrenner helped arrange, Anselm's *Requiem* rather than Schubert's was played. Schober's request that the Hüttenbrenners keep costs low to save money for Schubert's gravestone was a subtle reminder not to use the occasion to promote Anselm's work.

It is entirely typical, therefore, that Anselm's work rather than Schubert's is indicated as being 'new' on the concert advertisement and that his overture rather than Schubert's symphony opened the programme. As is often the case, any attempt at aggrandizement backfired. Reviews in the Viennese press not only bypassed the opening work while describing Schubert's 'Unfinished' in purple prose, but devoted a considerably long section to the story of its rediscovery, praising Herbeck 'for snatching the manuscript from the hands of an egoistic owner' and blaming Hüttenbrenner for hiding the work.[82] That it had taken Herbeck five years to obtain the work *quid pro quo* from Anselm is related in Herbeck's biography by the conductor's son and confirmed in Josef's correspondence with his brother Heinrich.[83] Josef never showed any remorse. Instead, he criticized his brother for handing over the symphony: 'He should not have let it go until Herbeck had performed ten of Anselm's overtures and a symphony as well – only then should he have handed over Schubert's symphony.'[84]

So while Schober has been portrayed as the reprobate in Schubert scholarship, perhaps the real villain is Josef Hüttenbrenner, who did not answer the biographer Ferdinand Luib's first letter in October 1857 and largely dodged Luib's specific questions in favour of self-indulgent reminiscences.[85] In contrast to Schober, who, unsolicited, handed over all of Schubert's manuscripts to Ferdinand on his brother's death, Josef gathered up a garland of manuscripts, all for his own personal gain. Was even Schober's handing over of the manuscripts to Schubert's family entirely innocent of the 200 Gulden his best friend owed him, which Franz Theodor promptly paid? Was Ferdinand's search to procure publishers after his brother's death entirely free of self-interest? Schubert loved Schober and Ferdinand. It must be remembered that he also loved Anselm and signed his last letter to him in 1828: 'I remain your faithful friend until death.'[86] It also must be acknowledged that Anselm handed over not a transcription but what was left of the original manuscript of D 759, which remained in Herbeck's possession until his death, when it was bought in turn by the collector Nikolaus Dumba, who bequeathed it to the Gesellschaft der Musikfreunde in 1900. At best this demonstrated a lazy lack of responsibility on Anselm's part rather than malice at a very deep level. But loved or hated, self-interested or self-sacrificing, the carelessness of the Hüttenbrenner brothers had serious consequences: it not only delayed the premiere of the 'Unfinished' Symphony but the work's subsequent influence on music history.

18

SONGS OF A WAYFARER (1822–1824)

'That which is to live immortally in song,
In life must founder.'

Immanuel Kant

PARADISE LOST, GOETHE REGAINED

Complete or incomplete, as Christmas 1822 approached, Schubert turned from symphony to song. Similarities in metric ambiguity between the song 'Suleika I' (D 720) – written in March 1821 but revised for publication in December 1822 – and the first movement of the 'Unfinished' B minor Symphony place Goethe at the heart of Schubert's self-citation.[1] In his settings of summation and farewell from December 1822 – 'Der Musensohn' (D 764), 'An die Entfernte' (D 765), 'Am Flusse' (D 766) and 'Willkommen und Abschied' (D 767) – Richard Kramer has identified a 'distant' cycle.[2] Certainly, in this Goethe quartet, the music of longing has been replaced by a music of meeting: one that cannot be granted fixity. In 'Willkommen und Abschied' (D 767) the expression of love that is completely communicated and shared by another is mirrored by the world which seems not only to share but to acquiesce in the lovers' experience. The terrors of the night give way to spring and even with the pain of parting there is gratitude for the miracle of reciprocal love, that ardent desire has been fulfilled. Most crucially, there is parting at the very moment when life's purpose seems clearest. The poem, as its title suggests, embodies a paradoxical truth: an experience of the absolute fullness of love which is perpetually contained and can only be experienced within the parameters of greetings and farewells.

At a time of crisis, Schubert sought stability, returning to his father's home and to his artistic fathers, Goethe and Salieri. Many gestures of 'Willkommen und Abschied' (D 767) pay homage to all he had learnt from Salieri. The combination of a reverberating chordal figuration in a quick tempo with a melodic line characterized by short phrases and frequent breaks, is found in many *agitato* arias, perhaps most notably in Cherubino's 'Non so più cosa son, cosa faccio' from Mozart's *Le nozze di Figaro*, Act 1. The recitative insertions and pronounced cantabile character of the vocal line are operatic tropes, as is the effective placing of the vocal climax at the apex of the closing phrase, a notated a" (first version, bars 43 and 101) that can easily be imagined as a high tenor a". The final textual repetitions, which Schubert partly employs in a closing sense – 'mit hundert schwarzen Augen sah' (bars 17–20), 'ihr Götter!/ich hofft' es, ich verdient' es nicht!' (bars 69–76), or as an expression of particular emphasis, even three times, 'und jeder Atemzug für Dich' (bars 55–61) – create an emphatic intensification in the song's closing bars (bars 94–104).[3] This antinomic coupling of Italian and German traditions, of the lyric and dramatic, is a phenomenon with which Schubert was preoccupied from his very first Goethe setting. His 1826 bilingual publication of 'Willkommen und Abschied' (D 767) with Italian parallel translation acknowledges this influence.

Was Schubert deliberately trying to recapture the urgency of the emotionally crowded days in which his Goethe settings were first conceived? Or was he acknowledging to himself even half consciously that an important epoch in his life was over? The 1822 Goethe settings are distinguished by a certain loss of innocence and the beginnings of a new commitment. Like many songs of the period – 'Die Liebe hat gelogen' (D 751), 'Du liebst mich nicht' (D 756) and 'Sei mir gegrüsst' (D 741) – 'An die Entfernte' (D 765) and 'Am Flusse' (D 766) are acknowledgements of lost love. In 'An die Entfernte' Schubert asks in disbelief, 'Have I really lost you? Have you fled from me, fairest love?', and his second setting of 'Am Flusse' suggests a chapter had closed in his life:

Verfließet, vielgeliebte Lieder	Flow away, beloved songs
Zum Meere der Vergessenheit!	Into the sea of oblivion!
Kein Mädchen sing' euch lieblich wieder,	No youth nor maiden in the springtime
Kein Jüngling in der Blütenzeit.	Of their lives will ever sing you again.
Ihr sanget nur zu meiner Lieben:	You sang only of my beloved:
Nun spricht sie meiner Treue Hohn	Now she pours scorn on my constancy
Ihr wart ins Wasser eingeschrieben;	You were inscribed upon water;
So fließt denn auch mit ihm davon.	Then with that water flow away.

INNOCENT GUILT: SCHUBERT'S OP. 12

When preparing his Harper cycle for publication in December 1822, Schubert was all too visibly suffering in his soul. If Eduard von Bauernfeld is to be believed, Schubert recognized his Doppelgänger in Goethe's Harpist. The importation – late in the day – of a whole new setting of 'Wer nie sein Brot mit Tränen aß' holds the key to his op. 12 cycle. The year in which he revisited this poem was the year in which it had become clear that the life he had lived could not be continued. The separation of his own emotional life from a formal social exterior left its mark on this quintessentially tragic setting sung by a bard-like figure who lives on the margins of society. Schubert knew what he was setting when he returned to these poems. When the Harper loses Sperata, he loses Hope. Schubert's setting is oppressed by a similar remorse.

SONGS OF A WAYFARER (1822–1824)

In a diary entry on 8 September 1816 – when Schubert first set these songs – he had compared the world to a stage 'on which each human being plays a part'. He continues: 'as a stage part is assigned so is our part assigned to us [. . .] Is it a bad producer who gives his actors parts they are unable to play?' For Schubert in 1816, 'Man resembles a ball, to be played with by chance', a notion of chance which comes up in the Harper's second lied:

Wer nie sein Brot mit Tränen aß,	He who has never eaten his bread with tears,
Wer nie die kummervollen Nächte	He who has never through nights of sorrow
Auf seinem Bette weinend saß,	Sat weeping on his bed,
Der kennt euch nicht, ihr himmlischen Mächte.	Such a man does not know you, you heavenly powers.
Ihr führt ins Leben uns hinein,	You lead us into life,
Ihr laßt den Armen schuldig werden,	You allow the wretched to become guilty and
Dann überlaßt ihr ihn der Pein;	Then deliver him to his torment;
Denn alle Schuld rächt sich auf Erden.	For all guilt is avenged on earth.

Two distinct elements relate the diary entry to the inception of the song and the need to revise it in 1822: firstly, the possibility that the gods are indifferent to the cries of weeping men, and secondly, that for the soul the only escape from the self-inflicted misery of guilt may be the misery of self-inflicted punishment that goes by chance. Taken together, the diary entry and the song provide the material of truly tragic paradoxes: that the gods hold aloof from men because of men's distance from the gods, or (as for Goethe's Harper) that our awareness of guilt is the crime for which we are punished. The self-destruction of a sensibility is not in itself tragic. It becomes tragic when the soul appeals to the gods for a relief that it is beyond its own powers to bring, and yet finds no relief, for the gods have punished the soul by leaving it to its own devices. This song tells us something of Schubert's emptiness of heart in December 1822. The hideous possibility, enacted by his experience, is that this state of being is a true one and that hope for anything else is a form of self-deception and hubris of the heart.

Fate's intentions seemed clear to Schubert as he prepared his op. 12 settings for publication. The cyclical element is endorsed through the overarching tonal unity of A minor as the governing tonic, and through the shared musical rhetoric and tempi directions between the first two songs. Thematic and motivic cross-references such as the falling dominant seventh motif in the opening verses of 'Wer sich der Einsamkeit ergibt' (bar 7) and 'Wer nie sein Brot mit Tränen aß' (bars 9–10), the recurring accompaniment harp motif exchanged for a journeying figure in the final song reinforce the cyclical coherence of Schubert's grief-stricken trilogy.

'Wer sich der Einsamkeit ergibt' opens dramatically on an inverted supertonic 7th: only in bar 3 is the tonality crystallized with the cadential 6-4 chord on A minor. The periodic charge declaimed over a dominant seventh chord establishes an unvarnished truth through the cadence (bar 8): the isolation of living a marginalized life. Unlike Schumann and Wolf, who recall some Romantic idyll, Schubert makes the lover's stealth the musical middlepoint (ll. 9–10). The sense of homecoming evoked through a Schubertian shift to the submediant, F major (bar 25), turns out to be a hollow gesture: the comparative metaphor 'so überschleicht bei Tag und Nacht' (underscored by the 'schleichen' motif) leads to unremitting pain, underscored by an unexpected *fortepiano* diminished seventh chord (bar 29). With an octave leap and the direction *mit leiser Stimme* (bar 32) the Harper enunciates his death wish triple *piano* (ll. 14–15) and chants 'einsam' contrary to the metrical stresses of the poem (bar 34). This ancient association between desire and death – underscored by a *lamento* bass (bars 47–50) – is the overarching metaphor of the cycle.

The A minor tonality of Schubert's 1822 setting of 'Wer nie sein Brot', which opens with a quiet and unassertive motif, is confirmed by a double cadence (bars 5–8), his common symbol of death (Example 18.1 online).

SONGS OF A WAYFARER (1822-1824)

The Harper's lamentation commences with a haunting melody and frequent 'sigh motifs' on 'Tränen' and 'kummervollen Nächte' ('tears' and 'nights of anguish'), at which point the piano, as if struck dumb, abandons the singer to face the terrors of his own soul (bars 11–12). The Harper's accusations are hurled at the gods in the Neapolitan key of B flat major (bar 35) and A major (bar 43), the second cry of dereliction shifting to B flat minor (bar 46) and A minor (bar 55). The Harper's inability to find relief is reinforced by diminished sevenths over a tonic pedal in a six-bar postlude which forms an arch of suspense leading to the final song.

In 'An die Türen' the deranged Harper is depicted as a modern-day Oedipus or Philoctetes, dragging out his existence as an outcast beggar – an uncanny harbinger of *Winterreise*'s 'Der Leiermann' (D 911/24). Here too the onset of madness is portrayed through a melody devoid of emotion. The intransigent bass, which emulates the dragging footsteps of the pilgrim Harpist, is a different manifestation of the inability to rest found in 'Der Musensohn' (D 764). Both songs raise interesting questions about the impossibility of human freedom and the course of one's life when essential freedom is constrained. In the op. 12 cycle, as the music is worn down to silence and mute grief, the arbitrariness of the connection between virtue and happiness, as it appears in Goethe's novel and as Schubert experienced it in his own life, is brought to the point of revelation.

The Harper's alter ego in 'Der Musensohn' (D 764), the best-known of the four Goethe settings composed in December 1822, is a self-characterization (in the third person) of extraordinary dispassionate clarity. The poem portrays an image of the artist which was very much in the air: Wilhelm Wackenroder and Ludwig Tieck speak of artists as 'a few chosen men whom God has appointed as His favourites', a phrase reminiscent of Kant's idea of the genius as nature's favourite.[4] The poem also presents the concept of *Steigerung*, an eighteenth-century belief in man's will to perfect himself as part of a universal tendency. The questing mind of the *Musensohn* is involved in never-ceasing formation and transformation in the midst of which a constant is revealed. The unlimited striving which he experiences in himself is operative around him in nature, where life is portrayed as a never-ending process of renewal and becoming.

From the opening waltz-like figuration in 6/8 time, Schubert's setting seizes the insatiable life urge as a driving force of the *Musensohn*'s personality, his relentless movement as the march of existence, of life. Although the direction, *ziemlich lebhaft*, is often interpreted in relation to speed, the song is an example of Schubert's use of expressive markings derived from the poem, which do not necessarily indicate speed but vivacity. Tempo alters meaning: a waltz taken too quickly evokes unease, a manic creativity, an inverse dance of death affirming life. Schubert's ABABA rondo formalizes Goethe's incessant movement. In the middle sections he shifts from G major to B major via a pivot note, B natural, which is common to both tonic chords, as the vocal line moves from the upbeat in one key to the downbeat in another (bars 29–30). Schubert underscores this change by altering the 'wandering' accompanying motif (bar 30) without ever slowing the rhythm. Instead, he waits to break the iambic rhythm to stress a central development in Goethe's *Wanderlied* – 'die erste Blüt' (bars 34–35) where winter finally yields to spring. This central Schubertian message hidden in the middle – the composer's ability to turn winter into spring through song – is reaffirmed in the final line of B which is rhythmically and musically embellished (bars 44–48), signalling a return to the frivolity of A where winter is 'schön blühend' (bars 54–57).

It has often been said that Schubert misinterprets the poet's 'Ariel-like longing for release',[5] whereas his setting affirms Goethe's closing question as rhetorical: for the *Musensohn*, as for nature, there is no repose, only eternal activity and creation. This movement is confirmed through the active verbs 'geben' and 'treiben' in the final verse, as the wanderer is driven far from home. His *piano* dynamic and *ritardando* underscore the poet's polarization of 'Musen' and 'Busen', the two poles of man's existence. 'When shall I at last rest on her breast?', the poet asks. The music affirms he never will. Like Goethe's Harper, Schubert has lost his Sperata, his Hope. In contrast to 'Mein Traum', the incessant movement undermines the myth of homecoming as symbol. Idea and phenomenon coincide and are grasped as one.[6]

'QUORUM PARS MAGNA FUI': *DIE SCHÖNE MÜLLERIN*

'Quaeque ipse miserrima vidi
et quorum pars magna fui.'
('All of which misery I saw
and a great part of which I was.')

Virgil[7]

'Soyons scandaleux sans plus nous gêner.'
('Let us not care and be scandalous.')

Paul Verlaine[8]

In the music of this period Schubert identifies with the wanderer forces operative in his own life: an inability to rest or be with the person he loves and, above all, existential solitude. We see this most poignantly in his first song cycle which tells the story of the beautiful miller-maid popularized by Paisiello's opera *La bella Molinara* (1788), widely performed in translation as *Die schöne Müllerin*. The romance at the mill is also a common trope in German literature, most famously in Goethe's sequence of four mill romance poems.

Wilhelm Müller's cycle of poems began as a party game played by a literary circle of young Berlin intellectuals in Privy Councillor Friedrich August von Stägemann's house in 1816. Each player wrote and recited their own part in a glorious send-up of their characters inspired by Goethe's mill romance, especially 'Junggeselle und Mühlbach' (The Journeyman and the Millstream) and 'Der Müllerin Verrat' (The Miller Maid's Betrayal). Over the years Müller added to his part until he published a cycle of twenty-three poems in a collection entitled *77 Poems from the Posthumous Papers of a Travelling Horn-player* with the ominous subtitle 'to be read in

Winter'. The imprint of Weimar Classicism is all over Müller's cycle. When poets take the 'contradiction between the actual and ideal as their subject matter,' Schiller wrote, 'the result will be satire', which Müller confirms through his 'Prologue' and 'Epilogue' written in rhyming couplets.[9]

When Schubert began composing these songs in 1823 he omitted these framing opening and closing poems, which deepens the social critique and makes a philosophical *conte* out of Müller's cycle. The first-person utterance is the means by which Schubert's protagonist becomes the central consciousness in a world of abstract symbols – the Miller, the Hunter, the Maid and the Brook – all examples of moral or spiritual conditions. By omitting 'Das Mühlenleben', a poem which realizes the miller maid's character, Schubert reduces her to a shadowy presence. In the tradition of Beethoven's *An die ferne Geliebte*, Schubert places the immortal beloved offstage, thereby accentuating what is pathological in the miller's obsessive love.

Metaphors abound in Müller's story of lost love. The central character falls in love with the miller's daughter, who prefers the Hunter (D 795/14), thereby setting nature against civilization. The brook (introduced in 'Wohin?', D 795/2) is a death-dealing force which is capable of exercising a hypnotic effect over the soul: the narcissistic hybrid of eros and self-preoccupation drawing the protagonist to his death (in 'Der Müller und der Bach', D 795/19). Through the miller's suicide, sensual love is at once shown as a destructive passion (*Vanitas*) and the basis of social institutions. The strength of the love story is that the miller's selfhood is not all-embracing but embedded in a particular social milieu. The cycle shows the fate of an individual struggling with particular social and cultural circumstances as symbolized by 'the monstrous mill driven by chance' ('Das Wandern', D 795, no. 1, 'Halt', no. 3), a negative metaphor in post-Reformation atheist philosophy.[10] The mill's *perpetuum mobile* is a symbol of the normality of everyday life which the miller is unable to navigate: the soulless grinding of Wilhelm Wackenroder's wheel of time, turned single-mindedly on and on by the saint of his tale.[11] The true genesis of the particularly Schubertian version of this fable is where these themes combine and the cycle becomes another manifestation of the composer's ability to turn experience into objective symbols of central truths about himself.

That the cycle was composed in a state of nervous debility during Schubert's hospital stay in 1823 makes the familiar 'I' all the more poignant. Not only was he enduring all the physical symptoms of syphilis – including the loss of his hair – but all the changes it wrought on his personal and private life: the isolation from friends, the veto placed on sexual intimacy, the realization that time to prove himself as a composer was limited. Unable to fit into the mores of marriage and permanent employment, Schubert must have felt like a complete outsider. The recognition of how marginal his life had become was the moment when he most needed to belong, and even Schwind reneged on promised vignettes for the published cycle.

'The greatest of evils is guilt', Schubert had conceded in his 1822 Harper songs, and at the height of his crisis the composer must have experienced excoriating self-recrimination.[12] Our awareness of guilt is the crime for which we are punished, but unlike Goethe's Harper, Schubert had it within himself to find relief.

In this position of extreme vulnerability, Schubert composed the first song cycle in European music to critique the self-destructiveness of Sentimentalism, which is both the secret of the cycle's modernity and the reason for its location in time and place. Never before in his compositional life had there been so exact a coincidence of personal and general concern. Schubert understood the crisis because it was his own: *Die schöne Müllerin* is Schubert's *Werther*. It is also his *Heiligenstadt Testament* and like Beethoven he was held back from self-destructive thoughts by the music he had to create. In 'Am Flusse', composed in December 1822, and 'Mein Gebet', written in May 1823, Schubert seeks to bathe in Lethe, the River of Forgetfulness, be incarnated and forget his past life. It is in this desire to be plunged into Lethean waters (to be reborn) that the connection with

Die schöne Müllerin and the miller's final act of despair in the millstream is most intense.[13] Goethe wrote suicide out of himself in *Werther*. In *Die schöne Müllerin* the miller dies so that Schubert can be reborn. Müller framed his cycle with a satirical prologue and epilogue because, after the reception of Goethe's *Werther*, it could not be seen to condone suicide. By removing this frame, Schubert's cycle becomes an emblem of the human call to love and be loved. We hear his own take on the cycle in the opening and closing songs: the folk-like gestures of 'Das Wandern' (D 795/1) distance the story from real life. 'Des Baches Wiegenlied' (D 795/20) is a Romantic epilogue on which he lavishes his most beautiful cradle music to bring his wayfarer home. This is music of sincerity, without any reservations, but still a warning is concealed. The excursion into the first-person narrative defines – and also limits – the miller's final metamorphosis. The miller dies of a shattered self but that cannot be isolated from the intellectual and social world.

As in 'Mein Traum', Schubert's *femme inconnue* also dies. From 1822 the desired object is consistently represented in music as lost, though unforgotten, in the past. If one reads *Die schöne Müllerin* merely as a lament for lost love, one misses its true theme: the acute suffering in which music has its origin. It is this closeness of relationship between the composer and the song cycle rather than between the composer and the miller upon which its special status among Schubert's works is grounded. Schubert has fashioned out of Wilhelm Müller's poems something so utterly his own that it bears testimony to his powers of spiritual healing and self-preservation.

SCHILLER'S PILGRIM

While Schubert was writing *Die schöne Müllerin*, Goethe was pondering the role of music in his *Trilogie der Leidenschaft* (1823) where the expression of human striving for profound fulfilment is found in the combination of music and love. The affinity between the two men's conceptions of the function of music in relation to the profound meaning of human existence, and the profound role that music plays in expressing the inexpressible, is found in the Goethe settings of Schubert's crisis years. How preoccupied Schubert was with Weimar Classicism is also found in his neighbouring compositions: 'Das Geheimnis' (D 793) and 'Der Pilgrim' (D 794) are among his best settings of Schiller's lyric poems.[14] 'Der Pilgrim' sets out the earthly, restless, obsessive, surging, despairing mind of the artist, and in 'Das Geheimnis' he seems to achieve his goal: Paradise, a sanctuary, where all desire is fulfilled and he has reached the goal of his innermost striving. Both manuscripts presuppose their preliminary work – an *erste Niederschrift* – was part of a periodic harvesting of earlier songs for publication because, unusually, neither revision resulted in a second *Reinschrift*.

The second last of his Schiller settings, 'Der Pilgrim' (D 794), confirms Schubert's *Weltanschauung* has changed. This hymnal lied is cleverly constructed to incorporate elements of strophic song, which the composer is ever present to modify and redirect. The deceptively simple narrative of this enigmatic song symbolizes the artist's search for authenticity, spirituality and self-knowledge. Part 1 (verses 1 to 4) establishes the wayfarer's youthful innocence and irrepressible exuberance as he leaves home and sets out on a pilgrimage to a sacred place. Verses 1 and 3 are musically identical, as are verses 2 and 4. Part 2 (verses 5–6) of the song's tripartite structure is a musical portrait of the pilgrim relentlessly driven in hopeless quest for the Golden Gate, the threshold between earthly and heavenly realms. The mythical names of the Golden Gate – the Gate of Repentance and the Gate of Mercy – raise the question as to how much the Face of Truth hides itself in song. At the very least, this Pilgrim's song offers a parallel world in which to explore the relationship between illusion and reality, memory and abstraction.

To be a pilgrim means travelling far from one's everyday life and home. Schubert depicts this musically as the tonally simple stanza five with its chain of close relationships through G minor, C major, F major (bars 53–56) gives way to the complex harmonic terrain of stanza six as the pathway over mountains, across turbulent rivers and through an abyss brings a dizzying sequence of modulations which climbs through F sharp minor, G minor, A flat minor, A minor (bars 57–65). This journey across geography, imaginary and real, is forestalled as vii7 of A minor is resolved onto C major with an appoggiatura from which we emerge into a more settled F major (bar 66) where, for a time, the pilgrim is happily carried along by the stream of life. Schubert imbues musical sensibility with mystical depth as the music for verses 1 and 3 comes around again transposed into F major for verses 7–8. The consequence of this transposition is immediately striking as it is followed by a vocal line we have already heard at the beginning of verse five transposed up a minor third (bars 49–52 and 76–79). By weaving contrasting melodic strands together in the manner of a rondo, Schubert appears to unify the structure, but on closer examination this proves to be a mirage. As he moves somnambulantly through quicksilver chords – E flat minor to F, D flat minor to E flat, G sharp minor to D7, to F sharp decorated with a French augmented 6th chord (bars 81–91) – Schubert conjures the mind of the pilgrim in the act of realization that his journey has been in vain and all hope has been utterly betrayed.

The apotheosis of thought in the final stanza – in the telling key of B minor – is searing in its intensity as the music gathers force (bars 92–106). The portentous pronouncement, 'Dort ist niemals hier' (There is never here) — is a moment of grave recognition: security is unattainable. And yet, in the midst of this calamity, in a final almost triumphant voicing of 'ist niemals hier' the third of the scale is raised. Resolute strength is regained by facing reality courageously. The ear anticipates the final piano chord (unequivocally in the minor), its sheer depth and isolation acknowledging this existential truth at the core of Schubert's composition. The song closes, the paradox returns, and we are left wondering whether the journey it depicts is a poetic reconstruction of some internal process: whether the feeling embodied in Schubert's lied contains a trace of life itself or is an artefact, an invention.

SONGS OF A WAYFARER (1822–1824)

GOETHE'S WANDERER

Many of Schubert's Lieder are moral exemplars which appear alongside – even in – his instrumental works and letters as a kaleidoscope of hidden experiences. 'Wandrers Nachtlied' (D 768), op. 96, no. 3, is one such setting in which layers of human history are hidden. Goethe wrote the poem on the wall of a hunting lodge on the Kickelhahn, a mountain in Thuringia, on 6 September 1780 at the age of thirty-one, the same age Schubert was when he died. The death-bound beauty of life is recorded in three simple images: the tranquillity of the hilltops, the stillness of the treetops, the silence of the birds in the forest as Goethe recognizes that man is part of this chain. This peaceful acceptance of his own mortality, when layers of distraction are peeled back, was easier at thirty-one than on the eve of his eighty-third birthday when Goethe returned to the Kickelhahn for the last time, re-read his own words in his youthful hand, and wept for himself.

Goethe's Wanderer is Schubert's incognito. Although the date of his night-song is uncertain, it was most likely written after Schubert's letter to Kupelwieser and before July 1825 when the poet's experience alone on the Kickelhahn, the highest mountain around Ilmenau, forms a striking parallel to Schubert in the mountains of Bad Gastein and Gmunden. In his letters from Zseliz in July 1824, Schubert admitted 'I am better able now to find peace within myself'.[15] His letter to his father and stepmother on 25 July 1825 confirms not only a new-found acceptance of death but a delight in being here at all.[16] It shows an extraordinary shift in his thinking from lamenting the years and months that are left to him in March 1824, to the wonder of being alive. Lied and letter register an important shift to an acceptance of his own mortality and a determination to make the most of the time remaining to him.

The *multum in parvo* miniaturism of Goethe's 'Wandrers Nachtlied' is perfectly realized in Schubert's setting. The composer's choice of tonality as B flat, his key of repose, suggested a pavane rhythm of the accompaniment

– one of Schubert's favourite symbols of death – the slow sustained melody of the opening couplet (bars 3–4) which hovers around the tonic, tonic pedal (bars 1–4), quiet recitation of the vocal line whose range lies within an octave, and slow harmonic pace, all capture the serenity of Goethe's sublime natural scene.[17] The countervailing forces of life and death, so central to Goethe's poem, are poignantly realized in Schubert's setting. Firstly, the melody, which rises from B flat (lines 1–3, bars 3–5) to C (line 4, bar 5) to D flat (line 5, bar 6), underscored by increased accompanimental movement and rising chromaticism in the bass (bars 5–6), beautifully underscores 'kaum einen Hauch' ('*hardly* a breath', bar 6). As in 'Der Musensohn', the syncopated accompaniment (bars 5–8) underscores that the Wanderer is (for now) precluded from the rest he seeks. Goethe's scene of repose is musically realized through Schubert's reiteration of 'schweigen' (bar 8) and the repetition this renders in the vocal line and perfect cadence. Schubert's restatement not only of 'Warte nur' (bar 9) but also the closing couplet (lines 7–8, bars 11–13), the caesura on 'balde' ('soon', bar 10) answered by a perfect cadence (bar 11), emphasize his own heightened awareness of the scene. By echoing the opening figure (E natural–E flat moving into the dominant, bar 2) in the final bars (bars 10, 13, 14), Schubert mirrors musically Goethe's intimate permeation of Self and World, where the accent on 'Ruh' ('repose', line 2) is echoed (line 8) as the peace of Nature is related to man. Like Goethe, Schubert does not philosophize about the harmony between Nature and man: his setting states it as a basic experience of being. By marking the long 'u' of 'Ruh' with a dotted crotchet (bar 4), which he echoes in the penultimate bar (bar 13), Schubert affirms the poet's concept of circularity.

In his hymn to Nature, Goethe celebrates life as the loveliest invention of Nature and 'death is her ploy to live fully'.[18] The experience of confronting his own mortality pointed Schubert back to life. Life became more productive, more meaningful, and for a while even more joyful.[19] Even Schubert's awareness of his own mortality became a bit more bearable than expressed in his letter to Kupelwieser, his finite time on earth a little less provisional

SONGS OF A WAYFARER (1822–1824)

and a lot more purposeful. Despite tragic life circumstances, Schubert's extraordinary resilience and dignified acceptance – even more extraordinary at age twenty-five – is voiced to perfection in 'Wandrers Nachtlied'.

Example 18.2: 'Wandrers Nachtlied' (D 768), op. 96, no. 3

19

HIGH WINDOWS OF ZSELIZ

'Writing is a gift from heaven; a substitute for unhappiness in love.'
Goethe, *Stella*

THE FLIGHT PATH: SCHUBERT AS TEACHER

One side of the composer's life which is often overlooked is Schubert as a piano teacher. Teaching was part of his upbringing, he had been trained as a teacher, and Zseliz provided the perfect opportunity for him to put his own mark on it. His salary was now 100 fl. KM (he had earned 75 fl. in 1818) for piano tuition and as an unofficial resident musician. Socially speaking, these were a quiet few months, but the duets he wrote for Karoline von Esterházy in Zseliz were a consolation prize for having to spend another summer in Hungary.

Schubert's *mésalliance* with a titled woman was the exact complement to his potentially real relationship with Therese Grob. Karoline was at once serious-minded and physically attractive, had more intelligence and more fibre than any other woman to whom he had openly given his affection. A decade earlier when desire had outpaced reality, he had remained uncommitted to Therese and out of this tension had created his music. But evasion is also a commitment and he had walked backwards into the arms of a clandestine affair, or prostitution, through which he had contracted syphilis. By 1824 his appetite was whetted for a love more perfect, which presented itself to him in a purely spiritual relationship with a noblewoman known to him only as his student. Schubert's relation with her was not really a relation with a woman: it was a relationship with an ideal possibility of endless holy love, which might bear her name. Here again was the Tantalus motif – Eros diverted – another unattainable object of desire and affection. Eduard von Bauernfeld and five others testify to Schubert's yearning love for Karoline von Esterházy.[1] Schwind, Baron Schönstein, Spaun, and a descendant of the family all confirm the romantic and unrequited passion that he conceived for her.[2] In his final years especially, Schubert's attraction to her was intoxicated with the hope of happiness – and was that not a great part of his happiness itself?

The pathological element in Schubert's obsession with Karoline von Esterházy inspired a sheaf of piano duets leading to the most celebrated of these pieces, the Fantasie in F minor (D 940). With its deeply sincere opening subject and dramatic double fugue, D 940 is one of Schubert's most important piano compositions and one of the great piano achievements of the early nineteenth century. The duet is dedicated to Karoline von Esterházy and there has been a fanciful suggestion that the notes C and F in the opening theme codify the names Karoline and Franz.[3] More broadly – and more likely – the motto communicates Schubert's need to love and be loved, and tells us something of the nature as well as the strength of emotion which he felt for her.[4] Four months after Schubert composed his F minor Fantasy, Schumann confided in his diary: 'Musical duets become duets of the heart and the conversation and language of kindred souls; that is when they are most beautiful and valuable.'[5] Certainly, the medium drew from Schubert one of his most intimate and imaginative creations. The emotional range of his late piano duets more broadly – which is largely missing in his operas – takes this repertoire far beyond its domestic origins.

By the time Schubert came to this medium, the one-piano duet was a central part of Viennese musical life, composed for the amateur and seasoned professional, and performed in private and semi-public contexts. Of the two types of piano duet, two pianists playing at one keyboard – piano four hands – was the popular domestic version of the more glamorous piano duo – two pianists performing on two separate pianos – where each pianist can display their virtuosity without compromising their freedom.[6] In Schubert's day, works for two pianos were rare, but Viennese drawing rooms abounded with music for piano four hands. The medium became a social medium, an intimate pastime shared by family and friends, and sometimes a 'substitute' medium because of its role in the dissemination of orchestral works. Schubert tapped into this market as early as December 1817 through his arrangement of two Overtures in Italian Style as four-hand piano works (D 592 and D 597) for Babette and Therese Kunz, two sisters with whom he gave two concerts in March 1818. He composed two overtures for piano duet in 1819: Overture in G minor (D 668) and the more interesting F major/F minor Overture (D 675). He also arranged his operatic overtures to *Alfonso und Estrella* (D 773) and *Fierabras* (D 796) in 1823, which were the last piano-duet overtures he transcribed. Despite the publication and popularity of D 675 and D 773, the vast majority of his duets were not transcriptions, but original works for piano four hands.[7]

EVERYDAY RENEWALS: SCHUBERT'S PIANO DUETS

From his piano lessons with his brother Ignaz, Schubert knew the vital significance of piano duets as a pedagogical tool and he wrote over forty piano duets between 1810 and 1828. His earliest surviving composition was a Fantasy in G major for Piano Four Hands (D 1, 1810), composed between 8 April and 1 May 1810 when Schubert was thirteen and attending the Stadtkonvikt in Vienna (Example 19.1 online). His very first composition, D 1 and D1b, along with his other three early duet fantasies, D 2e, D9 and D 48, 'Grand Sonata' 1810–13, hold a very special place in the history of the genre because Schubert was the first to explore the piano fantasy duet.

Schubert's Fantasy in G minor (D 9) is significant because he already cites his own work (rather than someone else's). In the slow introduction of D 9 he borrows from his first lied, 'Hagars Klage' (D 5) and weaves the Allegro around the fourth *geschwind* section of the song. His interruption of the Allegro with a *Tempo di Marcia* creates a characteristic tension between a controlling genre and a more popular genre and is one of the powerful ways in which Schubert surprises his audience. This friction between unity and disorder affirms the presence of a truly gifted improviser and raises tantalizing questions about Schubert's precocious play with genre conventions and audience expectations.

Five years after composing these early duet Fantasies, Schubert returned to the piano duet when teaching led him out of his first crisis and back into composition. Teaching piano went hand in hand with composing for it and in the summer of 1818 he wrote Four Polonaise Piano Duets (D 599), op. 75. These splendid national or pseudo-national dances eminently suited to the duet medium were composed for the two Esterházy sisters with parts of varying difficulty. The pieces were perfect for teaching as Marie and Karoline could learn how to perform together through tailor-made writing for four hands. The first set shows Schubert's ability to compose imaginative pedagogical material which does not pretend to unity between both performers. Here the second part provides the harmonic framework in a repetitive figuration, the first part presenting embellished thematic material.

Schubert returned to the medium in 1826 when he composed his cycle of Six Polonaises (D 824), op. 61, with alternating trios, whose main function is to provide a variety of texture, sonority and dynamic contrast within each paired dance. Most of his trios are in contrasting keys to the Polonaise to which they belong: D 599/2 and D 824/1 offer a contrast between major and minor modes, but many of his trios are cast in remoter keys such as F major/D flat major in D 824/2, in E major/C major in D 824/6, and E major/D flat major in D 599/3. The pomp and nobility of Polonaise D 824/2 resounds in percussive effects, which contrasts with a more lyrical trio. A similar pianistic bravura and poetic intensity is heard in a characteristically Viennese Polonaise and thoughtful Trio, D 824/3 (Example 19.2 online).

The passionate character and 'brilliant' idiom of the E major closing polonaise contrasts with the lighter texture of its accompanying C major Trio. Both sets contain the classic characteristics of the stylized court polonaise in binary form, with accompanying binary trio sections, the entire dance composed in a rounded *da capo* form. This rhetorical aspect of the polonaise made both cycles easy listening in Viennese drawing rooms. Schubert's second set (D 824) develops the dance to a more technical, harmonic and formal complexity announced by a richer sharing of musical material and moves closer to a Polonaise Fantasy.

Another form which Schubert began to explore on the second visit to Zseliz is the military march (Table 19.1). Many of the marches written during the Napoleonic Wars owe their continued familiarity to Schubert's imagination, as he transformed them into stylized marches for artistic purposes. There was a fashion for brilliant arrangements of marches of which Schubert wrote twenty, fourteen of which were published in his lifetime.

Table 19.1: Schubert's Marches for Piano Four Hands

			Publication (Composition) date
Trois Marches Héroiques	D 602	op. 27	December 1824
Six Grandes Marches et Trios	D 819	op. 40	May–September 1825
Grande Marche Funèbre	D 859	op. 55	February 1826
Trois Marches Militaires	D 733	op. 51	August 1826
Grande Marche Héroique	D 885	op. 66	September 1826
Kindermarsch in G	D 928		(12 October 1827)
Deux Marches Caractéristiques	D 968b	op. post. 121	December 1829

As many of the original manuscripts were either lost or destroyed, it is difficult to determine their exact date of composition. According to Spaun, many were written in Zseliz: the three *Marches Héroiques* (D 602), op. 27, six *Grandes Marches* (D 819), op. 40, and the three *Marches Militaires* (D 733), op. 51, of which D 733/1 is justly famous (Example 19.3 online). These three military marches epitomized the form into which the military march had evolved: typically about four minutes long, written in common time, an introductory fanfare followed by an opening section, a second theme followed by a trio featuring a broad lyrical melody. The military march tempo very much depends on its function whether it is performed as a processional theatrical march or as a functional piece played for weddings or written for the enjoyment of friends. Long before these marches for piano four hands were published, Schubert's friends were trying them out.[8] In a letter to Josef Spaun in 1821, Anton von Ottenwalt wrote: 'Marie practises Schubert's marches beside me. Although it is only the bass part on our aunt's piano, I have difficulty resisting such a charming pastime; even my fingers itch to follow the changing lines.'[9] Recognizing how exceptional Schubert's marches were, Schwind wrote to Schober in 1825, 'The character of the marches and unutterable inwardness and loveliness of their trios would astonish you.'[10]

Of the non-military marches, the funeral march was the most common, of which Schubert's *Grande Marche Funèbre* in C minor (D 859), op. 55, is an example. This *tombeau* was released on 8 February 1826 to mark the death of Tsar Alexander I on 1 December 1825. The Russian Tsar had been very popular during the Congress of Vienna (1814–15) and had visited the city between 1818 and 1822. It is likely that Schubert composed this march long before his death, but his dedication marks an important milestone through his politicization of the genre. Its orchestral effects are very much part of Schubert's early duet style and its accompanying trio in a contrasting key is very much the norm in nineteenth-century marches.

Pennauer seized a second political opportunity to increase Schubert's fame with the piano duet *Grande Marche Héroique* (D 885) to mark the crowning of Tsar Nicholas I of Russia. The publisher also released it in a solo piano version approved by the composer, which contributed to a wider circulation of both works. The A minor tonality – with its two accompanying trios in E minor (bars 49–83) and F major (bars 132–160) – is more characteristic of a funeral march than a heroic coronation march, which again suggests Schubert's selection of previously composed marches. The sense of grandeur in Schubert's slow march ($\decrescendo=60$) and its strong repetitive rhythms adhere to the march's uncomplicated style, but its recurring double trio (bars 49–83, 132–159), attack march in a more rapid tempo (Allegro giusto, bars 84–131 and 160–207) and expressive coda (bars 208–266) greatly expand the march form beyond convention.

Schubert's *Marche brillante* formed an integral first movement to *Divertissement sur des motifs originaux français* in E minor (D 823), op. 63 and op. 84. The march was published separately as op. 63 on 17 June 1826, its companion variations and rondo followed as op. 84 on 6 July 1827. As the didactic and commercial value of the *Divertissement* lay in three extended movements which did not yet demand the technical virtuosity of the sonata but exceeded the technical demands of Schubert's dance sets, it is not known why they were published separately. Schubert may not have had the second and third movements ready or Pennauer may have been impatient to cash in on the March craze.

According to Baron Karl von Schönstein, *Divertissement à l'hongroise* in G minor for Piano Four Hands (D 818) was composed in Zseliz in autumn 1824. The date, 2 September 1824, on the manuscript of his Hungarian Melody in B minor (D 817), and Schubert's incorporation of this theme into the third movement of his *Divertissement à l'hongroise*, has linked this work with more substantial piano duets written at the time, including the 'Grand Duo' Sonata (D 812). The work has also been connected with an ongoing interdisciplinary debate about a seventeenth-century Hungarian epic, *Szigeti veszedelem* (The Peril of Sziget), written by Miklós Zrinkyi and referred to by its Latin title *Obsidionis Szigetianae* (The Siege of Sziget).[11] Moritz von Schwind's 1825 drawing of the Siege of Sziget originated as a public protest against Peter Krafft's oil painting of the same battle. This repositioning of Schubert's *Divertissement* in autumn 1825 would not only remove it from its pedagogical context in Zseliz but would link the work more closely with Katharina von Lászny, to whom the duet is dedicated and who was married to the wealthy Hungarian nobleman, Ludwig Lászny von Folkusfálva. The duet was performed by Johann Jenger and Irene Kiesewetter in her salon in the Viennese suburb of Wieden

(7 Paniglstrasse), and is an example of how in later years Schubert's musical patronage began to shift to the upper classes.

Although the *Divertissement* form gives the impression of reduced aesthetic demands, neither work signals a reduction of the pianistic demands. Jenger refers to his duet partner in the Hungarian *Divertissement* (D 818) as 'the very dear and very capable pianist Irene', 'capable' here referring to her ability to surmount the works' technical challenges.[12] The pieces are clearly in the tradition of the divertimento as a chamber music sonata with a three-movement structure which is neither fantasy nor sonata but could be assigned to both forms. The freer rondo form of the Hungarian divertissement with a march in the middle could correspond to the fantasy, while the French divertissement is closer to a sonata with a first-movement sonata form in a *Tempo di Marcia* followed by an Andante variation movement and a Rondo-Allegretto. This sonata-form framework is veiled in the title 'Divertissement en forme d'une Marche brillante et raisonnée', where 'raisonnée' alludes to the structural logic underpinning the march. What is striking about both *Divertissements* is the lack of tonal variety within and between the three movements (D 818: g-c-g, D 823: e-b-e) and the exclusivity of even-beat metres in both sets. It is not only their sonata-fantasy form but also the thematic weight of their musical material which determines here the aesthetic criteria and frame of reference.

The piano duet comes up time and again in Schubert-Beethoven mythology, especially through the sets of variations that both composers improvised and published which were fashionable at the time.[13] Schubert famously called on Beethoven in 1822 to give him a fair copy of his Variations on a French Song (D 624), op. 10, for Piano Four Hands, which he dedicated from one composer to another, a gesture that was unusual at the time. Both composers became acquainted with each other's music via the medium of the piano duet: Beethoven through playing this set of variations, op. 10, with his nephew Karl, and Schubert through playing four-hand versions of Beethoven's symphonies, reminding us again how closely piano duets were bound up with symphonic repertoire.

One of Schubert's most striking duets is his Eight Variations on an original theme in A flat major (D 813), op. 35, composed in the summer of 1824, around the same time as the most ambitious of all his piano duets, the 'Grand Duo' in C (D 812), once believed to be the missing 'Gastein' symphony.[14] Writing from Zseliz to Moritz von Schwind, Schubert records the audience's warm reception of the premiere of his A flat Variations, which is one of his neglected masterworks.[15] The dotted march rhythm of its theme – which Schwind deems as grandiose as it is languorous – is transformed directly into the dactylic rhythm from the third variation onwards, performed with deep tenderness in Variations five and seven before it is finally returned in a dotted rhythm that dances in 12/8 time in the closing Variation eight (Example 19.4 online).[16] Such a transposition of an alla Marcia in a dance triple time is found in the final variation of the Hüttenbrenner Variations (D 576), which start from the dactylic rhythm and anticipate the later alienation of the dactylic rhythm in the scherzo of the 'Wanderer Fantasy'.

THE LOCAL AND THE UNIVERSAL

After he left his Zseliz hermitage, Schubert began to explore the ready-made market for performance and publication of his piano duets, which provided the impetus for him to develop the medium far beyond its didactic origins. Many of the duets he had written in Zseliz, Schubert tried out in Viennese salons with Josef von Gahy, Karl Maria von Bocklet and Franz Lachner. The brilliance of his duet partners and intelligence of his audiences invited the particular play on generic forms which distinguishes his contribution to the genre (see Table 19.2).

Even the last of Schubert's piano duets throw open the Sonata-Fantasy question, not through their chronology between the F minor Fantasy (D 940) and Schubert's sonata trilogy (D 958–D 960), but through their play on generic conventions. The impassioned A minor *Lebensstürme* (D 947), op. 144, composed in May 1828, and the beautiful four-hand

Table 19.2: Schubert's Complete Piano Duets Published During his Lifetime

1.	Eight Variations on a French Song in E minor	D 624, op. 10	Cappi & Diabelli, 19 April 1822
2.	Trois Marches Héroiques	D 602, op. 27	Sauer & Leidesdorf, 18 December 1824
3.	Sonata in B flat major	D 617, op. 30	Sauer & Leidesdorf 30 December 1823
4.	Overture in F major	D 675, op. 34	Cappi & Comp., 28 February 1825
5.	Variations on an original theme in A flat	D 813, op. 35	Sauer & Leidesdorf, 9 February 1825
6.	Six Grandes Marches et Trios	D 819, op. 40	Sauer & Leidesdorf, 7 May and 21 September 1825
7.	Trois Marches Militaires	D 733, op. 51	Diabelli, 7 August 1826
8.	Divertissement à l'hongroise	D 818, op. 54	Matthias Artaria, 8 April 1826,
9.	Grande Marche Funèbre in C minor à l'occasion de la mort de S. M. Alexandre I	D 859, op. 55	Pennauer, 8 February 1826
10.	Six Polonaises	D 824, op. 61	Cappi & Czerny, 8 July 1826
11.	Divertissement en forme d'une Marche brillante et raisonnée, composé sur des motifs originaux français	D 823/1, op. 63/1	Weigl, 17 June 1826
12.	Grande Marche Héroique, composée à l'occasion du Sacre de Sa Majesté Nicolas I	D 885, op. 66	Pennauer, 14 September 1826
13.	Overture Alfonso und Estrella	D 773, op. 69	Sauer & Leidesdorf, 20 February 1826
14.	Four Polonaises	D 599, op. 75	Diabelli, 6 July 1822
15.	Eight Variations on a Theme from Hérold's Opera *Marie*	D 908, op. 82	Haslinger, 3 September 1827
16.	Andantino varié et Rondeau brilliant, composés sur des motifs originaux français	D 823/2–3, op. 84	Weigl, 6 July 1827

A major Rondo (D 951), op. 107, composed in June 1828, have been considered as a two-movement Sonata (like Beethoven's op. 90) on account of their striking tonal and thematic analogy, which is more likely a coincidence of chronology.[17] Although the Rondo in A gives the impression of a possible final movement, it could not counterbalance the monumental Allegro opening movement, and no further movements or drafts for an orchestral work have been found. The opening movement's orchestral effects are very much part of Schubert's duet style from his earliest overtures and fantasies for Piano Four Hands and in the interconnections between piano duet and orchestral work in his Sinfonie in D (D 936A).

Schubert was the first major composer to write so extensively for the piano duet, though many have contributed to the genre.[18] As with the lied, he transformed the piano-duet genre into a force to be reckoned with which had an immediate impact on the duets of the next generation of composers. In the medium of piano duets he embraced a wide range of individual genres – including fantasies, overtures, sonatas, variations, rondos, divertissements, sets of marches, dance cycles including Polonaises, Ländler and Deutsche – through which he redefined generic meanings while remaining alive to their associations. The best of these duets offer didactic benefits which are still not widely availed of, as well as hours of private enjoyment between friends. The music holds tremendous value for professional performers willing to open an eye to a repertoire that has been consigned to amateur performances at home. In his mature duets especially, Schubert granted each voice a distinctive role which enables individual performers – when this is combined with music that is designed to show their strengths – to create duos that complement each pianist's personal talents and offer or offer a platform to showcase a gifted student within a solo recital, and themselves as pedagogue and performer. All of Schubert's late duets exemplify the rich texture of his mature instrumental style and characteristic emotional depth, which have raised the medium of the piano duet to a whole new level.

IV

ESSENCE

20

AFTER THE CRISES: THE SPIRIT OF BEAUTY AND ITS FATE

'Alles Vergängliche / Ist nur ein Gleichnis.'
('Everything transitory is only a likeness.')

Goethe, *Faust*

OLD FRIENDS AND NEW: EDUARD VON BAUERNFELD

In January 1825, Schubert was back in hospital. Even so, he was composing 'Der Einsame' (D 800), one of many new songs he then performed with Vogl at Sophie Müller's home on 7 March.[1] Schubert had first met 'the bewitching Sophie' (1803–1830), resident actress at the Burgtheater, at a lunch with Vogl and Jenger on 24 February. According to Anselm Hüttenbrenner, she sang Schubert's songs 'most movingly'.[2] Schubert was to visit her inner-city home (28 Graben) five more times in the spring of 1825 where they spent long afternoons together. Her diary records thirteen visits by Schubert between February 1825 and November 1826. She was smitten enough to purchase her own copy of Josef Teltscher's lithographed portrait of him directly from the artist. She survived Schubert by two years; her early death at twenty-seven was mourned by all of Vienna.

In the spring of 1825 Schubert's old triangle of friends – Spaun, Schober, Mayrhofer – had given way to an almost new one: Schober,

Schwind and Eduard von Bauernfeld (1802–1890). Bauernfeld had heard Schubert perform some of his songs at Professor Vincentius Weintridt's apartment (8 Bankgasse) in January 1822, but it was not until Schwind brought the composer to his home in February 1825 that their friendship blossomed. According to Bauernfeld, 'We were soon on familiar terms. At Schwind's insistence I had to recite some of my crazy early poems, then moved to the piano, Schubert sang, we played duets, and later repaired to the tavern where we stayed long into the night. Our friendship was sealed there and then; from that day on we were inseparable.' Unlike Schober, Bauernfeld wrote a chapter about his friendship with Schubert and Schwind in his memoirs, Aus Alt und Neu-Wien', an important source about Viennese life as they knew it.[3] In Schubert's friendship with Bauernfeld one recognizes a just and firm encounter, in thought and in feeling: the steps and forms of the gifted and true.

One of Schubert's commercial ventures in April 1825 was a collaboration with the poet and translator, Jacob Nicolaus Craigher de Jachelutta (1797–1855), who provided singing translations of a number of well-known English, Spanish, French and Italian texts to be published alongside the originals, thereby reaching a wider market. The first of these bilingual settings was 'Der blinde Knabe' (D 833), de Jachelutta's translation of Colley Cibber's *The Blind Boy*. Commercial as the venture was, Schubert's setting, 'Der blinde Knabe', reflects at least three personal strands. It resulted from Klein's integration of blind children with their sighted peers into Viennese classrooms,[4] which Schubert had experienced in his father's school. It masks a very real fear of ocular syphilis which could afflict Schubert – already a victim of eye trouble – at any stage. Thirdly, and most significantly, it shows his extraordinary empathy with those on the margins, and a new-found understanding of the inner radiance that emerges through suffering. His song is a musical tapestry of changing attitudes towards blindness in nineteenth-century Vienna and London, and belongs to a broader movement to give voice to the blind. Its opening stanzas challenge the bias that blindness was a ticket to misery and reflects contemporary educational debates surrounding how blind and newly sighted people relate to the world. Schubert's closing strophe affirms the kind of spiritual vision that mythically accompanies physical blindness and emerging recognition that the ability to see is not necessary for human understanding. One of the reasons why the significance of the song has been overlooked lies in its mawkish performance tradition which misunderstands the boy's radiance though the song underscores this through its dignified *Langsam* tempo and double-dotted rhythms on 'so glücklich', 'so reich'. Schubert had the quietude within himself not only to recognize great joy and love in the blind boy's bearing, but to realize it in his setting. It was this rapport rather than pathos that moved Hummel to tears as he listened to Schubert's and Vogl's rendering with its well-rehearsed *rallentandi* and perfectly paced interludes.

IN MEDIAS RES: PORTRAIT OF AN ARTIST

'Der blinde Knabe' is a good example of how music provided a release from the tyranny of life, but also how the money that Schubert received from his art released him financially. In February 1825, as a result of such publications, he was able to move out of his father's home into his own apartment beside the Karlskirche, in Vienna's Wieden suburb (9 Technikerstrasse). Schwind and his family were near neighbours. Not too far away lived another friend, Wilhelm August Rieder, a painter, whose father, Ambrois Rieder (1771–1855), was a composer of over 500 works and who came from a long lineage of schoolteachers. A warm understanding immediately arose between composer and painter, who gave Schubert access to the piano in his studio home (32 Wiedner Hauptstrasse).[5] The Schubert-Rieder axis was a family affair: Ferdinand described Rieder's brother, Johann, as his 'only true friend'.[6] Ambrois Rieder's keyboard preludes and fugues published by Diabelli in 1826 were 'respectfully dedicated to the esteemed composer Franz Schubert', the only such inscription he received in his lifetime.[7]

Through the good grace of Wilhelm Rieder's friendship, Schubert tried out his compositions in an apartment which was once inhabited by Gluck. The painter agreed a signal with Schubert that if the curtain was open, the piano was available for his use, but if it was closed, he did not want to be disturbed. There are various accounts of Schubert making his way to Rieder's home, looking up at the window joyfully, or disappointed if the curtain was drawn.[8]

Wilhelm Rieder's piano, made by the Viennese firm, Anton Walter, with its six octaves and two pedals (sustaining and una corda), reignited Schubert's interest in the piano sonata. His first venture was the unfinished 'Reliquie' Sonata in C major (D 840). A second piano sonata followed in May 1825, the composer choosing once again the key of A minor, but avoiding the starkness of the grim A minor Sonata (D 784) swiftly written in the first stages of his syphilis and just as swiftly rejected by his publisher. This new A minor Sonata (D 845) was accepted by the publisher Pennauer as Schubert's op. 42 and reviewed at length 'as his first Grand Sonata' in Leipzig's *Allgemeine musikalische Zeitung* on 1 March 1826.[9] A third sonata in D major (D 850), which followed in August 1825, was published as his second Grand Sonata, op. 53, by Artaria on 8 April 1826.

As well as providing a piano for his creative pleasure, Rieder painted the best-known and best-loved portrait of Schubert, considered by his friends to be an extremely good likeness (Figure 2). That Schubert was relaxed in Rieder's presence is central to the success of this deeply sympathetic portrait. It is truer and finer than other studies, which may have imitated the composer with punctilious precision, but captured nothing of his spirit. Schubert signed the sepia and watercolour versions as well as Rieder, thereby endorsing it as a realistic depiction or at the very least the image he wanted to portray of himself. That he is holding a small paperback book in his right hand illustrates how inextricably linked literature was with Schubert's creative process.[10] His seated gesture also allows him to be very naturally portrayed with his signature glasses. Rieder does not distract from the centrality of the composer by portraying his surroundings.

Instead, Schubert is foregrounded: alone and in his own world. His intelligent eyes are intensely focused, diverted away from the viewer; his stance is confident and unselfconscious, gestures shared by Friedrich Lieder's 1827 realistic sketch. In his 1825 watercolour, Rieder was free to create, to be a poet, an artist who does not paint things in a dry, analytical way. If Schubert's head, well observed and at leisure, is more beautiful than in other portraits, it captures the spirit of the composer in a physical likeness as his closest friends knew him. Rieder has expressed the poetry of new-found confidence in the summer of 1825, which was why his watercolour spoke to Spaun and to Sonnleithner more intimately and more personally than other portraits of Schubert.

SUMMER IN UPPER AUSTRIA AND THE APPREHENDING OF BEAUTY

Schubert played the Rieder Sonatas on his recital tour with Vogl in Upper Austria, a summer which marked a new era in his life. The end of an epoch was a time of opportunity, and before going on tour, he ordered special copies of his op. 19 Goethe settings ('An Schwager Kronos', 'An Mignon', 'Ganymede') on satined paper with a gold title, and asked Diabelli to send them to the poet. His accompanying letter is deferential, but this time he addressed the poet directly as artist:

> Your Excellency
>
> If I should succeed in giving evidence of my unbounded veneration of Your Excellency by the dedication of these compositions of your poems, and the possibility of gaining some recognition of my insignificant self, I should regard the favourable fulfilment of this wish as the fairest of my career.
>
> With the greatest respect, I am
> Your most devoted servant
> Franz Schubert

Op. 19 was published on 6 June and in his diary on 16 June 1825, Goethe noted receipt of Schubert's songs.

Schubert had left Vienna on 20 May to join Vogl on tour in Steyr and Linz. He needed someone of similar culture and comparable intellect with whom he could make sense of this welter of new and unexpectedly unmanageable impressions, and Vogl knew both towns intimately. From Linz, they visited the monastery of St Florian, where they performed Schubert's Lieder to Vogl's friends. On the way back to Steyr, on 26/27 May, they visited the Kremsmünster monastery, where Schubert played his Sonata in A minor (D 845), also the *Marche Militaire* (D 733) and Variations in A flat (D 813) with one of the Kremsmünster residents. After a few weeks in Steyr and Linz, they reached Gmunden on 4 June where they remained for five weeks (until 12 July). Here they resided with Ferdinand Traweger, in whose home there was a substitute for Schubert's baby brother, Andreas, in the person of Traweger's five-year-old son Eduard, with whom the composer played for hours.[11] Johann Nepomuk Wolf also invited Schubert into his home where he played duets with Wolf's seventeen-year-old daughter, Nanette. Vogl and Schubert were welcome visitors at Ebenzweier Castle on Lake Traun, three miles from Gmunden, owned by Florian Maxmilian Clodi, a widower who had married Spaun's aunt, Therese, now deceased. Their twenty-three-year-old daughter, Therese Clodi, Spaun's cousin, was eleven when her mother died. This orphaned *châtelaine* had gradually taken over running the castle and was deeply admired by the locals. By the time he met her, Schubert was already working on a set of seven songs based on Walter Scott's *Lady of the Lake*, prompted by Donizetti's *La Donna del Lago* which had been performed in Vienna the previous year. Scott's romantic drama and its landscapes now took hold of his imagination as Therese Clodi became Schubert's *Lady of the Lake*. It is his only song-set to contain Lieder for multiple voices (Ellen D 837–839, Norman D 846 and Malcolm D 843), including two choral songs (D 835–836). The deep religious feeling in 'Ellens Gesang III' (Ave Maria, D 839), which Schubert described as spontaneous prayer, was immediately popular with local audiences.¹² Around 12 July, Schubert and Vogl said goodbye to the Trawegers, and returned to Linz and Steyr (15 July–10 August), stopping at Püchelberg, near Wels, where Vogl had friends. Between 15 and 25 July, Schubert divided his time between Linz – where he stayed with Spaun's sister, Marie, and her husband Anton von Ottenwalt – and Steyregg Castle, where he was a guest of Count and Countess Weissenwolff.

Schubert's summer tour gave him the strength to continue on a new, exalted creative plane. Having soaked up rest and the care of others, his appearance and whole manner changed. The inner and outer man grew more communicative, he began to open up and out to the world again. In a letter to Spaun on 19 July 1825, Anton von Ottenwalt rejoiced in his recovery, 'he looks so well and strong, is so pleasantly cheerful and so genially communicative that one cannot but be inwardly delighted by it'.[13] He described Schubert's 'penetrating intelligence:

> I have never seen nor heard him like this: serious, profound and as though inspired. How he talked of art, of poetry, of his youth, of friends and other people who matter, of the relationship of ideals to life, etc. I was more and more amazed at such a mind, of which it has been said that its artistic achievement is so unconscious, hardly revealed to and understood by himself, and so on. Yet how simple was all this! – I cannot tell you of the extent and the unity of his convictions – but there were glimpses of a world view that is not merely acquired, and the share which worthy friends have in it by no means detracts from the individuality shown by all of this.[14]

Just how talkative, energetic and witty Schubert was can be glimpsed in his letter to Spaun two days later on 21 July:

> Here I sit at Linz, half dead with sweating in this frightful heat, with a whole book of new songs, and you are not here! Aren't you ashamed?

Linz without you is like a body without a soul, like a headless horseman, or like a soup without salt [. . .] As you see, I'm getting positively unjust towards the end of Linzdom, since after all I am quite happy in your mother's house and in the company of your sister, Ottenwalt and Max, and seem to see your spirit flash from the body of many another Linzer. Only I fear that this spirit will gradually flash itself away entirely, it is enough to make you burst.[15]

Between 11 August and 4 September, Vogl and Schubert moved back to Steyr and on to Salzburg where they were invited to perform for a prestigious aristocratic soirée. In Salzburg, Schubert made a pilgrimage to Michael Haydn's grave and described the visit at length in a letter to Ferdinand.[16] The urbane and overweight Vogl, suffering from gout, wanted to press on quickly to Bad Gastein, one of Austria's most famous spas where Vogl wished to take the cure. They reached Gastein on 13/14 August where they remained for almost three weeks. Staying there at the same time was Johann Ladislaus Pyrker, the great Patriarch of Venice with whom the composer engaged in fruitful collaboration. Rather to the irritation of Schubert, Vogl became impatient to move on again, this time back to Gmunden where they stayed one week (10–16 September) before travelling on to Steyr on 17 September. After a couple of weeks in Steyr, Vogl wanted to travel to Italy, so the two musicians parted company. Schubert set off towards Linz, with musical performances at the Ottenwalts, at Steyregg Castle and at Spaun's, where his Walter Scott songs were warmly received. Josef Gahy arrived in a hired carriage to perform duets with Schubert before accompanying him back to Vienna.

By the beginning of October, Schubert was much freer in himself than he had been at the beginning of the tour. This was not just due to the waft of the climate or the waiving of economic anxieties through recital fees. It had to do with the intellectual distinction of the people around him, the particular nurture that came from new friendships and an intellectually stimulating environment.

AFTER THE CRISES: THE SPIRIT OF BEAUTY AND ITS FATE

SCHUBERT'S 'SOMMERREISE' (D 944)

'In praise of the radiance of God's grace, the heart is seized!
Love draws the reign of peace over all the world!'
                            Schober and Schubert, *Alfonso und Estrella*

In the summer of 1825, Schubert experienced, with metaphysical keenness, feelings of restored health, perhaps even a belief that he was cured, but certainly a blossoming of his creativity. His mood bears witness to a transformative change of heart, a new-found ability to 'see things as they are'. It is unsurprising that he would see in his being spared further ill health the workings of a higher purpose, and he began questing for a vocation. The time was right for the task he had set himself the previous year: the largest symphony he had ever undertaken.

For six weeks when he was in Gmunden on the edge of Lake Traun, Schubert began to sketch a new symphony which he continued in Bad Gastein. The terrifying grandeur of the mountains and lakes he had seen in 1819 and 1823 beckoned to him: like old friends they held something of him captive which needed to be released in relation to his new-found self. In their familiar atmosphere, with the shadow of illness lifted, Schubert experienced reveries of immensity, of humanist joy, a tremendous sense of what had been achieved on earth and of which he was a part. His Symphony of Thanksgiving communicates this spiritual and physical élan, his acknowledgement of the healing forces of nature. It was the high point of the summer but also the culmination of all that Schubert had felt and suffered over the past three years. In the very same summer Beethoven was writing the second movement of his A minor String Quartet, 'a Hymn of thanksgiving to the divinity from a convalescent in the Lydian mode'. The fact that Schubert is doing this at the same time should not be attributed to influence but to two composers trying to make music the most it could be in 1825. As a symbol of renewal, the 'Great' C major Symphony (D 944) bears testimony to the fulfilment of creative ambition confided in that extraordinary letter to Kupelwieser on 31 March 1824,[17] two months before Beethoven's Ninth was premiered.

Schubert's desire to 'pave his way towards a grand symphony' was not just a private expression of personal ambition but a reflection of how the symphony had become a 'veritable touchstone for composers and listeners alike', as Adolf Bernhard Marx, Berlin's most influential critic of the time, had noted in 1824.[18] It was held to be the most serious of genres in that it avoided virtuosity and demanded skill in orchestration. Schubert's identification of this symphony as an example of his 'striving after the highest in art'[19] echoes E. T. A. Hoffmann's review of Beethoven's Fifth (*Allgemeine musikalische Zeitung*, Leipzig, 1810) in which he declared instrumental music to be the highest of all art forms and implies how the Absolute can be glanced through the agency of Beethoven's 'Eroica' Symphony no. 3. Ten years earlier, in *Kalligone* (1800), Herder had unambiguously declared instrumental music to be the highest of all arts 'because it provides a means of perceiving the Absolute, the realm in which distinctions between subjectivity and objectivity disappear'.[20] One could attach a similar poetically inspired metaphysics to Schubert's D 944, where listening becomes a way of knowing, where nature's grandeur and human experience are perceived as emanations of the divine.[21]

D 944 is an early example of a programmatic symphony in the sense of Mendelssohn's Italian Symphony. It is also a pastoral symphony 'in a higher sense' in that its broad canvas exudes a pantheistic message: Schubert's commitment to the Romantic doctrine of Nature as the vesture of God. It is implicit in the symphony, but explicit in his Leid and his elaborate choral and solo settings of 'Die Allmacht' (D 852 and D 875A) by Ladislaus Pyrker, whom Schubert had met for a second time in Gastein and whose pantheistic poem he set cheek by jowl with this symphony.[22]

Die Allmacht	Omnipotence
Groß ist Jehova, der Herr; denn Himmel	Great is Jehovah, the Lord! For heaven

und Erde verkünden
    Seine Macht!
Du hörst sie im brausenden
    Sturm, in des Waldstroms
 	
Laut aufrauschendem Ruf',
    in des grünenden
    Waldes Gesäusel;
Siehst sie in wogender
    Saaten Gold,
    in lieblicher Blumen
    Glühendem
Schmelz, im Glanz
    des sternbesäten Himmels.
Furchtbar tönt sie im
    Donnergeroll,
    und flammt in
    des Blitzes
Schnell hinzuckendem Flug; doch
    kündet das pochende Herz dir,
 	
Fühlbarer noch, Jehova's Macht,
    des ewigen Gottes,
Blickst du flehend empor,
    und hoffst auf Huld und
    Erbarmen![23]
	And earth proclaim
	    his might!
	You hear it in the
	    roaring storm,
	    In the
	loud, surging call of the forest stream,
	    In the greenwood's
	    rustling;
	You see it in the
	    golden waving wheat;
	    In the glowing brilliance of the
	    beautiful
	Flowers, in the radiance of the
	    Star-strewn heavens.
	It resounds terrifyingly in the
	    rolling
	Thunder and flames in the
	    lightning's
	Swiftly flickering flight; but
	    your beating heart will tell even
	
	More palpably of Jehovah's power,
	    the Eternal God,
	if you gaze up in prayer
	And hope for grace and
	    mercy!

Pyrker's and Schubert's world is one where the Divine is revealed. The song recognizes a fundamental identity between the concrete world and the Divinity: one is the external expression of the other, or to borrow Goethe's words, 'Alles Vergängliche ist nur ein Gleichnis'. Everything transitory is only a likeness, but a likeness of something real.

Here, in a quasi-theology of music, Schubert's election of a C major tonality to portray God as a majestic, animating force seems predetermined: the arrival of primal Light from Chaos in Haydn's *Creation*, the *locus classicus* of sublimity, and the Divine omnipotence in Mozart's 'Jupiter' Symphony both resound in C major. This Pastoral Symphony (D 944) is not so much a painting of nature as an expression of the feelings arising from a metaphorical identification with nature. In his travelogue to Ferdinand, Schubert records the deep impression made by this natural landscape outside the urban circle in Vienna within which he had hitherto lived.[24] While Schubert was not on the point of reverting to Catholicism, the renewal of contact with his former self made accessible again a religious position to which he had once held and which would become increasingly discernible in his work. The days were past when he would denounce religion. In the summer of 1825 Nature poured redemption. Schubert wrote home as if, in some sense, he believed in a God – though the nature both of the Divinity and of his belief in it require some subtle definition, as will be explored in the following chapter.

Schubert's Great C major Symphony was originally listed as Symphony no. 7 in Ferdinand's catalogue of works and in its first 1840 publication. Deutsch numbered it Symphony no. 8 when he catalogued Schubert's works until modern watermarking methods determined it was composed in 1825/26 and was the missing Gmunden-Gastein symphony (D 849).[25] The revised date is highly significant because it shows Schubert reaching his symphonic maturity three years before his death. The New Schubert Edition now numbers the 'Great' C major Symphony as no. 8 and the 'Unfinished' Symphony as no. 7, but perhaps the thermographic watermarking project DRACMarkS (Digitization, Recognition, and Automated Clustering of Watermarks in the Music Manuscripts of Franz Schubert), will resolve some of the remaining issues surrounding D 759. One of the reasons why there is so much confusion around the dating of D 944 is because the manuscript contains no title page. The interpolated date 'March 1828' on the score's first page is when the final corrections were made.[26]

AFTER THE CRISES: THE SPIRIT OF BEAUTY AND ITS FATE

George Bernard Shaw's belief that 'a more exasperatingly brainless composition was never put on paper' says more about the writer's ability to parrot popular opinion than it does about D 944, whose autograph shows how systematically Schubert conceived this score.[27] Through the use of various colours of ink for different phases of the work we eavesdrop on a mind *in medias res* as he sketched a continuous outline score, the leading voices filled in at appropriate places, leaving detailed scoring to be completed later. The sheer sweep of invention is no doubt related to the circumstances of Schubert's life, but the revised score – where folios are interpolated into the outer movements and trio – is proof positive of the radical rethinking of that original intention. Until the *NSA* edition, many published editions contained countless errors. The simple correction of the score's opening marking to the manuscript *alla breve*, for example, greatly changes the character of the opening movement, and by extension the entire symphony, from Brucknerian-like massiveness into something more Schubertian: lithe but no less heroic. At a very basic level, the symphony emerges a faster, tauter, more nervous composition than earlier performances would have us believe. Its driving power, dissonant harmonies, and striking trombone colouring take a giant step even beyond the highly original 'Unfinished'. Writing his memoir of Schubert in 1829, Bauernfeld identified this symphony as the one 'for which the composer had a vast preference'.[28]

Just as Schubert's 'Sommerreise' Symphony (D 944) is a companion work to *Winterreise* (D 911), the 'Unfinished' and 'Great' C major Symphonies depict 'two contrary states of the human soul'.[29] How different the symphonies are reflects the biographical circumstances in which they were written and how different the landscape looked on either side of the watershed. Both works are huge statements of Schubert's Janus-faced creativity in highly existential situations. Composed in a minor key, the 'Unfinished' is intensely personal, dramatic, concise, emotionally and thematically homogenous, its poetic tone is that of sombre passion, constantly interrupted by violent explosions of feeling. D 944 is in the *Ur*-key, C major: grand on account of its lyric monumentality and narrative weight, also its creative ambition. Except for the climax of the Andante con moto, the symphony is markedly extrovert, a magnificent human triumph and a work of profound sublimity.[30]

As expressions of human consciousness and self-overcoming, these companion symphonies display Schubert's humanity at its most noble. In his essay *Über das Erhabene* (Concerning the Sublime, 1796), Schiller acknowledges how, 'as sensual beings, we are never safe from disease, loss and death, but when we can face even our own annihilation with dignified calm', it is a manifestation of the sublime.[31] D 944 gives voice to Schubert's physical, mental and creative prowess, his ability to overcome what he fears. In different ways, both symphonies give voice to such moments of terror, his coming-to-knowledge and musical avowal of his chosen life as a composer. Individually and together, they are examples of Schubert's capacity to feel the sublime, which Schiller recognizes as 'one of the most glorious dispositions in human nature'.[32]

D 944 opens in an unprecedented way: two solo horns pronouncing a gesture of Divine Providence:

Example 20.1: Symphony no. 8 (D 944/i), introductory horn call, bars 1–8

This bold but quiet cantabile horn call with its evocations of Nature is singular among Schubert's introductions which more characteristically begin with an assertive long note, heavily accented, often an open octave (Symphonies no. 1, 3, 4 and 6), some with a fermata (Symphonies no. 3, 4 and 4). It is longer than slow introductions in any other Schubert work, auguring that the entire symphony will be one of comparable spaciousness.[33] The centrality of its introductory theme, which overshadows the main subjects (bars 78–94 and 134–141), intimately links the work with Schubert's B minor Symphony (D 759/i). The introductory material – in

AFTER THE CRISES: THE SPIRIT OF BEAUTY AND ITS FATE

particular its second bar – is extensively recalled throughout the sonata-allegro, including its triumphant return in the culminating bars in the coda at the end of the Allegro proper, clinching the music's architectural momentum (bars 650–685). This double excursion (of the introductory and main themes) is reminiscent of the coda in the finale of Schubert's Third Symphony. In his First Symphony he had restated his slow introduction in Allegro tempo. The 'Great' goes beyond this precedent: its Allegro redeploys material from the opening Andante theme – always in the current tempo – to build the last and principal climaxes of the exposition, development, recapitulation and coda. In the closing bars the return of the horn theme is a highly dramatic moment as a new six-bar wind version resounds in an orchestral *tutti* (bars 662–685) *ben marcato*. The *pianissimo* dynamic now resounds *fortissimo* with *sforzando* accents, the passage is marked double dotted, the tension heightened by a tonic pedal in the trombones. The repetition of the Andante theme lends a certain quality of stasis to the opening movement that suggests the timelessness or fixity of the natural order, of nature objectified (*natura naturata*). And yet, for all its repetitiveness this movement – and entire symphony – with its short rhythmic motifs endlessly recurring is more properly heard as an evocation of *natura naturans*, nature's vitality and growth. It is less that the symphony represents this than that this philosophy is embedded in its language.

Long associated with the supernatural, and in church music with spiritual awe, trombones rise to a new level of prominence in D 944.[34] Schubert had indicated them in the particell for the E major symphony (D 729) in August 1821, in the 'Unfinished' (D 759) in October 1822, but in D 944 they play their most significant role. He not only uses three trombones to reinforce orchestral *tutti* (bars 662–685), but takes advantage of their distinctive timbre in *pianissimo* passages where the alto and tenor trombones present thematic material.[35] Prior to this, for example, the trombones take up the introductory motif in the third and closing theme at the end of the exposition (bars 199–228). Further examples are the trombone passage in the development which moves from A flat minor to A flat major (bars 304–318) and the 'jubilus' closing theme in the recapitulation, which culminates *fff* where the tonic is finally reached (bars 517–558).

The rhythmic vitality of the Allegro contrasts with the Andante con moto second movement, which abounds in delicate orchestral colouring. This intimate, deeply lyrical movement opens with a plaintive, processional oboe solo (bars 8–16) which oscillates between A minor and C major – a characteristic modal shifting that carries tremendous weight (Example 20.2a online). This march-like melody plays itself out, finally yielding to a chorale-like expanse of majestic lyricism, largely centred in the strings. The first subject's rhythmic élan contrasts with the emotional intimacy of the F major second subject, full of longing and all the more powerful because of its restraint (Example 20.2b online).

Both themes unfold in a rondo (ABA′B′A″) whose tonal dramaturgy demonstrates divine power by mediant motion away from the tonic: A minor (bars 1–88)–F major (bars 93–144)–A minor (bars 160–250)–A major (bars 267–329)–A minor (bars 330–356, Coda 356–380). Lest anyone doubt that these are sacred matters, Schubert permeates the movement with plagal relationships. The sense of Divinity is evident in the mysterious transitions between sections, most famously the sublime moment when the horns, as if from the distance, quietly call everything into question with the repeated tolling of a single note (bars 148–160). Schumann heard the horn emerge 'from another sphere. Here everything listens, as if a heavenly spirit were wandering through the orchestra.' The reiterated horn Gs are harmonically reinterpreted by the strings between contrasting dominants of C major, F major alternating with D minor, to B flat as the Neapolitan sixth of A minor (bars 148–160). The emotional effect of these sudden shifts is heightened by the sudden emergence of the sublime, where we are suddenly thrust over the edge into new, ferocious territory (bars 214–250). At the end of this engulfing climax, a diminished seventh, strident with passion, is suddenly reduced to silence (bar 250), a gesture which is highly dramatic in its musical expression. The hushed pizzicato that breaks this silence, the cellos' attempts to steer us towards the Neapolitan key of B flat major (bars 253–56), along with the oboe's restorative pull back to A minor then to A major (bars 257–260, 264–267), are mature Schubert at his most inimitable.

The richly scored Scherzo and Trio combine orchestral weight with vitality in a way which is new to symphonic writing. Schubert's sonata form Scherzo has a precedent in his Sixth Symphony. Here the supercharged rhythm of the Scherzo springs to life with the full force of octave unison in the strings (bars 1–4), which makes the trio theme all the more powerful:

Example 20.3a: Symphony no. 8 (D 944/iii), Scherzo, first subject, bars 1–4

This opening figure later decorates the accompaniment of a broader, waltz-like second subject, which evolves into a retransition sweeping down and up the omnipresent unison strings (bars 30–56).

Example 20.3b: Symphony no. 8 (D 944/iii), Scherzo, second subject, bars 30–48

Another example of retransition is heard between the Scherzo and Trio where Schubert repeats a single note to the point at which it is removed from its harmonic context, allowing him to slip magically from a resounding C major close as the music pivots into A major for the Trio (bars 239–246).

Schubert's Trio is one of his most striking departures from symphonic tradition. Susan Youens traces a kinship between his setting of Pyrker's

'Das Heimweh' (D 851), also composed in the summer of 1825, and the revised Trio rescored and inserted as a musical inlay. For Youens, Schubert's Trio affords 'prime sites for nostalgia' where 'the impression is of something formerly beautiful and now lost, which can only be recovered by memory'.[36] Schubert's single-note reiterations herald our passage to and from this world whose waltz-like woodwind choral song transcends the simple tunefulness of the traditional trio (bars 247–294, 295–396). There is something unvarying in its texture, which is all part of Schubert's purpose and becomes the Trio's strength: long-reaching melodic spans, ample sonority, unyielding onward thrust, with its answering echo in the brass, all hold our rapt attention. The movement ends with a resounding cadence in C major. Its haunting reminiscence is essential for the Finale's effect.

The Scherzo gives way to a culminating *tour de force* Finale. Its opening gestures and their immediate sequels (bars 1–164), are all upwards-aspiring, inspired by Divine Providence and Schubert's naturalistic retreat from the dehumanizing perspectives of illness. Ascent, spiritual elation and redemption intermingle in the affirmative outburst that sets the Finale in motion. By the time he reaches his celebratory second subject (bars 169–340, principally G major), Schubert has already established the four-bar grouping as an almost invariable norm, the psychological effect of which is that this uplifting music now moves in long strides:

Example 20.4: Symphony no. 8 (D 944/iv), Finale, second subject, bars 170–85

The four repeated notes of the second subject, which most clearly symbolize the four-bar grouping, assume greater importance later on when they become a topic for development on their own and, at the end of the development, form a continuing backdrop against which the recapitulated first theme is superimposed. Later, in the coda, the same four notes, in deep and forceful octave-unison, become the four hammer-blows that call the finale's accumulated hyperactivity to account: a decisive part of the process of conclusion, after which the final sprint to the finish is unleashed (bars 973–1048). There is a marvellous rally in this final proclamation of God's greatness resounding in *fortissimo* C major cadences. Schubert's epilogue transforms its normal function and becomes the coda not just of the Finale but of the entire symphony, carrying its wordless message, communicating the liberation of Schubert's spirit after years of suffering. The sheer feat of carrying this symphony off is a showpiece of orchestral virtuosity.

Recognizing what he had achieved, Schubert wrote to the Directors of the Gesellschaft der Musikfreunde in autumn 1826, informing them of his decision to dedicate his most recent C major Symphony to the society.[37] At the Directors' meeting on 9 October, the Vice-President, Raphael Georg Kiesewetter (1773–1850), brought Schubert's proposal to the attention of the board.[38] Josef Sonnleithner, Leopold's uncle, was secretary of the society, Leopold and his father, Ignaz, were directors. The board had already been informed of the composer's straitened circumstances on an earlier occasion, and decided to grant him aid to tide him over a difficult period. They now awarded him 100 fl. KM as a token of appreciation for his past services to the society, which they swiftly paid before Schubert delivered the score. Kiesewetter informed Schubert of their decision, which the composer formally acknowledged on 20 October.[39] Between 28 November and 31 December he submitted the autograph to the society, which commissioned two professional copyists to prepare a set of orchestral parts.[40] When the orchestra of the society's performing members rehearsed the symphony with a view to including it in the Großer Redoutensaal concerts, they were unable to realize their aim. According to Leopold Sonnleithner, 'it was provisionally laid aside because of its difficulty and length', which was a tremendous blow to the composer. 'It was only on 15 December 1839 that a performance of this symphony, in its entirety, was planned for one of the Gesellschaft's concerts; but at the very first orchestral rehearsal the paid "artists" refused to carry out the necessary number of rehearsals, as a result of which the Concert committee had to confine themselves, for this occasion, to the first two movements.'[41]

Eight years after Schubert's death the world premiere of the 'Great' C major symphony by the Gewandhaus Orchestra under the direction of Felix Mendelssohn was an historic event, not only because of Mendelssohn's renown for conducting Bach's *St Matthew Passion*, but because Schubert's symphony was a similar revelation to the general public. The performance took place on 21 March 1839 and was part of the 'historical concerts' that Mendelssohn had instituted, each devoted to a group of composers from the past. These concerts encouraged the 'selfless immersion into a music' that manifested 'another world' and so formed an educative function: music was to be 'understood', not merely 'enjoyed'.[42] In 1839, Mendelssohn was thirty years old, two years older than Schubert was when he composed D 944.

At the beginning of the symphony's reception, Mendelssohn recognized D 944 as a symphony *sui generis*. Reports of the premiere lasting fifty-five minutes suggest that most of the repeats were observed; moreover, Mendelssohn's understanding of the score was communicated to the audience 'who received the work with tremendous applause [. . .] even more significantly all the musicians in the audience were moved and delighted by the splendid work'. Leipzig's *Allgemeine musikalische Zeitung* reported that the performance was 'as masterly as if the work had already been performed many times.' A further four performances – Schumann was at the second on 12 December, Liszt at the fourth on 23 March – established a Gewandhaus tradition and under Mendelssohn's direction the symphony was heard twelve times. Eager to secure a wider audience, Mendelssohn tried to procure a London premiere by the Philharmonic Society in 1839. Describing the work as 'a very extraordinary composition which has created an uncommon sensation among the musicians here', he cautioned 'I strongly recommend you not to repeat the first part of the last movement, perhaps also not the first and second part of the Scherzo.' The cuts that Mendelssohn suggested are very much in keeping with the kind of refinements Schubert made in rehearsals for his 'Death and the Maiden' Quartet (D 810) and Piano Trio in E flat (D 929), and which he might have made in D 944, had the planned performance by the Gesellschaft der Musikfreunde taken place.

Both posthumously and within Schubert's lifetime, D 944 marks a watershed. Death had always been on his horizon, but being confronted with his own mortality freed him up to live his life more fully 'until'. His final years are exemplary of the powerful paradoxical way in which the proximity of death charges living with life. Everything intensifies. Schubert's music too. He realized the importance of being alive; he knew how fragile life is and this charged his music with meaning and magnetism for future audiences. We hear this outward turning in D 944, which is one of the most pivotal works in Schubert's compositional career. His later dedication of his Piano Trio (D 929) to 'nobody save those who find pleasure in it' is another manifestation of this inner dichotomy and development, a direction of a very personal self towards an anonymous public.

AFTER LIBERATION

On his return to Vienna in October 1825, Schubert was in excellent spirits. As well as a decent income, the tour had brought him happiness and more recognition than he had ever known. As soon as he arrived in Vienna he took up residence in the Frühwirthaus and the warm welcome he received by friends is recorded in Bauernfeld's diary: 'Schubert is back. Inn and coffee-house gatherings with friends, often until 2 or 3 in the morning.'[43] In December an engraving of Wilhelm Rieder's watercolour made by Johann Nepomuk Passini was displayed and quickly sold by one of the city's leading art dealers. The impression is that of a successful composer on the threshold of an increasingly public career.

As usual on his return journeys, though, Schubert gradually withdrew into himself. Once again in support of him, the Schobers opened their home, but it was not a neutral environment. There was tremendous tension between

Schober and his mother, both of whom were grieving Sophie's death in 1825. Schober, who was now his mother's only remaining child, was struggling even more to make something of his gifts. Her patience was thinner than ever with him for squandering her inheritance. Bauernfeld and Kupelwieser had lived with the Schobers in late 1825, but swiftly moved out in favour of a more peaceful abode. Schubert moved in offering rent, support and musical distraction, as at the party that Schober hosted on 10 January 1826. Knowing that Schubert would be there, Bauernfeld had invited the poet Johann Gabriel Seidl to a gathering which he promised would be a 'feast of song'. The upshot of this reintroduction to the poet was at least six Seidl songs and three male-voice settings ('Widerspruch', D 865, 'Nachthelle', D 892 and 'Grab und Mond', D 893) in 1826, many in two versions (D 865 and 'Das Zügenglöcklein', D 871), with more to follow in Schubert's final year. One of these Seidl settings, 'Wiegenlied' (D 867), is a song of celebration in C major for the birth of Schubert's baby brother, Anton Eduard. The dominant theme of his songs is that of the divine woman, the transfigured image of an earthly woman, of which 'Die Sterne' (Leitner, D 939), 'Der Wanderer an den Mond' (D 870) and 'Im Freien' (D 880) are examples.

Shortly after Schober's Schubertiad, Schubert was out playing waltzes for a 'sausage ball' on 14 January and the number of performances and publications in January alone is a measure of Schubert's standing. On 20 January the *Wiener Zeitung* announced a new compilation of fifty New Waltzes, which included dances by Beethoven, Czerny, Hummel and Schubert among others. Five days later Schubert was performing his settings of Ernst Schulze's poems after a dinner party at Sophie Müller's home. A few days later the first rehearsal of the D minor 'Death and the Maiden' Quartet (D 810) took place in Franz Lachner's home, with Schubert correcting the freshly copied parts on 29 January; a second rehearsal was scheduled the following day, 30 January, at which Schubert cut part of the first movement. Thanks to the resident tenor at the Court Chapel, Josef Barth, the premiere took place in Prince Schwartzenberg's winter palace on 1 February, followed by a private perfor-

AFTER THE CRISES: THE SPIRIT OF BEAUTY AND ITS FATE

mance at Lachner's residence. Lachner, who was now assistant conductor at the Kärntnertortheater, wrote an account of their playing, which acknowledges Schubert composing in a very inward way, in direct comparison to the public chamber works that would follow.[44]

Between 20 and 30 June 1826, Schubert completed what is arguably the greatest of his String Quartets, no. 15 in G major (D 887), while elsewhere in the city Beethoven was coming to the end of his C sharp minor String Quartet, op. 131. In his last quartet Schubert is writing for a public audience, for a professional rather than a private quartet. The work shows him reacting to the changing environment, both audience and venue, through richly resonant writing, thicker textures, bold gestures along with a tightly knit structure and concentration of expression.

At first glance the quartet's formal structure seems conventional: an Allegro molto moderato in sonata form, an E minor Andante, a D major Scherzo, G major Trio and sonata-rondo Fnale. The opening meditation on the descending tetrachord, whereby the partimento schemata is refracted through Schubert's imagination in a novel way, announces this quartet as unprecedented Example 3.16a. The cataclysmic exchange of major and minor in this opening passage (bars 1–4) dominates the entire quartet, which is very tightly conceived through this inter-movement modal exchange, trading of themes and replications of form in the middle movements, and interconnecting triplets of the first and second subject groups of D 887/i.

Schubert's 'orchestral conception' of the work – one of the hallmarks of his early schoolhouse quartets – is confirmed by the end of the first movement when a D major chord vibrates across fifteen of the available sixteen strings, vastly extending the quartet's breadth of sonority (bar 428). Schubert's harmonic daring is heard in the prolongation of G major with an equal subdivision of the octave using major thirds (bars 414 and 429, Example 20.5 online). Passing seventh chords (in the bass) voice a whole-tone descent in the cello with major-third prolongations through G (bars 414–416), E flat (bars 417–418), B (bars 419–420), G (bars 421–422) and E flat (bars 423–426). Schubert enharmonically reinterprets this dominant-seventh structure (bar 426), resolving it as a German augmented 6th (bVI–V–I, bars 427–429) (Example 20.5 online).

Schubert's G major quartet offers a classic example of the (E minor) second movement violently interrupted by a G minor episode (bars 40ff). The emotional vulnerability of Schubert's music is also heard in the haven of the B minor Trio, but unearthly bliss is not a place in which we can stay. The Wanderer motif, never resting, resumes in the sudden tarantella rhythms, key shifts (frequently by half-step), and rapid G major–minor modal exchange of the Dionysian Fnale, reminding us there is no such certainty in life, no resolution. Schubert wrote this masterwork in ten days.

The public nature of Schubert's writing in his final string quartet is completely at one with his professional outreach. Although he had turned down the position of Court Organist which had been offered to him in 1825 (and for which his brother Ferdinand later competed unsuccessfully), Schubert sat down on 7 April to write to Emperor Francis, requesting that he be considered for Salieri's post as Musical Director at the Court Chapel, a position for which his teacher had trained him. In his stead, however, Josef Eybler, Salieri's assistant in his twilight years, was elevated to the position, which opened up the post of Deputy Court Kapellmeister, to which Josef Weigl was eventually appointed. Eybler's subsequent rejection of Schubert's request for a court performance of the A flat major Mass may well have been because Schubert's textual omissions would have been unthinkable within the context of the Imperial Chapel. Although Brahms later premiered this Mass in the Gesellschaft der Musikfreunde, Schubert's request to have it performed in the Court Chapel shows he saw it as a liturgical work.

If Schubert's spirits were raised by the prospect of this position, they swiftly sank with the police's raid on Ludlamshöhle in the spring of 1825. The arts club – named after a play by Adam Oehlenschläger performed at the Theater an der Wien in December 1817 – counted among its members distinguished international and local artists including Salieri, Ignaz Castelli, Adalbert Gyrowetz, Moscheles, Ludwig Rellstab, Rückert, Weber, Josef Götz, Ludwig Tietze, Grillparzer, Karl Pachler, Josef Kupelwieser and Seidl.

AFTER THE CRISES: THE SPIRIT OF BEAUTY AND ITS FATE

The innocuous nature of the society is reflected in the playful pseudonyms members were granted – Weber was Agathus, the Target and the Nobleman Samiel (after characters in *Der Freischütz*), and Grillparzer was Saphokles Istrianus (the Istrian Saphocles, a play on the philosopher Sophocles and his poetic drama, *Sappho*) – but the artists' intellectual interests soon attracted Foreign Minister Metternich's attention.[45] During the raid, members were placed under house arrest, their homes were searched and though nothing was found, the club was disbanded 'for endangering the state'. As Schubert and Bauernfeld were not formally enrolled, neither was involved, but their spirits were crushed by the draconian reality of Metternich's Vienna.

The absence of close friends for much of 1826 was also depressing for Schubert. After receiving the final payment for his Shakespeare translations commissioned for the German Shakespeare edition, Bauernfeld set out with Ferdinand Mayerhofer von Grünbühel on 15 April on a paid trip to survey and map parts of Carinthia.[46] At the end of his 1825 recital tour with Schubert, Vogl had travelled to Italy, and shortly after his return, announced his engagement to Kunigunde Rosa, whom he married in July 1826. Schubert was thereby left without the moral or material support which had proved essential to him from the time that they were first introduced in 1817. Schober was not good company for anyone nor was Schwind, whose love affair with Anna [Nanette] Hönig (1803–1888) was going badly.[47] Even Anselm Hüttenbrenner's visit to Vienna did little to lift the gloom which seasonally descended on Schubert every May, during which time he composed very little.

Writing to Bauernfeld at the end of that month, Schubert admitted 'I'm not working at all. The weather is truly appalling, the Almighty seems to have forsaken us altogether, for the sun simply refuses to shine. It is May, and we cannot sit in any garden yet. Awful! Appalling!! Ghastly!!! and the most cruel thing on earth for me!'[48] Bauernfeld immediately invited him to Gmunden where they could discuss the libretto for their opera, *Der Graf von Gleichen*, to which Schubert replied on 10 July, 'It is impossible for me to come to Gmunden or anywhere else, for I have absolutely no money, and everything else is going very badly with me. However, I am bearing up and in good spirits.' Short of funds, Schubert set a number of Shakespeare songs in translation for publication: Bauernfeld and Mayerhofer von Grünbühel's rendering of 'Trinklied: Bachus, feister Fürst des Weins' from *Antony and Cleopatra* (D 888), and Bauernfeld's translations, 'Horch, horch, die Lerch' (D 889) and 'Gesang: Was ist Sylvia' from *The Two Gentlemen of Verona* (D 891). The Shakespeare settings were a commercial venture and a good example of how Schubert took his friends' influence into himself.

When Bauernfeld returned to Vienna in late July 1826, Schubert and Schwind whisked him off to Schober's at Währing to celebrate. Schubert was very taken with Bauernfeld's libretto, *Der Graf von Gleichen*; though turned down by the Imperial Censorship Office in October 1826, he began composing it anyway the following June.[49] Its proposed ménage à trois suggests the experience of a man between two women, or two loves, had a certain topicality. Goethe's *Stella* had led to a similar furore: two marriages, one to an older woman, one to a younger, one rich, one poor. 'We are yours!' the two women exclaim at the end of Goethe's original version, which he subsequently revised for the censors. Schubert was, from the start, little concerned about the public reception of his opera: it was written out of personal need. Bauernfeld, who established himself as a successful writer of comedies of manners at the Burgtheater, attested to Schubert's intention to complete the work. Perhaps, had he lived, he would have succeeded. Opera was, after all, his dream.

FROM THE DUST-CLOUD OF A PASSIONATE EMPIRICISM INTO THE PURE CIRCLE OF HISTORICAL LIGHT: SCHUBERT AND HIS PUBLISHERS

'What would I be
Without you,
Friend public!
All my feelings, a monologue,
All my joy, dumb.'

Goethe, *The Author* (1773)

AFTER THE CRISES: THE SPIRIT OF BEAUTY AND ITS FATE

When he was away from Vienna in 1825, Schubert had been elected as an alternate member of the Gesellschaft der Musikfreunde and a full member of the Board of Representatives in 1827, a mark of his public presence and increasing prominence. That his membership enhanced his political and social standing can be seen from the increasing number of public performances of his music, which fed the developing interest of publishers, especially in his songs and male-voice settings.[50]

The paradox of so many of his songs coming into print is that they address large numbers of people in a language of intimacy. Schubert had made a conscious decision in 1821 not only to compose for a few dozen named friends, but to trust himself to the anonymous medium of print. Where was he to find a broader audience for his more ambitious works and how was he to address it? Was he to continue to commend himself in private gatherings to a few select though possibly influential patrons? Or was he to commit himself even further to the anonymous and bourgeois public? And if so, how?

On his return from his recital tour, Schubert turned to the Austrian public, no longer with opera and a plan to reform the stage, but through numerous songs, piano dances and duets in the form of printed music. The conscious effort to take himself in hand, discipline his life, and make himself an efficient social being, is evident in the tremendous energy he exerted on behalf of his manuscripts. Fifteen opus numbers were published in 1825, thirteen in 1826, eighteen in 1827 and eight in his final year.

Right from the beginning, Schubert's relationships with publishers had been problematic and remained so for the rest of his life. The root of his distrust of publishers came from his first interactions with Cappi & Diabelli in 1821–23 who had exploited lack of author's rights, profited from the lack of protection of intellectual property, whereby Schubert received no royalties. The whole fraudulent affair is read as Schubert's political ineptitude without examining the myriad details of his career in print. Schubert was gauche in his early negotiations with Diabelli, but immediately afterwards realized his mistake. On 21 February 1823 he complained about his first published dance set D 145, which he alleged had not been in accord with what they agreed. His request for compensation was ignored because the company was in dire financial straits and dissolved in December 1823.

Such problems were commonplace, even with eminent writers of Schubert's day. Goethe's publisher, Cotta, did not offer him royalties, though both men fought hard to protect artist's rights. At the Congress of Vienna in 1815, Cotta had presented a petition for the protection of authors and publishers which addressed issues of piracy that were particularly rampant in Vienna. While Schubert was writing D 944, Goethe was spending all of 1825 in single-minded pursuit of legal protection of his works against piracy because he wanted to hand down an authorized collection of his work whereby reprinting was prohibited and royalties were secured for himself and his heirs. Goethe had written a very carefully considered letter on 11 January 1825 requesting this privilege and protection. As a lawyer, he knew it was not enough to write a letter, but he had it handed to Metternich by von Nagler, with whom he was in correspondence. He also had Chancellor von Müller intervene with the Prussian government which led to King Frederick Wilhelm I signing Goethe's petition on 23 January 1826, granting him Prussian Privilege subsequently published in the 'Collection of Laws for the Prussian State'. On receipt of this privilege Goethe put together a 'society of younger and older friends' to edit the final authorized collection of his work.[51] In future years he emphasized not what he had secured for himself, but what he had gained for fellow artists and publishers.

While Goethe helped change the artist's role in the publishing process, it took years for such laws to become common practice. Many of the difficulties Schubert experienced in his negotiations with publishers were shared by his contemporaries. Surprisingly, though most music publishing companies were owned by composers, many did not safeguard original manuscripts. One of the biggest culprits was Josef Czerny who made little effort to preserve the originals. Pennauer was another publisher who did not safeguard autographs. When he opened a music shop in Leopoldstadt (1 Bräunerstrasse) on 1 July 1825, the firm published three of Schubert's songs and first editions of another thirteen compositions during his lifetime. As soon as Schubert's music was printed, fair copies were destroyed.[52]

From his first published dance set, Schubert recognized that his music was turned into a commodity which had to survive in the marketplace and which was subject to commercial practices, principles, even pressures. Despite his falling out with Diabelli in 1823, most of his dance sets were published by Cappi & Diabelli either jointly or by one of their firms.[53] As Schubert became more conscious of the material value of his music he offered the publisher Tobias Haslinger the Carnival Waltzes of 1827 and 1828 and requested honoraria for dances that appeared in anthologies.[54] Schubert was continually the victim of music piracy, a good example of which is the Galopp and eight Écossaises (D 735) which Lichtl had printed in Vienna at his own expense. Karl Theodor Müller published D 735 separately in Pest without Schubert's name on it, at which point Lichtl took him to court on 2 March and Müller was cautioned on 10 April. Schubert did not know about this lawsuit nor about the pirated copy of D 735 printed by Karl Gustav Förster in Breslau in 1826.[55]

Diabelli swindled Schubert, but he also gave him his first break and in time became his most prominent publisher. Reconciliation began with Diabelli's publication of Schubert's dance sets D 735, D 779 and D 734 for the Carnival in 1825 and 1826. Between March 1827 and October 1828, Schubert trusted Diabelli with the publication of numerous works including the last song issued in his lifetime, 'Glaube, Hoffnung und Liebe' (D 955), on 6 October 1828. After Schubert's death, the firm bought a significant part of his estate from his brother Ferdinand, thereby acquiring the rights to many printed works and unpublished compositions, also rights to compositions published in catalogues by Cappi, Czerny and the publisher's successor, Spina.[56] This amalgamation was lucrative because the family engraver Cappi had various branches. Between January and May 1825, Cappi & Co had published first editions of Schubert's dances D 783, op. 33, an Overture in F major for Piano Four Hands (D 675), op. 34, 'Mirjams Siegesgesang' (D 942), op. 36, and Kenner's 'Der Liedler' (D 209), op. 38.[57] Between June and November 1826, Cappi and Czerny issued first editions of Schubert's op. 60–1 and op. 65, which included Schubert's Six Polonaises for Piano Duet and various songs.[58] When he became sole owner of the firm, Josef Czerny published numerous posthumous first editions, which were negotiated before Schubert's death because they were announced by the *Wiener Zeitung* on 21 November, the day of the composer's funeral. On New Year's Eve 1828, Czerny announced that he had bought a further eighteen works from Schubert's estate, which were published in 1829–30 and eventually subsumed into the Diabelli estate.[59]

Schubert's initial dispute with Diabelli in 1823 caused him to change publisher frequently. Sauer & Leidesdorf subsequently released first editions of a considerable number of his compositions and played a very significant role in his career.[60] Schubert was on very friendly terms with Maximilian Leidesdorf, a prolific and popular composer, whom Beethoven nicknamed 'Dorf des Leidens' on account of his melancholic nature.[61] Leidesdorf's depression over the firm's financial difficulties, and his inability to pay Schubert in 1824, is mentioned in the composer's letter to Kupelwieser.[62] When he registered the company in his own name in May 1826, Leidesdorf continued to promote Schubert's work, including his Waltz in C major for piano (D 980D) and in July 1828 first editions of the Goethe settings 'Auf dem See' (D 543), 'Der Musensohn' (D 764) and 'Geistes-Gruß' (D 142), three choruses from *Rosamunde* (D 797/4, 7–8) and *Moments musicaux*, nos. 1–2, 4–5 (D 780/1–2, 4–5). Leidesdorf was another publisher who did not safeguard manuscripts and many were destroyed, including *Die schöne Müllerin* (D 795), op. 25, and the String Quartet in A minor (D 804), op. 29.

Schubert's first negotiations beyond Vienna were with the family engravers, Matthias Artaria in Mannheim, who paid Schubert 300 florins (WW) for his Piano Sonata in D Major (D 850), op. 53, and the

AFTER THE CRISES: THE SPIRIT OF BEAUTY AND ITS FATE

Divertissement à la hongroise (D 818), op. 54, both of which were published on 8 April 1826. Artaria also published his seven settings from Walter Scott's *The Lady of the Lake* (D 835–9, 843 and 846), following successful performances of these songs on Schubert's tour. A similar linkage of performance and publication is found in Schubert's dealings with the Viennese branch of Artaria & Co. Following a performance by Josef Slavík and Karl Maria von Bocklet of Schubert's Rondo in B minor for Violin and Piano (D 895) at a party in his home, Domenico Artaria commissioned and published the Rondo in A major for Piano Duet (D 951).[63]

Conscious of his own worth and ambitious to become known beyond Austria, Schubert looked increasingly to international publishers. On 12 August 1826 he wrote to Heinrich Albert Probst in Leipzig and sent the same letter to Breitkopf & Härtel.[64] Breitkopf never answered but Probst invited the submission of songs and piano pieces accessible for the general public. On 15 January 1827, Probst considered 80 fl rather high for each of the three manuscripts Schubert sent, but entered into negotiations with him in Vienna later that year. On 9 February 1828, Probst invited a second submission, again stressing that songs and piano pieces should not be too difficult. Instead, Schubert sent works that he wanted to see in print, most notably his Piano Trio in E flat (D 929), op. 100, on 10 April. When the six weeks' turn-around that Probst had promised became six months, Schubert expressed his frustration but still offered Probst his last three Piano Sonatas (D 958–60), the Heine songs from *Schwanengesang* (D 957) and his String Quintet (D 956), works he wanted to enter the commercial world of print.

Schubert's last publishing relationship was launched with the twelve Carnival Waltzes (D 969) of January 1827. Haslinger also published a number of first editions of opp. 77–83, 89, 90/1–2 and 91, including the G major Piano Sonata (D 894), Impromptus (D 899/1–2) and the songs 'Das Heimweh' (D 851), 'Das Zügenglöcklein' (D 871) and 'Der Wanderer an den Mond' (D 870). By far Haslinger's most important release was *Winterreise*, Part 1 (D 911, 1–12), and the posthumous publication of Part 2 (D 911, 13–24).[65] Payments for *Winterreise* were unlikely to have been very large, enough to eat up some of the debts that Schubert had incurred through medical expenses. From his first publications to his final proofs, economic necessity forced Schubert to accept less than was his due.

21

⬥
LATE SACRED MUSIC AS A SITE OF THEOLOGY?[1]

'As kingfishers catch fire, dragonflies draw flame;
As tumbled over rim in roundy wells
Stones ring; like each tucked string tells, each hung bell's
Bow swung finds tongue to fling out broad its name;
Each mortal thing does one thing and the same;
Deals out that being indoors each one dwells;
Selves – goes itself; myself it speaks and spells
Crying: *What I do is me: for this I came.*'
        Gerard Manley Hopkins, 'As Kingfishers Catch Fire' (c. 1877)

REVOLUTION AND RENUNCIATION: FINAL MASSES

Schubert knew that the Faustian contradictions which are central to human life and which he reflected in his music cannot be resolved except within Divinity itself. In his 1822 short story 'Mein Traum' redemption means reaching the state of being in death that is denied us in life: a state where all the contradictions and conflicts we experience in our lives are resolved in a symbolic circle which signifies full consciousness of, and being directly present to, the ultimately Real. He contemplated this circularity in 'Wandrers Nachtlied' (D 224, 1824), where God in Nature and Nature in God actively create in all eternity, and in 'Die Allmacht' (D 852, 1825), which challenges the myth of a god as a fixed Absolute. Here Divine Beauty is traditionally found 'in the flowers and the radiance of the star-strewn heavens', but it resounds just as 'terrifyingly in the roaring storm, in the rolling thunder and lightning's flames'. Schubert's God is Nature and as such is the foundation not only of everything good but everything that inspires horror, everything sublime, everything dark, nocturnal, desolate, intoxicatingly Dionysian, everything that confronts and shatters the deeper, more careful observer: 'Nemo contra deum nisi deus ipse.'[2] No one is in conflict with God except God himself. Schubert's God is Eternal Becoming.

How does this ethical imperative resound in Schubert's sacred music and how are his Lichtental masses different from these later proclamations? In all six masses Schubert's musical hermeneutics are a creative response to a contemporary crisis of faith. His last two masses were also written in the aftermath of a personal crisis when the renewal of contact with his former self made accessible again a religious position to which he had held when his mother died and which becomes discernible in his later works. This dialectic of public reform and private revolutions, for example the liberties he takes with the late masses, taking them beyond the church into the concert hall both musically and doctrinally, distinguish them from his early settings. His late religious works suggest a profound understanding of Christianity as a religion of redemption, of Divine revelation, and his view of religion is eirenic and aesthetic. We witness Schubert opening up to the philosophy of religion as evidenced in his Psalm 92 Hebrew setting for the Sabbath (D 953), which is all of one piece with his early distrust of Christian monotheism.

Whereas Schubert arrived at such a stance through his experience and education, how much he inherited from home can be detected in a letter from late June 1824 written by Franz Theodor, who despite their differences is still a father to him:

Dear Son
[. . .] We are all heartily glad that you are in good health [. . .] Try to take care of and maintain your health, the most important of all earthly

possessions, and make it your business to deserve the love and respect of all who mean well by you.

You know that, as a teacher to young people, I am prone to moralize; but believe me, it is not from habit, but from a profound conviction that nobody can be truly happy who is not continually in touch with God and keeps steadily to his Divine Will. We may, no we should even, moderately enjoy the innocent pleasures of life with grateful hearts, but we should not let our spirits sink in dark times either, for sorrows too are a Divine blessing and lead those who bravely endure them to the most glorious goal.

Where in history can we find a great man who did not triumph through suffering and unflinching perseverance? That is why I should like to persuade those I love best to such a disposition![3]

Although he draws substantially – yet loosely – on his father's representation of the Christian Absolute and belief that suffering is necessary for salvation – Schubert's God of Eternal Becoming reflects his own profound preoccupation with the fundamental meaning of life. His sacred music is a reflection of his fundamental situation – his aspirations, his striving for greatness, his limitations, his triumphs, even his ultimate need for some kind of redemption at the end of his life. Again and again music made him sense this redemption, in a kind of Divine revelation – lifting him inwardly far beyond the world of concrete experience. This is Schubert's mysticism which is heard just as immediately in his 'Great' C major symphony (D 944), his String Quintet (D 956) and *Winterreise* (D 911), as it is in the late sacred works, where text and music communicate his convictions about ultimate meaning.

Schubert's mysticism is evident in his last two masses, which transcend liturgical functionality and signal his desire to write music that challenges its own limits. In a letter to the publisher Schott's Söhne on 21 February 1828, Schubert singled out the A flat major Mass (D 678) as an example of his Faustian 'striving after the highest in art'.[4] Unlike his other masses, it was written without commission or a definite performance in mind. Its unusually long gestation period, his intention to dedicate it to the Kaiser or Kaiserin, his decision to revise it and the difficulty in securing a performance are all indicative of the efforts this work cost him. Although performance records are incomplete, we know from surviving parts and rehearsal markings on his manuscripts that his first five masses – and vernacular masses – were performed in various churches in Vienna and beyond, as Schubert himself confirms in his letter to Emperor Francis I on 7 April 1826.[5] Many of his liturgical works were in circulation in handwritten copy long before publication. In 1824, on an official visit as school inspector, his brother Ferdinand is surprised by a performance of Schubert's B flat major Mass at Pressburg, which the choirmaster had prepared for Ferdinand's visit, and for which he, impromptu, played the organ.[6] Schubert's 1826 revision of his *Missa solemnis* in A flat was one last bid to secure an official Church position.[7] Perhaps Josef Eybler, who succeeded Salieri as Court Kapellmeister in March 1824 and who would have been well familiar with Schubert's liturgical music, refused a Chapel Royal performance on account of its brilliance rather than its difficulty.[8]

How much of the *Missa solemnis* in A flat is unorthodox, both musically and liturgically? Certainly its extravagance challenges convention and is characteristic of the monumental growth in Schubert at a time of crisis. The orchestration is orthodox for a *Missa solemnis*: like Haydn, Schubert uses the flute occasionally but adds his own stamp with three trombones. His choice of key, A flat major, was uncommon though not exceptional, but the chain of thirds – which is only broken in the Sanctus – imprints a brazen originality on the architecture of the mass. The Kyrie establishes the key of A flat major, the Gloria is in E major, the Gratias in A major, the Credo in C major and the Incarnatus in A flat major, the Sanctus and Hosanna in F major, the Benedictus in A flat major and Agnus Dei in F minor. The effect of the E major Gloria after a prayerful Kyrie is dynamic and the contrast between these movements shows how tightly this mass was conceived.

Unorthodoxy proliferates in the Gloria and the Credo. Schubert's departure from generic norms is immediately apparent in both movements and in the five-part Kyrie – Kyrie (a), Christe (b), a', b', coda – which departs from the stock tripartite plea for mercy. The Gloria is divided into four rather than the customary five parts and recalls almost exactly the structure of his F major Mass. His handling of the Quoniam in the Gloria (D 678/ii), for example, where a long crescendo drops to *pianissimo* before the Cum Sancto Spiritu fugue, is the same plan as in the F major Mass. Such structural innovations – also evident in the Sanctus and Agnus Dei – arise through Schubert's symphonic conception of the mass and desire for greater textual expressivity. He achieves this through a variety of means. D 678 is written in the Neapolitan tradition of a Credo mass whereby the sparse texture of an *a cappella* treatment of the opening section gains intensity with each repetition. Its rising line gains figurative significance on its reappearance at 'et resurrexit tertia die secundum scripturas, et ascendit in coelum' (Credo, bars 187–200), where scriptural revelation and musical revelation are at one. At the centre of the Credo, he scores the 'Et incarnatus' for double choir in eight parts in 3/2 time (bars 131–182). The same Trinitarian symbol which one finds in a fifteenth- or sixteenth-century mass is underscored with the mass's characteristic tonality of A flat–C–A flat to capture the metamorphosis of God being made man (bars 131–154). Schubert's mature religiosity is evident in the double counterpoint of the 'Crucifixus', where each voice announces the figure familiar from Bach's Passions as a cruciform subject (Example 21.1).

The Credo closes with a powerful hymn in Schubert's Divinity key of C major ('Et vitam venturi saeculi', bars 350ff). Its sense of awe before the Infinite is continued in the bold labyrinthine opening phrases of the Sanctus, where the extreme tension of the harmony – which traverses from F major, F sharp minor, to C sharp major (bars 1–5), from D major, E flat minor, to B flat major (bars 6–11), from B major, C minor, to G major (bars 12–17) – characterizes this Eucharistic song of praise.

Example 21.1: Mass no. 5 in A flat major (D 678/iii), Credo, 'Crucifixus', bars 157–62

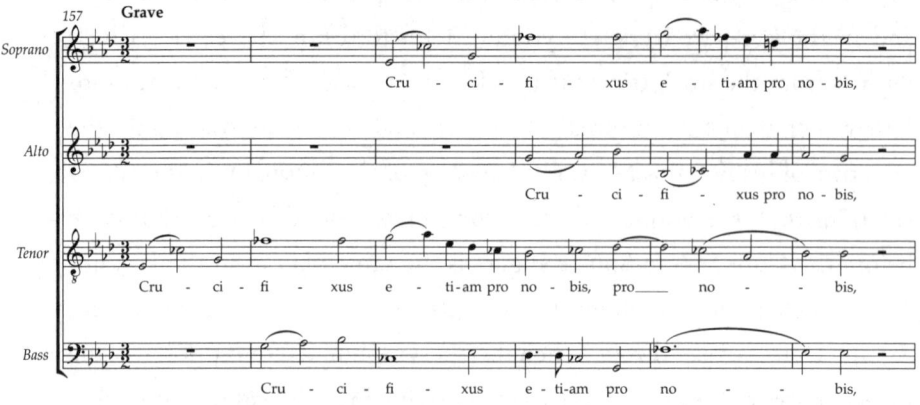

Schubert carries this textual expressivity into the Agnus Dei, where the solo quartet moves through extraneous keys, A flat major to E major (bars 1–11), and from E flat major to C flat major (bars 31–35), pleading for mercy, which is doubly effective after an arioso opening suggestive of Pergolesi.

Compositional unity through nuanced textual setting is extended across several movements in Schubert's E flat major Mass (D 950). By restraining the opening burst of praise in the Gloria (bars 1–16), he achieves a greater uniformity not only with other sections of the Gloria but also with the Credo. In the 'Domine Deus, Agnes Dei' section of the Gloria (bars 151–188), Schubert's dynamic extremes shift from *fortissimo* to *pianissimo* within 10 bars (bars 151–160) over an ostinato figure in the trombones' G–F sharp–G–A flat–G motif (bars 151–156), as tenors and basses implore mercy from the Lamb of God. Dynamic extremes and chromatic lines return in a tonally overwhelming Sanctus that musically depicts God's incomprehensibility and immensity. In the second part of the Sanctus (Osanna in excelsis Deo, bars 25–86), the choirs of heaven, souls in purgatory, and faithful on earth raise their voices in entreaty and spiritual connection. The chromatic motif, G–F sharp–G–A flat–G, returns in the Agnus Dei, transformed into a figure associated with the sign of the cross (C–B–E flat–D, bars 1–4). This is the only mass in which Schubert created compositional references between movements, where religious and symphonic thought are unified.[9]

STILE ANTICO FUGUES IN VOCAL STYLE

Fugues in vocal style abound in Schubert's late sacred music where he develops the *stile antico* fugue into a deeply symbolic thematic form. In his very first sacred music composition Schubert had tested his ability to write fugato passages in the Kyrie (D 31). His assimilation of the Neapolitan vocal fugue tradition and its acculturation had also been explored in the closing fugue of the Gloria of his first Mass in F major (D 105), which serves as a model for the large Cum Sancto Spiritu fugues in the A flat major and E flat major masses where Schubert raises this form to a higher level of perfection. In his 1826 revisions of D 678, inspired by his private study of Bach, he replaced the real response in the concluding fugue of the Gloria with a tonal response.[10] The astonishing 'Agnus Dei' of the E flat major Mass, which starts with a fine *fugato* and its deeply moving, extremely personal interpretation of the text, affirms Schubert's ability to compose truly sacred music, a Requiem for suffering humanity. Ultimately this *Lacrimae rerum* is composed for himself, a tragic Requiem 'in memory of me', to be conducted by his brother Ferdinand after his death. Its double fugue – whose first subject is identical to the subject of Bach's fugue in C sharp minor from *Das wohltemperierte Klavier*, Book 1 – shows Schubert at the height of his contrapuntal writing powers, just three months before his death. Both masses show an ever-deepening engagement with the fugue for a whole host of reasons, not least its intellectual, spiritual, expressive and even mystical properties.

When Schubert employs fugue as part of the sacred music tradition, he uses it as an allegory of Divine law and order through the deployment of chromaticism, which takes on thematic qualities and tonally stamps the fugue as a sign of suffering and sorrow. This tendency was already evident in nos. 7 and 12 of the *Stabat Mater* (D 383) and recurs with finesse in his final Mass in E flat major where he pushes back the boundaries of what is meant by the term 'fugue'. In the Cum Sancto Spiritu fugue at the end of the Gloria (D 950/ii), Schubert borrows the Magnificat subject which Bach made a figure of enquiry in the E major fugue of *Das wohltemperierte Klavier*, Book 2 (see Examples 21.2a and 21.2b).

Example 21.2a: Bach, *Das wohltemperierte Klavier*, Book 2, Fugue no. 9, subject, bars 1–3

Example 21.2b: Mass no. 6 in E flat major (D 950/ii), Gloria, fugue subject, bars 160–70

Schubert treats the subject chromatically and in dense combination with three hyperstretti, each entry separated from the next by a progressively shorter interval. Schubert's handling of the Credo fugue (D 950/iii) is just as engaging. After the exposition of themes there is only one single episode, the 'Et incarnatus' (D 950/iii, A flat major, 12/8), a rondo in canon form for soprano solo and two solo tenors into which is woven a deeply emotional and explosive Crucifixus (bars 134–198). This continuity with past style rather than modernist rupture is evident when Schubert is at his most innovative. It is interesting to compare the Crucifixus of the E flat and A flat major masses where counterpoint plays an equally important role. In the 'et incarnatus' section of the A flat major Mass it is an eight-part chorus in block chords (bars 131–182), whereas in the E flat major Mass it is a three-part solo canon for soprano and two tenors (bars 134–161). But perhaps the biggest surprise in the Credo (D 950/iii) is when the chromatic element already contained in the fugal countersubject leads to the lamento bass (bars 305–309), at which point the musical equivalent of the sign of the cross is recast ('et vitam venturi saeculi', bars 310ff). Here, in Schubert's final mass, chromaticism is given a formal function, whereby a traditional trope is deployed as a personal profession of faith. The E flat major Mass is a personal statement of ambition: a conscious compendium of musical styles from Palestrina's *stile antico* to the expressively free writing of the Crucifixus in the repose and sureness of Schubert's last liturgical composition.

LICHTENTALESQUE: *TANTUM ERGO* IN E FLAT (D 962) AND *INTENDE VOCI* IN B FLAT (D 963)

Regular commissions for occasional works in Schubert's final years testify to his standing as a composer of church music in Vienna. His most extraordinary *Tantum Ergo* settings, D 750 and D 962, were written for two of Ferdinand's close friends, Josef Mayssen, *maestro di cappella* in Hernals, and Johann Rieder (Wilhelm's brother) at Alsergrund's Church of the Holy Trinity. In his terrifying *Tantum Ergo* setting of 1822 (D 750), Schubert's juxtaposition of two modalities and descending and ascending tetrachords (D 750, bars 1–2) heralds deep inner conflict in which grace and guilt, the drama of last things – even terror of them – is present. Even if he was unaware of Monteverdi, which is unlikely given Salieri's and Kiesewetter's early interest in the composer, Schubert was a natural master of the *musica reservata* vocal style through his chromatic progressions and expressive word painting. His penultimate *Tantum Ergo* (D 750) is a work of singular expressivity, as is his final setting (D 962), whose gentle modulation from the dominant B flat to the minor mediant G flat at 'Praestet fides supplementum/Sensuum defectui' (bars 18ff) is an example of his ability to infuse a common text with uncommonness.

Schubert's early practice of writing occasional works which complement the architecture of his masses is realized with consummate perfection in his final year. The *Tantum Ergo* in E flat (D 962) and the Offertory *Intende voci* in B flat (D 963) were composed in October 1828, just one month before his death, as companion pieces to his final mass. The three compositions are for the same forces – a quartet of soloists, chorus and large orchestra but without an organ part because the organ in the Church of the Holy Trinity at Alsergrund was tuned to the older meantone temperament. Earlier in the year, 'Glaube, Hoffnung und Liebe' (D 954) had been commissioned for the unveiling of the new bell in the Minorite Church on 2 September. Beethoven's funeral had taken place at Alsergrund, and Schubert's wish to have his Mass in E flat major (D 950) performed there gives an uncanny sense of premonition, of writing his own commemorative mass in the summer of 1828. His choice of the Church of the Holy Trinity forms a conspicuous arch not only to Beethoven but to the Holy Trinity Chapel that his grandfather had built in Vysoká. Intended or not, this mass is a summation of his involvement with the Viennese church music tradition, a summary statement of his musical and artistic creed.

What is immediately noticeable is how differently Schubert approaches the companion settings D 962 and D 963, which partake of a musical diction that is much more directly emotional in impact and correspondingly less challenging to the liturgical status quo than the unorthodoxies of the E flat major Mass. Building on his earlier practice, the *Tantum Ergo* (D 962) and *Intende voci* in B flat (D 963) are complementary in mood, key and instrumental forces, but they are also harmonically interlinked, for example through Schubert's enrichment of the traditional plagal (minor subdominant) cadential formula which he uses in the final 'Dona nobis pacem' (Grant us peace) in the E flat major Mass (D 950; see Example 21.3a).[11] The originality of Schubert's musical thought is evident in these lines of supplication. In the 'dona nobis pacem' of his mass he surprises us by using ii7 with a flattened fifth, C flat (bar 252), with a very smooth transition into a diminished seventh chord in bar 253, and from there he slides into the minor subdominant:

Example 21.3a: Mass no. 6 in E flat major (D 950/vi), Agnus Dei, bars 250–6

How Schubert reaches the minor subdominant in the *Tantum Ergo* (D 962) also catches us by surprise. By using the German 6th in bars 30 and 31, followed by a typical Schubertian shift from E flat major to C flat major in bar 32, the C flat is announced well before it appears as chord iv as the final chord in the penultimate bar (Example 21.3b).

Example 21.3b: *Tantum Ergo* in E flat major (D 962), bars 29–33

In the *Intende voci* the resolution of the diminished seventh in bar 289 over a continuous tonic pedal is a further example of how Schubert varies a traditional plagal formula (Example 21.3c) and transcends liturgical function in an artistic expression of faith:

Example 21.3c: *Intende voci* in B flat major (D 963), bars 283–92

HISTORY AND HERMENEUTICS: SCHUBERT'S *CREDO*

It is clear from his late sacred music that the majesty of the Church never really left Schubert. Yet questions had emerged, fostered by his older brother's mockery of priests and the mindless worship of Christ's person and his cross.[12] If Ignaz – twelve years older than Schubert – became anti-clerical, Franz did not exceed him by become irreligious. As his faith in Catholicism faltered,[13] so his faith in Art grew considerably. Of the two ways of leaving the Church that were open to him, denial or transmutation, Schubert chose the second.

LATE SACRED MUSIC AS A SITE OF THEOLOGY?

Ferdinand Walcher von Uysdael (1799–1873), lawyer, civil servant, and fine amateur tenor, was on intimate terms with Schubert by 1827. His note to Schubert on 25 January, which opened with a citation of the Gregorian chant phrase 'Credo in unum Deum' that he immediately qualified 'you don't, I know that well',[14] has simplified the view of Schubert's unorthodox Christology. His distrust of religious dogma did not make him an atheist or a *faux dévot*. While he refused to recognize any Christian Church or the Bible itself as an ultimate authority in religious matters, there are accounts of him attending mass of his own volition in Zseliz in 1818 and with Franz von Hartmann at the University Church on 6 January 1827, three weeks before Walcher's note to him.[15] That Schubert continued to write uncommissioned sacred works until a month before his death calls into question his turning away from Catholicism with the kind of éclat normally attributed to him.[16] Numerous scholars have contemplated Schubert's Christian inheritance,[17] with Glenn Stanley recognizing the A flat major Mass as 'passionately religious'.[18] Is this mass a musical manifestation of the Godhead? Or is it an example of what Paul Ricoeur identified as the revelatory power of the text regardless of the author's intentions?[19] At the very least it bears the imprint of a composer who had reflected deeply on the liturgical texts that he was setting, on their universal as well as their personal significance. In contrast to the reactionary Catholicism of Schlegel and the Romantics, Schubert grew up steeped in Roman Catholic traditions and he rethought Biblical assumptions.

Schubert's reading of the Nicene Creed is illustrative of music's ability to give a realistic depiction of an individual in relation to the large-scale historical and social categories of his time.[20] Erich Benedikt has shown convincingly how in countless masses of Schubert's era large parts of the *Symbolum Nicenum* were missing,[21] while Hans Jaskulsky has argued equally convincingly that many of Schubert's omissions were done for reasons of musical form.[22] Yet they also provide a clear example of how music is a historically determined cultural artefact, as well as the product of individual and original creativity.

Writing to Friedrich von Müller, Goethe alludes to the European catastrophe of the spirit that characterizes Schubert's age: 'Humanity is faced with a religious crisis: how they will come through it, I do not know but they must and will see it through. Since people have realized how much nonsense has been fastened onto Him and since they began to believe that the Apostles and saints are also no better than such characters as Klopstock, Lessing and the rest of us [. . .], naturally it plays havoc with their thinking.'[23] This crisis of religion was occasioned by the rise of hermeneutics in eighteenth- and nineteenth-century Germany, which destabilized the sense of truth in Biblical utterances. A naïve understanding of the Book of Genesis and the Gospels as a 'realistic narrative' was eclipsed in the secular Enlightenment and replaced by a conception of these texts as (reliable or very unreliable) documentary evidence for historical purposes.[24] In Schubert's settings of the mass this principle of scriptural infallibility is clearly surrendered and the nature of his omissions suggests they were informed by contemporary criticism of the Evangelists.[25] Just beneath the surface of his six settings of the Nicene Creed, and sometimes not even beneath it, there is a systematic rejection of certain Christian claims. The consistency of these omissions makes for a welcome clarity. The seriousness in the position that Schubert adopts proves the process was conscious.

Firstly, his omission of the words 'et unam sanctam catholicam et apostolicam Ecclesiam' (and one Holy Catholic and Apostolic Church) from the Nicene Creed marks a point of difference between Christian inheritance and Schubert, who became increasingly ecumenical. There are two very different meanings contained in the expression 'credo in' I believe in, which can mean to accept the existence or the truth of something, or to devote oneself heart and soul to a person or a cause. This is what the profession of faith implies when it states 'I believe in one God', 'I believe in Jesus, the Son of God', 'I believe in one Holy Catholic and Apostolic Church'. Schubert's profession of faith could not accept Christian tenets, and the subtle distinctions in what he states he can 'believe' need to be understood as responses to the difficulties and dilemmas of his time and place. He viewed the institutional Church with a certain distrust but clearly identified with the ethical content of Christianity as a religion of love.

Secondly, Schubert's difficulty in believing in a life after death is evident in his inability to set the text 'et exspecto resurrectionem mortuorum' (I look forward to the resurrection of the dead) in his mass settings.[26] Enlightenment literature consciously propagated the impossibility of the 'resurrection of the flesh' which Christians took literally. Setting this part of the text, therefore, created a dilemma for Schubert as a modern believer: either he acknowledge the impossibility of the resurrection of Jesus, and thereby cease to be a believer, or he hold with the pious conviction that Jesus rose from the dead and exclude himself from modernity.

When he set the resurrection scene in 'Chor der Engel' (D 440), Schubert – like Faust in Goethe's *Nacht* scene – was drawing on his memory of childhood faith and remembering what it was like to believe. It is no coincidence that four years later his work on the oratorio, *Lazarus oder die Feier der Auferstehung* (D 689, February 1820), breaks off before the resurrection scene. August Hermann Niemeyer's text, which is based on St John's Gospel (chapter 11, 1–44), posed a problem for Schubert: How could he, as modern man, set to music this miracle of the waking of the dead in such a way that it appears as a meaningful message? The aesthetic crisis on which his fragment falters is not Schubert rejecting religion but an unrealistic narrative. Despite the impression of historical reality which Niemeyer's story gives by virtue of its concrete and lively character, it is, from beginning to end, a purely fictitious creation based on the story of the fourth evangelist.[27] In the whole of the New Testament, Lazarus's name occurs only in this episode. He is not even mentioned in the Synoptic Gospels, which were written before John and were closer to the narrated event.[28] Lazarus is not an historical figure and the easily imaginable physical resurrection which Schubert could not set argues against this truth. The cantata is a profound musical reflection on contemporary criticism of Christianity and a perfect image of Schubert's existence, caught in transition from one system of belief to another. *Lazarus* is not the music of an indifferentist but of a genuine spiritual pilgrim, determined to make his own way, in music and religion, as in other things.

Concomitant with the notion of the resurrection is the eschatological question of eternity and the human soul's immortality as opposed to eternity in the sense of God's everlasting presence. As early as his Mass no. 2 in G major and from his Mass no. 4 in C major, Schubert had omitted the phrases 'suscipe deprecationem nostram' (accept our prayer) and 'qui sedes [sedet] ad dexteram patris' (who sits at the right hand of the Father). Schubert's consistent omission of these passages suggests he was of a deistical disposition but not a theist. His rejection of an intervening God and a religious interpretation of suffering – namely that it is something deserved by humans for their wrongdoing – is confirmed in the opening line of the Nicene Creed in his fifth and sixth masses through his omission of 'Patrem omnipotentem' (Almighty Father) and 'in remissionem peccatorum' (for the remission of sins).

A fourth problem that Schubert had with the Nicene Creed was the idea of the Virgin Birth. One of the fundamental issues was that the Nicene Creed presented the historical Jesus of Nazareth as a mythological being: that he was 'conceived of the Holy Spirit' and 'born of the Virgin Mary'. A related dogmatic question is whether Christ arrives as the fulfilment of a prophecy suggested in Isaiah 7:14, namely that a virgin would conceive. If the Nicene Creed is right to say that Jesus Christ lived, died and rose again *secundum Scripturas*, then the Scriptures have to be read from beginning to end as the fulfilment of that prophecy. We detect Schubert's problem with this idea as early as his third mass, where the words 'consubstantialem patri' (of the same substance as the Father) are left out, and in the fifth and sixth masses where 'genitum, non factum' (begotten, not made) is omitted. Here, in the Nicean sense, 'Son of God' is no longer understood metaphorically but genetically as offspring. In Schubert's first working of the Mass in A flat major, he goes a step further and omits 'ex Maria virgine' (of the Virgin Mary) completely.[29] These omissions are not incidental: they are, unquestionably, manifestations of Schubert's belief which he shared

LATE SACRED MUSIC AS A SITE OF THEOLOGY?

with Goethe, who declared himself roundly, 'I for my part could not be persuaded by an audible voice from heaven that a woman has given birth without a man or that a dead man has risen again; on the contrary I regard these as blasphemies against the great God and His revelation in Nature.'[30] In contrast to Goethe's *Venetian Epigrams*, the poet's first explicitly and violently anti-Christian work, Schubert's omission of Christian mythology from the mass makes a very subtle but definite statement about Christianity as a series of illusions.

INTIMATIONS OF THE TRANSCENDENT

Was it Schubert's engagement with liturgy that led him to contemplate such issues? What was the relationship for Schubert between worship and belief? These are not easy questions to answer, and they open up even more sinewy and thorny ones. Does Schubert's music wrestle with such imponderables? In a purely logical cognitive sense we cannot know. But perhaps we can concede that Schubert was constitutionally heterodox and his sacred music opens up a path of enquiry into the nature of his belief in particular and the nature of his achievement more generally.

What can we conclude from Schubert's music about the nature of his belief? Firstly, his musical hermeneutics free the figure of Christ from its unhistorical patina, which the composer could not accept uncritically, and is a musical response to the contemporary quest for the historical Jesus that had continued for nearly a hundred years. That Schubert acknowledged the historical reality of Christ and could still look upon him with admiration is evident from his reflections on the terrible image of the crucifix commemorating the battle between Bavarian and Tirolian troops on the Pass Leug, which he passed when travelling in Upper Austria in the summer of 1825: 'O glorious Christ, to how many foul deeds must you lend your image? You yourself, the most terrible memorial of human depravity. They erect your image as if they wanted to say, "Look! We have trodden on the most perfect creation of God." '[31] The Christ with whom Schubert could identify was the Son of Man who suffered. But the nature of his identification is also telling because the penalty of crucifixion was not only death but degradation. In contrast to Pauline theology where the spilt blood of Jesus is the alpha and omega of the doctrine of salvation, Schubert highlights in his 21 September 1825 letter to Ferdinand the scandal that God's Messiah ended his life wretchedly on a cross. In the crucifixion scenes of his masses Schubert is deeply aware of the history of sin with which that event has marked humanity. By referring to 'glorious Christ' as the 'most perfect creation of God' he recognizes the Incarnation as the supreme moment in the unending process of God's self-revelation as the one who reveals Himself in human nature. Incarnation is here inseparable from Revelation if not identical with it.

Secondly, this sacred content is evident in many of Schubert's secular works.[32] Describing the experience of a great work of music, the philosopher Roger Scruton speaks of 'sacred' moments, moments 'outside time, in which the deep loneliness and anxiety of the human condition is overcome' and 'the human world is suddenly irradiated from a point beyond it'.[33] Schubert's experience of the mountains at Gmunden and Gastein in the summer of 1825 was among those 'transcendent' moments when the drab, mundane pattern of our ordinary routines gives way to something vivid and radiant, and we seem to glimpse something of the beauty and significance of the world we inhabit.[34] In 'The Prelude', William Wordsworth called such moments 'spots of time' when our mind is 'nourished and invisibly repaired' by our encounters with the natural world;[35] elsewhere, the poet speaks of how the mind can be impressed by the 'quietness and beauty' of nature, how we are lifted up by 'a cheerful faith that all that we behold is full of blessing'.[36] Schubert's music offers just as vivid a sense of the awe and wonder of the profound mystery of existence. A religious interpretation of his experience at Gmunden immediately points to its uplifting character, where the renovating power of nature transformed him into a deeper, richer, more joyful state of exaltation and thankfulness. Such manifestation is audible in the glory of Schubert's 'Great' C major

Symphony composed in the summer of 1825, which celebrates the natural and human world, and the majesty of the moral law that inspires the human race with awe and longing.[37] The bedrock of this experience was evident in the Klopstockian ode he wrote in boarding school on God's omnipotence in creation.[38] In this regard Schubert's religious position seems similar to the German Lutheran philosopher, Johann Georg Hamann (1730–1788), through his need to approach the supernatural by analogy with the natural, which attached him neither to deist nor orthodox parties. It was a belief to which Schubert remained true for the rest of his life.

Paul Ricoeur's transfer to non-Biblical writing of key characteristics of the pre-modern understanding of the Bible picks up and renews a tendency that was part of the invention, around 1800, of a sacred realm of human art as a compensation for the simultaneous secularization and humanization of religion. In his essay, 'Toward a Hermeneutic of the Idea of Revelation', Ricoeur distinguishes five forms of Biblical discourse, the fourth of which is the wisdom discourse, namely the reflections on human life in Proverbs, Ecclesiastes or Job, characterized by an absent God and the closest point of contact between sacred and secular scripture.[39] The existentialist's 'limit situations' of solitude, guilt, unjust suffering and death immediately gain a Divine dimension in *Winterreise* (D 911) when interpreted as manifestations of the incomprehensibility or silence of God and the emptiness of all humanly constructed meaning. The story of the Wanderer, perhaps the most striking reflection on the problem of suffering anywhere in Schubert's music, makes it clear that the horrible torments the protagonist undergoes, like those of Job, are undeserved. A whole world is 'manifested' in *Winterreise*: a world we recognize and share with one another. The Wanderer's encounter with the Leiermann in the last song is a reminder of our responsibility to each other, that our truth is everyone else's – which is one reason why after a performance of *Winterreise* there is not usually very much to say.

Winterreise embodies a truth known with certainty by our inner feeling that we are dependent, without qualification, on something outside ourselves. This certainty of unqualified dependence is the basic certainty of all religions, and it remained throughout Schubert's life the cornerstone of religion as he understood it. A passage from his diary on 28 March 1824 states: 'A person comes into the world with faith – it comes far ahead of understanding and knowledge; because in order to understand something, I must believe it first; [faith] is the higher basis on which understanding plants his first pillars of faith. Understanding is nothing other than analysed belief.'[40] Schubert's aphorism is reminiscent of the writings of Augustine and Anselm, where intellectual argument about a generous Absolute is part of the activity of 'faith seeking understanding', and it also embodies the Hegelian idea that God can be known by reason in conjunction with faith. Here, in this aphorism, faith constitutes for Schubert a universal religious certainty that is itself unmediated, not given to us by others, even prior to all language. It is a universal, natural religion beyond the reach of hermeneutics and history.

St Augustine describes this religious quest as proceeding via a descent into the 'interior' of the human psyche 'in which truth dwells'.[41] Certainly, Schubert's diary entries and correspondence bear testimony to a doxastic shift in 1825 in response to a deep and overwhelming crisis. Reading passages from his diaries and letters during these years, one cannot but notice correlations with the rich historical resources of scripture, religious tradition and praxis, where religion as a phenomenon arises from deep longings of the human heart, against a background of dire need and distress. Schubert's growth in experience and understanding during his years of crisis was not only an increase in self-knowledge, but also an escape from what had deceived him and held him captive. Such learning by suffering, in the process of undeception, deepened his recognition that the cosmos, with man as its preliminary high point, is the ever-richer self-expression of a fundamental spiritual reality. The sheer force of Schubert's creative engagement bears testimony to the belief that the true liberation of man consists in his growing humanization which is the fruit of constant endeavour.

LATE SACRED MUSIC AS A SITE OF THEOLOGY?

It is clear not only from the sheer volume of his sacred music, but from his transmission and transformation of that tradition, that Schubert experienced very intensely the impulse of the ultimate mystery to achieve self-revelation and that he sensed, in his psyche, the need to express it. The truth of this imperative resonates in music that is transcendent because Schubert attended to an inner voice that submitted him to ethical obligation: not merely to be something, but to do something. In the realm of church music this was for him to provide a personal contribution to the body of sacred music which was truly worthy of the liturgy for his fellow Viennese Catholics, possibly with a view to post-Christian humanity, and at a time when Catholic scriptures could be interpreted in a more sophisticated way. This latter claim is difficult to prove, but the sympathetic and non-dogmatic way in which Schubert set sacred texts provides some support for it and allows us to contemplate his sacred music as a religious activity made possible by a completely secularized world view. For as the great Catholic thinker and poet Gerard Manley Hopkins spelt out for us in the sonnet 'As Kingfishers Catch Fire',[42] the fundamental principle of natural existence applies in the moral world too: we are what we do, and our identity lies, not dormant and hidden within us, but in our interface with all other things.

22

DE PROFUNDIS: FINAL SONGS

> 'Most wretched men
> Are cradled into poetry by wrong.
> They learn in suffering what they teach in song.'
>
> Percy Bysshe Shelley, *Julian and Maddalo: A Conversation*

In 1826 Schubert had moved around Vienna with Odyssean rapidity. At the end of the year he moved out of Schober's to live alone near the Karolinentor, where he would remain until February 1827. Living in the Inner City connected him with friends. It also made it possible for him to maintain the usual round of Schubertiads, followed by drinks in favourite bars with friends and fellow musicians. Thanks to the von Hartmann brothers, Franz and Fritz, we have a more detailed account of the year in which Schubert turned thirty, which must have played some part in his decision to have a place of his own. On the surface, he gave the impression of good health, but telltale signs were frequent absences from performances of his own music and Bauernfeld's recognition that he was drinking too much.

Schubert's public life was laden with performances and publications. In early January, the pianist Josef von Gahy played two sonatas in Spaun's home – presumably the Sonata in A minor (D 845), op. 42, and Sonata in D major (D 850), op. 53 – which was one of two occasions when the composer was absent. The other was on 13 January when Gahy played

DE PROFUNDIS: FINAL SONGS

Schubert's *Valses nobles* (D 969) for their friends. Before that, on 11 January, 'An Schwager Kronos' (D 369) had been performed at the Gesellschaft der Musikfreunde. The following evening Ferdinand Walcher sang 'Drang in die Ferne' (D 770) and 'Auf dem Wasser zu singen' (D 774), before joining a large Schubertiad at Spaun's. There, in addition to Gahy and Schubert's rendering of the 'Grand Duo' Sonata (D 812) and *Divertissement sur des motifs originaux français* (D 823), Johann Vogl performed a sheaf of Schubert songs including 'Romanze des Richard Löwenherz' (D 907), 'Nacht und Traüme' (D 827), 'Erlkönig' (D 328) and 'Im Abendrot' (D 799). As often happened, Schubert ended the night in Bognor's café with Schober, Bauernfeld, Huber and the von Hartmann brothers. Another significant January house concert took place in Domenico Artaria's home, where Schubert heard his *Rondeau brillant* in B minor (D 895) performed by Josef Slavík (violin) and Karl Maria von Bocklet (piano), which prompted its April publication.

Already in January, Beethoven's death was anticipated in the *Allgemeine musikalische Zeitung*.[1] By the end of February, the fifty-five-year-old Beethoven had acknowledged to friends he was dying, which brought Hummel and Anselm Hüttenbrenner to Vienna to sit by his bedside when he took his last breath on 26 March. We do not know whether Schubert visited the dying Beethoven with Anselm. Anton Schindler's account of Beethoven reading Schubert's songs on his deathbed and proclaiming, 'Truly in Schubert there dwells a divine spark', sits uncomfortably with the blessing of an older composer passing the mantle. But Schubert was among the thirty-six artists who were torchbearers at his funeral, each of their torches draped with black crepe ribbons. Fritz von Hartmann's diaries record how he retired with Schubert, Schober and Schwind to the Castle of Eisenstadt Inn afterwards, where they stayed 'talking of nothing but Beethoven' into the early hours.[2]

In the weeks following the funeral a succession of private and public concerts took place in which works by Schubert and Beethoven were performed side by side. At a private gathering on 10 April at Eduard

Horstig's home, the tenor Ludwig Tietze and Schubert included Beethoven's 'Adelaide' in a recital of Schubert's songs. The public premiere of Schubert's Octet (D 803) was given on 16 April, in Ignaz Schuppanzigh's final subscription concert of the season. On the same evening, Beethoven's *An die ferne Geliebte* was programmed as well as his 'Emperor' Piano Concerto no. 5 in E flat major performed by Carl Czerny, the Schuppanzigh Quartet, and a second pianist supplying 'the orchestra'.

On account of all this performance activity, Schubert composed very little in May, though he may have been working on *Winterreise*. Certainly, around the anniversary of his mother's death, Schubert's mood and productivity were characteristically low. With wraith-like rapidity, he moved out to Dornbach, far enough to benefit from the necessary solitude to compose, yet close enough to Vienna to make periodic visits to the Castle of Eisenstadt Inn. Professionally things were going quite well for him. The first half of the year had brought many of his dances and songs into print, beginning on 5 January when Diabelli announced the publication of 'Der Einsame' (D 800) and 'An die untergehende Sonne' (D 457). In the same week Sauer & Leidersdorf announced a new collection of dances and waltzes for the Carnival to which Schubert had contributed. The release of his songs and piano works resulted in newspaper announcements in Vienna, Leipzig, Frankfurt and Berlin. In 1827 Schubert was in the ascendant.

HUMAN CHAIN:[3] *WINTERREISE* (D 911)

From the beginning of the year Schubert had been composing *Winterreise*, a high-water mark in nineteenth-century song. There are few song cycles written in the last 200 years which can move us in the same way as this. From its opening bars it conjures up a world that is mature, majestic, ascetic and virtuosic. Even its title is a totalizing image, in that so much is gathered into its orbit of meaning

Schober claims Schubert found Wilhelm Müller's poems in his private library, but what really drove the composer to set these twenty-four songs?

The autograph copy for Part One is dated February 1827. Fritz von Hartmann's diary entry for 4 March records how Schubert invited friends to Schober's to hear the *Ur-Winterreise*, but then he failed to show up.[4] Did he recoil anticipating their reaction or did he decide that the songs weren't ready? The toil involved in Schubert's creative process are imprinted on the manuscript. The autograph for Part One is a mixture of fair copies and first versions, which are sketched in a light brown ink, with the piano part and revisions added in a darker, clearer ink. The engraver's copy contains five different hands: an unknown hand for the title page, two copyists, Haslinger and Schubert. Before *Ur-Winterreise* was passed by the Central Book Censorship office on 24 October 1827 and published on 14 January 1828, Schubert was already preoccupied with Part Two. He delayed giving a very carefully transcribed fair copy of Part Two (in his own hand) to Haslinger until the end of September 1828, eleven months after he completed the cycle and just seven weeks before he died.

Long before Schubert composed or published a note of this work, the twenty-one-year-old Wilhelm Müller had consoled and assured himself in a journal entry of 1815, 'that the poems will find a kindred soul who hears the melody in the words and gives them back to me'.[5] If Müller heard Schubert's *Die schöne Müllerin* a decade later, he would have known his hopes had been fulfilled. On the surface their lives were so different: Müller was married with children, a well-travelled polyglot and literary translator, a writer and classics scholar whose life displayed all the trappings of success. But below that veneer, continuities and solidarities are easily elicited: both men survived in families where multiple siblings had died in infancy; both died of an infectious disease, Müller unexpectedly in his sleep on 30 September 1827, one week before his thirty-third birthday. He had lost his mother at fourteen; his father died on 13 June 1821. Like Book VI of Virgil's *Aeneid*, he descended into the underworld in search of the spirit of his father. That Müller spent two years recording and revising his winter's journey suggests it meant more to him than he was willing to admit. This Virgilian *pietà* for the dead contains an immediacy which is not present in his other work.⁶ Its integrity and distinction inheres in its poetic and narrative energy, which is laden with anthropological and eschatological interest.

Schubert's musical setting changed the way Müller's poems were received, initiating a new era and new terms of appreciation. Part of the poignancy of *Winterreise* (D 911) is the twilit fetch of Schubert's harmonic language and our posthumous knowledge that he was dying when he composed it. Long before he set these poems, the solitary wayfarer had been Schubert's sobriquet. From his very first composition, 'Lebenstraum: Gesang' (D 39, 1810), through 'Wandrers Nachtlied I and II' (D 224 and D 768), 'Der Wanderer' (D 489 and D 649) and 'Der Wanderer an den Mond' (D 870), he had continually cast himself in this role. Knowing how closely this figure shadowed the composer, Spaun's uneasiness about *Winterreise* grew to the point where he could no longer keep it to himself. He relates how Schubert issued a second invitation to Schober's for a private recital of 'terrifying songs which had affected him more than has ever been the case with any other songs. With a voice full of feeling Schubert sang [and played] the entire *Winterreise* for us. We were altogether dumbfounded by the sombre mood of these songs.'⁷ When Schober broke the silence, admitting he only liked 'Der Lindenbaum', Schubert jumped up from the piano and admitted, 'I like these songs more than all the rest, and in time you will too.' Like Spaun, Mayrhofer recognized the biographical connection: '[*Die schöne Müllerin*] opens with a joyous song of roaming, the mill songs depict love in its awakening, its deceptions and hopes, its delights and sorrows [. . .] Not so with *Winterreise*, the very choice of which shows how much more serious the composer had become. He had been long and seriously ill, had gone through shattering experiences and life for him had shed its rosy colour; winter had come for him.'⁸

The arc of Schubert's adult life is contained in *Winterreise*: the short-lived *Paradiso* and unforgiving winter were all too familiar. Yet the most striking thing about the cycle is how extraordinarily it beseeches, yet also rejects, a principally or exclusively autobiographical interpretation. It is not wrong to stress the degree of Schubert's self-identification with

Müller's solitary wayfarer, but it would be wrong to overlook the double nature of his role. The cycle *is* expressive of Schubert's spiritual state, it deals with crises, challenges, complexities which the composer certainly experienced, but the work is also an artistic triumph over the irrational passion the protagonist harbours. Schubert turned private suffering into a cycle of public significance: his art made his life worthy of attention.

Working on his translation of Virgil's *Aeneid*, Book VI, in the final summer of his life, Seamus Heaney recognized, 'All the great myths are consistent with what you need. You need a sense of moving on, crossing something – into the dark . . . into the unknown. The great mythical stories of the afterworld are stories which stay with you and which ease you towards the end, towards a destination and a translation.'[9] *Winterreise* is cast from the same mould as Heaney's poetry collection *Human Chain* and Yeats's *Spiritus Mundi* from 'The Second Coming', whereby human minds are linked to a single vast intelligence which causes certain universal symbols to reappear.[10] Like Homer's *Odyssey*, the cycle opens *in medias res*, its twenty-four Lieder reflecting the twenty-four books in Homer's *Odyssey*, its two sequences of twelve songs marking the passage of time. The monodrama possesses enormous mythic potency: it arrives from somewhere beyond the boundaries of our experience and, having fulfilled its purpose, passes back into the beyond. In the intervening time Schubert conjures up a musical world as remote, as commanding, as solid and dazzling as Homer's *Odyssey* and Virgil's *Aeneid*, in a non-linear plot where prior events are described through flashbacks.

This musical monologue can also be framed as a modern-day *Commedia*, though not in the medieval-Aristotelian sense in that it never leads from misery to a state of happiness. Schubert has composed a *Divine Comedy* of a soul in exile without the *lieto fine*. Its weight and heft has much in common with Wisdom literature from the ancient Near East and the existentialists' 'limit situations' in that it treats the world not as the place where God acts or speaks, but the place where he is absent and has to be sought. Like St John of the Cross's Dark Night of the Soul, the cycle draws our attention to the ineluctably wretched destinies some people face when neither earth nor heaven offers an adequate response to their heart's cry for love.

Turning to nineteenth-century cultural symbols, the cycle can be read as Schubert's *Werther*. The Wanderer is a highly intelligent individual and intensely artistic persona, who reveals an experiential energy so great that it threatens to overwhelm him. Across the twenty-four songs we witness in him a process of ever-greater disintegration through his inability to find some kind of sustaining balance between himself and the world. Like Goethe's epistolary novel, the songs present a necessarily episodic series of encounters. Werther's tendency to read his own emotions into his natural surroundings is mirrored in the interplay of feeling heart and nature in Part One where the forces are in perfect equilibrium. Right at the beginning Schubert symbolizes the dangerous weathercock of the soul in the daring unison writing of 'Die Wetterfahne (D 911/2), confined key areas of F minor and A flat major, and the cautious voice leading of 'Gefrorne Tränen (D 911/3). He traces his pilgrim's spiritual journey through the obsessional repetition of 'Erstarrung' (D 911/4), the major and minor (fantasy and reality) modalities of 'Wasserflut' (D 911/6), and the overflowing harmonies of 'Auf dem Flusse' (D 911/7). Freed from the control of any object, either natural or human, the traveller's emotions swirl into hysteria in Part Two where the clear Homeric vignettes of the opening song, 'Gute Nacht' (D 911/1), give way to wild but indefinite landscapes. The springtime of the Wanderer's heart heard in the diatonic passage of 'Frühlingstraum' (D 911/11, bars 1–14) contrasts with the violence of reality (bars 15–26, 59–70) and return of accentuated unison writing to invoke winter winds in 'Der stürmische Morgen' (D 911/18). The essence of debility is suggested through an ever-narrower focus and confinement of his world as the Wanderer pinpoints his hopes on a solitary leaf. His precarious position on the threshold of psychosis is symbolized by the song's metrical displacement, tonal and rhythmic disorder. In the last songs of the cycle, the wayfarer's mind races away in detachment from its object as he slips rapidly from delusion in 'Der greise Kopf' (D 911/14) into the despair of 'Im Dorfe' (D 911/17), and from there into the G minor *Todessehnsucht of* 'Der Wegweiser' (D 911/20). In the F major 'Das Wirthaus', Schubert cites the plainchant Kyrie from the *Requiem Mass*, which he had sung as a child in Lichtental and the Stadtkonvikt, and which he paraphrases in his *Deutsche Messe* (D 872).[11] His Dance of Death strikes up in the Ländler patterns of his last two Lieder as he remembers his beloved in heaven, whose eyes close in 'Die Nebensonnen' (D 911/23), and now he hopes to return to her 'when the third sun sets'. The repeated hollow fifths of 'Der Leiermann' (D 911/24), persistent diatonic A minor tonality, and trance-like repetitions capture the fate of one whose life goes on and on, beyond all bearing (Example 22.1 online).

What, then, are we to make of Schubert's identification with this solitary wayfarer? At one level our answer is framed in psychological terms. We register in Schubert's pilgrim the monstrosity of the uncompromising, intransigent self, yet we can also hear a protagonist who expresses a profound philosophical dilemma: that of an acutely self-aware, self-reflective spirit, who is in quest of a simple, unifying experience. The path the Wanderer takes seems too extreme for lost love and at the same time portrays an experience of love so strong that it throws everything into sharp relief. In this disquieting ambivalence at the heart of this cycle one hears the central issue as having very little to do with erotic entanglement and a great deal to do with the displacing force of human self-consciousness. As with Goethe's *Werther*, *Winterreise* suggests that passion which is denied any acknowledgement or any means of expression has broader socio-cultural implications than one individual's emotional inadequacy; it is only in philosophizing such a journey that the Platonic concept of Eros acquires its depth and human relevance.

During Schubert's lifetime German theology secularized itself into philosophy, and in some respects the cycle can also be read as a tributary to some of the resulting religious philosophies and an expression of 'post-Christian' consciousness. It illustrates the secularization and humanization of religion: the Wanderer is an 'unhoused man' ('Im Dorfe' and 'Täuschung', D 911/17 and 19), whose lack of any habitation or dwelling symbolizes the Biblical impermanence of human life (Hebrews 13:14). As soon as we are aware of these archetypal patterns and the cycle's three symbolic sites of fear – the ravens ('Die Krähe', D 911/15), the river ('Wasserflut', D 911/6), and the outcast ('Der Leiermann, D 911/24) – the question that Schubert's pilgrim faces is raised for us: Who or what is guiding his life, and to what end? Is the Leiermann a nineteenth-century Charon, the boatman waiting to take Aeneas across the River Styx? Or does the cycle end, like the *Aeneid*, Book VI, at that moment on the bank of the River Lethe where we are shown the soul of one about to be reborn – as Schubert continually sought in 1822 – and about to return to life on earth?

Schubert's most powerful and profound drama of the self opens out into at least three possible endings. Firstly, the word 'Tod', death, never appears in Müller's monodrama but is implied through its imagery and euphemisms. Schubert's cycle opens with the *Grußformel*, 'Gute Nacht', a literary trope expressing a leave-taking from life alluded to in the descending lines and hollow fifths (bars 1–2) which frame the cycle. It closes with the same musical gestures expressed by a mythic figure who takes the wayfarer to the other side and crosses into the unknown. In between the *gravitas* of these songs, Müller's cycle was consistent with Schubert's needs and his composition of it was a way of coming to terms with death, an easing towards the end. We sense an opening of his consciousness that is characteristic of his late works, but the ending suggests he had not reached a receptivity to what might be awaiting on the farther shore. Even Schubert, who was a master in dwelling in contradiction, could not grasp a time beyond his own existence. *Winterreise* suggests he was grief-stricken by its terminus, recoiling from admitting that this is all, and at the same time not demanding absolutes.

A second reading is a spiritual numbness or death, reaching a psychological realization or a loss of innocence, or the end of an era in one's life that is allegorically a kind of death.

A third reading is that Schubert's solitary Wanderer has lost his ability to reason, as suggested by his gradual withdrawal from personal relationships, from reality into fantasy and delusion. It is not simply that the Wanderer's imagination takes over his life and deludes him into seeing himself as an old man in 'Der greise Kopf' (D 911/14), a deception which is no part of ordinary experience, where he more or less ghostifies himself in the song's descending vocal lines and echoing cadences (bars 7–10, 32–35, 43–44). In 'Der Leiermann' (D 911/24) – in the figure of the hurdy-gurdy player mindlessly churning out music – Schubert depicts a death that corrupts the intellectual powers themselves: the loss of music as an instrument for the apprehension of truth. The Leiermann is an image of horror because death of the imagination is the worst possible pain for a composer, because it destroys his ability to lament or to express acute suffering. This fading grasp of organizing reason is horribly apparent in the Wanderer's final dialogue – or rather monologue – with the derelict hurdy-gurdy player he encounters, or imagines. *Winterreise* closes in this shadow region with one of the ghosts and shades of the dead. In this shadowland, Schubert conjures up his ancestral Moravian musicians, his great-grandfather and grandfather from the village of Vysoká whose improvisatory dance music with its plaintive melodic line, hollow fifths, minor tonality, and hypnotic repetition resound in the melodic, rhythmic, harmonic and formal gestures of 'Der Leiermann' (Example 22.1 online).[12] 'Strange old man, shall I join you?' gains real significance when we realize the hurdy-gurdy player churns out their song. Schubert leaves open the question of whether the last words of his cycle are to be understood as the last words his wayfarer is capable of uttering, or whether the silence that follows is that of a spiritual night, though much points in that direction.

But before the shadows close in, the Wanderer recovers enough composure to be able to identify with the humanity of another. Up to this point he has been surrounded by a dead, unresponsive world, which he no longer has the power to transform into a Golden Age.[13] Brought to the limit of his own mortality, he steps out of his isolation and recognizes his ethical responsibility to a person who has nothing. Standing barefoot on the ice, on the outskirts of the village, the Leiermann is a symbol of suffering humanity. The moment the Wanderer addresses him (bars 53–61) is a moment of Shakespearean complexity. It is as if Schubert has fully envisaged the possibility of a tragic conclusion for his cycle, but has not had the courage to render it explicit. The final song is frozen in this moment of horror, which expresses existential loneliness before death with such unforgiving truth. The isolation of human beings is the theme of 'Der Leiermann', though it seems to be describing a collective fate: the Wanderer reads his condition in the street musician, but neither of them speaks a word of it. The absence of dialogue in this little tableau is perhaps its most terrifying feature, which is what makes it an image not so much of a shared destiny as of individual isolation in the face of death.

But we also sense we are not alone. We are in the presence of the composer who is terrifying us, and for his own purpose. Schubert touched on this human condition in a wistful diary entry of 27 March 1824: 'There is no one who understands the pain or joy of others! We always imagine we are coming together, and we always merely go side by side. O what torture for those who recognize this!'[14] In 1827 he lures us back into the same dilemma: he is present as one who shares in the terror he has created and as the solitary Wanderer whose condition he shares. The silence of the Wanderer and the Leiermann about the horror they witness is never directly articulated. The composer of the cycle passes over their silence and thereby shares in it, so our situation as listeners is both solitary and shared. Schubert is playing a double role: he is with us in this scene and he is outside it, overstepping the boundaries of our desperately constricted condition, compelling us to see ourselves in the broader context of his apologetic cycle. We recognize the world we share with each other, this existential stance within ourselves. The desire to remain sitting quietly after a performance of *Winterreise* has to do with steadying and reorienting in the face of such harrowing truth.

The evaporation of the *liete fine* is something one rarely finds in Western art because of humankind's deep-seated need for resolution. *Winterreise* is a work of tragic recognition which does not betray the listener into simplicity or fake consolation. By the time he composed it, Schubert was familiar enough with individual tragic fate to know that he could not relate such experience to a more general order that would resolve or simply explain it, without falsifying its particular hurt or truth. The cycle frames the Wanderer's experience in the light of an original dependence on things, which relegates unity, harmony and perfection to the status of ideals that he cannot compel into reality. Schubert shows himself reduced to silence by the experience of his central character, whose fate is too appalling for anyone. On his deathbed, Schubert even recoiled from his original *Todessehnsucht* tonality of B minor, through which he had transfigured his most intense suffering.[15]

Winterreise is open-ended because philosophizing has so much to do with pure awareness that, in being aware, questioning falls silent. The best and most essential attribute of philosophical *theoria* is the speechless wonder that looks down into the abyss. At the end of this cycle lies a question at the heart of philosophy: 'What is it all about?' The open-ended nature of Schubert's exploration affirms his recognition that it poses an unanswerable question. The very act of questioning it in music is a way of remaining in pursuit of reality and of keeping it in sight. Schubert raises a question that cannot be precisely answered, for *philosophia* means anything but the possession of that comprehensive knowledge which we call wisdom. Instead, it is the loving search for it: a search that, while never-ending, is also not in vain. The musical resolution that underpins the uncertain ending of the cycle may be aimed at 'rescuing' in art the image of a world that, despite everything, is unified, and points to a totality which defies any final formulation. The gods may be silent, the Leiermann too, but Schubert's response is to say there has to be more than silence.

GATHERING UP FRAGMENTS: SCHUBERT'S *ITALIANITÀ*

In a radically different way to *Winterreise*, *Drei Gesänge* (D 902), op. 83, three Italian songs published on 12 September 1827, is Schubert's response to the pathology of the public mind, in this case Vienna's opera-loving public. These bilingual songs were also part of a commercial project that Schubert had been exploring since 1825 when he began collaborating with de Jachelutta, who had provided singing translations for Schubert's *Lady of the Lake* settings which were released in a bilingual German and English edition on 5 April 1826. A fortnight after op. 83 was published, 'Der blinde Knabe' appeared in German and English in the *Wiener Zeitschrift für Kunst, Literatur, Theater und Mode* on 25 September 1827, and it was one of the songs reprinted by Probst in the aftermath of Schubert's death. Even though German and Italian traditions were closely entwined in multicultural Vienna, publishing in two languages was still unusual for the time. Neither of his Viennese contemporaries, Franz Lachner and Conradin Kreutzer, both of whom were successful opera composers, crossed over into Italian composition. Beethoven's *Tremate, empi, tremate* op. 116 by the court librettist, Giovanni de Gamerra (1742–1803), was also composed as part of his lessons with Salieri (1801–1803) to commemorate de Gamerra's passing, and was intended for Vogl to sing. The former court opera singer was long experienced in the interweaving of Italian and German traditions on stage and in the salon through the Italian practice of *manieren*, improvised embellishments which he lavished on Schubert's songs.

Schubert wrote his *Drei Gesänge* not for Johann Vogl but for Luigi Lablache (1794–1858), one of the most celebrated basses in Vienna in the 1820s. Between 1823 and 1827 Lablache gave 130 performances of twenty-four different roles, thereby ranking among the most important singers during the reign of the Italian impresario Domenico Barbaja. When Schubert dedicated his *Drei Gesänge*, op. 83, to him in 1827, Lablache was at the pinnacle of his success. In the very same year Edward Holmes reported on his visit to Vienna the depth of feeling in Lablache's singing, his ability as an actor, the theatricality of his performances, along with a complete and serious absorption in his roles.[16] As early as 1823 Lablache had heard Schubert's 'Nachtigall' (D bracket) in an evening concert in celebration of Barbaja's name day. After this there were many opportunities for the two artists to get to know each other at the musical evenings in Raphael Kiesewetter's home. 'The singer took a great shine to Schubert, and once when the four-part song, "Der Gondelfahrer" [D 809], was sung at a party, he liked it so much that he asked for it to be repeated and then sang the second bass part himself.' In the *Dresdner Morgen-Zeitung* in February 1828, Lablache's fondness for Schubert's songs and the integration of Italian culture into Viennese musical life is very explicitly stated:

> The great Lablache – who understands and respects German music and values Schubert's songs very highly for example – repeatedly expresses his amazement at the complete absence of patriotism in Vienna and at the levels of praise, which [allow] foreigners to prosper here to the disadvantage of the locals, which is all the more remarkable at a time when people all over the world loudly proclaim their patriotism.

Music history would have us believe that Schubert wrote these Italian songs to procure Lablache's support of his application for the position of Hoftheaterkapellmeister in 1826. Certainly Lablache, who was as thick as thieves with Barbaja, would have been a much more effective advocate than Vogl, who had left the court theatre five years earlier, and appears to have had no further contact with it.[17] This reading has its origins in a controversial episode which Anton Schindler circulated whereby Schubert, on Vogl's recommendation, applied for a position replacing Karl Krebs in 1826, to which Josef Weigl was eventually appointed in early 1827. Schindler's task to determine the composer's suitability for the post was to ask him to set to music a libretto chosen by Georg von Hofmann, the court secretary, within a short period of time. Reputedly, Schubert managed it, but he was not prepared to accept alterations suggested by the soprano

Nanette Schechner, so he slammed the score shut and returned home. Schindler's anecdote is immediately suspect on account of his unreliability as a witness and the episode follows all too quickly the topos of favourite music myths.[18] It is also at odds with Schubert's lifelong practice of refining a performance.

Obviously, the music of op. 83 – and not just their Italian texts – has perplexed scholars, who located these Italian songs in Schubert's application to be resident composer at the Court Theatre in 1826, even though the dates don't add up. Lablache formally accepted Schubert's dedication on 30 April 1827 and Haslinger announced publication in the *Grazer Zeitung* on 1 September.[19] Klaus Pietschmann even suggests Schubert applied for an additional unadvertised position of Kapellmeister in 1827, to which Lachner was appointed. If Schubert applied for any additional positions (for which there are no records), it was more likely he would have done so in 1826 when he was applying for other posts.[20] Even then, Schubert turned down an offer as Court Organist in 1826, a position for which (as mentioned earlier) his brother Ferdinand unsuccessfully applied. In 1827, Schubert was far too absorbed in *Winterreise* and his own compositional development to sacrifice either for any position.

Evidence suggests that – independent of any application – Schubert was simply seeking to augment his income with a set of songs which were right up Haslinger's alley. The bilingual song set was ideal for consumerist purposes: the dedicatee was a celebrity, songs in the Italian language were all the rage, and the style of the music was accessible. Schubert's dedication of these songs to Lablache is characteristic of the friendships he cultivated with professional musicians in his final years and a recognition of the power of virtuosity in mediating his music. Opus 83 typifies the publishing habits of Schubert's final years as he sifted through songs, revised and reset them for publication.

What is special about this song set is not that they mix German and Italian texts and styles – which had been at the heart of Schubert's style since 'Der Jüngling am Bache' and 'Gretchen am Spinnrade' – but that he reached back into the first year of his partimento training with Salieri, revised and released apprentice settings of Metastasio's operatic texts into public life. This song set is singular among Schubert's resettings because his partimento training primed him perfectly to play to popular taste. Exactly as he had prepared his Harper songs, op. 12, for publication, Schubert composed one new song and revised two settings. Even the proximity of these ariette to an important landmark in Schubert's career suggests they were a commercial venture and concessions to popular taste, and entirely typical of his compositional habits: 'Al par del ruscelletto chiaro' was composed for Irene Kiesewetter after his completion of the E flat Piano Trio no. 2 (D 929), op. 100.

Schubert's 'Drei Gesänge', op. 83, exhibit a stylistic and generic versatility which testifies to his training in Italian opera seria, oratorio and opera buffa.[21] The first song is a da capo aria with ornamentation notated on the reprise. Every Italian operatic signifier is here: sudden shifts in dynamics, instantaneous leaps between high and low registers, rapid changes in mood between pathos and playfulness, but with harmonic gestures that are more subtle than Rossini.[22] The accompanimental figuration, which is typical of a Schubertian serenade, is equally subtle: not illustrative of textual meaning but supporting it.

The accompaniment of 'Il traditor deluso', a recitative and da capo aria which follows, is at once pianistic and orchestral. Even the form of the aria shows Schubert's familiarity with Salieri's opera, whereby the repetition of A is broken off by a return of B and new musical material drives it to a climax. From the opening bars of this dramatic setting the protagonist is in a state of nervous agitation, which is skilfully captured in the vocal line. In Metastasio's drama, the murderous female usurper Atalia, grandmother of Gioas, originally sings this aria, which Schubert now turns into an expressive showpiece for bass. The pathos of the song is typical of the *comédie larmoyante* introduced into Italian opera buffa by de Gamerra, whereby a virtuous heroine is placed in a dangerous situation in which the audience is asked to pity her. While this Italian duality of comedy and tragedy can be detected in the libretto, the tempo is central in conveying the emotional import in Schubert's song. The vocal line is skilfully underscored by the accompaniment from the defining opening gesture to the *crescendo–diminuendo tremolandi* (bars 24–27) and the accompanimental runs in A (bars 40–43). The bipartite form in two different tempi, portrayal of a very heightened emotional state, animated *stretto* virtuosic codetta and pulsing accompanimental rhythm, render it an early example of a cabaletta, in the manner of 'Non più mesta' in Rossini's *La Cenerentola* (1817). Laden with syncopation, an Italianate touch used so insistently as to verge on parody but not for exaggeration or comic effect, Schubert's setting is richly illustrative of a clever handling of multifarious Italian operatic tropes (Example 22.2 online).

The third setting, 'Il modo di prender moglie', breaks away from Salieri's models and reorientates itself to the formal spectrum of opera buffa in Schubert's Vienna. The structure of six strophes concluding with a *verso tronco* is typical for opera buffa of the late eighteenth century and is reminiscent of 'Udite, tutti, udite', Don Geronimo's entrance aria from *Il matrimonio segreto* (1792), Cimarosa's most popular opera in Vienna, which was one of Lablache's showpieces. That this aria was carefully composed for Lablache is subtly suggested in the textual parallels: 'Il modo di prender moglie' announces the decision of an old bachelor to marry for money: Geronimo does not have intentions of marriage for himself but for his daughter, whose motives are equally pecuniary. The unusual 6/8 metre, found in Figaro's opening Cavatina, 'Largo al factotum' in Rossini's *Il barbiere di Siviglia* (1816), also pays homage to one of the bass baritone's favourite roles.[23] In an early critique of these songs, Heinrich Marschner noted this connection in the Berlin *Allgemeine musikalische Zeitung*,[24] claiming Schubert was no way on a par with Rossini.

The songs, which were aimed at an Italian opera-loving audience, received a mixed reception in the press. In an enthusiastic notice (30 January 1828) one critic, G[eorg] W[ilhelm] Fink of the Leipzig *Allgemeine musikalische Zeitung*, recognized that the songs are 'well suited to social entertainments' and predicted that 'Signor Luigi Lablache, to whom these three numbers are dedicated, is sure to make a furore with them'. The rivalrous Heinrich Marschner, on the threshold of his own success as an opera composer, was far less impressed. Writing in the Berlin *Allgemeine musikalische Zeitung* on 19 March 1828 he criticized the songs for being 'neither fish nor fowl – neither sufficiently colourful and vital enough to be truly Italian, nor expressive enough to be truly German [. . .] The flow of his melodies is too intermittent, too heavy-handed; it is no glowing lava stream but only a somewhat cold, murmuring northern brooklet', and he concludes, 'Herr Schubert has not succeeded [. . .] in bringing about an alliance [. . .] between German and Italian music.' Marschner's critique completely missed the mark of Schubert's intentions, because through his Lieder and other works such as his Sixth Symphony (D 589) he had long achieved that aim. A forerunner to this publication is 'Willkommen und Abschied' (D 767), which successfully couples Italian and German traditions, as acknowledged in its 1826 bilingual publication with Italian parallel translation.[25]

The music of the Lablache settings problematizes the commercial motivation of appealing to an opera-loving public, at least insofar as the Metastasio settings are student exercises. The question is: Why would Schubert release these settings but turn down the opportunity to perform one of his male-voice settings at Vienna's Gesellschaft der Musikfreunde in 1821 for fear of reputational damage?[26] Why he would risk it in 1827? Was this a clever use of early settings with its dedication to Lablache, or a business move misplaced?

It is obvious that the real professional motivation underlying op. 83 was material survival and their publication reveals vital aspects of Schubert's commercial and public life. Firstly, their extravagant Italian manner throws the originality of *Winterreise* into even sharper relief. His use of striking harmonic progressions, especially the B minor to G minor progression for the dark fearful night in 'Il traditor deluso', op. 83/2, may well have suggested to Marschner Schubert's attempt to bridge Rossini-like melody and texture with German Romantic harmony, which was a touchstone from his lessons with Salieri. It is intriguing that the Marschner progression is found in Schubert's neighbouring composition, 'Der Wegweiser' (D 911/20) from *Winterreise*, with the same chords, B minor to G minor, where it expresses the dark and the gruesome. Secondly, the co-existence of *Winterreise* alongside Schubert's Italian settings typifies an essential aspect of his late style: meditative works for private reception versus compositions full of effect for public performance.[27] The internalized style of *Winterreise* (D 911), the last three Piano Sonatas (D 958–960), Piano Trios (D 898 and D 929) and Quintet (D 956) are all in direct contrast with the public virtuosity of the Violin Fantasy in C (D 934), Rondo in B minor for Violin and Piano (D 895) and Schubert's last commercial concert lied, 'Der Hirt auf dem Felsen' (D 965), which were all written for distinguished performers.

SCHUBERT'S WOMEN

Luigi Lablache was often accompanied by Irene Kiesewetter, 'one of the foremost female pianists in Vienna', and one of many women overlooked in Schubert's reception history. She performed Schubert's songs with Baron von Schönstein in her father's salon. Beyond the confines of her home she played Schubert's *Divertissement à l'hongroise* (D 818) with Johann Baptist Jenger in Sophie von Müller's salon on 26 October 1827. Schubert's friendship with Irene Kiesewetter resulted in two cantatas: the second, 'Der Tanz' (D 826), a humorous SATB cantata with piano accompaniment, was aimed at curtailing her love of dancing.

Schubert's regular participation in Kiesewetter's private house concerts in later years exemplifies how membership of the Gesellschaft der Musikfreunde offered a closer relationship to its directors and opened a door into aristocratic salons. Schubert's performance with Baron von Schönstein at the residence of Princess Karoline Charlotte von Kinsky in the summer of 1828 shows how he began to move in different circles. Schubert dedicated to the princess his op. 96 settings – 'Die Sterne' (D 939), 'Jägers Liebeslied' (D 909), 'Wandrers Nachtlied II (D 768) and 'Fischerweise' (D 881) – which he had privately printed at Schober's Lithographic Institute. The princess duly thanked him by enclosing money in her letter of 7 July 1828. The year before, Schubert had dedicated his Goethe-inspired *Gesänge aus Wilhelm Meister* (D 877), op. 62, to Princess Mathilde Schwarzenberg of Český Krumlov whose father maintained his own orchestra in Neuer Markt in Vienna. The Mignon songs were very sensitively selected for the princess, who in childhood had suffered a spinal deformation which robbed her of the ability to walk. In 1825, the year before the dedication, she was permanently cured of her paralysis by Prince Alexander Hohenlohe-Waldenburg-Schillingsfürst, a priest and controversial faith healer. In July 1828 Schubert dedicated three Goethe-Lieder – 'Der Musensohn' (D 764), 'Auf dem See' (D 543) and 'Geistes-Gruß' (D 142), op. 87, later op. 92 – to Frau Josephine von Franck. Her husband, Josef von Franck, owned the wholesale dealers, Franck & Co., which Schott Söhne mentioned would pay Schubert on receipt of compositions.[28] When negotating with Franck & Co. – who delivered Schott Söhne's letters straight into the composer's hands – Schubert dedicated op. 87 to Josephine von Franck, one of a number of distinguished female patrons at the end of his life whose influence is overlooked.

Schönfeld and Reichardt both noted the musical proficiency of women in Schubert's Vienna, including one of Ignaz Sonnleithner's daughters who is never mentioned.[29] Even the Fröhlich sisters, immortalized (and fictionalized) in Rudolf Bartsch's novel, *Schwammerl*, and H. Berté's operetta *Das Dreimädlerhaus* (The House of the Three Girls), have not been given their due recognition. After Schubert's death, a writer in the *Allgemeine Wiener Zeitung* recognized how 'the four Fröhlich sisters may well have done more for art, and particularly for singing, than many international singers' (Figure 1). After Anna Fröhlich's (1793–1880) death, Auguste von Littrow-Bischoff published a memorial article, 'Von Vieren die Letzte', in the *Neue freie Presse* (Vienna, 1880). From an early stage in Schubert's public career Anna Fröhlich had played an active role in the promotion of his music. It was her private performance of 'Erlkönig' with her sister Katharina that prompted August von Gymnich to give the public premiere with 'the vivacious Anna'. Anna, Nanette or 'Netti', as she was known to friends, was 'absolutely charming, typically Italian in appearance and spirit. Short, stout, tremendously lively, wholly mercurial in temperament, warm-hearted, quarrelsome, readily moved to laughter and as easily to tears. You just cannot help liking her'.[30] Schubert certainly did and often visited her in her home, 'Zum roten Apfel', on 18 Singerstrasse, not far from St Stephen's Cathedral. He also visited 21 Spielgasse where the three sisters moved in 1826, after Barbara married the flautist, Ferdinand Bogner, for whom Schubert wrote the 'Trockne Blumen' Variations (D 802), again illustrating the centrality of occasional works in Schubert's compositional career. Anna was a pioneer in professional vocal training for women at Vienna's Gesellschaft der Musikfreunde and Schubert wrote many of his SSAA settings for her students, who performed 'Psalm D 23' (D 706) on 30 August 1821, also with 'Gott in der Natur' (D 757) on 8 March 1827 and 28 February 1828. 'Netti' was a true friend to Schubert. When he was diagnosed with syphilis, was in need of money, and had to move home in November 1822, she mediated a commission of 50 Gulden for 'Des Tages Weihe' (D 763) for the Swiss banker and Baron Johann Heinrich Geymüller and his wife Barbara, who hosted one of the most important (and most neglected) music salons in their city home (8 Wallnerstrasse). Their house concerts promoted celebrated musicians including Beethoven, Rossini and Schubert, whose songs, choral works, dances and duet settings were performed on one of the five pianos.

Winterreise was received sympathetically at Anna Fröhlich's home at a time when it was misunderstood by Schubert's closest friends. Schubert paid tribute to 'Netti' in 'Mirjams Siegesgesang' (D 942), which was intended for her and her sisters to sing at his Benefit Concert. Barbara

(Babette) Fröhlich (1797–1879), a contralto, took part in many of the Gesellschaft der Musikfreunde concerts. Katharina (Kathi) Fröhlich (1800–1879), a competent pianist, 'was the most striking of the sisters, sensitive, highly intelligent, very lively, rather touchy, very well educated but never vaunting her knowledge, very beautiful in appearance [. . .] with a fine figure, a long oval face, and eyes that are limitless and wonderfully deep, almost unfathomable, and into which one would like to gaze forever, eyes of the blackest black'.[31] Josefine (Pepi), the youngest sister (1803–1878), a Danish Court chamber singer from 1829, enjoyed some international success in Prague (1826), Venice (1829) and Milan (1830).[32] Anna Fröhlich, Sophie von Müller and Katharina von Lásny were just three professional female musicians in Schubert's final years whose friendship was vital to his success.

GIFTS OF GRAZ

Another female patron, Marie Pachler née Koschak (1794–1855), lived in Graz. On Sunday 2 September 1827 at 9.30 a.m. Schubert set out on a 24-hour journey by express coach, in the company of Johann Baptist Jenger, to stay with her and her husband Karl from 3 to 20 September. Marie was a composer, an exceptional pianist, and a gifted interpreter of contemporary music. Her pianism inspired Schubert's first set of four Impromptus (D 899), op. 90, which are fantasies of the freest kind. Their counterpoint of genres which he built into the substance of his musical thought are clearly conceived for an educated audience and were undoubtedly tried out at one of numerous musical gatherings in their home. As the title suggests, the impromptus are pianistic reinterpretations of partimento principles, where a characteristic arpeggiated accompanimental figuration – an inner chord-outlining pattern found in the Impromptu in G flat major (D 899/3) – supports a freely intoned melody above. Hours improvising in the Pachler salon resulted in September 1827 in Schubert's *Grazer Galopp* (D 925) and twelve *Grazer Walzer* (D 924), op. 91, the most difficult of his dance cycles. The grace and maturity of his pianistic writing mark D 924 as the apotheosis of his dance sets.

During his stay Schubert composed the Lieder, 'Eine altschottische Ballade' (D 923) and 'Heimliches Lieben' (D 922). According to Karl Gottfried von Leitner, Marie Pachler brought his poems to Schubert's attention and gave him a copy of his *Gedichte* published in Graz in 1825, seven of which Schubert set. In spring 1828, Schubert privately published and dedicated to Marie his op. 106 which contained two of the new Leitner songs – 'Das Weinen' (D 926) and 'Vor meiner Wiege' (D 927) – as well as 'Heimliches Lieben' (D 922) composed in her home. Due to his failing health and a complete focus on the works he wanted to compose and release in his final year, Schubert overlooked sending Marie the published song set. She did not receive a printed copy until she negotiated with Diabelli to reissue the songs in Graz, a year after Schubert's death.

One of the highlights of the visit was a charity concert mounted in Schubert's honour by the Styrian Musical Society and local musicians, the proceeds of which were to be divided between victims of recent flooding and widows and orphans of local schoolmasters.[31] The pieces performed by this 'greatly celebrated composer from the metropolis' were 'Normans Gesang' (D 846), the male-voice quartet 'Geist der Liebe' (D 747) and the SSAA setting 'Gott in der Natur' (D 757), all of which Schubert accompanied on the piano. After the concert the Pachlers took Schubert and Jenger on a three-day excursion twenty miles west of Graz to Wildbach Castle, which was managed by Karl Pachler's aunt, Anna Massegg, for whom Schubert performed privately.

On 20 September, Schubert and Jenger began their return journey to Vienna, taking a leisurely four days to return home. On the first evening they stayed with Jenger's friends in Fürstenfeld before moving on to Harberg, then Friedberg where they climbed the Eselberg and stayed in an eighteenth-century home at Schloss Schleinz. For Schubert, Graz had proved a sort of haven from Vienna and when they arrived back in the capital, he expressed his profound gratitude to Frau Pachler:

DE PROFUNDIS: FINAL SONGS

Madam,

Already it became clear to me that I was only too happy at Graz and I cannot as yet get accustomed to Vienna . . . At Graz I soon recognized an artless and sincere way of being together, and a longer stay would have allowed me to take it even more readily. Above all, I shall never forget the kindly shelter where, with its dear hostess and sturdy 'Pachleros' [Karl] as well as little Faust, I spent the happiest days I have known for a long time. Hoping to be yet able to prove my gratitude in an adequate manner, I remain with profound respect

Most devotedly yours
Franz Schubert

PS The opera libretto I hope to send in a few days.[32]

The libretto to which he refers is *Alfonso und Estrella* which he had played for Josef Kinsky, Director of the Landständisches-Theater, still in hope of igniting his interest. Long after the rejection of Schober's opera by the Kärntnertortheater in 1823, Schubert retained his belief in this work and actively sought performances in 1825.[33] In 1826 he had told Bauernfeld that the Kärntnertortheater were looking for an opera from him and on his return from Graz in September 1827 requested that the libretto for *Alfonso* might be returned to him. The producer, Josef Gottdank, who tried out the opera in rehearsals before rejecting it, held onto the libretto long after Schubert's visit.[34]

The Pachler home, in which Schubert had been temporarily sheltered from the realities of life, had been yet another setting for Schubert to show his affection for young children. On 12 October he sent Marie Pachler the commissioned *Kindermarsch* in G (D 928), which he had written for her to perform with her son Faust on Karl Pachler's name day. On the reverse of the primo part Jenger wrote to Faust, 'think of friend Tubby and me'. In Schubert's letter to Marie he hoped Faust would be happy with the piece and admitted, 'I do not feel I am the right person for this kind of composition', though it is brilliantly written for the different pianistic abilities of

Marie Pachler and her son.[35] He confided to her that his usual headaches were assailing him again, an indication that his health was beginning to break down. Three days later he began to excuse himself from social gatherings on the grounds of ill health and being 'totally unfit for society', abandoning a visit to Anna Hönig on 15 October.[36] Declining health may not have been the only cause of the dark mood that descended on Schubert in October 1827 when he was working on *Winterreise*, the dark introversion of which is in direct contrast with his commercial and public life. 'From then on', recalled Spaun in 1858, 'Schubert was a sick man, although his condition gave no cause for anxiety.'[37]

23

THE FINAL YEAR (1828)

'We can make our minds so like still water that beings gather about us that they may see, it may be, their own images, and so live for a moment with a clearer, perhaps even with a fiercer life because of our quiet.'

W.B. Yeats

ALARMS WITHIN, THE UNIVERSE WITHOUT

As 1827 drew to a close, Schubert sat down at the piano to entertain the friends Schober had gathered around. On the stroke of midnight he raised a toast of Malaga wine and wished a Happy New Year to Spaun, Schwind, Bauernfeld, Gahy and the Hartmann diarists, Franz and Fritz, no doubt to their good health. For the absent audience with whom his soul was always in dialogue he wrote 'Der Winterabend' (D 938). The song is a perfect image of human existence, caught always in transition from one state to another, neither at one with the past nor beyond it altogether.

At the turn of the year Schubert was sad at heart, unsettled, already sensing his death. How long he had left was unknowable but his fate was certain. The year leading up to his death had contained some uncanny premonitions. The second movement of the Piano Trio in E flat major (D 929), op. 100, begun in November 1827 and published posthumously exactly one year later, quotes the *Marcia funèbre* from Beethoven's 'Eroica' Symphony and closes with a citation from a Swedish *Abschiedsgesang*, 'Se solen sjunker' ('See the sun is setting'), the words of which bear a codified message, 'Farewell, Farewell'. Although the work has been convincingly read as a tribute to Beethoven, we cannot rule out the possibility that Schubert was auguring his own farewell, the piano trio was crystallizing itself out of the inexorable and the elegiac. Here (as elsewhere in his E flat *Requiem* for his own mortality), Schubert is grieving for himself. His closest friends sensed this and cracks were already appearing in the commune: Bauernfeld's occasional poem augured his friend's departure and Schubert uncharacteristically signed off a letter to Anselm Hüttenbrenner, 'I remain your faithful friend until death'.[1] In January 1828 Schubert's mood was like the mood of other tragic wayfarers: Oedipus at Colonus, Hamlet in the last illuminations of his prophetic soul. 'No easy bargain is made in that place by any man. For everyone of us living in this world means waiting for our end.'[2]

The inwardness of Schubert's suffering and withdrawal from friends is evidenced on many occasions, even performances of his own music which he failed to attend. Schober re-established the reading group after many years, but even this did not capture Schubert's imagination. He was no longer found at his old haunts but headed for Zur Eiche, the Oak Tree pub frequented by professional musicians. There he drank with the violinists Schuppanzigh, Slavík, Böhm and Holz, the cellist Linke and horn-player Josef Lewy, who gave their services at his Benefit Concert. These professional friendships were increasingly at the neglect of others who had long promoted his music. Gerhard von Breuning recalls, 'On the birthday, for which the "Ständchen" was intended and on which it was to be performed for the first time [. . .] I had the piano carried secretly under the garden window and had invited Schubert to the performance. But he did not come. The next day, when I asked him why he had stayed away, he apologised, "'Oh dear! I forgot all about it.'" He also arranged a performance of 'Ständchen' at the Musikverein; again Schubert failed to appear but was found at the Oak Tree pub. 'But after the performance,' Breuning tells us, Schubert 'appeared quite transfigured and remarked, "Do you know, I had no idea it was so beautiful."' What looks like lack of responsibility on Schubert's part was complete responsibility to his art.

Whether in his presence or not, Schubert's work was performed in every single evening concert of the Gesellschaft der Musikfreunde in January 1828. The Sixth Evening Concert on 3 January even featured two works: the male-voice quintet, 'Mondenschein' (D 875) followed by Tietze's rendition of 'Normans Gesang' (D 846), which was applauded endlessly so it had to be repeated. The Seventh Concert premiered 'Gute Nacht' to mark the publication of *Winterreise* Part 1 (D 911), announced by Haslinger on 14 January. On 20 January, Josef Slavík and Karl Maria Bocklet premiered the C major Fantasy for Violin and Piano (D 934). This long virtuosic display piece was heedlessly placed at the very end of an overly packed programme. Schubert and his performers had to endure the audience emptying out before the premiere came to a close.

The last recorded Schubertiad in the composer's presence took place at Spaun's on 28 January 1828; ten months later Schubert would be dead. On this occasion fifty people were privy to a premiere of Schubert's E flat major Piano Trio (D 929), op. 100, by Schuppanzigh, Linke and Bocklet, as a dry run for Schubert's Benefit Concert. A couple of days later Schubert's music graced Josef Witteczek's private party, and throughout February he was again included in each of the Musikfreunde evening concerts. At the Eleventh Concert, Moses Mendelssohn's Psalm 23 (D 706) was premiered by Josefine Fröhlich with Anna Fröhlich's female pupils of the Conservatoire and conducted by their teacher, for whom it had been written. 'Ellens Gesang' (Ave Maria, D 839) graced the programme of the Twelfth Concert on 31 January 1828, Schubert's last living birthday marked by the Musikverein. At the Thirteenth Concert on 28 February the SSAA choral song 'Gott in der Natur' (D 757) was the last Gesellschaft der Musikfreunde performance of Schubert's work during his lifetime.

REDEFINING THE PUBLIC: SCHUBERT'S BENEFIT CONCERT

During these Winter months a mood of self-preoccupation enveloped Schubert, who was busy organizing a concert of his own. He knew if it were successful, the venture could prove personally and professionally profitable, whereby his music would reach an unknown public. After the premiere of his F major Mass, this was the most important concert of his life. New works were written, artists carefully chosen, and the programme well rehearsed. Schubert accompanied all of the vocal works, something he had refused to do in public performances before 1827. Being so actively involved in the hurly-burly of concert arrangements robbed him of the necessary detachment to complete Grillparzer's cantata 'Mirjams Siegesgesang' (D 942). He replaced it with 'Ständchen' (D 921), which he knew would be a guaranteed success. It had already been performed twice: at the garden birthday party for Louise Gosmar, for whom it was written, and later, on 24 January 1828, in the Musikverein.

The day of the concert became, in Schubert's mind, talismanic. Chance was too significant for him to allow it complete freedom. He finally resolved to hold the concert at the Gesellschaft der Musikfreunde on Wednesday, 26 March 1828 on the first anniversary of Beethoven's death. He paid private homage to Beethoven's death and funeral by composing an anniversary lied, 'Auf dem Strom' (D 943), for tenor, piano and horn in March 1828, a song of departure which Ludwig Rellstab had written for Beethoven to set.[3] The song is a typical journeying poem, taking the protagonist across the Styx, bringing him home to his beloved, uniting Heaven and Earth. In the final months of his life, Schubert took up this mantle in a very thoughtful way. He honoured Rellstab's original intention by composing the poem to variants of the funeral march from Beethoven's 'Eroica' Symphony and *An die ferne Geliebte*, a gesture inspired by the poet's intention and the simple texting of Beethoven's instrumental music which he had heard when he was torchbearer.

Table 23.1: Programme for Schubert's Benefit Concert, Wednesday, 26 March 1828[4]

1	First movement of a new string quartet [the first movement of his G major String Quartet, D 887 (premiere)], performed by Schuppanzigh's quartet [with Böhm replacing Schuppanzigh who was unwell]
2	Four Lieder performed by Vogl and Schubert: 'Der Kreuzzug' and 'Die Sterne' (Leitner, D 932 and D 939) 'Der Wanderer an den Mond' (Seidl, D 870) 'Fragment aus dem Aeschylus' (Mayrhofer, D 450)
3	'Ständchen' (Grillparzer, D 920), with Josephine Fröhlich (soprano) with SSAA female students from the conservatory
4	'New Trio' in E flat (D 929) for piano, violin and cello, performed by Bocklet, Böhm and Linke
5	'Auf dem Strom' (Rellstab, D 943), lied with horn and piano accompaniment, performed by Tietze, Lewy and Schubert
6	'Die Allmacht' (Pyrker, D 852), lied performed by Vogl and Schubert
7	'Schlachtlied' (Klopstock, D 912), Male-voice double chorus TTBB TTBB

By all accounts the concert was an artistic and financial triumph. According to Bauernfeld, Schubert benefited by 800 fl. WW.[5] The performance sold out and his friends tried to convince him to repeat it immediately, even preparing a petition for publication in the *Wiener Zeitschrift für Kunst, Literatur, Theater und Mode*, which the editor, Johann Schickh, sent directly to him.[6] Schubert himself singled out the Trio for the praise it had received in his correspondence with the publishers, Probst and Scott.[7] It has been readily accepted that the long version of the Trio was performed, despite evidence that the composer continually refined musical thought through performance. The parts from which the players performed have not been handed down and the fair copy once owned by Karoline Esterházy is our only source of the original version. Schubert's instruction to Probst, 'The cuts in the last manuscript are to be most scrupulously observed', is knowledge gained from performance.[8]

One of the most intriguing aspects of Schubert's Benefit Concert is his total grip on the home ground, his attentiveness to it and sense of musical and artistic responsibility reaching the furthest horizons. Reviews appeared in papers as far afield as Leipzig, Dresden and Berlin but – as is often the case – were scarcely noted in Vienna. The Viennese press instead devoted itself to details of Linke's private memorial concert for Beethoven. Schubert was unfortunate in at least one other respect: Paganini was in town and gave his opening concert on March 29. We do not know whether Schubert was there but we do know he took Bauernfeld to hear the virtuoso violinist on 9 May.

After the elation of his concert Schubert appears to have been exhausted and entered a period where he composed very little. Once again he turned to publication and, following an exchange of letters, Probst purchased the E flat Piano Trio in mid-April, paying him 60 fl in lieu of the requested 100 fl. Schubert reluctantly accepted the fee, though he was doubly disappointed with the publisher's rejection of the Violin and Piano Fantasy and request for ever-popular 'trifles'. Perhaps Probst's request prompted Schubert to turn to the piano: 'Drei Klavierstücke' (D 946) marked the renewal of his compositional activity at the end of May, followed by the impassioned four-hand *Lebensstürme* duet (D 947). At the beginning of June, Johann Schickh invited Schubert and Lachner to accompany him on an excursion to the Heiligenkreuz monastery in Baden, where the two composers performed fugues they had written for the organ. Schubert's Fugue in E minor for organ duet (D 952) is his only 'solo' organ work. Midsummer also marked the graceful four-hand Rondo in A (D 951) and the first stirrings of the E flat major Mass (D 950).

SONGS ON THE THRESHOLD: 'GLAUBE, HOFFNUNG UND LIEBE' (D 954 AND D 955)

Two companion settings to his *Requiem* are Schubert's 'Glaube, Hoffnung und Liebe' (D 954 and D 955) to different texts based on Paul's letter to the Corinthians (1:13). The first by Johann Anton Friedrich Reil is a

TTBB strophic setting with SATB chorus and wind ensemble commissioned for the consecration of the new bell at the Church of the Holy Trinity in Alsergrund on 2 September 1828. This commission attracted a great deal of public attention, as noted in the *Wiener allgemeine Theaterzeitung* on 27 September 1828, 'It was with great joy that the crowd gazed at the brightly shining work of art.' Schubert himself had taken this cue in his 6/8 *Langsam feierlich* setting with *Harmoniemusik* (for outdoors), marking the pealing of the bells below TTBB voices, with female voices lifting each refrain. His strophic setting extols the trinity of virtues, faith, hope and love, in three beautifully paced stanzas. D 954 was published by Tranquillo Mollo one month after Schubert's death to raise money for the Church. The wind parts were published as an optional supplement, as indicated on the manuscript in a note in the composer's hand.

Schubert's companion setting, 'Glaube, Hoffnung und Liebe' (D 955), is a setting of a different text to the very same theme, this time by Christoph Kuffner. This *pièce d'occasion* was released by Diabelli after the bell's inauguration and is a good example of Schubert's ability to situate himself commercially. Even the choice of text is commercial, having originally appeared in Castelli's almanac *Selam* in 1813, but more significantly in Johann Wilhelm Klein's anthology, *Lieder für Blinde und von Blinden*, published in 1827. The anthology, which featured poems by eminent blind poets, Homer, Milton and Ossian, was intended as a companion volume of musical settings whereby composers were assigned various poems. Schubert's name was originally pencilled in beside 'An Gott' (D 863), whereas Abbé Stadler was the named composer for 'Glaube, Hoffnung und Liebe'.

Schubert's Kuffner setting (D 955), which opens with a tolling bell, may well have been conceived for Alsergrund *before* the composer realized his more ambitious setting (D 954). The companion settings are unique because together they mark the only time in Schubert's output when he turns to a related poetic text to completely reimagine the commission in a much more successful and suitable resetting. This deeply felt but rarely performed lied deserves to be better known. Scored in E flat major,

Schubert's *Dreifaltigkeit* tonality, the song opens with its trinity of virtues, *Glaube, Hoffnung, Liebe*, beautifully proclaimed in the tonic major (bars 5–6). The tempo becomes *etwas geschwinder* as each stanza centres on a single virtue and cycles through three tonalities from E flat minor (bar 17) to G flat major (bar 20) to C flat major (bar 22) returning to E flat major (bar 36). The coda is conceived in the tradition of the Italian *Manieren*, an elegant embellishment of the opening affirming 'Love' as the greatest of virtues.[9] Written for a public inauguration, perhaps also for wedding ceremonies, D 955 is the last publication to appear in the composer's lifetime.

MYSTICISM, ECSTASY AND THE SUBLIME: STRING QUINTET IN C (D 956)

In the last eighteen months of his life Schubert revisited every genre he had cultivated and many of these works are central to his legacy.[10] Are they late works or 'middle works', as has been suggested, auguring even greater heights?[11] When appraising a life we cannot define style on the surmise of what might have been. His final works express a preternatural wisdom refined in the crucible of experience.[12]

So much of what Schubert writes in 1828 is bathed in an awareness that is sixth-sensed, but the truths that penetrate the deeper mental reserves which feed the creative process are deeply complex, so we can only intuit what the music is about. At the beginning of *Part II*, Faust describes how the play of the sun's light on the spray produced by the waterfall results in a brilliant rainbow, and in this phenomenon he sees a reflection of man's situation:

> Der spiegelt ab das menschliche Bestreben,
> Ihm sinne nach, und du begreifst genauer:
> Am farbigen Abglanz haben wir das Leben.[13]

> (It mirrors human striving.
> Think about it and you will understand more clearly
> that what we have is a colourful reflection of life.)

THE FINAL YEAR (1828)

In a similar vein the String Quintet in C (D 956), and other works, are a musical reflection of Schubert's life: the Quintet represents the metaphysical but can only allude to it. Written two months before his death, D 956 is Schubert's last completed instrumental work, for many his most compelling chamber work, and one in which he extends himself to the limits of his humanity. The richness of its sound world is announced in the static harmonic progression with which the Quintet opens (bars 1–25) and in its second subject where the two cellos reign supreme (bars 40–79). The almost static Adagio (bars 1–28) in E major – whose otherworldly tranquillity is shared with D 759/ii – is one of Schubert's most intimate utterances:

Example 23.1a: Quintet in C major (D 956/ii), first subject, bars 1–9

Its meditative serenity calls forth the lyrical sublimity of an ailing Schubert at the very height of his powers, but upon this beauty intrudes one of his most terrifying outbursts of pain, even brutality (bars 29–39), a gesture shared with the slow movements of the 'Great' C major Symphony, the A minor and G major String Quartets, the Octet, and late piano sonatas, most especially the A major Piano Sonata.

This rapid oscillation between Paradise and Inferno is central to Schubert's vision, whereby irreconcilable opposites are deliberately collapsed into each other, interrupting absolute serenity and untenable totalities. In the haunting presence of the outer E major sections and doom-laden atmosphere of the F minor middle interruption, the subjective and the inevitable are in perfect balance.

Neapolitan relations of the C major presto Scherzo are dramatically juxtaposed with the Andante sostenuto funereal Trio in D flat (bars 24–42) which abandons triple time. The four-squareness of this doleful Trio's utterance and frenzied Scherzo in one movement is an extraordinary example of Schubert's ability to live with uncertainty, opening up more and more to the richness of experience, embracing beauty and horror as twin realities of life. The Hungarian Dance of the finale (A, bars 1–45)

Example 23.1b: Quintet in C major (D 956/ii), bars 29–39

THE FINAL YEAR (1828)

gloriously manifests a more metaphysically tempered second subject (B, bars 46–53) and the cello duet (C, bars 87–106), interchanging conflicting realities of tonic major and minor, Neapolitan relations of C and D flat. As the spectre of syphilis hovered closer and closer to him, Schubert's creative vitality pulsed more vigorously through him, reverberating as it had in his letter to Kupelwieser in which he recognizes, without despair, there is no love of life.[14]

There is a sense, though, that Schubert writes from a place of even greater realization, a sense of the paradoxical reality of the edge of the precipice as the richest and most intense time. Schubert moved in with his brother Ferdinand in September 1828 and wrote the Quintet in the same month. In touch with the equilibrium of a bigger picture of which he is aware, he draws on this to create musical meaning in his current reality. In sympathy with the tragic, waiting, unredeemed phase of things, he writes music that exudes the greatest imaginative vitality.

Once again, music transported him to a better world and uplifted him when personal realities felt overwhelming. Wallace Stevens later defined poetry as 'a violence from within that protects us from a violence without [. . .] the imagination pressing back against the pressure of reality'. This confrontation between reality and the imagination is the determining factor in the Quintet's poetic character, which is one of the reasons why when listening to it we share in that raised consciousness. It is no coincidence that Robert Browning has Abt Vogler in his eponymous poem proclaim, 'hark, I have dared and done, for my resting-place is found./The C major of this life: so, now I will try to sleep.' The novelist Thomas Mann on his deathbed, like many others, named this Quintet as the music he preferred above all other works. Schubert's Quintet comforts and bolsters the courage of those facing slow departures; it helps us to order our thoughts, make sense of our lives. It connects us to Schubert's encounter with the violent realities that surrounded him and to his success in that struggle for spiritual survival.

ESSENCE

NEW TERRITORY, NEW DIRECTIONS: SYMPHONY IN D (D 936A)

In the final months and weeks of his life Schubert was preoccupied with the flawed torso of a tenth symphony left unfinished and the proofs of *Winterreise* (Part 2), suggestive of the Romantic condition of a fragment. Here 'unfinished' work in the Schlegelian sense depends on a text that is complete but whose ending resists closure. Where writing stops in Schubert's halted orchestral composition, we bear witness to a breach of thought. Its broken music challenges us to imagine a moment of departure. The last haunting melody he composed, a revised opening subject of the second movement (Example 21.2), was written down without indicating an instrument. This was, most likely, because death intervened, yet there is also a sense that what Schubert had to express went beyond the audible surface of the score.

Example 23.2: Symphony in D (D 936A/ii), revised first subject

There is nothing about this plaintive melody that suggests reality breaking through, rather transcendence of human dignity and the indignity of his death. There is heroism and intransigence in Schubert's endgames, in the composer working to the very end.

Schubert's 'Anfang' is not easy to decipher and is less defined than the second movement, which embodies a wonderful musical economy, calling to mind the striking opening horn passage of Schubert's 'Great' C major Symphony or the last song of *Winterreise*, 'Der Leiermann'. Schubert coupled this textural sparseness with free counterpoint. For the third movement, originally headed 'Scherzo', he sketched two contrasting, contrapuntal themes, yet in his development of this material he abandoned this sketch and began a fresh draft, this time omitting the 'Scherzo' title. There is nothing about this impressive polyphonic material that suggests art as a reflection of reality or the composer's recognition of his impending death. The work conveys a lack of revolt or desperation, a sense of tranquillity and peaceful acceptance of a new, other form of existence.

Schubert's piano score for his final symphony contains many structural innovations. Like Christian Cannabich, Carlo Toeschi and Ignaz Pleyel, he appears to return to the three-movement symphony with a central slow movement, the third movement combining the functions of scherzo and finale. His novel use of a slow tempo at the beginning of the development section in the opening movement – in lieu of a slow introduction – is unprecedented in a symphony. More centrally, the contrapuntal character of the second movement and double counterpoint, canon, augmentation and fugato passages of the scherzo-finale, memorialize the opening up of Schubert's consciousness right to the end. For Schubert, as for Goethe, the conviction of his continuance came from the concept of activity, the belief that if he worked without rest until his end, then Nature was bound to show him another form of being when his spirit could not endure the present one.[15]

FINAL JOURNEYS, FINAL GIFTS

As autumn 1828 drew in, the darkening landscapes of Schubert's final years were recognized by family and friends. To Jenger, with whom he had planned to return to the Pachlers, a crestfallen Schubert confided on 25 September: 'Nothing will come of the journey to Graz this year, as money and weather are wholly unfavourable.' Schubert had received an income from a greater than average number of publications, also substantial receipts from his March concert. The real cause of his reluctance to travel was a deterioration in his health. Recognizing the gravity of his illness, he may have been reluctant to spend money needed for future medical attention.

Schubert's relocation to Ferdinand's home in the Neue Wieden suburb of Vienna (today Kettebrückengasse 6, District 4) in September 1828 is always imagined as a temporary move because he left his manuscripts behind at Schober's. We never know how close we are to the precipice, but everything in the composer's life suggests ravaged health. Schubert's doctor, Ernst Rinna von Sarenbach, who had been treating him for chronic syphilis, was probably aware that he was in the terminal stages of illness. He recommended a period of convalescence and Schubert was fortunate in Ferdinand's kindness and intelligence. By this stage he probably had little faith in the group of doctors treating him, but he did follow their advice to relocate. As autumn closed in he also set out on a three-day walking tour in Lower Austria and the Burgenland, a round trip of 100 miles, with Ferdinand and some friends, making a pilgrimage to Joseph Haydn's grave in Eisenstadt 'at which he remained for a fairly long time'. What was the purpose of his expedition? What had been attained? Was the journey illustrative of the existential need to hold out hope during the whole slow-motion, self-deferring approach to death? On his return, uncertainly poised on Vienna's outer margins, Schubert started to work again.

LIGHTNINGS: 'DIE TAUBENPOST' (D 965A) AND 'DER HIRT AUF DEM FELSEN' (D 965)

Unburdened by this final pilgrimage and illuminated by natural settings, Schubert's spirit flared in two final songs. Intimations of his first masterpiece is contained in his last, an Italian bel canto display lied for Salieri's student, Pauline Anna Milder Hauptmann, whose voice had transported Schubert when he was sixteen. In October he composed his last solo song, Seidl's 'Die Taubenpost' (D 965A), one of his transcendent songs and the nearest thing to an idyll he ever wrote. The desire to go home to the beloved is also expressed in his last chamber lied and setting by Wilhelm Müller, 'Der Berghirt', known to us as 'Der Hirt auf dem Felsen (D 965), op. 129, for soprano, clarinet and piano:

THE FINAL YEAR (1828)

Wenn auf dem höchsten Fels ich steh',	When I stand on the highest rock,
In's tiefe Tal hernieder seh',	Look down into the deep valley,
Und singe,	And sing,
Fern aus dem tiefen dunkeln Tal	From far away in the deep dark valley
Schwingt sich empor der Widerhall	The echo from the ravines
Der Klüfte.	Rises up.
Je weiter meine Stimme dringt,	The further my voice carries,
Je heller sie mir wieder klingt	The clearer it echoes back to me
Von unten.	From below.
Mein Liebchen wohnt so weit von mir,	The one I love is so distant, so far away!
Drum sehn' ich mich so heiß nach ihr	I so long to be with her over there
Hinüber.	On the other side.
In tiefem Gram verzehr ich mich,	Deep grief consumes me,
Mir ist die Freude hin,	My joy has fled,
Auf Erden mir die Hoffnung wich,	All earthly hope has vanished,
Ich hier so einsam bin.	I am so lonely here.
So sehnend klang im Wald das Lied,	The song rang out so longingly through the wood,
So sehnend klang es durch die Nacht,	Rang out so longingly through the night,
Die Herzen es zum Himmel zieht	That it draws hearts to heaven
Mit wunderbarer Macht.	With wondrous power.
Der Frühling will kommen,	Spring is coming,
Der Frühling, meine Freud',	Spring, my joy,
Nun mach' ich mich fertig	I shall now make
Zum Wandern bereit.	ready to journey.[16]

The dying often use the metaphor of travel to alert those around them that it is time for them to depart and it is entirely characteristic of Schubert that he would express this in song. The journeying motif of 'Der Hirt auf dem Felsen', its shadow-line text, the deep valley in the shadow of death – a classic emblem – all reflect and exhibit an insight that is visionary. Death is inevitable. Schubert has not yet journeyed to his destined place, but he already has a beyond-the-grave, revenant quality to him. Schubert's musical metaphors – commencing on the third as an invocation of longing in bar 6; the clarinet obbligato whose opening cry follows the natural notes of the alphorn and whose answering echo suggests the reciprocity of love; the distant key of G flat to portray the distant beloved (bars 64–75); G minor as the tonality of desire (bars 126–148); and the G major modulation drawing hearts to heaven (bars 182–189) – bridge heaven and earth in his final setting. He has lost his Paradise but it is soon to be regained: all his yearnings seem here put to rest as he reaches the goal of his innermost striving.

In 'Die Taubenpost', Schubert holds the tragic in abeyance as art escapes reality and transcends existence in a depiction of serene, absolute love (Example 23.3a online). The upward lift of the five-bar piano introduction celebrates the vitality of longing, which lifts and carries us along.[17] Its recurring syncopation on the first two beats continues through most of the song, subtly suggesting – as in 'Der Musensohn' – there is no rest. The difference here is Schubert no longer seeks it: this valedictory song is born of acceptance. Although the grieving register is there, this is a song of celebration. The expression of desire is all the more vivid because of Schubert's restraint, his *ziemlich langsam* tempo signalling the pianist to slightly restrain the lilt and lift he had written into the accompanying figuration. The sudden shift to the flattened mediant, B flat (bar 38), indicates to the attentive listener that letters are no longer needed: his tears are to be carried instead. More poignant still is the *lamento* bass hidden below the double-dotted dominant pedal in the piano interlude (bars 47–51). 'Sehnsucht' is first indicated in A major (bars 78–80), the sudden shift to E flat major via a C minor chromatic chord accentuates the certainty of love's reciprocity (bars 89–90) before the homecoming is tonicized in G major (bar 93). Through these gestures we are offered a carefully crafted place to listen to Schubert's song of departure. Knowing it is his last lied is part of its truth, but its undeluded quality is what gives the setting its great emotional credibility. Schubert is aware of the perilous nature of life and is capable of seeing it steadily (Example 23.3b online).

PATRI ANTEVERTENS:[18] ILLNESS AND DEATH

The Christian celebration of All Saints' Day, 1 November, and All Souls' Day, 2 November, recognizes that powerful spiritual bond between those in heaven and those on earth. The Solemnity begins on All Hallows' Eve and, following the annual blessing of his mother's grave, Schubert had his last meal at his family's local tavern, Zum roten Kreuz, but found the fish nauseating and immediately felt poisoned. His toxophobia had first manifested itself in 1824 as a result of the traumatic experience of syphilis, which not only scarred him physically but threatened his self-esteem. It is unsurprising that his fear of contamination and nonentity was triggered at his last supper. Retrospectively, Ferdinand realized this marked the beginning of the end. Schubert's extreme anxiety, panic and nausea on this occasion was all part of a debilitating illness which brought on delusions of being poisoned and perhaps showed signs of syphilis taking a greater toll on the brain. It certainly marks Schubert's digestive system closing down. Over the next fortnight he couldn't eat anything.

The year darkened as it declined. On 3 November Schubert attended a performance of Ferdinand's *Requiem* in the Hernals district after which he went for a walk alone. Was it another occasion where Ferdinand passed off Schubert's *Requiem* as his own? Or did he feel he was staring into his own grave? Walking home with Ferdinand, Schubert complained of great tiredness.

In this terrible winter he took his first counterpoint class at Simon Sechter's home the following evening. They were not aware of it but this was to be their first and final meeting. His decision to study with Sechter was a natural outgrowth of his own private development starting with his attendance (through Sonnleithner) at Kiesewetter's historical house concerts of Renaissance and Baroque music as early as 1816 to his discovery of Handel which inspired the fugal writing in 'Mirjams Siegesgesang' (D 942, March 1828). In between, Schubert's own private study of Bach in 1824 had brought about his most extensive revisions of his A flat major Mass (1826) where the supreme contrapuntal writing of the Gratias makes one question what Schubert could ever have learnt from Sechter. His mastery of the keyboard fugue is clear through his dramatic use of fugue in the finale of his Fantasy in F minor for Piano Four Hands (D 940, 1828). Nonetheless, Schubert wanted to deepen his understanding of complex fugue such as triple fugue, diminution and augmentation for rectus and inversus versions of the theme, thematic and retrograde inversion which he had not learnt from Salieri when realizing partimenti fugues *extempore*. Schubert and Sechter had both grown up in the tradition of sacred music and were very familiar with the Viennese preference for contrapuntal textures, but Schubert had been trained in the Neapolitan tradition, Sechter in the Albrechtsberger school. Sechter was the nineteenth-century Viennese authority on fugue with an intimate knowledge of Marpurg, Kirnberger and Rameau's theories of fundamental bass, as evidenced in his three-volume treatise, *Die Grundsätze der musikalischen Komposition*.

Schubert's first lesson – with Sechter's corrections – confirm the composer's preoccupation with tonal answers. From the 1826 revisions of his A flat major Mass (D 678), it is clear Schubert had been interested in writing tonal answers, in challenging, chromatic subjects, and linear counterpoint inspired by his knowledge (through Kiesewetter and Salieri) of Palestrina and Bach. His Organ Fugue (D 952), composed for Lachner on 3 June 1828, is based on the F sharp minor fugue from *Das wohltemperierte Klavier* and Schubert's response is composed in three versions, the last of which is a tonal answer. The work is a fine example of how friendship influenced his aesthetic practice when a contrapuntal tournament inspired the composer to approach systematically real and tonal answers. Schubert's fair copy for Sechter records pairs of fugal openings, where each theme begins on a new degree of the scale, in strict order from the tonic to the octave, which suggest Marpurg's rules for a Dux response. Sechter's commentary is equally thorough: he illustrates the basic principle through a theme which embraces tonic and dominant, with a countermelody in double counterpoint and tonal response. Pace Marpurg, Sechter sets linear themes with a melodic range from a fourth to a seventh, thereby showing the range of possibilities for a real response. Arriving at a chordal theme within the octave, he returns to a tonal answer derived from the *stile antico* tradition, again illustrating a tonic-dominant relationship for theme and reply.[19] One of the exercises that Sechter set for the following week, 11 November, was a chromatic subject on Schubert's name. When Schubert did not live to complete this task, Sechter wrote a commemorative Fugue in C minor on the subject, which Diabelli published on 28 November, nine days after the composer's death. It is not only dedicated to Schubert's memory, but pays quiet tribute to the composer's thirst for knowledge to the end:

Example 23.4: Simon Sechter, Fugue in C minor on the name 'Schubert', op. 43, 'Dem Andenken des zu früh verblichenen Franz Schubert', November 1828, bars 1–15

By 11 November, the scheduled date of his second lesson, Schubert was bedridden, actively dying in Ferdinand's home. As he lay on his deathbed, wasting with disease, he wrote the last letter of his life to Schober on 12 November, seeking escape in the novels of Fenimore Cooper, confiding in

him 'I am ill. I have eaten nothing for eleven days and drunk nothing, and I totter feebly and shakily from my chair to bed and back again. [. . .] If ever I take anything, I bring it back up at once again.'[20] This was the second time Schober left his best friend in great solitude: by the time he arrived, Schubert no longer recognized him.

Instead, it was Karl Holz who brought relief. Holz had played Schubert's chamber music with Schuppanzigh, and arranged a private bedside performance of Beethoven's String Quartet in C sharp minor, op. 131, at Schubert's request, on 14 November, five days before his death. Although the validity of this performance has been questioned, it is all of a piece with Schubert's roots – the family performances of Beethoven's chamber music, Schubert's schoolhouse string quartets – and the quartet's performance at Beethoven's bedside a year earlier. Wagner believed its first movement was the most haunting expression of melancholia in music and Beethoven considered the quartet his most perfect work. According to Holz, as reported later by Ludwig Nohl, 'Schubert was sent into such transports of delight and enthusiasm and was so overcome that [we] feared for him . . . The quartet was the last music that he heard.'[21]

Emotionally and physically exhausted, Schubert was bled on 13 November. The following day a female nurse was employed to attend to skin lesions, as the account for his medical expenses shows medicine, ointments and powders were purchased every day except on 14 November, the day she was appointed. His final medical consultation took place on 16 November. Ernst Rinna von Sarenbach, who had been treating him for syphilis, was sick and was replaced by Josef von Vering. A second opinion was sought from Johann Baptist Wisgrill, a classmate of Schubert's at the Stadtkonvikt (1808–11) who had published a book on *Syphilitische Therapie* in 1826. Schubert's hair was shorn, most likely to attend to lesions on his head; a second, male nurse was employed to help turn him.

Schubert's death was almost certainly syphilitic in origin. Three of the four stages of syphilis have manifestations on the skin of the sufferer: on his deathbed he was clearly being treated for terrible abscesses and ulcers. One of the medical purchases for vesicatory-plaster (*Viskatur-Pflaster*) contained a blistering agent, cantharidinm, which was used to cauterize syphilitic skin lesions.[22] Tertiary syphilis can spread to the brain and central nervous system (neurosyphilis) or to the eye (ocular syphilis, causing changes to vision, even blindness). Given the pace of Schubert's work in autumn 1828, it is unlikely that he died of neurosyphilis. As hearing is the last sense we lose and music the last intelligence, we cannot completely rule out the possibility of syphilis becoming a neurological condition. During tertiary syphilis, the skin, bones and internal organ systems begin to be irreversibly damaged, resulting in death. On a body seriously weakened by chronic syphilis and the assimilation of mercury used in its treatment, the bacterial infection on Schubert's death certificate would have contributed to his immune system's rapid collapse.

The record of his symptoms directly relates to *typhus abdominalis*, a bacterial infection (*salmonella typhi*), which was raging in nineteenth-century Vienna and from which Schubert's mother had died. Schubert's weak constitution may also have been ravaged by the inclement conditions of Ferdinand's apartment where, even by the standards of the time, the water supply and sanitation were inadequate. Contracted by the hands, or indirectly through water and milk, with an incubation time of one to three weeks, typhoid fever typically develops in three stages over the course of three weeks, beginning with exhaustion, headaches, an inability to retain food, and a very gradual increase in temperature reaching a high fever of 40–41° C, all of which matches surviving accounts of Schubert's final fortnight.

Schubert's death was not, in Novalis's sense, a gentle transition to the other world. The stream of visits by his friends suggests they knew he was not long for the world. Spaun's account is a common experience of denial of a loved one's death. He found Schubert 'ill in bed, though his condition did not seem to me at all serious. He corrected my copy [of Psalm 23] in bed and was glad to see me, saying, "I am not in any pain, only I'm so exhausted I feel as if I were going to fall through the bed. [. . .] I left him without any anxiety at all, and it came as a thunderbolt when I heard of his death.'[23] Notably absent from his bedside were Schwind, who was in Munich, and Vogl, who was preoccupied with his new wife. Schubert's last visitors, on 17 November, were his duet partners, Lachner and Bauernfeld, who visited in the knowledge that his time was now limited. Lachner's morning visit obviously tired the composer, because in the afternoon Bauernfeld found him 'very flaccid, but quiet and not without hope of recovery'. Unable to face the terror of his own death, 'he expressed the wish to receive another libretto but on the same day became so violently delirious' that his restlessness had to be constrained. According to Spaun, Schubert sang ceaselessly in his delirium.[24] Schober recollected how Schubert 'lay in wild, feverish delirium', had lost consciousness and no longer recognized him. He recalled the pain he felt 'when the eyes, once so familiar, looked strangely and wildly at him'.[25] Schubert had begun his final withdrawal from friends and the greatest trial of his humanity.

The drama of the composer's last hours is recorded in Ferdinand's passion narrative as he reshaped his brother as the Christ-like figure their grandfather had portrayed in the Garden of Gethsemane fifty years earlier. First he has Schubert cry out to him for help. Restless, confused, and lacking the physical strength to project his voice, he asked him to put his ear to his mouth and then whispered, 'What is the matter with me?' Ferdinand tried to assuage the disorienting, fearful trials of his brother, who no longer recognized where he was and continually experienced being in a strange room. All day long, the dying composer struggled to get out of bed in an attempt to escape his fate. When the doctor arrived a few hours later, Schubert grasped at the wall with a feeble hand to steady his own recognition and released one final cry, 'This, this is my end'.[26]

We cry coming into the world. Sometimes we do the same leaving it. It must have been very difficult for Ferdinand to watch, being in almost constant attendance, providing the kind of family environment his brother needed and craved. On the threshold of death, most of Schubert's interactions with his family were non-verbal as his body gradually shut down. At Franz Theodor's request Schubert received the sacrament of extreme unction but not holy viaticum, being insufficiently conscious and unable to hold anything down.

On the eve of his death, delirious and disorientated, Schubert, presaging his own burial, called out to his brother, 'I implore you not to leave me here in this corner under the earth; do I not deserve a place above the earth? [. . .] Beethoven does not lie here.' Was this a final burst of lucidity before Schubert died? Was this the last time he opened his eyes to look at Ferdinand? His final invocation was taken by his brother as a wish to be buried beside Beethoven. If this is true, it suggests that in the closing moments of his life Schubert did not experience the tranquillity of a life well spent. Until he lost consciousness, an insistent inner voice, 'What did you do with your life?', 'What does it all amount to or ever will?', was there to the very end.

On Wednesday 19 November at 3 o'clock in the afternoon he took his final breath and reached a state of being that was denied him in life, where all the contradictions and conflicts were resolved.[27] Ferdinand was charged with breaking the news to their father. The Lichtental Church bells tolled his death.

The year 1828 was the one in which the dying Schubert gave so much to posterity. In his final days he kept himself sane by concentrating all the energy he could summon up on a single task. Five people – Bauernfeld, Spaun, Haslinger, Schindler and Ferdinand – all bear witness to Schubert finalizing the proofs for Part Two of *Winterreise* in the hours he was sitting out. Most likely the proofs were in his keeping when he died. The wayfarer had been a constant presence in Schubert's life from his first song to this final gesture. With Schubert the re-reading of proofs was a creative act. He kept the mills grinding to the end. Even in his final conscious moments, as he revised these proofs before he died, Schubert acted according to what he knew to be true and right and which defined him. As Socrates says, we take nothing with us into death but what we are, and Schubert was true to the creative impulse right to the end. Death merely dissolved the bonds that tied him to the ordinary world he knew. Like the image the composer conjured up of his dead mother in 'Mein Traum', Spaun said he looked peaceful. He richly deserved that *quietus*.

24

◈

LACRIMAE RERUM: BURIAL AT WÄHRING

'Sunt hic etiam sua praemia laudi;
sunt lacrimae rerum et mentem mortalia tangunt.
Solve metus; feret haec aliquam tibi fama salutem.'

('Here, too, the praiseworthy has its rewards; there are tears for things and our mortality cuts to the heart. Release your fear; this fame will bring you some safety.')

Virgil, Aeneid, II. 1, 461ff

On receiving the news of his son's untimely death, Franz Theodor may well have felt deeply the absence of his first wife of twenty-seven years, Maria Elizabeth, with whom he had shared the true tragedy of their relationship: the burial of eleven children. Losing children had been a cruelly disproportionate part of his existence and the cause of his emotional and physical breakdown across the next eighteen months. Once again Fate had overturned the natural order of human affairs as he closed the eyes of his 'dearly beloved Franz', as son gave way to his father. The steadiness of Franz Theodor's hand on 19 November, in comparison to Ferdinand's letter littered with mistakes, shows a resilience that had been hard won (Figure 21a and b).[1] But the impact of the blow soon manifested itself in ungainly sentences which question his capacity to endure (Figure 22a and b).[2] As the father of two teenage girls and two boys of five and two when his thirty-one-year-old son died, he soon had no interest in having yet another child, or even living on.

Morning after morning he would awake to recall that his favourite son had gone, the son with whom he had most in common. Both men had the imagination to free themselves from the bounds of family expectations. Both had the intelligence to know their lives were not predetermined. Both had the creativity and capacity to determine their life's meaning, knowing 'whatever is inherited can be reimagined'. Such wisdom was useless to him now. Everything seemed too overwhelming.

But his first task, a trademark of his life, was once more to bury his son, whose wasted body lay dressed in loose brown grave clothes. Responsible as ever, he took charge of the death notice while Ferdinand made arrangements for his brother's burial.[3]

In the spirit of the age, where singing was encouraged by adding new words to a familiar tune, the family invited Schober to write a *tombeau* commemorating Schubert's death. In the tradition of sixteenth- and seventeenth-century Italian memorial poems, Schober wrote new words to his tripartite 'Pax Vobiscum' (D 551), which Schubert had set to music in 1817, conjoining himself with his life's closest friend in one final artistic collaboration. When he originally set this text, Schubert had already composed many pavanes – most famously for Goethe's *Mignon* – but unknowingly he had here written his own.

Woven into the fabric of Schubert's chorale are the descending lines of the Italian *Lachrimae*, a metaphor for grief that had appeared in his earliest songs. The lament is embroidered with many expressive elements of mourning – the elegiac tempo in quadruple metre whose gravity is heightened by the expressive indication 'mit heilger Rührung' (with holy feeling), its dotted rhythms, particularly in repeated notes (bars 24 and 25), depicting Death knocking at the door, its slow-moving harmonies and ceremonious manner depicting the soul's transcendence – all communicating the composer's deep spirituality:

Example 24.1: 'Pax Vobiscum' (D 551), to Schober's text, 'An Franz Schubert's Sarge', 21 November 1828

Der Friede sei mit dir, du engelreine Seele!	May peace be with you, you pure angelic soul!
Im frischen Blüh'n der vollen Jugendkraft	In the fresh bloom of youth
hat dich der Strahl des Todes hingerafft,	Death ruthlessly claimed you
daß er dem reinen Lichte dich vermähle,	So Eternal Light would make you whole,
dem Licht, von dem hienieden schon durchdrungen	The light, which already penetrated
dein Geist in heil'gen Tönen uns gesungen,	Your spirit, which resounded in heavenly tones,
das dich geweckt, geleitet und entflammt,	Which awoke, guided, and inflamed
Dem Lichte, das von Gott nur stammt.	That spirit, which came from Heaven.
O sieh, verklärter Freund, herab auf unsre Zähren,	O transfigured friend, look down on our bitter tears,
vergib den Schmerz der schwachen Menschenbrust	Forgive the feeble human breast its sorrow:
wir sind beraubt, *wir* litten den Verlust;	We have been robbed, we suffer the loss as
du schwebst befreit in heimatlichen Sphären.	You soar home, released to better spheres.
Für viele Rosen hat dies Erdenleben	For the many roses which this early life gave
dir scharfe Dornen nur zum Lohn gegeben,	Fate in return has granted sharp thorns,
ein langes Leiden und ein frühes Grab –	Years of suffering, then an early grave –
dort fallen alle Ketten ab!	There all chains will fall away!

Und was als Erbteil du uns hast zurückgelassen:	And what a bequest you have left behind for us:
die Wirken heißer Liebe, reiner Kraft,	Manifestations of fervent love, of pure power,
die heilge Wahrheit, groß und unerschlafft,	That sacred, eternal noble truth,
wir wollen's tief in unsre Seelen fassen.	We want to hold forever inside.
Was du der Kunst, den Deinen du geworden,	What you have given to others through music
ist offenbart in himmlischen Akkorden.	Is evident in celestial song.
Und wenn wir nach den süßen Klängen gehen,	And if we follow each sweet note,
Dann werden wir dich wiedersehen!	We will encounter you again!

On Friday 21 November, pallbearers dressed in black and wearing red cloaks carried the upright coffin down the narrow winding stairs of Ferdinand's apartment in Neu-Wieden no. 694, and around the corner to St Josef's Church in the Margareten suburb (today Schönbrunner Strasse 50, Vienna 5), for a funeral mass at 2.30 p.m. The funeral was conducted with a certain propriety as Schubert's talent was reabsorbed into the Lichtental Parish and Catholic tradition. Johann Baptist Gänsbacher, Director of Music at St Stephen's Cathedral, conducted a chamber choir who sang a funeral motet that Gänsbacher himself had written. Schubert had come to the end of his life's work and in the tradition of *Trauermusik*, Schober's 'An Franz Schubert's Sarge' was accompanied by wind instruments.

After final prayers Schubert's coffin was carried from the church, family and friends walking for the three-mile slow incline from Neu-Wieden to Währing Cemetery in a cordoned-off procession through the side streets of Vienna, where the light was pewter in the afternoon rain. As the cortège passed, the air was heavy with rain and sadness. The women held their skirts as they made their way through the wet streets – and for those who loved him most, time seemed to stand still.

At dusk the troupe reached the church of St Lorenz and St Gertrud in Währing, for a second service which had been arranged to allow family and friends to rest and recover from the journey before the final parting. Listening to the standard *Miserere* and *Libera me* sung by local schoolchildren, they summoned their strength before laying his body in a grave neighbouring Beethoven's, just three graves away. Like Orpheus, Schubert had found a resting place after years of wandering. Now he lay and waited to become a hero in the fullest sense: a genius of his time and place, one who would have a cult following and be honoured as a kind of guardian spirit.

In the weeks that followed, the intensity and depth of feeling that Schubert's circle invested in their friendships was evident in many different ways. Grief-stricken, Moritz von Schwind confessed to Schober: 'I have wept for him as for a brother, but now I am glad for him that he has died in his greatness and done with his sorrows. The more I realize now what he was like, the more I see what he has suffered. To you I bring all the love they have not buried with him.'[4] Overwhelmed by Schubert's death, Bauernfeld wrote in his diary, 'Yesterday afternoon Schubert died. On Monday I still spoke with him. On Tuesday he was delirious, on Wednesday dead. [. . .] It all seems like a dream to me.' His poetic tribute, 'Schubert', and Mayrhofer's loyalty to Schubert so evident in his poem, 'Retrospective Feelings at F. Schubert's Decease', bear testimony to death as friendship's final closure. Anselm Hüttenbrenner published a musical expression of his grief in *Nachruf an Schubert in Trauerstimmen am Pianoforte*. Many years later, in 1861, he set to music a quatrain which Baron Schlechta had written on the occasion of Schubert's death. It had been published in the *Wiener Zeitschrift für Kunst, Literatur, Theater und Mode* on 9 December 1828, a private gesture of friendship that became public a century later. In the tradition of valedictory fugues, Simon Sechter embedded Schubert's name in memoriam (see Example 23.4). Such gestures show how variously and strangely Schubert's life had become intertwined with his friends, so that when their relationship ended there was a very deep sense of loss but also a readiness to understand that tears lie at the heart of things.[5]

DE BREVITATE VITAE: MEMORIALS AND REBURIALS[6]

Numerous Requiem masses were sung in Schubert's memory. The first took place one week after the funeral on Thursday 27 November at St Ulrich's Parish at 10.30 a.m. Mozart's *Requiem* was performed, organized by Ferdinand who had been part of that parish and by his sister Resi who lived there still. Invitations were sent out by the family. A second memorial service funded by the Gesellschaft der Musikfreunde was announced by the Viennese Press on 20 December, with an official invitation from Schubert's circle of friends to subscribe to a memorial tombstone for him. Three days later in Vienna, on 23 December in St Augustine's Court Chapel at 11 a.m., Josef Hüttenbrenner chose his brother Anselm's *Requiem*, instead of Schubert's *Requiem* in E flat major (D 950) or even his *Trauermesse*, in a service celebrating the composer's life.

The Gesellschaft der Musikfreunde were very active in their support. The first public professional performance of a Schubert symphony at the Redoutensaal took place on 14 December. Leopold von Sonnleithner was actively involved in securing the score of Schubert's 'Little' C major Symphony in C major (D 589) and arranged for the parts to be prepared by professional copyists. Schubert had known about the performance, which had been passed by the board on 24 October. It was one of the sad ironies of fate that he did not live to hear this landmark event.

On the eve of his birthday and less than three months after his death, Schubert's Piano Trio in E flat (D 929), 'Die Allmacht' (D 852) and 'Auf dem Strom' (D 943) were performed in a commemorative concert organized by Anna Fröhlich, whose loyalty to Schubert proved to be enduring. Her boundless energy and astonishing industry were in large part a financial imperative. Half of the funds raised went towards erecting a tombstone for the composer. Schubert's last song, 'Die Taubenpost', opened the concert. His cantata to Grillparzer's *Miriams Siegesgesang* – which he had been unable to finish on time for his own public concert – was now finally premiered. The concert was so successful that it had to be repeated on 5 March, at which more money for the memorial was raised.[7]

With Ludwig Förster's help, Schober designed Schubert's tombstone in Währing Cemetery – a memorial of how his friendship with the composer had consciously incorporated demonstrations of love, shared history and material support, along with other signs of enduring solidarity. The simply styled gravestone was carved by Anton Wasserburger. The artist Josef Alois Dialer was commissioned to sculpt the bust, which is said to be an excellent likeness of the composer. When the monument was erected on Schubert's grave in the summer of 1830, it gave his friends the illusion of closure (Figure 16).

Schubert lived at seventeen different addresses in his thirty-one years and the casualness of his lodgings continued after his death.[8] In 1863 his body was exhumed, sealed in a lead-lined ossuary and placed in a wooden casket while his grave was being repaired. Schubert's only surviving sibling, Maria Theresa, attended his reburial with her stepbrothers, Andreas Theodor and Anton Eduard, both of whom were alive for the second service of remembrance. Like the body of a king, Schubert was again taken up from his grave on 23 September 1888 as he made one last journey to his final resting place where his remains were re-interred in Vienna's Central Cemetery. He now lies in repose beside Beethoven, his parting wish to his brother Ferdinand finally granted:

> Alles entsteht und vergeht nach Gesetz; doch über des Menschen Leben, dem köstlichen Schatz, herrschet ein schwankendes Los.
>
> (Everything rises and passes away in accordance with laws, but over human life,
> that precious treasure, an uncertain lot holds sway.)

Grillparzer recognized this when he wrote his lament for Schubert's untimely death and the frustration of young promise. His epitaph is not a simplistic affair of unrealized potential: it also contains an historical and human truth. There *was* discontinuity of what is natural, as abrupt as any transition asserted by Schubert.

In Nature such change is part of an eternal cycle, as permanent as the music he has left us. At a fundamental and very profound level – reaching beyond the obvious issue of longevity – is there any difference between Schubert's and Beethoven's hopes and Goethe's far fairer hopes? Beethoven died with plans for a tenth symphony, a *Requiem* and a *Faust*. Two months before his death, after he completed *Faust II* (and his life's work), Goethe described how certain works lined up inside him 'like a queue in a baker's shop' for remaking. When we award all life its due dignity, youth as well as age, what difference lies between Schubert finalizing the proofs of *Winterreise* on his deathbed and Goethe's crying out for 'mehr Licht'? Robert Schumann was right: to talk of what Schubert might have composed – even to consider his final works as middle-period works – denies the historical contingency of his life. They *are* Schubert's final works. He *did* contract syphilis. It *did* have a bearing on the remainder of his life. What Schubert has left us was achieved by a human and historical person who composed what he might not have composed and who himself might not have been. Had he died one year earlier he would never have written the Quintet, *Winterreise*, the late piano sonatas, or the E flat major Mass. Had he died like his younger brother Joseph aged five in 1798 or his other ten siblings who did not survive infancy, Schubert the composer would never have been and this moment in our lives would never have been. But he lived, and what he achieved in the short time granted him and in the face of such suffering is truly inspiring. In the greater scheme of time and transcendent realities, what he achieved is like a grain of sand. But acknowledging his achievement allows us to understand the true meaning of an existence so fully lived and shared, and 'because there was a Schubert, maybe there is hope for the rest of us'.[9]

CHRONOLOGY

It is often said there is so little we know about Schubert's life, but a chronology of the occasions of his life, compositions and publications that we can date with absolute certainty shows we can, in fact, document if not a day-by-day account, at least a month-by-month account with great accuracy. Such a table is a good example of the truth of contingency, of events succeeding one another in a universe of accident and chance, but it also illustrates how systematically Schubert worked. The following is not a complete list of works, but of manuscripts which are dated or ones where the month can be ascertained.

1797

31 Jan	Schubert's birth, *Zum roten Krebsen* (The Red Crayfish), Himmelpfortgrund no. 72 (today Nussdorferstrasse no. 54, Vienna 9)
1 Feb	Schubert baptized

1801 Schubert's family move to *Zum schwarzen Rössel* (The Black Horse), Himmelpfortgrund no. 10 (today Säulengasse no. 3, Vienna 9)

1802 Schubert starts piano lessons with Ignaz, violin with Franz Theodor

CHRONOLOGY

1805   Singing, counterpoint and organ lessons with Michael Holzer

1808

30 Sept   Auditioned by Antonio Salieri, Court Kapellmeister, and Franz Innocenz Lang, Director of the Stadtkonvikt
Offered scholarship in the Court Kapelle and Stadtkonvikt
Boarding student at Stadtkonvikt, Universitätsplatz (today Dr.-Ignaz-Seipel-Platz 1, Vienna 1)

Oct   Joins Stadtkonvikt Orchestra and meets Josef von Spaun
Musical Instruction: Wenzel Ružička and Salieri
Becomes friends with Albert Stadler, Anton Holzapfel, Josef Kenner, Johann Chrisostomus Senn, Johann Leopold Ebner, Benedikt Randhartinger

1810   Earliest surviving composition: 'Lebenstraum' (Gabriele von Baumberg, D 39)

8 April–
1 May   First complete composition: Fantasia in G major for Piano Four Hands (D 1)
String Quartet in G minor (D 18)

1811

30 March   First complete song, 'Hagars Klage' (D 5)

29 June   Overture in C minor for String Quintet (D 8), dedicated to Ferdinand

29 June–
12 July   Overture in C minor for String Quartet (D 8A)

20 Sept   Fantasia in G minor for Piano Duet (D 9)

26 Dec   'Der Vatermörder' (D 10)
Begins first work for music theatre, *Der Spiegelritter* (Kotzebue, D 11); overture parts in Josef Doppler's possession

1812   12 Wiener Deutsche für Klavier (D 128)

28 May	Schubert's mother dies; Salieri takes him under his wing and gives him free, private lessons
18 June	Counterpoint exercises and improvised fugues (D 24A–D and D 25C)
26 June	Completes Overture in D major (D 26)
28 June	*Salve Regina* (D 27), composed to mark the first month anniversary of his mother's death
26 July	Schubert's voice breaks, last performance as a choirboy
27 July– 28 Aug	Begins composing chamber works for domestic performance: Piano Trio in B flat (D 28)
9 Sept	Andante in C for Piano (D 29)
24 Sept	'Der Jüngling am Bache' (Schiller, first version, D 30)
25 Sept	First stepping-stone to a mass: Kyrie in D minor (D 31)
Sept–Oct	String Quartet in C (D 32) First Metastasio resettings; Partimento exercises for Salieri: 'Quell' innocente figlio' (D 17) 'Entra l'uomo allor che nasce' (D 33)
Oct–Dec	'Serbate, o Dei custodi' (D 35)
5 Nov	'Te solo adoro' (D 34)
19 Nov– 21 Feb	String Quartet in B flat (D 36; parts dated 5 April 1813)
25–27 Dec	'Die Advokaten' TTB (Engelhart, D 37), op. 74, written for family entertainment at Christmas
1813	Schubert's Schillerjahr: 14 TTB Schiller canons Schoolhouse String Quartets
Jan/Feb	30 Minuets and Trios for Piano (D 41) for his brother Ignaz
19 Jan	'Totengräberlied' (Hölty, second version, D 44)
1 March	Kyrie in B flat (D 45)
3–7 March	String Quartet in C (D 46)
29 March	'Dithyrambe' (Schiller, first version, D 47)
12 April	'Die Schatten' (Matthisson, D 50)

15 April	Kyrie in D minor (D 49)
15 April	'Unendliche Freude durchwallet das Herz', TTB (Schiller, D 51)
15–17 April	'Sehnsucht' (Schiller, D 52)
18 April	'Vorüber die stöhnende Klage', TTB (Schiller, D 53)
19 April	Three TTB occasional works (for the Schubert brothers to perform at their father's wedding?): 'Unendliche Freude durchwallet das Herz', TTB (Schiller second version, D 54)
21 April	'Selig durch die Liebe', TTB (Schiller, D 55) and Sanctus in B flat (D 56), TTB canon: fair copy and 2 additional copies in Schubert's hand
25 April	Schubert's father marries Anna Kleyenböck
29 April	'Hier strecket der wallende Pilger', TTB (Schiller, D 57)
May 1813	'Dessen Fahne Donnerstürme wallte', TTB (Schiller, D 58)
4 May	'Verklärung' (Alexander Pope, trans. Herder, D 59)
8 May	'Ein jugendlicher Maienschwung', TTB (Schiller, D 61)
9 May	'Thronend auf erhabnem Sitz', TTB (Schiller, D 62)
10 May	'Wer die Steile Sternenbahn', TTB (Schiller, D 63) and 'Majestätische Sonnenrosse', TTB (Schiller, D 64)
11 May	Sketch for 'Schmerz verzerret ihr Gesicht', TTB (Schiller, D 65)
12 May	Kyrie in F (D 66)
15 May	'Frisch atmet des Morgens lebendiger Hauch', TTB (Schiller, D 67)
28 May	'Die Zeit', poem marking the first anniversary of his mother's death
April–10 June	Fantasie in C minor for Piano Four Hands (D 48)
8 July	'Dreifach ist der Schritt der Zeit', TTB (Schiller, D 43, 69, D 70), three versions composed the same day

CHRONOLOGY

15 July	'Die zwei Tugendwege', TTB (Schiller, D 71)
8 June–18 Aug	String Quartet in B flat (D 68)
18 Aug	Octet for Wind Instruments (D 72)
22–23 Aug	'Thekla' (Schiller, first version, D 73)
22 Aug– Sept	String Quartet in D (D 74)
29 Aug	'Trinklied' (Schäffer, D 75)
7 and 13 Sept	'Pensa, che questo istante' (Metastasio, D 76)
17 Sept	'Der Taucher' (Schiller, D 77, completed 5 April 1814; second version 1815)
18 Sept	'Son fra l'onde' (Metastasio from *Gli orti esperidi*, D 78)
19 Sept	Nonet for Wind, 'Franz Schuberts Begräbnis-Feyer' (D 79)
27 Sept	'Zur Namensfeier meines Vaters', TTB with guitar (Schubert's text, D 80)
3 Oct	'Hier umarmen sich getreue Gatten', TTB (Schiller, D 60)
22 Oct	Offered a Meerfeld Endowment which Schubert turns down; he leaves the Stadtkonvikt
	Schubert moves home to the Schoolhouse *Zum schwarzen Rössel*, Himmelpfortgrund no. 10 (today Säulengasse no. 3, Vienna 9)
28 Oct	Completes his First Symphony (D 82), two days before his mother's birthday
28 Oct–4 Nov	'Zur Namensfeier des Herrn Andreas Siller', soloist, violin and harp (Anon. text, D 83)
30 Oct–15 May 1814	Begins second Singspiel, *Des Teufels Lustschloß* (Kotzebue, D 84), on his mother's birthday
Nov	Commences teacher training at the St Anna Normalhauptschule, 3–3a Annagasse

15 Nov	'Verschwunden sind die Schmerzen', TTB (Anon., D 88)
19 Nov	5 Minuets, 6 Trios and 5 Deutsche with 7 Trios and a coda for String Quartet (D 89)
22 Nov	2 Minuets and 2 Trios for Piano (D 91)
Nov	Minuet in D for String Quartet (D 86)
	String Quartet in E flat (D 87)
	Andante in C for String Quartet (D 87A)
29 Dec	Completes as far as no. 10, *Des Teufels Lustschloß* (D 84)
1814	Meets Johann Mayrhofer and Leopold Kupelwieser
	Schubert's Matthissonjahr
11 Jan	Completes Act 1, *Des Teufels Lustschloß* (first version, D 84)
22 Jan	Schubert's sister, Maria Barbara Anna, is born
26 Feb	Arranges Matiegka's Notturno in G for Flute, Viola and Guitar (D 96), op. 21
16 March	Completes Act 2, *Des Teufels Lustschloß* (first version, D 84)
April	5 Matthisson Settings, 'Adelaide' (D 95), 'Trost' (D 97), 'Andenken' (D 99), 'Geisternähe' (D 100), 'Erinnerung' (D 101)
23 April	Quartettsatz in C minor for String Quartet (D 103)
15 May	Completes Act 3 and, thereby, first complete opera, *Des Teufels Lustschloß* (first version, D 84)
16 May	'Die Befreier Europas in Paris' (Mikan, D 104)
17 May–22 July	Composes first Mass (D 105)
16 June	Franz Theodor displays inscription on front door to celebrate return of Emperor Francis I from Paris
28 June–1 July	*Salve Regina* in B flat (D 106)

July	3 Matthisson settings: 'Lied aus der Ferne' (D 107), 'Der Abend' (D 108), 'Lied der Liebe' (D 109)
24–25 July	'Wer ist groß?' B, TTBB Choir, Orchestra (Anon., D 110)
19 Aug	Passes Exams at I&R Training College/St Anna Normalhauptschule, 3–3a Annagasse
5–13 Sept	String Trio in B flat major (D 111A) and String Quartet in B flat major (D 112): first movement 'completed in four and a half hours'
17 Sept	'An Emma' (Schiller, D 113, first version)
Sept	'Romanze' (Matthisson, D 114)
2–7 Oct	'An Laura, als sie Klopstocks Auferstehungslied sang' (Matthisson, D 115)
14 Oct	'Der Geistertanz' (Matthisson, D 116)
16 Oct	Premiere of first Mass in F major (D 105), Lichtental Parish Church
	'Das Mädchen aus der Fremde' (Schiller, first version D 117)
19 Oct	Schubert sets his first scene from Goethe's *Faust*, 'Gretchen am Spinnrade' (D 118)
26 Oct	Schubert conducts second performance of the Mass in F major (D 105), St Augustine's Church
	2 Matthisson settings, 'Erinnerungen (D 98) and 'Die Betende' (D 102)
	Teaching assistant at his father's school
30 Nov	3 Goethe settings: 'Nachtgesang' (D 119), 'Trost in Tränen' (D 120), 'Schäfers Klagelied' (D 121)
Dec	'Ammenlied' (Lubi, D 122)
3 Dec	'Sehnsucht' ('Was zieht mir das Herz so?', Goethe, D 123)
7 Dec	'Am See' (Mayrhofer, 2 versions, D 124)
	Meets Mayrhofer
12 Dec	Schubert sets his second scene from Goethe's *Faust*, Cathedral Scene (2 versions, D 126)

CHRONOLOGY

10 Dec–24 March	Sinfonie no. 2 in B flat (D 125)
1815	Spaun introduces Schubert to Franz von Schober, Josef Gahy, Josef Wilhelm Witteczek, Karl von Enderes Meets Anselm Hüttebrenner through Salieri Schubert's Liederjahr and Goethejahr
Jan	'Der Liedler' (Kenner, D 209)
Feb	'Der Sänger' (Goethe, 2 versions, D 149)
2 Feb	'Auf einen Kirchhof' (Schlechta, D 151)
8 Feb	'Minona' (Bertrand, D 152)
10 Feb	'Als ich sie erröten sah' (Ehrlich, D 153)
11 Feb	'Das Bild' (Anon., D 155), Piano Sonata in E (D 154/i fragment)
15 Feb	10 Variations in F for Piano (D 156)
18 Feb	Begins Sonata in E major (D 157, fragment)
21 Feb	Écossaise in D minor/F major for Piano (D 158)
27 Feb	4 Goethe settings: 'Am Flusse' (D 160), 'An Mignon' (D 161), 'Nähe des Geliebten' (D 162), 'Der Sänger' (D 149)
27 Feb	'Sängers Morgenlied' (Körner, first version, D 163)
1 March	3 Körner settings, 'Liebesrausch' (D 164), 'Sängers Morgenlied' (second version, D 165), 'Amphiaros' (D 166)
2–7 March	Mass in G major (D 167)
9 March	2 Klopstock settings: 'Begräbnislied' (Nun laßt uns den Leib begraben, D 168) and 'Jesus Christus unser Heiland, der den Tod überwand' (D 168A), SATB, piano
12 March	4 Körner settings: 'Trinklied vor der Schlacht' (D 169), 'Schwertlied' (D 170), 'Gebet während der Schlacht' (D 171), 'Der Morgenstern' (D 172)
26 March	'Das war ich' (Körner, D 174)

CHRONOLOGY

25 March–1 April	String Quartet in G minor (D 173)
4–6 April	*Stabat Mater* in G minor (D 175)
6 April	'Die Sterne' (Fellinger, D 176), 'Vergebliche Liebe' (Bernard, D 177)
8 April	2 Körner settings: 'Liebesrausch' (D 179), 'Sehnsucht der Liebe' (D 180)
8 April	Birth of Schubert's sister Josefa Theresia; Adagio in G for Piano (D 178)
9 April	Josefa Theresia's Christening
10–11 April	Offertorium in A minor ('Tres sunt, qui testimonium dant in coelo', D 181)
15–17 April	'Graduale' in C major (D 184), SATB, orchestra
12 April	'Die erste Liebe' (Fellinger, D 182) and 'Trinklied' (Zettler, Rundgesang for solo, unison choir and piano, D 183)
May	3 Matthisson settings: 'Die Sterbende (D 186), 'Stimme der Liebe' (D 187), 'Naturgenuß (D 188)
May	'An die Freude' (Schiller, D 189), for solo, unison choir and piano
15 May	'Des Mädchens Klage' (Schiller, D 191, second version), 'Der Jüngling am Bache' (Schiller, D 192, second version)
17 May	'An den Mond' (Hölty, D 193) and 'Die Mainacht (Hölty, D 194)
8–19 May	*Der vierjährige Posten* (Körner, D 190)
19 May	'Rastlose Liebe' (Goethe, 2 versions, D 138), 'Amalia' (Schiller, D 195)
22 May	3 Hölty settings: 'An die Nachtigall' (D 196), 'An die Apfelbäume, wo ich Julien erblickte' (D 197), 'Seufzer' (D 198)
24 May	'Mailied' ('Grüner wird die Au', Hölty, D 199, second setting)

24 May–19 July	Symphony no. 3 in D major (D 200)
25 May	'Auf den Tod einer Nachtigall' (Hölty, D 202)
26 May	'Mailied' ('Der Schnee zerrinnt', Hölty, D 199 resetting), 2 Körner settings: 'Der Morgenstern' (D 203) and 'Liebeständelei' (D 206); 2 Körner duets for unison voices or horns: 'Jägerlied' (D 204) and 'Lützows wilde Jagd' (D 205)
29 May	2 Hölty settings: 'Der Liebende' (D 207) and 'Die Nonne' (fragment and 2 versions, D 208)
3 June	'Klärchens Lied' from *Egmont* Act 2, Scene 2 (Goethe, D 210)
5–14 June	'Adelwold und Emma' (Bertrand, D 211)
17 June	2 Hölty settings: 'Der Traum' (D 213) and 'Die Laube' (D 214)
20 June	2 Goethe settings: 'Jägers Abendlied' (first version, D 215), 'Meeresstille' (first version, D 215A)
21 June	'Meeresstille' (second version, D 216)
22 June	'Kolmas Klage' (Ossian, D 217)
24 June	'Grablied' (Kenner, D 218)
25 June	'Das Finden' (Kosegarten, D 219)
26 June	Schubert's father applies unsuccessfullly for a teaching post at the Elementary School of the Monastery of the Prelate of the Scottish Order, Andreas
2 July	'Lieb Minna' (Stadler, D 222)
3–9 July	*Fernando* (Stadler, D 220)
5 July	*Salve Regina* (Offertorium) in F (first version, D 223); 3 Goethe Settings: 'Wandrers Nachtlied' ('Der du von dem Himmel bist', D 224), 'Der Fischer' (2 versions, D 225), 'Erster Verlust' (D 226)
7 July	4 Kosegarten songs: 'Idens Nachtgesang' (D 227), 'Von Ida' (D 228), 'Die Erscheinung' (D 229), 'Die Täuschung' (D 230)

8 July	'Das Sehnen' (Kosegarten, D 231)
11 July	'Hymne an den Unendlichen', SATB with piano (Schiller, D 232)
15 July	'Der Abend' (Kosegarten, D 221), 'Geist der Liebe' (Kosegarten, D 233), 'Tischlied' (Goethe, D 234)
20 July	'Das Abendrot' (Kosegarten, D 236)
24 July	2 Kosegarten songs: 'Abends under der Linde' (D 235, first version)
25 July	'Abends under der Linde' (D 237, second version) and 'Die Mondnacht' (D 238)
26 July	Begins *Claudine von Villa Bella* (Goethe, D 239)
27 July	2 Kosegarten songs: 'Huldigung' (D 240) and 'Alles um Liebe' (D 241)
Aug	3 Hölty TTB settings: 'Trinklied im Winter' (D 242), 'Frühlingslied' (D 243), 'Willkommen, lieber schöner Mai' (canon, D 244)
	'Die Bürgschaft' (Schiller, D 246), 'Die Spinnerin' (Goethe, D 247), 'Lob des Tokayers' (Gabriele von Baumberg, D 248)
1 Aug	'Die Schlacht' (Schiller, sketch for first working, D 249)
7 Aug	4 Schiller settings: 'Das Geheimnis' (first working, D 250), 'Hoffnung' (first working, D 251)
12 Aug	'Das Mädchen aus der Fremde' (D 252, second setting)
18 Aug	'Punschlied' (2 versions, D 253); 8 Goethe settings: 'Der Gott und die Bajadere' (D 254)
19 Aug	'Der Rattenfänger' (D 255), 'Der Schatzgräber' (D 256), 'Heidenröslein' (D 257), 'Bundeslied' (D 258), 'An den Mond' (first working, D 259)
20 Aug	'Wonne der Wehmut' (D 260)
21 Aug	'Wer kauft Liebesgötter' (D 261)
22 Aug	'Die Fröhlichkeit' (Prandstetter, D 262) and 3 Gabriele von Baumberg settings: 'Cora an die Sonne' (D 263), 'Der Morgenkuss' (D 264)

23 Aug	and 'Abendständchen. An Lina' (D 265)
24 Aug	'Morgenlied' (Stolberg-Stolberg, D 266)
25 Aug	9 settings in one day: 2 anonymous TTB settings: 'Trinklied' (D 267), 'Bergknappenlied' (D 268) and 'Das Leben', TTB (Wannovius, D 269). 'An die Sonne' (Baumberg, D 270), 'Der Weiberfreund' (from Abraham Cowley's *The Mistress*, trans. Ratschky, D 271), 'An die Sonne' (Tiedge, D 272). 2 anonymous Lieder: 'Lilla an die Morgenröte' (D 273) and 'Tischlerlied' (D 274), 'Totenkranz für ein Kind' (Matthisson, D 275)
28 Aug	'Abendlied' (Stolberg-Stolberg, D 276)
29 Aug	'Punschlied', TTB with piano (Schiller, D 277)
9–15 Sept	Piano Sonata in C (D 279, fragment), 'Das Rosenband' (Klopstock, D 280); 2 Ossian settings: 'Das Mädchen von Inistore' (D 281)
5 Sept	and 'Cronnan' (D 282)
6 Sept	Schiller settings: 'An den Frühling' (first version, D 283) and 'Lied' ('Es ist so angenehm, Schiller, D 284)
12 Sept	8 Klopstock settings: 'Furcht der Geliebten/An Cidli' (D 285)
14 Sept	'Selma und Selmar' (D 286), 'Vaterlandslied' (D 287), 'An Sie' (D 288), 'Die Sommernacht' (D 289), 'Die frühen Gräber' (D 290)
15 Sept	'Dem Unendlichen' (D 291)
15 Sept	Magnificat in C (D 486)
20 Sept	'Shilric und Vinvela' (Ossian, D 293)
27 Sept	'Namensfeier' für Franz Michael Vierthaler/'Gratulations-Kantate' (Anon., D 294)
Oct	'Erlkönig' (D 328)
	'Liane' (Mayrhofer, D 298)
3 Oct	12 Écossaise für Klavier (D 299)
12 Oct	'Lambertine' (Stoll, D 301)

15 Oct	8 love songs on Therese Grob's name day, the feast of St Theresa of Avila, 'Labetrank der Liebe' (Stoll, D 302) and 'An die Geliebte' (Stoll, D 303); 'Wiegenlied' (Körner, D 304), 'Mein Gruß an den Mai' (Kumpf, D 305), 'Skolie' (von Deinhardtstein, D 306), 'Die Sternenwelten' (Fellinger, D 307), 'Die Macht der Liebe' (Kalchberg, D 308), 'Das gestörte Glück' (D 309)
18 Oct	'Nur wer die Sehnsucht kennt' (Goethe, D 310, 2 versions)
19 Oct	'An den Mond' (D 311, fragment), 'Hektors Abschied' (Schiller, D 312), and 7 Kosegarten settings: 'Die Sterne' (D 313), 'Nachtgesang' (D 314), 'An Rosa I and II' ('Warum bist du nicht hier?', D 315, and 'Rosa, denkst du an mich?', D 316), 'Idens Schwanenlied' (D 317, 2 versions), 'Schwanengesang' ('Endlich stehen die Pforten offen', D 318), 'Luisens Antwort' (D 319)
23 Oct	'Der Zufriedene' (Reissig, D 320) and 'Mignon' (Goethe, 'Kennst du das Land?', D 321)
27 Oct	'Hermann und Thusnelda' (Klopstock, D 322)
9 Nov–June 1816	'Klage der Ceres' (Schiller, D 323)
11 Nov	Mass in B flat (D 324)
13 Nov	'Wer sich der Einsamkeit ergibt' (Goethe, D 325, first setting)
18 Nov–31 Dec	Singspiel, *Die Freunde von Salamanka* (Mayrhofer, D 326)
28 Nov	'Lorma' (Ossian, fragment, first version, D 327)
23 Dec	'Die drei Sänger' (Bobrik, D 329, fragment)
28 Dec	'Das Grab', SATB canon (von Salis-Seewis, fragment for a first version, canon, D 329A, and second version, SATB setting, D 330)

CHRONOLOGY

1816	Meets Anton von Spaun and Leopold Sonnleithner
7 Jan	4 komische Ländler in D for 2 violins (D 354), 8 Violin Ländler in F sharp minor (D 355), 9 Violin Ländler in D (D 370), 11 Ländler in B flat for Violin (D 374) composed for the carnival and perhaps Ferdinand's marriage
15 Jan	'An die Natur' (Stolberg-Stolberg, D 372) 'Mutter geht durch ihre Kammern' (Stolberg-Stolberg, D 373)
17 Jan	'Lodas Gespenst' (Ossian, D 150)
20 Jan	'Bardengesang (Ossian, D 147)
Jan	3 Goethe settings: 'Der König in Thule' (D 367), 'Jägers Abendlied' (D 368), 'An Schwager Kronos' (D 369); 'Klage' ('Trauer umfließt mein Leben', Anon., D 371)
Feb	'Der Tod Oskars' (Ossian, D 375)
10 Feb	'Lorma' (Ossian, second version, D 376)
11 Feb	'Das Grab' (third version, D 377)
13 Feb	8 Ländler in B flat for Piano (D 378)
21 Feb	German *Salve Regina* in F (D 379)
22 Feb	3 Minuets with 2 Trios for Piano (D 380)
24 Feb	2 anonymous settings: 'Morgenlied' (D 381) and 'Abendlied' (D 382)
28 Feb	Composes a German-language *Stabat Mater* (D 383), rare in Schubert's day
March	Sonata in D for Violin and Piano (D 384), Sonata in A minor for Violin and Piano (D 385); 6 Schiller settings: 'Die Schlacht' (D 387), 'Laura am Klavier' (two versions, D 388), 'Des Mädchens Klage' (third setting, D 389), 'Entzückung an Laura' (D 390), 'Die vier Weltalter' (D 391), 'Gruppe aus dem Tartarus' (D 396);

CHRONOLOGY

	5 Salis-Seewis settings: 'Pflügerlied' (D 392), 'Die Einsiedelei' (D 393), 'An die Harmonie' (D 394), 'Die Herbstnacht' (D 404), 'Abschied von der Harfe' (D 406); 'Lebensmelodien' (August Wilhelm von Schlegel, D 395)
13 March	'Ritter Toggenburg' (Schiller, D 397)
18 March	'Der Flüchtling' (Schiller, D 402)
March	'Die Erwartung (Schiller, D 159)
27 March	4 Salis-Seewis settings: 'Lied. Ins stille Land' (D 403), 'Die Herbstnacht' (D 404), 'Der Herbstabend' (first version, D 405) and 'Abschied von der Harfe' (D 406)
April	Meets Anton von Spaun
14 April	Schubert applies unsuccessfully for the position of music teacher at the teacher-training college in Laibach (Ljubljana)
16 April	3 Matthisson settings: 'Entzückung' (D 413), 'Geist der Liebe' (D 414), 'Klage' (D 415)
	2 August Wilhelm von Schlegel settings: 'Die verfehlte Stunde' (D 409) and 'Sprache der Liebe' (D 410);
	4 Stolberg-Stolberg settings: 'Daphne am Bache' (D 411), 'Stimme der Liebe' (D 412), 'Lied in der Abwesenheit' (D 416) and 'In der Väter Hallen ruhte' (D 144);
	Sonata in G minor for Violin and Piano (D 408)
17 April	Spaun writes to Goethe seeking permission to publish several volumes of Schubert's Goethe settings
27 April	Schubert finishes 'Tragic' Symphony no. 4 in C minor (D 417)
29 April	5 Matthisson settings: 'Stimme der Liebe' (D 418),
30 April	'Julius an Theone' (D 419)
1 May	TTB canon, 'Goldner Schein' (D 357)
May	'Andenken' (D 423, second version) and 'Erinnerungen' (D 427, second version)
	'Der Leidende' (Anon., D 432)
	6 Écossaises for Piano 'composed while confined to my room at Erdberg' (D 421)

Whitsun weekend	Schubert stays with Spaun at Prof. Heinrich Josef Watteroth's home in Landstrasse no. 97 (today Erdbergerstrasse 17, Vienna 3), where Josef Wilhelm Witteczek, his friend, former fellow student and important collector of his music, is also staying
2 May	*Die Bürgschaft* (Anon., D 435)
12 May	12 Hölty settings: 'Klage' (first version, D 436),
13 May	'Frühlingslied' (D 398), 'Auf den Tod einer Nachtigall' (D 399), 'Die Knabenzeit' (D 400), 'Winterlied' (D 401),
May	'Trinklied im Mai' (D 427), 'Widerhall' (D 428), 'Minnelied' (D 429), 'Die frühe Liebe' (D 430), 'Blumenlied' (D 431), 'Seligkeit' (D 433), 'Erntelied' (D 434)
	Requiem in C minor (D 453, fragment)
28 June –1 July	*Salve Regina* in B flat, SATB (D 106)
June	Rondo in A for Violin and String Orchestra (D 438)
	'Chor der Engel' (*Nacht* scene chorus from Goethe's *Faust*, D 440)
	4 Uz settings: 'An die Sonne', SATB with piano (D 439), 'Die Liebesgötter' (D 446), 'Gott im Frühlinge' (D 448), 'Der gute Hirt' (D 449)
	4 Klopstock settings: 'Das große Halleluja' (D 442), 'Schlachtlied' (D 443), 'Die Gestirne' (D 444), 'Edone' (D 445);
	'An den Schlaf' (Anon., D 447)
	'Fragment aus dem Aeschylus' (from *Eumenides*, trans. Mayrhofer, D 450)
13–17 June	First diary entries
16 June	Schubert participates in celebrations marking the 50th anniversary of Salieri's arrival in Vienna (D 407)

17 June	Completes his *Prometheus* cantata (Dräxler von Carin, D 451), his first paid commissioned composition
24 July	Conducts the premiere of *Prometheus* at Heinrich Watteroth's house, 17 Erdbergerstrasse; among the performers was Leopold von Sonnleithner, whose active promotion of Schubert's music was deeply influential on his career
June-July	Mass in C major (D 452)
July	'Grablied auf einen Soldaten' (Schubart, D 454)
	'Freude der Kinderjahre' (Köpken, D 455)
	'Das Heimweh' (Winkler, D 456)
30 July	'Aus Diego Manazares. Ilmerine' (Schlechta, D 458)
Aug	Schubert moves in with Schober, 'Zum Winter' (today Tuchlauben no. 26 at the corner of Landkrongasse, Vienna I)
Aug	Piano Sonata in E (D 459)
	Drei Klavierstücke (D 459A)
	Tantum Ergo in C (D 460), dedicated to Michael Holzer; parts Josef Doppler
	Tantum Ergo in C (D 461)
	6 Jacobi settings: 'Litanei auf das Fest aller Seelen' (D 343), 'An Chloen' (D 462), 'Hochzeitlied' (D 463), 'In der Mitternacht' (D 464), 'Trauer der Liebe' (D 465), 'Die Perle' (D 466)
	'Pflicht und Liebe' (Gotter, D 467)
7 Aug	'An den Mond' (Hölty, D 468)
Sept	'Mignon' ('So laßt mich scheinen', Goethe, D 469)
	Overture in B flat (D 470)
	String Trio in B flat (D 471)
	Cantata in honour of Josef Spendou (D 472)
	'Lied des Orpheus' (Jacobi, D 474)

	Goethe settings: 'Gesänge des Harfners aus Wilhelm Meister' (D 478, 7 versions of 3 songs), op. 12, dedicated to Ritter Johann Nepomuk von Dankesreither with respect; 'Nur wer die Sehnsucht kennt' (D 481, third setting), 'Gesang der Geister über den Wassern' (first version, D 484)
	2 Caroline Picher settings: 'Der Sänger am Felsen' (D 482) and 'Lied' ('Ferne von der großen Stadt', D 483)
	4 Mayrhofer settings: 'Liedesend' (2 versions, D 473), 'Abschied' (D 475), 'Rückweg' (D 476), 'Alte Liebe rostet nie' (D 477)
7 Sept	Schubertiad at Mayrhofers
8 Sept	Diary entry lamenting new Marriage Consent Law
Sept–3 Oct	Composition and premiere of Symphony no. 5 in B flat major (D 485) at Otto Hatwig's
Oct	Adagio and Rondo Concertante in F for Piano Quartet (D 487)
	'Auguste jam coelestium' (D 488)
	'Der Wanderer' (Schmidt, D 489, three versions catalogued as D 493, op. 4/1)
	3 Mayrhofer settings: 'Der Hirt' (D 490), 'Geheimnis' (D 491), 'Zum Punsche' (D 492)
6 Oct	Mayrhofer's 'To Franz'
Nov	'Der Geistertanz' (Matthisson, D 494) and 'Abendlied der Fürstin' (Mayrhofer, D 495)
	7 Claudius settings: 'Bei dem Grabe meines Vaters' (D 496), 'Klage um Ali Bay' (D 496A), 'An die Nachtigall' (D 497), 'Abendlied' (D 499), 'Phidile' (D 500), 'Zufriedenheit' (2 versions, D 501), 'Am Grabe Anselmos' (2 versions, D 504)
	'Herbstlied' (Salis-Seewis, D 502); 'Mailied' (Hölty, third working, D 503)
Dec	2 Matthisson settings: 'Skolie' (D 507) and 'Lebenslied' (D 508)

	2 Metastasio settings: 'Leiden der Trennung' (from *Artaserse*, trans. von Collin, D 509) and 'Vedi quanto adoro' (D 510)
15 Dec	Schubert's brother, Theodor Kajetan Anton, is born. 'Wiegenlied' ('Schlafe, schlafe, holder süßer Knabe' (Anon., D 498), and 1817 occasional settings 'Der Knabe in der Wiege' (Anton von Ottenwalt, 2 versions, D 579) and 'Lied eines Kindes' (Anon., D 596) composed for his siblings?
1817	Meets Josef Hüttenbrenner and Johann Michael Vogl, who will become the foremost interpreter of his songs
Jan	'Frohsinn' (Castelli, D 520), 'Jagdlied' (Werner, D 521), 'Die Liebe' (Leon, D 522), 'Trost' (unknown, D 523) 4 Mayrhofer settings: 'Der Alpenjäger' (D 524), 'Wie Ulfru fischt' (D 525), 'Fahrt zum Hades' (D 526), 'Schlaflied', also entitled 'Abendlied' and 'Schlummerlied' (2 versions, D 527) 'La pastorella al prato' (Gondoli, 2 versions, TTBB, D 513, and second version, a lied, D 528)
22 Jan	Premiere of Cantata for Spendau (D 472) at the 20-year Jubilee of the Orphanage founded by Josef Spendau
Feb	8 Piano Ecossaises for the Carnival (D 529) 5 Claudius settings: 'An eine Quelle (D 530), 'Der Tod und das Mädchen' (D 531), 'Das Lied vom Reifen' (D 523), 'Täglich zu singen' (D 533), 'Die Nacht' (D 534) 'Brüder, schrecklich brennt die Träne', (Anon., orchestrated song, D 535)
March	Piano Sonata in A minor (D 537) 4 Goethe settings: 'Gesang der Geister über den Wassern' (second working, D 538), 'Auf dem See' (2 versions, D 543), 'Ganymed' (D 544), 'Mahomets Gesang' (D 549) 6 Mayrhofer settings: 'Der Schiffer' (2 versions, D 536); 'Am Strome' (D 539), 'Philoktet' (D 540), 'Memnon' (D 541), 'Antigone und Oedip' (D 542), 'Orest auf Tauris' (D 548)

	'Der Jüngling und der Tod' (Spaun, D 545), 'Die Forelle' (Schubart, D 550)
	2 Schober settings: 'Trost im Liede' (D 546) and 'An die Musik' (2 versions, D 547)
April	'Der Schäfer und der Reiter' (La Motte Fouqué, second version, D 517), op. 13/1
	'Pax Vobiscum' (Schober, D 551)
	'Hänflings Liebeswerbung' (D 552)
	2 Mayrhofer settings: 'Auf der Donau' (D 553) and 'Uraniens Flucht' (D 554)
May	'An die untergehende Sonne' (Kosegarten, D 457), op. 44
	Sketch for a song without words in A minor (D 555)
	Overture in D (D 556)
	Piano Sonata in A flat (D 557)
	4 Goethe settings: 'Liebhaber in allen Gestalten' (D 558), 'Schweizerlied' (D 559), 'Der Goldschmiedsgesell' (D 560), 'Gretchen im Zwinger' (D 564), third dramatic scene from Goethe's *Faust*
	'Nach einem Gewitter' (Mayrhofer, D 561)
	4 Salis-Seewis settings: 'Fischerlied' (D 562), 'Die Einsiedelei' (D 563), 'Das Grab' (fourth version, a setting for unison male-voice choir, D 569) and 'Lied im Freien' (D 572)
June	Piano Sonata in E minor (D 566)
	Piano Sonata in E flat (2 versions, D 568)
July	Piano Sonata in F sharp minor' (D 571)
	Scherzo in D and Allegro in F sharp minor for Piano (D 570)
	'Iphigenia' (Mayrhofer, D 573)
30 July	Schubert's eight-month-old brother, Theodor Kajetan, dies.
Aug	Sonata in A for Violin and Piano (D 574)
	Piano Sonata in B (D 575)

	13 Piano Variations on a Theme in A minor by Anselm Hüttenbrenner (D 576)
	'Entzückung an Laura' (D 577)
24 Aug	'Abschied' (D 578) (text and music by Schubert) for Schober
Sept	Schubert moves back home to Säulengasse no. 3 and resumes teaching at his father's school
	Overture in B flat (D 470), parts by Ferdinand Schubert
	Polonaise in B flat for Violin and Orchestra (D 580)
	String Trio in B flat (D 581)
	2 Schiller settings: 'Gruppe aus dem Tartarus' (D 583) and 'Elysium' (D 584)
	2 Mayrhofer settings: 'Atys' (D 585) and 'Erlafsee' (D 586)
27 Sept	Schlechta's poem, 'An Herrn Franz Schubert (Als seine Kantata Prometheus aufgeführt ward)', printed in the *Wiener allgemeine Theaterzeitung*
	2 Schiller settings: 'An den Frühling' (D 587) and 'Der Alpenjäger' (D 588)
Oct	2 Matthisson settings: 'Vollendung' (D 579A) and 'Die Erde' (D 579B)
Oct–Feb 1818	Schubert composes Symphony no. 6 in C (D 589)
Nov	Two Overtures in the Italian Style in D (D 590) and in C (D 591)
	Overture in the Italian Style in D for Piano Four Hands (D 592)
	Overture in the Italian Style in C for Piano Four Hands (D 597)
	2 Scherzi for Piano (D 593)
	2 Schiller settings: 'Der Kampf' (D 594) and 'Thekla' (D 595)
	'Lied eines Kindes' (Anon., D 596)

CHRONOLOGY

Dec	'Das Dörfchen' (Bürger, D 598)
1818	Meets Marie and Karoline von Esterházy and Karl von Schönstein
	Schubert's family move to the new schoolhouse no. 147 in the suburbs of Rossau (today no. 11 Grünentorgasse)
	Rondo in D for Piano Four Hands (first version, D 608)
Jan	'Die Geselligkeit' (Unger, D 609), SATB with piano for performance at Schubert's 21st birthday?
29 Jan	First song to appear in print, 'Erlafsee' (D 586), published under the title 'Am Erlaf-See' as a supplement to *Mahlerisches Taschenbuch für Freunde interessanter Gegenden, Natur- und Kunst-Merkwürdigkeiten der österreichischen Monarchie* 6 (Vienna, 1818)
31 Jan	Schubert turns 21
6 Feb	Completes his Sixth Symphony (D 589) just after his 21st birthday; its premiere at Otto Hatwig's or at Pettenkofer's
Feb	'Trio, to be regarded as the prodigal son of a minuet by Franz Schubert written down expressly for his beloved brother' (D 610)
21 Feb	Dedicates a copy of 'Die Forelle' to Josef Hüttenbrenner after several bottles of Szegzárd, a red Hungarian wine
March	Otto Hatwig moves from the Schottenhof to the Gundelhof (Bauernmarkt no. 4/5 Brandstätte) and a private orchestra meets there. Hatwig falls ill shortly afterwards and the concerts are moved to Anton von Pettenkofer's apartment (1 Bauernmarkt)
1 March	First known public performance: Overture in the Italian Style (D 590 or D 591) is played at 'Zum römischen Kaiser' (Roman Emperor Inn)
March	'Auf der Riesenkoppe' (Körner, D 611)

CHRONOLOGY

5 March	Schubert applies unsuccessfully to become a member of the Gesellschaft der Musikfreunde (hereafter GdM)
12 March	Overture in the Italian Style arranged for eight hands (either D 592 or D 597) performed by Therese and Babette Kunz, Anselm Hüttenbrenner and Schubert at a private concert hosted by Karl Friedrich Müller, Roman Emperor Inn
14 March	Dedicates Trauerwaltz, op. 9/2, first to Anselm Hüttenbrenner, also to Ignaz Assmayr
17/18 March	Begs Anselm to be at home on 19 March at 3 p.m. so they can go to the Kunzs' home together
April	Adagio in E for Piano (D 612)
	Piano Sonata in C (D 613, fragment)
	'An den Mond in einer Herbstnacht' (Schreiber, D 614)
May	Sketch for two movements for a symphony in D (D 615)
June	'Grablied für die Mutter' (D 616)
July–21 Nov	Schubert is employed as music teacher to Count Esterházy's two daughters at Zseliz, Hungary (today Želiezovce, Slovak Republic)
July–Aug	4 Polonaises for Piano Four Hands (D 599)
	Sonata in B flat for Piano Four Hands (D 617)
	Deutscher in G with Trios and 2 Ländler in E (D 618)
	Polonaise in B flat for Piano Four Hands (D 618A)
	3 Marches Héroiques for Piano Four Hands (D 602)?
	3 Marches Militaires for Piano Four Hands (D 733)
	Solfeggio (D 619)
	'Einsamkeit' (Mayrhofer, D 620)
	2 Scheiber settings: 'Der Blumenbrief' (D 622) and 'Das Marienbild' (D 633)
	German *Requiem* in G minor, SATB and organ (D 621)
Sept	8 Variations on a French Song in E minor for Piano Four Hands (D 624)

	Piano Sonata in F minor (D 625)
	'Blondel zu Marien' (D 626)
29 Sept	Performance Polonaise for Violin and Orchestra (D 580) – and German *Requiem* (D 621) – Orphanage
11 Oct	Overture by Schubert played at the County Hall
Nov	'Das Abendrot' (Schreiber, D 627)
	3 Sonnets by August Wilhelm von Schlegel (D 628, D 629, D 630)
19 Nov	Schubert arrives back in Vienna and moves in with Mayrhofer, inner city no. 420 (today Wipplingerstrasse, no. 2, Vienna I)
Dec	Petrarchan Sonnet (D 630)
	4 Friedrich von Schlegel settings: 'Blanka' (D 631), 'Vom Mitleiden Mariä' (D 632), 'Der Schmetterling' (D 633) and 'Die Berge' (D 634)
1819	Meets Anton von Ottenwalt and Moritz von Schwind
8 Jan	Second performance of *Prometheus* (D 451) in Ignaz von Sonnleithner's apartment at the Gundelhof
	'Abend' (Tieck, D 645, fragment)
	Die Zwillingsbrüder (Hofmann, D 647)
Feb	Overture in E minor (D 648)
	3 Friedrich von Schlegel settings: 'Die Gebüsche' (D 646), 'Der Wanderer' (D 649) and 'Das Mädchen' (D 652)
	2 Silbert settings: 'Abendbilder' (D 650) and 'Himmelsfunken' (D 651)
	'Bertas Lied in der Nacht' (Grillparzer, D 653)
28 Feb	First public performance of a Schubert song: 'Schäfers Klagelied, (D 121) sung by by Franz Jäger, Roman Emperor Inn
March	'An die Freunde' (Mayrhofer, D 654)

14 March	Schubert Overture (D 648?) performed by Society of Amateurs, Müller's Hall
25 March	'Schäfers Klagelied' performed by Jäger at a Benefit Concert for the Poor, Theater an der Wien
April	Der Jüngling am Bache' (Schiller, third working, D 638) Piano Sonata in C sharp minor (Fragment, D 655) 'Sehnsucht' (Goethe, fourth version, SATB, D 656) 'Ruhe, schönstes Glück der Erde' (Anon., D 657)
6 April	Schubert takes part in a performance of Joseph Haydn's oratorio, *Die sieben Worte des Erlösers am Kreuze*, at Anton von Pettenkofer's 'Schäfers Klagelied' performed by Jäger at County Hall
May	5 Novalis Settings: 'Marie' (D 658) and 'Hymne I–IV' (D 659–662)
June	Psalm no. 13 (Moses Mendelssohn, D 663)
July–Sept	Schubert spends the summer in Upper Austria with Vogl; visits Steyr where he stays with Alberg Schellmann, and Linz, where he meets Anton von Ottenwalt
10 Aug	Cantata for Johann Michael Vogl (D 666) performed at Steyr by Josefine von Koller, Bernhardt Benedict, Albert Stadler and Schubert
Sept	Return to no. 2 Wipplingerstrasse, Vienna
Oct	Overture in G minor for Piano Four Hands (D 668) 4 Mayrhofer settings: 'Beim Winde' (D 669), 'Die Sternennächte' (D 670), 'Trost' (D 671), 'Nachtstück' (D 672) 2 Goethe settings: 'Die Liebende schreibt' (D 673) and 'Prometheus' (D 674)
Nov	*Salve Regina* (D 676) 'Strophe aus Die Götter Griechenlands' (Schiller, 2 versions, D 677) Begins Mass in A flat (D 678)

19 Nov	Performance of 'Das Dörfchen' (D 598) at Ignaz von Sonnleithner's
1820	Meets Anna and Josefine Fröhlich, Franz Grillparzer and Franz Lachner Matthäus von Collin's Salon (7 Teinfaltstrasse), at which Schubert is introduced to some of the most influential and distinguished Viennese music lovers. Vogl sings several Schubert songs, including 'Der Wanderer' (D 489); Schubert and Anselm Hüttenbrenner perform Eight Variations on a French Song (D 624)
Jan	'Nachthymne' (Novalis, D 687) 4 Canzoni for voice and piano (Vittorelli and Metastasio, D 688)
Feb	*Lazarus* (Niemeyer, D 689)
March	Schubert is present when the police search Johann Senn's rooms; alleged to have behaved offensively, no action is taken against Schubert; Senn is arrested
2 March	Overture (D 648?) played at Anton von Pettenkofer's
March	5 Friedrich von Schlegel settings: 'Abendröte' (D 690), 'Die Vögel' (D 691), 'Der Knabe' (D 692), 'Der Fluß' (D 693), 'Der Schiffer' (D 694)
19 March	'Namentagslied' ('Vater, schenk mir diese Stunde', Albert Stadler, D 695), for Josef von Kollers
26 March	6 Antiphons for Palm Sunday (D 696) conducted by Ferdinand, Alt-Lerchenfeld Church
4 April	Schubert conducts Haydn's *Nelson Mass* in Alt-Lerchenfeld Church, Vienna's sixth district, on Easter Sunday
7 April	First known public performance of a work by Schubert outside Vienna: Overture (D 648?), Assembly Hall, Graz
May	6 Écossaises in A flat for Piano (D 697)

CHRONOLOGY

14 June and 21 July	*Die Zwillingsbrüder* (D 647) premiered at the Kärntnertortheater; 6 performances
July	Schubert stays at Atzenbrugg Castle near Tulln as a guest of Schober and his uncle Josef Derffel
19 Aug	*Die Zauberharfe* (D 644), melodrama produced at the Theater an der Wien; 8 performances
Sept	'Frühlingsglaube' (Uhland, D 686), 'Des Fräuleins Lebenslauschen' (Schlechta, D 698)
	2 Mayrhofer settings: 'Der entsühnte Orest' (D 699) and 'Freiwilliges Versinken' (D 700)
21 Sept	Therese Grob marries Johann Bergmann
28 Sept	Publication of 'Widerschein' (D 639) as a supplement to *Taschenbuch zum geselligen Vergnügen*, (Leipzig, 1821)
Oct	Begins *Sakuntala* (fragment, D 701)
Nov	'Der Jüngling auf dem Hügel' (Heinrich Hüttenbrenner, D 702)
1 Dec	August von Gymnich sings 'Erlkönig' (D 328) at Leopold von Sonnleithner's
9 Dec	Publication of 'Die Forelle' (D 550) as a supplement to the *Wiener Zeitschrift für Kunst, Literatur, Theater und Mode*
Dec	String Quartet in C minor (Quartettsatz, D 703)
	'Gesang der Geister über den Wassern' (D 705)
	Psalm no. 23 (Moses Mendelssohn, D 706)
	'Der zürnenden Diana' (Mayrhofer, D 707)
	'Im Walde' (Friedrich von Schlegel, D 708)

1821

Jan	Schubert moves from Mayrhofer's apartment into new lodgings in the same street (21 Wipplingerstrasse); Vogl pays the rent
	The first time he lives alone

Jan	'Die gefangenen Sänger' (August Wilhelm von Schlegel, D 712)
	'Der Unglückliche' (Caroline Pichler, D 713)
16, 24 and 27 Jan	Schubert obtains testimonials respectively from Ignaz Franz von Mosel, Count Dietrichstein, and a joint testimony from Salieri and Josef Weigl perhaps with the intention of seeking a post at the court theatre or seeking a commission at the opera
19 Jan	Gymnich sings 'Der Wanderer' (D 489) at Ignaz von Sonnleither's
25 Jan	Gymnich sings 'Erlkönig' (D 328) at an evening entertainment, GdM
26 Jan	Schubert sings a number of his songs at a party at Schober's
Feb	Schubert briefly employed as *répétiteur* at the court theatre where he coaches Karoline Unger in the part of Isabella (Dorabella) in Mozart's opera *Mädchentreue* (*Così fan tutte*)
	'Gesang der Geister über den Wassern' (D 714, second working)
	'Versunken' (D 715)
8 Feb	Josef Götz sings 'Sehnsucht' (D 636) at an evening entertainment, GdM
2 March	Sophie Linhart sings 'Gretchen am Spinnrade' (D 118) at Ignaz von Sonnleithner's
7 March	First public performance of 'Erlkönig' (D 328) by Vogl, 'Das Dörfchen' (D 598) and 'Gesang der Geister über den Wassern' (D 714) at the Kärntnertortheater
March	5 Goethe settings: 'Grenzen der Menschheit' (D 716), 'Suleika I' (D 720), 'Suleika II' (D 717), 'Geheimes' (D 719), 'Mahomets Gesang' (D 721)
	Piano Variations in C minor on a waltz by Diabelli (D 718)
8 March	'Gruppe aus dem Tartarus' (Schiller, D 583), premiered GdM
	Deutscher in G flat for Piano (D 722) composed on Ignaz Schubert's birthday

2 April	Publication (on sale or return) of 'Erlkönig' (D 328), Schubert's op. 1 dedicated to Count Moritz von Dietrichstein with respect 'Linde Lüfte wehen' duet, ST (Anon., D 725, fragment) 3 Goethe settings: Mignon I (D 726), Mignon II (D 727), 'Johanna Sebus' (D 728)
8 April	Performance of 'Erlkönig' (D 328) by Vogl, 'Das Dörfchen' (D 598), at a concert Large Assembly Hall, GdM
22 April	First public performance of the TTBB quartet, 'Die Nachtigall' (Unger, D 724), Kärntnertortheater
30 April	Publication (on sale or return) of 'Gretchen am Spinnrade' (D 118), op. 2, dedicated to Count Moritz von Fries (with respect)
29 May	Publication (on sale or return) of 4 Goethe Lieder as Schubert's op. 3 dedicated to Ignaz Mosel with high regard: 'Schäfers Klagelied' (D 121), 'Meeresstille' (D 216), 'Heidenröslein' (D 257), 'Jägers Abendlied' (D 368) Publication (on sale or return) of Schubert's op. 4 dedicated to Johann Ladislav Pyrker with respect: 'Der Wanderer' (von Lübeck, D 493), 'Morgenlied' (Werner, D 685), 'Wanderers Nachtlied' (Goethe, D 224)
20 June	Premiere of Duet and Aria for L. J. F. Hérold's comic opera *Das Zauberglöckchen* (D 723), Kärntnertortheater
30 June	Psalm no. 23 ('The Lord is my Shepherd', D 706) performed by Anna Fröhlich's pupils at the Gundelhof, GdM Publication of 'An Emma' (D 113) as a supplement to *Wiener Zeitschrift für Kunst, Literatur, Theater und Mode*
9 July	Publication (on sale or return) of 5 Goethe songs dedicated to Salieri: 'Rastlose Liebe' (D 138), 'Nähe des Geliebten' (D 162), 'Der Fischer' (D 225), 'Erster Verlust' (D 226), 'Der König in Thule' (D 367), op. 5
10 July	Leopold Kupelwieser sketches Schubert

Aug	Symphony in E (D 729)
16 Aug	*Tantum Ergo* in B flat (D 730)
23 Aug	Publication (on sale or return) of Schubert's op. 6 dedicated to Johann Michael Vogl in high regard: 'Memnon' (Mayrhofer, D 541), 'Antigone und Oedip' (Mayrhofer, D 542) and 'Am Grabe Anselmos' (Claudius, D 504); Spaun moves to Linz
30 Aug	Premiere of Psalm 23, GdM
Sept	'Der Blumen Schmerz' (Majláth, D 731)
mid-Sept–mid-Oct	Schubert and Schober spend four weeks at St Pölten and at nearby Ochsenburg Castle, where they are guests of Schober's relative Johann Nepomuk von Dankesreither, Bishop of St Pölten
20 Sept	Begins *Alfonso und Estrella* (D 732)
30 Aug	'Erlkönig' is performed at Kärntnertortheater by Vogl and Karl Schunke
Nov	Schubert is invited to write an opera for the Court Theatre
18 Nov	Public premiere of Schubert's Overture in E minor (D 648) conducted by Leopold von Sonnleithner, Large Assembly Hall, GdM; Schubert made a member of the GdM Premiere of 'Der Wanderer' (Schmidt, D 493/D 489), Roman Emperor Inn
27 Nov	Publication (on sale or return) of Schubert's op. 7 dedicated to Count Ludwig Széchényi with high regard: 'Die abgeblühte Linde' (Széchényi, D 514), 'Der Flug der Zeit' (Széchényi, D 515), 'Der Tod und das Mädchen' (Claudius, D 531)
29 Nov	Publication by Cappi & Diabelli of Schubert's op. 9: 36 Piano Dances in 2 Books (D 365)
2 Dec	Premiere of 'Der Jüngling auf dem Hügel' (Heinrich Hüttenbrenner, D 702), Roman Emperor Inn

CHRONOLOGY

8 Dec	Publication of 'Der Blumen Schmerz' (D 731) as a supplement to *Wiener Zeitschrift für Kunst, Literatur, Theater und Mode*

1822

Jan	Schubert moves in with Schober (Göttweigerhof, today 9 Spiegelgasse at the corner of Göttweigergasse, Vienna I)
	'Herrn Josef Spaun, Assessor in Linz' (D 749), a humorous recitative and aria about not being in contact
	'Geist der Liebe', TTBB (Matthisson, D 747)
21 Jan	Schubert sings some of his songs, accompanied by Schwind, at a party hosted by Prof. Vincentius Weintridt
	Eduard von Bauernfeld is present but they will not become friends until 1825
11 Feb	Private publication and premiere of the cantata *Am Geburtstage des Kaisers* (D 748), SATB and orchestra, text by von Deinhardtstein, one of the teachers, premiered by the pupils of the Imperial Theresian Academy, conducted by Leopold von Sonnleithner
27 Feb	Completes *Alfonso und Estrella* (D 732)
3 March	'Geist der Liebe' (D 747) sung by Barth, Tietze, Nejebse and Nestroy, concert conducted by Leopold von Sonnleithner, Large Assembly Hall, GdM
5 March	Schubert sings some of his songs in Karoline Pichler's home
20 March	*Tantum Ergo* in D (D 750)
7 April	'Frühlingsgesang' (Schober, D 740), Kärntnertortheater
15 April	'Geist der Liebe' performed by Barth, Tietze, Nejebse and Nestroy at the County Hall
17 April	'Die Liebe hat gelogen' (von Platen-Hallermünde, D 751), composed before 17 April
	3 Mayrhofer settings: 'Nachtviolen' (D 752), 'Heliopolis I' (D 753), 'Heliopolis II' (D 754)

CHRONOLOGY

19 April	Publication by Cappi & Diabelli of 8 Variations on a French Song dedicated to Beethoven in admiration (D 624), op. 10
May	Fragment of a Kyrie for a Mass in A minor 'for my brother Ferdinand' (D 755)
7 May	Publication of 'Die Rose' (D 745) as a supplement to *Wiener Zeitschrift für Kunst, Literatur, Theater und Mode*
9 May	Publication (on sale or return) of 5 of Schubert's op. 8: 'Der Jüngling auf dem Hügel' (Heinrich Hüttenbrenner, D 702), with 3 settings by Mayrhofer, 'Sehnsucht' (D516), 'Erlafsee' (D 586) and 'Am Strome' (D 539) dedicated to Count Johann Esterházy with respect
26 May	'Geist der Liebe' sung by Barth, Tietze, Nejebse and Nestroy at the Kärntnertortheater
3 June	'Geist der Liebe' Liebe' sung by Barth, Tietze, Nejebse and Nestroy at the County Hall
12 June	Publication by Cappi & Diabelli of Schubert's op. 11 dedicated to Josef Barth (in friendship): 'Das Dörfchen' (D 598), 'Die Nachtigall' (D 724) and 'Geist der Liebe' (D 747), TTBB with *ad libitum* guitar accompaniments
Summer	Schubert moves back temporarily to the Schoolhouse in Rossau, Grünentorgasse no. 11, Vienna 9 Sends a note to Josef Hüttenbrenner which implies he is staying temporarily at the schoolhouse in Rossau and asking him to see to his account with Diabelli as he needs money
July	'Selige Welt' (Senn, D 743) 'Du liebst mich nicht' (von Platen-Hallermünde, D 756)
3 July	Writes 'Mein Traum'
30 July	'Der Wachtelschlag' (Sauter, D 742) published as a supplement to *Wiener Zeitschrift für Kunst, Literatur, Theater und Mode*
Aug	'Gott in der Natur' (Kleist, D 757)

CHRONOLOGY

6 and 7 Aug	Prokesch has supper at the Komödiengässchen inn, beside the Kärntnerertortheater, and meets Schubert on both nights
27 Aug	Performance of 'Geist der Liebe' by Jäger, Spitzeder, Rauscher, Ruprecht and the guitarist Josef Schmidt
Autumn	Weber writes to Josef Hüttenbrenner saying Schubert's opera *Alfonso und Estrella* is 'very promising'
Sept	'Todesmusik' (Schober, D 758)
	Completion of the A flat major Mass (D 678)
8 Sept	'Das Dörfchen' performed by the Styrian Music Society, Graz
13 Sept	'Erlkönig' sung by Herr Ruess, 'Die Nachtigall' performed by the Styrian Music Society, Graz
15 Sept	'Die Nachtigall' performed at the Linz Musical Society
24 Sept	'Geist der Liebe' with guitar accompaniment at Kärntnerertortheater
30 Oct	'Unfinished' Symphony, fair copy of the score begun on his mother's birthday (D 759)
Nov	*Alfonso und Estrella* Overture (D 759A) for Piano Four Hands
	'Wandererfantasie' (D 760)
	'Schatzgräbers Begehr' (Schober, D 761)
	'Schwestergruss' (von Bruchmann, D 762)
12 Nov	'Das Dörfchen' performed in the County Theatre, Graz
22 Nov	'Des Tages Weihe', SATB with piano (Anon., D 763)
28 Nov	Josef Hüttenbrenner in correspondence with Peters about publishing Schubert's songs
1 Dec	Schubert quotes Martin Luther in the Album Leaf for Albert Schellmann: 'Whoever does not love wine, girls and song/ Remains a fool his entire life', and also from Goethe's *Beherzigung*, 'One thing will not do for all/Let each live in his tradition/Each consider his own mission/And who stands, beware a fall'

Dec	4 Goethe settings: 'Der Musensohn' (D 764), 'An die Entfernte' (D 765), 'Am Flusse' (second working, D 766) and 'Willkommen und Abschied' (first working, D 767)
13 Dec	'Frühlingsgesang', private music concert at the Roman Emperor Inn
13 Dec	Publication (on sale or return) of Schubert's Harper Songs (D 478), op. 12
	Publication (on sale or return) of Schubert's op. 13, 'Der Schäfer und der Reiter' (D 517, Fouqué), 'Lob der Tränen' (D 711, August Wilhelm von Schlegel) and 'Der Alpenjäger' (Mayrhofer, D 524), dedicated to Josef von Spaun in friendship
	Publication (on sale or return) of Schubert's op. 14 'Suleika I' (D 720) and 'Geheimnis' (D 719), dedicated to Schober
	'Gruppe aus dem Tartarus' performed by Herr von Preisinger, Zum roten Igel (The Red Hedgehog), GdM
1823	Meets Fritz and Franz von Hartmann, August Wilhelm Rieder
Jan	Schubert listed in Anton Ziegler's *Directory of Musicians*
	12 Écosaisses for Piano (D 781)
	'Drang in die Ferne' (Leitner, D 770)
	7 Rückert settings: 'Sei mir gegrüt' (D 741), 'Das sie hier gewesen' (D 775), 'Du bist die Ruh' (D 776), 'Lachen und Weinen' (D 777), 'Greisengesang' (D 778), 'Die Wallfahrt' (D 778A), 'Ich hab in mich gezogen' (D 778B)
9 Jan	'Geist der Liebe' performed by Barth, Tietze, Leschetitzki and Kiesewetter, The Red Hedgehog, GdM
10 Jan	3 Deutsche Tänze (D 971) in the *Carnival 1823* Dance Collection Book 2, edited by Czerny, published by Leidesdorf
28 Jan	*Salve Regina* (Offertorium) in F (second version, D 223)

5 Feb	Publication of Schubert's op. 18: 12 Walzer, 17 Ländler and 9 Écossaises for Piano (D 145)
Feb	Piano Sonata in A minor (D 784)
	'Der zürnende Barde' (Bruchmann, D 785)
	Begins *Die Verschworenen* (Castelli, D 787)
20 Feb	'Gretchen am Spinnrade' (D 118) performed at Zum roten Igel, GdM
24 Feb	Publication of the 'Wanderer Fantasy' (D 760), op. 15, dedicated to Lord Carl Emanuel von Liebenberg
28 Feb	Schubert informs Ignaz von Mosel that he is too ill to leave his room; living with Schober at Göttweigerhof no. 1155 (today Spiegelgasse no. 9, Vienna 1)
	Composes Waltzes D 779, nos. 8, 9, 12 and 14 during this time
6 March	'Die abgeblühte Linde' (D 514), The Red Hedgehog, GdM
March	'Viola' (Schober, D 786), 'Nacht und Träume' (von Collin, D 827)
	12 'Deutsche für Klavier' (D 790)
25 March	'Drang in die Ferne' (Leitner, D 770) published as a supplement to *Wiener Zeitschrift für Kunst, Literatur, Theater und Mode*; MS in the Pachler family's possession
6 April	The Styrian Music Society confer honorary membership on Schubert
10 April	Publication of Schubert's op. 20: 'Sei mir gegrüst' (D 741), 'Frühlingsglaube' (D 686) and 'Hänflings Liebeswerbung' (D 552), dedicated to Frau Justine von Bruchmann
April	'Die Mutter Erde' ('Des Lebens Tag ist schwer und schwül', Stolberg-Stolberg, D 788), 'Pilgerweise' (Schober, D 789)
end April	*Die Verschworenen* (D 787)
8 May	Schubert writes poem, 'Mein Gebet'
May	*Rüdiger* (von Mosel, D 791), sketch for 2 operatic numbers
	'Vergißmeinnicht' (Schober, D 792)

	2 Schiller settings: 'Das Geheimnis' (D 793) and 'Der Pilgrim' (D 794)
25 May–2 Oct	Begins *Fierabras* (Josef Kupelwieser, D 796)
27 May	Publication of 2 von Collin settings as Schubert's op. 22: 'Der Zwerg' (D 771) and 'Wehmut' (D 772), dedicated to the poet
30 May	Completes Act 1, *Fierabras* (D 796)
31 May	Begins Act 2, *Fierabras*
5 June	Completes Act 2, *Fierabras*
7 June	Begins Act 3, *Fierabras*
19 June	Publication of 3 Mayrhofer settings: 'Auf der Donau' (D 553), 'Der Schiffer' (D 536), 'Wie Ulfru fischt' (D 525), op. 21, dedicated to the poet in friendship
22 July	Libretto for *Fierabras* is presented to censors
25 July–mid Sept	Trip to Linz and Steyr. At Linz, on 28 July, Schubert is introduced by Spaun and Albert Stadler to Friedrich Ludwig von Hartmann and his family, who will become fervent Schubertians; in August he spends some time with Vogl at Steyr; return journey to Vienna via Linz
Aug	Schober moves to Breslau
Autumn	Schubert moves in with 'Tall' Huber, inner city no. 1187 (today Stubentorbastei no. 14, Vienna 1)
	Rosamunde (Helmina von Chézy, D 797)
	Linz Musikverein confers honorary membership on Schubert
4 Aug	Publication of Schubert's op. 23: 'Die Liebe hat gelogen' (von Platen-Hallermünde, D 751), 'Selige Welt' (Senn, D 743), 'Schwanengesang' (Senn, D 744) and 'Schatzgräbers Begehr' (von Schober, D 761)
19 Aug	*Fierabras* is passed by censors
26 Sept	Completion of *Fierabras*, Act 3 (D 796)
2 Oct	Completes Overture for *Fierabras* (D 796)
	In Vienna General Hospital, Alserstrasse 4, Vienna 9

CHRONOLOGY

	Composing *Die schöne Müllerin* (Müller, D 795)
9 Oct	Publication of Schubert's op. 16, TTBB: 'Frühlingslied' (Schober, D 740) and 'Naturgenus' (Matthisson, D 422) Publication of Schubert's op. 17, TTBB: 'Jünglingswonne' (Matthisson, D 983), 'Liebe' (Schiller, D 983A), 'Zum Rundetanz' (Salis-Seewis, D 983B) and 'Die Nacht' (Krummacher, D 983C)
27 Oct	Publication of Schubert's op. 24: 'Gruppe aus dem Tartarus' (D 583) and 'Schlummerlied' (Mayrhofer, D 527)
7 Nov	Schubert's brother, Andreas Theodor, is born
9 Nov	Schwind informs Schober that Schubert is well on the way to recovery
11 Nov	Schubertiad at the Bruchmanns' house
13 Nov	'Der Zwerg' (von Collin, D 771)
19 Dec	'Moment Musical' (D 780/3) Publication of *Air russe*, op. 94/3 and 2 'Deutsche' for Piano (D 769) in *Album musicale I*, Leidesdorf
20 Dec	Premiere of Helmina von Chézy's play *Rosamunde, Fürstin von Zypern* with music by Schubert (D 797), with the overture for *Alfonso und Estrella* (D 732), Theater an der Wien
30 Dec	Publication of 'Auf dem Wasser zu singen' as a supplement to *Wiener Zeitschrift für Kunst, Literatur, Theater und Mode* Publication by Leidesdorf of the Sonata in B flat major for Piano Four Hands (D 617), op. 30, dedicated to Count Ferdinand Pálffy
1824	Meets Anna Hönig
15 Jan	'Die Nachtigall' performed by Barth, Tietze, Nejebse and Rotter, The Red Hedgehog, GdM
Jan	Variations in E minor for Flute and Piano (D 802)
19 Jan	Schubertiad at Mohn's

22 Jan	Schubert stops wearing his wig
17 Feb	Publication by Leidesdorf of *Die schöne Müllerin*, 20 songs in 5 Books. Book 1 (D 795), op. 25, dedicated to Karl von Schönstein
21 Feb	Publication of 3 Écossaises (D 781/3 and 6, and D 782) in *Nouvelles Galoppes Favorites et Écossaises pour la Pianoforte seule par Fr. Schubert et M. J. Leidesdorf*
	Publication of 'Zwei Ländler' (op. 127/2 and D 366/6) in *Halt's enk z'samm!* (Leidesdorf), vol. 2
24 Feb	Schubert attends reading circle
Feb–1 March	Octet in F (D 803)
March	String Quartet in A minor (D 804)
	String Quartet in D minor (D 810)
start March	5 Mayrhofer settings: 'Der Sieg' (D 805), 'Abendstern' (D 806), 'Auflösung' (D 807), 2 settings of 'Gondelfahrer' (Lied, D 808 and TTBB, D 809)
14 March	Premiere of String Quartet in A minor (D 804) by the Schuppanzigh Quartet, The Red Hedgehog, GdM
21 March	'Die Nachtigall' performed at County Hall
24 March	Publication of *Die schöne Müllerin*, Book 2 (D 795), op. 25 (Leidesdorf)
24 March	Publication of songs from *Rosamunde* (aria and 3 choruses), op. 26
Spring	Private premiere of the Octet in F major (D 803) at Count Troyer's
25–29 March	Schubert resumes his journal as healing and reflection leading to the famous Kupelwieser letter
31 March	Letter to Kupelwieser where he tells him he is the unhappiest creature in the world
1 April	'Die Nachtigall' performed by Barth, Tietze, Nejebese and Rotter, The Red Hedgehog, GdM

April	*Salve Regina* (D 811)
	Completes Singspiel, *Die Verschworenen* (D 787)
1 May	'Die Nachtigall' performed at Schuppanzigh's May Day concert
5 May–16 Oct	Schubert's second escape to Zseliz
9 June	Schubert is one of 50 composers to compose a variation on a theme by Diabelli (D 718) published (alongside Beethoven's Diabelli Variations) in *Vaterländlischer Künstlerverein*, II
June	'Grand Duo' Sonata in C for Piano Four Hands (D 812)
26 June	Publication of 'An den Tod' (Schubart, D 518) as a supplement to *Allgemeine musikalische Zeitung mit besonderer Rücksicht auf den österreichischen Kaiserstaat*
July	8 Variations on a Theme in A flat for Piano Four Hands (D 813)
	4 Ländler for Piano Four Hands
July – Nov	17 Ländler for Piano (D 366)
Before 7 July	'Wandrers Nachtlied' ('Über allen Gipfeln ist Ruh', D 768)
2 Aug	Publication by Lithographic Institute of 'An den Tod' (D 518)
12 Aug	Publication by Leidesdorf of 'Der Gondelfahrer', TTBB (D 809), op. 28
12 Aug	Publication by Leidesdorf of *Die schöne Müllerin*, Books 3–5 (D 795), op. 25
2 Sept	Hungarian Melody in B minor for Piano (D 827)
7 Sept	Publication by Leidesdorf of String Quartet in A minor (D 804), op. 29, dedicated to Ignaz Schuppanzigh in friendship
Sept	'Gebet' (La Motte Fouqué, D 815)
	3 Écossaises for Piano (D 816)
	Divertissement in G minor for Piano Four Hands (D 818)
	6 'Grandes Marches' for Piano Four Hands (D 819)

21 Sept	'Klage an den Volk'
Oct	6 'Deutsche' for Piano (D 820)
12–16 Oct	Schubert travels back from Zseliz to Vienna with Baron von Schönstein and moves back home to the schoolhouse in Rossau (Grünentorgasse no. 11, Vienna 9)
3 Nov	Karl, Ferdinand's son, is born
Nov	Sonata in A minor for Arpeggione and Piano (D 821) and premiere by Vincenz Schuster
5 Dec	'Die Nachtigall' performed in County Hall by Jäger, Seipelt, Wächter and Webert
11 Dec	*Moments musicaux* (D 780/3)
	Publication of *Plaintes d'un Troubador* (D 780/6) and 'Die Erscheinung' ('Erinnerung', D 229) in *Musical Album*, 2
12 Dec	Anna Milder Hauptmann corresponds with Schubert
18 Dec	Publication of 3 'Marches Héroiques' for Piano Four Hands (D 602), op. 27
22 Dec	Publication by Leidesdorf of D 366/17 in *Musikalisches Angebinde zum neuen Jahren*, a compilation of 40 Waltzes released for Christmas
31 Dec	'Lied eines Kriegers', TTBB with piano (Anon., D 822)

1825

Jan	Schubert becomes friends with Edward von Bauernfeld and Josef Jenger
8 Jan	Publication by Cappi & Co of 16 German Dances and 2 Écossaises for Piano (D 783), op. 33
13 Jan	Publication by Cappi & Co of 'Die Forelle' (D 550), op. 32
13 Jan	'Erlkönig' performed by Tietze, The Red Hedgehog, GdM
27 Jan	Schubert is part of a Dance Music collection, *Halt's enk z'samm!*, published by Leidesdorf
27 Jan	Josefine Fröhlich performs Schiller's setting of 'Sehnsucht' (D 636), The Red Hedgehog, GdM

29 Jan	Beginning of weekly Schubertiads in Karl von Enderes and Josef Witteczek's homes
Feb	Schubert hires a room from Georg Kellner in the Wieden suburbs, no. 100, apartment 26 (today Technikerstrasse no. 9, Vienna 4)
	Lives alone for the second time
	Friendship with Bauernfeld blossoms
3 Feb	'Der Blumen Schmerz' (Majláth, D 731), The Red Hedgehog, GdM
Feb	2 Lappe settings: 'Im Abendrote' (D 799) and 'Der Einsame' (D 800)
	'Lied der Anne Lyle' (Andrew McDonald, D 830), 'Gesang der Norma' (Scott, trans. Spiker, D 831), 'Des Sängers Habe' (Schlechta, D 832)
	Schubert becomes friends with Bauernfeld
7 Feb	Schubert contributes to *Terpsichore*, a collection of dances published by Mechetti
9 Feb	Publication by Leidesdorf of 8 Variations on an Original Theme for Four Hands (D 813), op. 35, dedicated to Count Anton Berchtold
11 Feb	Publication by Cappi of 'Der zürnenden Diana' (D 707) and 'Nachtstück' (D 672), op. 36, dedicated to Katharina von Lászny
24 Feb	Schubert, Vogl and Johann Baptist Jenger are invited to lunch by Sophie Müller, who will visit on several occasions in 1825 and 1826
	Premiere of 'Der zürnenden Diana' (D 707) performed by Johann Hoffmann (baritone), The Red Hedgehog, GdM
28 Feb	Publication by Cappi of 'Der Pilgrim' (D 794) and 'Der Alpenjäger' (D 588), op. 37, dedicated to Ludwig Ferdinand von Schnorr in friendship

	Publication by Cappi of Overture in F for Piano Four Hands (D 675), op. 34
12 March	Publication of 'Der Einsame' (D 800) as a supplement to *Wiener Zeitschrift für Kunst, Literatur, Theater und Mode*
March	'Im Walde' (D 834)
20 March	Premiere of 'Die Flucht' (D 825/3), County Hall
April	2 de Jachelutta settings: 'Der blinde Knabe' (D 833) and 'Totengräbers Heimwehe' (D 842) 5 Walter Scott settings: Ellens Gesang I, III and III (D 837, D 838 including 'Ave Maria', D 839), 'Lied des gefangenen Jägers' (D 843) and 'Normans Gesang' (D 846)
April	Piano Sonata in C (D 840), 2 Deutsche (D 841), Piano Sonata in A minor (D 845)
10 April	'Der Alpenjäger' (Schiller, D 588), The Red Hedgehog, GdM
16 April	Waltz in G for Piano (Album Leaf for Anna Mayerhofer von Grünbühel)
Early May	Wilhelm August Rieder paints Schubert's portrait
7 May	Publication by Leidesdorf of Book 1 of 6 'Grandes Marches et Trios' for Piano Four Hands (D 819), op. 40, dedicated to J. Bernhardt (in gratitude and friendship)
9 May	Publication by Cappi of 'Der Liedler' (D 209), op. 38, dedicated to Kenner
20 May– early Oct	Schubert undertakes a lengthy trip during which time he visits Steyr (26/27 May) and Linz more than once, spends nearly six weeks at Gmunden (4 June–12 July), three weeks in Linz (15 July–10 Aug), Steyr again (11 Aug–4 Sept), visiting Salzburg and spending three weeks in Bad Gastein (from 13/14 Aug) where he meets Johann Ladislaus Pyrker, one week in Gmunden (10–16 Sept), returning to Steyr (17 Sept); during most of this time he is in Vogl's company, returning to Vienna in Oct

6 June	Publication of 3 Goethe settings as op. 19: 'An Schwager Kronos' (D 369), 'An Mignon' (D 161) and 'Ganymed' (D 544), dedicated to the poet with veneration. A special copy on satin paper with a gold title is sent from Diabelli to the poet with Schubert's accompanying letter
9 June	Anna Milder Hauptmann performs 'Erlkönig' (D 328) and 'Suleika II' (D 717) with her sister Jeannette Bürde, Jagor's Hall, Berlin
16 June	Goethe notes receipt of Schubert's op. 19 in his diary
17 June	'Divertissement sur des motifs originaux français' in E minor for Piano Four Hands (D 823), op. 63
23 June	Publication of *Tantum Ergo* in C (D 739), op. 45
	Publication of 'Offertorium' no. 1 ('Totus in corde langueo') in C (D 136), op. 46, dedicated to Ludwig Tietze
June – Sept	Symphony in C major (D 944)
July	'Trinklied aus dem 16. Jahrhundert' (Gräffer, D 847) and 'Nachtmusik' (Seckendorf, D 848), TTBB, Gmunden
25 July	Publication by Pennauer of 'Die junge Nonne' (Jachelutta, D 828) and 'Nacht und Träume' (von Collin, D 827), op. 43
	Publication 'Offertorium' no. 2 (*Salve Regina*) in F (D 223), op. 47
July	Schober returns to Vienna from Breslau
Aug	Piano Sonata in D (D 850) and 2 Pyrker settings, 'Das Heimweh' (D 851), 'Die Allmacht' (D 852), dedicated to Pyrker
	'Auf der Bruck' (Schulze, D 853), 'Fülle der Liebe' (Friedrich von Schlegel, D 854)
12 Aug	Publication by Pennauer of 'Suleika II' (D 717), op. 31, dedicated to Anna Milder Hauptmann

CHRONOLOGY

3 Sept	Publication by Diabelli of Mass in C (with new Benedictus, D 452), op. 48, in memory of Michael Holzer
8 Sept	Premiere of Mass in C (D 452), 'Offertorium, Totus in corde' (D 136), Offertorium in F, *Salve Regina* (D 223) and *Tantum Ergo* in C (D 739), St Ulrich (Maria Trost)
Sept	2 August Wilhelm von Schlegel settings: 'Wiedersehen' (D 855) and occasional work, 'Abschied für die Entfernte' (D 856)
	2 Scenes from *Lacrimae* (Schütz, D 857)
Sept	Schubert is elected a substitute representative (Ersatzmann) of the GdM
21 Sept	Publication of Book 2 of 6 'Grandes Marches et Trios' for Piano Four Hands (D 819), op. 40
17 Nov	Premiere of 'Der Gondelfahrer' (D 809) TTBB, The Red Hedgehog, GdM
21 Nov	Publication by Diabelli of Galopp and 8 Écossaises for Piano (D 735), op. 49, and 34 *Valses sentimentales* (D 779), op. 50
1 Dec	'Grande March Funèbre' in C for Piano Four Hands (D 859)
Dec	3 Schulz settings: 'An mein Herz' (D 860), 'Der liebliche Stern' (D 861) and 'Um Mitternacht' (D 862)
29 Dec	Publication of Waltz (D 978) in *Seid uns zum zweiten Mal willkommen!*
	Cotillon in E flat for Piano (D 976) published in *Ernst und Tändelei*, a compilation by Leidesdorf of 44 Dances by different composers
1826	Schubert lives with Schwind at Schober's intermittently in spring, and summer in Währing (exact location unknown) and during the autumn in the city (today Bäckerstrasse no. 6, Vienna 1)
Jan	'Wehmut' (Heinrich Hüttenbrenner, D 825)

	4 Seidl settings: 'Widerspruch' (D 865), 'Wiegenlied' (D 867), 'Der Wanderer an den Mond' (D 870), 'Das Zügenglöcklein' (D 871)
	2 Schulze settings: 'Im Jan 1817' (D 876) and 'O Quell, was strömt du rasch und wild' (D 874)
	Gesänge aus *Wilhelm Meister* (D 877)
	TTBB settings: 'Mondenschein' (Schober, D 875), 'Die Allmacht' (Pyrker, D 875A)
6 Jan	Galopp and 8 Écossaises (D 735), anonymously arranged for orchestra for the Carnival Ball, Seven Elector's Hotel, Pest, and repeatedly performed until Ash Wednesday
12 Jan	'Rastlose Liebe' (D 138), The Red Hedgehog, GdM
8 Feb	Publication of op. 39, 'Die Sehnsucht' (Schiller)
	Publication by Pennauer of 'Grande March Funèbre' in C for Piano Four Hands (D 859), op. 55
1 Feb	Performance of Quartet in D minor ('Death and the Maiden', D 810) at Franz Paul Lachner's
17 Feb	Performance of the melodrama 'Abschied' ('Leb wohl, du schöne Erde', Josef Pratobevera, D 829), commissioned by the family for Pratobevera to perform on his birthday. The text is the final monologue from an epic poem, 'Der Falke', written by his son, Adolf
20 Feb	Publication by Diabelli of Overture to *Alfonso und Estrella* for Piano Four Hands (D 759A and D 773), op. 69, dedicated to Anna Hönig
25 Feb	Schubert's father is granted citizen rights
March	3 Seidl settings: 'Am Fenster' (D 878), 'Sehnsucht' (D 879) and 'Im Freien' (D 880)
	4 Schulze settings: 'Fischerweise' (D 881), 'Im Frühling' (D 882), 'Lebensmut' (D 883) and 'Über Wildemann (D 884)
1 March	Publication of the premiere of the Grand Sonata for Piano in A minor (D 845), op. 42

5 April	Publication of 7 Songs from Walter Scott's *Fräulein vom See* (5 Lieder and 2 Gesänge in 2 books), op. 52, dedicated to Countess Sophie Weissenwolff
6 April	Publication of 2 August Wilhelm von Schlegel songs: 'Der Schmetterling' (D 633), 'Die Berge' (D 634) and 'An den Mond' (Hölty, D 193), op. 57
	Publication of 3 Schiller Lieder: 'Hektors Abschied' (D 312), 'An Emma' (D 113) and 'Des Mädchens Klage' (D 191), op .58
7 April	Schubert applies for the vacant post of Deputy Court Kapellmeister
8 April	Publication of the Second Grand Sonata in D for Piano (D 850), op. 53, dedicated to Karl Maria von Bocklet
	Publication of *Divertissement à l'hongroise* for Four Hands (D 818), op. 54, dedicated to Katharina von Lásny
April	6 Polonaises (D 824)
31 May	Schubert at Karl Enderes's home
10 June	Publication by Cappi and Czerny of 'Greisengesang' (Rückert, D 778) and 'Dithyrambe' (Schiller, D 801), op. 60
17 June	Publication by Weigl of *Divertissement en forme d'une marche brillante et raisonnée, composé sur des motifs originaux français* in E minor for Piano Four Hands (D 823/i), op. 63, no. 1
20–30 June	String Quartet in G (D 887)
1 July	Spaun returns to Vienna where he will remain in intimate contact with Schubert until the latter's death
	Occasional setting of 'Trinklied' (Shakespeare, trans. Bauernfeld, D 888) to mark his return, in Spaun's MSS collection
July	'Gesang: Was ist Silvia, saget an' (Shakespeare, trans. Bauernfeld, D 891)

	'Ständchen' (Shakespeare, trans. August Wilhelm von Schlegel, D 889), 'Hippolits Lied' (von Gerstenberg, D 890)
8 July	Publication by Cappi and Czerny of 6 Polonaises for Piano Four Hands (D 824), op. 61
14 July	Publication by Pennauer of 'Wilkommen und Abschied' (Goethe, D 767) and 2 Bruchmann settings, 'An die Leier' (D 737) and 'Im Haine' (D 738), op. 56, dedicated to Karl Pinterics in friendship
Autumn	Schubert and Schober move back into the city (Bäckerstrasse no. 6, Vienna 1)
7 Aug	Publication of 3 'Marches Militaire' for Four Hands (D 733), op. 51
Sept	'Nachthelle', TTBB (Seidl, D 892), 'Grab und Mond', TTBB (D 893)
14 Sept	Publication by Pennauer of the 'Grande March Héroique' in A minor for Piano Four Hands (D 885), op. 66
21 Sept	Publication of 3 Rückert songs, 'Daß sie hier gewesen' (D 775), 'Du bist die Ruh' (D 776), 'Lachen und Weinen' (D 777), and 'Du liebst mich nicht' (von Platen-Hallermünde, D 756), op. 59
Oct	Piano Sonata in G (D 894)
	Rondo in B minor for Violin and Piano (D 895)
9 Oct	The GdM, on learning that Schubert intends to present a new symphony, awards him 100 florins. The award is not linked to the proposed gift but is described as a token of appreciation for his part contributions to the society's activities
end Nov/ Dec	Schubert presents the autograph of D944 to the GdM
23 Nov	Performance of 'Der Einsame' (D 800), The Red Hedgehog, GdM

CHRONOLOGY

24 Nov	Publication of 2 Mayrhofer songs, 'Lied eines Schiffers an die Dioskuren' (D 360), 'Heliopolis I' (Mayrhofer, D 753) and 'Der Wanderer (Friedrich von Schlegel, D 649), op. 65
8 Dec	Schwind sings Schubert's songs accompanied by the composer at an evening spent at Spaun's
15 Dec	Schubertiad at Spaun's at which Schubert plays duets with Josef von Gahy and Vogl sings about 30 of his songs Publication by Diabelli of 'Wiener Damen-Ländler (und Ecossaisen)', 18 Dances for Piano (D 734), op. 67
21 Dec	Performance of 'Der Zwerg' (D 771), The Red Hedgehog, GdM
23 Dec	Waltz in A flat for Piano (D 978) Waltz in G for Piano (D 979) in *Moderne Liebes-Walzer* 2 Piano Waltzes in G major and B minor (D 980) in *Neue Krähwinkler Tänze*, a compilation of 50 Waltzes published by Leidesdorf
28 Dec	Performance of 'Die junge Nonne' (D 828), The Red Hedgehog, GdM
1827	Meets Marie Pachler
Jan–Feb	For the third time Schubert lives alone near Karolinentor (opposite the Stadtpark)
5 Jan	Publication by Diabelli of 'Der Einsame' (Lappe, D 800), op. 41 Publication by Diabelli of 'An die untergehende Sonne' (Kosegarten, D 457), op. 44
Jan	Josef Weigl is appointed Deputy Court Kapellmeister
Jan	3 Rochlitz settings: 'Zur guten Nacht' TTBB (D 903), 'Alinde' (D 904) and 'An die Laute' (D 905) 'Der Vater mit dem Kind' (Bauernfeld, D 906)
11 Jan	Premiere of 'An Schwager Kronos' (D 369), The Red Hedgehog, GdM

593

22 Jan	Publication by Haslinger of *Valse nobles* (D 969), op. 77
	Publication of Overture from *Fierabras* (D 796) arranged for Piano Four Hands by Carl Czerny, op. 76
25 Jan	Premiere of 'Nachthelle' (D 892), The Red Hedgehog, GdM
early 1827	Karl Maria Bocklet and Josef Slavík play the Rondo for Violin and Piano (D 895) at Domenico Artaria's
8 Feb	'Lied des gefangenen Jägers' (D 843), The Red Hedghog, GdM
Feb	8 Variations on a theme from Hérold's opera *Marie* for Piano Four Hands (D 908)
	'Jägers Liebeslied' (Schober, D 909), op. 96/2, and 'Schiffers Scheidelied' (D 910)
	Starts composing *Winterreise*, Part 1 (D 911)
19 Feb	Publication by Antaria of *Rondeau brillant* in B minor for Piano and Violin (D 895), op. 70
28 Feb	'Schlachtlied' for double choir, TTBB TTBB (Klopstock, D 912), piano part added by Ferdinand
March	Schubert once more takes up residence at Schober's 'Zum blauen Igel' (The Blue Hedgehog, today Tuchlauben, no. 18, near Zum roten Igel, The Red Hedgehog, GdM, and former residence 'Zum Winter') where he has a music room and two other rooms at his disposal; except for a short break he will live here until August 1828
2 March	Publication by Diabelli of *Gesänge aus Wilhelm Meister* (Goethe, D 877), op. 62, dedicated to Princess Mathilde Schwarzenberg
	Publication by Diabelli of 'Drang in die Ferne' (von Leitner, D 770), op. 71
	Publication by Diabelli of 'Auf dem Wasser zu singen' (D 774), op. 72
4 March	Schwind and Schober perform Schubert's songs at Schober's

8 March	Premiere of 'Gott in der Natur' (D 757) and 'Normans Gesang' (D 846) accompanied by Schubert, The Red Hedgehog, GdM
20 March	Schubert possibly visits the dying Beethoven with Anselm Hüttenbrenner
	At Katharina Lásny's, Vogl and Schubert perform some of Schubert's songs including 'Der blinde Knabe' in the presence of Johann Nepomuk Hummel, who is very moved by them
29 March	Schubert is a torchbearer at Beethoven's funeral
April	'Nachtgesang im Walde' (Seidl, D 913) and 'Frühlingslied' (D 914)
11 April	Publication by Haslinger of the Piano Sonata in G (D 894), op. 78, dedicated to Josef von Spaun
16 April	Premiere of the Octet in F major (D 803) by the Schuppanzigh Quartet and others, The Red Hedgehog, GdM
19 April	Publication by Antaria & Co of the Rondo in B minor for Violin and Piano (D 895), op. 70
21 April	Schubertiad at Spaun's
22 April	At a concert given at the Landhaus by the violinist Leopold Jansa, Schubert accompanies an unidentified singer in 'Normans Gesang' (D 846). On the same day the quartet 'Nachtgesang im Walde' (D 913) is performed at Josef Lewy's concert, The Red Hedgehog, GdM
26 April	Allegretto in C minor for Piano (D 915)
29 April	Performance of 'Der Einsame' (D 800), County Hall
May	'Das stille Lied' (Seegemund, D 916)
6 May	Performance 'Im Freien' (D 880), University Aula Maxima
16 May	Publication of 'Der Wachtelschlag' (Sauter, D 742), op. 68
	Publication of 'Die Rose' (Friedrich von Schlegel, D 745), op. 73

CHRONOLOGY

	Publication of *Die Advokaten*, parody of a work by Anton Fischer (Engelhart, D 37), TTB with piano, op. 74
	Publication by Haslinger of 2 Pyrker settings: 'Das Heimweh' (D 851) und 'Die Allmacht' (D 852), op. 79
25 May	Publication by Haslinger of 3 Seidl settings: 'Der Wanderer an den Mond' (D 870), 'Das Zügenglöcklein' (D 871) and 'Im Freien' (D 880), op. 80, dedicated to Josef Weigl in friendship
28 May	Publication on the 15th anniversary of his mother's death of 3 Rochlitz Lieder: 'Alinde' (D 904), 'An die Laute' (D 905), 'Zur guten Nacht' (D 903), op. 81
before June	'Wein und Liebe' (Haug, D 901)
May–June	Schubert stays for a few weeks at Zur Kaiserin von Österreich (Austrian Empress) Inn, Dornbach suburb of Vienna (today Dornbacherstrasse 101, Vienna 17)
Summer/ Autumn	*Deutsche Messe* (D 872) 4 Impromptus (D 899)
June	'Das Lied im Grünen' (Reil, D 917)
12 June	In a letter to the GdM, Schubert accepts the position of representative to which he had recently been elected
19 June	Begins *Der Graf von Gleichen* (D 918)
23 June	Publication of 'Trost im Liede' (D 546) and 'Wandrers Nachtlied II, (D 768) in a supplement to *Wiener Zeitschrift für Kunst, Literatur, Theater und Mode*
5 July	Publication officially passed by the censor for 8 Variations on a theme from Hérold's opera *Marie* for Piano Four Hands (D 902)
6 July	Publication by Diabelli of 4 Polonaises for Piano Four Hands (D 599), op. 75
	Publication by Weigl of *Andantino varié et Rondeau brillant, composés sur des motifs originaux français* in E minor for Piano Four Hands (D 823/ii and ii), op. 84, nos 2 and 3

	Publication by Pennauer of 2 Schiller settings, 'Hoffnung' (D 637) and 'Der Jüngling am Bache' (D 638), and 'Der Unglückliche' (Pichler, D 713), op. 87
July	'Ständchen', TTBB (D 920) and SSAA (D 921)
11 Aug	Premiere of 'Ständchen' (D 920) on Louise Gosmar's birthday
3 Sept	Publication by Haslinger of 8 Variations on a theme from Hérold's opera *Marie* for Piano Four Hands (D 908), op. 82, dedicated to Kajetan Neuhaus
Sept	'Heimliches Lieben' (Karoline von Klenke, D 922), 'Eine altschottische Ballade' (Percy, trans. Herder, D 923)
	12 'Grazer Walzer für Klavier' (D 924), 'Grazer Galopp für Klavier' (D 925)
12 Sept	Publication by Haslinger of 3 Italian Songs (D 902), op. 83, dedicated to Luigi Lablache
14 Sept	Publication of 'Grande Marche héroïque, composée à l'occasion du Sacre de Sa Majesté Nicolas I' for Piano Four Hands (D 885), op. 66
2–24 Sept	Schubert and Jenger travel to Graz where they are guests of Karl and Marie Leopoldine Pachler; Schubert returns to Vienna to live with Schober again, Zum blauen Igel (The Blue Hedgehog, today Tuchlauben, no. 18)
25 Sept	Publication of 'Der blinde Knabe' (D 833) as a supplement to *Wiener Zeitschrift für Kunst, Literatur, Theater und Mode*
Oct	Starts composing *Winterreise*, Part 2 (D 911)
8 Oct	Publication of TTBB, 'Grab und Mond' (D 893) and 'Wein und Liebe' (D 901) in *Die deutschen Minnesänger*, vols. 1 and 4
12 Oct	March in G for Piano Four Hands (D 928)
18 Oct	Schwind performs Schubert's piano dances at Ottenwalt's

Nov	Piano Trio in E flat (D 929)
	'Der Hochzeitsbraten', STB with piano (Schober, D 930)
	3 von Leitner settings: 'Der Wallensteiner Lanzknecht beim Trunk' (D 931), 'Der Kreuzzug' (D 932) and 'Des Fischers Liebesglück' (D 933)
6 Dec	Premiere of 'Der Kampf' (D 594), The Red Hedgehog, GdM
Dec	Fantasie in C for Violin and Piano (D 934)
	4 Impromptus for Piano (D 935)
10 Dec	Publication by Haslinger of Piano Impromptus (D 899 nos. 1 and 2), op. 90
12 Dec	Publication by Weigl of Schubert's op. 88: 'Abendlied für die Entfernte' (August Wilhelm von Schlegel, D 856), 'Thekla' (Schiller, D 595), 'Um Mitternacht' (Schulze, D 862) and 'An die Musik' (Schober, D 547)
26 Dec	Premiere of a 'new' piano trio (perhaps D 929), The Red Hedgehog, GdM
	Cantata for Katharina Kiesewetter (D 936), TTBB quartet, SATB choir and Piano Four Hands
1828	String Trio in B flat (D 898)
3 Jan	'Mondenschein' (D 875)
5 Jan	Publication by Haslinger of 12 *Grazer* Waltzes for Piano (D 924), op. 91
	Grazer Galopp for Piano (D 925) issued separately as no. 10 in *Favorit-Galoppe*
10 Jan	'Gute Nacht' (D 911/1) performed by Ludwig Tietze, The Red Hedgehog, GdM
Jan	Reading sessions, suspended since 1824, resume at Schober's 'Der Tanz' (D 826), SATB and piano, occasional work commissioned by Raphael Kiesewetter for his daughter, Irene

Jan	2 Leitner settings: 'Der Winterabend' (D 938) and 'Die Sterne' (D 939)
Jan–April	Fantasy in F minor for Piano Four Hands (D 940)
14 Jan	Publication by Haslinger of *Winterreise*, Part 1 (D 911), op. 89
20 Jan	Slavík and Bocklet give the first performance of the Fantasy for Violin and Piano (D 934) at Slavík's private concert at the Landhaussaal
24 Jan	Premiere of 'Ständchen', SSAA (D 921), The Red Hedgehog, GdM, soloist: Josefine Fröhlich
26 Jan	Waltz in C for Piano (D 980D)
28 Jan	Schubertiad at Spaun's, Bocklet, Schuppanzigh, and Josef Linke perform a Piano Trio (D 929) by Schubert, who also plays one of his sets of variations for piano duet with Bocklet
30 Jan	Schubertiad at Josef Wilhelm Witteczek's
31 Jan	Performance on Schubert's 31st birthday of 'Ellens Gesang III' (D 839), The Red Hedgehog, GdM
2 Feb	Premiere of 'Romanze des Richard Löwenherz' (D 907) by Ludwig Tietze, County Hall
1 March	Deutscher for Piano (D 944A)
March	'Mirjams Siegesgesang' (Grillparzer, D 942) Soprano solo, SATB choir and piano 'Auf dem Strom' (Rellstab, D 943) Sinfonie in C (D 944), dated March 1828
14 March	Publication by Diabelli of 3 Scott settings: 'Lied der Anne Lyle' (D 830) and 'Gesang der Norna' (D 831), op. 85 Publication by Diabelli of 'Romanze des Richard Löwenherz' (Scott, D 907), op. 86
16 March	'Normans Gesang' accompanied by Schubert, GdM

26 March	Schubert gives his only public concert in which he performs 7 works; on the programme the first movement of a 'new' string quartet in G (D 887/i), a 'new' piano trio (D 929); the part-song for double choir TTBB and TTBB 'Schlachtlied' (D 912) and 'Ständchen' (D 920); the songs 'Auf dem Strom' (D 943), 'Der Kreuzzug' (D 932), 'Die Allmacht' (D 852), 'Die Sterne' (D 939), 'Fischerweise' (D 881) and 'Fragment aus dem Aeschylus' (D 450), The Red Hedgehog, GdM
April	'Herbst' (Rellstab, D 945)
14 April	Spaun marries Franziska Roner von Ehrenwerth
20 April	'Auf dem Strom' (Rellstab, D 943)
May	3 Klavierstücke (D 946)
	Allegro in A minor for Piano Four Hands (*Lebensstürme*, D 947)
	'Hymnus an den heiligen Geist' (D 948)
Summer	Premiere of Psalm 92 (D 953), Synagogue, Vienna
4 May	Schubert at Zur Schnecke (The Snail) Inn with Enk, Schober and Enderes
10 May	Schubert sends his Piano Trio in E flat major (D 929) to the Leipzig publisher Probst, who releases it in October
30 May	Publication by Diabelli of 2 Schulze Settings: 'Im Walde' (D 834) and 'Auf der Bruck' (D 853), op. 93
3–4 June	Johann Schickh invites Schubert and Lachner to accompany him on an excursion to Baden and thence to Heilgenkreuz Monastery, where the two musicians play fugues they have specially written for the famous organ there. Schubert's Fugue in E minor for organ duet (D 952) is his only composition for 'solo organ'
June	Rondo in A for Piano Four Hands (D 951)
June	Mass in E flat (D 950)
9 July	Katharina von Lásny dies

CHRONOLOGY

Summer	Private Publication of Schubert's op. 96: 'Die Sterne' (von Leitner, D 939), 'Jägers Liebeslied' (Schober, D 909), 'Wandrers Nachtlied II' (Goethe, 'Über allen Gipfeln', D 768), 'Fischerweise' (Schlechta, D 881) dedicated to Princess Karoline von Kinsky with respect; the first edition was without opus number
	Private publication of Schubert's op. 96: 'Heimliches Lieben' (Klenke, D 922), 'Das Weinen' (D 926), 'Vor meiner Wiege' (D 927) and 'Was ist Sylvia' (D 891), op. 106, dedicated to Maria Pachler; this first edition was without opus number
July	Psalm no. 92 (D 953)
11 July	Publication by Leidesdorf of 3 Goethe Lieder: 'Der Musensohn' (D 764), 'Auf dem See' (D 543) and 'Geistes-Gruß' (D 142), dedicated to Frau Josefine von Franck, op. 87, later op. 92
	Publication by Leidesdorf of 6 *Moments musicaux* (D 780), op. 94
Aug	'Glaube, Hoffnung und Liebe' (Reil, D 954)
13 Aug	Publication by Weigl of 'Vier Refrainlieder' (Seidl, D 866), op. 95, dedicated to the poet in friendship
Aug	Schubert begins *Schwanengesang* (D 957)
1 Sept	On the advice of his doctor Ernst Rinna von Sarenbach, Schubert moves to his brother's lodgings in the Neu-Wieden suburb (today 6 Kettenbrückengasse, Vienna 4)
2 Sept	'Glaube, Hoffnung und Liebe', TTBB with SATB choir and wind or piano (D 954), Dreifaltigkeitskirche (Church of the Holy Trinity)
6 Sept	Jenger informs Marie Leopoldine Pachler that Schubert hopes to visit her family in Graz in the near future
Sept	String Quintet in C (D 956)
	Piano Sonata in C minor (D 958), Piano Sonata in A (D 959)

16 Sept	Publication of 'Im Frühling' (D 882) as a supplement in *Wiener Zeitschrift für Kunst, Literatur, Theater und Mode*
26 Sept	Piano Sonata in B flat (D 960)
Sept	Schubert and his brother Ferdinand make a three-day excursion, in part or entirely on foot, to Unter-Waltersdorf and Eisenstadt, where they visit Joseph Haydn's grave
6 Oct	Publication by Diabelli of 'Glaube, Hoffnung und Liebe' (Kuffner, D 955), op. 97
6 Oct	Publication by Pennauer of 3 TTBB settings: 'Wehmut' (Heinrich Hüttenbrenner, D 825), 'Ewige Liebe' (Schulze, D 825A), 'Flucht' (Lappe, D 825B), op. 64
Oct	Publication by Probst of the Piano Trio in E flat (D 929), op. 100
Oct	'Der Hirt auf dem Felsen' (Wilhelm Müller and Helmina von Chézy, D 965) and 'Die Taubenpost' (Seidl, D 965A)
31 Oct	Schubert is seized by nausea during a meal in the Zum roten Kreuz restaurant (today 50 Nussdorferstrasse)
3 Nov	Attends a performance at Hernals parish church of a *Requiem* composed by his brother Ferdinand
4 Nov	Schubert and Josef Lanz receive a joint lesson in advanced counterpoint from Simon Sechter; Exercises D 965B
11 Nov	Schubert takes permanently to his bed
12 Nov	In his last letter, written to Schober, he writes that he has not eaten or drunk anything for 11 days
13 Nov	Schubert is bled
14 Nov	Beethoven's String Quartet in C sharp minor, op. 131, is reportedly performed for Schubert, at his request, in Ferdinand's apartment
15 Nov	Spaun visits Schubert for what will be their final meeting
16 Nov	Dr Josef von Vering, who has taken over from the indisposed Rinna von Sarenbach, confers at Schubert's bedside with Dr Johann Baptist Wisgrill

17 Nov	Bauernfeld and Lachner visit Schubert; in the evening, on his mother's name day, Schubert becomes violently delirious
19 Nov	Schubert dies at 3 p.m.
20 Nov	First performance of 'Dithyrambe' (Schiller, D 801), Musikverein, Vienna, to mark Schubert's death
21 Nov	Schubert's funeral at St Josef's Church in the Margareten suburb and at the Church of St Lorenz and St Gertrud in the Währing district, close to Beethoven's grave
27 Nov	First Memorial Service, St Ulrich's (Maria Trost), Mozart's *Requiem* is performed
11 Dec	'Der Alpenjäger' (D 524), GdM
14 Dec	Symphony no. 6 in C (D 589), GdM
23 Dec	Second Memorial Service at St Augustine's Court Chapel, Vienna, at which Anselm Hüttenbrenner's *Requiem* in C minor is performed; in the evening there is a Schubert Concert at Spaun's
30 Dec	Publication by Haslinger of *Winterreise*, Part 2 (D 911), op. 89

1829–

10 Jan	First performance of *Winterreise* (D 911), Ludwig Tietze, Musikverein
22 Jan	Second performance of *Winterreise* (D 911), Johann Karl Schoberlechner
30 Jan and 5 March	Two private concerts organized by Anna Fröhlich at the Musikverein: one half of the receipts are used for the erection of a funeral monument
23 Feb	Mayrhofer memorializes Schubert in 'Erinnerungen an Franz Schubert', *Neues Archiv für Geschichte, Staatenkunde, Literatur und Kunst* (Vienna)
16 March	Publication by Diabelli of the Fantasy in F minor for Piano Four Hands (D 940), op. 103, dedicated to Karoline Esterházy

27, 30 March and 3 April	Spaun's 'Über Franz Schubert' appears anonymously in *Österreichisches Bürgerblatt für Verstand, Herz und gute Laune* (Linz)
9, 11 and 13 June	Bauernfeld's 'Über Franz Schubert' is published in the *Wiener Zeitschrift für Kunst, Literatur, Theater und Mode* (Vienna)
29 Nov	Premiere of 'Gott im Ungewitter' (D 985)
Summer 1830	Schubert's tombstone, designed by Schober with Ludwig Förster, is erected at Schubert's grave, with a bust of the composer by Josef Alois Dialer
21 March 1839	Premiere of the 'Great' C major Symphony (D 944) by the Leipzig Gewandhaus Orchestra conducted by Felix Mendelssohn
23 April–3 May 1839	Ferdinand Schubert's *Aus Franz Schuberts Leben* published with works listed by *Neue Zeitschrift für Musik* (Leipzig)
1861	Heinrich Kreisle von Hellborn, *Aus Schuberts Leben*
Oct 1863	The GdM restores Schubert's grave; on this occasion his body is exhumed, examined and re-interred in a stronger coffin for better preservation
1865	Publication of *Franz Schubert*, Kreissle's second and far more substantial study of Schubert's life and works (English translation by Arthur Duke Coleridge, published in London in 1869)
17 Dec 1865	Premiere of the B minor Symphony (D 759)
12 Oct 1868	Foundation stone of Karl Kundemann's Schubert statue is laid in the Stadtpark
15 May 1872	Unveiling of Kundemann's statue

CHRONOLOGY

	Publication of the First Collected Edition of Schubert's Works (Breitkopf & Härtel)
23 Sept 1888	Schubert's remains are transported to the Grave of Honour in the new cemetery and interred in a grave near Beethoven's
1963	International Schubert Society founded with the purpose of bringing a new and updated collection of Schubert's works
1965–in progress	*Neue Schubert-Ausgabe* (Bärenreiter)
2010	www.schubert-online.ie, database of Schubert's music manuscripts, first and early editions, IAMP in co-operation with Vienna City Library, Institute of Musicology, University of Vienna, funded by WWFT and hosted by the Department of Musicology, Austrian Academy of Sciences
2021	Schubert Research Centre, Austrian Academy of Sciences, Vienna
1 Sept 2021 – 31 August 2024	Interdisciplinary project DRACMarkS (Digitization, Recognition, and Automated Clustering of Watermarks in the Music Manuscripts of Franz Schubert)

NOTES

The following are abbreviations used in the Notes.

AGA	Franz Schubert's Werke. Kritisch durchgesehene Gesamtausgabe (Leipzig 1884–1897); Alte Gesamtausgabe.
BN	Bibliothèque Nationale, Paris
Brille	*Schubert durch die Brille*, IFSI, ed. Ernst Hilmar (1988–2003)
Cahiers F. Schubert	*Cahiers F. Schubert. Bulletin de la Société Franz Schubert* ed. Xavier Hascher (1992–2001)
Cambridge Companion to Schubert	*The Cambridge Companion to Schubert*, ed. Christopher Gibbs (Cambridge University Press, 1997)
D	Otto Erich Deutsch, *Thematisches Verzeichnis seiner Werke in chronologischer Folge* (Kassel: Bärenreiter, p. 1978)
Dok	Otto Erich Deutsch, *Franz Schubert: Die Dokumente seines Lebens und Schaffens* (Wiesbaden and Leipzig: Breitkopf & Härtel, 1996)
Erinn	Otto Erich Deutsch, *Schubert. Die Erinnerungen seiner Freunde* (Wiesbaden, Leipzig and Paris: Breitkopf & Härtel, rev. 1983)
fl.	Florin – Gulden (1 fl. was 60 kr.)
FSD	Waidelich, Till Gerrit (ed), *Franz Schubert, Dokumente, 1817–1830. Erster Band – Texte: Programme, Rezensionen, Anzeigen, Nekrologe, Musikbeilagen und andere gedruckte Quellen* (Tutzing: Hans Schneider, 1993). In two parts: Texte, Kommentar.
GdM	Gesellschaft der Musikfreunde, Vienna
Jahre der Krise	Franz Schubert, *Jahre der Krise, 1818–1823*. Festschrift Arnold Feil ed. Werner Aderhold, Walther Dürr and Walburga Litschauer (Kassel: Bärenreiter, 1985)
Johnson	Graham Johnson, *Franz Schubert: The Complete Songs*, 3 vols (Yale University Press, 2014)
Kreissle	Heinrich Kreissle von Hellborn, *Franz Schubert* (Vienna, 1865)
kr.	Kreuzer
Lexikon	Ernst Hilmar and Margret Jestremski, *Schubert-Lexikon* (Graz, 1997)
MA	*Münchner Ausgabe*: Johann Wolfgang Goethe, *Sämtliche Werke nach Epochen seines Schaffens*, 20 vols (Munich: Carl Hanser Verlag, 1985–98)
MGG	*Die Musik in Geschichte und Gegenwart*
M&L	*Music & Letters*

MMR	*Monthly Musical Record*
MQ	*Musical Quarterly*
MR	*Music Review*
MT	*The Musical Times*
NA	*Schillers Werke, Nationalausgabe*, Julius Petersen et al. (eds), 43 vols (Weimar: Herman Böhlaus Nachfolger)
NCM	*19th-Century Music*
NCMR	*Nineteenth-Century Music Review*
ND	*Neue Dokumente zum Schubert-Kreis*, 2 vols, ed. Walburga Litschauer (Vienna, 1986 and 1983)
NSA	*Neue Schubert-Ausgabe*; Franz Schubert. *Neue Ausgabe sämtlicher Werke*, ed. International Schubert-Gesellschaft (Kassel: Bärenreiter, 1965–in progress)
NSA, KB	Franz Schubert. *Neue Ausgabe sämtlicher Werke (Neue Schubert-Ausgabe)*, Kritischer Bericht
ÖNB	Österreichische Nationalbibliothek (Austrian National Library, Vienna)
Rethinking Schubert	*Rethinking Schubert*, ed. Lorraine Byrne Bodley and Julian Horton (Oxford University Press, 2016)
Schubert Handbuch	*Schubert Handbuch*, ed. Walther Dürr and Andreas Krause (Kassel: Bärenreiter, 1997)
Schubert Jahrbuch	*Jahrbuch der Schubert Gesellschaft* (Duisberg, 1997–2013)
Schubert's Late Music	*Schubert's Late Music: History, Theory, Style*, ed. Lorraine Byrne Bodley and Julian Horton (Cambridge University Press, 2016)
Schubert: Perspektiven	*Schubert: Perspektiven* (Stuttgart: Steiner Verlag, 2001–2016)
Schubert-Studien	*Schubert-Studien. Festgabe der Österreichischen Akademie der Wissenschaft zum Schubert-Jahr 1978*, ed. Franz Grasberger and Othmar Wessely (Vienna, 1978)
Schubert Studies	*Schubert Studies: Problems of Style and Chronology*, ed. Eva Badura-Skoda and Peter Branscombe (Cambridge University Press, 1982),
Staatsbibl. Preuß. Kulturbes. Berlin	Staatsbibliothek Preußischer Kulturbesitz, Berlin
WA	*Weimar Ausgabe. Goethes Werke*, ed. Gustav von Loeper, Erich Schmidt, Hermann Grimm et al. (Weimar: Böhlau, 1887–1912)
WB	Wien Bibliothek
W.W.	Wiener Währung (Austrian currency)

PROLOGUE: BECOMING SCHUBERT

1. The citation is taken from Carmen heroicum, line 1,286 of Tertianus Maurus's poem *De litteris, syllabis et metris Horatii*. Just like the reader who takes them up, books have their own fate. The translation is Goethe's, *Maximen und Reflexionen*.
2. *Schumann on Music: A Selection from the Writings*, trans. and ed. Henry Pleasants (New York: Dover, 1988), 142.
3. Heinrich Kreissle von Hellborn, *Franz Schubert* (Vienna. Carl Gerold's Sohn, 1865), trans. A. D. Coleridge as *The Life of Franz Schubert* (London: Longmans, Green & Co., 1869).
4. George Grove, 'Schubert' in the *Dictionary of Music and Musicians* (London: Macmillan, 1883).
5. Oscar Wilde, *In Praise of Disobedience: The Soul of Man under Socialism* (London and New York: Verso, 2018).
6. Ernst Kris and Otto Kurz, *Die Legende vom Künstler: Ein historischer Versuch* (Vienna: Krystall Verlag, 1934); trans. Alastair Laing and republished as *Legend, Myth and Magic in the Image of the Artist: A Historical Experiment* (New Haven, CT, and London: Yale University Press, 1979), 11. See also Ira Bruce Nadel, who debates 'To what extent is

fact necessary in a biography?', *Biography: Fiction, Fact and Form* (London: Macmillan, 1984), 5.
7. Maynard Solomon, 'Franz Schubert and the Peacocks of Benvenuto Cellini', *19th-Century Music*, 12/3 (1989), 193–206; Scott Messing, *Schubert in the European Imagination*, vol. 1, *The Romantic and Victorian Eras*, and vol. 2, *Fin-de-Siècle Vienna* (New York: University of Rochester Press, 2007–08).
8. Eduard von Bauernfeld, 'Über Franz Schubert', *Wiener Zeitschrift für Kunst, 9, 11, 13 June 1829*, cited in Otto Erich Deutsch, *Schubert. Die Erinnerungen seiner Freunde* (Wiesbaden: Breitkopf & Härtel, 1957, rpt. 1983), 40.
9. *Mit meinen heißen Tränen* directed by Fritz Lehner, produced by ORF, ZDF, SRG Films, cinematography by Gernot Roll (released 31 October 1986 in Germany, Austria and the Netherlands). The film's lead actor, Udo Samel, was nominated for the 1986 European Film Award for Best Actor.
10. Solomon, 'Franz Schubert and the Peacocks of Benvenuto Cellini', 193–206; cf. Maynard Solomon, 'Taboo and Biographical Innovation: Mozart, Beethoven, Schubert', *American Imago* 64/1 (2007), 7–21. Solomon's biographical work is also relevant; see, for example, his 'Thoughts on Biography', *19th-Century Music* 5/3 (1982), 268–76, and his entry on 'Biography' in *Grove Music Online* (http://www.oxfordmusiconline.com.jproxy.nuim.ie/grovemusic/view/10.1093/gmo/9781561592630.001.0001/omo-9781561592630-e-0000041156?rskey=joWuXc&result=1, last accessed 24 March 2018) and his *Beethoven* biography (London: Macmillan, 1977, and New York: Schirmer Trade Books, 1977, rev. 1998 and 2001), and his *Mozart: A Life* (New York: HarperCollins Perennial, 1995 and 2005).
11. *Schubert: Music, Sexuality, Culture*, in *19th-Century Music* 17/1 (1993). Contributors were: Kofi Agawu, David Gramit, Susan McClary, Kristina Muxfeldt, Maynard Solomon, Rita Steblin, James Webster and Robert Winter.
12. See also Susan McClary, 'Constructions of Subjectivity in Schubert's Music', in *Queering the Pitch: The New Gay and Lesbian Musicology*, ed. Philip Brett, Elizabeth Wood and Gary C. Thomas (New York: Routledge, 1994), 205–34.
13. Lisa Feurzeig, 'Heroines in Perversity: Marie Schmidt, Animal Magnetism, and the Schubert Circle', *19th-Century Music* 21/2 (1997), 223–43.
14. Rita Steblin, 'Schubert's Love Affair with Marie von Spaun and the Role Played by Helene Schmith, the Wife of Mozart's First Violinist', *Schubert: Perspektiven* 8 (2008), 49–87, and 'Schubert's Pepi: His Love Affair with the Chamber Maid Josepha Pöcklhofer and her Surprising Fate', *Musical Times* 149 (2008), 47–69.
15. Philip Brett, 'Piano Four-Hands: Schubert and the Performance of Gay Male Desire', *19th-Century Music*, 21/2; *Franz Schubert: Bicentenary Essays* (1997), 149–76.
16. Lawrence Kramer, *Schubert: Sexuality, Subjectivity, Song* (Cambridge University Press, 1998); 'The Schubert Lied: Romantic Form and Romantic Consciousness' in *Schubert: Critical and Analytical Studies*, ed. Walter Frisch (Lincoln, NE: University of Nebraska Press, 1986), 200–36.
17. This question has most recently been raised by Robert Winter, 'Whose Schubert?', *19th-Century Music* 17/1 (1993), 94–101, and Gernot Gruber, *Schubert. Schubert?* (Kassel, Basel, London, New York and Prague: Bärenreiter, 2010).
18. Thomas Carlyle, Review of Croker's edition of Boswell's *Life of Johnson* (April 1832), cited by Hermione Lee in *Biography: A Very Short Introduction* (Oxford University Press, 2009), 3.
19. A very entertaining read is found in May Byron, *A Day with Franz Schubert* (New York: Hodder & Stoughton, 1900), which opens: 'Time – A Cloudy April Day in the Year 1824. Scene – a gloomy, dusty, ill-furnished apartment in a back street in Vienna. Enter a short, round-shouldered, podgy-looking man, unbrushed, unwashed, unshaven – who, without a glance at the coffee going cold on the extremely dubious table-cloth, drops clumsily upon the broken chair before the piano, and flings himself into an animated rendering of the song which he has composed during his so-called toilet', 5.

NOTES to pp. 4–6

20. Grove 'Schubert', *Dictionary of Music and Musicians*. Grove gives the source for the two anecdotes as Schindler, *Beethoven*, vol. 2, 176, and Kreissle, *Franz Schubert*, 261.
21. Newman Flower, *Franz Schubert: The Man and his Circle* (London: Cassell & Co., 1928; New York: Tudor Publishing, rpt. 1935).
22. Arthur Hutchings, *Schubert* (London: Dent & Son [=Dent Master Musicians Series], 1945, rpt. 1973).
23. A very detailed and thorough study of Beethoven and Schubert mythology is found in Christopher Mark Wiley, *Re-Writing Composers' Lives: Critical Historiography and Musical Biography*, vol. 1 (Royal Holloway, University of London: unpublished PhD dissertation, 2008), esp. ch. 4, 102–24.
24. Anton Schindler, *Life of Ludwig van Beethoven*, 3rd edn (Münster: Aschendorff, 1860), 522.
25. This began as early as Henry Frederic Frost, *Schubert*, The Great Musicians Series (London: Sampson Low, Marston, Searle & Rivington Ltd, 1881, rpt. 1885), 48; see also Ralph Bates, *Franz Schubert* (Edinburgh: Peter Davies Ltd, 1934), 67; Marcel Schneider, *Schubert* (Paris: Seuil, 1959), 90.
26. Maurice Brown, *Schubert: A Critical Biography* (New York: St Martin's Press, 1958), trans. Gerd Severs as *Schubert. Eine kritische Biographie* (Wiesbaden: Breitkopf & Härtel, 1969), 258–60, 329 and 332–33.
27. George Grove, *Beethoven, Mendelssohn, Schubert* (London: Macmillan, 1951).
28. See, for example, McKay's discussion of Schindler's account, 273–75.
29. Otto Eric Deutsch, ed., *Schubert: Die Dokumente seines Lebens und Schaffens* (Kassel: Bärenreiter Verlag, 1964, rpt. 1980 and 1996), 160.
30. This anecdote is repeated continually in biographies. See, for example, Henry Frederic Frost, who has a collection of Schubert's songs placed into Beethoven's hands on his deathbed, where he expresses 'the utmost admiration and astonishment at their exceeding beauty exclaiming, "Truly Schubert possesses a spark of the divine fire" and "Some day he will make a noise in the world". The prophecy of the dying man has been amply fulfilled', *Schubert*, The Great Musicians Series (1885), 49; for a twentieth-century biography, see Arthur Hutchings, *Schubert*, The Master Musicians (London: Dent and New York: Farrar, Straus and Cudaby Inc, 1945, rpt. 1956), 74. The songs Beethoven reputedly admired included the Ossian songs; 'Die Bürgschaft' (D 435), 'Die junge Nonne' (D 828) and 'Grenzen der Menschheit' (D 716).
31. In Schubert's day the Mehlgrube was an elite venue where composers and visiting virtuosi performed for aristocrats; today it is the Hotel Ambassador near the Musikverein and Vienna State Opera.
32. Alfred Einstein (1951), 178, Brown (1958), 331. As Deutsch noted (1946), 623, the anecdote is contradicted by Fritz von Hartmann's diary entry for 29 March 1827, the day of Beethoven's funeral, where he records, 'I went to the "Castle of Eisenstadt", where I remained with Schober, Schubert and Schwind until almost 1 a.m.', *Dok*, 419.
33. Lee, *Biography*, 7.
34. John Gingerich, *Schubert's Beethoven Project* (Cambridge University Press, 2014).
35. For more on this argument, see Leon Edel, author of *Writing Lives: Principia Biographica* (New York: W. W. Norton, 1987). For reference books on musical biography see Hans Erich Bödeker, 'Biographie. Annaherungen an den gegenwärtigen Forschungs- und Diskussionsstand' in *Biographie schreiben*, ed. Hans Erich Bödeker (Göttingen: Wallstein, 2003), 9–63; *Musical Biography: Towards New Paradigms*, ed. Jolanta Pekacz (Aldershot: Ashgate, 2006); Melanie Unself, *Biographie und Musikgeschichte: Wandlungen biographischer Konzepte in Musikkultur und Musikhistoriographie* (Cologne: Böhlau, 2014).
36. Joseph Conrad, *Under Western Eyes* (1911) in *The Cambridge Edition of the Works of Joseph Conrad*, ed. Roger Osborne and Paul Eggert (Cambridge University Press, 2013), 9.
37. Edward Wilberforce, *Schubert* (London, 1866).
38. For an overview of English-language publications on Schubert see Edmondstone Duncan, *Schubert*, rev. edn (London: Dent & Sons, 1921 [1912?]), 229–38.

39. Frost, *Schubert*, 10.
40. Letter to William Knight, 24 June 1889 in Percy M. Young, *George Grove, 1820–1890: A Biography* (London: Macmillan, 1980), 283, cited in David Gramit, 'Constructing a Victorian Schubert: Music, Biography, and Values', *19th-Century Music* 17/1 (1993), 65–78.
41. This is an aspect which is not present in the French reception, even though Kreissle's biography was also influential and contributed to a distorted image of Schubert as an untutored semi-amateur.
42. George Lowell Austin, *The Life of Schubert* (Boston: Shepard and Gill, 1873).
43. Max Friedlaender, *Beiträge zur Biographie Franz Schuberts* (Berlin: unpublished PhD dissertation, 1887).
44. August Reissmann, *Franz Schubert. Sein Leben und Seine Werke* (Berlin: J. Guttentag, 1873).
45. See, for example, George Austin, 'The story of his career reads like an elegy . . . It is, in truth, the elegy of the dying swan, the sweetness of whose song grows even sweeter as it nears its final dissolution', *The Life of Schubert*, 10.
46. Wiley, *Rewriting Composers' Lives*, II, 'The Master Musicians Series', 275.
47. Richard Heuberger, *Schubert* [= Berühmte Musiker Series] (Berlin: Harmonie, 1902, rpt. 1907).
48. Wilhelm Klatte, *Franz Schubert* (Berlin: Marquardt & Co., 1907).
49. Alfred Einstein, *Schubert* (London: Cassel & Co., 1951).
50. Hans Joseph Fröhlich, *Schubert. Eine Biographie* (Munich: Paul Zsolnay, 1978, rev. end 1996).
51. John Reed, *Schubert*, Master Musicians Series (London: J. M. Dent & Sons, 1987, rev. 1997).
52. Maurice J. E. Brown, *Schubert* (London: Macmillan and New York: St Martin's Press, 1958).
53. Otto Erich Deutsch, ed., *Schubert: Die Dokumente seines Lebens* (Kassel: Bärenreiter Verlag, 1964, rpt. 1980 and 1996), trans. Eric Blom as *Schubert: A Documentary Biography* (J. M. Dent & Sons, 1946) and as *The Schubert Reader: A Life of Franz Schubert in Letters and Documents* (New York: W. W. Norton, 1947).
54. Earlier English-language attempts of objectivity in biography, outlining the events of Schubert's life and misunderstood genius, include the chapters on Schubert in Frederick Crowest, *The Great Tone Poets: Being Short Memoirs of the Greater Musical Composers* (London: Richard Bentley & Son, 1874), and in Robert Farquharson Sharp, *Makers of Music: Biographical Sketches of the Great Composers* (London and New York: C. Scribner's Sons, 1898, rev. 1901).
55. Deutsch, ed., *Schubert. Die Erinnerungen seiner Freunde*; trans. Rosamond Ley and John Nowell as *Schubert: Memoirs by his Friends* (London: Adam and Charles Black, 1958).
56. Elizabeth Norman McKay, *Franz Schubert: A Biography* (Oxford: Clarendon Press, 1998).
57. Brian Newbould, *Schubert: The Music and the Man* (Berkeley and Los Angeles: Victor Gollancz, 1999).
58. Christopher Gibbs, *The Life of Schubert* (Cambridge University Press, 2000).
59. Robert Winter, 'Schubert', *Grove Music Online* [http://www.oxfordmusiconline.com.jproxy.nuim.ie/grovemusic/view/10.1093/gmo/9781561592630.001.0001/omo-9781561592630-e0000025109?rskey=h1Orw1&result=1, last accessed 28 March 2018]. See also Robert Winter's earlier engagement around reception issues with Harry Goldschmidt in 'The Continuing Schubert Controversy', *19th-Century Music* 9/1 (1985), 70–77.
60. Hans-Joachim Hinrichsen, *Franz Schubert* (Munich: C. H. Beck, 2011).
61. Gernot Gruber, *Schubert. Schubert? Leben und Musik* (Kassel: Bärenreiter Verlag, 2010). See too Harry Goldschmidt, *Franz Schubert. Ein Lebensbild* (Berlin: Henschel, 1954, rev. 1980); Peter Gülke, *Franz Schubert und seine Zeit* (Regensburg: Laaber-Verlag, 1991); Ernst Hilmar, *Franz Schubert in seiner Zeit* (Vienna and Graz: Akademische Druck- und Verlagsanstalt, 1985); and *Franz Schubert* (Hamburg: Rowohlt Taschenbuch Verlag, 1997).

62. Deutsch, ed., *Schubert: Die Erinnerungen seiner Freunde*, O. E. Deutsch, ed., trans. Rosamond Ley and John Nowell as *Schubert: Memoirs by his Friends* (London: Adam and Charles Black, 1958), and *Schubert: Die Dokumente seines Lebens* (Kassel: Bärenreiter Verlag, 1964, rpt. 1980 and 1996), trans. Eric Blom as *Schubert: A Documentary Biography* (J. M. Dent & Sons, 1946) and as *The Schubert Reader: A Life of Franz Schubert in Letters and Documents* (New York: W. W. Norton, 1947).
63. Walburga Litschauer, ed., *Neue Dokumente zum Schubert-Kreis aus Briefen und Tagebüchern seiner Freunde* (Vienna, 1986).
64. Ernst Hilmar and Werner Bodendorff, *Franz Schubert. Dokumente, 1801–1830*. Vol. 1: *Texte, Programme, Rezensionen, Anzeigen, Nekrologe, Musikbeilagen und andere gedruckte Quellen. Addenda und Kommentar* (Tutzing: Veröffentlichungen des IFSI, 2003).
65. Till Gerrit Waidelich, ed., *Franz Schubert: Dokumente, 1817–1830*. Vol. 1: *Texte, Programme, Rezensionen, Anzeigen, Nekrologe, Musikbeilagen und andere gedruckte Quellen* (Tutzing: Hans Schneider Verlag, 1993).
66. Eduard von Bauernfeld, 24 November 1857, *Erinn*, 53.
67. *Erinn*, 268.
68. Josef Kenner, 21 April 1858, *Erinn*, 96. As Kreissle von Hellborn cursorily acknowledged in his biography, it is not known whether he had seen all the material that Luib gathered for his aborted biography which Deutsch makes available to us, 51–200.
69. *Erinn*, 100.
70. Johann Wolfgang von Goethe, *Faust 1*, Vor dem Tor, ll. 1,112–1,116 in *Johann Wolfgang von Goethe Sämtliche Werke*, Münchner Ausgabe 6.1, ed. Victor Lange (Munich and Vienna: Carl Hanser Verlag, 1986), 565.
71. Joyce Carol Oates, 'Adventures in Abandonment', *New York Times*, 28 August 1988.
72. James Boswell, *The Life of Samuel Johnson*, 2 vols (London: Henry Baldwin, 1791), vol. 2, 111. Cited in Maxwell Jones, 'Boswell, Johnson and the Birth of Modern Biography', *Newsweek*, 28 October 2009.
73. Oscar Wilde, 'The Butterfly's Boswell' in *The Critic as Artist: Critical Writings of Oscar Wilde*, ed. Richard Ellmann (University of Chicago Press, 1968), 65.
74. Lorraine Byrne Bodley, *Goethe and Zelter: Musical Dialogues* (Aldershot: Ashgate, 2008), Letter no. 6, Goethe to Zelter, 29 May 1801.
75. Schubert to Leopold Kupelwieser, 31 March 1824, *Dok*, 234.
76. Schubert, Journal Entry, 27 March 1824, *Dok*, 233.
77. Wiley, *Re-Writing Composers' Lives*, 350.
78. Gibbs, *The Life of Schubert*.
79. Graham Johnson, *Franz Schubert: The Complete Songs* (New Haven, CT, and London: Yale University Press, 2000).

CHAPTER ONE: THE FAMILY BEFORE SCHUBERT

1. He died in Hanušovice, Šumperk District, Olomouc Region, Czech Republic. Cf. Richard Heuberger, 'Der Stammort der Familie Schubert', *Der Merker* 2 (1910), 452–53; Franz Köhler, 'Zur Abstammung Schuberts', in: *Bericht über den internationalen Kongress für Schubertforschung Wien 25. bis 29. November 1928*, ed. Robert Haas and Alfred Orel (Augsburg: Benno Filser Verlag, 1929), 79–80.
2. Malá Morava, near the Moravian-Schönberg (Šumperk) District, Olomouc Region, Czech Republic.
3. Sibille Schubert died in December 1678 during childbirth.
4. And three stepsons (dates unknown): Andreas, Johann and Josef (b. 1704).
5. Karl Schubert's memorial on the Schubertweg is acknowledged in the little museum in the Church of St Ludmila. The last of Schubert's ancestors buried in Vysoké Žibřidovice, Moravia, are Johann and Marie Schubert, 19 October 1917.
6. Vojtěch Kyas, 'K historii rodu Schubertú na severní Moravě' in *Morava v česke hudbě, sborník z hudebněvědné konference 1984*, ed. Rudolf Pečman (Brno, 1985), pp. 55–57.

7. A memorial plaque (written in Czech) in the Chapel acknowledges that the chapel was his initiative and also thanks to his financial aid.
8. This date and the following information is taken from a plaque in the Schubert chapel, which was renovated in consolidation of Czech-Austrian cultural relations. The chapel was completely destroyed between 1948 and 1989. Karl Schubert's great-great-great-granddaughter and Schubert's great-great-grandniece, Martha Böhm Schubert, led the renovation project funded by the Franz Schubert Institute in Vienna, the Czech, Austrian and German governments with private funding from the Bierenta, Bíny, Jablončíka, Reichla, Straky and Winklera families. The church was newly plastered, electric lighting and a new floor fitted, and wooden pews installed. The paintings and ceiling frescoes which had been badly damaged were also restored. In order to complete the project on time for the 200th anniversary of Schubert's birth, sponsorship was secured from Vienna and the Austrian-Bohemian Memorial Foundation was founded in 1996. Its benefactors were Martha Böhm-Schubert; V. Dostál, professor, University of Vienna; E. Harant, Director of Compressverlag, Vienna; P. Jajtner, Ambassador for the Czech Republic; M. Poiger, Director of the Austrian Cultural Institute in Prague; F. Spurný, researcher, Šumperk; S. Šikula, Deputy Mayor of Malá Morava; F. Winter, Marwin's farm manager; H. Zilk, President of the Austrian-Czech Society, former Mayor of Vienna and Culture, Austria; V. Zmeškal, Major of Hanušovice, Šumperk.
9. In addition to Karl, Schubert's three uncles on his father's side were Franz Anton Schubert (6 January 1757, death and location of death unknown); Gottfried Schubert (12 February 1774–12 October 1857), Johann Josef Schubert (4 October 1775, death and location of death unknown). The baptismal certificate of Schubert's father from the church in Hohenseibersdorf in 1783 is in the private possession of the Hofbauer family in Kritzendorf.
10. Katalin Kim-Szacsvai, *Dokumente über das Musikleben der Jesuiten. Instrumenten- und Musikalienverzeichnisse zur Zeit der Auflösungen. Studia Musicologica Academiae scientiarum Hungaricae* 39 (1998), 351, 360–66.
11. The college is the sixth oldest in the Czech Republic and the second oldest in Moravia. It is the only remnant of a Jesuit college from the sixteenth and seventeenth centuries, with the interior added in the eighteenth century. The organ is by Riga (1728). For further information on the church (and college) see Eugen Dostál, *Umělecké památky Brna* (Prague: Jan Štenc, 1928), 92–100; Bohumil Samek, *Umělecké památky Moravy a Slezska I, A–J* (Prague: Czech Academie of Sciences, 1994), 199–204; Josef Koláček, *200 let jezuitů v Brně* (Velehrad: Refugium Velehrad-Roma, 2002); Hana Jordánková and Vladimír Maňas, *Jezuité a Brno. Sociální a kulturní interakce koleje a města (1578–1773)* (Brno: Česko, 2008); cf. Jiří Sehnal, 'Obsazení kúru u brněnských jezuitů v letech 1676–1770', 171–84, and Vladimír Maňas, 'Feriální mše na brněnském jezuitském gymnáziu a latinský písňový repertoár v 17. a 18. století', in Hana Jordánková and Vladimír Maňas, *Jezuité a Brno. Sociální a kulturní interakce koleje a města (1578–1773)*, vol. 1 (Brno: Archiv města Brna, 2013), 185–93, 199–210. Suplementum BMD č. 19. I am indebted to Jiří Kopecký for the many hours he devoted to reading through this literature, translating it and discussing it with me. No friend or fellow scholar could have been more generous.
12. Vojtěch Kyas, *Franz Schubert. Mýty a nové pohledy* (Brno: Moravské zemské muzeum, 2014), p. 31. The house marked with a centenary plaque in 1928; by 1978 the site on which Karl Schubert had built the family home in 1759 was merely marked by its ruins; its commemorative plaque hangs today at the back of the Kapelle der heiligen Dreifaltigkeit church. The last traces of the family in Neudorf are marked by a final grave with the name 'Schubert' in Hohenseibersdorf, 1917.
13. *Album Caesarei Regiique, Gymnasii Brunensi Societatis Jesu*, Archiv města Brna. The details are researched by Ann Schilbauer and reproduced in a catalogue for the exhibition, *Franz Schubert und seine mährisch-schlesischen Wurzeln* (Klosterneuburg: Mährisch-Schlesischen Heimatmuseum, 1997).

14. For further reading, see Diarmuid MacCulloch, *A History of Christianity* (London: Penguin, 2010).
15. Jan Klein and Norman Klein, *Solitude of a Humble Genius – Gregor Johann Mendel*. Vol. 1, *Formative Years* (Berlin and Heidelberg: Springer Verlag, 2013), 247.
16. Jiří Sehnal, 'Obsazení kůru u brněnských jezuitů v letech 1676–1770' in *Jezuité a Brno*, ed. Jordánková and Maňas, 159–70, here 168.
17. KKKP Strahov, Praha, sign. JK X 56. Sources of the German State Gymnasium in Brno became part of Brno library, see MZK Brno, rkps č1156.019, 11.268 and 11.269 (original signatures Deutsches Staatsgymnasium in Brünn, Lehrerbibliothek, 5179a, 5179b and 5180).
18. Vladimír Maňas, 'Feriální mše na brněnském jezuitském gynmáziu a latinský písňový repertoár v 17. a 18. století' in *Jezuité a Brno*, ed. Jordánková and Maňas, 171–81, here 174.
19. *Manuale Marianum*, 2nd edn (Brno, 1698).
20. 'Prvni tři písne z jezuitského rukopisu pravdépodobné brněnského púvodu. Ukázka z rukopisu určeného pro varhanni doprovod'. MZK Brno, rukopis c.1156.019.
21. Sehnal, 'Obsazení kůru u brněnských jezuitů v letech 1676–1770', 159–60.
22. For the composition of the school orchestra, see Sehnal, 'Obsazení kůru u brněnských jezuitů v letech 1676–1770', ed. Jordánková and Maňas, 159–70, here 163–64.
23. *Catalogus Seminaristarum et Convictorium Seminarii Brunensis*. NA Prague, MS JS III, 439, 437. See Sehnal, 'Obsazení kůru u brněnských jezuitů v letech 1676–1770', 159–60.
24. Rita Steblin, 'Franz Schubert – das dreizehnte Kind', *Wiener Geschichtsblätter* 56/3 (2001), 245–65.
25. *Schubert Franc: moravus Neodorensis parvista in collegio civitas*, Archiv der Universität Wien, Matr. fac. art., Ph. 2, Anno 1778, lit S (Mikrofilm 063), cited by Steblin, 'Franz Schubert – das dreizehnte Kind', 252.
26. Archiv der Universität Wien, Matr. fac. art., Ph. 2, Anno 1775, lit S (Mikrofilm 062), cited by Steblin, 'Franz Schubert – das dreizehnte Kind', 252.
27. Ernst Hilmar, 'Ferdinand Schuberts Skizze zu einer Autobiographie', in *Schubert-Studien*, ed. Franz Grasberger and Othmar Wessely (Vienna: Österreichische Akademie der Wissenschaft, 1978), 85–117, here 86.
28. Herwig Knaus, *Franz Schubert. Vom Vorstadtkind zum Compositeur* (Vienna: Löcker, 1997), 24. Niederösterreichisches Landesarchvi, K-Indices, vol. 11 (1786), folio 18r.
29. *Instructionen für die deutschen Schulen* (Vienna, 1806), 3.
30. Lichtental Taufbuch 6 fol.3978, Steblin, 'Franz Schubert – das dreizehnte Kind', 245.
31. Steblin, 'Franz Schubert – das dreizehnte Kind', 245–65.
32. Erich Benedikt, 'Die "Meldezettel" von Schuberts Eltern', *Schubert durch die Brille* 10 (1993), 42–44.
33. Ibid, 42.
34. Hans Dietrich Kiemle, 'Die landschaftliche Prägung des Franz Schubert und seiner Musik über die Eltern und deren Herkunft aus dem Altvatergebirge mit seiner speziellen Mundart' in *Sborník prací Filozofické fakulty brněnské university* (Musicologica Brunensia) 35 (2000), ed. Jiří Fukac, Masarykova univerzita v. Brne, 2001, 33–41.
35. Robert Arthur v. Lemm, 'Franz Hohann Vietz (Franz Schuberts Großvater) und seine baltischen Nachkommen in *Adler-Zeitschrift für Genealogie und Heraldik* 16/2 (1950–2), 56–68.
36. *Dok*, xxxi.
37. Two scholars have questioned if the Franz Johann Vietz who died on that evening was, in fact, Schubert's grandfather, and it remains uncertain: cf. Bruno Hampel, 'Neues zu Franz Schuberts mütterlicher Verwandtschaft' in Adler, *Zeitschrift für Genealogie und Heraldik* 16/2 (1950–2), 242, and Steblin, 'Franz Schubert – das dreizehnte Kind', 255.
38. Niederösterreichisches Landes Archiv, Particular Indices der N. Ö. Landesregierung, K-Indices 23/11 (1786), folio 18r.

39. *Dok*, 4.
40. For further appointment details see *Lexikon*, 406.
41. *Dok*, 36.
42. *Dok*, 55.
43. The certificate is in the private possession of the Hofbauer family in Kritzendorf. See also Otto Biba, 'Franz Schubert und die Gesellschaft der Musikfreunde' in O. Brusatti (ed.), *Schubert Kongress Wien 1978* (Graz: Akademische Druck- und Verlagsanstalt, 1979), 30.
44. This was part of the rehabilitation programme led by Johann Wilhelm Klein (1764–1855), who had founded a school for the blind in Vienna in 1804 and was instrumental in the debate as to what and how blind children could learn. While some educators believed that it was more beneficial to teach the blind a trade, Klein argued that a classical education would propel the blind into more esteemed professions. The programme, which was government-funded, was part of an educational debate for enabling a marginalized group to become contributing citizens within the community and about the potential of the human capacity for learning. His textbook for the instruction of the blind was published in Vienna in 1819 and his Institute for the employment of the blind was erected in Josefstadt in 1826.
45. O. E. Deutsch, 'Schuberts Vater', *Altwiener Kalender für das Jahr 1924* (Wiener Drucke, 1924), 134–48.
46. Josef Graf Sedlnitzky Odrow von Choltitz (8 January 1778–24 June 1855) was court official and head of the police during the Vormärz in Vienna. Emperor Francis I of Austria entrusted censorship to his care (1815–48), as a result of which he was extremely unpopular among Austrian artists.
47. For literature on Ferdinand Schubert see: Ernst Hilmar, 'Ferdinand Schuberts Skizze zu einer Autobiographie' in *Schubert-Studien* (Vienna: Österreichische Akademie der Wissenschaften, 1978), 86–117; Alexander Weinmann, *Ferdinand Schubert. Eine Untersuchung* [=*Beiträge zur Geschichte des Alt-Wiener Musikverlages* series 1, vol. 4] (Vienna: Krenn 1986); Martha Böhm-Schubert, *Ferdinand Schubert und das Schulwesen. Ferdinand Schuberts Nachkommen. 400 Jahre Familienchronik Franz Schubert's Bruder*, vols 1–4 (Vienna: privately published, 1998–2001); Irmtraud Löwy, *Ferdinand Schuberts Kompositionen für Kinderstimmen im historischen Zusammenhang seiner Zeit* (Vienna: unpublished dissertation, 2002); Till Gerrit Waidelich, *Ferdinand Schubert (1794–1859) und seine Überlieferung innerfamiliärer Korrespondenzen* in *Schubert und die Nachwelt. 1. International Arbeitstagung zur Schubert-Rezeption Wien 2003*, ed. Michael Kube, Walburga Litschauer and Gernot Gruber (Munich and Salzburg: Katzbichler, 2007).
48. Steblin, 'Franz Schubert – das dreizehnte Kind', 245–65.
49. Pfarre Lichtental, Taufbuch 7, folio 107.
50. Conventions-Munze (CM) is Austrian Currency: 1 Gulden = 80 Kreuzer; the sale of the house was agreed by Franz Theodor on 5 October 1826, Steblin, 'Franz Schubert – das dreizehnte Kind', 265.

CHAPTER TWO: THE ORIGINS OF A COMPOSER (1797–1813)

1. Kreissle, 4.
2. Ibid.
3. *Erinn*, 244.
4. Kreissle, 5.
5. L. J. Wetzl, *Drei vergessene Lichtentaler. Aus Franz Schuberts Zeit* (Vienna, 1930), and Werner Bodendorff, 'Zur Genealogie Michael Holzers', *Brille* 9 (1992).
6. *Erinn*, 72.
7. *Erinn*, 44; Kreissle, 5.
8. Document in private possession in Switzerland. See Reinhard van Hoorickx, 'Schubert: Further Discoveries since 1978', *MR* 80 (1989), 117–18.
9. *Dok*, 8 and 9.
10. *Dok*, 8.

NOTES to pp. 36-43

11. *Dok*, 9.
12. *Dok*, 9.
13. Benedikt Randhartinger, *Erinn*, 113.
14. *Erinn*, 45.
15. McKay, *Franz Schubert: A Biography*, 15–16.
16. *Erinn*, 404.
17. Josef Tranz, *Versuch eines Leitfadens der christlichen Religion nach der im Jahre 1808 entworfenen und vorgeschriebenen Skizze bearbeitet* (Vienna and Trieste: Geistingerischen Buchhandlung, 1813, rev. 1815). The book opens with an explanation of the Apostolic Creed, the seven Sacraments, the ten Commandments, the five Commandments of the Church and the Lord's Prayer. Tranz's study contemplates the creation of the world in six periods, not necessarily six 24-hour days, the Fall of Man and prophecy of a Saviour. The main thrust of the book contemplates the Life of Christ, and Christianity.
18. For recent research see Maria Benediktine Pagel, *Die kk Hofsängerknaben zu Wien 1498 bis 1918* (Vienna, Cologne and Weimar: Böhlau Verlag, 2009).
19. *Erinn*, 404.
20. *Erinn*, 67.
21. *Erinn*, 45.
22. *Erinn*, 40 and 147.
23. *Dok*, 18.
24. *Erinn*, 311.
25. *Erinn*, 24.
26. *Erinn*, 147.
27. *Erinn*, 407.
28. *Erinn*, 25.
29. *Erinn*, 67.
30. *Erinn*, 150.
31. Eduard Hanslick, *Geschichte des Concertwesens in Wien*, 2 vols (Vienna: W. Braumüller, 1869 and 1870; rpt. Hildesheim, 1979), vol. 1.
32. *Erinn*, 407.
33. *Erinn*, 407.
34. *Erinn*, 147.
35. Kreissle, 9.
36. Alfred Einstein, *Schubert* (London: Harper Collins, 1971), 24.
37. The *NSA* records the date of the first public performance of D 26 as 18 March 1838 in the Musikvereinsaal Vienna, conducted by Ferdinand Schubert.
38. *Erinn*, 24.
39. *Erinn*, 24.
40. Salieri's approach to choral training is outlined in his treatise, *Scuola di canto, in versi, e i versi in musica*, Sig. H 25124, Gesellschaft der Musikfreunde, Vienna. Rudolph Angermüller, 'Antonio Salieri und seine "Scuola di Canto"', *Beethoven-Studien*, ed. Erich Schenk (Vienna: Böhlaus, 1970), 37–50. For further reading on the *Hofkapelle* see Ludwig Köchel, *Die Kaiserliche Hof-Musikkapelle in Wien von 1543 bis 1867* (Vienna [publisher name:], 1976); Cölestin Wolfsgruber, *Die k. u. k. Hofburgkapelle und die k. und k. geistliche Hofkapelle* (Vienna: Mayer & Comp, 1905); *Musica Imperialis: 500 Jahre Hofmusikkapelle in Wien 1498–1998*, ed. Günter Brosche et al. (Tutzing: Hans Schneider, 1998); and Richard Steurer, *Das Repertoire der Wiener Hofmusikkapelle im 19. Jahrhundert* (Tutzing: Hans Schneider Verlag, 1998).
41. See, for example, Johann Georg Albrechtsberger, Graduale, Offertorium, GdM, Sign. I 67260; Michael Haydn, Graduale, GdM, Sign. I 37988 and 76551; Adalbert Gyrowetz, Missa Solemnis in F, Sign. I 7613 and Missa Brevis in B GdM, Sign. I 79055; Leopold Hofmann, Missa in C. Alla Capella GdM, Sig. I 11623. Wagenseil's Missa a Quattro da Capella is included in *Three Masses from Vienna: A Cappella Masses by Georg Christoph Wagenseil, Georg Reutter and Leopold Hofmann*, ed. Jen-yen Chen (Middleton, WI: A-R Editions, 2004).

42. Cf. J. S. Hettrick, 'A Thematic Catalogue of Sacred Works by Antonio Salieri: an Uncatalogued Holograph of the Composer in the Archive of the Vienna Hofkapelle', *Fontes artis musicae* 33 (1986), 226–35. Rudolf Angermüller and R. Ofner, 'Aspekte Salierischer Kirchenmusik', *Mitteilungen der Internationalen Stiftung Mozarteum* 21/1–2 (1973), 1–18; E. E. Swenson, *Antonio Salieri: A Documentary Biography* (Cornell University: unpublished dissertation, 1974); R. Nützlader, *Salieri als Kirchenmusiker* (University of Vienna: unpublished dissertation, 1924).
43. Jane Schatkin Hettrick, 'Antonio Salieri's Mass in B flat (1809)', *Studien zur Musikwissenschaft* 39 (Gesellschaft zur Herausgabe von Denkmälern der Tonkunst in Österreich (*DTÖ*, 1988), 141–57.
44. Antonio Salieri, Mass in D minor, ed. Jane Schatkin Hettrick (Madison, WI: A-R Editions, 2002).
45. Handschriften (HSS) Hofburgkapelle, Vienna; Moravské Zemské Muzeum, Oddělení Dějin Hudby, Brno.
46. HSS Hofburgkapelle, Vienna; Klosterneuburg, Augustiner-Chorherrenstift, Stiftsbibliothek.
47. HSS Hofburgkapelle, Vienna; Moravské Zemské Muzeum, Oddělení Dějin Hudby, Brno.
48. HSS Hofburgkapelle, Vienna; ÖNB; Klosterneuburg, Augustiner-Chorherrenstift, Stiftsbibliothek; Kremsmünster, Benediktinerstift; Moravské Zemské Muzeum, Oddělení Dějin Hudby, Brno and Sächsische Landesbibliothek- Staats- und Universitäts-Bibliothek, Dresden.
49. *Erinn*, 24.
50. *Erinn*, 54.
51. *Erinn*, 67.
52. *Erinn*, 59.
53. *Erinn*, 66.
54. *Erinn*, 59.
55. *Erinn*, 170.
56. *Erinn*, 99.
57. *Erinn*, 54.
58. See, for example, the remarkable 'Lebenstraum' fragment (D 39, 1810?), a sprawling work of 40 pages/400 bars of a vocal line to a text by Gabriele von Baumberg composed at the age of 13, where Schubert's favourite diatonic stepwise descent spanning a diminished fourth between the mediant and leading note in the minor is already very much in evidence.
59. The title pays homage to Richard Kramer's thought-provoking contemplation of C. P. E. Bach's musical heritage in *Unfinished Music*, 25–46, which made me radically rethink my understanding of these songs. I am deeply inspired by his scholarship.
60. Walther Vetter, *Der Klassiker Schubert* (Leipzig: C. F. Peters, 1953), I, 209.
61. I am citing Kramer's brilliant reading of C. P. E. Bach's relationship to his father, which perfectly - and uncannily - describes the forces at play in this song, *Unfinished Music*, 37.
62. *Erinn*, 361, also 33.
63. Two months after her death, in July 1812, each of her children, with the exception of Ignaz, her eldest living son, received an inheritance of 204 fl. from the home she owned in Zuckmantel.
64. *Dok*, 158–59.
65. The title of this section is taken from a collection of 5 Greek and 14 Latin poems, in a variety of metres, published in 1627 alongside John Donne's commemoration of George Herbert's mother, Lady Danvers. Both are reproduced in a modern edition: *George Herbert: Memoriae matris sacrum = To the Memory of my Mother: A Consecrated Gift. A Critical Text, Translation, and Commentary* (Fairfield, CT: George Herbert Journal, 2012). Like Schubert's commemorative pieces for his mother, the poems are remarkable for their musical imagery and emotional intensity.
66. The parts are marked 'Ad Usum 1812'.
67. Chapter 7, 156–160 and Chapter 9, 214–17.

68. Chapter 1, 26–27.
69. *Dok*, 22.
70. *Erinn*, 148.

CHAPTER THREE: SALIERI, PARTIMENTO AND THE BEGINNINGS OF CREATION

1. *Lexikon*, 383. Michael Lorenz gives the address at which Salieri lived for the rest of his life as inner city 1115 (today Spiegelgasse 11), 'Antonio Salieri's Early Years in Vienna', *Musicological Trifles and Biographical Paralipomena*, http://michaelorenz.blogspot.ie/2013/03/antonio-salieris-early-years-in-vienna.html (accessed July 2017).
2. *Erinn*, 68.
3. *Erinn*, 131. Cf. Brian Newbould, who refers to him as second rate, *Schubert: The Music and the Man*, 22.
4. *Erinn*, 131.
5. *Erinn*, 18.
6. *Erinn*, 68.
7. *Erinn*, 68. The method by which Salieri instructed his students is outlined by Anselm Hüttenbrenner in an obituary he wrote for Salieri in 1825 which was published in the *Musikalische Zeitung*.
8. BN, Ms. 306 [PhA 1058].
9. The extant counterpoint exercises (along with Salieri's corrections), the exercises in double counterpoint, fugue, studies in vocal setting, also the exercises Schubert undertook with Simon Sechter, are edited by Alfred Mann in *Schubert Studien NSA* VIII (Kassel, Basel and London: Bärenreiter Verlag, 1986).
10. Walburga Litschauer, 'Schubert und sein Lehrer Salieri', *Schubert-Perspektiven* 1 (2001), 74–83, here 74 and 77.
11. This is evident in Alfred Mann's commentary in the *NSA*, VIII, 2, 15–16. Mann recognizes that Haydn and Beethoven received a similar training to that of Schubert when he very helpfully draws up the different cantus firmus with which all three composers worked. Yet he fails to mention Haydn's lifelong loyalty to Italian teaching methods and to his teacher Porpora, who had been a teacher in the Naples Conservatoires of Sant' Onofrio and Santa Maria di Loreto, and a student of Gaetano Greco, another celebrated Neapolitan teacher and partimenti author; nor does Mann mention Beethoven's subscription to Italian compositional theory. Giorgio Sanguinetti, *The Art of Partimento: History, Theory and Practice* (Oxford University Press, 2012), 7–8.
12. *Intero studio di Partimenti del Sig. P. Martini Conventuale*.
13. *Lezioni di accompagnare date al nobil uomo Federico Bernardini dal Sig. re Pasqual'Antonio Lotti* (1758).
14. *NSA*, VIII, 2. Deutsch Verzeichnis, Appendix I, 32. Cf. Schubert's figured bass in 'Evangelium Johannes 6', v. 55–56.
15. To make both examples more legible for readers, I have transcribed the top staff into the G clef and merely indicate the C clef at the beginning as in Baroque scores. Schubert's solid grounding in all clefs should, however, be noted. Salieri's correction in Example 3.3a overlooks issues in voice-leading and the parallel fifths and octaves between bars 22 and 23.
16. Robert Gjerdingen, *Music in the Galant Style* (Oxford University Press, 2007), 369; Sanguinetti, *The Art of Partimento*, 14.
17. Sanguinetti, *The Art of Partimento*, 142.
18. It is likely Schubert had finished not only the Kyrie and Gloria but also the continuation: there are ten bars of the Credo.
19. The ending, for example, is completely out of style, including the modulation to G flat. The soaring exposition (bars 48ff) is one of the hallmarks of the Neapolitan tradition.

20. This is a problem in recent fugal analysis more broadly which Julian Horton discusses with characteristic brilliance in his reading of 'J. S. Bach's Fugue in C sharp minor, *Well-Tempered Clavier*, Book I and the Autonomy of the Musical Work' in *Music Preferred: Essays in Musicology, Cultural History and Analysis in Honor of Harry White*, ed. Lorraine Byrne Bodley (Vienna: Hollitzer Verlag, 2016), 41–66. Cf. David Ledbetter, *Bach's Well-Tempered Clavier: The 48 Preludes and Fugues* (New Haven, CT, and London: Yale University Press, 2002), and also the pedagogical texts of Thomas Benjamin, *The Craft of Tonal Counterpoint* (New York and London: Routledge, 2003), and especially Peter Schubert and Christoph Neidhöfer, *Baroque Counterpoint* (Upper Saddle River, NJ: Pearson, 2006).
21. Peter Kivy, *Music Alone: Philosophical Reflections on the Purely Musical Experience* (Ithaca, NY: Cornell University Press, 1990), 206.
22. *NSA*, Appendix 3, 12.
23. Manuscripts are held in the GdM; 25 of Salieri's canons were published in the *Scherzi armonici vocali* (Vienna, 1795) and 15 in the *Continuazione de' Scherzi armonici* (Vienna, n.d.).
24. The parts, formerly held by GdM, are lost. The bass part for D 51, D 57, D 61, D 62, D 64, D 67 and D 71 are the bequest of Ludwig Ritter von Köchel.
25. *Erinn*, 206–07.
26. For further reading on the topical associations of the descending tetrachord see Ellen Rosand, 'The Descending Tetrachord: An Emblem of Lament', *MQ* 65 (1979), 346–59.
27. Christoph Wolff, 'Schubert's *Der Tod und das Mädchen:* Analytical and Explanatory Notes on the Song D 531 and the Quartet D 810', *Schubert Studies*, 143–71, here 164.
28. *Erinn*, 26.
29. Walther Dürr recognizes this as Salieri instructing Schubert in opera in the *Schubert Handbook*, 11.
30. *Erinn*, 26.
31. *Erinn*, 26 and 152.
32. GdM, Signatur A517.
33. *Sechs deutsche Lieder für das Pianoforte von Beethoven, Grosheim, Salieri, Hummel, Giuliani und Moscheles in Musik gesetzt und dem Herrn Joseph Pargfrieder von dem Verfasser [Christian Ludwig Reissig] gewidmet* (Vienna: Tranquillo Mollo, 1815), WZ (29.11.1815), no. 333/3.
34. The settings are discussed in Orel, *Der junge Schubert*, 5–6 and 14–20 (see 17–27).
35. John Reed, *Schubert* (Oxford University Press, 1987), 9.
36. *Dodici Divertimenti Vocali con accompagnamento di Piano Forte composti per il Sigre Conte di Browne [. . .] dal Sigre Antonio Salieri [. . .] Parte prima* (Vienna: Thadé Weigl, 1803), 26–29.
37. Hilmar, *Verzeichnis der Schubert-Handschriften in der Musiksammlung der Wiener Stadt- und Landesbibliothek* [=Catalogus musicus VIII] (Kassel: Bärenreiter, 1978), 1, 65.
38. WB, Signatur MH 106c.
39. Hans-Joachim Hinrichsen, 'Schuberts Ouvertüre, im italienischen Stile' D-Dur D 590 – Druckfassung und Originalgestalt' in *IFSI. Mitteilungen* 5 (1990), 7–14 and 'Auf dem Weg zur "tondichterischen" Ouvertüre. Die kleineren Orchesterwerke' in *Schubert-Handbuch*, 513–47. See also Walther Dürr, 'Schubert in seiner Welt', in *Schubert-Handbuch*, 1–76, and Manuela Jahrmärker, 'Les ouvertures de Schubert. Champ d'expérimentation ou esthétique spécifique?' in *Le Style Instrumental de Schubert. Source, Analyse, Évolution* (Paris: Sorbonne, 2007). Ferdinand Schubert was the first to designate these overtures as being 'Italian in style' and they were described by Schubert's first biographer, Kreissle von Hellborn, as 'Rossini amulets'.
40. *Erinn*, 26.
41. Chapter 22, 498–503.

CHAPTER FOUR: THE MAKINGS OF A COMPOSER (1812–1813)

1. *Erinn*, 167.
2. *NSA* 6/3 viii.

3. For detailed readings see Brian Black, *Schubert's Apprenticeship in Sonata Form: The Early String Quartets* (McGill University, Montreal: PhD dissertation, 1996) and Salome Reiser, *Franz Schuberts frühe Streichquartette. Eine klassische Gattung am Beginn einer nachklassischen Zeit* (Heidelberg: PhD dissertation, 1995).
4. For a detailed discussion of Schubert's quartets see Stephen E. Hefling and David S. Tartakoff, 'Schubert's Chamber Music', in Hefling (ed.), *Nineetenth-Century Chamber Music* (New York: Routledge, 1998, rev. 2003), 39–101.
5. Hilmar, *Verzeichnis der Schubert-Handschriften in der Musiksammlung der Wiener Stadt- und Landesbibliothek, Catalogus Musicus* 8 (Kassel: Bärenreiter, 1978), 94.
6. *Dok*, 234–235. See Chapter 16, 371–372.
7. Walther Dürr, 'Von Modellen und Rastern. Schubert studiert Mozart?', *Mozart Studien* 1 (1992), 455–69.
8. For a brilliant and characteristically perceptive reading of Schubert's early string quartets, see Hans-Joachim Hinrichsen, '"Bergendes Gehäuse" und "Hang ins Unbegrenzte": Die Kammermusik', *Schubert Handbuch*, ed. Walther Dürr and Andreas Krause (Kassel: Bärenreiter, 1997), 455–465, here 458. My understanding of Schubert's early string quartets is informed by Hinrichsen's perceptive research and by Anne Hyland's writing on Schubert's String Quartets (CUP, 2023).
9. For a comprehensive discussion of this topic see Hans-Joachim Hinrichsen, *Untersuchung zur Entwicklung der Sonatenform in der Instrumentalmusik Franz Schuberts* (Tutzing: Hans Schneider Verlag, 1994). For earlier readings see: Richard A. Coleridge, 'Form in the String Quartets of Franz Schubert', *MR* 32 (1971), 309–25; Carl Dahlhaus, 'Formenprobleme in Schuberts frühen Streichquartetten (Graz, 1979), 191–97, and Felix Salzer, 'Die Sonatenform bei Franz Schubert', *Studien zur Musikwissenschaft* 14 (1927), 86–125.
10. Although it is generally agreed that Schubert was familiar with Bach's works through Raphael Kiesewetter's historical concerts as early as 1816, it is likely this acquaintance began much earlier; for further discussion see Walther Dürr, 'Über Schuberts Verhältnis zu Bach' in *Johann Sebastian Bach. Beiträge zur Wirkungsgeschichte*, ed. Ingrid Fuchs and Susanne Antonicek (Vienna: Verband der wissenschaftlichen Gesellschaften Österreichs (VWGÖ), 1992), 69–79, and Arfried Edler, 'Hinweise auf die Wirkung Bachs im Werk Franz Schubert', *Die Musikforschung* 33 (1980), 279–91.
11. WB MH 125/c.
12. Hinrichsen, '"Bergendes Gehäuse"' in *Schubert Handbuch* 451–511, here 459.
13. Martin Chusid, *The Chamber Music of Schubert* (University of California, Berkeley: PhD dissertation, 1961), 303, and 'Das "Orchestermäßige" in Schubert's früher Streicherkammermusik' in *Aufführungspraxis* (1981), 77–86, here 79; Hinrichsen, '"Bergendes Gehäuse"', 459.
14. I am grateful to Xavier Hascher for his discussion of the absence of thematic contrast in this passage and the whole issue of monothematicism, most famously in Haydn's Symphony no. 104/i.
15. Paul Griffiths reads them as being intended as the missing movements for Haydn's op. 103, *The String Quartet: A History* (New York: Thames & Hudson, 1983), 96.
16. Dahlhaus's identification of this quartet as a path of inquiry into Schubert's reinterpretation of sonata principles has been problematized by Hinrichsen, '"Bergendes Gehäuse"', who pinpoints how difficult it is to access the early works analytically, 460 61. For recent readings see Anne Hyland, 'Rhetorical Closure in the First Movement of Schubert's Quartet in C Major, D. 46: A Dialogue with Deformation', *Music Analysis* 28/1 (2009), 111–42; 'The "tightened bow": Analyzing the Juxtaposition of Drama and Lyricism in Schubert's Paratactic Sonata-form Movements', *Irish Musical Studies* 11, *Irish Musical Analysis*, ed. Gareth Cox and Julian Horton (Dublin: Four Courts Press, 2014), 17–40.
17. For discussion of this repertoire see Jean Mongrédien, *French Music from the Enlightenment to Romanticism 1789–1830*, trans. Sylvain Frémaux (Portland, OR: Amadeus Press, 1996), 289–99.
18. Richard Kramer, *Unfinished Music* (Oxford University Press, 2008), 375.

19. *Erinn*, 26.
20. See, for example, the programme notes to the Hohenems Schubertiade, 2 May 2018, at which these works were performed by the Orfeo Baroque Orchestra, conducted by Michi Gaigg. Dr Michael Kube, Member of the *NSA*, led an extraordinary lecture-recital with the orchestra; the collaboration between orchestra and musicologist made the performance possible. See also Wolfram Steinbeck, '"Und über das Ganze eine Romantik ausgegossen" Die Sinfonien', *Schubert Handbuch*, 550–666, here 617–18.
21. For further discussion see Hans Joachim Hinrichsen, 'Schubert und das Orchester' in 'Auf den Weg zur "tondichterischen Ouvertüre". Die kleineren Orchesterwerke', *Schubert Handbuch*, 514–49, here 514–18.
22. Kreissle, 29.
23. John Irving, 'The Viennese Symphony 1750 to 1827' in *The Cambridge Companion to the Symphony*, ed. Julian Horton (Cambridge University Press, 2013), 27. Irving, at the same time, acknowledges the individuality of Schubert's 'Unfinished' and 'Great' C major symphonies in the continuation of this passage: 'While there are no voices in Schubert's symphonies, the vocality of his personal symphonic genre is unmistakable. In his hands, as in Beethoven's, the Viennese symphony had travelled far.'
24. For further reading see Helmut Weil, 'Frühwerk und Innovation, Studien zu den "Jugendsinfonien" Franz Schuberts' (Kassel: Kieler Schriften zur Musikwissenschaft, 1994), and Steinbeck, '"Und über das Ganze eine Romantik ausgegossen"', here 557–92.
25. The sheer volume of unexplored symphonies by his contemporaries in the Vienna archives bears testimony to the prolificacy of the domestic and social character of the symphony in Schubert's Vienna. See, for example, Gassmann's B minor Symphony (Vienna: Universal Edition, 1933), GdM, Sign. XIII 45265; Wagenseil's Symphony in C major, GdM, XIII 77396, and Symphony in D major (Berlin: Bernouli, 1927), GdM, Sign. XIII 41087 and XIII 77288; Václav Pichl, Symphony in G, GdM, Sign. XIII 19068; Franz Krommer, Symphony no. 1 in F Dur, Sign XIII 8119, Symphony no. 2 in D, Sign. XIII 6666, and Symphony in C minor, Sign. XIII 2453. Chronological accounts of the symphony, which include some of Schubert's forgotten contemporaries, are available in such studies as D. Kern Holoman's *The Nineteenth-Century Symphony* (New York: Schirmer, 1997) and A. Peter Brown, *The First Golden Age of the Viennese Symphony: Haydn, Mozart, Beethoven, and Schubert* (Bloomington, IN: Indiana University Press, 2002), *The Symphonic Repertoire*, vol. III part A: *The European Symphony c. 1800–c1900: Germany and the Nordic Countries* (Bloomington, IN: Indiana University Press, 2007), Mary Sue Morrow and Bathia Churgin (eds), *The Symphonic Repertoire*, vol. 1: *The Eighteenth-Century Symphony* (Bloomington, IN: Indiana University Press, 2012). Important essays include John Irving, 'The Viennese Symphony 1750 to 1827', and Mary Sue Morrow, 'Other Classical Repertoires' in *The Cambridge Companion to the Symphony*, 15–28, 29–60, but a comparative analysis of Schubert's symphonies with forgotten, prominent contemporaries living in Vienna is still waiting to be written.
26. *Erinn*, 103. A report on the incident from the curator of the seminary to the Emperor on 29 August 1813, now lost, was printed in *Die Quelle* in April 1928, 485–87.
27. *Dok*, 32.
28. *Dok*, 28–32, here 29.
29. *Dok*, 32.

CHAPTER FIVE: PLACE AND DISPLACEMENT (1813–1814)

1. *Dok*, 34.
2. Chapter 2, 46–51 and Chapter 5, 113, 117–120.
3. Although Schubert only used the guitar in one other composition – the cantata in celebration of his father's name's day on 27 September 1813, some of his male-voice quartets – Opus 11 ('Das Dörchen', 'Die Nachtigall', 'Geist der Liebe') and op. 16 ('Frühlingslied', 'Naturgenuß') — were arranged and published with guitar accompaniment by the composer and publisher, Anton Diabelli.

NOTES to pp. 113-126

4. The 1805 model is in Vienna Museum and the Staufer guitar, held by the Vienna Schubertbund, is exhibited in his birthplace.
5. Although the autograph, which is an *Überlieferungsfragment*, is cut off on page 32 at the opening three bars of the fifth variation of the fifth movement, it is still possible to give a very successful performance, as given by John Feeley (guitar), William Dowdell (flute), John Lynch (viola) and William Butt (cello) at Maynooth University, 27 April 2003. Like everyone who now writes on fragments, I am indebted to Richard Kramer's *Unfinished Music* (Oxford University Press, 2008).
6. Kreissle, 71.
7. That Schubert had *Des Teufels Lustschloß* (D 84) copied in 1822 and had Josef Hüttenbrenner seek performances in Prague, Munich and elsewhere shows his belief in this flawed but fascinating work.
8. Uta Hertin-Loeser, Hans-Joachim Hinrichsen, 'Die Entwicklungsstufen von "Des Teufels Lustschloß" D 84', *Brille* 9 (1992), 43–64, and Till Gerrit Waidelich 'Vielleicht hielt er sich zu streng an das französische Original. Ein Plagiat Kotzebues als Libretto für Walter, Reichardt und Schubert', *Brille* 16/17 (1996), 95–109.
9. Against this background, it is understandable why the director Marco Arturo Marielli in Zurich's Stadttheater production in 1995 portrayed Knight Oswald as Schubert, who stands apart from the cheering crowd – the very antithesis of Schubert's *Schwammerl* in Heinrich Berté's Operetta *Das Dreimäderlhaus* (1916). Nikolaus Harnoncourt, the conductor of this widely acclaimed performance, was not the only one to take this opera seriously. Bruno Weil conducted a concert performance in Vienna in 1986 and again four years later in New York.
10. *Dok*, 33.
11. His other political settings are the cantata *Am Geburtstage des Kaisers* (D 748, commissioned by Leopold Sonnleithner) in January 1822 and *Grand Marche Funèbre* (D 859) and *Grande Marche Héroique* (D 805), Chapter 19, 425–426.
12. It is an interesting coincidence of life and art that two days after the allied victory at the Battle of Leipzig, which this setting commemorates, Emperor Franz Josef signed the Imperial Resolution outlining the terms of Schubert's continuing scholarship, which the composer rejected, *Dok*, 29.
13. Chapter 10, 249.
14. Chapter 6, 145–48.
15. Kreissle, 34.
16. GdM, A239.
17. Examples illustrate chordal balance in D 82/i (bb. 9–10), how hard he works the orchestra in *tutti* sections (which is really only a measure of his ambition) or his persistent placing of the trumpets at a high register more than in any of his later symphonies.
18. In contrast to the support Mendelssohn received from his father hiring members of the royal orchestra to perform his string symphonies at the family's Sunday musicales, the comparable example within Schubert's family is never acknowledged.

CHAPTER SIX: SCHUBERT AS A CHURCH MUSIC COMPOSER

1. Erich Benedikt, 'Schubert und das Kirchenmusik-Repertoire in Lichtental', *Brille* 12 (1994), 107–11. Cf. Erich Benedikt, 'Die alten Notenarchive der Schubertkirche in Lichtental und der Klosterkirche der Barmherzigen Brüder in Wien', 51–98, in '*Musik muss man machen*'. *Eine Festgabe für Josef Mertin zum neunzigsten Geburtstag am 21. März 1994*, ed. Michael Nagy (Vienna: Pasqualatihaus, 1994); Erich Benedikt and Michael Jahn, *Die Musikhandschriften des Pfarrarchivs Wien-Lichtental* (Vienna: Der Apfel [=Veröffentlichungen des rism-österreich, Band/Reihe: 3/A], 2006).
2. *Erinn*, 18.
3. Schubert acknowledges this direction on 7 April 1826, *Dok*, 354.

4. The virtuoso clarinet part was written for his friend, Josef Doppler, and later published as op. 46 by Diabelli in 1825 with a dedication to the tenor, Ludwig Tietze, an admired interpreter of Schubert's songs.
5. Otto Biba, 'Kirchenmusikalische Praxis zu Schuberts Zeit', *Jahre der Krise*, 113–20, here 118.
6. *Dok*, 74.
7. Maurice J. E. Brown, 'Schubert's Setting of the *Salve Regina*', *M&L* 37/4 (1956), 424.
8. Friedrich Nietzsche, *Jenseits von Gut und Böse* in *Werke in 3 Bänden* (Cologne: Könemann, 1994), 259.
9. Martin Heidegger, *Sein und Zeit* (Tübingen: Max Niemeyer Verlag, 1972); Jean-Louis Chrétien, *L'Appel et la Réponse* (Paris: Minuit, 1992), 1.
10. John Milton, 'Eikonoklastes' in *Complete Prose Works of John Milton*, vol. 3, *1648–1649*, ed. Merritt Y. Hughes (New Haven, CT, and London: Yale University Press, 1962), 547.
11. *Dok*, 299.
12. The *commemorationis dies* – or 'month's mind' as we call it in Ireland – is a Requiem mass celebrated one month after a person's death, in memory of the deceased.
13. WB, MH 18.
14. For early reception of the work see Leopold Hirschberg, 'Franz Schuberts deutsches "Stabat Mater"', *Deutsche Musikerzeitung* 59 (1928), 388–90.
15. Benedikt, 'Schubert und das Kirchenmusik-Repertoire in Lichtental', 111.
16. I warmly acknowledge Giorgio Sanguinetti's knowledge of the partimento tradition and his visits to Maynooth when he discussed my work of Schubert's appropriation of such topics. One of the lectures he gave at Maynooth, 'The Stabat Cadence', was subsequently published by Giorgio Sanguinetti, *Kazan Conservatoire Magazine: Music, Art, Science and Practice*, 2/18, (2017), 21–26. The Ultimate Stabat Mater Site https://www.stabatmater.info (accessed 2 March 2019) offers a wealth of information.
17. See Glenn Stanley, 'Schubert's Religious and Choral Music: Toward a Statement of Faith', *Cambridge Companion to Schubert*, 211–15.
18. A representative selection of twenty *Tantum Ergo* settings, some with orchestral and some with organ accompaniment, by Ignaz Aßmeyer, Joseph Blahack, Anton Bruckner, Anton Diabelli, Michael Haydn, Conradin Kreutzer, Sigismund Neukomm, Ambros Rieder, Ludwig Rotter, Ferdinand Schubert, Franz Schubert and Simon Sechter is published in Karl Pfannhauser (ed.), *Österreichische Kirchenmusik* 3/i–iii (Vienna: Doblinger, 1947).
19. Crawford Howie, 'Small Is Beautiful: Schubert's Smaller Works' in Lorraine Byrne Bodley and Barbara Reul (eds), *The Unknown Schubert* (Aldershot: Ashgate, 2008), 67.
20. Howie, 'Small Is Beautiful', 67.
21. Chapter 21, 473–476.
22. *Erinn*, 46.
23. Erich Benedikt, 'Notizen zu Schuberts Messen, mit neuem Aufführungsdatum der Messe in F-Dur', *Österreichische Musikzeitschrift* 52/1–2 (1997), 64–66.
24. *Erinn*, 46.
25. Kreissle, 36.
26. For discussion of Schubert's liturgical music and Latin masses see: Maurice J. E. Brown, 'Schubert's Setting of the *Salve Regina*', *M&L* 37 (1956), 234–49; Robert S. Stringham, *The Masses of Franz Schubert* (Ithaca, NY: PhD dissertation, Cornell University, 1964); Kenneth Nafziger's *The Masses of Haydn and Schubert: A Study in the Rise of Romanticism* (Portland, OR: University of Oregon Press, 1970); Karl Gustav Fellerer, 'Franz Schuberts geistliche Musik', *Musica Sacra*, 98 (1978), 73–80; Reinhard van Hoorickx, 'Schubert and the Bible', *MT* 119 (1978), 953–55; Hans Jaskulsky, *Die lateinischen Messen Franz Schuberts* (Mainz: Schott, 1986); Stanley, 'Schubert's Religious and Choral Music, 207–23; Manuela Jahrmärker, 'Von der liturgischen Funktion zum persönlichen Bekenntnis: Die Kirchenmusik', *Schubert Handbook*, 345–78; Werner Bodendorff, *Die kleineren Kirchenmusikwerke Franz Schuberts* (Augsburg: Wissner, 1997).
27. *Dok*, 336–37.

CHAPTER SEVEN: AWAKENINGS

1. Hans-Georg Gadamer, *Truth and Method*, trans. Joel Weinsheimer and Donald Marshall, 2nd rev. edn (New York: Continuum, 1989), 281.
2. Pierre Boulez, *Orientations: Collected Writings*, trans. Martin Cooper, ed. Jean-Jacques Nattiez (Cambridge, MA: Harvard University Press, 1986), 454.
3. Ralph Waldo Emerson, 'Quotation and Originality' in *The Collected Works of Ralph Waldo Emerson*, vol. 8, *Letters and Social Aims*, ed. Ronald A. Bosco, Glen M. Johnson and Joel Myerson (Cambridge, MA: Belknap, 2010), 91.
4. Kristina Muxfeldt, 'Schubert's Songs: The Transformation of a Genre', *Cambridge Companion to Schubert*, 121; Ewan West, *Schubert's Lieder in Context: Aspects of Song in Vienna 1778–1828* (University of Oxford: D.Phil dissertation, 1989); see also West, 'The Musenalmanach and Viennese Song 1770–1830', *M&L* 67 (1986), 37–49; Ernst Hilma, 'Schuberts Lieder im Kontext: Einige Bemerkungen zur Lied-komposition in Wien nach 1820', *Brille* 12 (1994), 5–19.
5. *Erinn*, 72.
6. There are many links between the Schubert and Grob families: the Grobs introduced Franz Theodor to his second wife, Anna Kleyenböck, and in 1836 Franz's brother, Ignaz, married Therese's aunt Wilhelmine, a widow whose son, Heinrich Hollpein, became a very competent painter and bequeathed to us portraits of Ignaz Schubert and Therese Grob.
7. *Erinn*, 69.
8. *Erinn*, 209. As Therese Grob's father was deceased, Therese was advised by her mother.
9. *Erinn*, 69–72.
10. For an alternative reading of the Grob relationship see Rita Steblin, 'Schubert's Beloved Singer Therese Grob: New Documentary Research', *Brille* 28 (2002), 55–100.
11. Following Amalia Grob's death on Christmas Eve 1886, the songbook was given to the Meangya family, descendants of Marianne Grob, granddaughter of Therese Grob's brother, Heinrich. Dr Wilhelm purchased the songbook at an auction in 1958 and it is now in the Wilhelm family's private collection in Bottmingen in Basel, Switzerland. Reinhard van Hoorickz privately printed a facsimile edition of the collection in 1967.
12. Rita Steblin, 'Franz Schubert und das Ehe-Consens Gesetz von 1815', *Brille* 9 (1992), 32–42.
13. *Dok*, 49. See Chapter 9, 212–217.
14. I thank Xavier Hascher with whom I discussed the technical details of this passage for my book on *Music in Goethe's Faust: Goethe's Faust in Music* (Woodbridge: Boydell & Brewer, 2017), and in the early stages of writing this book.
15. I have traced the reception history of this idea in my first monograph, *Schubert's Goethe Settings* (Surrey and Burlington: Ashgate, 2003; Routledge reprint 2016), 3–57.
16. Johann Peter Eckermann, *Gespräche mit Goethe* (Stuttgart: Reclam, 1994), 12 February 1829, 325.
17. The 335-page document (*Criminalia 1771*, no. 62) is in the Institute for the History of Frankfurt. The scissors with which Brandt is said to have mutilated the corpse of her child are on display in the Institute for the History of Frankfurt. For literature on the case see: Ruth Berger, *Gretchen. Ein Frankfurter Kriminalfall* (Reinbek: Kindler, 2007); Siegfried Birkner, *Das Leben und Sterben der Kindsmörderin Susanna Margaretha Brandt. Nach den Prozeßakten dargestellt* (Frankfurt: Insel Verlag, 1973); Rebekka Habermas (ed.), *Das Frankfurter Gretchen. Der Prozeß gegen die Kindsmörderin Susanna Margaretha Brandt* (Munich: C. H. Beck, 1999).
18. Steblin, 'Franz Schubert und das Ehe-Consens Gesetz von 1815', 259.
19. Ferdinand Schubert, 'Aus Franz Schubert's Leben', *Neue Zeitschrift für Musik* 10 (1839), 129.
20. For further discussion see Nicholas Boyle, 'Wagering on Modernity: Goethe's Eighteenth-Century Faust' in Byrne Bodley, *Music in Goethe's Faust: Goethe's Faust in Music*, 45–60.
21. *Dresdener Abendzeitung*, 30 January 1821; *Wiener Zeitung*, 30 April 1821; *Wiener Allgemeine musikalische Zeitung*, 19 January 1822; *Wiener Zeitschrift für Kunst, Literatur, Theater und Mode*, 23 March 1822; *Leipziges Literarisches Konversations-Blatt*, 18 January 1823.

22. Herder, *Volkslieder*, vol. II (Leipzig: Weygand: 1779). It was included in *Des Knaben Wunderhorn*, ed. Achim von Arnim and Clemens Brentano (Heidelberg: Mohr und Zimmer, 1805–1808). Other translations appeared in Wilhelm Grimm's *Altdänische Heldenlieder, Balladen* (Heidelberg: Mohr und Zimmer, 1811). Goethe's masterpiece awoke a new interest in the theme, but in the lyrics it inspired – Matthesons 'Die Elfenkönigin' and Uhland's 'Die Elfin', for example – the seducer is usually female.
23. Walter Pater, *Greek Studies* (London: Macmillan and Co., 1910), 91.
24. *Egmont*, II, 'Egmonts Wohnung', MA, 3.1, 276–77.
25. *Dichtung und Wahrheit*, MA, 16, 831–32.
26. *Wilhelm Meisters Wanderjahre, Padagögische Provinz* II/1, MA, 17, 381.
27. *Dok*, 40.
28. For a detailed study of both manuscripts, see Byrne Bodley, *Schubert's Goethe Settings*; Walther Dürr, 'Aus Schubert's erstem Publikationsplan: Zwei Hefte mit Liedern von Goethe' in *Schubert-Studien*, ed. Franz Grasberger and Othmar Wessely (Vienna [missing publr name:], 1978), 43–55.
29. For an account of Goethe's response to Schubert's dispatch and his later acknowledgement of the composer, see Lorraine Byrne Bodley, *Schubert's Goethe Settings*, 15–22.
30. WA III 5, 189.
31. WA III 5, 6 June 1816, 239.
32. For further discussion of this topic see 'In Pursuit of a Single Flame?: Schubert's Settings of Goethe's Lyrics', in Lorraine Byrne Bodley and James Sobaskie (eds), *Schubert Familiar and Unfamiliar: Continuing Conversations*, NCMR 13/1 (2016), 11–34. The article was written in response to Robert Hatten's article 'A Surfeit of Musics: What Goethe's Lyrics Concede When Set to Schubert's Music', NCMR 5/2 (2008), 7–18; Hatten in turn published a response to my article in 'Reflections Inspired by a Response', NCMR 13 (2008), 35–38.
33. *Briefe über die ästhetische Erziehung des Menschen*, Letter no. XXII, SA, 20, 380.
34. Schiller, 'Über Matthissons Gedichte', SA, 16, 259.
35. Schiller, 'Die Künstler', SA, 1, 201.
36. Schiller's letter to Körner, 23 February 1794.
37. For an alternative reading of this see R. M. Longyear, *Schiller and Music* (University of North Carolina Press, 1966), 105.
38. Schiller's letter to Körner, 3 February 1794.
39. Schiller, 'Über Matthissons Gedichte', SA, 22, 272.
40. *Das gegenwärtige teutsche Theater*, SA, 11, 87
41. See Chapter 20, 449.
42. Körner to Schiller, 30 July 1797, 29 September 1795.
43. Körner to Schiller, 10 February 1802.
44. Johnson, CDJ33034.
45. A brilliant reading of this work is found in Susan Youen's 'Reentering Mozart's Hell: Schubert's "Gruppe aus dem Tartarus" D 583', *Drama in the Music of Franz Schubert* (Woodbridge, Boydell & Brewer, 2019), 171–204.
46. See Chapter 3, 72–75.
47. NA, XII, 83–85.
48. Andreas Dorschel, ' "Like from a thousand nerve strands": The Piano in Schubert's Lied Texts' in *Schubert's Piano*, ed. Christine Martin and Matthew Gardner (Cambridge University Press, 2023).
49. Lydia Goehr, *The Imaginary Museum of Musical Works* (Oxford University Press, 1992); Jim Samson, 'The Practice of Pianism' in *The Musical Work: Reality or Invention*, ed. Michael Talbot (Liverpool Musical Symposium, 2010), 110–27; Edward Said, *Beginnings, Intention, Method* (New York: Columbia University Press, 1985), xii–xiii.
50. For further reading on this topic see Max Friedländer, 'Fälschungen in Schubert's Liedern', *Vierteljahresschrift für Musikwissenschaft* 9 (1893), 166–85; Walther Dürr, 'Schubert and Johann Michael Vogl: A Reappraisal', NCM 3/2 (1979), 126–140; Andrea Lindmayr-Brandl, 'Schuberts Erlkönig: Entstehung, Werkgestalt und Dramatisierung des Werkkonzepts' in

NOTES to pp. 188–192

Musikgeschichte als Verstehensgeschichte. Festschrift für Gernot Gruber zum 65. Geburtstag, ed. Joachim Brügge, Franz Födermayr, Wolfgang Gratzer, Thomas Hochradner and Siegfried Mauser (Tutzing: Schneider 2004), 261–77; Suzannah Clark, 'A Gift to Goethe: The Aesthetics of the Intermediate Dominant in Schubert's Music and Early Nineteenth-Century Theoretical Thought', *NCMR* 13/1 (2016), 39–70, and more generally Rebecca Herrisone, *Musical Creativity in Restoration England* (Cambridge University Press, 2013), 209.

51. Although *Werther* had been published in 1774, he revised it in 1782, 1783, 1785, finally settling on revisions in 1786.
52. A further example is 'Klage' (D 436 and D 437) where the piano introduction of the first edition is not in Schubert's manuscript (and most likely was added by the publisher).
53. Timothy L. Jackson, 'Schubert's Revisions of "Der Jüngling und der Tod", D 545a–b and "Meeresstille", D 216a–b', *MQ* 75/3 (1991), 336–61; cf. Marius Flothius, 'Schubert Revises Schubert' in *Schubert Studies*, ed. Eva Badura-Skoda and Peter Branscombe (Cambridge University Press, 1982), 61–84; Sterling Lambert, *Rereading Poetry: Schubert's Multiple Settings of Goethe* (Woodbridge: Boydell & Brewer, 2009), 34–56.

CHAPTER EIGHT: UNSUNG SCHUBERT: APPRENTICESHIP IN OPERA

1. See Christine Martin, 'Die Particell-Entwürfe zu Schuberts Fierabras und ihre Bedeutung für den Kompositionsprozess der Oper', *Schubert-Perspektiven* 8/1 (2008), 1–16.
2. Alan Armstrong, 'Gilbert-Louis Duprez and Gustav Roger in the Composition of Meyerbeer's *Le Prophète*', *Cambridge Opera Journal* 8/2 (1996), 147–65, here 164.
3. Roger Parker, 'A Donizetti Critical Edition in the Postmodern World', *L'opera teatrale di Gaetano Donizetti*, ed. Francesco Bellotti (Bergamo: Comune di Bergamo-Assessorato allo Spettacolo, 1993).
4. It is only in the last century that scholars have even considered this repertoire, initially around both the 100th and 150th anniversary years, 1928 and especially 1978, but more noticeably in the 1990s when opera studies emerged as a discipline. The first serious studies of Schubert's operas were written by Rudolfine Krott, *Die Singspiele Schuberts* (Vienna: unpublished dissertation, 1921) and W. van Endert, *Schubert als Bühnenkomponist* (Leipzig: PhD dissertation, 1925). Examples of centenary publications include Helmut Wolter, 'Schubert als Opernkomponist', *Der Auftakt* 8 (1928), 241–44; Alfred Orel, 'Schuberts Bühnenschaffen', *Der neue Pflug* 3 (1928), 35–40; P. Stefan, 'Schubert und die Oper', *Neue Zürcher Zeitung*, 18 November 1928; Hugo Leichtentritt, 'Schubert's Early Operas', *MQ* 14 (1928), 620–38. Important articles between both anniversary include: Maurice Brown 'Schubert's Two Major Operas: A Consideration of the Possibility of Actual Stage Production', *MR* 20 (1959), 104–18; Reinhard van Hoorickx, 'Les Opéras de Schubert', *Revue Belge de Musicologie* 28–30 (1974–76), 238–59; George R. Cunningham, *Franz Schubert als Theaterkomponist* (Freiburg im Breisgau: PhD dissertation, 1974); and Elizabeth Norman McKay, 'Schubert as a Composer of Operas' in *Schubert Studies*, 85–104; Walter Thomas made this claim in 'Bild und Aktion in Fierabras. Ein Beitrag zu Schuberts musikalischer Dramaturgie', *Jahre der Krise*, 85–112; Christian Pollack, *Franz Schubert: Bühnenwerke: Kritische Gesamtausgabe der Texte* (Tutzing [missing publr name:], 1988); Christian Pollack, 'Problemstellung zum dramatischen Schaffen Schuberts', *Brille* 1 (1988), 5–10. Important landmarks in the 1990s include Elizabeth Norman McKay, *Franz Schubert's Music for the Theatre* (Vienna: Hans Schneider, 1991); Till Gerrit Waidelich, *Franz Schubert: Alfonso und Estrella. Eine frühe durchkomponierte deutsche Oper. Geschichte und Analyse* (Tutzing: Schneider, 1991); Walther Dürr, 'Bühnenwerke' in *Musikführer* (1991), 163–191, and 'Schuberts Opern als Ideentheater' in *Zeichen-Setzung. Aufsätze zur musikalischen Poetik*, ed. Werner Aderhold and Walburga Litschauer (Kassel: Bärenreiter, 1992), 282–84; Thomas A. Denny, 'Schubert's Operas: "the judgment of history?"', *Cambridge Companion to Schubert*, 224–40; Brian Newbould, 'Music for the Theatre' in

Schubert: The Music and the Man (London: Victor Gollanz, 1997), 185–210. The most recent study broadly addressing the topic with two chapters on opera is Joe Davies and James W. Sobaskie, *Drama in the Music of Franz Schubert* (Woodbridge: Boydell & Brewer, 2019): Lorraine Byrne Bodley, 'Opera that Vanished: Goethe, Schubert and *Claudine von Villa Bella*', 11–34, and Christine Martin, 'Pioneering German Musical Drama: Sung and Spoken Word in Schubert's *Fierabras*', 35–50.

5. *Erinn*, 28.
6. Johann Friedrich Reichardt, *Vertraute Briefe, geschrieben auf einer Reise nach Wien und den Österreichischen Staaten zu Ende des Jahres 1808 und zu Anfang 1809*, Confidential Letters, 1808–1809, 2 vols (Amsterdam: Kunst- und Industrie-Comptoir, 1810).
7. *Erinn*, 150.
8. *Erinn*, 150–51.
9. BN, Slg MS 306 [PhA 1058].
10. *Erinn*, 26.
11. Other fragmentary sketches include a lost setting of *Der Minnesänger* (D 981), sketches for three numbers (SSTB Quartet, Ariette and SSB Terzet) for *Sophie* (D 982, 1821?) and sketches for two numbers (and Introduction and TT Duet) for Ignaz von Mosel's *Rüdiger* (D 791) from *c.* May 1823, completed and premiered by Johann Herbeck on 5 January 1868.
12. Goethe, *Aesthetische Schriften 1806–1815, Proserpina*, FA I, 19, 714.
13. See Goethe's essay on the production of his own work, 'Proserpina, Melodram von Goethe, Musik von Eberwein', first printed in *Morgenblatt für gebildete Stände* no.136, Tübingen, 8.6.1815, 41–54.
14. Chapter 16, 375–379.
15. Goethe to Philipp Christoph Kayser, 23 January 1786, FA II, 2, 622.
16. Elmar Bötcher, *Goethes Singspiele 'Erwin und Elmire' und 'Claudine von Villa Bella' und die Oper Buffa* (Marburg: Elwert, 1912).
17. Goethe to Philipp Friedrich Seidl, 14 March 1788, *Johann Wolfgang Goethe, Italien – Im Schatten der Revolution. Briefe, Tagebücher und Gespräche von 3.9.1786–12.6.1794* (Frankfurt: Deutscher Klassiker Verlag, 1991), FA II, 3, 393.
18. See for example Klinger's *Die Zwillinge*, Leisewitz's *Julius von Tarent* both of which were published in 1776, the same year as Goethe's *Ur-Claudine*, and Schiller's *Die Räuber* of 1781. Scholarly literature on the topic is reviewed by Stefanie Wenzel, *Das Motif der feindlichen Brüder im Drama des Sturm und Drang, Marburger Germanistische Studien* 14 (Frankfurt am Main: Peter Lang, 1993). Wenzel does not mention *Claudine* but on this see Michael Mann, 'Die feindlichen Brüder', Germanisch-romanische Monatschrift 49 (1968), 225–47 and Alain Préaux, 'Le motif des frères ennemis', *Revue de littérature comparée* 53 (1979), 470–89. See also Margaret Stoljar, 'The *Sturm und Drang* in Music' in David Hill (ed.), *Literature of the Sturm und Drang*, Camden House History of German Literature 6 (Rochester, New York and Woodbridge: Camden House, 2003), 289–308.
19. The extensive changes Goethe made in character, song and scene are analysed by Schubert's Goethe Singspiel ed. Lorraine Byrne Bodley and Dan Farrelly (Dublin), 161–192, and Christine Martin and Dieter Martin in their foreword to *Claudine von Villa Bella*, NSA II/14 (Kassel: Bärenreiter Verlag, 2011), ix–xxii, especially xiii–xv.
20. This motif of rival brothers in love takes its cue from the story of jealous sons of Duke Cosimo di Medici in J.-A. de Thou, *Historiae sui temporis*, 1604ff, book 32. The text is available in German translation in Heinz Nicolai (ed.), *Sturm und Drang, Dichtungen und theoretische Texte* (Munich: Winkler, 1971), 2, 1917.
21. See, for example, Eberhard von Zezschwitz, *Komödienperspektiven in Goethes Faust I* (Frankfurt am Main: Peter Lang, 1985), 71. Zezschwitz's book contains one of the fullest and most interesting discussions of *Claudine*. See also Nicholas Boyle, *Goethe. The Poet and the Age* I (Oxford University Press, 1990), 214, 494, 522 and 601.
22. The three German-language monographs on Goethe's operas, all written in the last twenty years, are the product of German literary criticism: Benedikt Holtbernd, *Die dramaturgischen Funktionen der Musik in den Schauspielen Goethes*. 'Alles aufs Bedürfnis der lyrischen

Bühne gerechnet' (Frankfurt: Lang, 1992); Thomas Frantzke, *Goethes Schauspiele mit Gesang 1773–1782* (Frankfurt: Lang, 1988) and Tina Hartmann, *Goethes Musiktheater. Singspiele, Opern, Festspiele,* 'Faust' Hermaea Germanistische Forschungen Neue Folge (Tübingen: Max Niemeyer Verlag, 2004).
23. Kreissle, 70.
24. Otto Biba, 'Schubert's Position in Viennese Musical Life', *NCM* 3/2 (1979), 106–13, here 112. See also Otto Biba, 'Public and Semi-Public Concerts: Outlines of a Typical 'Biedermeier' Phenomenon in Viennese Music History' in *The Other Vienna. The Culture of Biedermeier Austria,* ed. Robert Pichl and Clifford A. Bernd in collaboration with Margarete Wagner (Vienna [publisher name:], 2002), 257–70. Schubert's friends were also familiar with the overture, see Dok, 72–73.
25. For a brief performance history, both in Schubert's day and posthumously, see Bodley, 'Revisiting *Claudine*' in *Goethe and Schubert: Across the Divide,* 161–93. The aforementioned North-South performance in Dublin of *Claudine von Villa Bella* in 2003 is outlined in Byrne Bodley, 'Goethe and Schubert: *Claudine von Villa Bella* - Conflict and Reconciliation', 126–33.
26. Lorraine Byrne Bodley, *Claudine von Villa Bella. Goethe's Singspiel set by Franz Schubert,* Piano Reduction with German Text and English Translation (Dublin: Carysfort Press, 2002), 80–84.
27. Edmund Goehring, *Three Modes of Perception in Mozart: The Philosophical, Pastoral, and Comic* (Cambridge University Press, 2004).
28. Dieter Borchmeyer, *Johann Wolfgang Goethe, Dramen 1776–1790* (Frankfurt: Deutscher Klassiker Verlag, 1988), I, 5, 718.
29. Goethe thanked Reichardt for at least keeping the dialogue in verse form on 29 June 1789, WA IV, 9, 136. To Polzelli on 24 May 1814, he expresses the same preference for the dialogue to be set as recitative, WA IV, 32, 288.
30. 'The intention is to have Faust recite his lines with a strange musical accompaniment. The approach and apparition of the Spirit is treated melodramatically', cited in Rose Unterberger (ed.), *Johann Wolfgang Goethe. Napoleonische Zeit, Briefe, Tagebücher und Gespräche 10.5.1805–6.6.1816.* II: Von 1812 bis zu Christianes Tod, Frankfurter Ausgabe II/7, 433. Eberwein too speaks in this vein: 'Strolling up and down with Goethe on the broad garden paths I reported to him that I had, indeed, finished the Easter songs but that the composition's melodramatic sections were in no way satisfactory. The text did not seem to me suitable for introducing the music effectively, for developing it and concluding it. Goethe then asked, "Is the moment where Faust opens the Book of Nostradamus not the right one for melodrama?", Carl Eberwein, 'Die Musik zum Goetheschen Faust' in Wilhelm Bode/Carl Eberwein, *Goethes Schauspieler und Musiker* (Berlin: Mittler, 1912), 99–100.
31. The presence given to the protagonist through the soloist and his stagecraft, stage design and costume have been performed by Ian Bostridge (tenor) and Julius Drake (piano), staged by David Alden, produced by Peter West and Gordon Baskerville in a Channel 4 documentary (1997), and in a different way the many filmic realizations with natural tableaux. For recent interpretations see *Schubert: Winterreise,* performed by Matthias Goerne and Markus Hinterhäuser (piano), visualized by the director, set designer and theatre artist, William Kentridge, recorded live at the Festival d'Aix-en-Provence, 8 and 14 July 2015, video director Christian Leblé; *Schubert: Die Winterreise* realized by Jorma Hynninen and Ralf Gothoni. For a recent contemporary response see Franz Zender, Schubert's *Winterreise,* performed at the Zurich Opera House by Mauro Peter (tenor), Ballett Zürich, Philharmonia Zürich, cond. Benjamin Schneider [Accentus Music ACC20545].

CHAPTER NINE: THE PROMISE OF FREEDOM (1816–1818)

1. All of the June diary entries are from *Dok,* 42–45.
2. See Chapter 3, 58.

3. *Dok*, 49–50.
4. *Dok*, 38.
5. *Dok*, 39.
6. *Dok*, 40.
7. Eduard Hanslick, *Aus dem Concertsaal. Kritiken und Schilderungen aus den letzten 20 Jahren des Wiener Musiklebens* (Vienna: Wilhelm Braumüller, 1870), 206.
8. See, for example, discussion of symphonies nos 5 and 6, Chapter 9, 217–232; Schubert's more conservative E flat major Mass after a performance of his most adventurous A flat major Mass was denied a performance in the *Hofkapelle*, Chapter 21, 466–471 and Chapter 14, 323–321, or his refusal to accept an offer for one of his male-voice settings to be performed at the Gesellschaft der Musikfreunde after the negative response to 'Gesang der Geister über den Wassern'.
9. For further reading see Horst Weber, 'Schuberts IV. Symphonie und ihre satztechnischen Vorbilder bei Mozart', *Musica* 32 (1978), 147–51.
10. Walther Dürr, Schubertiade Hohenems, 28 April to 5 May 2018, programme notes, 81–82.
11. Mark Evan Bonds, *Music as Thought: Listening to the Symphony in the Age of Beethoven* (Princeton University Press, 2006), 52.
12. *Erinn*, 392.
13. Johann Wolfgang Goethe, *Wilhelm Meisters Wanderjahre*, Book Two, Chapter Eight, *Pädagogische Provinz*, *Sämtliche Werke Münchner Ausgabe*, vol. 17 (MA: Carl Hanser Verlag, 1991).
14. For development of this theme more broadly, see Julian Horton, 'Tonal Strategies in the Nineteenth-Century Symphony' in *The Cambridge Companion to the Symphony*, (Cambridge University Press, 2013), 232–67.
15. Brian Newbould, *Schubert and the Symphony*, 123.
16. Arnold Feil, *Studien zu Schuberts Rhythmik* (Munich: Fink, 1966), 47–62; see also Feil, 'Zur Satztechnik in Schuberts VI. Sinfonie. Interpretation und Analyse', *Schubert-Studien*, 69ff.
17. 26 February 1818, 21 March, 6 June and 17 October 1818, *FSD* 7–12.
18. Bauernfeld 'Über Franz Schubert', *Wiener Zeitschrift für Kunst*, 9–13 June 1829, *Erinn*, 40–43; *FSD*, 454–57. Otto Biba, 'Schubert und die Gesellschaft der Musikfreunde' in *Schubert Kongress Wien* 1978 ed. Otto Brusatti (Graz: Akademische Druck- und Verlagsanstalt, 1979), 31–32.
19. I am inspired to use this term, also the notion of intra-movement strategies, through conversations with Julian Horton. For related published work see, 'Tonal Strategies in the Nineteenth-Century Symphony', in *The Cambridge Companion to the Symphony*, 232–67, here 235.
20. The work has been recorded many times, for example John Del Carlo, Teresa Ringholz, Richard Croft, Delores Ziegler, Jake Gardner, Claus Viller, Agnes Meth, Stuttgart Radio Symphony Orchestra conducted by Arnold Östmann (Stuttgart: Arthaus Musik, 31 July 2000). It has also been been recorded by Chiara Chialli, Fernando Luis Ciuffo, Filippo Bettoschi, Romano Franceschetto et al., with the Madrigalists of Milan and Guido Cantelli Orchestra Milan conducted by Alberto Veronesi (Essex: Chandos, 17 March 1998). The other recording is by József Gregor, Mária Zempléni, Dénes Gulyás, Istvan Gáti, Eva Pánczél et al., Salieri Chamber Orchestra and Chamber Chorus, conducted by Tamás Pál (Hungaroton, 27 September 2003).
21. For an entirely different reading see Brian Newbould, who traces the roots of this introduction in Beethoven's *Prometheus* Overture, *Schubert and the Symphony*, 127.
22. Peter Gülke, *Franz Schubert. Drei Sinfonie-Fragmente D 615, D 708A, D 936A. Partitur und Kommentar* (Leipzig: Peters, 1982), also 'Neue Beiträge zur Kenntnis des Sinfonikers Schubert. Die Fragmente D 615, D 708A und D 936A', *Musik-Konzepte*, ed. Heinz-Klaus Metzger (Munich [publisher name:], 1979), 187–220.
23. Robin George Collingwood, *Speculum Mentis* (Oxford: Clarendon Press, 1924).

CHAPTER TEN: *ARS AMICITIA:* ART OF FRIENDSHIP

1. David Gramit, *Cultivating Music: The Aspirations, Interests, and Musical Limits of German Musical Cuture, 1770–1848* (Berkeley and Los Angeles: University of California Press, 2002); cf. Gramit, 'The Intellectual and Aesthetic Tenets of Franz Schubert's Circle: Their Development and their Influence on his Music' (Duke University: PhD dissertation, 1987), and Gramit; ' "The passion for friendship": Music, Cultivation, and Identity in Schubert's Circle', *Cambridge Companion to Schubert*, 56–71; Michael Kohlhäufl, *Poetisches Vaterland. Dichtung und politisches Denken im Freundeskreis Franz Schuberts* (Kassel: Bärenreiter, 1999); Rita Steblin, *Die Unsinnsgesellschaft: Franz Schubert, Leopold Kupelwieser und ihr Freundeskreis* (Vienna: Böhlau, 1998); John Gingerich, ' "Those of us who found our life in art": The Second-Generation Romanticism in the Schubert-Schober Circle, 1820–1825' in *Franz Schubert and His World*, ed. Christopher H. Gibbs and Morten Solvik (Princeton University Press, 2014), 67–114.
2. Eckardt Meyer-Krentler, *Der Bürger als Freund. Ein solzialethisches Programm und seine Kritiker in der neueren deutschen Erzählliteratur* (Munich: Fink, 1984); Wolfram Mauser and Barbara Becker-Cantarino (eds), *Frauenfreundschaft–Männerfreundschaft. Literarische Diskurse im 18. Jahrhundert* (Tübingen: Niemeyer, 1991); Georg Simmel, 'Soziologie der Gesellschaft' in *Verhandlungen des Ersten Deutschen Soziologentages* (Tübingen: J. C. B. Mohr, 1911); Albert Salomon, *Die Freundschaftskult des 18. Jahrhunderts in Deutschland: Versuch zur Soziologie einer Lebensform* (Heidelberg: PhD dissertation 1922).
3. For literature on the topic see *Ars et Amicitia: Beiträge zum Thema Freundschaft in Geschichte, Kunst und Literatur. Festschrift für Martin Bircher zum 60. Geburtstag*, ed. Ferdinand van Ingen and Christian Juranek (Amsterdam: Rodopi, 1998); Wolfgang Adam, *Freundschaft und Geselligkeit im 18. Jahrhundert*, on Goethezeitportal.de, https://www.yumpu.com/de/document/view/21474108/freundschaft-und-geselligkeit-im-18-jahrhundert-das- (accesssed 4 April 2019); Albert Salomon's 'Der Freundschaftskult des 18. Jahrhunderts in Deutschland: Versuch zur Soziologie einer Lebensform', ed. Richard Grathoff, *Zeitschrift für Soziologie* 8 (1979), 279–308; *Frauenfreundschaft – Männerfreundschaft: Literarische Diskurse im 18. Jahrhundert*, ed. Mauser and Becker-Cantarino. I am very grateful to Laura Tunbridge for directing me to the following literature: Ursula Nötzing-Linden, *Freundschaft. Zur Thematisierung einer vernachlässigten soziologischen Kategorie* (Opladen: Westdeutscher Verlag, 1994); Emanuel Peter, *Geselligkeiten. Literatur, Gruppenbildung und kultureller Wandel im 18. Jahrhundert* (Tübingen: Niemeyer, 1999); Tobias Heinrich, 'Communicative Identity in the Eighteenth Century', *Gender & History* 13/2 (2002), 224–48; and Johann Wilhelm, 'Ludwig Gleim's Epistolary Network and the Cult of Friendship', *European Journal of Life Writing* 3 (2014), 100–22.
4. Samuel Gotthold Lange and Georg Friedrich Meier (eds), *Der Gesellige: eine moralische Wochenschrift*, newly edited by Wolfgang Martens (Hildesheim: G. Olms, 1987).
5. *Das Jahrhundert der Freundschaft: Johann Wilhelm Ludwig Gleim und seine Zeitgenossen*, ed. Ute Pott (Göttingen: Wallstein, 2004). See also Frauenfreundschaft – M.nnerfreundschaft: Literarische Diskurse im 18. Jahrhundert, ed. Mauser and Becker-Cantarino.
6. Christian Fürchtegott Gellert, *Moralische Vorlesung* (Biel: Heilmann Verlag, 1771).
7. Johann Joachim Winckelmann, *Gedanken über die Nachahmung der griechischen Werke in der Malerei und Bildhauerkunst* (Dresden: Walther, 1756).
8. WA 46: 27–28.
9. *Beyträge zur Bildung für Jünglinge*, 2 vols, ed. Anton Spaun and Johann Mayrhofer (Vienna: Härter, 1816 and 1817); for discussion of the journal see Walther Dürr, 'Der Linzer Schubert-Kreis und seine Beiträge zur Bildung für Jünglinge', *Historisches Jahrbuch der Stadt Linz* (1985), 51–59.
10. Peter Brown, 'The Saint as Exemplar in Late Antiquity', *Representations* 1 (1983), 1.
11. There is a profusion of literature on this topic. See, for example, Martin Kagel, 'Brothers or Others: Male Friendship in Eighteenth-Century Germany', *Colloquia Germanica* 40, 3/4

(2007), 213–35; Daniel Wilson, 'But Is It Gay? Kissing, Friendship and Pre-Homosexual Discourses in the Eighteenth Century', *Modern Language Review* 103 (2008), 767–83.
12. WB Inv. No. 36525.
13. Josef Kenner, 21 April 1858, *Erinn,* 96; Prologue, 2.
14. *Dok,* 574.
15. For further discussion, see Karen V. Hansen, ' "Our eyes should behold each other": Masculinity and Intimate Friendship In Antebellum New England' in *Men's Friendships,* ed. Peter M. Nardi (California: SAGE Series on Men and Masculinity, 1992) 35–58, here 54.
16. Jonathan Ned Katz, *Gay American Almanac: A New Documentary* (New York: Harper Colophon, 1983), 450.
17. See, for example, Edward Carpenter, *Ioläus: An Anthology of Friendship* (London: Swan Sonnenschein, 1902, Manchester: self-publication by the author, 1902, and Boston, MA: Charles Goodspeed, 1902).
18. Henry Clay Trumbull, *Friendship the Master-Passion or The Nature and History of Friendship, and its Place as a Force in the World* (Philadelphia, PA: J. D. Wattles, 1892).
19. Elisar von Kupffer, *Lieblingminne und Freundesliebe in der Weltliteratur* (Adolf Brand 1900, rpt. Max Spohr, 1903). *Lieblingminne* translates as 'preferred form of love' or the Greek form of pederastic relationships; von Kupffer's preface argues for homosexuality that is not just tolerated by society but is an integral part of its social fabric.
20. *Dok,* 73.
21. *Dok,* 479.
22. *Dok,* 67.
23. *Dok,* 298–300.
24. *Dok,* 250.
25. Gramit, 'The Intellectual and Aesthetic Tenets of Franz Schubert's Circle', and Illija Dürhammer, 'Zu Schuberts Literaturästhetik. Entwickelt anhand seiner zu Lebzeiten veröffentlichten Vokalwerke', *Brille* 14 (1995), 5–99.
26. *Von der innigsten Vereinigung der Liebe mit der Achtung in der Freundschaft* (sections 46 and 47 of *Metaphysische Anfangsgründe der Sitten* (The Doctrine of Virtue, 1797), 134.
27. Anton von Ottenwalt's letter to Schober, 17 March 1814, WB, MS 36511.
28. Kreissle, 34.
29. *Kalliasbriefe, NA* 26, 191; *Erinn,* 151.
30. Johann Gottfried Herder's *Kalligone* (1800) awards music a religious veneration and reverence (Andacht) and Wilhelm Friedrich Wackenroder goes as far as to claim that 'music is certainly the ultimate mystery of faith, the mystique, the fully revealed religion', *Werke und Briefe* (Heidelberg: Lambert Schneider, 1967), 251.
31. See Chapter 15, 341–347.
32. *NA* 20: 412.
33. *NA* 20: 412.
34. *NA* 20, 424.
35. See Chapter 8, Chapter 21, 476–481.
36. See Chapter 20, 439.
37. *Dok,* 290.
38. *Erinn,* 199.
39. For a richly informative view of Viennese musical life in Schubert's time, see Leopold von Sonnleithner, 'Musikalische Skizzen aus Alt-Wien' in: *Recensionen und Mittheilungen über Theater und Musik* 7–9 (1861–63), 7: 737–47, 753–78, 8: 4–7, 177–80, 369–75, 9: 305–07, 322–25.
40. *Erinn,* 136.
41. *Erinn,* 206, 157–58.
42. *Dok,* 537–38.
43. *Erinn,* 389.
44. *Erinn,* 331.
45. This idea is first raised in Montaigne, 'De l'amitié', from his *Essais,* I XXVIII (1580).

CHAPTER ELEVEN: *ARS AMICITIAE*: ART BORN OF FRIENDSHIP

1. Among the many valuable contacts Schubert made through Spaun were the poet, Matthäus von Collin (1779–1824); Karl von Enderes (1787–1861); the pianist and duet partner, Josef von Gahy (1793–1864); Josef Kenner (1794–1868); Theodor Körner (1791–1813); Leopold Kupelwieser (1796–1862); Johann Baptist Mayrhofer (1787–1836); Franz von Schober (1796–1882); Moritz von Schwind (1804–1871); and Josef Wilhelm Witteczek (1787–1859).
2. *Dok*, 149.
3. *SA* 23: 178.
4. *Erinn*, 215.
5. *Erinn*, 235.
6. *Dok*, 79.
7. *Dok*, 479.
8. Mayrhofer, *Gedichte* (1824), 43–44.
9. Deutsch concludes that the poem was written for Schober because it was in his bequest after his death, but all of Schubert's possessions, personal and artistic, remained with Schober. After Schubert's death, he swiftly handed over most of Schubert's manuscripts and papers to Ferdinand unsolicited. Schubert set the second poem from this trilogy, 'Fels aufs Felsen hin gewälzet', which contains textual variants from the 1821 and 1824 versions.
10. For literature on Mayrhofer see: Fritz List, *Johann Mayrhofer, ein Freund und Textdichter Franz Schuberts* (Munich: unpublished dissertation, 1921, later published in Nittenau: Kangler 1991); David Gramit, 'Schubert and the Biedermeier: The Aesthetics of Joh. Mayrhofer's "Heliopolis"', *M&L* 74/3 (1993), 355–82; Susan Youens, *Schubert's Poets and the Making of Lieder* (Cambridge University Press, 1996), 151–227; Ilja Dürhammer, '"Was ich gefühlt, hast Du gesungen", Neue Dokumente zu Johann Mayrhofers Leben und Schaffen', *Mitteilungen der Österreichischen Gesellschaft für Musikwissenschaft* 31 (1997), 13–45; Ilja Dürhammer, *Schuberts lit. Heimat, Dichtung und Literatur-Rezeption der Schubert-Freunde* (Wein: Böhlau Wien, 1999); Michael Kohlhäufl, *Poetisches Vaterland, Dichtung und politisches Denken im Freundeskreis Franz Schuberts* (Kassel: Bärenreiter, 1999); Michael Lorenz, 'Dokumente zur Biographie Johann Mayrhofers', *Brille* 25 (2000), 21–50, and 'Johann Mayrhofer's real date of birth', 7 September 2012, http://michaelorenz.blogspot.com/2012/09/johann-mayrhofers-real-date-of-birth.html (accessed 3 April 2019).
11. For the posthumous diagnosis of Mayrhofer's case by the twentieth-century psychiatrist, Wilhelm Gail, see Moritz Bauer, 'Johann Mayrhofer' in *Zeitschrift für Musikwissenschaft* 5 (October 1922–September 1923), ed. Alfred Einstein (Leipzig: Breitkopf & Härtel, 1923), 83–84; an extract is cited by Youens, *Schubert's Poets*, 152.
12. Ernst Freiherr von Feuchtersleben, 'Errinnerungen an Johann Mayrhofer' in *Lebensbilder aus Österreich*, ed. Andreas Schumachers (Vienna: Tauer & Sohn, 1843).
13. Youens, *Schubert's Poets*, 159.
14. *Beiträge zur Bildung für Jünglinge* 2 (Vienna: 1817) in Walther Dürr, 'Der Linzer Schubert-Kreis und seine Beiträge für Jünglinge' in *Historisches Jahrbuch der Stadt Linz 1985*, 51–59.
15. *SA* 23: 79.
16. *Dok*, 49; for an example of Mayrhofer's views on marriage see *Neue Sammlung* (1843), 247.
17. *Erinn*, 121.
18. *Mahlerisches Taschenbuch für Freunde interessanter Gegenden, Natur- und Kunst-Merkwürdigkeiten der Österreichischen Monarchie* (Vienna, 1818).
19. Mayrhofer, *Neue Sammlung* (1843), 227. See also 'Die Hyacinthenflor', Mayrhofer, *Gedichte* (1824), 128.
20. Mayrhofer, *Neue Sammlung* (1843), 107–8.
21. Mayrhofer, 'Tillisberg', *Gedichte* (1843), 53.
22. Mayrhofer, 'An Eccho', *Gedichte* (1843), 63.

23. Mayrhofer, *Neue Sammlung* (1843), 99; Youens, *Schubert's Poets*, 151–227.
24. *Erinn*, 19.
25. Youens, *Schubert's Poets*, 154.
26. Adam Haller (1858) in Rabenlechner, 'Nachwort', 233, cited by Youens, *Schubert's Poets*, 158.
27. The manuscript which remained in Schober's possession for the rest of his life is now in the WB, MS 34965. For a discussion of this cycle see *Franz Schubert: die Texte seiner einstimmig komponierten Lieder und ihre Dichter*, ed. Maximilian Schochow and Lily Schochow (Hildesheim and New York: Georg Olms, 1974), and David Gramit, 'Schubert and the Biedermeier: The Aesthetics of Johann Mayrhofer's "Heliopolis"', *M&L* 74/3 (1993), 355–82.
28. Mayrhofer, *Sammlung* (Vienna: Ignaz Klang, 1843), 11.
29. For discussion of Mayrhofer's final settings see Blake Howe's 'The Allure of Dissolution: Bodies, Forces and Cyclicity in Schubert's Final Mayrhofer Settings', *Journal of the American Musicological Society* 62/2 (2009), 271–322. See also David T. Bretherton, 'The Shadow of Midnight in Schubert's "Gondelfahrer" Settings', *M&L* 92/1 (2011), 1–42.
30. For a comparison of Mayrhofer's published texts with those of Schubert's songs, see Schochow and Schochow, *Franz Schubert: die Texte*, I, 318–58.
31. *Dok*, 336.
32. Eduard Bauernfeld, 'Ein Wiener Censor' in *Gesammelte Schriften* xi Reime und Rhythmen (Vienna: Wilhelm Braumüller, 1873).
33. Mayrhofer, *Neue Sammlung* (1843), 54
34. Goethe, 'Harzreise im Winter', ll. 35–42.
35. Mayrhofer, *Neue Sammlung* (1843), 296.
36. Franz Grillparzer, 'Mayrhofers Texte sind immer wie Text zu einer Melodie', *Sämtliche Werke* 3 (Munich: Hanser Verlag, 1960–1965), 843.
37. 'Still-Leben', Mayrhofer, *Neue Sammlung*, 101.
38. Youens, *Schubert's Poets*, 164.
39. The fiercest denunciation of Schober as a veritable Mephisto was pronounced by Josef Kenner, whose condemnation is all the more remarkable for having been made not in the heat of the moment but several decades later, 22 May 1858, *Erinn*, 101–02.
40. Schober, *Paligensien aus den heiligen Büchern des alten Bundes* (1826), the poems of which were included in his *Gedichte* (Leipzig: J. J. Weber, 1865).
41. *Dok*, 351.
42. *Dok*, 160–61.
43. Ernst Schulze, Die bezauberte Rose (Leipzig: Brokhaus 1818), I, 90. Schober did not include 'An die Musik' in his collected poems (1865); for further discussion on this see Johnson, 'An die Musik', Track 11 on CDJ33021; Track 12 on CDS44201/40 CD18.
44. *Erinn*, 239.
45. Thekla von Schober (née von Gumpert, 1810–1897), *Unter fünf Königen und drei Kaisern* (Glogau, 1891), p. 123. If Schober did in fact respond to Schubert's request for escape, he might have brought more volumes from the same edition with him as the following works were published in 1828: *Lionel Lincoln* (vols 25–30), *The Steppe* (vols 31–36) and *The Red Rover* (vols 37–42).
46. For the most recent biography of Vogl see Andreas Liess, *Johann Michael Vogl* (Graz, Cologne: Hermann Böhlaus Nachf., 1954).
47. *Dok*, 154.
48. *Dok*, 160.
49. David Gramit, ' "The passion for friendship": Music, Cultivation, and Identity in Schubert's Circle', 57–58.
50. *Dok*, 227; Fritz von Hartmann's diary, *Dok*, 413 and 461.
51. *Erinn*, 130.

CHAPTER TWELVE: ART BORN OF IMPROVISATION

1. For further reading on improvisation in the early decades of the nineteenth century see Dana Gooley, 'Saving Improvisation: Hummel and the Free Fantasia in the Early Nineteenth Century' in Benjamin Piekut and George E. Lewis (eds), *The Oxford Handbook of Critical Improvisation Studies* 2 (Oxford University Press, 2016); Angela Esterhammer, *Romanticism and Improvisation, 1750–1850* (Cambridge University Press, 2008); Robert Wangermée, 'L'improvisation pianistique au début du XIXe siècle', in *Miscellanea Musicologica: Floris van der Mueren* (Ghent: L. van Melle, 1950), 227–53; John Rink, 'Chopin and Improvisation' in *Chopin and his World*, ed. Jonathan D. Bellman and Halina Goldberg (Princeton University Press, 2018), 249–70.
2. Carl Dahlhaus, *Nineteenth-Century Music*, trans. J. Bradford Robinson (Berkeley and Los Angeles: University of California Press, 1989), 9.
3. Ferdinand Schubert, *Aus Franz Schuberts Leben, Neue Zeitschrift für Musik* 10 (1839), 139.
4. *Erinn*, 149.
5. Charlotte Moscheles, *Recent Music and Musicians as Described in the Diaries and Correspondence of Ignaz Moscheles* (New York: [s.n.], 1879), 9–10.
6. See, for example, André Ernest Modeste Grétry, *Méthode simple pour apprendre à préluder* (Paris: l'Imprimerie de la République, 1802), and Carl Czerny, *A Systematic Introduction to Improvisation on the Pianoforte* (1829), ed. and trans. Alice L. Mitchell (New York and London: Longman, 1983).
7. *Erinn*, 131.
8. *Erinn*, 255–56.
9. *Erinn*, 303.
10. *Erinn*, 316–17; *Dok*, 401.
11. *Erinn*, 324.
12. *Erinn*, 46–47.
13. *Erinn*, 207.
14. *Erinn*, 379–80.
15. Johann Mattheson, *Johann Mattheson's Der vollkommene Capellmeister*, trans. Ernest Charles Harriss (Ann Arbour, MI: UMI Research Press, 1981), 298.
16. For recent research on this topic see Scott Messing, *Self-Quotation in Schubert: 'Ave Maria', the Second Piano Trio and Other Works* (Woodbridge: Boydell and Brewer, University of Rochester Press, 2020).
17. *Erinn*, 100.
18. *Erinn*, 211–12.
19. *Erinn*, 184. Carl Czerny's variations were published in *The Harmonicon* 10 (London, 1823), 143–146, and are reproduced by Walburga Litschauer in *NSA* VII/Tänze II, 129; *FSD* I, 164–65.
20. *Erinn*, 318.
21. For a full list of published dances in Schubert's lifetime see Walburga Litschauer and Walter Deutsch, *Schubert und das Tanzvergnügen* (Vienna: Holzhausen, 1997), 155; Schwind's illustration for the 1824 cover page is on page 2.
22. *Erinn*, 130.
23. *Erinn*, 32, 141, 156, 211–12.
24. Walburga Litschauer, 'Franz Schuberts Tänze: Zwischen Improvisation und Werk', *Musiktheorie* 10/1 (1995), 3–9.
25. Mark Knowles, *The Wicked Waltz and Other Scandalous Dances* (North Carolina and London: McFarland and Co, 2009).
26. Other favourites include: D 366, nos 1, 4, 6, 9 10 and 13; D 783, nos 2 and 6, Litschauer and Deutsch, *Schubert und das Tanzvergnügen*, 125–32.
27. *Dok*, 343.
28. In other cycles Schubert breaks the tonal chains, for example in his 8 Écossaises in D major (D 529), no. 3 is in G major. Another pattern is found in his Deutsche D 820 where the first three are in A flat, the second three in B major.

29. All of Schubert's waltz sets are tonally closed: see D 779, op. 50; D 734, op. 67; D 924, op. 91; D 969, op. 77. Further examples of cycles include D 420 and D 421.
30. Litschauer and Deutsch, *Schubert und das Tanzvergnügen*, 56.
31. Ibid, 125–32.
32. Schubert's violin Ländler, which were written for family as well as commercial gain, were also arranged in chains, for example his 4 komische Ländler (D 354) for two violins or three Ländler chains for violin: 9 Ländler in D (D 370) and 8 Ländler in F sharp minor (D 355). His 11 Ländler in B flat for solo violin (D 374) served as a model for his 8 Ländler in B flat for piano (D 378).
33. Walburga Litschauer, 'Neue Dokumente zu Schubert in Oberösterreich' in Bruckner-Symposion, 'Musikstadt Linz – Musikland Oberösterreich' Bericht (Linz, 1993), 222.
34. Hartmann Diaries, fol. 67v; *Dok*, 407.
35. *FSD* I, 238. Josef von Spaun, Familien-Journal der Familie Spaun, Wien, Privatbesitz, 259f.
36. WB, IN 39 725, fol.70r.
37. *Erinn*, 262.
38. WB, IN 39 725, fol. 67v–68r.
39. Josef-Horst Lederer, 'An original Manuscripten, die dann im Stich erschienen sind, besitze ich . . .' – Anselm Hüttenbrenners "andere" Schubert-Autographe', *Musicologica Austriaca* 13 (1994), 55.
40. *NSA* KB IV/1, 103.
41. *Erinn*, 267.
42. Silesian folk songs with which Schubert was familiar include: 'Aničko děvečko, poviz mi věrně'; 'Usnula děvečka pod lelujem'; 'Zdalo se mi zdalo'; 'Jezerečko vyschlo'; 'Oj, vim ti ja v poli lisku'; 'Pověz mi, děvucho, ežli budeš moja'; 'Holubičko bila'; 'Idě děvucha od Bohumina'; 'Dy sem jel do Prahy'; 'Mladošť, mila mladošť'. Walburga Litschauer and Walter Deutsch trace Schubert's German folk-music inheritance in depth in *Schubert und das Tanzvergnügen*, 133–48, here 136–37.
43. *Dok*, 515. See Joe Davies, *Interpreting the Expressive Worlds of Schubert's Late Instrumental Works* (University of Oxford: PhD dissertation, 2018), Epilogue, 185, and ch. 2, 66–84.
44. For discussion of this work see Lorraine Byrne Bodley, 'Between Society and Solitude: Schubert's Improvisations' in *Schubert's Piano*, ed. Matthew Gardner and Christine Martin (Cambridge University Press, 2023, forthcoming). For a contrary reading, see David Brodbeck, 'Dance Music as High Art: Schubert's Twelve Ländler, op. 171 (D790)', in Walter Frisch (ed.), *Schubert: Critical and Analytical Studies* (Lincoln, NE, and London: University of Nebraska Press, 1986), 31–47, here 44.
45. Raymond MacDonald, Gunter Kreutz and Laura Mitchell, 'What is Music, Health, and Wellbeing and why is it Important?' in Raymond MacDonald, Gunter Kreutz and Laura Mitchell (eds), *Music, Health and Wellbeing* (Oxford University Press, 2012), 3–12; Tony Wigram, 'Evidence and Effectiveness in Music Therapy', *British Journal of Music Therapy* 20/2 (2007), 93–95; Dorothy Miell, Raymond MacDonald and David J. Hargreaves (eds), *Musical Communication* (Oxford University Press, 2005).

CHAPTER THIRTEEN: IN THE DOLDRUMS (1817–1818)

1. *FSD*, 3–6.
2. Reed, *Schubert. The Final Years*, 67.
3. See Schubert's letter to Ferdinand, 16–18 July 1824, *Dok*, 250.
4. See Franz Theodor's letter to Karl in July 1818 where he rejoices in the affectionate tone of Schubert's letter and his son's well-being, *Dok*, 65; the postscript in Ferdinand's letter where he conveys his request not to send money home without keeping a receipt, *Dok* 73, or the way he parents and strengthens and expresses his love for him in his 1824 letters to Zseliz, *Dok*, 245–46, 253–54.
5. *Erinn*, 19.
6. See Chapter 1, 32.

7. *Register of Births and Deaths in the Family of the Schoolmaster, Franz Schubert*, *Dok*, 4–7, 19, 24, 33, 50, 53, 203, 548.
8. *Dok*, 65.
9. *Dok*, 71.
10. *Dok*, 62–63.
11. Walter Salmen, 'Social Obligations of the Emancipated Musician in the 19th Century' in *The Social Status of the Professional Musician from the Middle Ages to the 19th Century*, ed. Walter Salmen (New York: Pendragon, 1983), 270.
12. The paintings are illustrated and discussed by Krisztina Ilko, *Stredoveké nástenné maľby Kostola svätého Jakuba staršieho v Železovciach* (in Slovak, with English summary entitled 'The Medieval Wall Paintings of the Church of St James in Železovce' (Rožňava: Georgius Bubek, 2018), 153.
13. *Dok*, 67.
14. *Dok*, 66.
15. *Dok*, 71.
16. *Dok*, 66.
17. Johnson, 478–88.
18. For an outstanding chapter on this song see Susan Youens, 'The "Problem" of Solitude and Critique in Song: Schubert's Loneliness', *Schubert's Late Music: History, Theory, Style*, ed. Lorraine Byrne Bodley and Julian Horton (Cambridge University Press, 2016), 309–30.
19. *Dok*, 74.
20. *Dok*, 74.

CHAPTER FOURTEEN: SCHUBERT'S 'DOUBLE NATURE' (1819–1822)

1. Schubert, 'Mein Traum', in *Dok*, 227.
2. Goethe, 'Klärchens Lied', *Egmont*, lines 25–34, *MA* 3.1, 286.
3. *Erinn*, 53, 268.
4. *Erinn*, 96, 100.
5. Wilhelm von Humboldt, *Ideen zu einem Versuch, die Gränzen der Wirksamkeit des Staats zu bestimmen* (Breslau: Trewendt, 1851).
6. Otto Biba, 'Franz Schubert und die Gesellschaft der Musikfreunde in Wien', in *Schubert-Kongress Wien 1978: Bericht*, ed. Otto Brusatti (Graz: Akademische Druck- und Verlagsanstalt, 1979), 23–36; 'Franz Schubert in den musikalischen Abendunterhaltungen der Gesellschaft der Musikfreunde', in *Schubert-Studien: Festgabe der Österreichischen Akademie der Wissenschaften zum Schubert-Jahr 1978*, ed. Franz Grasberger and Othmar Wessely (Vienna: Österreichische Akademie der Wissenschaften, 1978), 7–31; and 'Schubert's Position in Viennese Musical Life', *NCM* 3 (1979), 106–13.
7. Alexander Wheelock Thayer, *Life of Beethoven*, trans. Henry Edward Krehbiel, ed. Elliot Forves (Princeton University Press, 1967), 576; Lewis Lockwood, *Beethoven's Symphonies: An Artistic Vision* (New York: W. W. Norton & Co, 2015), 148.
8. The one female part-song to appear in print during Schubert's lifetime was 'Coronach' (SSA with piano, D 836, op. 54, no. 4).
9. Walther Dürr, 'Zwischen Liedertafel und Männergesangverein. Schuberts mehrstimmige Gesänge' in *Logos Musicae. Festschrift für Albert Palm* (Wiesbaden [publisher name:], 1982), 36–54.
10. *Dok*, 116–17.
11. *FSD* I, 63.
12. *Dok*, 117; *FSD* I, 64 and 65. The negative reception contrasts with the reception of his other part-songs. The only other mention of a negative audience response is the review of the performance of 'Geist der Liebe' on 26 May 1822 published by the *AMZ* on 15 June 1822, 'This quartet, *although it seems to have been frequently heard*, failed to rise to the occasion, in spite of a very fine performance.'
13. *Dok*, 182.

14. *Erinn*, 127. Rosenbaum's diary entry for 7 March 1821 also registers the failure of this performance, *Dok*, 117.
15. *Dok*, 120, 375–76. *FSD* I, 66. Half the octet remained the same, four singers were replaced this time by Josef Barth, August Ritter von Gymnich, Johann Karl Umlauff, Georg Krebner, Josef Nejebse, Josef Götz, Josef Preysinger and Hardt.
16. *Erinn*, 432–33.
17. *Dok*, 185; *Erinn*, 396.
18. *Erinn*, 126–27.
19. *Erinn*, 292 and 220.
20. *Erinn*, 128.
21. *Erinn*, 304.

CHAPTER FIFTEEN: SECRETS OF THE SELF

1. I am referring to Goethe's *Wilhelm Meisters Lehrjahre* and in particular its first version, *Wilhelm Meisters Theatralische Sendung*, where the protagonist has false hopes of succeeding in the theatre.
2. In the *Odyssey*, Homer portrayed the Garden of Alcinous as a lost paradise of abundant fertility and beauty.
3. *Dok*, 158–59.
4. Schumann did not have much to say about Schubert's 'dream' when he published it with four letters and two poems) as part of 'Reliquien von Franz Schubert', *Neue Zeitschrift für Musik*, 10/6, 5 February 1839, 44. Since then it has received numerous readings by biographers, psychoanalysts and musicologists. Grove was amongst the first to describe it as an 'autobiographical sketch' (Grove 1883, 336), followed by Walter Dahms, *Schubert* (Berlin, 1912), 137, while Kreissle von Hellborn had more cautiously remarked that the interpretation is to be left to the reader, *The Life of Franz Schubert*, trans. Coleridge (London 1869), 16. See Eduard Hitschmann, 'Franz Schuberts Schmerz und Liebe', *Internationale Zeitschrift für ärztliche Psychoanalyse* 3 (1915), 287–92; Maynard Solomon, 'Franz Schubert's "My Dream"', *American Imago* 38 (1981), 137–54; Walther Dürr, 'Franz Schuberts Wanderjahre. Einführung in das Generalthema', *Jahre der Krise*, 11–21; Till Gerrit Waidelich, 'Zur Überlieferung des Textes "Mein Traum"', 5/2 (2005), 138–61; Gingerich, *Schubert's Beethoven Project*, 13.
5. *Dok*, 159. The statement was allegedly made to the early Schubert biographer Alois Fellner and has been accepted as fact by many biographers beginning with Walter Dahms's *Schubert* (Berlin and Leipzig: Schuster & Loeffler, 1912). It was one of many interpretations that Maurice Brown dismisses, on the grounds that Anton was too young even though familial stories are handed down, 'Schubert's "Dream"', *MMR* 83 (1953), 39–43.
6. *Dok*, 186.
7. Deutsch was the first to recognize this, *Dok*, 159.
8. Schubert's original story is in the private possession of Dr Friedrich Georg Zeileis. Photos of Schwind's copy are held in the Staatsbibl. Preuß. Kulturbes. Otto Erich Deutsch's bequest 143, Schubert-Archiv Tübingen. A copy made by Wilhelmine Witteczek is in GdM, Vienna.
9. Ilija Dürhammer, 'Zu Schuberts Literaturaesthetik', *Brille* 14 (1995), 5–99.
10. For discussion of the tropes see Michael Kohlhäufl, 'Ton und Traum – Schubert und die literarische Frühromantik', *Schubert: Perspektiven* 5/2 (2005), 127–37, here 128.
11. *Noli foras ire, in te ipsum redi: in interiore homine habitat veritas* ('Go not outside, but return within thyself; in the inward man dwelleth the truth'), Augustine, *De vera religione*, XXXIX, 72.
12. Jean Chevalier and Alain Gheerbrant, *Dictionary of Symbols*, trans. John Buchanan-Brown (London: Penguin Classics, 1982), 1,014.
13. Dahms, *Franz Schubert*, 184.
14. See, for example, Walther Dürr, 'Franz Schuberts Wanderjahre. Einführung in das Generalthema', *Jahre der Krise 1818–1823*, 11–21.

15. *Dok*, 49–50, Chapter 9, 213–214.
16. They had four children: Theresia (1821–1894), Johann Baptist (1822–1875), Amalia (9 July 1824–24 December 1886) and Carolina (b. 1828). Amalia Grob inherited the Grob Songbook on her mother's death and on her demise it was passed to the Meangya family.
17. Theodor Körner, cited in Peter Clive, *Schubert and his World* (Oxford University Press, 1997), 113.
18. Hans J. Fröhlich, *Schubert* (Munich and Vienna: Hanser 1978), 89; Hans D. Kiemle, 'Woran starb Schubert eigentlich?', *Brille* 16/17 (1996), 41–51.
19. For a quick introduction to the topic see Anne Hanley's opinion piece in the *Guardian*, https://www.theguardian.com/science/blog/2017/oct/16/itvs-victoria-illustrates-how-19th-century-sexism-helped-syphilis-to-spread (accessed 19 December 2018). For further reading see A. Hanley and J. Meyer (eds), *Patient Voices in Britain, 1840–1948* (Manchester University Press, 2021).
20. *Dok*, 274–76.
21. For studies in Paris with comparisons across Europe see Romain Jaquen, 'Male Prostitution, 19th–20th Centuries', *Encyclopédie d'histoire numérique de l'Europe*; Robert A. Nye, 'Sex Difference and Male Homosexuality in French Medical Discourse, 1830–1930', *Bulletin of the History of Medicine* 63 (1989): 32–51; Ambroise Tardieu, *Les attentats aux moeurs* (Paris: Jérôme Millon, 1857, rev. 1995); and Andrew Israel Ross, *Public City/Public Sex: Homosexuality, Prostitution, and Urban Culture in Nineteenth-Century Paris* (Philadelphia, PA: Temple University Press, 2019). For more recent studies see Trevon D. Logan, *Male Sex Work: Antiquity to Online* (Cambridge University Press, 2017); *Male Sex Work in Society*, ed. Victor Minichiello and John Scott (Harrington Park Press, 2014); Eve Kosofsky Sedgwick, *Epistemology of the Closet* (University of California Press, 1990).
22. *Erinn*, 417. See also Constant von Wurzbach's objection in his entry on Schubert, *Biographisches Lexikon des Kaisertums Österreich*, vol. 32 (Vienna, 1876), 98–99; Rita Steblin, 'Schubert's Pepi: His Love Affair with the Chambermaid Josepha Pöcklhofer and her Surprising Fate', *MT* 149 (2008), 47–69.
23. Schober's estate, WB-HSS, H.I.N 36:340.
24. *Erinn*, 236.
25. Antonio Baldassarre, *The Iconographic Schubert: The Reception of Schubert in the Mirror of his Time* (1997).
26. A *ghazal* is a poem made up like an odd-numbered chain of couplets, with an inline rhyme that precedes the recurring refrain: AA bA cA dA eA.

CHAPTER SIXTEEN: THE WATERSHED (1822–1824)

1. For a recent study of their friendship see Reinhard Göltl, *Franz Schubert und Moritz von Schwind. Freundschaft im Biedermeier* (Munich: Nymphenburger, 1989).
2. *Dok*, 229.
3. *Dok*, 275.
4. *Dok*, 460.
5. *Dok*, 173.
6. *Dok*, 186.
7. *Dok*, 458.
8. Einstein, *Schubert*, 218.
9. *Dok*, 197.
10. *Dok*, 192.
11. *Dok*, 197.
12. *Dok*, 204.
13. *Erinn*, 306. Heinrich Josef Hölzl, a colleague of Mayrhofer at the Book Censorship Office. Eric Sams prefers a May date for Schubert's hospitalization and the popular eruption in July, 'Schubert's Illness Re-Examined', *MT* (1980), 15–22, here 15. A letter from Bruchmann to Schober on 30 April 1823 invites Schubert to their summer residence

at Hütteldorf, which he accepted, along with Josef Kupelwieser; the letter also enquires about a Schubertiad on 13 May. Reed, *Schubert*, 109, suggests a June or July date. June/July is possible before he went to Steyr, but his head was not shorn before he went away with Vogl. McKay, *Franz Schubert*, 184, also places Schubert's hospitalization in October 1823. For examples of medical literature on the treatment of syphilis in the nineteenth century, see C. Franzen, 'Syphilis in Composers and Musicians', *European Journal of Clinical Microbiology & Infectious Diseases* 27 (2008), 1,151–57.

14. *Dok*, 203.
15. *Dok*, 207, 204.
16. *Dok*, 209. Leopold Kupelwieser, painter and graphic artist, is the younger brother of Josef Kupelwieser, theatre administrator, playwright, librettist and translator. As is evident from his correspondence, Schubert was closest to Leopold, whom he most likely met through his brother Karl, though the first documented evidence of their friendship is in 1820 and 1821 through Leopold's two watercolours of Schubert's circle at Atzenbrugg Castle.
17. *Dok*, 219.
18. *Dok*, 221.
19. Peter Gilroy Bevan, 'Adversity: Schubert's Illnesses and their Background' in *Schubert Studies*, ed. Brian Newbould (Aldershot: Ashgate, 1998), 244–66, here 246.
20. *Dok*, 186, 203 and 458.
21. *Dok*, 237.
22. *Dok*, 209.
23. *Dok*, 226.
24. *Dok*, 228.
25. *Dok*, 228–29.
26. *Dok*, 237.
27. *Dok*, 238–39.
28. *Dok*, 250.
29. For an alternative reading of this setting see Dietrich Berke, 'Franz Schuberts Vokalquartett "Gebet" D 815 als Schlüsselwerk für Gesellschaftsmusik', *Musica* 48 (1994), 219–25.
30. I am playing on the title of an exhibition which Seóirse and I attended at the Joseph D. Carrier Gallery in Toronto (2005): Timothy Verdon, 'Broken Beauty, Shattered Heart', in *A Broken Beauty*, ed. Theodore L. Prescott (Grand Rapids, MI: Eeerdmans, 2005), 25.
31. Thomas Mann (1950), in *The Thomas Mann Reader*, ed. Joseph Warner Angell (New York: Knopf), 443.
32. For alternative readings see Hans-Joachim Hinrichsen, who draws a sharp distinction between last and late works in 'Is There a Late Style in Schubert?', *Rethinking Schubert*, 17–28, and Ben Korstvedt, who situates this debate in Schubert's socio-cultural time and argues that his late instrumental music is the expression of a new, distinctly modern consciousness in '"The prerogative of late style": Thoughts on the Expressive World of Schubert's Late Works', *Schubert's Late Music*, 404–25, here 412.
33. A sense of Kupelwieser's character and distinction in his own right is well captured in Rupert Feuchtmüller, *Leopold Kupelwieser und die Kunst der österreichischen Spätromantik* (Vienna: Österreichischer Bundesverlag, 1970).
34. Christopher Gibbs identifies it as 'the key document of Schubert's life', *The Life of Schubert*, 115.
35. *Dok*, 339.
36. *Dok*, 336–37.
37. *Dok*, 250.
38. Daniel A. Siedell, *God in the Gallery: A Christian Embrace of Modern Art* (Grand Rapids, MI: Baker Academic, 2008), 29.
39. Jonathan Bellman, *The 'Style Hongrois' in the Music of Western Europe* (Boston, MA: Northeastern University Press, 1993), especially ch. 7, and Hefling and Tarakoff, 'Schubert's Chamber Music', p. 71.
40. W. Dean Sutcliffe, 'Haydn, Mozart and their Contemporaries', *The Cambridge Companion to the String Quartet*, ed. Robin Stowell (Cambridge University Press, 2003), 185–209. See

also Mary Hunter, who shows that the line between the private and public was tenuous in 'Haydn's London Piano Trios and his Solomon Quartets. Private vs. Public?', in Elaine Sisman, *Haydn and his World*, 103–30, especially 105–09.
41. Analytical discourse on both quartets includes Stephen E. Hefling, 'The Austro-Germanic Quartet Tradition in the Nineteenth Century' in *The Cambridge Companion to the String Quartet*, 230–31; Stephen E. Hefling and David S. Tarakoff, 'Schubert's Chamber Music' in Hefling (ed.), *Nineteenth-Century Chamber Music* (New York: Routledge, 2003), 39–101.
42. Schwind wrote to Schober immediately after the performance that D 804 was, in Schubert's opinion, performed very slowly 'but very purely and sensitively', *Dok*, 230.
43. Paul Griffiths, *The String Quartet: A History* (New York: Thames & Hudson, 1983), 110. Schubert's works were regularly reviewed in the *Musikalische Eilpost* in Weimar, such as the pirated copy of Galopp and 8 Ecossaises (D 735) published in Breslau in 1826.
44. Gingerich, *Schubert's Beethoven Project*, 54.
45. For a reading of the 'Knight' symbol in Gay culture, see Robert K. Martin, 'Knights-Errant and Gothic Seducers: The Representation of Male Friendship in Mid-Nineteenth-Century America' in *Hidden from History: Reclaiming the Gay and Lesbian Past*, ed. Martin Duberman, Martha Vicinus and George Chauncey (New York: Meridan, 1989), 169–82.
46. For an appraisal of what they achieved in this opera see Till Gerrit Waidelich, *Franz Schubert. Alfonso und Estrella. Eine frühe durchkomponierte deutsche Oper – Geschichte und Analyse* (Tutzing: Schneider, 1991).
47. *Dok*, 161. For available DVD performances see the production of *Alfonso und Estrella* conducted by Nikolaus Harnoncourt, directed by Brian Large and filmed at the Theater an der Wien, May 1997 (Naxos, 2009), and the performance by the resident orchestra and choir at the Teatro Lirico di Cagliari conducted by Gerard Korsten, directed by Luca Ronconi and filmed by Marco Scali (Genoa: Dynamic, 2004).
48. Aidan Lang on staging Schubert's *Fierabras* in Alfred Hickling, *Guardian*, 7 July 2000, https://www.theguardian.com/friday_review/story/0,3605,340405,00.html (accessed 17 September 2021).
49. For available DVD performances see the performance at Zurich opera house conducted by Franz Welser-Möst, directed by Gudrun Hartmann and produced by Claus Guth (EMI Classics, 2007) and the performance directed by Peter Stein in association with the Salzburg Festival and the Vienna Philharmonic (Unitel Classica, Cmajor Entertainment, 2015).
50. For a deeply informed reading of Schubert's achievement in this opera written by one of the editors of the *NSA* edition of *Fierabras*, see Christine Martin, 'Pioneering German Musical Drama: Sung and Spoken Word in Schubert's *Fierabras*', *Drama in the Music of Franz Schubert*, 35–50. Earlier appraisals which pondered whether it could be successfully staged include: Ernst Hilmar, 'Kann Schuberts "Fierabras" eine Lebensfähige Oper sein?', *Österreichische Musikzeitschrift* (1988), 241–44, and Thomas Werner, 'Bild und Action in "Fierabras"', *Jahre der Krise*, 85–112.

CHAPTER SEVENTEEN: 'ART BORN OF SORROW': SCHUBERT'S 'UNFINISHED'

1. Andrea Lindmayr-Brandl, 'The Myth of the Unfinished', *Rethinking Schubert*, 116, 120–21.
2. The autograph, is in the Gesellschaft der Musikfreunde (A 244), see *Sinfonie in h-Moll, 'Die Unvollendete': Franz Schubert: Vollständiges Faksilime der autographen Partitur und der Entwürfe*, ed. Walther Dürr and Christa Landon, Publikationen der Sammlungen der Gesellschaft der Musikfreunde in Wien, ed. Otto Biba, vol. III (Munich, 1978). Schubert's particell and facsimile of the scherzo fragment is included in Peter Gülke (ed.), *Symphony Nr. 7 (Die Unvollendete) h-moll, D 759* (Wiesbaden: Breitkopf & Härtel, 1990).
3. For an engaging analytical reading on why Schubert left the scherzo unfinished in D 708A, D 729 and D 759, but was able to complete a scherzo in D 944, see Yusuke Takamatsu, 'Warum blieb die "Unvollendete" von Franz Schubert D 759 unvollendet? Das Scherzo als

möglicher Schlüssel zur Erklärung', *Schweizer Jahrbuch für Musikwissenschaft* 37 (2017), 59–80.
4. Deutsch emphatically rejected the idea of a two movement work, see 'The Riddle of Schubert's Unfinished Symphony', *The Music Review* (1940), reprinted in Martin Chusid's *The Norton Critical Score*, ed. Martin Chusid (1968).
5. See, for example, John Gingerich, 'Unfinished Considerations: Schubert's "Unfinished" Symphony in the Context of his Beethoven Project', *NCM* 31/2 (2007), 99–112; Andrea Lindmayr-Brandl, *Franz Schubert. Das fragmentarische Werk* (Stuttgart: Franz Steiner, 2003), 242; Rudolf Weber, 'Mythen und Legenden um die Entstehung von Schuberts Unvollendeter' in Claudia Bullerjahn and Wolfgang Löffler (eds), *Musikermythen: Alltagstheorien, Legenden und Medieninszenierungen* (Hildesheim and New York: Georg Olms Verlag, 2004), 191–122, and for earlier studies see Arnold Schering, *Franz Schuberts Symphonie in h-moll und ihr Geheimnis* (Würzburg: Konrad Triltsch Verlag, 1938).
6. Amadeus Wendt, 'Über den Zustand der Musik in Deutschland. Eine Skizze', *Allgemeine musikalische Zeitung mit besonderer Rücksicht auf den österreichischen Kaiserstaat* 6 (1822), 762.
7. Maynard Solomon, 'Schubert's Unfinished Symphony', *NCM* 21/2 (1997), 111–33, here 112.
8. *Dok*, 172.
9. Schubert's interest in the valve horn is well known in 'Nachtgesang im Walde', and then in 'Auf dem Strom'; but there were no valve horns in Vienna in 1822 nor when Schubert wrote the 'Great' C major symphony in 1825. I am immensely grateful to Trevor Herbert for placing his immense knowledge at my disposal.
10. The argument that the B minor Entr'acte was originally the final movement of Schubert's B minor Symphony is based on it being in the same key, requiring the same orchestral forces; the music is also highly original, the entr'acte is longer, more developed than most operatic overtures, and Schubert had little time to fulfil the *Rosamunde* commission. Although you can immediately hear it is not the symphony's finale, the tradition of playing it as D 759/iv goes back well into the nineteenth century. George Grove was among the first to endorse the idea and Maurice Brown was one of the first to repudiate the claimed connection between the two works on the grounds that their scores were written on paper of different types with different watermarks, *Schubert: A Critical Biography* (London: Macmillan 1958), 123.
11. See Chapter 6, 149–150.
12. Arnold Schering was the first to suggest 'Mein Traum' as an extra-musical programme for D 759 in *Franz Schuberts Symphonie in h-moll ('Unvollendete') und ihr Geheimnis* (Würzburg-Aumühle: Triltsch, 1939).
13. Andrea Lindmayr-Brandl traces the reception of this idea in 'The Myth of the Unfinished', 115.
14. Chapter 3, 64; Montgomery, *Unfinished History: A New Account of Schubert's B Minor Symphony* (New York: Brown Walker Press, 2017), 122-23.
15. Xavier Hascher, 'Narrative Dislocations in the First Movement of Schubert's "Unfinished" Symphony', *Rethinking Schubert*, 131.
16. Peter Andraschke, *Franz Schubert. Sinfonie Nr. 7 h-Moll 'Unvollendete' Einführung und Analyse* (Munich: Goldmann, 1982), 71–127; Stefan Kunze's *Franz Schubert. Sinfonie h-moll. Unvollendete* (Munich: W. Fink, 1965).
17. Hascher, 'Narrative Dislocations', 130.
18. Hugh MacDonald, 'Schubert's Volcanic Temper', *MT* 119 (1978), 949–52; Michael Spitzer, 'Mapping the Human Heart: A Holistic Analysis of Fear in Schubert', *Music Analysis* 29/1–3 (2010), 149–213; Hascher, 'Narrative Dislocations', 138.
19. Edmund Burke, *On the Sublime and the Beautiful* (London: R. and J. Dodsky, 1757), Part I, Section VII, 'A Philosophical Enquiry into the Origin of our Ideas of the Sublime and the Beautiful', 36.
20. Jean Paul, *Vorschule der Ästhetik, Sämtliche Werke*, V, 106–09.
21. Johann Georg Sulzer, *Allgemeine Theorie der schönen Künste* (1771–74).

22. Schiller, 'Über das Erhabene', *Werke und Briefe*, VIII, 830.
23. Burke, *On the Sublime and the Beautiful*, 36.
24. Mark Evan Bonds, 'Idealism and the Aesthetics of Instrumental Music at the Turn of the Nineteenth Century', *Journal of the American Musicological Society* 50/2 (1997), 387–420, here 406.
25. Wendt, 'Über den Zustand der Musik in Deutschland, 762.
26. John Irving, who also concedes 'in his hands the Viennese symphony had travelled far', 'The Viennese Symphony 1750 to 1827' in *The Cambridge Companion to the Symphony* (Cambridge University Press, 2013), 15–28, here 27.
27. Carl Reinecke (1824–1910) conducted the Leipzig premiere with the Gewandhaus Orchestra on 13 December 1866. The programme booklet states it was played from the original score, and from the same set of parts as there are no copies of parts in the Gewandhaus archive, Montgomery, *Unfinished History*, xxxiii.
28. Kreissle, 255–56.
29. Eduard Hanslick, *Aus dem Concert-Saal. Kritiken und Schilderungen aus 20 Jahren des Wiener Musiklebens. 1848–1868*, 2nd edn (Vienna and Leipzig: Braumüller, 1897), 391–93; cited in Lindmayr-Brandl, 'The Myth of the Unfinished', 113.
30. *Dok*, 189–91. The letter is co-signed by Jenger and Johann Nepomuk Ritter von Kalchberg, chairman of the Society's executive committee; Ignaz Count Attems, Govenor of Styria, is the third signatory on the diploma.
31. *Dok*, 199–200.
32. For forensic research on Schubert's manuscript and complexity of the symphony's reception history, see Montgomery, *Unfinished History*. The study has not gained the prominence it deserves; ch. 1, 1–38, re-examines the history and reproduces copies of these letters. Earlier studies include Renate Bozic, 'Franz Schubert, die "Unvollendete" und der Steiermärk. Musikverein' in *175 Jahre Musikverein für Steiermark*, ed. Erika Kaufmann (Graz [publisher name:], 1990), facsimile, 34. A facsimile was published by the artistic director of the Graz Verein, Richard Wickenhausser, 'Der steiermärkische Musikverein in Graz', *Neue Zeitschrift für Musik* 72 (1905), 466–69; it is reproduced in Montgomery, *Unfinished History*, 13.
33. The most recent, most detailed account is given in Montgomery, *Unfinished History*, 1–38. Otto Erich Deutsch, *Franz Schubert Briefe und Schriften* (Vienna: Hollinek, 1954), 72. Hellmut Federhofer, *Deutsches Jahrbuch der Musikwissenschaft für 1965* (Leipzig: Peters, 1965), 83, 95. Alois A. Chalus was the first to claim the entire cover page of the B minor Symphony as well as the *Dankschreiben* were forged by Josef Hüttenbrenner in 'Franz Schubert, der Musikus des Biedermeiers', *Der Kollege* 5/6 (1963), 6–8. *Franz Schubert und seine h-moll-Sinfonie im Blickpunkt seiner Freundschaft mit Anselm und Josef Hüttenbrenner* (Vienna: private publication held at the Österreichische Nationalbibliothek, 1965).
34. Universität für Musik und darstellende Kunst, Graz, MS 1813, Montgomery, *Unfinished History*, xxix. The report was commissioned by Felix Hüttenbrenner and updated in 1965. For Felix Hüttenbrenner's account of the report see 'Franz Schubert und die Brüder Hüttenbrenner', Universität für Musik und darstellende Kunst, Graz, MS 1875. See entries on 'Fälschungen', 'Anselm Hüttenbrenner', 'Josef Hüttenbrenner' and 'Unvollendete' in Ernst Hilmar, *Schubert Lexikon*, 118, 202–03, 476–78.
35. *NSA*, V/3, 11. Wickenhauser, 'Der steiermärkische Musikverein in Graz', 467.
36. See, for example, the two copies of his letter to Schober on 30 November 1823 where he writes in Schulschrift (Sig. HIN 104189), which is like his letter to Diabelli on 10 April 1823 (Sig. HIN 043020), and then transcribes it in Kurrentschrift (Sig. HIN 104188).
37. See, for example, his letter to Breitkopf & Härtel, 12 August 1826, Sig. HIN 004878.
38. Sig. HIN 223234.
39. Montgomery, *Unfinished History*, xxvii; the signatures are superimposed on p. 26.
40. Montgomery, *Unfinished History*, 1–38, esp. 13–14.
41. Ibid.; Wickenhauser, 'Der steiermärkische Musikverein in Graz', 467.

42. Josef Hüttenbrenner to Johann Herbeck, *Erinn*, 430.
43. Josef Hüttenbrenner to his brother, Andreas, 11 February 1867, Herbeck, 164–65, *Erinn*, 512.
44. Deutsch connects this letter with Ferdinand Luib's biography and dates it 1858, *Erinn*, 91–93; Montgomery, *Unfinished History*, xxv.
45. Montgomery, *Unfinished History*, xxv. Felix Hüttenbrenner, 'Anselm Hüttenbrenner und Schuberts H-moll-Symphonie', *Zeitschrift des historischen Vereins für Steiermark* 52 (1961), 126. The note had already appeared in the first edition of Deutsch, *Erinn*, 88.
46. Montgomery, *Unfinished History*, xxxv.
47. See for example, Felix Hüttenbrenner 'Zur Geschichte der h-Moll Symphonie', *Zeitschrift des Steiermärkischen Sängerbundes* 2 (1928), 31–32, and 'Anselm Hüttenbrenner und Schuberts H-moll Symphonie', *Zeitschrift des historischen Vereins für Steiermark* 52 (1961), 122–37.
48. *Erinn*, 510.
49. *Erinn*, 90.
50. Solomon, 'On the Subject of Schubert's "Unfinished" Symphony', 111–33, here 113.
51. Einstein, *Schubert*, 202; Solomon, 'On the Subject of Schubert's "Unfinished" Symphony', 111–33.
52. *Sinfonie in h-Moll*, 'Die Unvollendete': *Franz Schubert: Vollständiges Faksimile der autographen Partitur und der Entwürfe*, ed. Walther Dürr and Christa Landon, Publikationen der Sammlungen der Gesellschaft der Musikfreunde in Wien, ed. Otto Biba, vol. III (Munich, 1978).
53. Schubert's undated letter to Josef Hüttenbrenner acknowledges his possession of a symphony, which Deutsch reads as D 82, *Dok*, 76.
54. *Dok*, 120–21.
55. *Dok*, 121–22, 126.
56. Till Gerrit Waidelich, 'Josef Hüttenbrenners Entwurf eines Aufsatzes mit der ersten biographischen Skizze Schuberts (1823) und zwei Fragmente seines ungedruckten Schubert-Nachrufs (1828)', *Schubert: Perspektiven* 1 (2001), 37–73.
57. Margaret Jestremski, 'Unveröffentlichte Dokumente aus dem Nachlaß Anselm Hüttenbrenners', *Brille* 15 (1995), *Dok*, 169–71.
58. *Dok*, 185, 186, 188–89.
59. *Dok*, 200.
60. Paragraph 9 of the statutes of the Society, of which Schubert received a copy with the Diploma, states that members 'are expected to do their best to further the Society's welfare, even at a distance', *Dok*, 190.
61. *Dok*, 80.
62. Schober purchased an autograph for Schubert's setting of his own poem, 'Jägers Liebeslied' (D 909), when he published it in his Lithographic Institute while the composer was living with him.
63. See Chapter 16, 371–72.
64. *Dok*, 253–54.
65. Kreissle, 130.
66. *Dok*, 167, 158.
67. *Dok*, 121, 126, 168.
68. O. E. Deutsch, 'Anselm Hüttenbrenners Erinnerungen an Schubert', *Grillparzer Jahrbuch* 16 (1906), 126–27; *Erinn*, 201.
69. *Erinn*, 210.
70. For details of the Hüttenbrenner Schubert-Manuscript collection, see Wolfgang Suppan, 'Schubert-Autographe im Nachlass Weiss, Ostborn, Graz', *Studia Musicologica Academiae Scientiarum Hungaricae* VI (1964).
71. *Erinn*, 515–16.
72. *Erinn*, 207.
73. *Erinn*, 512.
74. Cf. Werner Aderhold, *NSA*, xi.

75. Ferdinand Schubert placed two announcements on 26 April 1835 and 23 April 1839.
76. *Dok*, 464. Anton Hüttenbrenner, *Bruchstücke aus dem Leben des Liederkomponist Franz Schubert* (Vienna, 1854); *Erinn*, 151–61.
77. Universität für Musik und darstellende Kunst, Graz, MS 1848.
78. *Erinn*, 204–14, 76–81.
79. Waidelich, 'Josef Hüttenbrenners Entwurf', 43.
80. Renate Bozić, 'Franz Schubert und die "Unvollendete" und der Steiermärkische Musikverein', 175 Jahre Musikverein für Steiermark (Graz, 1990), 36; Susanne Flesch, 'Die Ehrenmitglieder des Musikvereins für Steiermark' in *Im Jahrestakt. 200 Jahre Musikverein für Steiermark*, ed. Michael Nemeth and Susanne Flesch (Vienna, Cologne and Weimar: Bohlau Verlag, 2015), 223–57; Erika Kaufmann (ed.), *175 Jahre Musikverein für Steiermark. Graz 1815–1990* (Graz, 1990).
81. *Erinn*, 497.
82. Lindmayr-Brandl, 'The Myth of the Unfinished', 123.
83. Ludwig Herbeck, *Johann Herbeck. Ein Lebensbild von seinem Sohne* (Vienna: Albert J. Gutmann, 1885), 164–69.
84. *Erinn*, 512.
85. *Erinn*, 83–91.
86. *Dok*, 479.

CHAPTER EIGHTEEN: SONGS OF A WAYFARER (1822–1824)

1. Richard Kurth, 'On the Subject of Schubert's "Unfinished Symphony": *Was bedeutet die Bewegung*', *NCM* 23/1 (1999), 3–32.
2. Richard Kramer, *Distant Cycles: Schubert and the Conceiving of Song* (University of Chicago Press, 1994), 85–101.
3. *Schubert Jahrbuch* (2000–2002), 19.
4. Wilhelm Heinrich Wackenroder and Ludwig Tieck, *Herzensergiessungen eines kunstliebenden Klosterbruders* (Berlin: Unger, 1797), *Outpourings of an Art-Loving Friar*, trans. Edward Mornin (New York: Frederick Ungar, 1975), 59.
5. John Reed, *The Schubert Song Companion* (Manchester: Manchester University Press, 1985), 120; Richard Capell, *Schubert's Songs*, ed. M. Cooper (New York: Da Capo Press, rev. 1977), 181.
6. For further reading see Lorraine Byrne Bodley, 'Challenging the Context: Reception and Transformation in Schubert's "Der Musensohn"', *Rethinking Schubert*, 437–55; also 'Wandermotive in Schuberts Goethe Liedern', *Schubert Jahrbuch* (2010–2013), 125–41.
7. Virgil, *The Aeneid*, Book 2, ll. 5–6.
8. Paul Verlaine, *Chansons pour elle* (1891).
9. *Über naïve und sentimentalische Dichtung, NA* 20, 442.
10. Novalis, 'Die Christenheit oder Europa' (1799).
11. Wackenroder, 'Ein wunderbares morgenländisches Märchen von einem nacktem Heiligen' (1797).
12. The closing line of Schiller's controversial *Die Braut von Messina* (1803).
13. Johnson, Hyperion, CDA30020.
14. See Chapter Chapter 7, 178–188.
15. *Dok*, 250.
16. *Dok*, 300.
17. See Lorraine Byrne Bodley, 'In Pursuit of a Single Flame? On Schubert's Settings of Goethe's Poems', which responds to Robert Hatten's 'A Surfeit of Musics: What Goethe's Lyrics Concede when Set to Schubert's Music', *NCMR* 5/2 (Cambridge University Press, 2008), 7–18, and Hatten's 'Reflections Inspired by a Response', *NCMR* 13/1 (Cambridge University Press, 2016), 11–38.
18. *Fragment über die Natur, MA* 12, 385.
19. See Chapter 20, 437–453.

CHAPTER NINETEEN: HIGH WINDOWS OF ZSELIZ

1. *ND* I, 68; *Erinn*, 267.
2. *Erinn*, 116–17 (Schönstein); 417 (Spaun); Gabriele Eder, 'Schubert und Caroline Esterházy', *Brille* 11 (1993), 13. For literature on Caroline Esterházy, see Rita Steblin, 'Le mariage malheureux de Caroline Esterházy. Une histoire authentique, telle qu'elle est retracée dans les lettres de la famille Crenneville', *Cahiers F. Schubert* 5 (October 1994), 17–34.
3. Rita Steblin, 'Neue Forschungsaspekte zu Caroline Esterházy', *Brille* 11 (1993), 21–34.
4. The F minor Fantasy can just as convincingly be associated with Schubert's impending death. William Kinderman traces this death-like narrative, including D 940/1's second 'funereal' subject', in 'Schubert's Piano Music: Probing the Human Condition', *Cambridge Companion to Schubert*, 171.
5. Robert Schumann, Diary Entry, 17 August 1828.
6. Frank Dawes, 'Piano Duet' in *Grove Music Online*. https://www-oxfordmusiconlinecom.jproxy.nuim.ie/grovemusic/view/10.1093/gmo/9781561592630.001.0001/omo-9781561592630-e-0000021629?rskey=6IEANJ&result=1 (accessed 18 April 2021).
7. Dallas A. Weekley, *The One-Piano, Four-Hand Compositions of Franz Schubert* (Indiana: PhD dissertation, 1968); Hermann Wetzel, 'Schubert's Werke für Klavier zu vier Hände', *Die Musik* 6 (1906–7), 36–44.
8. *Dok* 125, 295, 368, 382 and 388.
9. *Dok*, 125.
10. *Dok*, 275.
11. Mária Domokos, 'Über die ungarischen Charakteristiken der "Divertissement à l'hongroise" D 818', *Brille* 11 (1993), 53–64.
12. *Dok*, 461.
13. Philip Brett, 'Schubert and the Performance of Gay Male Desire', *NCM* 21/2 (1997), 149–76; Christopher Wiley, *Re-Writing Composers' Lives: Critical Historiography and Musical Biography* (University of London: PhD dissertation, 2008).
14. For recent research on Schubert's variation technique see Caitlin G. Martinkus, *The Urge to Vary: Schubert's Variation Practice from Schubertiads to Sonata Forms* (University of Toronto: PhD dissertation, 2017).
15. *Dok*, 255.
16. *Dok*, 275.
17. For an interesting comparative reading of the serene recording of the Rondo in A major (D 951) by Paul Lewis and Stephen Osborne on a Steinway piano and the tempestuous, troubled rendering by Andreas Staier and Alexander Melnikov on an 1827 Graf piano, see Julian Dodd, *Being True to Works of Music* (Oxford University Press, 2020), 8–9.
18. Theodor Adorno recognized this in his article, 'Four Hands, Once Again', trans. Jonathan Wipplinger, *Cultural Critique* 60 (2005), 1–4.

CHAPTER TWENTY: AFTER THE CRISES: THE SPIRIT OF BEAUTY AND ITS FATE

1. Reed, *The Final Years*, 133.
2. *Erinn*, 79.
3. Eduard von Bauernfeld, 'Aus Alt und Neu-Wien' in *Gesammelte Schriften*, vol. 12 (Vienna: Braumüller, 1873).
4. Fanny Arnstein, founder of the Gesellschaft adeliger Frauen zur Beförderung des Guten und Nützlichen (in whose benefit concerts Schubert's music was performed), also worked tirelessly to financially aid Klein's educational reform and the training of ocular specialists. See ch. 1, n. 44.

5. Josef Mertin, 'Gedanken zu einem "Schubert-Instrument" dem Tafelklavier des Malers Rieder', *Zur Aufführungspraxis der Werke Franz Schuberts*, vol. 4 (Graz: Beiträge zur Aufführungspraxis, 1994) 111–17.
6. *Dok*, 248.
7. Johnson, 606.
8. *Erinn*, 253–54.
9. *Dok*, 348.
10. Graham Johnson has identified – from the shape of the volume and ornamental border – that the book in Schubert's hand is Gabriel Seidl's *Dichtungen* (*Lieder der Nacht*), published in 1826 but advertised in the *Wiener Zeitschrift* and available in October 1825, Johnson, 606.
11. *Erinn*, 199; see Chapter 10, 247–248.
12. See Chapter 6, 130.
13. *Dok*, 295–96, 303–04.
14. *Dok*, 304.
15. *Dok*, 296.
16. *Dok*, 314.
17. *Dok*, 234.
18. Adolf Bernhard Marx's concert review of 13 December 1824, *Berliner allgemeine musikalische Zeitung* 1 (29 December 1824), 444.
19. *Dok*, 495.
20. Herder, *Kalligone*, II, *Sämmtliche Werke*, XXII, 187; Mark Evan Bonds, *Music as Thought: Listening to the Symphony in the Age of Beethoven* (Princeton University Press, 2006), 25.
21. For an invaluable study which traces these shifts in attitude towards reception of the symphony and draws on a wide range of philosophical, literary, political and musical sources is Bonds, *Music as Thought*.
22. For a richly informative and marvellously entertaining account of this character see ch. 2, 'Ego, *Ehrgeiz* and the Lied: Schubert and "the Homer of the Habsburg"', Johann Ladislaus Pyrker', from Youens, *Schubert's Late Lieder*, 93–201.
23. Johann Ladislaus Pyrker, *Sämtliche* Werke, vol. 3, *Perlen der heiligen Vorzeit* (Stuttgart and Tübingen: J. G. Cotta, 1855), 218; cited by Youens, *Schubert's Late Lieder*, 191.
24. *Dok*, 313–16, 319–21.
25. John Reed, 'The "Gastein" Symphony Reconsidered', *Music and Letters* 40/4 (October 1959), 341–49; John Reed, *Schubert: The Final Years* (New York: St Martin's Press, 1972), and John Reed, 'How the "Great" C Major was Written', *Music and Letters* 56/1 (1975), 18–25.
26. Ernst Hilmar, 'Datierungsprobleme im Werk Schuberts' in Otto Brusatti (ed.), *Schubert-Kongreß Wien 1978 veranstaltet von der Österreichischen Gesellschaft für Musikwissenschaft gemeinsam mit der Wiener Festwochen* (Graz: Akademische Druck- und Verlagsanstalt, 1979), 45–60.
27. George Bernard Shaw's review of a concert in London on 23 March 1892, cited in *Music in London 1890-1894*, vol. 2 (London: Constable and Company Limited, 1932), 53.
28. *Erinn*, 40.
29. William Blake's *Songs of Innocence and Songs of Experience Shewing the Two Contrary States of the Human Soul* (1794).
30. For an engaging reading of D 944's poetry see Walther Dürr, 'Zyklische Form und "Poetische Idee": Schuberts grosse C-Dur-Symphonie' in *Probleme der symphonischen Tradition im 19. Jahrhundert Internationales Musikwissenschaftliches Colloquium*, Bonn, 1989 : Kongressbericht (Tützing: H. Schneider, 1990), 455–69.
31. *NA* 20, 185.
32. *NA* 20, 52.
33. Mark DeVoto, *Schubert's Great C Major: Biography of a Symphony* (Hillsdate: Pendragon Press, 2006), 41.
34. For the cultural backdrop to Schubert's writing for trombone, see Trevor Herbert, *The Trombone* (New Haven, CT: Yale University Press, 2006), 127–203.

35. Klaus Aringer, 'Zur musikalischen Funktion der Posaunen in Franz Schuberts letzten Sinfonien', *Schubert Jahrbuch* (1998), 87–101.
36. Youens, *Schubert's Late Lieder*, 186.
37. *Dok*, 380.
38. For a fuller portrait of this influential figure in Schubert's musical development see Herfrid Kier, *Raphael Georg Kiesewetter (1773–1850), Wegbereiter des musikalischen Historismus* (Regensburg: Studien zur Musikgeschichte des 19. Jahrhunderts 13, 1968).
39. *Dok*, 381–82.
40. Otto Biba, 'Franz Schubert und die Gesellschaft der Musikfreunde in Wien' in *Schubert-Studien* (Graz: Verlag der Österreichischen Akademie der Wissenschaft, 1978), 23–36, here 30.
41. Leopold von Sonnleithner to Selmar Bagge, editor of the *Deutsche Musikzeitung*, Vienna, 26 January 1861, *Erinn*, 498; the first performance at the GdM took place on 1 December 1850.
42. Carl Dahlhaus, *Die Musik des 19. Jahrhunderts* (Laaber, 1980), 41; Andreas Krause, 'Unbekannte Dokumente zur Aufführung von Franz Schuberts großer C-Dur-Symphonie durch Felix Mendelssohn Bartholdy', *Beiträge zur Musikwissenschaft* 29 (1987), 240–50.
43. *Dok*, 321.
44. For writing on this topic and also D 887 see Anne Hyland, 'In What Respect Monumental? Schubert's Quartettsatz and the Dialectics of Private and Public' in *The String Quartet from the Private to the Public Sphere*, Speculum musicae 27 (2016), and 'In Search of Liberated Time, or Schubert's Quartet in G Major, D 887: Once More Between Sonata and Variation', *Music Theory Spectrum* 38/i (2016), 85–108.
45. Prince Klemens Wenzel Metternich (1773–1859), Austrian statesman, one of the organizers of the Congress of Vienna (1814–15) which devised the settlement of Europe after the Napoleonic Wars.
46. William Shakespeare: *William Shakespeare's sämmtliche dramatische Werke, übersetzt im Metrum des Originals* (Vienna: Sollinger 1825–27), 43 vols. Eduard von Bauernfeld contributed to vols 2: *Love's Labours Lost*; 18: *Henry the Eighth*; 31: *Troilus and Cressida*; 32: *The Comedy of Errors*; 42 and 43: Shakespeare's poetry.
47. Anna Hönig was a member of Schubert's circle, where she was nicknamed 'die süsse Anna Page' after the character in Shakespeare's *Merry Wives of Windsor*. Schwind became engaged to her in the spring of 1828 but the engagement was broken off the following year, when her fervent Catholicism finally became too much for him.
48. *Dok*, 360.
49. Walter Obermeier, 'Schubert und die Zensur' in *Schubert-Kongress Wien 1978*, ed. Otto Brusatti (Graz: Auftrag der Österreichischen Gesellschaft für Musikwissenschaft, 1979), 117–25.
50. Otto Biba, 'Franz Schubert in den musikalischen Abendunterhaltungen der Gesellschaft der Musikfreunde' in *Schubert-Studien. Festgabe der Österreichischen Akademie der Wissenschaften zum Schubert-Jahr 1978*, ed. Franz Grasberger and Othmar Wessely (Vienna: Veröffentlichungen der Kommission für Musikforschung, 1978), vol. 19, 7–31.
51. Goethe's editorial/advisory board included Friedrich Riemer (advisor in literary and philological questions), Karl Wilhelm Göttling (authority on correct orthography), Johann Heinrich Meyer (painter and art historian), Fréderic Jacques Soret (advisor on scientific writings), Johann Peter Eckermann (Goethe's secretary and most intense collaborator and editor), Chancellor von Müller (one of Goethe's closest legal advisors), Wilhem Reichel (Cotta's manager and proof-reader).
52. Pennauer first editions: D 568, 636, 637, 638, 713, 717 Suleika II, 737–8, 767 ('Willkommen und Abschied'), 786, 825, 825A–B, 827–8 ('Nacht und Träume' and 'Die junge Nonne'), 845 (Sonata in A minor), 857, 859 (*Grande Marche Funèbre* in C minor for Piano Four Hands), 885 (*Grande Marche Héroique* in A minor for Piano Four Hands).
53. D 365, op. 9 (Cappi & Diabelli, November 1821); D 145, op. 18 (Cappi & Diabelli, February 1823); D 783, op. 33 (Cappi & Co, January 1825); D 735, op. 49 (Diabelli &

NOTES to pp. 461-468

Co, November 1825); *Valses sentimentales*, D 779, op. 50 (Diabelli & Co, November 1825); D 734, op. 67 (Diabelli & Co, December 1826).

54. Haslinger published his *Valses nobles* (D 969, 1827), op. 77, and *Grazer Walzer* (D 924, 1828), op. 91. Dances which appeared in anthologies: D 971, 769/2, 366/6, 146/2, 366/17, 779/8, 779/9, 976, 978, 979, 980, 980D.

55. For further examples of piracy and duplicate printing, see the numerous manuscripts for D 365, but also D 145 and D 783.

56. Diabelli first editions: D 37, 59, 75, 77, 95, 102, 115–16, 119–20, 123, 126, 136, 140, 143, 146, 150–1, 153, 161, 171, 174, 182, 184, 197, 210, 217–19, 223, 246, 255, 259, 261, 263–4, 269, 274, 278, 280–2, 286, 290–1, 293, 297, 300–1, 321–2, 343, 352, 358, 361, 369, 375, 384–6, 393, 397, 403, 408, 412, 432, 434, 436, 442, 444–5, 450, 452, 457, 472, 473, 474, 492, 497–8, 506, 508, 520, 526, 530, 534, 540, 544, 548, 551, 560, 564, 573, 574, 575, 578, 584–5, 599, 608, 611, 614, 616, 620–3, 621 (*Trauermesse* in G minor), 623, 626, 632, 639, 650–4, 666, 671, 674, 676–7, 684, 690, 694, 696, 698–700, 706, 708, 710, 712, 715–16, 718, 727, 732, 733–6 (733, 3 *Marches Militaires*; 734, 17 Ländler and 2 Écossaises, 735, Galopp and 8 Écossaises), 739 (*Tantum Ergo* in C), 746, 749, 754, 757, 759A, 762–3, 779 (*Valses sentimentales*, nos 5–7, 10, 11, 13, 15–32), 784–5, 788–9, 792, 799, 802, 805–7, 811–12, 815, 822, 830, 831–2, 834, 842, 847–8, 853, 860–1, 869, 875–6, 877/1–4, 883, 887–90, 892, 897, 898 (Piano Trio in B flat), 906–7, 910, 912, 920, 930, 933–5, 938, 940, 942, 947 (*Lebensstürme*), 952, 955, 958–60 (last piano sonatas), 968B. A considerable number of first editions of Schubert's works were published posthumously under the imprint of J. P. Gotthard (Bohumil Pazdírek): D 48, 76, 122, 165, 168, 168A, 176, 179, 206, 237, 250–1, 264, 267–8, 272, 295, 309, 359, 366, 371, 377, 402, 409, 420, 439, 449, 454, 458, 466, 476, 494, 502, 509, 528–9, 545, 561, 572, 579, 592–3, 597, 609, 657, 659–62, 687–8, 692–3, 726, 752, 766, 808, 814, 821, 872, 915, 928, 937.

57. Cappi & Co first editions: D 209, 588, 672, 675, 707, 781, 783 and 794.

58. Cappi & Czerny first editions: D 360, 649, 753, 778, 801, 824.

59. Josef Czerny first editions: D 23, 87, 134, 141, 148–9, 189, 221, 232–4, 247–8, 270, 353, 391, 395, 594, 664, 667 ('Trout' Quintet), 810, 865, 867, 878–9, 985–6.

60. Leidesdorf first editions: D 142, 159, 260, 410, 543, 758, 764, 780, 797, 884, 917, 943, 980D.

61. *Dok*, 209, 221.

62. *Dok*, 259.

63. Matthias Artaria first editions: D 818 (*Divertissement à l'hongroise* for Piano Four Hands), 835–9, 843, 846 (Walter Scott songs), 850; Domenico Artaria & Co first editions: D 606, 895, 951.

64. *Dok*, 371–72.

65. Haslinger first editions: D 324, 379, 851, 870–1, 880, 893–4, 899/1–2, 899/3–4, 901–3, 908, 911, 913, 924–5 (*Grazer Walzer* and *Grazer Galopp*), 957, 965, 965A, 969 (*Valses nobles*).

CHAPTER TWENTY-ONE: LATE SACRED MUSIC AS A SITE OF THEOLOGY?

1. The question is drawn from Nicholas Boyle's discussion of this theme in *Sacred and Secular Scriptures: A Catholic Approach to Literature* (Notre Dame, IN: University of Notre Dame, 2005), 7.
2. *Dichtung und Wahrheit*, Part 4, Chapter, *MA*, 812.
3. *Dok*, 245–6.
4. *Dok*, 495.
5. *Dok*, 354.
6. *Dok*, 260.

7. *Dok*, 173; *Jahre der Krise*, 121–9.
8. Stanley, 'Schubert's Religious and Choral Music', 219; Kreissle, 380.
9. Cf. Walther Dürr, 'Dona nobis pacem. Gedanken zu Schuberts späten Messen', *Zeichen-Setzung* (1992), and James William Sobaskie, 'The Dramatic Monologue of Schubert's Mass in A flat Major', in *Drama in the Music of Franz Schubert*, ed. Joe Davies and James William Sobaskie (Woodbridge: Boydell & Brewer, 2019), 51–84 Jahrmärker, 372–76.
10. See Chapter 23, 529–531.
11. For an alternative reading of these works, see Howie, 'Small is Beautiful', 76–77.
12. *Dok*, 71. See also Schubert's reply, 74–75.
13. *Dok*, 34.
14. *Dok*, 403.
15. *Dok*, 397.
16. A starting point to understanding cultural shifts in Jewish 'toleration' in Vienna towards the end of Schubert's life is Joshua R. Jacobson, 'Franz Schubert and the Vienna Synagogue', *The Choral Journal: Official Publication of American Choral Directors Association* 38/1 (1997), 9–15.
17. In one of the earliest studies of Schubert's masses, Otto Wissig makes the claim that they were a 'spiritual necessity', *Franz Schubert Messen* (Leipzig: doctoral dissertation, 1909). Recent scholars who have written on Schubert's sacred music include Glenn Stanley, 'Schubert's Religious and Choral Music', 207–23; John Gingerich, ' "To how many shameful deeds you must lend your image": Schubert's Pattern of Telescoping and Excising in the Texts of his Latin Masses', *Current Musicology* 70 (2000), 61–99; John Gingerich, ' "Those of us who found our life in art": The Second Generation Romanticism of the Schubert–Schober circle 1820–1825', in Christopher H. Gibbs and Morten Solvik (eds), *Franz Schubert and his World* (Princeton University Press, 2014), 67–114, and James William Sobaskie, 'Contextual Processes in Schubert's Late Sacred Music', *Rethinking Schubert*, 295–332.
18. Stanley, 'Schubert's Religious and Choral Music', 219.
19. Paul Ricoeur, 'Herméneutique de l'idée de Révélation', in Paul Ricoeur et al., *La Révélation* (Brussels: Facultés Universitaires Saint-Louis, 1977), vol. 7, 15–54. English translation by D. Pellauer, 'Toward a Hermeneutic of the Idea of Revelation', *Harvard Theological Review* 70/1–2 (January–April 1977), 1–37.
20. For discussion of this theme see Erich Auerbach's *Mimesis: The Representation of Reality in Western Literature*, trans. Willard Trask (Princeton University Press, 1953; originally Bern: Francke, 1946). See also Erich Auerbach's essay, 'Figura', in Erich Auerbach, *Scenes from the Drama of European Literature* (New York: Meridian, 1959), 11–76.
21. Erich Benedikt, 'Notizen zu Schuberts Messen. Mit neuem Uraufführungsdatum der Messe in F Dur', *Österreichische Musikzeitschrift* 52 (1997), 64–66.
22. Hans Jaskulsky, *Die lateinischen Messen Franz Schuberts* (Mainz: Schott, 1986), 52–72. See also Gingerich, ' "To how many shameful deeds must you lend your image": Schubert's Pattern of Telescoping and Excision in the Texts of His Latin Masses', in *Current Musicology* (Fall, 2000), 61–99; Stanley, 'Schubert's Religious and Choral Music', 207, and Otto Biba, 'Schubert's Position in Viennese Musical Life', *NCM*, 3/2 (1979), 106–13.
23. C. A. H. Burkhardt (ed.), *Goethes Unterhaltungen mit dem Kanzler Friedrich von Müller, 8.6.1830* (Paderborn: Salzwasser Verlag, 2015), 143.
24. Hans Frei, *The Eclipse of Biblical Narrative: A Study of Eighteenth- and Nineteenth-Century Hermeneutics* (New Haven, CT: Yale University Press, 1974).
25. It is hard to surmise what Schubert could have read, but possible sources include Lessing's publication of the critical investigation of the Gospels by Hermann Samuel Reimarus in *Wolfenbüttel Fragments* (1774–78); Johann Gottfried Herder's *Vom Erlöser der Menschen* (1796), *Von Gottes Sohn, der Welt Heiland* (Riga: Johann Friedrich Hartknoch, 1797); Johann Jacobi's *Die Geschichte Jesu für denkende und gemutvolle Leser* (Gotha: Carl Steudel, 1816); and Karl Heinrich Georg Venturini, *Natürliche Geschichte des großen Propheten von Nazareth* (Jena: Bethlehem, rev. 1806).

26. I do intend 'inability to set' certain parts of the mass in contrast to discussion of different parts of the mass text which Schubert 'did not set'; see, for example, ch. 5, 'Zur Problematik der Texthandlung in Schuberts Messen' in Jaskulsky, *Die lateinischen Messen Franz Schuberts*, 52–72, especially 60–66 where Schubert's textual omissions are listed.
27. Roger Lenaers, *Jesus of Nazareth: A Person Like Us?*, trans. Dan Farrelly (Dublin: Carysfort Press, 2016), 56.
28. Lenaers, *Jesus of Nazareth*, 56.
29. On Schubert's request for a performance of this work at the Imperial Court Chapel, see Chapter 20, 456.
30. Goethe to Lavatar, 9 August 1782, *HA*, I, 403.
31. *Dok*, 320. The tone of his reflections echoes one of the most famous passages in Goethe's novel, *Wilhelm Meisters Wanderjahre*, where the protagonist and his son visit the Pedagogical Province and the Elder remarks of the crucifix, 'Wir halten es für eine verdammungswürdige Frechheit, jenes Martergerüst und den daran leidenden Heiligen dem Anblick der Sonne auszusetzen, die ihr Angesicht verbarg, als eine ruchlose Welt ihr dies Schauspiel aufdrang.' (We consider it a damnable impertinence to expose that martyr's scaffold and the saint who is suffering on it to the light of the sun which hid its countenance when a ruthless world forced this spectacle upon it.) Johann Wolfgang von Goethe, *Wilhelm Meisters Wanderjahre, oder Die Entsagenden* (Stuttgart: Cotta, 1821, rev. 1829), *MA* 17, 395.
32. Nicholas Boyle, *Sacred and Secular Scriptures: A Catholic Approach to Literature* (Notre Dame, IN: University of Notre Dame, 2005), 7.
33. Roger Scruton, 'The Sacred and the Human', http://www.st-andrews.ac.uk/gifford/2010/the-sacred-and-the-human (accessed 19 September 2018); see also Scruton, *The Face of God* (London: Continuum, 2012).
34. See Schubert's letter to his father and stepmother, 25 (28?) July 1825, Steyer, *Dok*, 298–300.
35. William Wordsworth, *The Prelude*, Book 11, l. 265, in S. Gill (ed.), *William Wordsworth: A Critical Edition of the Major Works* (Oxford: Oxford University Press, 1984).
36. Wordsworth, *Lines Written a Few Miles above Tintern Abbey*, ll. 135–46, in *William Wordsworth: A Critical Edition of the Major Works*.
37. See Chapter 20, 441–451.
38. *Erinn*, 67.
39. Ricoeur, 'Toward a Hermeneutic of the Idea of Revelation', 1–37.
40. *Dok*, 233.
41. *Noli foras ire, in teipsum redi: in interiore homine habitat veritas.* ('Go not outside, but return within thyself; in the inward man dwelleth the truth.') Augustine, *De vera religione*, XXXIX, 72.
42. Gerard Manley Hopkins, 'As Kingfishers Catch Fire' (c. 1877), in *The Poems and Prose of Gerard Manley Hopkins* (Harmondsworth: Penguin, 1953), no. 34.

CHAPTER TWENTY-TWO: *DE PROFUNDIS*: FINAL SONGS

1. *Allgemeine musikalische Zeitung*, 28, no. 8 (21 February 1827), column 139.
2. See Prologue, 3–5.
3. The title is from Seamus Heaney's last collection, *Human Chain* (2010).
4. *Dok*, 613.
5. Wilhelm Müller, *Diary and Letters of Wilhelm Müller*, ed. Philip Schuyler and James Taft Hatfield (University of Chicago Press, 1903), 5.
6. Cecilia C. Baumann and M. J. Luetgert. ' "Die Winterreise": The Secret of the Cycle's Appeal', *Mosaic: An Interdisciplinary Critical Journal* 15, no. 1 (1982), 41–52.
7. *Erinn*, 160–61.
8. *Erinn*, 20.

9. Seamus Heaney, *Aeneid*, Book VI (London: Faber & Faber, 2016).
10. Seamus Heaney, *Human Chain* (London: Faber & Faber, 2010), an autobiographical sequence in 12 sections, where events from Heaney's own life were plotted against episodes from the *Aeneid*, Book VI. The poetic conceit *Spiritus Mundi* is from the poem 'The Second Coming' by W. B. Yeats, who believed that individual human minds are linked to a single vast intelligence, which causes certain universal symbols to reappear. Jung called this 'the collective unconscious'.
11. Thrasybulus Georgiades, '"Das Wirthaus" von Schubert und das Kyrie aus dem Gregorianischen Requiem', in *Gegenwart im Geiste: Festschrift für Richard Benz*, ed. Walther Bulst and Arthur von Schneider (Hamburg: C Wegner 1954), 126–35; Youens, *Retracing a Winter's Journey: Schubert's Winterreise* (Cornell University Press, 1991) 281.
12. See Chapter 12, 297.
13. See Chapter 18, 409–411.
14. *Dok*, 336.
15. See Chapter 17, 384–385.
16. Edward Holmes, *A Ramble among the Musicians of Germany* (London: Hunt and Clark, 1828).
17. Andreas Liess, *Johann Michael Vogl. Hofoperist und Schubertsänger* (Graz-Köln: Verlag Herman Böhlaus Nachf., 1954), fn. 6.
18. Schindler also had Schubert fleeing Beethoven's home when the older composer pointed out a harmonic solecism in the Variations on a French Song (D 624), which Schubert dedicated to him in 1822; Wiley, *Re-Writing Composers' Lives*, 104.
19. *FSD*, 353.
20. For forensic research on court appointments made at the time, and an alternative reading of these songs, see Klaus Pietschmann, 'Italianità bei Schubert' in *Schubert: Interpretationen*, ed. Ivana Rentsch and Klaus Pietschmann (Stuttgart: Franz Steiner Verlag, 2014), 41–56, here 43–47.
21. This argument has already been established. See Vito Levi, 'Le arie e ariette di Schubert su testo italiano' in *Festschrift für Erich Schenk* (Graz [=Studien zur Musikwissenschaft 25] 1962), 307–14; Walburga Litschauer, 'Das Wort-Ton-Verhältnis in den italienischen Liedern von Franz Schubert' in *Wort und Ton im europäischen Raum. Gedenkschrift für Robert Schollum* (Vienna and Cologne: Böhlau, 1989), 115–32. See too Walther Dürr's introductory remarks in the *NSA*, IV, 4b, and Susanne Koopmann, 'Schubert und Metastasio. Zur Textvorlage von Franz Schuberts opus 83 aus dem Jahr 1827' in *Franz Schubert. 15 Nachtkonzerte mit Liedern, Szenen und Ensembles. 19. Aug.–6. Sept. 1991, Liederhalle Stuttgart* (Stuttgart: Internationale Hugo-Wolf-Gesellschaft, 1991), 198–213.
22. Litschauer, 'Das Wort-Ton-Verhältnis in den italienischen Liedern von Franz Schubert' (fn. 4), 126–27.
23. Pietschmann, 'Italianità bei Schubert', 48–49.
24. *Dok*, 501; Litschauer, 'Das Wort-Ton-Verhältnis in den italienischen Liedern von Franz Schubert' (fn. 4), 129.
25. See Chapter 18, 405.
26. See Chapter 14, 330.
27. I am responding to scholarship by and inspired by Hans-Joachim Hinrichsen. The Lablache songs were first brought to my attention through Klaus Pietschmann's 'Italianità bei Schubert' (41–56) when reviewing the Hinrichsen Festschrift, *Schubert: Interpretationen*, ed. Ivana Rentsche and Klaus Pietschmann (Stuttgart: Franz Steiner Verlag, 2014), in 'Door into the Dark: Another Look at Franz Schubert', *German Quarterly* 88/3 (2015), 379–83. I am also responding to one of Hinrichsen's arguments in 'Is There a Late Style in Schubert's Oeuvre', which I translated for *Rethinking Schubert*, 17–28, here 19.
28. *Dok*, 493, 495, 498, 509, 514, 544–45.
29. Johann Ferdinand von Schönfeld, *Jahrbuch von Wien und Prag* (Vienna: Schönfeld Verlag, 1796), and Johann Friedrich Reichardt, *Vertraute Briefe geschrieben auf einer Reise nach*

Wien und den österreichischen Staaten zu Ende des Jahres 1808 und zu Anfang 1809 (Leipzig: Kunst- und Industrie-Comtoir, 1810).
30. Körner, cited in Peter Clive, *Schubert and his World*, 53.
31. Körner, cited in Peter Clive, *Schubert and his World*, 53.
32. Otto Biba suggests Schubert is singing with Anna Fröhlich and Johann Vogl in 'Einige neue und wichtige Schubertina im Archiv der Gesellschaft der Musikfreunde', *Österreichische Musikzeitschrift* 33 (1978), 604–05. It is much more likely that the male singer is Ludwig Tietze, who premiered numerous Lieder, especially in 1827, or Baron von Schönstein, who was a regular performer in Kiesewetter's salon.
33. *Dok*, 448.
34. *Dok*, 451–52.
35. *Dok*, 208 and 308.
36. Till Gerrit Waidelich, *Schubert, Alfonso und Estrella: Eine frühe durchkomponierte deutsche Oper: Geschichte und Analyse* (Tutzing: Hans Schneider Verlag, 1991), 34.
37. *Dok*, 457.
38. *Dok*, 458.
39. *Erinn*, 161.

CHAPTER TWENTY-THREE: THE FINAL YEAR (1828)

1. *Dok*, 703 and 714.
2. Seamus Heaney, *Beowulf*, xv, ll. 2,415–16, 1,386–87.
3. Rufus Hallmark, 'Schubert's "Auf dem Strom"', *Schubert Studies*, 25–46; Alfred Einstein, *Schubert: A Musical Portrait* (Oxford University Press, 1951), 302–03.
4. Dok, 503. In this final draft of the programme 'Der Wanderer an dem Mond' replaces 'Fischerweise' (D 881), *FSD* I, 412.
5. *Erinn*, 271.
6. *Dok*, 508. The most detailed discussion of this concert is in Gingerich, *Schubert's Beethoven Project*, 271–301.
7. *Dok*, 509–10.
8. *Dok*, 516. The cuts are extensively discussed by Gingerich, *Schubert's Beethoven Project*, 278–301.
9. For further reading on this Italian practice of extempore embellishments see Livio Marcaletti, 'Improvisation and Essential Ornamentation in Vocal Music (1600–1900)', in *The Routledge Handbook of Philosophy and Improvisation in the Arts* (London and New York: Routlege, 2021); Livio Marcaletti, 'IL CANTAR SODO: Le Manieren di canto nella didattica tedesca di Sette e Ottocento' (Amsterdam: Ensemble Stile Galante 2022); Thomas Seedorf (ed.), *Aufführungspraxis. Solo-Gesang* (Stuttgart: Bärenreiter-Verlag, 2019).
10. Examples include Schubert's piano dances for the carnival (Grazer Walzer, D 924, Grazer Gallop, D 925, Valse nobles, D 969); works for violin and piano (Fantasy in C, D 934); chamber works (String Quintet in C, D 956), Piano Trio in E flat (D 929); Piano Four Hands (Fantasy in F minor, D 940); 4 Impromptus for Piano (D 935); last three Piano Sonatas (D 958–60); Song (*Winterreise*, D 911); TTBB and SATB works ('Ständchen', D 920 and D 921); Mass in E flat (D 950); opera (*Der Graf von Gleichen*, D 918); sketch for a symphony (D 936A).
11. See, for example, Hans-Joachim Hinrichsen, 'Is There a Late Style in Schubert's Oeuvre', and Walther Dürr, 'Compositional Strategies, *Rethinking Schubert*, 17–28 and 29–40.
12. See Chapter 16, 372–373.
13. *MA* 18/1, ll. 4,725ff, 108.
14. See Chapter 16, 369–373.
15. Goethe to Eckermann, 4 February 1829.
16. Translation by Richard Stokes except for verse 4 which is my own.
17. For a masterly reading of this song, see Susan Youens, *Schubert's Late Lieder* (Cambridge University Press, 2000), 404–14.

18. 'Preceding his father', the inscription Goethe decided on when he erected a gravestone for his son, August von Goethe, who is buried in the cemetery at the Pyramid of Cestius.
19. For a detailed reading of Schubert's exercises for Sechter see *NSA* VII/2.
20. *Dok*, 820. For an interesting reading see Laura Sewell Matter, 'Franz Schubert Dreamt of Indians', *Georgia Review* (2010), 111–29. The record of Schubert attending a supper party given by Baron Schönstein, who described him as 'unusually merry [. . .] almost restrained in his gaiety, a mood which might well have been induced by the large amount of wine he drank that evening', is believable because such hyperactivity was characteristic of Schubert's fasting. It is, however, contradicted by Schubert's letter to Schober.
21. *Erinn*, 344.
22. Elizabeth Norman McKay, *Franz Schubert: A Biography* (Oxford: Clarendon Press, 1996), 327.
23. *Erinn*, 162.
24. *ND*, 717.
25. *Erinn*, 242.
26. *Erinn*, 48.
27. *Erinn*, 43.

CHAPTER TWENTY-FOUR: *LACRIMAE RERUM*: BURIAL AT WÄHRING

1. *Dok*, 549, 550.
2. His final papers, written just two hours before his death, are in the private possession of the Hofbauer family in Kritzendorf.
3. WB HIN218365; *Dok*, 548.
4. *Dok*, 829.
5. From Seamus Heaney's translation of Virgil's *Aeneid*, 1, ll. 461ff.
6. The subtitle is borrowed from Seneca's *De Brevitate Vitae*, a moral essay he wrote to his friend Paulinus on the brevity of life and how we use (or waste) our time.
7. *ND* 705.
8. I borrow this phrase from Richard Ellmann's *James Joyce* (Oxford University Press, rev. 1982) 743.
9. George Steiner, *Language and Silence: Essays 1958–1966* (London: Penguin, 1967).

SELECT BIBLIOGRAPHY

PRIMARY SOURCES

Franz Schubert, *Neue Ausgabe sämtlicher Werke*, New Schubert Edition (*NSE*)/*Neue Schubert-Ausgabe* (*NSA*) (Kassel: Bärenreiter, 1956–in progress)

SECONDARY SOURCES

Aderhold, Werner, 'Kritscher Bericht': Sinfonie in H-moll. Supplement to *Neue Schubert-Ausgabe* V/3 (Tübingen, 2008)
—— 'Vorwort': Sinfonie in H-moll, *Neue Schubert-Ausgabe* V/3 (Tübingen, 1996)
Aderhold, Werner, Dürr, Walther and Litschauer, Walburga (eds), *Franz Schubert. Jahre der Krise 1818–1823. Festschrift Arnold Feil* (Kassel: Bärenreiter, 1985)
Adorno, Theodor W., 'Schubert (1928)', trans. Beate Perrey and Jonathan Dunsby, *19th-Century Music* 29/1 (Summer 2005), 3–14
Agawu, V. Kofi, 'On Schubert's "Der greise Kopf"', *Theory Only* 8/1 (1984), 3–22
Aldrich, Richard, 'The Heavenly Lengths in Schubert', *New York Times* (9 November 1919), 95
Aringer-Grau, Ulrike, ' "Im Gegenwärtigen Vergangenes" – Zu Schuberts Goethe-Vertonung in der Tradition des Männerquartetts von Johann Michael Haydn', *Schubert-Jahrbuch* (2000–2002), 49–59
Aschauer, Michael, 'Drei Stationen einer Auseinandersetzung mit dem System Metternichs. Franz Schuberts politische und weltanschauliche Haltung', *Studien zur Musikwissenschaft* 48 (2002), 373–88
Badura-Skoda, Eva, Gruber, Gerold W., Litschauer, Walburga and Ottner, Carmen (eds), *Schubert und seine Freunde* (Vienna: Böhlau, 1999)
Badura-Skoda, Paul, 'Possibilities and Limitations of Stylistic Criticism in the Dating of Schubert's "Great" C major Symphony' in Eva Badura-Skoda and Peter Branscombe (eds), *Schubert Studies: Problems of Style and Chronology* (Cambridge University Press, 1982), 187–208
Barry, Barbara, ' "Sehnsucht" and Melancholy: Explorations of Time and Structure in Schubert's *Winterreise*' in *The Philosopher's Stone: Essays in the Transformation of Musical Structure* (Hillsdale, New York: Pendragon Press, 2000), 181–202
Bartsch, Rudolf Hans, *Schwammerl. Ein Schubert-Roman* (Leipzig: L. Staackmann, 1912)
Bauernfeld, Eduard von, *Bilder und Persönlichkeiten aus Alt-Wien* ed. Wilhelm Zentner (Altötting: Verlag 'Bücher der Heimat', 1948)
Baumann, Cecilia and Luetgert, M. J., ' "Die Winterreise": The Secret of the Cycle's Appeal', *Mosaic: A Journal for the Interdisciplinary Study of Literature* 15/1 (1982), 41–52

SELECT BIBLIOGRAPHY

Beckerman, Michael, *Classical Music: Contemporary Perspectives and Challenges* (New York: Open Book Publishers, 2021)

—— *New Worlds of Dvořák: Searching in America for the Composer's Inner Life* (New York: Norton, 1991)

Bendikt, Erich and Jahn, Michael, *Die Musikhandschriften des Pfarrarchivs Wien-Lichtental* (Vienna: Der Apfel [=Veröffentlichungen des rism-österreich, Band/Reihe: 3/A], 2006)

Biba, Otto, 'Schubert's Position in Viennese Musical Life,' *19th-Century Music* 3 (1979), 106–12

Binder, Benjamin, 'Disability, Self-Critique and Failure in Schubert's "Der Doppelgänger"' in Lorraine Byrne Bodley and Julian Horton (eds), *Rethinking Schubert* (Oxford University Press, 2016), 418–36

Bischoff, Ferdinand, *Chronik des Steiermärkischen Musikvereines* (Graz: Verlag des steiermärkischen Musikvereines, 1890)

Black, Brian, 'Remembering a Dream: The Tragedy of Romantic Memory in the Transitional Process of Schubert's Sonata Forms', *Intersections* 25/1–2 (2005), 202–28

—— 'The Sensuous as a Constructive Force in Schubert's Late Works' in Lorraine Byrne Bodley and Julian Horton (eds), *Rethinking Schubert* (Oxford University Press, 2016), 77–110

Black, Leo, *Franz Schubert: Music and Belief* (Woodbridge: Boydell and Brewer, 2003)

Blaha, Johanna, *Die Schwestern Fröhlich* (Vienna: unpublished dissertation, University of Vienna, 2002)

Blanken, Christine *Franz Schuberts 'Lazarus' und das Wiener Oratorium zu Beginn des 19. Jahrhunderts, Schubert: Perspektiven – Studien 1* (Stuttgart: Steiner, 2002)

Bonds, Mark Evans, *Music as Thought: Listening to the Symphony in the Age of Beethoven* (Princeton University Press, 2015)

—— *The Beethoven Syndrome: Hearing Music as Autobiography* (Oxford University Press, 2020)

—— *Beethoven: Variations on a Life* (Oxford University Press, 2020)

Bostridge, Ian, *Schubert's Winter Journey: Anatomy of an Obsession* (London: Faber and Faber, 2015)

Botstein, Leon, 'Realism Transformed: Franz Schubert and Vienna' in Christopher H. Gibbs (ed), *The Cambridge Companion to Schubert* (Cambridge University Press, 1997), 15–17

Božić, Renate, 'Franz Schubert, die "Unvollendete" und der Steiermärkische Musikverein', *175 Jahre Musikverein für Steiermark, Graz. 1815–1990* (Graz: Mur-Kapfenberg, 1990)

Böhm, August, *Geschichte des Singvereines der Gesellschaft der Musikfreunde in Wien* (Vienna: Holzhausen, 1908)

Böttcher, Helmuth M., *Der Unvollendete. Franz Schubert und sein Kreis* (Rudolstadt: Greifenverlag, 1954)

Boyle, Nicolas, *Goethe: The Poet and the Age*, Vol.1, The Poetry of Desire, 1749–1790 (Oxford University Press, 1991) and Vol.2 Revolution and Renunciation, 1790–1803 (Oxford University Press, 2000)

Branscombe, Peter, 'Schubert and the Ungers: A Preliminary Study' in Brian Newbould (ed), *Schubert Studies* (2006), 209–19

Brendel, Alfred, 'Schubert's Last Sonatas', in *Music Sounded Out: Essays, Lectures, Interviews, Afterthoughts* (London: Robson, 1990), 72–141

Bretherton, David T., 'In Search of Schubert's Doppelgänger', *Musical Times* 144 (2003), 45–50

—— 'The Poetics of Schubert's Song-Forms' (Oxford: unpublished PhD dissertation, 2007)

—— 'The Shadow of Midnight in Schubert's "Gondelfahrer" Settings', *Music and Letters* 92/1 (2011), 1–42

Brett, Philip, 'Piano Four-Hands: Schubert and the Performance of Gay Male Desire', *19th-Century Music*, 21/2 (1997), 49–76

Brinkmann, Reinhold, *Franz Schubert, Lindenbäume und deutsch-nationale Identität: Interpretation eines Liedes* (Vienna: Pictus, 2004)

—— 'Schubert's Political Landscape' in David E. Wellbery (ed), *A New History of German Literature* (Cambridge, MA/London: The Bellknap Press of Harvard University, 2004), 540–46

SELECT BIBLIOGRAPHY

Brodbeck, David, 'Dance Music as High Art: Schubert's Twelve Ländler, Op. 171 (D 79)', in Walter Frisch (ed), *Schubert: Critical and Analytic Studies* (Lincoln, NE, and London: University of Nebraska Press, 1986), 31–47

Brown, Maurice J., *Schubert: A Critical Biography* (London: Macmillan, 1966)

Brown, Peter, 'Performance Tradition, Steady and Proportional Tempos, and the First Movements of Schubert's Symphonies', *The Journal of Musicology* 5/2 (1987), 296–307

Brusatti, Otto, *Schubert in Wiener Vormärz: Dokumente 1829–1848* (Graz: Adeva, 1978)

Burnham, Scott, 'Beethoven, Schubert and the Movement of Phenomena' in Lorraine Byrne Bodley and Julian Horton (eds), *Schubert's Late Music: History, Theory, Style* (Cambridge University Press, 2016), 35–51

—— 'Landscape as Music, Landscape as Truth: Schubert and the Burden of Repetition', *19th Century Music* (2005), 31–41

—— 'Schubert and the Sound of Memory', *Musical Quarterly* 84/4 (2000), 655–63

Burstein, Poundie, 'Lyricism, Structure and Gender in Schubert's G major String Quartet', *Musical Quarterly* 81/1 (1997), 51–63

—— 'Devil's Castles and Schubert's Strange Tonic Allusions', *Theory and Practice* 27 (2002), 69–84

Byrne Bodley, Lorraine, 'A Place at the Edge: Reflections on Schubert's Late Style', Invited Article for Special Edition 'Writing *in extremis*, *Oxford German Studies* 44/1 (2015), 18–29

—— *Claudine von Villa Bella: Goethe's Singspiel Set to Music by Franz Schubert* (Dublin: Carysfort Press, 2002)

—— *Goethe and Schubert: Across the Divide* (Dublin: Carysfort Press, 2001)

—— *Goethe and Zelter: Musical Dialogues* (London: Ashgate, 2009)

—— *Goethe: Musical Poet, Musical Catalyst* (Dublin: Carysfort Press, 2004)

—— 'In Pursuit of a Single Flame?: Schubert's Settings of Goethe's Lyrics', in Lorraine Byrne Bodley and James Sobaskie, Guest Editors of *Schubert Familiar and Unfamiliar: Continuing Conversations*, Special Schubert Edition of *Nineteenth Century Music Review* 13/1 (Cambridge University Press, May 2016), 11–34

—— 'Late Style and the Paradoxical Poetics of the Schubert-Berio Rendering' in Barbara Reul and Lorraine Byrne Bodley (eds), *The Unknown Schubert* (Aldershot: Ashgate, 2008), 233–50

—— *Music in Goethe's Faust: Goethe's Faust in Music* (Woodbridge: The Boydell Press, 2017)

—— 'Music of the Orphaned Self: Schubert and Concepts of Late Style' in Lorraine Byrne Bodley and Julian Horton (eds), *Schubert's Late Music: History, Theory, Style* (Cambridge University Press, 2016), 331–57

—— 'Opera that Vanished: Goethe, Schubert and *Claudine von Villa Bella*' in Joe Davies and James William Sobaskie (eds), *Drama in the Music of Franz Schubert* (Woodbridge: The Boydell Press, 2018), 11–34

—— *Proserpina: Goethe's Melodrama with Music by Carl Eberwein* (Dublin: Carysfort Press, 2007)

—— 'Revisiting Claudine: Schubert's Goethe Singspiel', in Lorraine Byrne and Dan Farrelly (eds), *Goethe and Schubert Across the Divide* (Dublin: Carysfort Press, 2003), 161–92

—— *Schubert's Goethe Settings* (Aldershot: Ashgate, 2002)

—— 'Schubert Sacred Music: Influence, Anxiety, Myth' in Harry White and Kerry Houston (eds), *A Musical Offering: Festschrift for Gerard Gillen* (Dublin: Four Courts Press, 2017), 256–84

—— *The Unknown Schubert* (Aldershot and Burlington: Ashgate, 2007)

—— 'Wandermotive in Schuberts Goethe Liedern', *Schubert-Jahrbuch* (2010–2013), 125–41

Byrne Bodley, Lorraine and Horton, Julian, *Schubert's Late Music: History, Theory, Style* (Cambridge University Press, 2016)

—— *Rethinking Schubert* (Oxford University Press, 2016)

Capell, Richard, *Schubert's Songs*, 3rd edn (New York: Collier Books, 1977)

Caplin, William E., *Classical Form: A Theory of Formal Functions for the Instrumental Music of Haydn, Mozart and Beethoven* (Oxford University Press, 1998)

SELECT BIBLIOGRAPHY

Chalus, Alois, *Franz Schubert und seine h-moll-Sinfonie im Blickpunkt seiner Freundschaft mit Anselm und Josef Hüttenbrenner* (Vienna: unpublished typescript, Vienna Library, 1965)

Chusid, Martin (ed), *Schubert, Symphony in B minor ('Unfinished')* (New York: W. W. Norton, 1968)

—— 'The Chamber Music of Schubert' (PhD dissertation, University of California, 1961)

Clark, Suzannah, *Analyzing Schubert* (Cambridge University Press, 2011)

—— 'On the Imagination of Tone in Schubert's *Liedesend* (D473), *Trost* (D523), and *Gretchens Bitte* (D564)' in Edward Gollin and Alexander Rehding (eds), *The Oxford Handbook of Neo-Riemannian Theories* (Oxford University Press, 2011), 294–321

—— 'Schubert, Theory and Analysis', *Music Analysis* 21 (2002), 209–43

Clive, Peter, *Schubert and his World: A Biographical Dictionary* (Oxford: Clarendon Press, 1997)

Cohn, Richard, '"As Wonderful as Star Clusters": Instruments for Gazing at Tonality in Schubert', *19th-Century Music* 22/3 (1999), 213–32

—— *Audacious Euphony: Chromaticism and the Triad's Second Nature* (Oxford University Press, 2012), 17–42

Cone, Edward T., 'Schubert's Promissory Note: An Exercise in Musical Hermeneutics', in Walter Frisch (ed), *Schubert: Critical and Analytical Studies* (Lincoln, NE, and London: University of Nebraska Press, 1986), 13–30

—— 'Schubert's Unfinished Business', *19th-Century Music* 7/3 (1984), 222–32

Dahlhaus, Carl, 'Die Sonatenform bei Schubert: Der Erste Satz des G-dur-Quartetts D. 887', *Musica* 32 (1978), trans. Thilo Reinhard as 'Sonata Form in Schubert: The First Movement of the G major String Quartet, Op. 161 (D. 877)' in Walter Frisch (ed), *Schubert: Critical and Analytic Studies* (Lincoln, NE, and London: University of Nebraska Press, 1986), 13–30

—— 'Franz Schubert und das "Zeitalter Beethovens und Rossinis"' in *Franz Schubert: Jahre der Krise 1818–1823* (Kassel: Bärenreiter, 1985) 22–28

Dahms, Walter, *Franz Schubert* (Berlin and Leipzig: Schuster & Loeffler, 1912)

Damschroder, David, *Harmony in Schubert* (Cambridge University Press, 2010)

Davies, Joe and Sobaskie, James William, *Drama in the Music of Franz Schubert* (Woodbridge: The Boydell Press, 2019)

Denny, Thomas A., 'Schubert's "Fierrabras" and Barbaja's Opera Business' in *Schubert: Perspektiven* 5 (2005), 19–45

—— 'Too Long? Too Loose? And Too Light? Critical Thoughts about Schubert's Mature Finales', *Studies in Music*, 23 (1989), 25–52

DeNora, Tia, *Beethoven and the Construction of Genius: Music and Politics in Vienna 1792–1803* (Berkeley and Los Angeles: University of California Press, 1995)

Deutsch, Otto Eric (ed), *Schubert: Die Erinnerungen seiner Freunde* (Wiesbaden: Breitkopf & Härtel, 1957, repr. 1983), trans. Rosamond Ley and John Nowell as *Schubert: Memoirs by his Friends* (London: Adam and Charles Black, 1958)

—— *Franz Schubert: Thematisches Verzeichnis seiner Werke in chronologischer Folge* (Kassel: Bärenreiter, 1978)

—— *Schubert: Die Dokumente seines Lebens* (Kassel: Bärenreiter, 1964, reprint 1980 and 1996) trans. Eric Blom as *Schubert: A Documentary Biography* (J. M. Dent & Sons, 1946) and as *The Schubert Reader: A Life of Franz Schubert in Letters and Documents* (New York: W. W. Norton, 1947)

De Voto, Mark, *Schubert's Great C major: Biography of a Symphony* (Hillsdale, NY: Pendragon Press, 2011)

Dittrich, Marie-Agnes, 'The Lieder of Schubert', in James Parsons (ed), *The Cambridge Companion to the Lied* (Cambridge University Press, 2004), 85–100

Dürhammer, Ilija, 'Der Wandel des Schubert-Bildes im 20. Jahrhundert' in Otto Kolleritsch (ed), '*Dialekt ohne Ende . . .*' *Franz Schubert und das 20. Jahrhundert* (Vienna, 1998), 238–58

—— 'Homoerotische Chiffren im Schubert-Kreis', *Kunstpunkt* 24 (2002), 19–20

—— '"Um Schuberts Schädel . . . eine ziemlich dichte Hülle seines bekanntlich sehr üppigen Haares". Beethovens und Schuberts Exhumierungen (1863/1888). Reflexionen über die

SELECT BIBLIOGRAPHY

Bedeutung von deren Sterben und Tod' in Ilija Dürhammer und Pia Janke (eds), 'Erst wenn einer tot ist, ist er gut', *Künstlerreliquien und Devotionalien* (Wien: Brandstätter, 2002), 53–62

—— 'Zu Schuberts Literaturaesthetik. Entwickelt anhand seiner zu Lebzeiten veröffentlichten Vokalwerke' in *Schubert durch die Brille* XIV (1995), 5–99

Dürr, Walther, 'Compositional Strategies in Schubert's Late Music' in Lorraine Byrne Bodley and Julian Horton (eds), *Rethinking Schubert* (Oxford University Press, 2016), 29–40

—— 'Denkmal oder Werk – Theorie und Praxis: Zu editorischen Verfahrensweisen im Lied um 1800' in Martin Staehlin (ed), *Musikalische Überlieferung und musikalische Edition. Gesammelte Aufsätze von Walther Dürr, Andreas Haug, Wolfgang Horn, Martin Just und Martin Staehelin* (Göttingen: Vandenhoeck & Ruprecht 2006) (Nachrichten der Akademie der Wissenschaften zu Göttingen. I. Philolosophisch-historische Klasse. Jahrgang 2006, no. 2), 135–48

—— 'Notation und Aufführungspraxis: Artikulation und Dynamik bei Schubert', in Helga Lühning (ed), *Musikedition. Mittler zwischen Wissenschaft und musikalischer Praxis* (Tübingen: Max Niemeyer, 2002), 313–27

—— 'Schuberts romantisch-heroische Oper *Alfonso und Estrella* im Kontext französischer und italienischer Tradition' in Erich Wolfgang Partsch and Oskar Pausch (eds), *Der vergessene Schubert: Franz Schubert auf der Bühne* (Vienna: Exhibit Catalogue, 1997), 79–105

—— 'Schuberts Dynamik – Beobachtungen am Manuskript', *Schubert: Perspektiven* 7/1 (2007), 1–21

—— 'Über Schuberts Verhältnis zu Bach' in Ingrid Fuchs (ed), *Johann Sebastian Bach: Beiträge zur Wirkungsgeschichte* (Vienna: Kongressbericht Wien, 1992), 69–79

Dürr, Walther, Arnold Feil, Christa Landon et al. (eds), *Franz Schubert: Thematisches Verzeichnis seiner Werke in chronologischer Folge* (Kassel: Bärenreiter, 1996)

Dürr, Walther and Krause, Andreas, *Schubert Handbuch* (Kassel, Basel, London, New York, Prague: Bärenreiter, 1997 also Stuttgart and Weimar: Metzler, 1997)

Dürr, Walther, Michael Kube, Uwe Schweikert and Stefanie Steiner (eds), *Schubert-Liedlexikon* (Kassel: Bärenreiter, 2012)

Einstein, Alfred, *Schubert. Ein musikalisches Porträt* (Zurich: Pan-Verlag, 1952), trans. *Schubert: A Musical Portrait* (Oxford University Press, 1951)

Erikson, Raymond (ed), *Schubert's Vienna* (New Haven, CT, and London: Yale University Press, 1997)

Everett, Walter, 'Grief in *Winterreise*: A Schenkerian Perspective', *Music Analysis* 9 (1990), 157–75

Federhofer, Helmut, 'Terzverwandte Akkorde und ihre Funktion in der Harmonik Franz Schuberts', in Otto Brusatti (ed), *Schubert-Kongress Wien 1978: Bericht* (Graz: Akademische Druck- und Verlagsanstalt, 1979), 61–70

Feil, Arnold, *Franz Schubert: Die schöne Müllerin, Winterreise* (Stuttgart: Reclams Musikführer, 1975)

Feurzeig, Lisa, 'Heroines in Perversity: Marie Schmidt, Animal Magnetism, and the Schubert Circle', *19th-Century Music* 21/2 (1997), 223–43

—— 'The Queen of Golconda, the Ashman, and the Shepherd on a Rock: Schubert and the Vienna Volkstheater,' in Christopher H. Gibbs and Morten Solvik (eds), *Franz Schubert and his World* (Princeton University Press, 2014), 157–82

Fischer Dieskau, Dietrich, *Auf den Spuren der Schubert-Lieder: Werden-Wesen-Wirkung* (Kassel: Bärenreiter, 1977)

—— *Schubert's Songs: A Biographical Study*, trans. Kenneth A. Whitton (New York: Alfred A. Knopf, 1977)

Fisk, Charles, 'Edward T. Cone's "The Composer's Voice": Questions about the Persona of Schubert's "Wanderer" Fantasy', *College Music Symposium* 29 (1989), 19–30

—— *Returning Cycles: Contexts for the Interpretation of Schubert's Impromptus and Last Sonatas* (Berkeley and Los Angeles: University of California Press, 2001)

—— 'Schubert's Last Finales', *TASI Journal: A Publication of the American Schubert Institute* 1 (1997), 3–17

SELECT BIBLIOGRAPHY

—— 'What Schubert's Last Sonata Might Hold', in Jenefer Robinson (ed), *Music and Meaning* (Ithaca, NY, and London: Cornell University Press, 1997), 179–200

Flothius, Marius, 'Schubert Revises Schubert' in Eva Badura-Skoda and Peter Branscombe (eds), *Schubert Studies* (Cambridge University Press, 1982), 61–84

Frisch, Walter, *Schubert: Critical and Analytical Studies* (Lincoln, NE, and London: University of Nebraska Press, 1986)

—— '"You Must Remember This": Memory and Structure in Schubert's String Quartet in G major, D. 887', *Musical Quarterly* 84/4 (2000), 582–603

Georgiades, Thrasybulos, 'Schubert. Lyric as Musical Structure: Schubert's "Wandrers Nachtlied" (Über allen Gipfeln D 768)', trans. Marie Louise Göllner in Walter Frisch (ed), *Schubert: Critical and Analytical Studies* (Lincoln, NE, and London: University of Nebraska Press, 1986), 84–103

Gibbs, Christopher H. (ed), *Cambridge Companion to Schubert* (Cambridge University Press, 1997)

—— '"Poor Schubert": Images and Legends of the Composer' in *The Cambridge Companion to Schubert* (Cambridge University Press, 2000), 36–55

—— *The Life of Schubert* (Cambridge University Press, 2000)

—— 'Writing Under the Influence? Salieri and Schubert's Early Opinion of Beethoven' in *Current Musicology* 75 (2003), 117–44

Gingerich, John M., 'Remembrance and Consciousness in Schubert's C-major String Quintet, D 956', *Musical Quarterly*, 84/4 (2000), 619–34

—— *Schubert's Beethoven Project* (Cambridge University Press, 2014)

—— '"To how many shameful deeds must you lend your image": Schubert's Pattern of Telescoping and Excision in the Texts of his Latin Masses', *Current Musicology* 70 (2000), 61–99

—— 'Unfinished Considerations: Schubert's "Unfinished" Symphony in Context of His Beethoven Project', *19th-Century Music* 31/2 (2007), 99–112

Gjerdingen, Robert, *Music in the Galant Style* (Oxford University Press, 2007)

Godel, Arthur, *Schubert's letzte drei Klaviersonaten* (Baden-Baden: Valentin Koerner, 1985)

—— 'Zum Eigengesetz der Schubertschen Fantasien', in Otto Brusatti (ed), *Schubert-Kongress Wien 1978* (Graz: Akademische Druck- und Verlagsanstalt, 1979)

Goethe, Johann Wolfgang von, *Sämtliche Werke nach Epochen seines Schaffens. Münchner Ausgabe*, 20 vols, ed. Karl Richter in collaboration with Herbert G. Göpfert, Norbert Miller and Gerhard Sauder (Munich: Carl Hanser Verlag, 1990)

Goldschmidt, Harry, *Franz Schubert. Ein Lebensbild* (Berlin: Henschel, 1954, rev. 1980)

Gottdang, Andrea, '"Ich bin unsern Ideen nicht untreu geworden": Moritz von Schwind und der Schubert-Freundeskreis', *Schubert: Perspektiven* 4 (2004), 1–48

Gramit, David, *Cultivating Music: The Aspirations, Interests, and Musical Limits of German Musical Cuture, 1770–1848* (Berkeley and Los Angeles: University of California Press, 2002)

—— 'Schubert and the Biedermeier: The Aesthetics of Johann Mayrhofer's "Heliopolis"', *Music and Letters* 74/3 (1993), 355–84

—— 'The Intellectual and Aesthetic Tenets of Franz Schubert's Circle: Their Development and teir Influence on his Music' (PhD dissertation, Duke University, 1987)

—— '"The passion for friendship": Music, Cultivation, and Identity in Schubert's Circle' in Christopher Gibbs (ed), *The Cambridge Companion to Schubert* (Cambridge University Press, 1997), 56–71

Griffel, L. Michael, 'A Reappraisal of Schubert's Methods of Composition', *Musical Quarterly*, 63/2 (1977), 186–210

Grove, George, *Beethoven, Schubert, Mendelssohn* (London: Macmillan, 1922)

Gruber, Gernot, *Schubert. Schubert? Leben und Musik* (Kassel: Bärenreiter, 2010)

—— 'Text und Kontext in der Musik. Zum "Gesang der Geister über den Wassern"' in Panagl, Oswald and Ruth Wodak (eds), *Text und Kontext. Theoriemodelle und methodische Verfahren im transdisziplinären Vergleich* (Würzburg: Königshausen & Neumann, 2004), 235–42

Gülke, Peter, *Franz Schubert und seine Zeit* (Laaber: Laaber-Verlag, 1991)

SELECT BIBLIOGRAPHY

—— 'In What Respect a Quintet? On the Disposition of Instruments in the String Quintet, D 956', in Eva Badura-Skoda and Peter Branscombe (eds), *Schubert Studies: Problems of Style and Chronology* (Cambridge University Press, 1982), 173–85

—— 'Neue Beiträge zur Kenntnis des Sinfonikers Schubert . . .' in Heinz-Klaus Metzger and Rainer Riehn (eds), *Musik-Konzepte. Sonderband Franz Schubert* (Munich: Edition Text+kritik, 1979), 187–220

—— 'Zum Bilde des späten Schubert', in Heinz-Klaus Metzger and Rainer Riehn (eds), *Musik-Konzepte. Sonderband Franz Schubert* (Munich: Edition Text+kritik, 1979), 107–66

Hall, Michael, *Schubert's Song Sets* (Aldershot and Burlington: Ashgate, 2003)

Hallmark, Rufus, 'The Literary and Musical Rhetoric of Apostrophe in *Winterreise*', *19th-Century Music* 35/1 (2011), 3–33

Hallmark, Rufus and Fehn, Ann C., 'Text and Music in Schubert's Settings of Pentameter Poetry' in Jürgen Thym (ed), *Of Poetry and Song: Approaches to the Nineteenth-Century Lied* (Rochester, NY: University of Rochester Press, 2010), 156–57

Hanslick, Eduard, *Geschichte des Concertwesens in Wien* (Vienna: Wilhelm Braumiller 1869–70)

Hanson, Alice, *Musical Life in Biedermeier Vienna* (Cambridge University Press, 1985)/*Die zensurierte Muse. Musikleben im Wiener Biedermeier* (Vienna: Böhlau, 1987)

—— 'The Significance of the *Ludlamshöhle* for Franz Schubert' in Barbara Haggh (ed), *Essays on Music and Culture in Honor of Herbert Kellman* (Paris and Tours: Minerve, 2001), 496–502

Hascher, Xavier, *Schubert, la forme sonate et son évolution* (Bern, Berlin and Paris: Peter Lang, 1996)

—— *Symbole et fantasme dans l'adagio du quintette à cordes de Schubert* (Paris, Budapest and Turin: l'Harmattan, 2005)

—— (ed), *Le style instrumental de Schubert, sources, analyse, évolution* (Paris: Publications de la Sorbonne, 2007)

Hatten, Robert S., *A Theory of Virtual Agency for Western Art Music* (Bloomington, IN: Indiana University Press, 2018)

—— *Interpreting Musical Gestures, Topics, and Tropes: Mozart, Beethoven, Schubert* (Bloomington, IN: Indiana University Press, 2004)

—— 'Interpreting Personal Motivations: Responses to Life Crisis in Later Works of Beethoven, Schubert and Chopin' in Mieczyslaw Tomaszewski and Magdalena Chrenkoff Beethoven Studien 2 (Krakow: Akademia Muzyczna W Krakowie, 2003), *Beethoven* 2, 203–20

—— 'Schubert's Alchemy: Transformative Surfaces, Transfiguring Depths' in Lorraine Byrne Bodley and Julian Horton (eds), *Schubert's Late Music: History, Theory, Style* (Cambridge University Press, 2016), 91–110

—— 'Schubert the Progressive: The Role of Resonance and Gesture in the Piano Sonata in A D 959', *Intégral* 7 (1993), 38–81

Haydn, Deborah, *Pox, Genius, Madness, and the Mysteries of Syphilis* (New York and Oxford: Basic Books and Publicity Partnership, 2003)

Herbeck, Ludwig, *Johann Herbeck. Ein Lebensbild von seinem Sohne* (Vienna: Gutmann, 1885)

Hetenyi, G. R, 'The Terminal Illness of Franz Schubert and the Treatment of Syphilis in Vienna in the Eighteen Hundred and Twenties', *Canadian Bulletin of Medical History* 3 (1986)

Hilmar, Ernst, 'Datierungsproblem im Werk Schuberts' in *Bericht über den Schubert-Kongress Wien 1978* (Vienna: Akademische Druck- und Verlagsanstalt, 1978)

—— 'Ferdinand Schuberts Skizze zu einer Autobiographie' in *Schubert-Studien* (Vienna: Österreichische Akademie der Wissenschaften, 1978), 86–117

—— *Franz Schubert: Drei große Sonaten für das Pianoforte, D 958, D 959 und D 960 (frühe Fassungen): Faksimile nach den Autographen in der Wiener Stadt- und Landesbibliothek* (Tutzing: Hans Schneider, 1987)

—— *Schubert* (Graz: Akademische Druck- und Verlagsanstalt, 1989)

—— *Verzeichnis der Schubert-Handschriften in der Musiksammlung der Wiener Stadt- und Landesbibliothek*, *Catalogus Musicus* 8 (Kassel: Bärenreiter, 1978)

SELECT BIBLIOGRAPHY

——— (ed), *Franz Schubert. Dokumente 1801–1830*. Vol. 1: *Texte, Programme, Rezensionen, Anzeigen, Nekrologe, Musikbeilagen und andere gedruckte Quellen. Addenda und Kommentar* (Tutzing: Veröffentlichungen des IFSI, 2003)

——— (ed), *Schubert durch die Brille*, vols 1–3 (Vienna: Mitteilungen des Internationalen Franz Schubert Instituts, 1988/89)

——— (ed), *Schubert durch die Brille*, vols 4–30 (Tutzing: Hans Schneider, 1990–2003)

Hilmar, Ernst, and Jestremski, Margret (eds), *Schubert-Enzyklopädie*, 2 vols (Tutzing: Schneider, 2004)

Hinrichsen, Hans-Joachim, '"Bergendes Gehäuse" und "Hang ins Unbegrenzte": Die Kammermusik' in Walther Dürr and Andreas Krause (eds), *Schubert-Handbuch* (Kassel: Bärenreiter, 1997), 451–511

——— 'Der Weg zur grossen Symphonie', *Schubert: Perspektiven* 10/1 (2010), 106–12

——— 'Die Sonatenform im Spätwerk Franz Schuberts' in *Schubert: Perspektiven* 4 (2004), 16–49

——— 'Durchkreuzte und eingelöste Erwartung. Schuberts Kammermusik' in Andreas Dorschel (ed), *Dem Ohr voraus. Erwartung und Vorurteil in der Musik* (Vienna, London and New York: Universal Edition für Institut für Wertungsforschung an der Universität für Musik und darstellende Kunst Graz, 2004), *Studien zur Wertungsforschung* 44, 112–33

——— 'Is There a Late Style in Schubert's Oeuvre' in Lorraine Byrne Bodley and Julian Horton (eds), *Rethinking Schubert* (Oxford University Press, 2016), 17–28

——— '"Rendering per orchestra". Luciano Berios komponierter Essay über Schuberts Spätwerk', *Schubert: Perspektiven* 2 (2002), 135–66

——— *Schubert* (Munich: C. H. Beck, 2011)

———*Untersuchung zur Entwicklung der Sonatenform in der Instrumentalmusik Franz Schuberts* (Tutzing: IFSI 11, 1994)

——— "Unvollendet" oder abgebrochen? Werkstatus und Manuskripttypologie bei Franz Schubert', *Schubert: Perspektiven* 5 (2005), 183–203

Hinrichsen, Hans-Joachim and Waidelich, Till Gerrit (eds), *Schubert: Perspektiven* (Stuttgart: Franz Steiner Verlag, 2001ff.)

Hirsch, Marjorie W., *Romantic Lieder and the Search for Lost Paradise* (Cambridge University Press, 2007)

——— *Schubert's Dramatic Lieder* (Cambridge University Press, 1993)

Horton, Julian, *The Cambridge Companion to the Symphony* (Cambridge University Press, 2013)

Howat, Roy, 'Reading between the Lines of the A major Sonata (D 959)', *The Schubertian* 50 (2006), 31–32

Howe, Blake, 'Bounded Finitude and Boundless Infinitude: Schubert's Contradictions of the "final barrier"' in Lorraine Byrne Bodley and Julian Horton (eds), *Schubert's Late Music: History, Theory, Style* (Cambridge University Press, 2016), 357–82

——— 'The Allure of Dissolution: Bodies, Forces, and Cyclicity in Schubert's Final Mayrhofer Settings', *Journal of the American Musicological Society* 62 (2009), 271–322

Howie, Crawford, 'Small is Beautiful: Schubert's Smaller Sacred Works' in Barbara Reul and Lorraine Byrne Bodley (eds), *The Unknown Schubert* (Aldershot: Ashgate, 2008), 59–80

Hyland, Anne M., 'In Search of Liberated Time or Schubert's Quartet in G major D 887: Once More Between Sonata and Variation', *Music Theory Spectrum* 38/1 (2016), 85–108

——— 'Rhetorical Closure in the First Movement of Schubert's Quartet in C major D 46: A Dialogue with Deformation', *Music Analysis* 28/1 (2009), 111–42

——— 'Tautology or Teleology? Towards an Understanding of Repetition in Franz Schubert's Instrumental Chamber Music' (Cambridge: PhD thesis, 2010)

——— 'The "Tightened Bow": Analysing the Juxtaposition of Drama and Lyricism in Schubert's Paratactic Sonata-Form Movements' in Gareth Cox and Julian Horton (eds), *Irish Musical Studies*, vol. 11: *Irish Musical Analysis* (Dublin: Four Courts Press, 2014), 17–40

SELECT BIBLIOGRAPHY

—— 'Unhimmlische Länge: Editorial Intervention as Reception History' in Lorraine Byrne Bodley and Julian Horton (eds), *Schubert's Late Music: History, Theory, Style* (Cambridge University Press, 2016), 52–76

—— 'Zumsteeg Ballads without Words: Inter-Generic Dialogue and Schubert's Projection of Drama through Form' in Joe Davies and James William Sobaskie, *Drama in the Music of Franz Schubert* (Woodbridge: The Boydell Press, 2018), 205–32

Hüttenbrenner, Anselm, [Auto]Biographische Notizen [mit Werkverzeichnis, für Gesellschaft der Musikfreunde] (Vienna, 1835), 91–138

—— 'Der Erlkönig', ed. Andreas Holzer (Graz: Akademische Druck- und Verlagsanstalt [=*Musik alter Meister* 59], 1993)

—— Klaviersonate zu zwei Händen E-Dur op. 16, Klaviersonate zu vier Händen A-Dur op. 22 ed. Michael Aschauer (Graz: Akademische Druck- und Verlagsanstalt [= *Musik alter Meister* 59] 2001)

—— 'Kleiner Beitrag zu Salieri's Biographie', *Leipziger Allgemeine musikalische Zeitung* 27 (1825), column 7961–99

—— *Lieder für eine Singstimme mit Klavierbegleitung*, 3 vols. ed. Ulf Bästlein, Alice and Michael Aschauer (Warngau: Accolade, 2008–10)

—— *Sämtliche Streichquartett*, ed. Michael Kube (Munich and Salzburg: Katzbichlers Kammermusik Bibliothek, 2003)

Hüttenbrenner, Felix, 'Anselm Hüttenbrenner und Schubert's H-moll-Symphonie', *Zeitschrift des historischen Vereins für Steiermark* LII (Graz, 1961/62)

—— 'Franz Schubert und die Brüder Hüttenbrenner', *Zeitschrift des historischen Vereines für Steiermark* 57 (1966), 127–39

—— 'Zu Anselm Hüttenbrenners 100. Todestag', *Mitteilungen des steirischen Tonkünstlerbundes* 35/36 (1968)

—— 'Zur Geschichte der H-moll-Symphonie' in *Zeitschrift des Steiermärkischen Sängerbundes* 2 (Graz, 1928)

Hyland, Anne M. and Litschauer, Walburga, 'Records of Inspiration: Schubert's Drafts for the Last Three Piano Sonatas Reappraised' in Lorraine Byrne Bodley and Julian Horton (eds), *Rethinking Schubert* (Oxford University Press, 2016), 173–206

Jahrmärker, Manuela, 'Von der liturgischen Funktion zum persönlichen Bekenntnis. Die Kirchenmusik' in Walther Dürr und Andreas Krause, *Schubert Handbuch* (Kassel, Basel, London, New York, Prague: Bärenreiter, 1997 also Stuttgart and Weimar: Metzler, 1997) 345–377

Jary-Janecka, Friederike, 'Franz Schubert als Bühnenfigur' in Michael Kube, Walburga Litschauer and Gernot Gruber (eds), *Schubert und die Nachwelt. I. Internationale Arbeitstagung zur Schubert-Rezeption Wien 2003. Kongreßbericht* (Munich, Salzburg: Katzbichler, 2007), 281–290

—— *Franz Schubert am Theater und im Film* (Salzburg: Müller-Spieser, 2000)

Jaskulsky, Hans, *Die lateinischen Messen Franz Schuberts* (Mainz, London and New York, Tokyo: Schott, 1986)

Jestremski, Margret, 'Unveröffentlichte Dokumente aus dem Nachlaß Hüttenbrenners', *Schubert durch die Brille* 15 (1995), 94–99

Johnson, Graham, *Franz Schubert: The Complete Songs* (New Haven, CT, and London: Yale University Press, 2014)

—— *The Hyperion Schubert Edition*, vols 1–37 (London: Hyperion, 2005)

—— 'A New Schubert Poet', *The Schubertian* 62 (2009), 4–6

Jurgenmeister, Charles, 'Salomon Sulzer and Franz Schubert: A Musical Collaboration' in Leonard J. Greenspoon (ed), *Studies in Jewish Civilisation* 19 (Omaha, NE: Creighton University Press, 2008), 27–42

Kahl, Willi, *Verzeichnis des Schrifttums über Franz Schubert 1828–1928* (Regensburg: Bosse, 1938)

Kerner, Dieter, 'Der kranke Schubert', *Neue Zeitschrift für Musik* 119 (1958), 645–47

SELECT BIBLIOGRAPHY

Kier, Herfried, *Raphael Georg Kiesewetter (1773–1850): Wegbereiter des musikalischen Historismus* (Regensburg: Gustav Bosse Verlag, 1968)

Kiesewetter, Raphael Georg, *Geschichte der Euopaisch-Abendländischen oder unser heutigen Musik* (Leipzig: Breitkopf und Härtel, 1846)

Kinderman, William, 'Schubert's Piano Music: Probing the Human Condition', in Christopher Gibbs (ed), *The Cambridge Companion to Schubert* (Cambridge University Press, 1997), 155–73

—— 'Wandering Archetypes in Schubert's Instrumental Music', *19th-Century Music*, 21 (1997), 208–22

—— 'Schubert's Tragic Perspective' in Walter Frisch (ed), *Schubert: Critical and Analytical Studies* (University of Nebraska Press, 1986), 65–83

Kobald, Karl *Schubert and His Times*, trans. Beatrice Marshall (New York: Associated Faculty Press, 1970; London: Alfred A. Knopf, 1928)

Koczirz, Adolf, 'Franz Schuberts Stiefbruder Andreas', *Der neue Pflug* 3/7 (1928), 25–29

Kohlhäufl, Michael, *Poetisches Vaterland. Dichtung und politisches Denken im Freundeskreis Franz Schuberts* (Kassel: Bärenreiter, 1999)

Kolleritsch, Otto, *'Dialekt ohne Erde . . .' Franz Schubert und das 20. Jahrhundert* (Vienna, Graz: Universal Edition, 1998)

—— 'Franz Schuberts literarische Kultur', *International Review of the Aesthetics and Sociology of Music* 32/1 (2001), 33–46

Kopp, David, *Chromatic Transformations in Nineteenth-Century Music* (Cambridge University Press, 2002)

Korstvedt, Benjamin M., ' "The prerogative of late style": Thoughts on the Expressive World of Schubert' in Lorraine Byrne Bodley and Julian Horton (eds), *Schubert's Late Music: History, Theory, Style* (Cambridge University Press, 2016), 404–25

Kramer, Lawrence, *Franz Schubert: Sexuality, Subjectivity, Song* (Cambridge University Press, 1998)

—— 'Performance and Social Meaning in the Lied: Schubert's "Erster Verlust"' *Current Musicology* 45 (1994), 5–23

Kramer, Richard, 'Against the Grain: The Sonata in G (D 894) and a Hermeneutics of Late Style' in Lorraine Byrne Bodley and Julian Horton (eds), *Schubert's Late Music: History, Theory, Style* (Cambridge University Press, 2016), 35–51

—— *Cherubino's Leap: In Search of the Enlightenment Moment* (University of Chicago Press, 2016)

—— *Distant Cycles: Schubert and the Conceiving of Song* (University of Chicago Press, 1994)

—— *From the Ruins of Enlightenment: Beethoven and Schubert in teir Solitude* (University of Chicago Press, 2023)

—— 'Gradus ad Parnassum: Beethoven, Schubert, and the Romance of Counterpoint', *19th-Century Music* 11 (1987/88), 107–20

—— 'The Hedgehog: Of Fragments Finished and Unfinished', *19th-Century Music* 21/2 (1997), 140

—— *Unfinished Music* (Oxford University Press, 1980)

Krause, Andreas, *Die Klaviersonaten Franz Schuberts: Form, Gattung, Ästhetik* (Kassel: Bärenreiter, 1991)

Krause, Peter, 'Unbekannte Dokumente zur Uraufführung von Franz Schuberts großer C-Dur-Sinfonie durch Felix Mendelssohn Bartholdy', *Beiträge zur Musikwissenschaft* 29 (1987), 240–50

Krautwurst, Franz, 'Zu den Autographen von Schuberts Liederzyklus "Die schöne Müllerin" D 795' in Stephan Hörner and Bernhold Schmid (eds), *Festschrift für Horst Leuchtmann zum 65. Geburtstag* (Tutzing: Hans Schneider, 1993), 253–59

Krebs, Harald, 'Alternatives to Monotonality in Early Nineteenth-Century Music', *Journal of Music Theory* 25 (1981), 1–16

—— 'Functions of Metrical Dissonances in Schubert's Songs', *Musicological Explorations* 14 (2014), 1–26

SELECT BIBLIOGRAPHY

—— 'Tonart und Text in Schuberts Liedern mit abweichenden Schlüssen', *Archiv für Musikwissenschaft* 47 (1990), 264-71
—— 'Wandern und Heimkehr. Zentrifugale und zentripetale Tendenzen in Schuberts frühen Liedern', *Musiktheorie* 13 (1998), 111-22
Kreeton, Monica, 'Schubert's Handwriting', *The Schubertian* 60 (2008), 6-9
Kreissle von Hellborn, Heinrich, *Franz Schubert* (Vienna: Carl Gold's Sohn, 1865), trans. Eduard Wilberforce, *Franz Schubert: A Musical Biography* (London, 1866), and trans. A. D. Coleridge as *The Life of Franz Schubert* (London: Longmans Green & Co, 1869)
Krenek, Ernst, *Franz Schubert – Der Fortschrittliche? Analysen – Perspektiven – Fakten*, ed. Erich Wolfgang Partsch (Tutzing: Hans Schneider [=Veröffentlichungen des Internationalen Franz Schubert Instituts, Band/Reihe: 4], 1989)
Kreutzer, Hans Joachim, 'Freundschaftsbünde – Künstlerfreunde' in Arnfried Edler (ed), *Schubert und Brahms. Kunst und Gesellschaft im frühen und späten 19. Jahrhundert* (Augsburg: Wißner, 2001), 69-82
Kris, Ernst and Kurz, Otto, *Die Legende von Künstler: Ein historischer Versuch* (Vienna, 1934), trans. Alastair Laing, *Legend, Myth and Magic in the Image of the Artist: A Historical Experiment* (New Haven, CT, and London: Yale University Press, 1979)
Kube, Michael, Aderhold, Werner and Litschauer, Walburga (eds), *Schubert und das Biedermeier. Beiträge zur Musik des frühen 19. Jahrhunderts. Festschrift für Walther Dürr zum 70. Geburtstage* (Kassel: Bärenreiter, 2002)
Kube, Michael and Aderhold, Werner, *Neue Schubert-Ausgabe: Mehrstimmige Gesänge für gemischte Stimmen und Klavier, Kritischer Bericht*, Neue Schubert-Ausgabe III/2 (Tübingen: Internationale Schubert-Gesellschaft, 2013)
Kube, Michael, Litschauer, Walburga and Gruber, Gernot, 'Ferdinand Schubert (1794-1859) und seine Überlieferung innerfamiliärer Korrespondenzen' in *Schubert und die Nachwelt. 1. International Arbeitstagung zur Schubert-Rezeption Wien 2003* (Munich and Salzburg: Katzbichler, 2007)
—— '". . . mir zum freundlichen Angedenken". Schöpferische Wechselwirkungen in Franz Schuberts "Dreizehn Variationen über ein Thema von Hüttenbrenner" (D 576)', *Schubert-Perspektiven* 7/1 (2007), 94-106
—— '". . . lieber in Grätz der Erste, als in Wien der zweyte." Zu den Streichquartetten von Anselm Hüttenbrenner' in Werner Aderhold, Michael Kube, Walburga Litschauer (ed), *Schubert und das Biedermeier. Beiträge zur Musik des frühen 19. Jahrhunderts. Festschrift für Walther Dürr zum 70. Geburtstag* (Kassel: Bärenreiter, 2002), 147-59
—— 'Unsicherheiten ohne Ende. Zu Schuberts frühesten sinfonischen Versuchen', *Schubert: Perspektiven* 10 /1 (2010), 71-77
—— 'Zur Satztechnik in Schuberts Sonate für Klavier, Violine und Violoncello, B-Dur, D 28 (Triosatz)' in *Bach und Schubert. Beiträge zur Musikforschung* (Munich: Katzbichler [=Jahrbuch der Bachwochen Dill], 1999), 15-22
Kube, Michael and Dürr, Walther, *Schubert. Familie: Franz Theodor, seine Kinder Ferdinand (1) Die Musik in Geschichte und Gegenwart. Allgemeine Enzyklopädie der Musik begründet durch Friedrich Blume. Zweite, neubearbeitete Ausgabe. Personenteil* 15 (Schoo-Stran) ed. Ludwig Fischer (Kassel: Bärenreiter, 2006), 73-75
Kube, Michael, Dürr, Walther, Raab, Michael, 'Vom "Erlafsee" zur Gesamtausgabe: Die Ausgaben der Werke Franz Schuberts' In Reinmar Emans and Ulrich Krämer (eds), *Musikeditionen im Wandel der Geschichte* (Berlin: De Gruyter, 2015), 431-51
Kurth, Richard, 'Music and Poetry, a Wilderness of Doubles: Heine—Nietzsche—Schubert—Derrida', *19th-Century Music* 21 (1997), 3-37
—— 'On the Subject of Schubert's "Unfinished" Symphony: *Was bedeutet die Bewegung?*', *19th-Century Music* 23/1 (1999), 3-32
Lange, Fritz, 'Schuberts letzte Pläne: Bisher unbekannte Reminiszenzen von Schubert', *Neues Wiener Journal* 6 (22 May 1910)
Latham, Edward D, 'Drei Nebensonnen: Forte's Linear-Motivic Analysis, Korngold's *Die tote Stadt*, and Schubert's *Winterreise* as Visions of Closure', *Gamut* 2/1 (2009), 299-346

SELECT BIBLIOGRAPHY

Lewin, David, '*Auf dem Flusse*: Image and Background in a Schubert Song', *19th-Century Music* 6 (1982), 47–59
—— *Studies in Music with Text* (Oxford University Press, 2006)
Lindmayr-Brandl, Andrea, *Franz Schubert. Das fragmentarische Werk*, Schubert: Perspektiven – Studien 2 (Stuttgart: Steiner, 2003)
—— 'The Myth of the Unfinished and the Film *Das Dreimädlerhaus* (1958)' in Lorraine Byrne Bodley and Julian Horton (eds), *Rethinking Schubert* (Oxford University Press, 2016), 111–26
Litschauer, Walburga, 'Franz Schuberts Tänze – zwischen Improvisation und Werk', *Musiktheorie* 10 (1995), 3–9
—— (ed), *Neue Dokumente zum Schubert-Kreis aus Briefen und Tagebüchern seiner Freunde* (Vienna, 1986)
—— 'Schubert und sein Lehrer Salieri', *Schubert: Perspektiven* 1 (2001), 74–83
—— 'Unbekannte Dokumente zum Tanz in Schuberts Freundeskreis', *Studien zur Musikwissenschaft. Beihefte der Denkmäler der Tonkunst in Österreich* (SMw) 42 (1993), 243–49
—— 'Unknown Versions of Schubert's Early Piano Sonatas' in Brian Newbould (ed), *Schubert the Progressive: History, Performance Practice, Analysis* (Aldershot: Ashgate, 2003), 101–06
—— 'Zur Aufführungspraxis von Schuberts Tänzen' in Barbara Boisits and Klaus Hubmann (eds), *Musizierpraxis im Biedermeier. Spezifika und Kontext einer vermeintlich vertrauten Epoche* (Vienna: Mille Tre Verlag Robert Schächter, 2004), 219–27
—— 'Zu Fritz Lehners Schubert-Film "Notturno"', *Schubert durch die Brille* 2 (1989), 26–29
Litschauer, Walburga and Deutsch, Walter, *Schubert und das Tanzvergnügen* (Vienna: Holzhausen, 1997)
Løberg Code, David, 'Listening for Schubert's "Doppelgängers"', *MTO A Journal of the Society for Music Theory*, 1 (1995) http://www.mtosmt.org (accessed 11 April 2016)
Lockwood, Lewis, 'Schubert as formal Architect: The "Quartettsatz" D 703' in Stephen A. Crist and Roberta Montemorra Marvin (eds), *Historical Musicology. Sources, Methods, Interpretations* (Rochester, NY, and Woodbridge: University of Rochester Press, 2004), 204–18
Lodes, Birgit, 'Nach Beethoven: Musik und Text in Schuberts Es-Dur-Messe', *Schubert-Jahrbuch* (1997), 155–76
Lohmann, Mario, 'Die Sinfoniefragmente D 615, D 708 A und D 729', *Schubert durch die Brille* 30 (2003), 69–90
Lorenz, Michael, 'Die Familie Schober und ihr genealogisches Umfeld', *Schubert durch die Brille* 30 (2003), 129–92
—— 'Dokumente zur Biographie Johann Mayrhofers', *Schubert durch die Brille* 25 (2000), 21–50
—— *Studien zum Schubert-Kreis* (Vienna: unpublished PhD dissertation, 2001)
Löwy, Irmtraud, *Ferdinand Schuberts Kompositionen für Kinderstimmen im historischen Zusammenhang seiner Zeit* (Vienna: unpublished dissertation, 2002)
Lück, Hartmut, 'Die symphonischen Fragmente Franz Schuberts zwischen wissenschaftlichem Eifer und Kommerzialismus', *Österreichische Musikzeitschrift* (ÖMZ) 40 (1985), 431–35
Lux, Joseph August, *Franz Schubert. Ein Lebensbild aus deutscher Vergangenheit* (Berlin: Fleming und Wiskot, 1922)
Macdonald, Hugh, 'Schubert's Pendulum' in *Beethoven's Century: Essays on Composers and Themes* (Rochester, NY: University of Rochester Press, 2008), 16–27
—— 'Schubert's Volcanic Temper', *Musical Times* 119 (1978), 949–52
Mak, Su Yin, 'Et in arcadia ergo: The Elegiac Structure of Schubert's *Quartettsatz* in C Minor (D 703)' in Barbara Reul and Lorraine Byrne Bodley (eds), *The Unknown Schubert* (Aldershot: Ashgate, 2008), 145–53
—— 'Formal Ambiguity and Generic Reinterpretation in the Late Instrumental Music' in Lorraine Byrne Bodley and Julian Horton (eds), *Schubert's Late Music: History, Theory, Style* (Cambridge University Press, 2016), 282–306

SELECT BIBLIOGRAPHY

—— *Schubert's Lyricism Reconsidered: Structure, Design and Rhetoric* (Saarbrücken: Lambert Academic Press, 2010)
—— 'Schubert's Sonata Forms and the Poetics of the Lyric', *Journal of Musicology* 23/2 (2006), 263–306
Mann, Alfred, 'Schubert's Lesson with Sechter', *19th-Century Music* 6 (1982), 159–65
—— *Schuberts Studien, NSA* VIII/2 (Kassel: Bärenreiter, 1986)
Marston, Nicholas, 'Schubert's Homecoming', *Journal of the Royal Musical Association*, 125/2 (2000), 248–70
—— '"Wie aus der Ferne": Pastness and Presentness in the Lieder of Beethoven, Schubert, and Schumann', *Schubert durch die Brille* 21 (1998), 126–42
Martin, Christine, 'Pioneering German Music Drama: Sung and Spoken Word in Schubert's *Fierabras*' in Joe Davies and James William Sobaskie, *Drama in the Music of Franz Schubert* (Woodbridge: The Boydell Press, 2018), 35–50
Martin, Christine and Martin, Dieter, *Claudine von Villa Bella* D 239, *NSA* II/14 (Kassel: Bärenreiter, 2011)
Martin, Nathan and Vande Moortele, Steven, 'Formal Functions and Retrospective Reinterpretation in the First Movement of Schubert's String Quintet', *Music Analysis* 33/2 (2014), 130–55
Matter, Laura Sewell, 'Franz Schubert Dreamt of Indians', *Georgia Review* 64/1 (2010), 111–29
Mayer, Andreas, 'Der Psychoanalytisches Schubert', *Schubert durch die Brille* 9 (1992), 7–31
Mayrhofer, Johann, *Gedichte von Johann Mayrhofer. Neue Sammlung*, ed. Ernst Freiherr von Feuchtersleben (Vienna: Ignaz Klang, 1843)
McClary, Susan, 'Constructions of Subjectivity in Schubert's Music', in Philip Brett, Elizabeth Wood, and Gary C. Thomas (eds), *Queering the Pitch* (New York: Routledge, 1994), 205–09
McClelland, Clive, 'Ombra Music in the Eighteenth Century: Context, Style and Signification' (Leeds: unpublished PhD dissertation, 2001)
McKay, Elizabeth Norman, *Franz Schubert: A Biography* (Oxford: Clarendon Press, 1996)
—— 'Schubert and Classical Opera: The Promise of Adrast', in Oskar Pausch (ed), *Der vergessene Schubert: Franz Schubert auf der Bühne* (Vienna: Böhlau 1997), 61–76
Messing, Scott, *The Life of Schubert's Marche Militaire. Marching to the Canon* (Rochester, NY: University of Rochester Press, 2014)
—— *Schubert in the European Imagination*, vol. 1, *The Romantic and Victorian Eras*, and vol. 2, *Fin-de-Siècle Vienna* (Rochester, NY: University of Rochester Press, 2007–8)
Metzger, Heinz-Klaus and Riehn, Rainer (eds), *Musik-Konzepte. Sonderband Franz Schubert* (Munich: Edition Text+kritik, 1979)
Montgomery, David, *Franz Schubert's Music in Performance: Compositional Ideals, Notational Intent, Historical Realities, Pedagogical Foundations* (Hillsdale: Pendragon Press, 2003)
—— *Unfinished History: A New Account of Schubert's B Minor Symphony* (New York: Brown Walker Press, 2017)
Mühlhäuser, Siegfried, *Die Handschriften und Varia der Schubertiana-Sammlung Taussig in der Universitaetsbibliothek Lund*. Quellenkataloge zur Musikgeschichte 17 (Wilhelmshaven: Nötzel, 1981)
Muxfeldt, Kristina, 'Schubert, Platen, and the Myth of Narcissus', *Journal of the American Musicological Society* 49/3 (1996), 480–527
—— *Vanishing Sensibilities: Schubert, Beethoven, Schumann* (Oxford University Press, 2012)
Newbould, Brian, *Schubert: The Music and the Man* (Berkeley and Los Angeles: University of California Press, 1997)
—— *Schubert Studies* (Aldershot and Burlington: Ashgate, 1998)
—— *Schubert and the Symphony* (London: Toccata Press, 1992)
—— 'Schubert's Last Symphony', *Musical Times* 126/1707 (1985), 272–75
Noeske, Nina, 'Schubert, das Erhabene und die letzte Sonate D 960 – oder: Die Frage nach dem Subjekt', *Schubert: Perspektiven* 7 (2007), 22–36

SELECT BIBLIOGRAPHY

Notley, Margaret, 'Schubert's Social Music: The "Forgotten Genres"' in Christopher Gibbs (ed), *The Cambridge Companion to Schubert* (Cambridge University Press, 1997), 138–54

Osborne, Charles, *Schubert and his Vienna* (New York: Alfred A. Knopf, 1985)

Perry, Jeffrey, 'Schubert's "Aus Goethe's Faust", D. 126: The "Scena" as Fragment', *Indiana Theory Review* 26 (2005), 105–21

—— 'The Wanderer's Many Returns: Schubert's Variations Reconsidered', *Journal of Musicology* 19 (2002), 375

Pesic, Peter, 'Schubert's Dream', *19th-Century Music* 23 (1999), 136–44

Pfitzner, Jozef, *Geschichte der Bergstadt Zuckmantel in Schlesien bis 1742* (Zuckmantel: Verlag der Stadtgemeinde, 1924)

Plantinga, Leon, 'Schubert, Social Music and Melancholy' in Lorraine Byrne Bodley and Julian Horton (eds), *Rethinking Schubert* (Oxford University Press, 2016), 237–52

Radcliffe, Philip, *Schubert Piano Sonatas* (London: Faber and Faber, 1967)

Rast, Nicholas, '"Schöne Welt wo bist du?": Motive and Form in Schubert's A Minor String Quartet' in Brian Newbould (ed), *Schubert the Progressive: History, Performance Practice, Analysis* (Aldershot: Ashgate, 2003), 81–88

—— 'Une déclaration d'amour en code? La Fantaisie en *fa* mineur D 940 de Schubert et la comtesse Caroline Esterházy', *Cahiers Franz Schubert* 13 (1998), 5–16

Reed, John, *Schubert* (New York: Schirmer, 1997)

—— *Schubert: The Final Years* (London: Faber and Faber, 1972)

—— *The Schubert Song Companion* (Manchester University Press, 1985)

Reiser, Salome, *Franz Schuberts frühe Streichquartette: Eine klassische Gattung am Beginn einer nachklassischen Zeit* (Kassel: Bärenreiter, 1999)

Rentsch, Ivana and Pietschmann, Klaus, *Schubert: Interpretationen* (=Schubert: Perspektiven – Studien 3) (Stuttgart: Franz Steiner Verlag, 2014)

Rosen, Charles, *The Classical Style* (London: Faber and Faber, 2005)

Salzer, Felix, 'Die Sonatenform bei Franz Schubert', *Studien zur Musikwissenschaft* 15 (1928), 86–125

Sams, Eric, 'Schubert's Illness Re-Examined', *Musical Times* (1980), 15–22

Sanguinetti, Giorgio, *The Art of Partimento* (Oxford University Press, 2012)

Schering, Albert, *Franz Schuberts Symphonie in H-Moll ('Unvollendete') und ihr Geheimnis* (Würzburg: Konrad Triltsch Verlag, 1938)

Schiff, Andreas, 'Schubert's Piano Sonatas: Thoughts about Interpretation and Performance' in Brian Newbould (ed), *Schubert Studies* (Aldershot and Burlington: Ashgate, 1998), 191–208

Schmalfeldt, Janet, *In the Process of Becoming: Analytic and Philosophical Perspectives on Form in Early Nineteenth-Century Music* (Oxford University Press, 2011)

Schnebel, Dieter, 'Klangräume-Zeitklänge. Zweiter Versuch über Schubert', in H. K. Metzger und R. Riehn, *Musik-Konzepte Sonderband: Franz Schubert* (Munich: Edition Text+kritik, 1979), 89–106

Schroeder, David, 'Feminine Voices in Schubert's Early Laments', *Music 6 Review* 55/3 (1994), 183–201

—— *Our Schubert: His Enduring Legacy* (Plymouth: The Scarecrow Press, 2009)

Schumann, Christiane et al. (eds), *Schubert–Jahrbuch* (Kassel: Bärenreiter, 1996–2013)

Schumann, Robert, 'Die 7te Symphonie von Franz Schubert', *Neue Zeitschrift für Musik* (*NZfM*), 12/21 (10 March 1840), 81–83

Shamgar, Beth, 'Schubert's Classic Legacy: Some Thoughts on Exposition–Recap. Form', *Journal of Musicology* 18/1 (2001), 150–69

Sobaskie, James William, 'Contextual Processes in Schubert's Late Sacred Music' in Lorraine Byrne Bodley and Julian Horton (eds), *Rethinking Schubert* (Oxford University Press, 2016), 295–333

—— 'The "Problem" of Schubert's String Quintet', *Nineteenth-Century Music Review* 2/1 (2005), 57–92

—— 'Tonal Implication and the Gestural Dialectic in Schubert's A Minor Quartet' in Brian Newbould (ed), *Schubert the Progressive: History, Performance Practice, Analysis* (2003), 53–80

SELECT BIBLIOGRAPHY

—— 'Schubert's Self-Elegies', *Nineteenth-Century Music Review* 5/2 (2008), 71–105
Solomon, Maynard, 'Franz Schubert and the Peacocks of Benvenuto Cellini', *19th-Century Music*, 12/3 (1989), 193–206
—— 'Franz Schubert's "My Dream"', *American Imago*, 38/2 (1981), 137–54
—— 'Schubert: Family Matters', *19th-Century Music* 28 (2004/05), 3–14
—— 'Schubert's Unfinished Symphony', *19th-Century Music* 21/2 (1997), 111–33
Spitzer, Michael, 'Axial Lyric Space in Two Late Songs: "Im Freien" and "Der Winterabend"' in Lorraine Byrne Bodley and Julian Horton (eds), *Rethinking Schubert* (Oxford University Press, 2016), 253–74
—— 'Mapping the Human Heart: A Holistic Analysis of Fear in Schubert', *Music Analysis* 28 (2010), 149–213
—— *Metaphor and Musical Thought* (University of Chicago Press, 2004)
—— 'Sad Flowers: Affective Trajectories in Schubert's "Trockne Blumen"' in T. Cochrane, B. Fantini, and K. R. Scherer (eds), *The Emotional Power of Music: Multidisciplinary Perspectives on Musical Arousal, Expression, and Social Control* (Oxford University Press), 7–22
Stanley, Glenn, 'Schubert's Religious and Choral Music: Toward a Statement of Faith' in Christopher Gibbs (ed), *The Cambridge Companion to Schubert* (Cambridge University Press, 1997), 205–21
Steblin, Rita, *A History of Key Characteristics in the 18th and Early 19th Centuries*, 2nd edn (Rochester, NY: University of Rochester Press, 2002)
—— *Die Unsinnsgesellschaft. Franz Schubert, Leopold Kupelwieser und ihr Freundeskreis* (Vienna: Böhlau Verlag, 1998)
—— 'Franz Schubert – das dreizehnte Kind', *Wiener Geschichtsblätter* 56/3 (2001), 245–65
—— 'Schubert's Love Affair with Marie von Spaun and the Role played by Helene Schmith, the Wife of Mozart's first violinist', *Schubert: Perspektiven* 8 (2008), 49–87
—— Schubert's Pepi: His Love Affair with the Chamber Maid Josepha Pöcklhofer and her Surprising Fate', *Musical Times* 149 (2008), 47–69
—— 'Who commissioned Schubert's Oratorio *Lazarus*? A Solution to the Mystery. Salieri and the Tonkünstler-Societät', *Schubert-Perspektiven* 9/2 (2009), 145–81
Steblin, Rita and Stocken, Frederick, 'Studying with Sechter: Newly Recovered Reminiscences about Schubert by his Forgotten Friend, the Composer Joseph Lanz', *Music & Letters* 88 (2007), 226–65
Stefan, Paul, *Franz Schubert* (Berlin: Volksverband der Bücherfreunde, Wegweiser-Verlag, 1928)
Stein, Deborah, 'The End of the Road in Schubert's *Winterreise*: The Contradiction of Coherence and Fragmentation' in Lorraine Byrne Bodley and Julian Horton (eds), *Rethinking Schubert* (Oxford University Press, 2016), 253–74
Steinbeck, Wolfram, 'Lied und Sonatensatzform bei Schubert. Zum Kopfsatz der Klaviersonate A-Dur D 644', in Wolfgang Horschmann (ed), *Aria. Eine Festschrift für Wolfgang Ruf* (Hildesheim: Olms, 2011), 590–602
—— 'Und über das Ganze eine Romantik ausgegossen' in Walther Dürr und Andreas Krause, *Schubert Handbuch* (Kassel, Basel, London, New York, Prague: Bärenreiter, 1997 also Stuttgart and Weimar: Metzler, 1997) 345–377
Steiner-Daviau, Gertraud, 'Opposing Views: Franz Schubert in the Films of Willi Forst (1933) and Fritz Lehner (1986)' in Robert Pichl and Clifford A. Bernd (eds), *The Other Vienna: The Culture of Biedermeier Austria. Österreichisches Biedermeier in Literatur, Musik, Kunst und Kulturgeschichte* (Vienna: Lehner, 2002), 315–22
Stillmark, Alexander, '"Es war alles gut und erfüllt". Rudolf Hans Bartsch's *Schwammerl* and the Making of the Schubert Myth' in Ian F. Roe and John Warren (eds), *The Biedermeier and Beyond: Selected Papers from the Symposium held at St. Peter's College, Oxford from 19–21 September 1997* (Bern: Peter Lang, 1999), 225–34
Strahan, Barbara, *(De)Constructing Paradigms of Genre: Aesthetics, Identity and Form in Franz Schubert's Four-Hand Fantasias* (Maynooth: unpublished doctoral dissertation, 2013)

SELECT BIBLIOGRAPHY

Suurpää, Lauri, *Death in Winterreise: Musico-Poetic Associations in Schubert's Song Cycle* (Indiana University Press, 2014)

—— 'Longing for the Unattainable: The Second Movement of the "Great" C major Symphony' in Lorraine Byrne Bodley and Julian Horton (eds), *Schubert's Late Music: History, Theory, Style* (Cambridge University Press, 2016), 219–40

Szabó-Knotik, Cornelia, 'Franz Schubert und die österreichische Identität im Tonfilm der 1930er Jahre' in Michael Kube, Walburga Litschauer and Gernot Gruber (eds), *Schubert und die Nachwelt. I. Internationale Arbeitstagung zur Schubert-Rezeption Wien 2003. Kongreßbericht* (Munich and Salzburg: Katzbichler, 2007), 309–19

Taylor, Benedict, 'Schubert and the Construction of Memory: The String Quartet in A Minor, D 804 ('Rosamunde')', *Journal of the Royal Musical Association*, 139/1 (2014), 41–88

Thomas, Werner, 'Der Doppelgänger von Franz Schubert', *Archiv für Musikwissenschaft* 11 (1954), 252–67

—— 'Die fast verlorene Zeit: Zum Adagio in Schuberts Streichquintett in C' in Werner Thomas (ed), *Schubert-Studien* (Frankfurt am Main: Peter Lang, 1990), 137–58

Thym, Jürgen, 'Invocations of Memory in Schubert's Last Songs' in Lorraine Byrne Bodley and Julian Horton (eds), *Schubert's Late Music: History, Theory, Style* (Cambridge University Press, 2016), 383–403

Tovey, Donald Francis, 'Franz Schubert', in Hubert J. Foss (ed), *Essays and Lectures on Music* (Oxford University Press, 1949), 103–33

Trost, Alois, 'Franz Schuberts Bildnisse', *Berichte und Mittheilungen des Alterthums-Vereines zu Wien* 33/2 (1898), 85–95

Tunbridge, Laura, 'Saving Schubert: The Evasions of Late Style', in Gordon McMullan and Sam Smiles (eds), *Late Style and its Discontents* (Oxford University Press, 2016)

van Hoorickx, Reinhard, 'The Chronology of Schubert's Fragments and Sketches' in Badura-Skoda and Branscombe (eds), *Schubert Studies* (1953), 297–326

Waidelich, Till Gerrit (ed.), 'Ferdinand Schubert (1794–1859) und seine Überlieferung innerfamiliärer Korrespondenzen' in Michael Kube, Walburga Litschauer and Gernot Gruber (eds), *Schubert und die Nachwelt. I. International Arbeitstagung zur Schubert-Rezeption Wien 2003* (Munich and Salzburg: Katzbichler, 2007)

—— *Franz Schubert: Dokumente, 1817–1830*, vol. 1: *Texte, Programme, Rezensionen, Anzeigen, Nekrologe, Musikbeilagen und andere gedruckte Quellen* (Tutzing: Hans Schneider Verlag, 1993)

—— 'Joseph Hüttenbrenners Entwurf eines Aufsatzes mit der ersten biographischen Skizze Schuberts (1823) und zwei Fragmente seines ungedruckten Schubert-Nachrufs (1828)', *Schubert: Perspektiven* 1 (2001), 37–73

—— 'Unbekannte Schubert-Dokument aus Breslau', *Schubert-Perspektiven* 8 (2008), 17–48

—— 'Zur Überlieferung des Textes "Mein Traum"', *Schubert-Perspektiven* 5 (2005), 138–61

Waldbauer, Ivan, 'Recurrent Harmonic Patterns in the First Movement of Schubert's Piano Sonata in A major, D 959', *19th-Century Music* 12 (1989), 64–73

Weber, Rudolf, 'Mythen und Legenden um die Entstehung von Schubert Unvollendeter' in Claudia Bullerjahn and Wolfgang Löffler (eds), *Musikermythen. Alltagstheorien, Legenden und Medieninszenierungen* (Hildesheim: Georg Olms Verlag, 2004), 191–221

Webster, James, 'Schubert's Sonata Form and Brahms's First Maturity', *19th-Century Music* 2 (1978), 18–35, and 3 (1979), 52–71

Weinmann, Alexander, *Ferdinand Schubert. Eine Untersuchung* [=*Beiträge zur Geschichte des Alt-Wiener Musikverlages*, series 1, vol. 4] (Vienna: Krenn 1986)

Wen, Eric, 'Schubert's *Wiegenlied*: The Andante sostenuto from the Piano Sonata in B flat D 960' in Lorraine Byrne Bodley and Julian Horton (eds), *Schubert's Late Music: History, Theory, Style* (Cambridge University Press, 2016), 134–48

Whaples, Miriam, 'On the Structural Integration in Schubert's Instrumental Works', *Acta Musicologica* 40 (1968), 186–95

Whittall, Arnold, 'The Sonata Crisis: Schubert in 1828', *Music Review* 30 (1969), 124–29

SELECT BIBLIOGRAPHY

Wiley, Christopher, *Re-Writing Composers' Lives: Critical Historiography and Musical Biography* (PhD dissertation, Royal Holloway, University of London, 2008) VII, 396 pp; II, 203 pp. esp. chapter 4, 'Mythology in Musical Biography: Correspondences in the Lives of Great Composers'

Willfort, Manfred, 'Das Urbild des Andante aus Schuberts Klaviertrio Es-dur, D 929', *Österreichische Musikzeitschrift* 33 (1978), 277–83

Winter, Robert, 'Paper Studies and the Future of Schubert Research', in Eva Badura-Skoda and Peter Branscombe (eds), *Schubert Studies: Problems of Style and Chronology* (Cambridge University Press, 1982), 209–75

—— 'Whose Schubert?' *19th-Century Music* 17/1 (1993), 94–101

Wollenberg, Susan, 'Schubert and The Dream', *Studi musicali*, 9 (1980), 135–50

—— *Schubert's Fingerprints: Studies in the Instrumental Works* (Surrey and Burlington: Ashgate 2011)

—— 'The C major String Quintet D 956: Schubert's "Dissonance Quartet"', *Schubert durch die Brille* 28 (2002), 45–54

Wyn Jones, David, *Music in Vienna 1700, 1800, 1900* (Woodbridge: The Boydell Press, 2016)

—— *The Symphony in Beethoven's Vienna* (Cambridge University Press, 2006)

Youens, Susan, 'A Gauntlet Thrown: Schubert's "Einsamkeit" D 620 and Beethoven's *An die ferne Geliebte*' in Lorraine Byrne Bodley and Julian Horton (eds), *Rethinking Schubert* (Oxford University Press, 2016), 456–85

—— *Die schöne Müllerin* (Cambridge University Press, 1992)

—— *Heine and the Lied* (Cambridge University Press, 2007)

—— 'Reentering Mozart's Hell: Schubert's "Gruppe aus dem Tartarus"' in Joe Davies and James William Sobaskie, *Drama in the Music of Franz Schubert* (Woodbridge: The Boydell Press, 2018), 171–201

—— *Retracing a Winter's Journey: Schubert's* Winterreise (Cornell University Press, 1991)

—— *Schubert's Late Lieder: Beyond the Song Cycles* (Cambridge University Press, 2002)

—— *Schubert, Müller and Die schöne Müllerin* (Cambridge University Press, 1997)

—— *Schubert's Poets and the Making of Lieder* (Cambridge University Press, 1996)

—— 'The "problem of solitude" and critique in song: Schubert's loneliness' in Lorraine Byrne Bodley and Julian Horton (eds), *Schubert's Late Music: History, Theory, Style* (Cambridge University Press, 2016), 309–30

—— 'Wegweiser in Winterreise', *Journal of Musicology* 5/3 (1987), 357–79

INDEX OF SCHUBERT'S WORKS

A minor *Lebensturme* (D 947), 428
'Abends unter der Linde' (D 235 and D237), 84
'Abendstern' (D 806), 267
'Abschied von einem Freunde' (D 578), 307, 385
Adagio and Rondo Concertante in F for piano quartet (D 487), 157, 305
Adrast (D 137), 196, 199, 261
Alfonso und Estrella (D 732), 197, 199, 274–5, 276, 278, 280, 336, 337, 375, 377–9, 422, 441, 509
Allegro assai in C minor (D 703), 89
'Am Bach im Fruhlinge' (D 731), 274
'Am ersten Maimorgen' (D 344), 157, 158
'Am Flusse' (D 766), 404, 405, 406, 413
'Am Grabe Anselmos' (D 504), 158, 159, 278, 333
'Am See' (D 746), 261
'Am Tage aller Seelen' (D 343), 152–4, 159
'An den Frühling' (D 283), 86
'An den Frühling' (D 587), 306
'An den Mond' (D 259, D296), 85, 176
'An die Entfernte' (D 765), 404, 405–6
'An die Freunde' (D 654), 270
'An die Geliebte' (D 303), 157
'An die Musik' (D 547), 245, 274, 306
'An die Nachtigall' (D 497 and D 724), 256, 327, 334, 499
'An die Natur' (D 372), 158, 159
'An die untergehende Sonne' (D 457), 488
'An Emma' (D 113), 186–7
'An Gott' (D 863), 517
'An mein Herz' (D 860), 250
'An Mignon' (D 161), 174, 437
'An Schwager Kronos' (D 369), 169, 437, 487

'Andenken' (D 99), 85, 157, 158, 159
'Antigone und Oedip' (D 542), 278, 333
'Atys' (D 585), 306
'Auf dem See' (D 543), 462, 505
'Auf dem Strom' (D 943), 250, 388, 514, 515, 543
'Auf dem Wasser zu singen' (D 774), 487
'Auf den Sieg der Deutschen' (D 81), 118–19
'Auf den Tod einer Nachtigall' (D 196 and D 399), 53, 53–4
'Auf der Donau' (D 553), 262, 266
'Auflösung' (D 807), 267, 372
'Augenlied' (D 297), 277
'Auguste jam coelestium' (D 488), 127

Beitrag zur fünfzigjährigen Jubelfeier des Herrn von Salieri (D 407), 58, 116, 209
'Blondel zu Marien' (D 626), 130, 319
'Bundeslied' (D 258), 176

'Chor der Engel' (D 440), 479
Claudine von Villa Bella (D 239), 57–8, 194, 195, 199–206, 257, 400

'Das Abendrot' (D 627), 318–19
'Das Dörfchen' (D 598), 116, 256, 325–8, 332, 334
'Das Geheimnis' (D 250), 185–6, 334
'Das Geheimnis' (D 793), 415
'Das Heimweh' (D 851), 463
'Das Mädchen aus der Ferne' (D117 and D252), 84
'Das Marienbild' (D 623), 130, 319
'Das Wandern' (D 795), 412, 414
'Das Weinen' (D 926), 273, 508

INDEX OF SCHUBERT'S WORKS

'Das Zügenglöcklein' (D 871), 454, 463
'Der Alpenjager' (D 588), 306, 334
'Der blinde Knabe' (D 833), 250, 434–5, 498
'Der Einsame' (D 800), 250, 433, 488
'Der entsuhnt Orest' (D 699), 262
'Der Fischer' (D 225), 168, 174, 333
Der Flüchtling (D 402), 84
'Der Flug der Zeit' (D 515), 333
'Der Gondelfahrer' (D 808 and D 809), 261, 267, 372
'Der Gott und die Bajadere' (D 254), 176
'Der Graf von Gleichen' (D 918), 193, 197, 280, 457, 458
'Der Herbstabend' (D 405), 158, 159
'Der Hirt auf dem Felsen' (D 965), 504, 526–8
'Der Jüngling am Bache' (D 30, D 192, D 638), 82, 84, 182, 500
'Der Jüngling auf dem Hugel' (D 702), 333, 348
'Der Jüngling und der Tod' (D 545), 79, 306
'Der Kampf' (D 594), 182, 306
'Der König in Thule' (D 367), 174, 333
'Der Kreuzzug' (D 932), 277, 515
'Der Leidende' (D 432), 158, 159, 385
'Der Leiermann' (D 911), 297, 385, 409
'Der Liedler' (D 209), 248, 462
'Der Lindenbaum' (D 911), 389
'Der Morgenstern' (D 172), 85
'Der Müller und der Bach' (D 795/12), 412
'Der Musensohn' (D 764), 387, 404, 409–10, 418, 462, 505, 528
'Der Pilgrim' (D 794), 415–16
'Der Rattenfänger' (D 255), 176
'Der Sänger' (D 149), 176
'Der Schafer und der Reiter' (D 517), 334
'Der Schiffer' (D 536), 266
'Der Sieg' (D 805), 267, 372
Der Spiegelritter (D 11), 61, 193, 195
'Der Tanz' (D 826), 504
'Der Taucher' (D 77), 182
'Der Tod und das Mädchen' (D 531), 55, 168, 306, 333
'Der Unglückliche' (D 713), 385
'Der Vatermörder' (D 10), 47–51, 52, 78, 79
Der vierjährige Posten (D 190), 173, 194, 195
'Der Wanderer an den Mond' (D 870), 454, 463, 490, 515
'Der Wanderer' (D 489, D 493 and D 649), 55, 256, 286, 324, 333, 490
'Der Wegweiser' (D 911), 79

'Der Winterabend' (D 938), 511
'Der Zufriedene' (D 320), 82
'Der zürnenden Diana' (D 707), 399
'Des Baches Wiegenlied' (D 795), 388, 414
'Des Mädchens Klage' (D 6, D 191 and D 389), 78, 84, 182
Des Teufels Lustschloß (D 84), 57, 114–17, 118, 122, 195, 399, 400
'Deutsche für Klavier '(D 790), 298
Deutsche Messe (D 872), 151, 493
Deutsche Tänze (D 971), 288, 289
Deutsche Trauermesse (D 621), 128
Deutscher in C sharp minor (D 643), 296–7
Deutscher Tänze (D 365 and D 779), 297
Deutsches Requiem (D 621), 165, 337
Deutsches Salve Regina (D 379), 131, 134, 151, 165, 319
Deux Marches Caractéristiques (D 968b), 424
'Die abgeblühte Linde' (D 514), 333
'Die Allmacht' (D 852), 85, 277, 465, 543
'Die Allmacht' (D 875), 442–3, 465–6, 515
'Die Befreier Europas in Paris' (D 104), 120–1
Die Bürgschaft (D 246 or D 435), 182, 195
'Die Forelle' (D 550), 306
Die Freunde von Salamanka (D 326), 58, 194–7, 261, 280
'Die Geselligkeit' (D 609), 280
'Die liebe Farbe' (D 795), 385
'Die Liebe hat gelogen' (D 751), 352, 405
'Die Nacht' (D 983C), 334
Die schöne Müllerin (D 795), 250, 291–2, 362, 363, 398, 411–14, 462, 489
'Die Spinnerin' (D 247), 174
'Die Sterne' (D 939), 273, 277, 454, 505, 515
'Die Sternennächte' (D 670), 261
'Die Taubenpost' (D 965A), 277, 526, 528–9, 544
Die Verschworenen (D 787), 197, 199, 375
Die Zauberglöckchen (D 723), 196, 199
Die Zauberharfe (D 644), 196, 198, 325, 396
'Die zürnende Diana' (D 707), 348, 349
Die Zwillingsbrüder (D 647), 196, 198, 323, 324–5, 337
Divertissement a l'hongroise in G minor for Piano Four Hands (D 818), 349, 426–7, 463, 504
Divertissement sur des motifs originaux francais in E minor (D 823), 426, 487

INDEX OF SCHUBERT'S WORKS

'Drang in die Ferne' (D 770), 250, 344, 487
Drei Gesange fur Basstimme mit Klavier (D 902), 86, 498–9, 500–4
'Drei Klavierstucke' (D 946), 516
'Dreifach ist der Schritt der Zeit' (D 43, D 69 and D 70), 54, 72–3, 74–5, 84, 183
'Du liebst mich nicht' (D 756), 337, 352, 405
Duo Sonata in A major for Violin and Piano (D 574), 110, 307

Écossaises in E flat for Piano (D 529), 305
'Edone' (D 445), 158, 159
Eight Variations in A flat (D 813), 364, 428
'Ein jugendlicher Maienschwung' (D 61), 71–2
'Eine altschottische Ballade' (D 923), 508
'Einsamkeit' (D 620), 318
'Ellen' (D 837–839), 438
'Ellens Gesang III' (Ave Maria, D 839), 130, 438–9, 513
'Elysium' (D 584), 388
'Entra l'uomo allor che nasce' (D 33), 61, 83
'Erinnerung: Die Erscheinung' (D 229), 388
'Erinnerungen' (D 98), 85
'Erlafsee' (D 586), 262, 306, 333
'Erlkönig' (D 328), 166–71, 175, 188, 205, 249, 256, 257, 277, 279, 324, 329, 332–3, 396, 487, 506
'Ernst und Tandeley' (D 328) (D 976), 289, 296
'Erster Verlust' (D 226), 174, 333
'Es reden und träumen die Menschen viel' (D 251), 86
'Evangelium Johannes' (D 607), 388–9

'Fahrt zum Hades' (D 526), 79
Fantasy for Violin and Piano (D 934), 287, 513
Fantasy in F minor for Piano Four Hands (D 940), 251, 287, 298, 421, 428, 513, 530
Fantasy in G major for Piano Four Hands (D 1), 107, 422
Fantasy in G minor (D 9), 286, 422–3
Fernando (D 220), 57, 173, 194, 195, 248
Fierabras (D796), 109, 197, 199, 280, 325, 361, 375, 376, 378, 398, 422
'Fischerweise' (D 881), 273, 277, 505
Four Polonaise Piano Duets (D 599), 316, 423
'Fragment aus dem Aeschylus' (D 450), 277, 515
'Freiwilliges Versinken' (D 700), 261, 262

'Frisch atmet des Morgens lebendiger Hauch' (D 67), 84
'Frühlingsgesang' (D 709), 85
'Frühlingsgesang' (D 740), 327, 334, 352
Fugue in C major (D 24 d), 78
Fugue in E minor for organ duet (D 952), 251, 516
Fugues (juvenalia), 66–8

Galopp und 8 Ecossaisen (D 735), 289, 295–6, 461
'Ganymed' (D 544), 49, 277, 437
'Gebet' (D 815), 367–8
'Geist der Liebe' (D 747), 327, 334, 352
'Geistes-gruß' (D 142), 175, 462, 505
'Gesang der Geister uber den Wassern' (D 714), 329–30, 332
'Gesang: Was ist Sylvia' (D 891), 273
Gesänge aus Wilhelm Meister (D 877), 505
'Glaube, Hoffnung, Liebe' (D 955), 289, 516, 517–18
'Glaube Hoffnung und Liebe' (D 954), 474, 516–17
Gmunden-Gastein symphony (D 849), 444
'Gott im Frühling' (D 448), 158, 159
'Gott in der Natur' (D 757), 337, 506, 508, 513
'Grab und Mond' (D 893), 454
'Grablied für die Mutter' (D 616), 152, 309, 310–11, 385
Gradual, *Benedictus es, Domine* in C major (D 184), 142
'Grand Duo' Sonata in C (D 812), 364, 426, 428, 487
Grande Marche Funébre (D 859), 424, 425
Grande Marche Héroique (D 885), 424, 425–6
Grandes Marches (D 819), 424
'Gratulations-Kantata' (D 294), 165
Grazer Gallop (D 925), 295–6, 507–8
'Grazer Walzer' (D 924), 291, 298
'Great' C major symphony (D 944), 7, 90, 180, 382, 401–2, 441–2, 444–53, 460, 467, 482–3, 520
'Grenzen der Menschheit' (D 716), 389
'Gretchen am Spinnrade' (D 118), 155–6, 160–3, 165–6, 171, 175, 188, 205, 216, 333, 396, 500
'Gretchen im Zwinger' (D 564), 306
'Grüner wird die Au' (D 129), 85
'Gruppe aus dem Tartarus' (D 65, D 396 and D 583), 79, 183, 306
Guitar Quartet (D 96), 111–14, 129
'Gute Nacht' (D 911/1), 250

'Hagars Klage' (D 5), 46, 78–9, 286, 423
'Harfenspieler I' (D 478), 79, 334
'Heidenröslein' (D 257), 168, 174, 188–9, 333
'Heimliches Lieben' (D 922), 273, 508
'Hektors Abschied' (D 312), 182
'Heliopolis I' (D 753), 262
'Hier umarmen sich getreue Gatten' (D 60), 53
Hungarian Melody in B minor (D 817), 426
Hunter (D 795), 412
'Hymne an den Unendlichen' (D 232), 183

'Ihr Grab' (D 736), 345
'Im Abendrot' (D 799), 487
'Im Freien' (D 880), 250, 454
Impromptus (D 899), 463, 507
'Ins stille Land' (D 403), 158, 159
Intende voci in B flat (D 963), 474, 475–6
'Iphigenia' (D 573), 261, 306

'Jägers Abendlied' (D 368), 174, 333
'Jägers Liebeslied' (D 909), 273, 505
'Jünglingswonne' (D 983), 334

Kantata zum Geburtstag des Sangers Johann Michael Vogl (D 666), 248, 278
Kantate für Irene Kiesewetter (D 936), 86
'Kennst du das Land' (D 321), 176
Kindermarsch in G (D 928), 424, 509–10
Klage' (D 292), 385
'Klage an das Volk' (Complaint to the Nation), 365–6
'Klage an den Mond' (D 436), 157, 158, 159
'Klage der Ceres' (D 323), 170
'Klarchens Lied' (D 210), 322
'Kriegers Ahnung' (D 957), 79
Kyrie (D 755), 165, 337
Kyrie no. 1 in D minor (D 31), 143–4, 147, 152, 471
Kyrie no. 2 in B flat major (D 45), 129, 143, 144
Kyrie no. 3 in D minor (D 49), 143, 144
Kyrie no. 4 in F major (D 66), 61, 143, 144

Lacrimas (D 607), 388
Ländler (D 146), 288, 297
Ländler (D 980B), 297
Ländler in D for violin (D 370), 217
Ländler in E for Piano Four Hands (D 618), 316
Ländler in F sharp minor for violin (D 355), 217

'Laura am Klavier' (D 388), 183–4
Lazarus oder die Feier der Aufstehung (D689), 196, 199, 338, 479–80
Lebensturme duet (D 947), 516
'Lebenstraum: Gesang' (D 1), 490
'Lebenstraum'(D 39), 33
Legnani, Luigi (1790–1877), 112
'Leichenfantasie' (D 7), 46–7, 78, 171
'Liebe rauscht der Silberbach' (D 983A), 183, 334
'Liebesbotschaft' (D 957/1), 250
'Lied aus der Ferne (D 107), 157, 158, 159
'Lied der Mignon' (D 489 and D 877), 79, 165–6
'Lied eines Schiffers an die Dioskuren' (D 360), 277
'Litanei auf Fest Aller Seelen' (D 343), 157, 158
'Lob der Thranen (D 711), 334

'Mailied' (D 503), 85, 157, 158, 159
Major Duo Sonata in B flat (D 617), 316
Marche Militaire (D 733), 438
Marches Heroiques (D 602), 424
Marches Militaires (D 733), 424–5
'Marie' (D 658), 130, 319
Mass in A flat major (D 678), 79, 149, 150, 151, 191, 281, 337, 384, 385, 456, 467–71, 477, 480, 530
Mass in B flat (324), 149, 150, 468
Mass in C major (D 452), 35, 127–8, 134, 149, 151
Mass in E flat (950), 149, 150, 151, 471, 472–3, 474, 475, 512, 516, 543
Mass in F major (D 105), 67, 121, 122, 142, 145–8, 149, 151, 156, 191, 471, 514
Mass in G major (D 167), 122, 149–50, 151–2, 480
'Meeresstille' (D 215A and D 216), 84, 174, 189–90, 333, 337
'Mein Gebet' (My Prayer, 1823), 360–1
'Mein Traum' (My Dream) (short story), 52, 322, 341–7, 349–50, 357, 379–80, 414, 465, 536
'Memnon' (D 541), 277, 278, 333
Messe in F (D 24E), 68–9
'Mignon I' (D 394 and D 726), 79, 165–6
'Mignon II' (D 395 and D 727), 79, 165–6
minuets (D 30), 291, 298
'Mirjams Siegesgesang' (D 942), 250, 462, 506, 514, 530, 544
Missa solemnis in F major (D 104), 142
Moments musicaux, nos 1–2, 4–5 (D 780), 462

INDEX OF SCHUBERT'S WORKS

'Mondenschein' (D 875), 513
'Morgenlied' (D 685), 333
'Mutter geht durch ihre Kammern' (D 373), 170

'Nacht und Träume' (D 827), 365, 487
'Nachtgesang' (D 119), 176
'Nachthelle' (D 892), 454
'Nachthymne' (D 687), 343
'Nachtstuck' (D 672), 261, 348–9
'Nähe des Geliebten' (D 162), 175, 299, 333, 351, 352
'Naturgenus' (D 422), 334
'Normans Gesang' (D 846), 250, 438, 508, 513

Octet (D 803), 372, 488
Offertory, *Tres sunt, qui testimonium dant in coelo* in A minor (D 181), 142
Offertory in C major (D 136), 127, 250
op.12 cycle, 409–11, 413
'Orestes auf Tauris' (D 548), 262
Organ Fugue (D 952), 530
'Original Dances' for Piano (D 365), 289, 290
Overture in D (D 2a), 41
Overture in D (D 12), 92
Overture in D (D 26), 41–2, 61
Overture in D major (D 4), 101
Overture in D minor (D 12), 41–2
Overture in E minor (D 648), 324
Overture in F major/F minor (D 675), 422, 462
Overture in G minor (D 668), 86, 422
Overtures in Italian Style as four-hand piano works (D 592 and D 597), 422
Overtures in the Italian style (D 590–1), 308

'Pax Vobiscum' (D 551), 306, 538–41
'Pensa, che questo istante' (D 76), 61
'Pflugerlied' (D 392), 158, 159
Piano Fantasy (D 1), 282
Piano Trio in B flat (D 28), 88
Piano Trio in E flat (D 929), 453, 463, 501, 513, 515, 516
Piano Trio in E flat major (D 929), 511–12
Piano Trios (D 898 and D 929), 504
Piano Variations (D 576), 256, 285–6
'Pilgerweise' (D 789), 274
Polonaise in B flat for Violin and Orchestra (D 580), 307
'Prometheus' (D 674), 47
Prometheus Cantata (lost), 210, 211–12, 323

Psalm 92 Hebrew setting for the Sabbath (D 953), 465
'Psalm D 23' (D 706), 506
'Punschlied' ('Vier Elemente,' D 277), 183

Quartetsatz in C minor (D 703), 79, 338
'Quell' innocente figlio' (D 17), 61, 82, 83, 131

'Rastlose Liebe' (D 138), 175, 250, 297, 333, 454
'Reliquie' Sonata in C major (D 840), 436
Requiem (D 453), 151
Rollengedichte (D 536), 261
'Romanze des Richard Löwenherz' (D 907), 487
Rondo in A (D 438), 217
Rondo in A major for Piano Duet (D 951), 430, 463, 516, 521
Rondo in B minor for Violin and Piano (D 895), 463, 487, 504
Rosamunde, Fürstin von Cypern (D 797), 197, 325

Sakuntala (D 701), 193, 196
Salve Regina (D 379), 128
Salve Regina in A major ('Offertorium,' D 676), 131, 135–7
Salve Regina in B flat (D 386), 129, 131, 134–6, 151
Salve Regina in B flat major (D 106), 127, 129, 131, 132, 319
Salve Regina in C major (D 811), 131, 136–8, 151
Salve Regina in F (D 27), 53, 131–2, 152, 319
Salve Regina in F major (D 223), 127, 131, 133–4, 319
Sanctus (D 56, 21 April 1813), 60–1
'Schäfers Klagelied' (D 121), 174, 324, 333
Scherzo and Trio in D and Allegro in F sharp minor for Piano (D 570), 305
'Schiffers Scheidelied' (D 910), 274
Schiller canons, 70, 71–3, 83
'Schlachtgesang' (D 912), 515
'Schmerz verzerret ihr Gesicht' (D 65), 71
'Schön wie ein Engel' (D 195), 182
'Schwanengesang' (D 744), 353
Schwanengesang (D 957), 463
'Schwestergruss' (D 762), 152
Sechs Antiphonen zum Palmsonntag (D 696), 128, 151
'Sehnsucht' (D 52 and D 636), 182
'Sehnsucht' (D 586), 333

675

INDEX OF SCHUBERT'S WORKS

'Sehnsucht' ('Nur wer die Sehnsucht kennt,' D 310), 176
'Sehnsucht' ('Was zieht mir das Herz so?', D 123), 176
'Sei mir gegrüsst' (D 741), 287, 405
'Seligkeit' (D 433), 389
'Serbate, o Dei custodi' (D35), 61, 83
'Seufzer' (D 198), 53–4
17 Ländler und 2 Ecossaisen (D 734), 289, 461
Six Ecossaises for piano (D 421), 210–11
Six Grandes Marches et Trios (D 819), 364–5
Six Polonaises (D 824), 423–4
16 Deutsche und 2 Ecossaisen (D 783), 289, 461
'Solfeggio' (D 619), 77
Sonata for Piano in B major (D 575), 305
Sonata for Piano in D flat major (D 567), 305
Sonata for Piano in E flat (D 568), 305
Sonata for Piano in G major (D 894), 463
Sonata in A flat (D 557), 305
Sonata in A minor (D 537), 305
Sonata in A minor (D 784), 436
Sonata in A minor (D 845), 80, 436, 438, 486
Sonata in D major (D 850), 436, 462–3, 486
Sonata in E minor (D 566), 305
Sonata in F sharp minor (D 571), 305
Sonata No. 1 in D major (D 384), 217
Sonata No. 2 in A minor (D 385), 217, 398
Sonata No. 3 in G minor (D 408), 217, 398
sonnets of solitude, (D 628–D 630), 319
Stabat Mater (D 383), 128, 135, 139–41, 472
Stabat Mater in G minor (D 175), 53, 139, 319
'Ständchen' (D 920), 279–80, 512, 515
'Ständchen' (D 921), 514
'Stimme der Liebe' (D 187), 157
String Quartet in A minor (D 804), 16, 90, 372–3, 374–5, 462, 520
String Quartet in B flat (D 112), 97, 122
String Quartet in B flat major (D 36), 88, 93
String Quartet in D (D 94), 61
String Quartet in D major (D 74), 58, 88, 90, 95–7, 518
String Quartet in D major (D 94), 92
String Quartet in D minor ('Death and the Maiden' D 810), 16, 55, 90, 251, 372–5, 453, 454–5

String Quartet in E flat major (D 87), 97, 110–11
String Quartet in G minor (D 173), 96, 122
String Quartet no. 1 in G minor/B flat major (D 18), 91–2
String Quartet no. 2 in C major (D 32), 7, 88, 92–3
String Quartet no. 5 in B flat major (D 68), 94
String Quartet no. 5 in C major (D 46), 78, 94–5, 110
String Quartet no. 7 in D major (D 74), 98–9, 101, 373
String Quartet no. 11 in E major (D 353), 314
String Quartet no. 15 in G major (D 887), 80, 81, 91, 455–6, 515, 520
String Quintet (D 8), 93
String Quintet in C major (D 956), 463, 467, 504, 519–23
'Suleika I' (D 720), 334, 404
Symphony in D (D 2b), 41
Symphony in D (D 936A), 119, 524–5
Symphony in D major (D 615), 232–3
Symphony in E major (D 729), 232, 338, 384, 447
Symphony no. 1 in D major (D 82), 90, 101, 102–3, 104–6, 107, 114, 121, 396, 447
Symphony no. 2 in B flat (D 125), 122–3
Symphony no. 3 in D major (D 200), 123–4
Symphony no. 4 in C minor (D 417) (the 'Tragic' symphony), 217, 218–22, 228
Symphony no. 5 in B flat (D 485), 222–6, 229
Symphony no. 6 (*Grosse Sinfonie*) (D 589), 226–32, 308, 337, 503, 543

Tantum Ergo (D 739), 142
Tantum Ergo (D 750), 473
Tantum Ergo in C (D 461), 142, 143
Tantum Ergo in C (D 739), 142
Tantum Ergo in C major (D 460), 127, 142, 143
Tantum Ergo in C major (D 739), 142
Tantum Ergo in D major (D 750), 127, 142
Tantum Ergo in E flat major (D 962), 473–4, 475
'Thekla' (D 73 and D 595), 84, 306
Thirty Minuets (D 41), 35
'Tischlied' (D 234), 176
'Todesmusik' (D 758), 274, 353
'Totengräberlied' (D 38), 84

INDEX OF SCHUBERT'S WORKS

'Totengräberlied' (D 44), 84
'Trauer der Liebe' (D 437), 158, 159
Trauerwalzer (D 365), 256, 288
'Trinklied' (D 148), 82
'Trockne Blume' Variations (D 802), 363, 506
Trois Marches Héroiques (D 602), 316
'Trost in Tränen' (D 120), 176
twelve Carnival Waltzes (D 969), 463
twelve *Grazer Walzer* (D 924), 507–8
twelve Waltzes, seventeen Ländler and nine Écossaises for piano (D 145), 289, 291–5, 334, 460, 461
12 Wiener Deutsche (D 128), 296

'Unendliche Freude durchwallet das Herz' (D 51), 84
'Unendliche Freude durchwallet das Herz' (D 54), 71, 183
'Unfinished' Symphony in B minor (D 759), 7, 338, 382–95, 397–8, 400–2, 404, 444–5, 446–7
'Uraniens Flucht' (D 554), 306

Valses nobles (D 969), 289, 291, 487
Valses sentimentales (D 779), 289, 290–1, 297, 461
Variations for piano (D 156), 58
Variations in A flat (D 813), 438
Variations on a French Air (D 624) op. 10, 4, 256, 285, 316, 333
'Vedi quanto adoro' (D 510), 83–4
'Verschwunden sind die Schmerzen' (D 81), 85, 119
'Vom Mitleiden Maria' (D 632), 130, 319
'Vor meiner Wiege' (D 927), 273, 385, 508

Waltz in C major for piano (D 980D), 462
'Wanderer Fantasy' (D 760), 286, 287, 384
'Wandrers Nachtlied I and II' (D 224 and D 768), 174, 333, 416–19, 465, 490, 505
'Wehmut' (D 772), 353–4
'Wer kauft Liebesgötter' (D 261), 176
'Widerspruch' (D 865), 454
'Wie Ulfru fischt' (D 525), 261–2, 266
'Wiegenlied' (D 867), 454
'Willkommen und Abschied' (D 767), 404–5, 503
Wind Nonet in E flat (D 79), 98
Wind Octet in F (D 72), 98
Winterreise (D 911), 55, 409, 444, 463–4, 467, 483–4, 488–97, 503, 504, 506, 510, 513, 524, 535–6, 545
'Wohin?' (D 795), 412
'Wonne der Wehmut' (D 260), 174

'Zufriedenheit' (D 501), 157, 158, 159
'Zum Rundetanz' (D 983B), 334
Zur Namensfeier des Herrn Andreas Siller (D 83), 98
'Zur Namensfeier meines Vaters' (D 80), 98–9
'Zwei Ländler' (D 366), 288, 289
'Zwerg, Der' (D 771), 354–5

INDEX

Full references to Schubert's works are to be found in the separate 'Index of Works'.

Adams, Henry Brooks, 57
aesthetics
   aesthetic distance and audience reception, 331
   aesthetic education, 13–14
   creativity and, 13
   friendship and, 243–7
   of listening, 180
   Schiller's aesthetic theory, 13–14, 71, 178–9, 180, 245–7, 351–2
Albrecht, Johann Friedrich Ernst (1752–1814), 101
Albrechtsberger, Johann Georg (1736–1809), 35, 43, 62, 67, 125
Alexander I, Tsar, 425
Allgemeine Musikalische Zeitung (AMZ), 329–30, 436, 442, 452, 487, 502–3
Artaria, Domenico, 436, 463, 487
Artaria, Matthias, 462–3
Assmayr, Ignaz, 255
audiences
   access to via publications, 459
   aesthetic distance and, 331
   the anonymous public, 453, 459
   composition for public audiences, 113, 330, 331, 455, 456
   improvisation and, 282–3, 285
   small educated elite audiences, 113, 223–4, 282–3, 459, 507
Augustine, 252, 339, 484
Austin, George Lowell, 7

Bach, J. S., 91, 472
Bacher, Johann, 106

Barbaia, Domenico, 375, 498, 499
Baroque Landhaussaal (County Hall), 324
Barth, Josef (1781–1865), 325, 329, 454–5
Bauernfeld, Eduard von (1802–1890)
   Der Graf von Gleichen (D 918), 457, 458
   friendship with Schubert, 38, 227, 351, 421, 434, 454, 486, 487, 511
   last visit to Schubert, 534
   musical ability, 279
   reaction to Schubert's death, 542
   on Schubert's double nature, 12, 297, 322, 406
   Shakespeare translations, 458
   trip to Carinthia, 457
Becker, Andreas, 25
Beethoven, Ludwig van (1770–1827)
   A minor String Quartet, 441
   counterpoint studies, 35
   critical dominance of, 382–3
   cross-referenced in Schubert's Sixth Symphony, 227–8, 230
   death of, 474, 487, 514, 542
   Egmont overture, 181
   'Eroica' Symphony no. 3., 442, 511–12, 514
   Fidelio, 115, 116
   Fifth Symphony, 442
   Fourth Symphony, 103
   improvisational brilliance, 282, 285
   memorial concerts, 487–8
   Schubert–Beethoven mythology, 3–5, 7, 11, 427
   Schubert's wish to be buried alongside, 535, 544

INDEX

Seventh Symphony, 123
String Quartet in C sharp minor, op. 131, 455, 532
Symphony no. 2 in D major, 40, 95, 96, 103
Tremati, empi, tremati, 498
waltzes, 454
works in C minor, 218, 219
Benedikt, Erich, 477
Benefit Concert, 506, 512, 513, 514–16
Bergmann, Johann, 160, 347
Bernhardt, Jacob (1790–1846), 362, 363, 364, 365
biographies
  of Beethoven, 4
  challenges of, 3, 5–6, 15–16, 17–18
  counter-images of Schubert, 1–3, 12–15
  cult of genius, 7
  of the late nineteenth century, 1–2, 3–4, 6–7
  primary sources, 9
  role of myth, 1–5
  Schubert–Beethoven connections, 3–5, 7
  Schubert's artistic career in, 9–10
  of the twentieth century, 2–3, 7, 17
  the works of Schubert in, 7–8, 9, 15–18
Blake, William, 347
Bocklet, Karl Maria von, 428, 513, 515
Bodendorff, Werner, 9
Bodmer, Johann Jakob (1698–1783), 239
Bogner, Ferdinand, 506
Böhm, Joseph, 512, 515
Boieldieu, Francois-Adrien, 192
Brandt, Susanna Margaretha (1746–1772), 163–4
Brett, Philip, 2
Breuning, Gerhard von, 335, 512
Brown, Maurice, 4, 8, 290
Bruchmann, Franz Seraph Josef Vincenz von (1798–1867), 152, 251, 268

Call, Leonhard von (1767–1815), 112
Cappi & Diabelli, 332, 333–4, 396, 459–60, 461–2; *see also* Diabelli, Anton
Castelli, Iganz Franz von (1781–1862), 82, 199, 517
Cherubini, Luigi, 40, 116, 192, 405
Chrétien, Jean-Louis, 129
Church of the Assumption of the Virgin Mary (kostel Nanebevzeti Panny Marie), 23
Cibber, Colley, 434
Clodi, Florian Maxmilian, 438
Clodi, Theresa, 438

Collin, Heinrich von (1771–1811), 41
Collin, Mätthaus von, 249, 256, 275, 353–5
commissions
  audience specificity in, 279–80
  choral works, 279
  by individuals, 249, 463
  Mass in F major (D 105), 121, 145–6
  occasional works, 127, 180, 217, 230, 279, 473–4, 506, 509–10
  Prometheus Cantata (lost), 211–13
  of sacred works, 35, 121, 142, 145–6, 474, 517
  theatrical commissions, 198, 199, 278, 323, 325
composition
  alongside improvisation, 281–2, 286–7, 507–8
  in biographies of Schubert, 7–8, 9
  canonic writing, 70–6, 83
  a capella masses, 43
  critiques of Sentimentalism, 413–14
  dedications to female patrons, 504–5, 508
  domestic music making, 89, 90–1, 98–9, 110, 111–12, 119
  during the fallow years (1818–22), 308, 313–14, 337–9
  following the death of his mother, 52–5, 87, 88–9, 90, 99–100, 130, 131–2, 138–9, 144, 152, 345, 353, 386, 488
  il filo concept, 64–5, 82
  imitatio technique, 129
  influence of Beethoven's Symphony no. 2 in D major, 40, 96
  influence of Mozart's Symphony no. 40 in G minor, 40
  influences from Eastern Europe, 40–1, 43, 113, 285
  influences from the Stadtkonvikt orchestra, 40–2
  innovation in Schubert's career, 156, 161
  intertextualities in the symphonies, 103–4
  Italianate influences, 62, 65–6, 67, 82, 83–4, 86, 132, 156, 228, 229, 405, 498–504
  Juvenilia, 43, 45–6, 47
  Lichtental liturgical works, 125, 126–8
  Lieder for multiple voices, 438–9
  lost children in, 165, 166–72
  love for the departed, 152–3, 345–7, 355–7, 454
  male-voice settings, 313, 325
  military marches, 424–6
  music for piano four hands, 422
  myth of a self-reflective art, 15–16

679

INDEX

on the occasion of Schubert's death, 542–3
occasional works, 127, 180, 217, 230, 279, 473–4, 506, 509–10
for orphans, 165–6
patriotism in, 118–21
piano duets, 421–30
piano sonatas, 436
Pietism and, 318–19
productivity of 1815, 172–4, 244
revision and resetting, 113, 332
role of tradition in, 155–6
schoolhouse string quartets, 88–98, 100
during Schubert's illness, 361, 363–6, 367–8, 372–5, 376, 380
self-borrowing, 116, 194, 286–7
for small groups of connoisseurs, 113, 223–4, 283, 459, 507
socio-historical contexts of, 9–12
songs borne of solitude, 318–20, 352–3
songs for Therese Grob, 157–8, 173–4
speed of, 121, 122
symphonic sketches, 100–1
theme of time, 412–13
themes of death, 48, 78–9, 152, 166–9, 309, 345, 348–9, 352–4, 385, 417
themes of journeying/wandering, 343–7, 406–11, 415–16, 417–19, 456, 483, 488–97, 504, 514, 526–8
themes of paternity, 46–51, 52, 78, 79, 98–9, 110, 113
unfinished works, 545
Conrad, Joseph, 6
Cotta, 460
counterpoint studies
compositional training, 59–60
early exercises in, 59–60
figured bass, 60–1, 63, 77
ground bass exercises, 62–3
scale-based counterpoint, 64–5
under Michael Holzer, 35–6
under Salieri, 64–5
under Sechter, 59, 529–31
see also partimento
Craigher de Jachelutta, Jacob Nicolaus (1797–1855), 434, 498
Czerny, Carl, 288, 454, 488
Czerny, Josef, 460, 461–2

dances
commercial market for, 288, 300, 461
Deutsche, 296–7
Impromptus (D 899), 507–8
improvisation, 281, 283, 288–99, 507–8

influences from folk songs, 297
popularity of, 288
publication of dance cycles, 288–9, 295, 300, 333–4, 461–2, 488
death
compositions following the death of his mother, 52–5, 87, 88–9, 90, 99–100, 130, 131–2, 138–9, 144, 152, 345, 353, 386, 488
Italian *Lachrimae*, 538
in 'Mein Traum', 343, 345–6, 465
'Pax Vobiscum' (D 551), 538–41
Requiem masses in Schubert's memory, 543
Schubert's acceptance of mortality, 379–80, 381, 417–19, 445–6, 453
Schubert's funeral and burial at Währing, 541–2
themes of death in Schubert's works, 48, 78–9, 152, 166–9, 309, 345, 348–9, 352–4, 385, 417
Deutsch, Otto Erich, 4, 8, 9
Diabelli, Anton (1781–1858), 4, 112, 129, 141, 165, 217, 295, 396, 435, 437, 461, 488, 517; *see also* Cappi & Diabelli
Doblhoff-Dier, Count Anton von, 361, 363, 364
domestic music making, 89, 90–1, 99, 223, 227, 249, 250, 279, 325, 330, 454, 456, 487, 512, 513, 532
Donizetti, Domenico, 191, 376–7, 438
Doppler, Josef, 102, 122
Dräxler von Carin, Philipp, 211
Dreifaltigkeitskirche (Church of the Holy Trinity), 362
Dresdener Morgen-Zeitung, 499

Eberl, Anton (1765–1807), 104
Eberwein, Carl, 198, 204, 206
Ebner, Johann Leopold (1791–1870), 40, 46, 248
Eckel, Georg Franz (b. 1797), 40, 44–5
Einstein, Alfred, 7
Enlightenment, 237, 238, 239, 478, 479
Esterházy, Karoline (1805–1851), 77, 297, 315, 364, 367–8, 420–1, 423
Esterházy, Marie, 77, 315, 367–8, 423
Evangelicalism, 478
Eybler, Josef Leopold (1765–1846), 36, 43, 143, 468, 500
eyesight
blind poets, 517
blindness, 434–5

INDEX

'Der blinde Knabe' (D 833), 250, 434–5, 498
ocular syphilis, 434, 533
short-sightedness, 45

Fellinger, Johann, 172
Fenaroli, Fedele, 65
Feurzeig, Lisa, 2
Feyerer, Karl, 112
Feyerer, Marianne, 112
Flower, Newman, 4
Francis I, 29, 37, 118, 119, 120, 145
Franck, Josephine von, 505
Friedlaender, Max, 7
friendship
  aesthetic education and, 243–7
  with Albert Stadler, 239
  with Anna Fröhlich, 505–7, 543–4
  with Anselm Hüttenbrenner, 249–50, 251, 254–7, 457
  art and musical achievement, 244–5
  with artists, 251
  concepts of friendship, 237–8, 252, 260, 276
  epistolary, 242–4
  with Franz von Schober, 239, 240–1, 251, 271–6, 336, 433–4, 457, 487
  with Johann Mayrhofer, 211, 239, 242, 257–71, 323, 350
  with Josef Hüttenbrenner, 242, 335, 336
  with Josef von Spaun, 39–40, 112, 239, 251, 253–4, 511
  with Katharina Lászny von Folkusfálva, 348–50, 426
  lack of in 1826, 457
  with Leopold Kupelwieser, 109, 239, 251, 362, 364
  with Moritz von Schwind, 251, 358–9, 363–4, 398, 434, 457, 511
  musical friendships, 249–52
  nineteenth-century homosociality, 240–2, 257–9, 260, 262–3, 267
  poetic friendship, 248–9, 259–60
  role of male friendship, 238–9
  during Schubert's illness, 340–1, 512–13
  in Schubert's musical practice, 278–80
  significance of for Schubert, 237, 252, 313, 323
  with Sophie von Müller, 433, 454, 504, 507
  at the Stadtkonvikt, 239–40, 248
  during the years of crisis, 303–6
Frischling, Franz, 122, 223

Fröhlich, Anna, 249, 279–80, 332, 505–7, 513, 543–4
Fröhlich, Barbara (Babette) (1797–1879), 505, 506, 507
Fröhlich, Hans Joseph, 7
Fröhlich, Josefine (Pepi) (1803–1878), 505, 507, 513, 515
Fröhlich, Katharina (Kathi) (1800–1879), 505, 506, 507
Frost, Henry F., 6–7
Frühwald, Josef, 329
Fux, Johann Joseph, 62, 65, 70

Gahy, Josef von, 288, 428, 486–7, 511
Gamerra, Giovanni de (1742–1803), 498
Gassmann, Florian Leopold (1729–1774), 62, 103
Gellert, Christian Fürchtegott, 238
Gesellschaft adeliger Frauen zur Beforderung des Guten und Nutzlichen (the Noblewomen's Society for the Advancement of Good and Benevolence), 329
Gesellschaft der Musikfreunde
  access to aristocratic salons from, 504–5
  dedication of C major symphony to, 451–2, 453
  establishment of, 172, 249
  memorial concerts for Schubert, 251, 543
  Musikalischen Abendunterhaltungen, 324
  performances of Schubert's works, 223, 227, 250, 279, 325, 330, 454, 456, 487, 512, 513
  public concerts, 223
  Schubert manuscripts bequeathed to, 395, 402
  Schubert's Benefit Concert, 506, 512, 513, 514–16
  Schubert's membership of, 459
  vocal training for women, 506, 507
Gewandhaus Orchestra, 448
Geymüller, Baron Johann Heinrich, 506
Gibbs, Christopher, 8, 17
Gingerich, John, 5
Giuliani, Mauro (1781–1829), 112
Gleim, Johann Wilhelm Ludwig (1719–1803), 238, 239
Gluck, Christoph Willibald, 192, 209
Goethe, Johann Wolfgang von (1749–1832)
  The Author, 458
  on Beethoven's deafness, 4–5
  Claudine, 199–201
  conflicted soul, 12–13
  Das Marchen, 340
  'An den Mond', 85

INDEX

Divan ghazals, 357
Egmont, 169
Erlkönig, 168–70
Faust I, 12–13, 162–3, 188, 205–6, 306, 321
Faust II, 518, 545
'Ganymed', 49, 437
Harper cycle, 409–11, 413
'Heidenröslein', 189
importance of letters, 242
knowledge of the Brandt case, 163–4
Lieder settings by Schubert, 85, 172, 173, 174–8, 201–2, 277, 404–6, 417, 437–8, 462, 505
Maximen und Reflexionen, 212
'Meeres Stille', 84
Mignon, 165, 437, 505, 538
mill romance poems, 411
music theatre, 198
on obituaries, 14–15
'Prometheus', 47
Proserpina, 198
royalty payments for publications, 460
Schubert's gift of the op. 19 Goethe settings, 437
Stella, 458
Trilogie der Leidenschaft, 414–15
Urfaust, 164, 188
Venetian Epigrams, 481
Werther, 414, 493
Göschen, 200
Götz, Josef (1787–1822), 326, 329, 456
Graz
  and the disputed ownership of the 'Unfinished' symphony manuscript, 392–6, 399, 401
  performances of Schubert's works, 255, 256
  Schubert's stay at the Pachlers, 507–9
Grillparzer, Franz (1791–1872), 271, 456, 457
Grob, Heinrich (1800–1855), 157, 217
Grob, Therese (1798–1875), 112, 113
  appearance, 156, 157
  marriage to Johann Bergmann, 160, 347
  Mass in F major (D 105), 145, 147–8, 156
  sacred music for, 127, 132, 133–4, 136, 139, 150, 319
  Schubert's love for, 156–7, 159–60, 194, 214, 215–17, 218, 303, 308, 347–8
  Schubert's song compositions for, 157–8, 173–4
  as a soprano, 112

Großer Redoutensaal (Large Assembly Hall), 324, 392, 451, 543
Grove, George, 1, 4, 6, 7
Gruber, Gernot, 8
Grünentorgasse no. 147, 30, 307, 308, 314
Gymnich, August von, 249, 332, 506
Gyrowetz, Adalbert (Vojtěch Matyás Jírovec, 1763–1850), 41, 43, 104, 456

Haller, Adam, 268
Hamann, Johann Georg (1730–1788), 483
Hanslick, Eduard, 39, 218
Hanslischek, Peter Anton, 215
harmonic theory, 11–12, 47
Hartmann, Franz von, 251, 283, 288, 296, 359, 361, 477, 486, 487, 511
Hartmann, Fritz von, 283, 486, 487, 489, 511
Haslinger, Tobias, 295, 461, 463–4, 500, 513
Hatwig, Otto (1766–1834), 217, 218, 223, 227
Hauer, Anton (b. 1796), 40
Hauptmann, Anna Milder, 192, 526
Hausmusik, 89
Haydn, Joseph (1732–1809), 42, 93, 103, 125, 140, 144, 526
Haydn, Michael (1737–1806), 42, 70, 73, 104, 125, 143, 144, 440
Heidegger, Martin, 129
Herbeck, Johann, 397, 400, 401, 402–3
Herder, Johann Gottfried, 168, 189, 238, 442
Heuberger, Richard, 7
Hilmar, Ernst, 9
Himmelpfortgrund no. 72 (today Nussdorferstrasse no. 54) cray, 25, 28, 33, 34, 114, 119, 307
Hinrichsen, Hans-Joachim, 8
Hofmann, Georg von, 198, 499
Hoffmann, E. T. A., 442
Hofmann, Leopold (1738–1793), 43, 104
Hölty, Ludwig, 53, 84, 85, 159, 172, 173
Holz, Karl, 512, 532
Holzapfel, Anton (1792–1868), 35, 38, 40, 42, 44, 45, 46, 59, 87, 145, 156, 239
Holzer, Michael (1772–1826), 35–6, 88, 121, 125, 145
Hölzl, Josef, 362
Hönig, Anna [Nanette] (1803–1888), 360, 457, 510
Hopkins, Gerard Manley, 465, 485
Horstig, Eduard, 487–8
Huber, Josef, 361, 369

INDEX

Humboldt, Wilhelm von, 322–3, 351
Hummel, Johann Nepomuk, 282, 283–4, 435, 454, 487
Hutchings, Arthur, 4
Hüttenbrenner, Anselm (1794–1868)
  and the alleged meeting with Beethoven, 4
  compositions, 255, 285–6, 306
  death of Beethoven, 487
  friendship with Schubert, 249–50, 251, 254–7, 457
  loss of Schubert's manuscripts, 114, 257
  membership of the Styrian Music Society, 397
  musical training under Salieri, 76
  ownership of the 'Unfinished' Symphony manuscript, 392–3, 394–6, 401, 402–3
  performances of Schubert's Lieder, 256
  performances of Schubert's works, 329
  personal collection of Schubert manuscripts, 399
  popularity of Schubert's dances, 288
  protection of Schubert's privacy, 351
  reaction to Schubert's death, 542
  Schubert's letters to, 242–3, 402
  on Schubert's love for Therese Grob, 157
  self-promotion, 402
  on Sophie Müller, 433
  waltz dedicated to, 297
Hüttenbrenner, Heinrich, 348, 397
Hüttenbrenner, Josef (1794–1868)
  alleged Schubert–Beethoven meeting, 4
  break with Schubert, 396–7
  Deutscher in C sharp minor (D 643) for, 296–7
  friendship with Schubert, 242, 335, 336
  memorial service for Schubert, 543
  ownership of the 'Unfinished' Symphony manuscript, 394–6, 397–9, 401–3
  personal collection of Schubert manuscripts, 201, 257, 399–400
  professional relationship with Schubert, 396, 399
Hymnodiae a Scholastica Juventute (1741), 24

illness *see* syphilis
improvisation
  alongside composition, 281–2, 286–7, 507–8
  commercial market for, 300
  dances, 281, 283, 288–99
  in fantasies, 286–7
  Impromptus (D 899), 507–8
  during partimento training, 11, 62, 63, 281, 282–3, 299
  rapport with the audience, 282–3, 285
  Schubert's skills in, 282–4, 287–8, 300
  variations and themes, 285–6
Isouard, Nicolas, 192

Jacobi, Friedrich Heinrich, 153, 172
Jaskulsky, Hans, 477
Jenger, Johann Baptist (1793–1856), 250, 251, 397, 401, 426–7, 433, 504, 507–10, 525
Jesuit Gymnasium, Brno, 23–4
Johann, Franz (1720–1768), 21
Johnson, Graham, 17, 352, 357
Joseph II, 23, 37, 165, 249
Joubert, Joseph, 129

Kalchberg, Johann, 172
Kant, Immanuel, 243, 323
Kapelle der heiligen Dreifaltigkeit (Chapel of the Most Blessed Trinity), 22
Kärntnertortheater (Carinthian Gate Theatre), 192, 198, 228, 256, 277, 323, 324, 325, 327–8, 348, 375, 455, 509
Kenner, Josef (1794–1868), 12, 13, 14, 46, 106, 239, 241, 242, 248, 271, 288, 322, 380, 462
Kiesewetter, Irene, 86, 426–7, 501, 504, 530
Kiesewetter von Wiesenbrunn, Raphael Georg (1773–1850), 86, 451,499
Kinsky, Princess Karolina Charlotte, 504–5
Klatte, Willhelm, 7
Kleindl, Johann Wilhelm, 517
Kleindl, Josef (b. 1796), 40, 42
Kleyenböck, Anna (1783–1860)
  children, 30, 32, 52, 109, 170, 313, 362
  marriage to Franz Theodor, 52, 93, 100, 108
Klopstock, Friedrich Gottlieb, 38, 140, 172, 173, 183, 239, 478
Körner, Christian Gottfried, 178, 181, 244
Korner, Philipp (1761–1831), 36, 122
Körner, Theodor, 85, 172, 173, 244
Kosegarten, Ludwig, 84, 172, 173, 353
Kotzebue, August von (1761–1819), 114–15, 116, 193, 203
Kozeluch, Leopold (Jan Antonín Koželuh, 1747–1818), 40–1
Kramer, Lawrence, 2
Kramer, Richard, 97, 404
Kreissle von Hellborn, Heinrich, 1, 4, 6, 7, 102, 160, 350–1, 392, 395, 399
Kreutzer, Konradin, 255, 376, 498
Kris, Ernst, 2

INDEX

Krommer, Franz (František Vincenc Kramá, 1759–1831), 41, 104
Kuffner, Christoph, 517
Küfstein, Johann Ferdinand Graf (b. 1752), 39
Kunz, Babette, 422
Kunz, Therese, 422
Kupelwieser, Josef, 109, 361, 375–6, 378–9, 456
Kupelwieser, Leopold (1796–1862)
  friendship with Schubert, 109, 239, 251, 362, 364
  at the Schobers, 454
  Schubert's despairing letter to, 16, 90, 219, 370–3, 376, 379, 418, 442
Kurz, Otto, 2

Lablache, Luigi (1794–1858), 498–9, 500, 502–3, 504
Lachner, Franz von (1803–1890), 5, 251–2, 298, 428, 454–5, 498, 530–1, 534
Lang, Franz Innocenz (1752–1835), 38, 96, 102, 122
Lange, Samuel Gotthold (1711–1781), 238
Lászny von Folkusfálva, Katharina (1789–1828), 348–50, 426
Lehner, Fritz, 2
Leidesdorf, Maximilian, 288, 363, 462
Leitner, Karl Gottfried von, 508, 515
Lewy, Josef, 512, 515
Lichtental Parish
  centenary celebrations, 121, 145
  Franz Theodor as Imperial Almoner, 29–30
  Maria Elisabeth's commemorative service, 132
  performances in, 127, 142
  sacred music for, 125, 126–8
  Schubert family connections with, 26, 27, 28, 34, 35
Liebenberg, Carl Emanuel von (1796–1856), 398
Lieder
  composed between 1814-1817, 172–4
  early compositions under Salieri, 46–7, 76, 79, 82, 83–4
  Liedertafel tradition, 76
  manuscript dissemination, 188
  for multiple voices, 438–9
  performances of, 249–50, 277, 324, 359, 438
  publications of, 188
  setting's from Goethe, 85, 172, 173, 174–8, 201–2, 277, 404–6, 417, 437–8, 462, 505
  settings from Mayrhofer, 172, 261–2, 266, 267, 277, 306, 318, 372
  settings of, 84–5, 172–4, 178–85, 188, 261–2, 266, 267, 306, 352–5, 372
  themes of absence and loss, 385, 406
  themes of death, 79, 493
  themes of time, 491
  for Therese Grob, 157–9, 173–4
  see also setting
Lieder, Friedrich, 437
Linke, Joseph, 512, 513, 515
Lithographisches Institut, 273
Litschauer, Walburga, 9
Littrow-Bischoff, Auguste von, 505–6
Lotti, Antonio (1667–1740), 62
Ludlamshöhle, 456–7
Luib, Ferdinand, 14, 45, 351, 401

Malcom (D 843), 438
male-voices settings (TTB), 71, 84–5, 98, 313, 325–6
Mann, Thomas, 369, 523
Maria Trost Church, 134
Marschner, Heinrich, 503
Martini, Padre Giovanni Battista (1706–1784), 62
Marx, Adolf Bernhard, 442
masses
  companion pieces to, 474–6, 516–18
  Latin masses, *149–50*
  Mass in A flat major (D 678), 467–71
  Mass in E flat major as Schubert's Requiem, 471, 474, 512
  mysticism in, 465, 467–8
  omissions from the Nicene Creed and, 477–81
  principle of scriptural infallibility, 478
  Requiem masses in Schubert's memory, 543
  see also sacred music
Matiegka, Wenzel (1773– 1830), 111, 112, 129
Mattheson, Johann (1681–1764), 286
Matthisson, Friedrich von, 70, 85, 172, 179, 180
Mayerhofer von Grünbuhel, Ferdinand, 457, 458
Mayrhofer, Johann (1787–1836)
  as a census official, 259, 262, 269
  Franz Theodor's concerns for Schubert, 306, 312

684

friendship with Schubert, 211, 239, 242, 257–71, 323, 350
homoeroticism in the works of, 257–9, 262–3, 267
Lieder settings, 172, 261–2, 266, 267, 277, 306, 318, 372
misrepresentation of Schubert, 59
obituary for Schubert, 261
personality, 259, 265–6, 269–71
poetry, 259–60, 261, 515
portrayals of Schubert, 257–9, 262–3, 268–9
reaction to Schubert's death, 542
Mayssen, Josef, 142, 473
McClary, Susan, 2
McKay, Elizabeth Norman, 8
Mehlgrube tavern, 5
Méhul, Étienne-Nicolas, 40
Meier, Georg Friedrich (1718–1777), 238
Mendelssohn, Felix, 4, 9, 401, 442, 452–3
Messing, Scott, 2
Metastasio, Pietro (1698–1782), 64, 80, 82, 83–4, 86, 131, 156, 205, 501
Metternich, Klemens von, 242, 261, 370, 457, 460
Meyerbeer, Giacomo, 191, 282, 376–7
Mikan, Johann Christian (1769–1844), 120–1
Milton, John, 129
Molitor, Simon (1766–1848), 111–12
Mosel, Ignaz Franz (1772–1844), 39, 83–4, 282, 456
Mozart, Wolfgang Amadeus (1756–1791)
  C minor movements, 218
  cross-referenced in Schubert's Fourth Symphony, 224, 225, 226
  Die Zauberflöte, 115, 116, 181, 192
  Don Giovanni, 83, 192
  'Jupiter' Symphony no. 41, 105
  Le nozze di Figaro, 405
  'Prague' Symphony, 103
  Requiem, 543
  Schubert's identification with, 208
  Schubert's musical training and, 40, 42, 46, 70, 73
  String Quartets, 95
Müller, Friedrich von, 478
Müller, Karl Theodor, 461
Müller, Sophie von (1803–1830), 433, 454, 504, 507
Müller, Wilhelm, 411–12, 488–90, 526–8
Müllner, Franz (b. 20 August 1797), 37
musical training
  canon, 70–6, 83

cantus firmus exercises, 64–5
as a chorister at the Stadtkonvikt, 36–8, 42–4, 87–8, 98, 125–6
church music, 131–2
in composition, 57
early exercises, 59–66
early years, 35–6
fugues, 64, 66–70
keyboard fugues, 66–8, 69, 516, 530–1
in opera composition, 114–15, 121, 193, 194, 195, 202–3
in *partimento*, 11
resetting, 53, 80–6
under Salieri, 36, 57–9, 62–8, 80–2, 83, 111, 282–3, 304, 368
schemata, 77–80
socio-historical contexts of, 11–12
solfeggios, 76–8
the Stadkonvikt orchestra, 39–42, 44, 87–8
stile antico fugues, 66, 67, 68–9, 471–3, 531
thoroughbass, 57
see also counterpoint studies
Musikalische Eilpost, 374

Napoleon, 40, 120
Nejebse, Wensel (1796–1865), 326, 329
Neudorf (Vysoká, Malá Morava), 21–2, 23, 25
Neue Schubert Ausgabe, 9
Newbould, Brian, 8
Nicholas I, Tsar, 425
Niemeyer, August Hermann, 479
Nietzsche, Friedrich, 129
Novalis (Georg Freiherr von Hardenberg), 130, 319, 343, 344–5, 357, 534

Oates, Joyce Carol, 14
opera
  apprenticeship on the Viennese Stage, 196–7, 198
  Italian opera in Vienna, 375, 502
  performances of, 191–2
  potential career in, 198–9, 324–5, 375–7
  Salieri's opera compositions, 59, 62
  Schubert–Goethe constellation in, 199–205
  Schubert's training under Salieri, 114–15, 121, 193, 194, 195, 202–3
  Schubert's working methods, 193–4
  self-borrowing in Schubert's operas, 194
  Singspiel (operettas), 192

INDEX

Ottenwalt, Anton von, 240–1, 271, 425, 439, 440

Pachler, Faust, 509–10
Pachler, Karl, 456
Pachler, Marie (née Koschak, 1794–1855), 507–10
Paër, Ferdinando, 192
Pantheism, 442–3
partimento
  canon, 70–6, 83
  church music, 127
  instruction in under Salieri, 62–8
  instrumental fugal writing, 66–7, 69
  keyboard improvisation and, 11, 62, 63, 281, 282–3, 299
  opera training, 194
  resetting, 53, 80–6
  of the *Stabat Mater*, 140
  vocal (*stile antico*) fugal writing, 66–9
  see also resetting
Pennauer, 425, 436, 460–1
performances/concerts
  Benefit Concert, 506, 512, 513, 514–16
  church music, 128
  deathbed performance of Beethoven's String Quartet in C sharp minor, 532
  'Der blinde Knabe' (D 833), 434–5
  'Der Wanderer' (D489), 324
  domestic music making, 89, 90–1, 99, 223, 227, 249, 250, 279, 325, 330, 454, 456, 487, 512, 513, 532
  early 1826, 454
  during 1827, 486–7
  'Erlkönig' (D 328), 249, 256, 257, 277, 279, 324, 329, 332–3, 487, 506
  at Franz Frischling's residence, 223
  at Franz von Lachner's home, 251
  'Gesang der Geister uber den Wassern' (D 714), 329–30
  at the Gesellschaft der Musikfreunde, 223, 227, 250, 279, 325, 330, 454, 456, 487, 512, 513
  of Goethe, 277
  'Great' C major symphony (D 944), 401, 451–3
  at the Gundelhof (Bauernmarkt no. 4/5 Brandstatte), 249
  at the Imperial Palace, 227
  at Leopold von Sonnleithner's soirées, 249
  in the Lichtental Parish, 127, 142
  of male-voice trios, 325–7
  Mass in A flat major (D 678), 456
  Mass in F major (D 105), 121, 145–8

memorial concerts for Beethoven, 487–8
memorial concerts for Schubert, 276, 402, 543–4
Octet (D 803), 488
of the operas, 191–2
orchestral, 223
at Otto Hatwig's home, 223, 227
Piano Trio in E flat (D 929), 513
Prometheus Cantata (lost), 211–12
publications following, 463
recital tour of Austria with Vogl, 437–40, 457
revision and resetting, 515
Schubertiade, 268, 273, 290, 454, 486, 487, 513
at the Stadtkonvikt, 41, 122
Symphony no. 1 in D major (D 82), 102–3, 543
Symphony no. 3 in D major (D 200), 123
Symphony no. 4 in C minor (D 417), 218
Symphony no. 5 in B flat (D 485), 223
Symphony no. 6 (*Grosse Sinfonie*) (D 589), 227, 543
'Unfinished' Symphony in B minor (D 759), 392
in Vienna 1819–22, 323–4
Vogl's performances of Schubert's works, 256, 277, 329, 487
by women in chapels, 127
see also audiences
Pergolesi, Giovanni, 139–40
Pescetti, Giovanni Battista (1704–1766), 62
Pettenkofer, Anton, 227
Pfeffel, Gottlieb Conrad, 47
Pichl, Wenzel (Václav Pichl, 1741–1805), 41, 104
Pietism, 238, 318–19
Pilgrims Progress, 347
Pinterics, Karl (d. 1831), 248
Pozzo, Andrea (1642–1709), 42
Probst, Heinrich Albert, 463, 515, 516
prostitution, 350
publications
  audiences for, 339, 459, 463
  bilingual settings, 434–5, 498–504
  commercial markets for, 517
  dance cycles, 288–9, 295, 300, 333–4, 461–2, 488
  'Erlkonig' (D 328), 332–3, 396
  'Gretchen am Spinnrade' (D 118), 396
  international publishers, 462–3
  in journals, 324
  loss of original manuscripts, 460–1, 462
  the op. 19 Goethe settings, 437–8

piracy, 461
royalty payments for, 459, 460
by Schober, 273
of Schubert's Lieder, 188
Schubert's relations with Diabelli, 334, 459–60, 461
of Shakespeare songs in translation, 458
textual fluidity, 188–9
Pyrker, Johann Ladislaus, 85, 440, 442–3, 449–50

Randhartinger, Benedikt (1802–1893), 5, 40
Reed, John, 7
Reichardt, Johann Friedrich, 114, 202
Reil, Johann Anton Friedrich, 516–17
Reissing, Christian Ludwig, 82
Reissmann, August, 7
religious faith
'Die Allmacht' (D 875), 442–3
'Ellens Gesang III' (Ave Maria, D 839), 438–9
of Franz Theodore, 313, 467
God is Nature, 444, 465–6, 482
'Mein Gebet' (My Prayer, 1823), 360–1
nineteenth-century crisis in, 22, 477–8
religious philosophy, 493–4
Schubert's engagement with, 318, 360–1, 372, 466
Schubert's God of Eternal Becoming, 466–7
Schubert's mysticism, 467–8
Schubert's quasi-theology of music, 442–4
Schubert's renewed religious faith, 444
Schubert's sacred music and, 481–5
Schubert's transmutation of faith, 476–8
see also sacred music
Rellstab, Ludwig, 456, 514
resetting see setting
residences
Grünentorgasse no. 147, 30, 307, 308, 314
Karolinentor, 486
with Mayrhofer, 259, 261, 264–5, 266, 323, 335
Schubert's relocation and death at Ferdinand's home (Kettebrückengrasse, 6), 523, 526, 531–2, 533–4
Schubert's time in Schober's home, 273–4, 304–7, 454, 526
Wieden suburb (9 Technikerstrasse), 435
Zum roten Krebsen (The Red Crayfish), Vienna, 25, 28, 33, 34, 114, 119, 307
Zum schwarzen Rossel, 108, 214, 304, 307, 313
see also Zseliz

Reutter the younger, Georg (1708–1772), 42
Ricoeur, Paul, 477, 483
Rieder, Ambrois (1771–1855), 435
Rieder, August, 251
Rieder, Johann, 435, 473
Rieder, Wilhelm August, 435–7, 453
Roman Emperor Inn, 324
Romanticism, 7, 10, 112, 180, 245, 322, 344, 442
Romberg, Bernhard Heinrich (1767–1841), 41
Roner von Ehrenwerth, Franziska, 86
Rosamunde (D 797), 462
Rosner, Ignaz, 112
Rossini, Gioachino, 501
Rückert, Friedrich, 355–7, 456
Rueskäfer, Michael von (1794–1872), 106
Ružička, Wenzel (1785–1823), 39, 44, 60

sacred music
Latin masses, 149–50
Lichtental liturgical works, 125, 126–8
Marienbild (Marian hymns), 129–39, 319
Mass in F major (D 105), 145–8, 151
performances of, 128
Salieri's compositions, 43–4, 59, 143
Salve Regina settings, 319
Schubert as a composer of, 473
Schubert's childhood exposure to, 125–6
Schubert's religious faith and, 481–5
secular texts, 152–4
Stabat Mater settings, 139–41, 151, 319, 472
stile antico fugues, 151–2, 471–3
Tantum Ergo texts, 127, 131, 141–3, 473–4
training in under Salieri, 61, 114, 126, 131–2, 143, 149
written for Therese Grob, 127, 132, 133–4, 136, 139, 150, 319
see also masses
Salieri, Antonio (1750–1825)
canonic repertoire, 71
church music composition, 43–4, 59, 143
church music training for Schubert, 61, 114, 126, 131–2, 143, 149
counterpoint instruction, 64–5
50th anniversary in Vienna, 58, 116, 209, 210
imitatio technique, 129
improvisational skills, 282
job reference for Schubert, 215
on the Mass in F major (D 105), 146

INDEX

membership of Ludlamshöhle, 456
musical training, 62
opera composition, 59, 62
opera training for Schubert, 114–15, 121, 193, 194, 195, 202–3
partimento knowledge, 62–5, 67
referenced in 'Willkommen und Abschied' (D 767), 405
Schubert's musical training under, 36, 57–9, 62–8, 80–2, 83, 111, 282–3, 304, 368
textual declamation, 83–4
Salieri, Francesco, 62
Sarenbach, Ernst Rinna von, 526, 532
Sauer & Leidesdorf, 288, 462, 488
Scarlatti, Alessandro, 140
Scarlatti, Domenico, 140
Schaefer, August von, 361
Schauff, Jakob, 215
Schiedermayr, Johann Baptist (1779–1840), 288
Schiller, Friedrich (1759–1805)
  aesthetic theory, 13–14, 71, 178–9, 180, 245–7, 351–2
  on the creative spirit, 255
  'An den Fruhling', 86
  Die Huldigung der Künste, 180
  'Dreifach ist der Schritt der Zeit', 84
  Elysium, 84
  'Frisch atmet des Morgens lebendiger Hauch', 84
  'Hoffnung', 86
  'Klage der Ceres', 170
  'Leichenfantasie', 46–7
  on Matthisson's poetry, 179, 180
  Schubert's Schiller canons, 70, 71–5, 83
  setting of poems, 82–3, 84–5, 172, 173, 178–85, 306, 415
  on the sublime, 446
Schindler, Anton, 4, 499–500
Schlechta, Franz, 211
Schlegel, Friedrich, 130, 180, 275, 319, 343, 355, 388, 477, 478
Schlösser, Louis, 284–5
Schober, Franz von (1796–1882)
  collaboration on *Alfonso und Estrella* (D 732), 274–5, 276, 278, 336, 377–8
  design of Schubert's tombstone, 276, 544
  family background, 271–2, 453–4
  friendship with Schubert, 239, 240–1, 251, 271–6, 336, 433–4, 457, 487
  friendship with Schwind, 358–9
  last visit to Schubert, 532, 534
  ownership of Schubert manuscripts, 403

  personality, 271–3, 274–5
  Schubert's deathbed letter to, 531–2
  during Schubert's illness, 275, 340–1, 362, 363–4, 366–7
  on Schubert's lifestyle choices, 335
  Schubert's time living with, 273–4, 304–7, 454, 526
  setting of poems, 85, 274, 538–41
  tombeau commemorating Schubert's death, 538
  transcription of 'Mein Traum', 343, 349–50
  on the *Winterreise* (D 911), 490
Schönstein, Baron Karl von (1796–1876), 249–50, 367–8, 369, 426, 504–5
Schreiber, Aloys Wilhelm, 130, 318–19
Schubert, Christoph (5 December 1632–1693), 21–2
Schubert, Elisabeth (d. 5 July 1751), 22
Schubert, Ferdinand Lukas (1794–1859)
  ambitions as a composer, 129
  appropriation of Schubert's compositions, 128–9, 165
  as a church organist, 127–8, 145, 147
  curatorship of Schubert's sacred music, 128
  domestic music making, 90–1, 99
  friendship with the Rieders, 435
  irreligiosity, 476
  marriage, 216, 217, 314
  Mass in E flat major as Schubert's Requiem, 471
  musical instruction to Schubert, 35, 38
  mythology around Schubert, 88
  obituary for Schubert, 284
  'Pastoral Mass', 129
  performances of Schubert, 223
  relationship with Schubert, 109, 128–9
  Requiem, 529
  Schubert's death at Kettebrückengrass, 6, 523, 526, 531–2, 533–4
  on Schubert's early compositions, 46
  Schubert's letters to, 243, 365, 366, 379, 440, 444
  Schubert's request for a monthly allowance, 55–6
  Tantum Ergo texts, 141
  teaching career, 128
  unsuccessful application for the Court Organist position, 456, 500
  visit to Pressburg, 468
  work in a orphanage, 165, 217, 307
Schubert, Franz Karl (1795–1855), 30, 99, 109, 208–9

INDEX

Schubert, Franz Peter (1797–1828)
  affection for children, 247–8, 438, 509–10
  antinomies, 8
  appearance, 38, 349, 355
  application for a teaching position in Laibach, 157, 160, 212, 214–15
  application for Musical Director at the Court Chapel, 456
  aspirations as a composer, 194, 307, 308, 313–14, 338
  birth of, 33
  childhood loneliness, 34, 44
  Dankschreiben letter to Graz, 392–6
  death of, 30, 531–5
  deathbed performance of Beethoven's String Quartet in C sharp minor, 532
  depressive episodes, 217–18, 219, 272, 308, 457, 488, 510
  double nature, 12–15, 297, 321–3, 406
  early musical ability, 35–7, 39, 42
  education, 34–8
  effeminateness, 6, 7, 8
  eyesight, 434
  family name, 21
  Faustian portrayals, 12–13
  final pilgrimage to Haydn's grave, 526
  financial insecurities, 334–5, 435, 440, 451, 453, 458, 464, 525
  forename, 21
  in Graz, 507–10
  improvisation and, 282–4, 287–8, 300
  introspective nature, 44–5, 87
  as Kapellmeister, 121, 128
  love for Therese Grob, 156–7, 159–60, 194, 214, 215–17, 218, 303, 308, 347–8
  love of music theatre, 192, 194
  myth and narrative of, 1–5
  obituary, 261
  as a pianist, 283–5
  as a piano teacher, 420, 423
  portraits, 435, 436–7
  reaction to his mother's death, 51–5, 87, 88–9, 90, 99–100, 131, 138–9, 488
  reburials, 544
  refusal of the Court Organist position, 456, 500
  relationship with Ferdinand, 109, 128–9
  relationship with his father, 46–51, 52, 78, 79, 98–9, 122, 309–14, 315, 466–7
  repetiteur job, 198–9
  Requiem for, 268, 306
  return to the family home, 369–70, 385, 405
  scepticism over happiness through marriage, 115, 216–17, 260
  schoolteaching career, 303, 307–8, 314
  self-contradictory inclinations, 12–15, 44–5
  self-reflection in his journals, 207–10
  sense of humour, 210–11
  short stature, 349, 355
  sociable disposition, 87
  spirituality, 22
  at the Stadtkonvikt, 36–46, 55–6, 87–8, 98, 106–7, 125–6
  supposed meeting with Beethoven, 3–4, 427
  teacher training, 108, 110, 111, 121–2, 420
  tombstone, 251, 276, 543, 544
  vocal qualities, 35, 36
  wish to be buried alongside Beethoven, 535, 544
  years of crisis, 212, 303–9, 313–15
  see also friendship; musical training; religious faith; sexuality; syphilis

Schubert, Franz Theodor Florian (11 July 1763–9 July 1830)
  children with Anna, 32, 52, 109, 170, 313, 362
  children with Maria Elisabeth, 21, 25–6, 30–1, 33–4, 265, 537
  concerns for Schubert, 306, 312
  'Die Kunstler', 179
  education, 23–5, 35
  fiftieth birthday celebrations, 95–6
  friendships, 31–2
  generosity to orphans, 29–30
  as Imperial Almoner, 29–30
  interest in philosophy, 24, 25
  lifestyle choices, 335–7
  marriage to Anna, 30–1, 52, 93, 100, 108
  marriage to Maria Elisabeth, 27
  move to Vienna, 25
  on music and form, 179–80
  musical ambitions for Schubert, 35, 108, 109–10, 145, 312
  patriotic fervour, 118–19
  personality, 28, 30, 32, 49, 119, 309–13, 314
  publication of Schubert's works, 273
  reaction to Schubert's death, 537–8
  relationship with Schubert, 46–51, 52, 78, 79, 98–9, 122, 309–14, 315, 466–7

689

INDEX

religious faith/personal strength, 313, 467
schoolteaching career, 25, 28–9, 30, 34, 307, 312–13
Schubert's letters to, 365, 366, 417
as a seminary choirboy, 24
Schubert, Franz Wagner (22 June 1785–27 January 1786), 31
Schubert, Ignaz Franz (1785–1844), 26, 28, 30, 35, 36, 99, 314, 315, 476
Schubert, Johann Karl Alois (3 April 1755–29 December 1804), 23, 25, 27, 28–9, 34, 165
Schubert, Johannes 'Hans' (17 December 1678–27 November 1760), 22
Schubert, Karl Josef (6 May 1723–24 December 1787), 21, 22, 23, 27, 28, 208, 297
Schubert, Kaspar (1593–26 March 1657), 21
Schubert, Maria Anna (née Becker), 25, 165
Schubert, Maria Magdalena (24 August 1797–9 October 1820), 34
Schubert, Sibille, 22
Schubert, Susann (née Möck, 19 January 1733–2 August 1806), 22, 27
Schulze, Ernst, 454
Schumann, Robert, 1, 7, 408, 421, 448, 452
Schuppanzigh, Ignaz, 374, 488, 512, 513, 515, 532
Schwarzenberg of Cesky Krumlov, Princess Mathilde, 505
Schwind, Moritz von (1804–1871)
  absence at Schubert's death, 534
  on Caroline von Esterházy, 421
  friendship with Schubert, 251, 358–9, 363–4, 398, 434, 457, 511
  illustrations for publications, 248, 288, 426
  on Katharina Lászny von Folkusfálva, 349–50
  on the military marches, 425, 428
  performances of Schubert's works, 279
  reaction to Schubert's death, 542
Scott, Walter, 438, 440, 463, 498
Scruton, Roger, 482
Sechter, Simon (1788–1867), 59, 69–70, 252, 529–31, 542–3
Seidl, Johann Gabriel, 454, 457, 515, 526
Senn, Johann (1785–1857), 106, 239
setting
  bilingual settings, 434–5, 498–504
  in compositional practice, 113, 332
  friends's texts, 248–9, 306
  ghazal, 355–7

Goethe poetry, 85, 172, 173, 174–8, 201–2, 277, 404–6, 417, 437–8, 462, 505
Italian memorial poems, 538
Kryie movements, 143–4
Kufffner, 517–18
Lady of the Lake (Scott), 438, 440, 463, 498
Leitner poetry, 508, 515
Lieder settings, 84–5, 172–4, 178–85, 188, 261–2, 266, 267, 306, 352–5, 372
Mayrhofer's poetry, 172, 261–2, 266, 267, 277, 306, 318, 372
Metastasio's texts, 80, 82, 83–4, 131, 205, 501
Müller's poetry, 488–9
musical training, 53, 80–6
the Nicene Creed in the masses, 477–81
Noavlis's poetry, 343
Pyrker's poetry, 440, 442–3, 449–50
Salve Regina text, 130–9, 319
Schiller's poetry, 82–3, 84–5, 172, 173, 178–85, 306, 415
Schober's texts, 85, 274, 538–41
Schubert's gift of the op. 19 Goethe settings, 437
Seidl's poetry, 454, 515, 526
Stabat Mater, 139–40
Tantum Ergo texts, 127, 131, 141–3, 473–4
textual fluidity, 189–90, 191
sexuality
  the androgyne, 351–2
  attraction to Caroline Esterházy, 420–1
  attraction to Therese Grob, 159–60
  in biographies, 6, 7, 8
  bisexuality, 156
  in 'Erlkonig' (D 328), 166–8, 171
  in 'Gretchen am Spinnrade' (D 118), 160–3, 171
  hedonistic portrayals of Schubert, 2–3
  nineteenth-century homosociality, 240–2
  prostitution, 350
  relationship with Katharina Lászny von Folkusfálva, 348–50, 426
  relationship with Mayrhofer, 257–9, 262–3, 267
  relationship with Sophie Müller, 433
  Schubert's sexual orientation, 156, 350–2
Silesia, 26, 27, 54–5, 297
Simoni, Giuseppe, 62
Slawjk, Josef, 512, 513
Smirsch, Johann Carl (1793–1869), 370

INDEX

Söhne, Schott, 505
solfeggios, 64
Solomon, Maynard, 1, 8
Sonnleithner, Josef, 451
Sonnleithner, Leopold von (1797–1873), 57, 59, 211, 223, 249, 250, 279, 323, 324–5, 330, 332–3, 334, 451, 530
Spaun, Anton von, 268, 271, 273
Spaun, Josef von (1788–1865)
  on the alleged Beethoven meeting, 4
  friendship with Schubert, 39–40, 112, 239, 251, 253–4, 511
  at Josef Watteroth's home, 210, 211
  last visit to Schubert, 534–5
  move to Linz, 340
  musical ability, 39, 145
  protection of Schubert's privacy, 350–1
  Schubertiad, 268
  on Schubert's family relations, 52
  Schubert's letters to, 439–40
  on Schubert's musical training under Salieri, 80, 82, 86
  on Schubert's talent, 42, 125–6, 166, 282
  setting of Goethe's poetry, 174–6
  at the Stadtkonvikt, 38, 39
  visits to the opera, 192
  on the *Winterreise* (D 911), 490
Spaun, Max von (1797–1844), 40
Spendou, Josef, 215
Spieglitzer Schneeberg (Kralicky Sněžnik), 22
Spina, 461
St Ludmilla (c. 860–921), 22
Stadler, Albert (1794–1888), 45, 46, 239, 248, 361, 517
Stadler, Anton, 173, 211, 361, 517
Stadtkonvikt (Wiener Kaiserliches-königliches Stadtkonvikt)
  friendships at, 239–40, 248
  performances at, 41, 122
  Schubert as a chorister, 36–8, 42–4, 87–8, 98, 125–6
  Schubert's time at, 36–46, 55–6, 87–8, 98, 106–7, 125–6
  the Stadtkonvikt orchestra, 40–2
Stanley, Glen, 477
Steblin, Rita, 2
Steigerung (concept), 409
Stenzl, Friedrich, 112
stile antico, 43, 66–9, 151–2
Stolberg-Stolberg, Friedrich Leopold zu, 172
Stoll, Josef, 172
Strauss, Anton, 201
Streinsberg, Josef Ludwig von, 152, 309

Styrian *Musikverein* (Styrian Music Society), 251, 392–3, 394, 395, 397, 398, 401, 508
Sulzer, Johann, 178
Süssmayr, Franz Xaver (1766–1803), 43
symphonies
  disputed ownership of the 'Unfinished' Symphony manuscript, 392–6, 397–9, 401–3
  'Great' C major symphony (D 944), 7, 90, 180, 382, 401–2, 441–2, 444–53, 460, 467, 482–3, 520
  influences from Beethoven and Mozart, 40, 96
  intertextualities in the symphonies, 103–4
  performances of, 102–3, 123, 218, 223, 227, 392, 401, 451–3, 543
  symphonic sketches, 100–1
  'Unfinished' Symphony in B minor (D 759), 7, 338, 382–95, 397–8, 400–2, 404, 444–5, 446–7
  see also the separate *Index of Works*
syphilis
  connection between sickness and creativity, 369–70, 441, 484
  contraction of syphilis, 347–52
  diagnosis and treatments, 340, 347–52, 359–60, 361–4, 413, 506, 510, 532–3
  enforced celibacy, 352–7
  money for medical bills, 525
  ocular syphilis, 434, 533
  preconceptions over transmission, 349
  premonitions of death, 511–12
  public ostracism, 340, 341, 360
  relocation to Ferdinand's home, 523, 526, 531–2, 533
  restored health, 439–40, 441
  return to the family home, 369–70, 405
  Schubert's acceptance and wisdom, 379–80, 381, 417–19, 445–6, 453, 518
  Schubert's acknowledgement of the inseparability of hope and despair, 370–3, 406–8, 410, 434
  Schubert's despairing letter to Kupelwieser, 16, 90, 219, 370–3, 376, 379, 418, 442
  toxophobia, 369, 529

Tandler, Franz (1782–1806), 112
Tartini, Giuseppe (1692–1770), 62
Taschenbuch zum geselligen Vergnügen, 324
Teltscher, Josef, 4, 251, 433
Thaa, Georg, 40
Theater an der Wien, 324
Tieck, Ludwig, 275, 409

INDEX

Tietze, Ludwig (1797–1850), 250, 456, 488, 513, 515
Tranquillo Mollo, 517
Traweger, Eduard, 247, 438
Traweger, Ferdinand, 247–8, 438
Tritto, Giacomo, 65
Trumbull, Henry Clay, 242

Umlauf, Johann Karl (1796–1861), 325–6, 329
Umlauff von Frankwell, Victor, 331
Unger, Johann Karl, 315

Vering, Josef von, 532
Vienna Court Theatre, 199, 376, 378, 499
Vienna Mannergesang-Verein, 326
Vietz, Felix (b. 1748), 27
Vietz, Franz Johann (4 October 1720–24 January 1772), 26–7
Vietz, Maria Elisabeth Catharina (30 October 1756–28 May 1812)
  children, 25–6, 27, 30–1, 33–4, 537
  compositions following the death of, 52–5, 87, 88–9, 90, 99–100, 130, 131–2, 138–9, 144, 152, 345, 353, 386, 488
  death of, 32, 51, 87, 99, 130, 345, 353, 386, 533
  family background, 26–7, 55
  illegitimate child with Franz Theodor, 25–6, 165
  marriage to Franz Theodor, 27
  musical background, 26
  religious faith/personal strength, 27
  Schubert's reaction to the death of, 51–5, 87, 88–9, 90, 99–100, 131, 138–9, 488
  Silesian roots, 26, 27, 54–5
Vietz, Maria Elisabeth (née Riedel, 1724–1772), 27
Vietz, Maria Magdalena (1763–1829), 27, 34, 108, 165
Vogl, Johann Michael (1768–1840)
  absence at Schubert's death, 534
  friendship with Schubert, 251, 266, 306, 457
  marriage to Kunigunde Rosa, 457
  musical partnership with Schubert, 182, 188, 192, 198, 249, 277, 278, 323, 336, 350, 361, 433
  performances of Schubert's works, 256, 277, 329, 487
  personality, 276–7
  recital tour with Schubert, 437–40, 457
  at Schubert's Benefit Concert, 515
Vranitzký, Antonín (1761– 1820), 43
Vysoké Žibřidovice, 22

Wackenroder, Wilhelm Heinrich (1773–1798), 180, 344, 409, 412
Wagenseil, Georg Christoph (1715–1777), 43, 104, 228
Wagner, Elisabeth, 32
Wagner, Ignaz (1756–12 February 1826), 26, 27, 31, 32, 114, 313
Wagner, Klara, 31–2, 313, 345
Waidelich, Till Gerrit, 9
Walcher von Uysdael, Ferdinand (1799–1873), 477, 487
Wanhal, Johann Baptist (Jan Krtitel Vanhal, 1739–1813), 103, 125
Watteroth, Heinrich Josef, 210, 211
Weber, Carl Maria von, 115, 255, 376, 456
Weigl, Josef, 192, 499, 500
Weimar classicism, 10, 412, 415
Weinkopf, Michael, 329
Weisse, Maximilian (1798–1863), 37, 42
Whistling, Carl Friedrich, 112
Wiener Kaiserliches-königliches Stadtkonvikt see Stadtkonvikt
Wiener Zeitschrift fur Kunst, Literatur, Theater und Mode, 324, 498
Wilberforce, Edward, 6
Wilde, Oscar, 1–2, 14
Winckelmann, Johann Joachim (1717–1768), 238, 242
Winter, Peter von (1754–1825), 43, 87
Winter, Robert, 8
Wisgrill, Johann Baptist, 532
Witt, Friedrich Jeremias (1770–1836), 104
Witteczek, Josef Wilhelm (1787–1859), 210, 211, 248, 513
Wolf, Johann Nepomuk, 438
Wöß, Josef, 215
Wranitzky, Paul (Pavel Vranický, 1756–1808), 41
writings
  'Die Zeit', 54
  'Klage an das Volk' (Complaint to the Nation), 365–6
  'Mein Gebet' (My Prayer, 1823), 360–1
  'Mein Traum' (My Dream) (short story), 52, 322, 341–7, 349–50, 357, 379–80, 414, 465, 536

Youens, Susan, 449–50

INDEX

Zelter, Carl Friedrich (1758–1832), 14, 76, 177, 178

Zseliz
- compositions, 77, 285, 305, 315–16
- friendship with Baron von Schönstein, 249
- open letters from, 243, 315, 316–18, 319–20, 417
- piano teaching in, 420
- second stay in, 364–9, 398, 424–8
- solitude of, 318–19

Zuckmantel (Zlaté Hory), 26

Zum goldenen Ring (At the Golden Ring), Lichtental, 26

Zum roten Krebsen (The Red Crayfish), Vienna, 25, 28, 33, 34, 114, 118, 307

Zum schwarzen Rössel (The Black Horse), 28–9, 32, 34, 108, 117, 214, 304, 307, 313

Zumsteeg, Johann Rudolf (1760–1802), 46, 70, 82